D1115875

# LIFE
# APPLICATION®
# BIBLE
# COMMENTARY

## MATTHEW

Bruce B. Barton, D. Min.
Mark Fackler, Ph.D.
Linda K. Taylor
David R. Veerman, M. Div.

Series Editor: Grant Osborne, Ph.D.
Editor: Philip Comfort, Ph.D.

Tyndale House Publishers, Inc.
WHEATON, ILLINOIS

© 1996 by The Livingstone Corporation
All rights reserved

Contributing Editors: James C. Galvin, Ed.D., and Ronald A. Beers

*Life Application* is a registered trademark of Tyndale House Publishers, Inc.

Scripture quotations marked NIV are taken from the *Holy Bible,* New International Version®. Copyright © 1973, 1978, 1984 by International Bible Society. Used by permission of Zondervan Publishing House. All rights reserved. The "NIV" and "New International Version" trademarks are registered in the United States Patent and Trademark Office by International Bible Society. Use of either trademark requires permission of International Bible Society.

Scripture quotations marked NKJV are taken from The New King James Version. Copyright © 1979, 1980, 1982, Thomas Nelson, Inc., Publishers.

Scripture quotations marked NRSV are taken from the New Revised Standard Version of the Bible, copyrighted, 1989 by the Division of Christian Education of the National Council of the Churches of Christ in the United States of America, and are used by permission. All rights reserved.

(No citation is given for Scripture text that is exactly the same wording in all three versions—NIV, NKJV, and NRSV.)

Scripture quotations marked KJV are taken from the *Holy Bible,* King James Version.

**Library of Congress Cataloging-in-Publication Data**
Matthew / Bruce B. Barton . . . [et al.].
     p.    cm.—(Life Application Bible Commentary)
  Includes bibliographical references and index.
  ISBN 0-8423-3034-8 (sc : alk. paper)
  1. Bible. N.T. Matthew—Commentaries.  I. Barton, Bruce B.
BS2575.3.M28  1996                96-15075
226.2'077—dc20

Printed in the United States of America
00  99  98  97  96
8   7   6   5   4   3   2   1

# *CONTENTS*

*Gospels*

MATTHE
MARK: betw
LU

AC
*Paul's Epistles*
ROMANS: about
1 CORINTHIANS: abou
2 CORINTHIANS: about 56-
GALATIANS: about 49

EPHESIA
PHILIPPIA
COLOSSIA
1 THESSALONIANS: about 51
2 THESSALONIANS: about 51-
1 TIMOT
2 TIMOT
TITU
PHILEMO

*General Epistles*   JAMES: about 49

1 PET
2 PET

JUI

NEW   TESTAMEN

| AD 30 | 40 | 50 | 60 |
|---|---|---|---|

The church begins (Acts 1)

35 Paul's conversion (Acts 9)

46 Paul's first missionary journey (Acts 13)

Jerusalem Council and Paul's second journey (Acts 15)

54 Paul's third journey (Acts 18) Nero becomes emperor

58 Paul arrested (Acts 21)

64 Ror bur

61–63 Paul's Roma impris ment (Acts

ween 60–65

–65

ut 60

JOHN: probably 80–85

ut 63–65

ut 61

ut 62

ut 61

ut 64

ut 66–67

ut 64

ut 61

HEBREWS: probably before 70

ut 62–64

ut 67

1 JOHN: between 85–90
2 JOHN: about 90
3 JOHN: about 90

ut 65

REVELATION: about 95

MELINE

| 70 | 80 | 90 | 100 |

–68
ul and
ter
ecuted

*Jerusalem
destroyed*

79 *Mt. Vesuvius
erupts in Italy*

68
Essenes hide
heir library
of Bible
manuscripts
n a cave
n Qumran
by the
Dead Sea

About 75
*John begins
ministry in
Ephesus*

75
*Rome begins
construction
of Colosseum*

*About 98
John's
death
at Ephesus*

# FOREWORD

The *Life Application Bible* Commentary series provides verse-by-verse explanation, background, and application for every verse in the New Testament. In addition, it gives personal help, teaching notes, and sermon ideas that will address needs, answer questions, and provide insight for applying God's Word to life today. The content is highlighted so that particular verses and phrases are easy to find.

Each volume contains three sections: introduction, commentary, and reference. The introduction includes an overview of the book, the book's historical context, a timeline, cultural background information, major themes, an overview map, and an explanation about the author and audience.

The commentary section includes running commentary on the Bible text with reference to several modern versions, especially the New International Version and the New Revised Standard Version, accompanied by life applications interspersed throughout. Additional elements include charts, diagrams, maps, and illustrations. There are also insightful quotes from church leaders and theologians such as John Calvin, Martin Luther, John Wesley, A. W. Tozer, and C. S. Lewis. These features are designed to help you quickly grasp the biblical information and be prepared to communicate it to others. The reference section includes an index and a bibliography.

# *INTRODUCTION*

Predictions, projections, and best guesses—everyone likes to state what they think the future will hold. Meteorologists forecast the daily weather, sports journalists predict the outcome of a championship series, pollsters project the probable winner of an election, news commentators declare the direction of the nation, and futurists explain what the world will be like a few decades hence. In addition, our daily conversations are sprinkled with future talk: "Who do you think will win?" "What are your retirement plans?" "What will your son do after graduation?"

Often these amateur prophecies are not fulfilled exactly as stated: Partly sunny turns into a downpour, the underdog becomes an upset victor, a technological breakthrough changes the way we live, and an unexpected event alters our plans.

With biblical prophets, the story reads quite differently. Inspired by God, each of their predictions would come true, in exact detail.

The Gospel of Matthew provides amazing examples of the power and accuracy of God's prophets who had foretold the coming of the Messiah. From his humble birth by a virgin (see Isaiah 7:14) in Bethlehem (see Micah 5:2), to his crucifixion (see Psalm 22:14, 16-17) with criminals (see Isaiah 53:12) and resurrection from the dead (see Psalm 16:10), Jesus did what the prophets had predicted—he fulfilled every prophecy and fit every description of the Jewish Savior.

As you read this Gospel, follow the dramatic story, predicted in detail centuries before, of Jesus, the Messiah, King of kings and Lord of lords . . . and *your* Savior too.

## AUTHOR

Matthew (Levi): former tax collector and one of the original twelve disciples

Although the text of this Gospel names no author, the early church nearly unanimously ascribed authorship to Matthew the apostle. The *Didache,* the *Epistle of Barnabas,* and the writings of Ignatius (bishop of Antioch), Papias (the second-century bishop of Hierapolis), Irenaeus (the bishop of Lyons), Origen (third century), and Eusebius (fourth century) all attest to Matthew as the author of this Gospel that bears his name.

A unique statement in the book provides a clue to its authorship. After Matthew was called to be a disciple (9:9), the text states that Jesus ate a meal with tax collectors and sinners "in the house," which could also be rendered "in his house." Since the parallel passage, Mark 2:15, states that this was "Levi's [Matthew's] house," it seems safe to say that the author of the first Gospel was speaking of his own home.

Another hint of Matthew's authorship comes from the references to taxes. For example, 17:24-27 describes the incident when the temple tax collectors asked Peter whether Jesus paid taxes. This incident is found only in Matthew, and it is the kind of story that a former tax collector would include.

The content of this Gospel certainly points to a Jewish author, thus including Matthew as a leading candidate. The following evidence indicates that this book was written by a Jew primarily to a Jewish audience.

**The vocabulary and style of writing.** The term *kingdom of heaven* occurs thirty-three times, compared to *kingdom of God* which occurs only four times. *Kingdom of heaven,* a distinctly Jewish description, appears in no other Gospel. The phrase *Son of Man* refers to the prophecy in Daniel 7:13 and would have been understood and appreciated by Jewish readers. In addition, Jerusalem is called the "holy city" (4:5; 27:53) and the "city of the great King" (5:35), and the Jewish people are called "the lost sheep of the house of Israel" (10:6; 15:24).

**The highlighted topics.** This book places great emphasis on the law, religious defilement, keeping the Sabbath, the kingdom, Jerusalem, the temple, David, the Messiah, fulfillment of Old Testament prophecies, and Moses—all of these would be highly interesting topics for Jewish readers.

**The genealogy.** Jesus' ancestry is traced from a Jewish perspective, from Abraham (the father of the Jewish nation) and through David (the greatest king of Israel).

**Old Testament references.** This Gospel is saturated with citations from the Old Testament Scriptures. Fifty-three of these references are quotations and seventy-six are allusions. Usually these references are used to prove a point, especially regarding Jesus as the Messiah who fulfills Old Testament prophecies.

**Jewish customs.** The book refers to a number of Jewish customs and leaves them unexplained; for example, the reference to ceremonial cleansing (15:2). The author knew that Jewish readers would understand these customs and need no explanations.

**Emphasis on Peter.** This Gospel tells much about Peter's calling, his interaction with Jesus, and his denial. Peter was known as the apostle to the Jews because that is where he concentrated his ministry. Jewish readers would have been very aware of Peter and would have appreciated the references.

Many scholars have disputed Matthew as the author of this Gospel, yet no strong evidence has surfaced to support any other candidate. Some say, for example, that an unknown, anonymous author used a collection of sayings compiled by Matthew, thus identifying Matthew with this work. But this is entirely speculative—there is no proof.

Matthew makes few appearances in Scripture. We first meet him when Jesus calls him to be an apostle: "As Jesus went on from there, he saw a man named Matthew sitting at the tax collector's booth. 'Follow me,' he told him, and Matthew got up and followed him" (9:9 NIV). In the parallel accounts in Mark 2:14-17 and Luke 5:27-32, Matthew is called Levi. Luke reports that when Jesus called him, Matthew (Levi) "got up, left everything and followed him" (Luke 5:28 NIV). Some scholars think that "Matthew," which means "gift of God," may be a new name given by Jesus, just as he had renamed Simon, Peter.

As a "tax collector," Matthew worked for the hated Roman government, having paid Rome for the right to collect taxes from his own people; thus, he would have been seen as a collaborator with the enemy. In addition to make their living, tax collectors (also called "publicans") were allowed to add their commission to the taxes. Many were quite wealthy, having increased their personal worth at the expense of their countrymen. Thus, tax collectors were viewed as dishonest swindlers. Zacchaeus, another tax collector, came to Christ through a dramatic confrontation (Luke 19:1-9). Scholars surmise that Matthew may have collected tolls and customs from those crossing the Lake of Gennesaret at Capernaum. When Jesus called him, Matthew immediately left this lucrative tax-collection career and followed the Lord.

Soon after this dramatic calling, Matthew hosted a dinner for Jesus and the other disciples. The dinner guests also included "many tax collectors and 'sinners'" (9:10 NIV). Evidently Matthew wanted to introduce Jesus to his friends and associates. This disturbed the Pharisees and teachers of the law (the religious establishment), who wondered why Jesus would associate with such undesirables. Jesus answered that he had not come "to call the righteous, but sinners" (9:13 NIV).

Matthew is next mentioned in the list of the twelve disciples, where he is called "Matthew the tax collector" (10:3—see also

Mark 3:18 and Luke 6:15). The only other reference to Matthew is in another list of the disciples in Acts 1:13. After Jesus' ascension into heaven, the disciples gathered regularly with others for prayer. At one of these gatherings, they chose a man to take the place of Judas among the Twelve. After this incident, the Bible records nothing more about Matthew, and nothing is known for sure about him. Tradition holds that he preached the gospel for eight years throughout Judea and then traveled to Persia, Parthia, and Ethiopia, where he died as a martyr in about A.D. 62.

## DATE AND SETTING

Probably written from Antioch (in Syria) in about A.D. 60

Jerusalem was totally destroyed in A.D. 70 by the Romans. That there is no mention in Matthew of this terrible event having already occurred (24:1-22 is a prediction by Jesus of this event) clearly indicates that the Gospel must have been written before that time. On the other hand, it could not have been written much earlier if, as many scholars believe, Mark was the first Gospel to be written and Matthew and Luke relied on his writings and compared their records to his (see Luke 1:1-4). In this case, Mark would have written his account in approximately A.D. 55–60, with Matthew and Luke following soon thereafter in approximately A.D. 60.

The place of writing is also unknown. Many surmise that Matthew wrote from Antioch, but neither the Gospel nor Acts provides any clues. Some, such as Ignatius, chose Antioch, a Gentile city, over Palestine because Matthew wrote in Greek instead of Hebrew. It is difficult to know, however, whether the Gospel was originally written in Greek or written in Aramaic and then translated into Greek. Some scholars point out that because the book contains several untranslated Aramaic terms, it is unlikely that it was originally written in Aramaic (otherwise those terms would have been translated or explained).

The Jewishness of this Gospel suggests that it was written in Palestine. But many of the original disciples had migrated to Antioch (Acts 11:19-27). Also, the great concern in the book for Gentiles tends to confirm this as the city.

## AUDIENCE

Greek-speaking Jews who believed in Jesus as Messiah

Matthew mentions no specific audience. It seems clear, however, that his primary audience was the Jews because, as stated above, the book has a distinctly Jewish flavor. Note especially the scores of references to words, statements, and stories in the Old Testament. The very first chapter sets the tone: "All this took place to fulfill what the Lord had said through the prophet: 'The virgin will be with child and will give birth to a son, and they will call him Immanuel'—which means, 'God with us'" (1:22-23 NIV). Throughout the Gospel, Matthew carefully pointed to Old Testament prophecies that had found fulfillment in statements, circumstances, and actions surrounding Jesus.

It seems, however, that the Jews to whom this book was written were expected to understand Greek because Matthew may have written in Greek, the common language of commerce, and not in Hebrew or Aramaic. Matthew doesn't take time to explain Jewish customs (for example, ceremonial cleansing and Passover)—that would be expected for a Jewish audience. But he does stop to interpret words like "Immanuel" (1:23), "Golgotha" (27:33), and Christ's prayer on the cross ("About the ninth hour Jesus cried out in a loud voice, 'Eloi, Eloi, lama sabachthani?'— which means, 'My God, my God, why have you forsaken me?'"— 27:46 NIV). This also indicates that the primary language of these readers probably was Greek.

## OCCASION AND PURPOSE

To prove that Jesus is the Messiah, the eternal King

Neither Matthew nor the other Gospels give any indication of a special occasion or specific incident that motivated Matthew to write. Early church fathers, Irenaeus (fl. c. 175–195) and Origen (c. 185–251), wrote that Matthew had been written for converts from Judaism, Jews who had embraced Jesus as their Messiah. Actually, until the dramatic conversion of Cornelius through Peter (Acts 10) and the missionary journeys of Paul (Acts 13–28), nearly all of the converts to Christianity were Jews. These new believers needed confirmation that Jesus had indeed met the messianic requirements and had fulfilled the ancient prophecies. Matthew's Gospel gave that confirmation.

In addition to encouragement and assurance of Jesus' true identity, Matthew's account helped believers to refute unbelieving Jews who would argue against them and persecute them. Matthew showed how Christ's death and resurrection fulfilled the promises made to Abraham and David.

While Luke and John clearly gave their purpose for writing (see Luke 1:4 and John 20:31), Matthew has no such purpose statement. But the very first verse provides a strong hint of the focus of the content of this book: "A record of the genealogy of Jesus Christ the son of David, the son of Abraham" (NIV). Note that "Christ," the Greek word for Messiah, follows "Jesus" and that Jesus is immediately identified with the royal line of David and with Abraham, the father of all Jews. Matthew's Jewish readers would have immediately caught the significance of that reference to their great and revered ancestors.

In addition to the opening, Matthew's style and method indicate his aim. Throughout his Gospel, he presents the various incidents in the life of Jesus as fulfillments of messianic prophecies, providing a cumulative demonstration that Jesus was the Messiah foretold in the Old Testament. Matthew, the Hebrew tax collector, knew how Jews thought and felt; he wrote for the Hebrew mind.

Matthew also wrote to explain Jesus' kingdom program. Surely these first-century believers who had left all to follow Christ must have wondered what would become of them and what would happen in the future. So Matthew explained how and why Jesus was rejected by Israel and God's program following that rejection.

In addition to being placed strategically at the beginning of the New Testament, the content of Matthew's Gospel makes an ideal historical connecting link between the two Testaments.

## RELATIONSHIP TO THE OTHER GOSPELS

Although this is not an exhaustive list of all the events in the Gospels (see the Harmony of the Gospels), the following lists of miracles provide a good indication of what the Gospels have in common.

Miracles unique to Matthew:
- healing the two blind men—9:27-31
- casting the demon out of the mute man—9:32-33
- healing the sick in Jerusalem—14:14
- paying tribute with money found in a fish—17:24-27

Miracles common to Matthew and Mark:
- healing in Galilee—9:35; Mark 7:24-30
- healing the Syrophoenician's daughter—15:21-28; Mark 6:5-6
- healing the multitudes in Galilee—15:29-31; Mark 7:31-37
- feeding the four thousand—15:32-39; Mark 8:1-9
- cursing the fig tree—21:18-21; Mark 11:13-14

Miracles common to Matthew and Luke:
- healing the centurion's servant—8:5-13; Luke 7:1-10
- healing the blind and dumb man—12:22; Luke 11:14

Miracles common to Matthew, Mark, and Luke:
- healing the leper—8:1-4; Mark 1:40-42; Luke 5:12-14

- healing Peter's mother-in-law—8:14-15; Mark 1:29-31; Luke 4:38-39
- quieting the wind and waves—8:23-27; Mark 4:36-41; Luke 8:22-25
- curing the demon-possessed man—8:28-33; Mark 5:1-20; Luke 8:26-39
- healing the paralyzed man—9:1-2; Mark 2:3-5; Luke 5:18-25
- healing Jairus's daughter—9:18-25; Mark 5:22-42; Luke 8:41-55
- healing the woman with the bleeding problem—9:20-22; Mark 5:25-34; Luke 8:43-48
- healing the man with the shriveled hand—12:9-13; Mark 3:1-6; Luke 6:6-11
- being transfigured—17:1-8; Mark 9:2-9; Luke 9:28-36
- healing the demon-possessed boy—17:14-18; Mark 9:14-29; Luke 9:37-43
- healing the blind men—20:29-34; Mark 10:46-52; Luke 18:35-43
  A miracle common to Matthew, Mark, and John:
- walking on water—14:22-27; Mark 6:48-51; John 6:19-21
  A miracle common to Matthew, Mark, Luke, and John:
- feeding the five thousand—14:15-21; Mark 6:30-44; Luke 9:10-17; John 6:1-14

## MESSAGE

Jesus Christ the King, the Messiah, Kingdom of God, Jesus' Teachings, Resurrection

**Jesus Christ the King (1:1–2:12; 8:1–10:42; 11:20–12:13; 14:13-36; 15:21-28, 32-39; 17:1-13; 21:12-17, 23-27; 27:37; 28:16-20).** Jesus is revealed as the King of kings: He was conceived by the Holy Spirit and born of a virgin (1:18-25); as a baby, he received gifts and worship from the kings of the east (2:1-12); he was endorsed and affirmed by God the Father (3:16-17); he defeated Satan (4:1-11); he taught with authority (7:28-29); he demonstrated his power over sickness (8:1-13), death (9:23-26), nature (8:23-27), and demons (8:28-34); he triumphed over death (28:1-10). These dramatic and profound incidents show Jesus' true identity.

*Importance for today.* Jesus cannot be equated with any person or power. He is above all as the supreme ruler of time and eternity, heaven and earth, humans and angels. He lives today, sitting at the right hand of the Father, and he will return as the Judge of all the earth (25:31-46). Too often we live as though Jesus were merely an impressive historical figure, or we treat him as just a traveling companion on our journey through life. Instead, we should give him his rightful place as king of our lives, our sovereign ruler to whom we give our total devotion and obedience.

Who sits on the throne of your life? Submit to your Lord and King.

**The Messiah (2:14-15, 21-23; 3:1–4:11; 4:13-16; 12:15-21; 13:13-15; 16:1-4, 13-20; 20:29–21:11; 22:41-46; 24:1-35; 26:1–27:66).** Jesus fulfilled the inspired predictions of the prophets concerning the Messiah, the one for whom the Jews had been waiting for centuries. Yet tragically, they didn't recognize their Messiah when he came because they were expecting a conquering king, one who would deliver them from Roman oppression. If they had read deeper, they would have realized that the "Son of Man" must first suffer and die (17:22-23) as the "suffering Servant" (Isaiah 53) before returning in power and glory. They would have realized that the true purpose of God's anointed deliverer was to free people from sin's oppression, not merely to defeat the Romans and rule an earthly empire.

*Importance for today.* Because Jesus fulfilled the prophecies recorded in the Old Testament, we can see that the Bible is true and reliable. Because Jesus was sent by God, we can know that we can trust him with our lives. It is worth everything we have to acknowledge Jesus as Lord and give ourselves to him because he came to be our Messiah, our Savior. Jesus is the *Christ!* Jesus knows us totally and loves us perfectly. He became one of us to bring us to God. Now that's good news!

Do you understand and feel Christ's love? He wants only the best for you—trust him.

**Kingdom of God (4:17, 23-25; 5:17-20; 9:35; 11:1-19; 12:22-37; 13:10-52; 16:24-27; 18:1-6; 19:13–20:16; 20:20-28; 21:28–22:14; 24:36–25:46).** Jesus came to earth, as God in the flesh, the Messiah, to begin his kingdom. This kingdom, however, is not earthly, determined by geography, military might, political power, or financial influence. God's kingdom is a kingdom of the heart, and his subjects include all who submit to him and acknowledge Christ as their sovereign Lord. Eventually, God's full kingdom will be realized at Christ's return when he comes to annihilate the forces of evil and gather his loyal subjects to himself.

*Importance for today.* Because Christ's kingdom is first a kingdom of the heart, we enter the kingdom through heartfelt faith—believing in Christ as God's Son and our Savior, trusting in him alone to save us from sin and to change our lives. Once we belong to him, we must do the work of his kingdom, living for him and spreading the good news about Christ to others. And we must always be prepared for his return.

If Jesus were to return today, would you be ready? Live with the expectation that Christ might return at any moment.

**Jesus' Teachings (5:1-9; 12:38-58; 15:1-20, 29-31; 16:5-12; 17:14-21, 24-27; 18:7-12; 21:18-22; 22:15-22, 34-40; 23:1-39; 28:20).** Jesus was a master teacher, teaching with authority and reaching people at their point of need. Jesus taught the people through sermons, illustrations, parables, and personal example. Through these teachings, he revealed the true ingredients of faith, how to be fruitful, and how to guard against hypocrisy. Those who were listening and were open and ready understood Jesus and gladly received and responded to the truth.

*Importance for today.* We can know what God is like by looking at Jesus (see John 14:6-10). And we can know how God wants us to live by listening carefully to what Jesus taught. His teachings show us how to live for him right now and how to prepare for life in his eternal kingdom. Jesus lived what he taught, providing the perfect example for us to follow.

Take a close look at Jesus and check out his teachings: "He who has ears, let him hear" (11:15 NIV).

**Resurrection (16:21-23; 17:22-23; 20:17-19; 22:23-33; 28:1-15).** When Jesus rose from the dead, conquering sin and death, he rose in power as the true King. With this incredible victory, the most important event in history, Jesus proved that he truly was the Son of God and that what he lived and taught was true. He also established his credentials as King with power and authority over evil. Jesus does not lie in a grave in Palestine—he is alive!

*Importance for today.* Christ's resurrection shows that not even death could stop God's plan of offering eternal life. Jesus is true and alive; we serve a risen Savior! The Resurrection also gives hope to all who believe in Jesus—we know that we will live with him and that one day we will experience a resurrection like his. No matter how bleak the outlook or difficult and painful our situation, we can hope in him. In the meantime, our role is to tell his story to all the earth so that everyone may share in his victory. This world is dying and passing away, but Jesus is alive and people can live forever.

What can you do to remember the Resurrection? To whom can you tell this glorious news?

# VITAL STATISTICS

**Purpose:** To prove that Jesus is the Messiah, the eternal King

**Author:** Matthew (Levi)

**To Whom Written:** Matthew wrote especially to the Jews

**Date Written:** Probably between A.D. 60–65

**Setting:** Matthew was a Jewish tax collector who became one of Jesus' disciples. This Gospel forms the connecting link between the Old and New Testaments because of its emphasis on the fulfillment of prophecy.

**Key Verse:** "Do not think that I have come to abolish the Law or the Prophets; I have not come to abolish them but to fulfill them" (5:17 NIV).

**Key People:** Jesus, Mary, Joseph, John the Baptist, the disciples, the religious leaders, Caiaphas, Pilate, Mary Magdalene

**Key Places:** Bethlehem, Jerusalem, Capernaum, Galilee, Judea

**Special Features:** Matthew is filled with messianic language ("Son of David" is used throughout) and Old Testament references (53 quotes and 76 other references). This Gospel was not written as a chronological account; its purpose was to present the clear evidence that Jesus is the Messiah, the Savior.

# OUTLINE OF MATTHEW

A. Birth and Preparation of Jesus, the King (1:1–4:11)

B. Message and Ministry of Jesus, the King (4:12–25:46)

    1. Jesus begins his ministry

    2. Jesus gives the Sermon on the Mount

    3. Jesus performs many miracles

    4. Jesus teaches about the kingdom

    5. Jesus encounters differing reactions to his ministry

    6. Jesus faces conflict with the religious leaders

    7. Jesus teaches on the Mount of Olives

C. Death and Resurrection of Jesus, the King (26:1–28:20)

Jesus' earthly story begins in the town of Bethlehem in the Roman province of Judea (2:1). A threat to kill the infant king led Joseph to take his family to Egypt (2:14). When they returned God led them to settle in Nazareth in Galilee (2:22-23). At about age 30, Jesus was baptized in the Jordan River and was tempted by Satan in the Judean desert (3:13; 4:1). Jesus set up his base of operations in Capernaum (4:12-13) and from there ministered throughout Israel, telling parables, teaching about the kingdom, and healing the sick. He traveled to the region of the Gadarenes and healed two demon-possessed men (8:28ff); fed over 5,000 people with five loaves and two fish on the shores of Galilee near Bethsaida (14:15ff); healed the sick in Gennesaret (14:34ff); ministered to the Gentiles in Tyre and Sidon (15:21ff); visited Caesarea Philippi, where Peter declared him as the Messiah (16:13ff); and taught in Perea, across the Jordan (19:1). As he set out on his last visit to Jerusalem, he told the disciples what would happen to him there (20:17ff). He spent some time in Jericho (20:29) and then stayed in Bethany at night as he went back and forth into Jerusalem during his last week (21:17ff). In Jerusalem he would be crucified, but he would rise again.

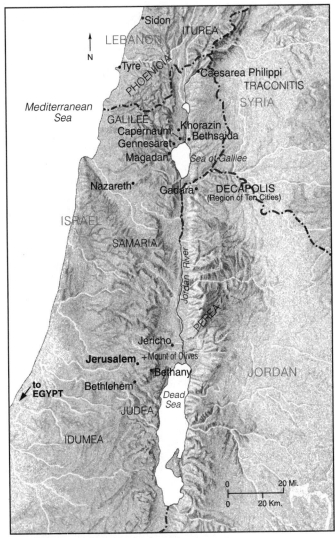

The broken lines (—·—·—) indicate modern boundaries.

# Matthew 1

Jesus entered human history when the land of Palestine was an insignificant outpost of the vast and mighty Roman Empire. The rule of Rome brought military peace to the whole world, and thus to Palestine; however, it did not eliminate oppression, slavery, injustice, and immorality. The Jews resented the Roman intrusion into their daily and religious life. Into this world of conflict and sin, Jesus came as the promised Messiah.

More than four hundred years had passed since the last Old Testament prophecies, and faithful Jews all over the world were still waiting for the Messiah (Luke 3:15). Under the inspiration of the Holy Spirit, Matthew wrote this book to Jews to present Jesus as King and Messiah, the promised descendant of David who would reign forever (Isaiah 11:1-5). The Gospel of Matthew links the Old and New Testaments, containing many references to show how Jesus fulfilled Old Testament prophecies.

Believers should not be put off by this long list of names at the beginning of the New Testament. Present-day Christians, like their early counterparts, should remember that the roots of their faith lie in Judaism. Jesus was a Jew, lived among the Jews, and followed their laws (insofar as they were truly God's laws); and he fulfilled the Old Testament Scriptures as he did so. Matthew's many quotations from and allusions to the Old Testament should cause believers to stand in awe at the unfolding of God's wonderful plan from ages past.

God's plan continues to unfold, and we are part of it. The end of Matthew's Gospel records Christ's Great Commission to the apostles, that they should "make disciples of all the nations" (28:19 NKJV). We believe because others obeyed Christ and carried the message to us. We fulfill the Great Commission today when we take part in sharing the gospel message with unreached people and nations.

**1:1 A record of the genealogy of Jesus Christ the son of David, the son of Abraham.**NIV The first seventeen verses of Matthew's Gospel present Jesus' ancestry. Giving *a record of the genealogy* *of Jesus Christ* was the most interesting way that Matthew could begin a book for a Jewish audience. The Old Testament contains several genealogies: See Genesis 5; Ruth 4:18-22; and 1 Chronicles 1–9. Genealogies served several purposes in Bible times. They traced ancestral claims to land and positions of authority, they were outlines for tracing history, and they revealed ancestral origins. Because a person's family line proved his or her standing as one of God's chosen people, Matthew began by showing that Jesus was a descendant of Abraham, the father of all Jews, and a direct descendant of David, fulfilling Old Testament prophecies about the Messiah's line ("son of" can also mean "descendant of"). The facts of this ancestry were carefully preserved. This is the first of many proofs recorded by Matthew to show that Jesus was the true Messiah. Matthew traced the genealogy back to Abraham, while Luke traced it back to Adam. Matthew wrote to the Jews, so Jesus was shown as a descendant of their father, Abraham. Luke wrote to the Gentiles, so he emphasized Jesus as the Savior of all people.

---

GOOD NEWS
Matthew's first sentence communicates the banner headline. He holds nothing back. Jesus is the Christ (God's long-promised Messiah)! He's the Savior of Israel (David's son)! He's the hope of all nations (Abraham's son)! Call a press conference, roll the videotape, this is big news.

People with news as good as this should get prickly with excitement to tell others. Don't be one of those who holds it in. Let the world know. Like Matthew, share the excitement. Be a missionary wherever God has put you. With your life and by your words, tell others the Good News: Jesus, the Savior, has come and he's here today.

---

This family line was traced through Joseph, who is listed in 1:16 as "the husband of Mary" not the father of Jesus. Because Mary was a virgin when she became pregnant, Joseph was not Jesus' father by sexual union, although Joseph was certainly Jesus' father by law and by paternal care. Matthew's genealogy gives Jesus' legal (or royal) lineage through Joseph, a descendant of King David. Jesus was first of all called *son of David.* God had promised to King David, "Your house and your kingdom will endure forever before me; your throne will be established forever" (2 Samuel 7:16 NIV). That verse was fulfilled in Jesus Christ who will reign as king forever: "I, Jesus, . . . am the Root and the Offspring of David" (Revelation 22:16 NIV). Prophesying Jesus' coming and reign, Isaiah wrote,

■ *For to us a child is born, to us a son is given, and the govern-*
*ment will be on his shoulders. . . . Of the increase of his govern-*
*ment and peace there will be no end. He will reign on David's*
*throne and over his kingdom, establishing and upholding it with*
*justice and righteousness from that time on and forever. The zeal*
*of the Lord Almighty will accomplish this.* (Isaiah 9:6-7 NIV)

Jesus was called *son of Abraham,* indicating more than just his
heritage among the Jews. God had told Abraham,

■ "All peoples on earth will be blessed through you" (Genesis
12:3 NIV).
■ "I will establish my covenant as an everlasting covenant
between me and you and your descendants after you for the
generations to come, to be your God and the God of your
descendants after you" (Genesis 17:7 NIV).
■ "Through your offspring all nations on earth will be blessed,
because you have obeyed me" (Genesis 22:18 NIV).

---

QUALIFICATIONS
In the first 17 verses we meet 46 people whose lifetimes span
2,000 years. All were ancestors of Jesus, but they varied
considerably in personality, spirituality, and experience. Some
were heroes of faith—like Abraham, Isaac, Ruth, and David.
Some had shady reputations—like Rahab and Tamar. Many
were very ordinary—like Hezron, Ram, Nahshon, and Akim.
And others were evil—like Manasseh and Abijah. God's work
in history is not limited by human failures or sins, and he works
through ordinary people. Just as God used all kinds of people
to bring his Son into the world, he uses all kinds today to
accomplish his will. Consider the following questions:
  ■ Whatever your background, have you put your trust wholly
    in Christ and turned from your sins?
  ■ Whichever your gender, have you opened your mind and
    heart to God's instruction, and do you depend on God for
    guidance each day?
  ■ Whatever your talents, have you committed your life to God
    so that, whether you're a carpenter or an executive, you do
    everything for God's glory?
God wants to use you.

---

Jesus Christ will reign forever, and he will also reign over
a kingdom of greater scope than only a Jewish kingdom. He
will reign over faithful believers from all the nations. While
Matthew seems to have written this book for the Jewish Christians to give them further assurance in their faith, in the first
verse he stated that the gospel was meant for all people, Jews

and Gentiles alike. As Jesus fulfilled God's covenant with David, so he also fulfilled God's covenant with Abraham. Through faith in Jesus Christ, anyone from any nation will be blessed through Abraham's covenant, will find salvation, and will "be blessed" with eternal life.

**1:2 Abraham was the father of Isaac, and Isaac the father of Jacob, and Jacob the father of Judah and his brothers.**NRSV Starting with *Abraham,* the recognized father of the Jewish nation, Matthew continued to list Jesus' ancestors to prove that Jesus was the "son" (or descendant of) both Abraham and David. The phrase "was the father of" can also mean "was the ancestor of." Thus, there need not be a direct father-and-son relationship between all those listed in a genealogy.

In ancient times, genealogies were often arranged to aid memorization. Matthew recorded his genealogy in three sets of fourteen generations (see 1:17 and explanation there): the first set from Abraham to David; the second from David's son Solomon to the Exile in Babylon; the third from the return from exile to Jesus' birth. God's plan unfolded across the generations; he controlled history in preparation for the arrival of his Son.

Abraham, as noted above in 1:1, was called by God, received God's covenant promises, and believed the Lord—so "the LORD reckoned it to him as righteousness" (Genesis 15:6 NRSV). His story is told in Genesis 11–25. (He is also mentioned in Exodus 2:24; Acts 7:2-8; Romans 4; Galatians 3; Hebrews 2; 6; 7; 11.)

Abraham *was the father of Isaac.* Abraham and Sarah wondered if God would ever send them the promised son. (If Abraham's descendants were to be too numerous to count, he certainly needed to start with one descendant!) But God always keeps his promises. Genesis records the story of Isaac's birth (and his near sacrifice) in chapters 21 and 22.

Isaac became *the father of Jacob.* These three men—Abraham, Isaac, and Jacob—are often named together as the "patriarchs," fathers of the nation and receivers of God's covenant (see Genesis 50:24; Exodus 3:16; 33:1; Numbers 32:11; Deuteronomy 1:8; 6:10; 9:5, 27; 29:13; 30:20; 34:4; 2 Kings 13:23; Jeremiah 33:26; Matthew 8:11; Luke 13:28; Acts 3:13; 7:32).

Jacob had many sons by his wives Rachel and Leah, including Joseph, whose coat of many colors caused great envy among his older brothers. Jacob's twelve sons became the twelve tribes of Israel (see Genesis 49:1-28). Matthew, desiring to trace Jesus' royal lineage, made special note of *Judah* because the royal line was to continue through him. In Jacob's blessing upon Judah, he had said, "The scepter shall not depart from Judah, nor the ruler's staff from between his feet" (Genesis 49:10 NRSV). King David was from the tribe of Judah (2 Samuel 2:4; 1 Chronicles 28:4).

The mention of Judah's *brothers* may have served to remind Matthew's readers of the twelve tribes of Israel that corresponded with the twelve apostles chosen by Jesus to continue his work. Later in his book, Matthew would record Jesus' words to the Twelve: "I tell you the truth, at the renewal of all things, when the Son of Man sits on his glorious throne, you who have followed me will also sit on twelve thrones, judging the twelve tribes of Israel" (19:28 NIV).

**1:3 Judah the father of Perez and Zerah, whose mother was Tamar, Perez the father of Hezron, Hezron the father of Ram.**NIV An interesting sidelight appears in this verse. One might expect a genealogy to avoid mention of less reputable ancestors, but Judah's sons were born by Tamar, who had prostituted herself to her father-in-law. The story of Judah and Tamar is told in Genesis 38—an intriguing tale of evil, judgment, lies, deceit, and ultimate vindication. While Judah was *the father of Perez and Zerah,* he was not married to their mother, *Tamar.* Perez and Zerah were twins (see also 1 Chronicles 2:4). The line tracing Perez to King David is also recorded in Ruth 4:12, 18-22.

Matthew's inclusion of four particular women in his genealogy reveals his concern to do more than relay historical data. While we might have expected him to include Sarah and Rebekah (wives of Abraham and Isaac, respectively), he chose instead Tamar (who had seduced her father-in-law), Rahab and Ruth (who were not Jews; also, Rahab had been a prostitute), and Bathsheba, called "Uriah's wife" in 1:6 (who had committed adultery). In other words, these women were less-than-sterling examples to have in one's ancestral line. Yet this was the line into which God's Son was born. The suspicion of illegitimacy surrounded these four women's sexual activity; this fits with the suspicion surrounding Mary, Jesus' mother—a suspicion that Matthew spent much time refuting. These were normal people, sometimes caught up in their own sin, all of them in need of God's mercy and grace. God sent his Son as Savior of *all* people—Jews, Gentiles, men, women—those pretty good and those very evil. No matter what the sins of the people, God's plan was never thwarted, and God's Son was born according to his plan.

Not much is known about *Hezron* and *Ram.* Hezron is mentioned in Genesis 46:12 and 1 Chronicles 2:5. Ram (or Aram) is mentioned in 1 Chronicles 2:9.

DYSFUNCTIONAL FAMILIES
In Jesus' family tree, we don't find all sports heroes and presidents. Some very bad-news characters formed his past. But Matthew does not hide them, and Jesus' parents, for all we know, never let the past determine the present.
    Overcoming a dysfunctional past is not easy, but never adopt the past as your excuse. With Jesus, life starts over with new energy, new purpose, and new love. Start your day with prayer, live it by the promises of God's Word, and use your church's resources and friendships to mend, heal, and overcome. No excuses!

**1:4 Ram the father of Amminadab, Amminadab the father of Nahshon, Nahshon the father of Salmon.**<sup>NIV</sup> *Amminadab* and *Nahshon* are mentioned in Exodus 6:23—Amminadab's daughter and Nahshon's sister, Elisheba, married Aaron, who became Israel's high priest. Mentioned in Numbers 1:7, Nahshon was chosen to help Aaron number the men of Israel who could fight in the army. Then in Numbers 2:3, Nahshon is called "the leader of the people of Judah," meaning that he was in charge of that tribe. He also was in charge of bringing an offering for the dedication of the altar in God's tabernacle—and he brought his offering on the first day (Numbers 7:12-17). *Salmon* is mentioned again only in the genealogy in Ruth 4:18-22. These men are also listed in 1 Chronicles 2:10-11.

**1:5 Salmon the father of Boaz, whose mother was Rahab, Boaz the father of Obed, whose mother was Ruth, Obed the father of Jesse.**<sup>NIV</sup> *Rahab* is the woman of Jericho who hid Israel's spies and eventually was saved by them when the Israelites destroyed Jericho. Rahab was a prostitute (Joshua 2:1) who operated an inn on the city wall. She came to believe in Israel's God, and she protected the spies and helped them in their mission: "'The Lord your God is God in heaven above and on the earth below. Now then, please swear to me by the Lord that you will show kindness to my family, because I have shown kindness to you.' . . . So she let them down by a rope through the window, for the house she lived in was part of the city wall" (Joshua 2:11-12, 15 NIV). Rahab is included in the Hall of Faith in Hebrews 11. She is the only non-Jew mentioned there by name.

There is a chronological problem in making Rahab the actual mother of Boaz, however. As with the phrase "father of," those listed as mothers in a genealogy may be ancestors rather than actual mothers.

However, chronology was not a concern with the next three people. The book of Ruth tells the story of *Boaz* and a young woman named *Ruth,* who had come to Israel from the nearby nation of Moab. Boaz married Ruth, and they became the parents of *Obed* (Ruth 4:13-17). Obed later became the father of *Jesse* (Ruth 4:21-22). See also 1 Chronicles 2:12.

**1:6 And Jesse the father of King David. David was the father of Solomon, whose mother had been Uriah's wife.**NIV *Jesse* had several sons, one of whom had been anointed by the prophet Samuel to be the next king of Israel after King Saul (see 1 Samuel 16:5-13). Placing the word *King* with *David* reminded Matthew's Jewish audience of the glorious reign of King David, the promises that God had given to David, and the fulfillment of those promises in the appearance of an even greater King—the Messiah himself. The story of David is told in 1 and 2 Samuel, with the transfer of his throne to his son Solomon recorded in 1 Kings 1.

*Solomon* was born to David and Bathsheba (described here as having *been Uriah's wife*). The story, recorded in 2 Samuel 11, describes David's murder plot against Uriah in order to get Uriah's wife for himself. God was very displeased with David's evil actions, and the first child born to David and Bathsheba died (2 Samuel 11:27–12:23). The next child born was Solomon, who later ruled Israel during a reign that would be described as the golden age of the nation. His God-given wisdom became known worldwide, and he wrote many of the proverbs in the book of Proverbs, as well as Ecclesiastes and Song of Solomon. His story is told in 1 Kings 1–11 and 2 Chronicles 1–9.

**1:7 Solomon the father of Rehoboam, Rehoboam the father of Abijah, Abijah the father of Asa.**NIV At the end of Solomon's glorious reign, his evil son *Rehoboam* split the kingdom because of a prideful and ill-advised decision (see 1 Kings 12:1-24). Two kingdoms emerged: The southern kingdom, called Judah, was ruled by Rehoboam; the northern kingdom, called Israel, was ruled by Jeroboam. But the kingdom of Israel had a succession of evil kings. Eventually Israel was conquered by Assyria, and many of its people were taken away into exile. The kingdom of Judah had both good and bad kings. This genealogy traces only the line of the kings of Judah.

Rehoboam's son *Abijah* (also called Abijam) was also an evil king who "committed all the sins that his father did before him; his heart was not true to the Lord his God, like the heart of his father David. Nevertheless for David's sake the Lord his God gave him a lamp in Jerusalem, setting up his son after him, and establishing Jerusalem" (1 Kings 15:3-4 NRSV). This son was the godly king *Asa* who "did what was right in the sight of the Lord, as his father David had done" (1 Kings 15:11 NRSV).

No particular pattern appears—sometimes an evil king had a godly son (as Abijah and Asa); other times a godly king had an evil son (as Jehoshaphat and Jehoram). They were often judged by the standard of King David, who, despite all his mistakes, was considered a great and God-honoring king.

---

HELPING CHILDREN FIND FAITH
For all his reputed wisdom, Solomon wasn't much of a dad. Solomon's kids were rebels who never seemed to understand the importance of faith in God. They messed up all he had built, but not all the fault was theirs.

To build your children in faith, start with the simple steps. Don't skip church; be there with them. Don't convey how hard you've worked; rather, convey how much God has blessed. Pray at meals, at bedtime, whenever it's right, which is usually when you're most tired. Don't be a deadbeat: Give to missions and to the homeless—time and money. *Show* them how to love God, before you start the lecture.

---

**1:8 Asa the father of Jehoshaphat, Jehoshaphat the father of Jehoram, Jehoram the father of Uzziah.**[NIV] Good King Asa was the father of another good king, *Jehoshaphat.* King Jehoshaphat "walked in all the way of his father Asa; he did not turn aside from it, doing what was right in the sight of the LORD" (1 Kings 22:43 NRSV). However Jehoshaphat's son *Jehoram* (also called Joram) "did what was evil in the sight of the LORD" (2 Kings 8:18 NRSV). Still, God's promise would not be deterred. For even as the evil king Jehoram led Judah into evil, "the Lord would not destroy Judah, for the sake of his servant David, since he had promised to give a lamp to him and to his descendants forever" (2 Kings 8:19 NRSV).

That Jehoram is called *the father of Uzziah* provides an example of how this phrase did not always mean actual "father of." According to the same genealogy in 1 Chronicles 3:10-12, Matthew omitted three names between Jehoram and Uzziah (also called Azariah): These three kings were Ahaziah, Joash, and Amaziah. Scholars have offered various opinions for why these names were excluded—such as the fact that all three men had connections with Ahab and Jezebel (the exceedingly evil king and queen of the northern kingdom of Israel) and with Athaliah, a wicked usurper (see 2 Kings 8:26-27 and 11:1-20). But it is more likely that Matthew did not include these names in order to keep his pattern of three sets of fourteen generations in this genealogy.

After the reign of evil king Jehoram, his son *Uzziah* (Azariah) assumed the throne. Uzziah followed God for most of his reign and became very powerful and successful. However, "after Uzziah became powerful, his pride led to his downfall. He was unfaithful to the Lord his God, and entered the temple of the Lord to burn incense on the altar of incense" (2 Chronicles 26:16 NIV), a job only the priests were entitled to do. God struck Uzziah with leprosy, and he "had leprosy until the day he died. He lived in a separate house—leprous, and excluded from the temple of the Lord. Jotham his son had charge of the palace and governed the people of the land" (2 Chronicles 26:21 NIV). The next verse tells of Jotham.

**1:9 Uzziah the father of Jotham, Jotham the father of Ahaz, Ahaz the father of Hezekiah.**NIV Apparently *Jotham* had learned from his father *Uzziah*'s mistake, for the Bible tells us that he "grew powerful because he walked steadfastly before the Lord his God" (2 Chronicles 27:6 NIV). But Jotham's good influence did not extend to his son, for *Ahaz* "walked in the ways of the kings of Israel and even sacrificed his son in the fire, following the detestable ways of the nations the Lord had driven out before the Israelites. He offered sacrifices and burned incense at the high places, on the hilltops and under every spreading tree" (2 Kings 16:3-4 NIV). Following the exceedingly evil reign of Ahaz came the prosperous reign of the good king *Hezekiah*. Scripture tells us that "Hezekiah trusted in the Lord, the God of Israel. There was no one like him among all the kings of Judah, either before him or after him" (2 Kings 18:5 NIV).

**1:10 Hezekiah the father of Manasseh, Manasseh the father of Amon, Amon the father of Josiah.**NIV *Hezekiah* obeyed God, but his son was the most evil king who reigned over the southern kingdom. "Manasseh led Judah and the people of Jerusalem astray, so that they did more evil than the nations the Lord had destroyed before the Israelites" (2 Chronicles 33:9 NIV). At the end of his life, however, *Manasseh* repented of his horrible sins (2 Chronicles 33:13).

Unfortunately, Manasseh's son *Amon* assumed too much of his father's character. Amon "did evil in the eyes of the Lord, as his father Manasseh had done. Amon worshiped and offered sacrifices to all the idols Manasseh had made. But unlike his father Manasseh, Amon did not humble himself before the Lord; Amon increased his guilt" (2 Chronicles 33:22-23 NIV).

Once again, God had mercy on the nation, and Amon's son *Josiah* attempted to undo all his father's evil deeds. "Neither before nor after Josiah was there a king like him who turned to the Lord as he did—with all his heart and with all his soul and with all his strength, in accordance with all the Law of Moses" (2 Kings 23:25 NIV).

---

**MAKE A DIFFERENCE**
Josiah might have said, "Hey, what's the use? Nothing can straighten out this mess." Or he could have said, "Whoa, I'm just one little guy in a big, big country. Gimme a break!" Or, "It's the old man's problem. Let him solve it!"

But Josiah did not look for excuses. He did what one faithful believer could do, and his world was better for it. Discover stories of other heroes of faith—men and women who did all that one person could and turned the tide. Be that person yourself, despite obstacles. One person with God can make a big, big difference. Be quick to take a stand against evil or to take the first step to bring about change.

---

**1:11 And Josiah the father of Jeconiah and his brothers at the time of the exile to Babylon.**<sup>NIV</sup> Matthew omitted another name from the lineage. *Josiah* was the father of Jehoiakim, who was deported to Babylon when he rebelled against Nebuchadnezzar. After Jehoiakim was taken away, his son *Jeconiah* (also called Jehoiachin) reigned in Jerusalem. Jeconiah reigned for only three months before Nebuchadnezzar laid siege to Jerusalem, causing the city to surrender. The phrase *and his brothers* refers to Jeconiah's brother Zedekiah whom Nebuchadnezzar placed on the throne of Jerusalem as a puppet ruler. Zedekiah's name was not mentioned because the royal line did not go through him, but through Jeconiah. However, Zedekiah made the grave mistake of also rebelling against Nebuchadnezzar, and this brought down the final wrath of Babylon. On his third visit to Jerusalem for battle, Nebuchadnezzar conquered Judah completely, destroying Jerusalem including its beautiful temple. The entire nation of Judah was taken into *exile to Babylon* (2 Kings 24:16–25:21). This occurred in 586 B.C.

The exile marked the end of David's line and kingdom. It must have looked like all the promises had come to nothing. But in approximately 735 B.C., the prophet Isaiah foretold that "a shoot will come up from the stump of Jesse; from his roots a Branch will bear fruit" (Isaiah 11:1 NIV). Judah (the royal line of David) would be like a tree chopped down to a stump. But from that stump a new shoot would grow—the Messiah. He would be greater than the original tree and would bear much fruit. The

Messiah is the fulfillment of God's promise that a descendant of
David would rule forever (2 Samuel 7:16).

**1:12** **After the exile to Babylon: Jeconiah was the father of Shealtiel, Shealtiel the father of Zerubbabel.**NIV In this final group-
ing, *Jeconiah* (also called Jehoiachin) is listed as *the father of
Shealtiel,* agreeing with 1 Chronicles 3:17. In listing Shealtiel
as *father of Zerubbabel,* Matthew departed from the genealogy
in 1 Chronicles 3:19 which lists Pedaiah as Zerubbabel's father.
However, Matthew agrees with several other Scriptures that
list Shealtiel as Zerubbabel's father (Ezra 3:2; 5:2; Nehemiah
12:1; Haggai 1:1; 2:2, 23). Why are there differences among
these genealogies? Scholars have offered various opinions, the
most likely being that a "levirate" marriage took place—the
marriage of a widow to the brother of her dead husband. The
purpose of such a marriage was to carry on the dead man's
name and inheritance. Family ties were an important aspect of
Israelite culture. The best way to be remembered was through
your line of descendants. If a widow married someone outside
the family, her first husband's line would come to an end. Thus,
Shealtiel may have died childless, and his brother Pedaiah may
have married Shealtiel's widow. Pedaiah would have been truly
Zerubbabel's father (as noted in 1 Chronicles), but Zerubbabel's birth, according to the laws of levirate marriage, would
have carried on Shealtiel's name.

Zerubbabel figured prominently in Judah's history *after the
exile.* When the people of Judah were finally allowed to return
to their nation, Zerubbabel became their governor (Haggai 1:1)
and "set to work to rebuild the house of God in Jerusalem. And
the prophets of God were with them, helping them" (Ezra 5:2
NIV). God greatly blessed his servant Zerubbabel, reaffirming
and guaranteeing his promise of a Messiah through David's
line, noted by the words of the prophet Haggai: "'On that day,'
declares the Lord Almighty, 'I will take you, my servant Zerubbabel son of Shealtiel,' declares the Lord, 'and I will make you
like my signet ring, for I have chosen you,' declares the Lord
Almighty" (Haggai 2:23 NIV).

**1:13-15** **And Zerubbabel the father of Abiud, and Abiud the father of
Eliakim, and Eliakim the father of Azor, and Azor the father
of Zadok, and Zadok the father of Achim, and Achim the
father of Eliud, and Eliud the father of Eleazar, and Eleazar
the father of Matthan, and Matthan the father of Jacob.**NRSV
Nothing is known from Scripture about any of these men because

they lived during the intertestamental period. Matthew probably got their names from Jewish genealogical records.

**1:16 And Jacob the father of Joseph, the husband of Mary, of whom was born Jesus, who is called Christ.**<sup>NIV</sup> According to Luke 3:23, Joseph's father was Heli. The royal line continued through *Joseph,* who, though he was not Jesus' father, was *the husband of Mary.* Mary was the mother of Jesus. The words *of whom* are in the feminine gender, meaning that Matthew was referring specifically to Jesus being born of Mary, but not of Joseph (as Matthew will explain in 1:18-25). Jesus *is called Christ;* he is the Messiah. Matthew had completed his goal in listing this genealogy—showing, beyond any doubt, that Jesus was a descendant of David, thus fulfilling God's promises.

**1:17 Thus there were fourteen generations in all from Abraham to David, fourteen from David to the exile to Babylon, and fourteen from the exile to the Christ.**<sup>NIV</sup> The Gospel breaks Israel's history into three sets of fourteen generations, but there were probably more generations than those listed here. Genealogies often compressed history, meaning that not every generation of ancestors was specifically listed. What was Matthew's point in mentioning fourteen generations? There are three possibilities (some or all may have been true):

1. Some scholars propose that Matthew used the "perfect number" (seven) and made three groups of twice seven. (The Jews regarded "seven" as the number denoting completeness, wholeness, as in the seven days of creation.)
2. Some note that in making three groups, Matthew was focusing on significant points in Jewish history: the arrival of King David on the throne of Israel, the loss of David's throne to the Babylonian exile, and the restoration of the throne and promises in the birth of the Messiah.
3. Others point out the use of David's name in this genealogy because Matthew wanted to prove that Jesus descended from David. The Hebrew numerical value of David's name is fourteen. The "numerical value" refers to the values of the Hebrew consonants in David's name (DVD = 4+6+4=14), accounting for the focus on three sets of fourteen generations. Some are concerned that in counting these generations, each section doesn't add up to fourteen. However, ancient counting would alternate between inclusive and exclusive reckoning. A duplicated name from one set to the next may or may not count with either the previous or following set. The same sort of reckoning was true with Jesus being in the grave for three days—the

three days included part of Friday, all of Saturday, and part of
Sunday, but not three twenty-four hour periods. This reckoning
was standard to Matthew's day.

A problem also seems to arise in comparing Matthew's genealogy with Luke's (recorded in Luke 3:23-38). Matthew's differences
can be explained by his omitting names in order to achieve his
symmetry of three sets of fourteen generations. Also, most likely
Luke was tracing Jesus' natural human ancestry through Joseph,
while Matthew was focusing on the legal and royal names to
emphasize the succession of the throne of David and Jesus' arrival
as the promised King. Matthew stressed Israelite history. Luke's
longer genealogy traces Jesus' ancestry through David's son
Nathan, not through Solomon, as Matthew did. Matthew also
includes the names of four women, which Luke does not.

To his Jewish audience, Matthew gave a documented genealogical record of Jesus' ancestry so they could see for themselves that
Jesus did indeed fulfill the requirements as the Son of David.

## AN ANGEL APPEARS TO JOSEPH / 1:18-25 / 8

The fact that Jesus was born to Mary even though she had not
had sex with Joseph (as noted in 1:16) needed to be explained
to Matthew's readers. In this section, Matthew relates the story
behind Jesus' birth and how all attempts to thwart God's plan
go awry when God gets involved. We can appreciate God's miraculous working in both Joseph and Mary. Although God's actions
were beyond their comprehension, and although they may have
faced misunderstanding and questioning looks from those around
them, Mary and Joseph willingly followed God's guidance. How
willing are we to do what God wants, no matter what? Can we
follow God's guidance without question?

**1:18 This is how the birth of Jesus Christ came about: His mother
Mary was pledged to be married to Joseph, but before they
came together, she was found to be with child through the
Holy Spirit.**[NIV] In 1:16, Matthew had stated that Mary was
Jesus' mother, but Joseph was not his father. This needed some
explanation, for, taken at face value, it sounded immoral.

Jesus' mother Mary *was pledged to be married to Joseph.*
Modern readers need to understand the traditions involved in
ancient Jewish marriages. First, the two families would agree
to the union and negotiate the betrothal, including a price for
the bride that would be paid to the bride's father. Next, a public
announcement would be made. At this point, the couple was

"pledged." This is similar to engagement today, except that it was much more binding. At this point, even though the couple was not officially married, their relationship could be broken only through death or divorce. Sexual relations were not yet permitted. This second step lasted for a year. During that time, the couple would live separately, with their parents. This waiting period would demonstrate the bride's purity. If she were found to be pregnant during that time, the marriage could be annulled. Otherwise, the couple would be married and begin living together.

Because Mary and Joseph were pledged to be married, they had not yet had sexual relations (the meaning of the phrase "before they came together"). Yet she *was found to be with child.* Mary was pledged and pregnant, and Joseph knew that the child was not his own. Mary's apparent unfaithfulness carried a severe social stigma. According to Jewish civil law, Joseph had the right to divorce her. The law also explained that the penalty for unchastity was death by stoning (Deuteronomy 22:23-24), although this was rarely carried out at this time. That Mary was "found" to be pregnant indicates that she may not have immediately told Joseph, but had waited until her condition could be seen. This probably occurred after her return from visiting her pregnant cousin Elizabeth (mother of John the Baptist) with whom she had stayed for three months (see Luke 1:39-56).

Removing any doubt of Mary's purity, Matthew explained that Mary was pregnant *through the Holy Spirit.* During Old Testament times, the Spirit acted on God's initiative (for example, see Genesis 1:2). Thus, the divine initiative in Mary's conception was made clear. Luke 1:26-38 records this part of the story. When the angel announced to Mary that she was chosen to be the mother of the promised Messiah, Mary asked the obvious question: "How will this be . . . since I am a virgin?" (Luke 1:34 NIV). The angel's amazing answer both surprised and reassured Mary: "The Holy Spirit will come upon you, and the power of the Most High will overshadow you. So the holy one to be born will be called the Son of God" (Luke 1:35 NIV). Mary humbly accepted the angel's words, "I am the Lord's servant. . . . May it be to me as you have said" (Luke 1:38 NIV). Surely Mary's mind must have tumbled with concern over how Joseph would respond. She chose to trust the Lord, however, and the Lord took care of Joseph, as we see in the following verses.

**FULLY HUMAN, FULLY GOD**
Why is the virgin birth important to the Christian faith?
Jesus Christ, God's Son, had to be free from the sinful nature
passed on to all other human beings by Adam. Because
Jesus was born of a woman, he was a human being; but as
the Son of God, Jesus was born without any trace of human
sin. Jesus is both fully human and fully divine. The infinite,
unlimited God took on the limitations of humanity so he could
live and die for the salvation of all who believe in him.

Because Jesus lived as a man, we know that he fully
understands our experiences and struggles (Hebrews 4:15-
16). Because he is God, he has the power and authority to
deliver us from sin (Colossians 2:13-15). We can tell Jesus all
our thoughts, feelings, and needs. He has been where we are
now, and he has the ability to help.

**1:19 Her husband Joseph, being a righteous man and unwilling
to expose her to public disgrace, planned to dismiss her
quietly.**NRSV Joseph was called Mary's *husband,* even though
they were not yet officially married. However, they were
"pledged" (see explanation on 1:18), which was as legally
binding as marriage. Joseph had a difficult decision to make.
Being a *righteous man,* he did not want to go against God's
laws. To marry Mary would have been an admission of guilt
when he was not guilty. To have a public divorce would have
exposed Mary *to public disgrace,* and apparently Joseph's
compassion would not allow him to expose her to public
humiliation. Therefore, he chose the option to have a private
divorce before two witnesses and *dismiss her quietly.* This
way he could keep his reputation, while still showing compassion.

Evidently, Mary had not explained her visit from the angel to
Joseph at this time. Joseph only resolved to dismiss Mary after
her condition had become visible (1:18). And the angel's words
in 1:20 indicate that Joseph did not know the Holy Spirit's role in
Mary's pregnancy. So, Joseph thought he had only two options:
divorce Mary publicly or dismiss her quietly, but God had
another option for Joseph.

God often shows us that we have more options than we think.
Although Joseph seemed to be doing the right thing by breaking
the engagement, God helped him make the best decision. We
should always seek God's wisdom, especially when our decisions
affect others.

**1:20 But just when he had resolved to do this, an angel of the Lord
appeared to him in a dream and said, "Joseph, son of David,**

**do not be afraid to take Mary as your wife, for the child conceived in her is from the Holy Spirit.**" NRSV As Joseph began to move forward on his decided course of action, God intervened. The conception of Jesus Christ was a supernatural event beyond human logic or reasoning. Because of this, God sent angels to help certain people understand the significance of what was happening (see 2:13, 19; Luke 1:11, 26; 2:9). In this case, an angel *appeared to him in a dream.* Dreams function in the Bible as a means to convey God's message to people. They occur in three major portions of the Bible: Genesis 20–41; Daniel 1–7; Matthew 1–2. Based on Numbers 12:6, Jews believed that God communicated his will in dreams. In Matthew, dreams are used repeatedly to guide people (2:12-13, 22; 27:19). God used dreams in a special way during these key times. We can benefit spiritually from our dreams, but there is no certainty that they are authoritative messages from God.

Angels are spiritual beings, created by God, who help carry out his work on earth. They bring God's messages to people (Luke 1:26), protect God's people (Daniel 6:22), offer encouragement (Genesis 16:7ff.), give guidance (Exodus 14:19), carry out punishment (2 Samuel 24:16), patrol the earth (Zechariah 1:9-14), and fight the forces of evil (2 Kings 6:16-18; Revelation 20:1-2). Both good and evil angels exist (Revelation 12:7), but because evil angels are allied with the devil, or Satan, they have considerably less power and authority than good angels. Eventually the main role of angels will be to offer continuous praise to God (Revelation 7:11-12). The angel who appeared to Joseph was one of God's messengers, sent to correct Joseph in his dealings with Mary.

The angel called Joseph *son of David,* signifying that Joseph had a special role in a special event. The angel explained that Joseph was to take Mary as his wife, for the child was to be in the royal line of David. Joseph, as "son of David," would establish that royal lineage. Joseph was not to *be afraid* to take Mary as his wife—no matter what the social repercussions might be. Of course, she was already his wife because they were pledged, but the angel told Joseph that instead of divorcing Mary, he should complete the marriage process and take her home as his wife. Mary had committed no sin. Instead, the angel explained that *the child conceived in her is from the Holy Spirit.* God himself had caused this pregnancy, and the child would be very special— God's Son. He would also be the fulfillment of prophecy, as described in the next verse.

MAKING GOOD DECISIONS
When facing big decisions, some people freeze with fright.
What if I decide wrong? What if I miss God's will? What if . . . ?
   To make good decisions, first take all these worries and put
them under God's promise: God cares for you, watches over
you, and guides your steps.
   Joseph came to the best decision he could, but God had
other plans and made them clear. Most of our decisions will
not be overruled by angels, but that's no reason for lack of
confidence. To make good decisions, pray, evaluate all the
options, talk with trusted friends, then act in faith. God is with
you, every step.

**1:21** **"And she will bring forth a Son, and you shall call His name
JESUS, for He will save His people from their sins."** NKJV
The angel's message included telling Joseph what was to come
and what he should do. There seems to have been no doubt that
Joseph would hear and obey. Mary would give birth to a baby
boy. Joseph was to name the child *Jesus.* "Jesus" is the Greek
form of "Joshua." The name means "the Lord saves." Jesus'
name identified him as the one who would bring God's promised salvation. The baby Jesus would be born to *save His
people from their sins.* From the very start, the book explains,
to a Jewish audience, that Jesus would not save the people
from Rome or from tyranny, nor would he set up an earthly
kingdom. Instead, Jesus would save people from sin. The
words "his people" form a mystery to be unfolded in the pages
of Matthew's Gospel. Who were "his people," and how would
Jesus save them from their sins? The answers to these questions
will be found in the unfolding story of Jesus' life, death, and
resurrection.

A NEW LIFE
Jesus came to earth to save us because we can't save ourselves from sin and its consequences. No matter how good we
are, we can't eliminate our alienation from God. Only Jesus can
do that. Jesus didn't come to help people save themselves; he,
and he alone, came to be their Savior from the power and
penalty of sin. Thank Jesus for his death on the cross for your
sin, and then ask him to take control of your life. Your new life
begins at that moment.

**1:22-23** **All this took place to fulfill what the Lord had said through the
prophet: "The virgin will be with child and will give birth to a
son, and they will call him Immanuel"—which means, "God**

**with us.**" NIV Throughout his Gospel, Matthew delighted in quoting or alluding to Old Testament Scripture to show how Jesus fulfilled it. Jesus was to be called *Immanuel—which means "God with us,"* as predicted by Isaiah the prophet (Isaiah 7:14). Jesus was God in the flesh; thus, God was literally "with us." The point was not that Jesus would ever bear the name "Immanuel," but rather this name described Jesus' role—to bring God's presence to people. Jesus Christ, who was himself God (John 1:1), brought God to earth in his human body—living, eating, teaching, healing, dying. Matthew closed his Gospel with the same promise of "God with us" because, before his ascension, Jesus promised his followers, "I am with you always, even to the end of the age" (Matthew 28:20 NKJV). Perhaps not even Isaiah understood how far-reaching the meaning of "Immanuel" would be.

Matthew quoted Isaiah 7:14 probably from the Greek version of the Hebrew Old Testament (the Septuagint). In Isaiah 7:14, "virgin" is translated from a Hebrew word used for an unmarried woman old enough to be married, one who is sexually mature (see Genesis 24:43; Exodus 2:8; Psalm 68:25; Proverbs 30:19; Song of Solomon 1:3; 6:8). Some have compared this young woman to Isaiah's young wife, who gave him a son (Isaiah 8:1-4). This is not likely because she had already borne a child, Shear-Jashub, and her second child was not named Immanuel. Some believe that Isaiah's first wife may have died, and so this is his second wife. It is more likely that this prophecy had a double fulfillment. (1) A young woman from the house of Ahaz who was not married would marry and have a son. Before three years passed (one year for pregnancy and two for the child to be old enough to talk), the two invading kings would be destroyed. (2) Matthew 1:23 quotes Isaiah 7:14 to show a further fulfillment of this prophecy in that a virgin named Mary conceived and bore a son, Immanuel, the Christ.

**1:24** **When Joseph awoke from sleep, he did as the angel of the Lord commanded him; he took her as his wife.**NRSV The angel had spoken to Joseph "in a dream" (1:20), so immediately *when Joseph awoke from sleep, he did as the angel of the Lord commanded him.* Joseph had been faced with a difficult choice after discovering that Mary was pregnant. Although he knew that taking Mary as his wife might be humiliating, Joseph chose to obey the angel's command to marry her. He did not hesitate. The decision was no longer difficult, for he simply did what he knew God wanted him to do. His action revealed four admirable qualities: (1) righteousness (1:19), (2) discretion and sensitivity (1:19), (3) responsiveness to God (1:24), and (4) self-discipline (1:25).

Apparently Joseph broke with tradition and *took her as his wife,* even though the customary one-year waiting period had not passed. However, Joseph did as God commanded and "completed" their marriage by taking Mary to live with him. No matter what the social stigma, no matter what the local gossips thought about this move, Joseph knew he was following God's command in marrying and caring for Mary during her pregnancy.

---

**"BUT WHAT WILL EVERYONE THINK?"**
Joseph changed his plans quickly after learning about God's plan for his life from the angel. He obeyed God and proceeded with the marriage plans. Although others may have disapproved of his decision, Joseph went ahead with what he knew was right. Sometimes we avoid doing what is right because of what others might think. Like Joseph, we must choose to obey God rather than seek the approval of others.

---

**1:25 But had no marital relations with her until she had borne a son; and he named him Jesus.**<sup>NRSV</sup> To squelch any doubts about the conception and birth of Jesus while Mary was still a virgin, Matthew explained that Joseph *had no marital relations with her* until after the son was born. These words also set aside the notion that Mary lived her whole life as a virgin; after Jesus' birth, Joseph and Mary consummated their marriage, and Jesus had several half brothers (12:46). Two of Jesus' half brothers figured in the early church—James, leader of the church in Jerusalem, and Jude, writer of the book that bears his name.

Traditionally, baby boys were circumcised and named eight days after birth. Luke records that "on the eighth day, when it was time to circumcise him, he was named Jesus" (Luke 2:21 NIV). Joseph did everything that God had told him through the angel (1:21), naming the baby his God-given name: *Jesus.*

# Matthew 2

Only Matthew has a record of the visit of the wise men. These men
traveled thousands of miles to see the king of the Jews. When they
finally found him, they responded with joy, worship, and gifts. This
is so different from the approach people often take today. Some
expect God to come looking for us, to explain himself, prove who
he is, and give *us* gifts. But the truly wise still seek and worship
Jesus today for who he is, not for what they can get.

**2:1 Now after Jesus was born in Bethlehem of Judea in the days
of Herod the king.**NKJV Matthew did not record the details of
Jesus' birth, as did Luke in the well-known chapter 2 of his
Gospel. Instead, after stating that Mary had given birth to a son
(1:25), Matthew moved to the time *after Jesus was born in
Bethlehem of Judea.* Most scholars believe that the traditional
nonbiblical picture of the wise men arriving at the manger is
incorrect based on clues given in this chapter. More likely, the
wise men arrived some time after Jesus' birth—Jesus is called
a child (*paidion,* 2:9, 11) rather than a baby or infant (*brephos,*
used in Luke 2:12), and the wise men went to a house (2:11),
not to a stable. The fact that Herod had all the baby boys under
two years old killed (2:16) may mean that a couple of years
had passed between Jesus' birth and this visit. If so, apparently
Mary and Joseph decided to remain for a time in Bethlehem
instead of returning after the census taking (Luke 2:1-5) to
Nazareth. Matthew 13:55 and Mark 6:3 describe Joseph as a
*tekton,* that is, a builder and possibly contractor, not just a
carpenter. This may have involved a lot of travel, which would
explain his mobile lifestyle.

While we cannot know exactly when this story took place, we
do know more details about other elements. The tiny village of
*Bethlehem* is located about five miles south of Jerusalem and sits
on a high ridge more than two thousand feet above sea level.
This little village held great significance for the Jews. Jacob had
buried his beloved wife Rachel in Bethlehem (Genesis 35:19);

## GOSPEL ACCOUNTS FOUND ONLY IN MATTHEW

Matthew records nine special events that are not mentioned in any of the other Gospels. In each case, the most apparent reason involves his purpose in communicating the gospel to Jewish people. Five cases are fulfillments of Old Testament prophecies (marked with asterisks below). The other four would have been of particular interest to the Jews of Matthew's day.

| Passage | Subject |
|---------|---------|
| 1:20-24 | Joseph's dream* |
| 2:1-12 | The visit of the Magi |
| 2:13-15 | Escape to Egypt* |
| 2:16-18 | Slaughter of the children* |
| 27:3-10 | The death of Judas* |
| 27:19 | The dream of Pilate's wife |
| 27:52 | The other resurrections |
| 28:11-15 | The bribery of the guards |
| 28:19-20 | The baptism emphasis in the Great Commission* |

Ruth had met Boaz in Bethlehem (Ruth 1:22–2:6); King David had grown up in Bethlehem (1 Samuel 16:1; 17:12). Even more important, the prophet Micah had prophesied that the Messiah would be born there: "But you, Bethlehem Ephrathah, though you are small among the clans of Judah, out of you will come for me one who will be ruler over Israel, whose origins are from of old, from ancient times" (Micah 5:2 NIV).

To distinguish this Bethlehem from other towns with the same name, Matthew added *of Judea*. The land of Israel was divided into four political districts and several lesser territories. Judea (also called Judah) was to the south, Samaria in the middle, Galilee to the north, and Idumea to the southeast.

Jerusalem was also in Judea and was the seat of government for *Herod the king*. While many Herods are mentioned in the Bible, this was Herod the Great, named king over all four political districts of Palestine by the Roman Senate. He ruled from 37 to 4 B.C. The history of the Herod family is filled with lies, murder, treachery, and adultery. Although Herod the Great was a ruthless, evil man who murdered many in his own family, he also supervised the renovation of the temple, making it much larger and more beautiful, as well as overseeing other building projects. This made him popular with many Jews. After Herod's death, the districts were divided among three separate rulers. We later read about Herod the Great's son, Herod Antipas, who killed John the Baptist (Mark 6:26-28) and taunted Jesus (Luke 23:6-12).

**Behold, wise men from the East came to Jerusalem.**NKJV Not much is known about these *wise men.* Also called Magi, they may have interpreted dreams and had other special knowledge and abilities; they specialized in astronomy. They may have been from the priestly caste in Persia; they were *not* kings. We don't know where they came from; the Bible just says *from the East.* Tradition says they were men of high position from Parthia, near the site of ancient Babylon (the book of Daniel refers to the wise men of Babylon; see Daniel 2:12, 18; 4:6, 18). The traditional view that there were three wise men comes from the three gifts presented to Jesus (2:11), but the Bible doesn't say how many wise men came. These men came from the East *to Jerusalem.* If they traveled from Parthia, they had covered thousands of miles in their quest to find a newborn king.

**2:2 Saying, "Where is He who has been born King of the Jews? For we have seen His star in the East and have come to worship Him."** NKJV The wise men said they had seen Jesus' star (*His star*). In the Old Testament, through a man named Balaam, God had referred to "a star" coming out of Jacob (Numbers 24:17 NIV). How did these wise men know that the star represented the Messiah, the one who was *born King of the Jews?* (1) They could have been Jews who remained in Babylon after the Exile and knew the Old Testament predictions of the Messiah's coming. (2) They may have been eastern astrologers who studied ancient manuscripts from around the world. Because of the Jewish exile centuries earlier, a large Jewish population still existed there, and they would have had copies of the Old Testament. (3) They may have had a special message from God directing them to the Messiah.

Some say this star may have been a conjunction of Jupiter, Saturn, and Mars in 6 B.C.; others offer many other explanations. However, no explanation accounts for the star moving as described in 2:9. We don't know if the miraculous element took the form of the timely conjunction of the planets, or if God, who created the heavens, created a special event to signal the arrival of his Son, just as he had created a pillar of cloud and of fire to lead the nation of Israel to the Promised Land (Exodus 13:21-22). Based on the significance of the star, these wise men traveled thousands of miles searching for the one who had been born King of the

> Worship is a meeting between God and His people when the worshiper is brought into personal contact with the one who gives meaning and purpose to life; from this encounter the worshiper receives strength and courage to live with hope in a fallen world. *Robert Webber*

Jews. When they found him, they worshiped him. While their worship was probably meant to be no more than homage to royalty (notice that Jesus did not "become" king of the Jews, he was "born" king of the Jews), the homage paid to this young king was more respect than he received from many of his own people.

Astrology and those who practiced the art were held in contempt by the Bible and by God-fearing Jews (Isaiah 47:13-15; Jeremiah 10:1-2; Daniel 2:10; 4:7). Matthew made a significant point in highlighting the worship of these wise men (who were pagan astrologers, wise in the ways of secular science, diviners, and magicians) in contrast to the Jewish religious leaders who knew the Holy Scriptures and did not need to travel far to find their Messiah. The Jewish leaders directed the wise men to Bethlehem but apparently did not go themselves (2:4-6). Some scholars say these wise men were each from a different land, representing the entire world bowing before Jesus. These men from faraway lands recognized Jesus as the Messiah when most of God's chosen people in Israel did not. Matthew pictures Jesus as King over the whole world, not just Judea.

---

LOOKING FOR GOD?
How can we learn about God? Some people say, "I find God on a nature hike when the wind whistles through trees and the stars shine brightly." Others say, "Read the Bible and you'll discover God." And yet others, "Only by believing in Jesus can a person ever know God."

Here we learn that all three ways of knowing God are important. The wise men were drawn to worship by a bright heavenly radiance. They came close (Jerusalem) and got specific instruction from people who knew the Old Testament well. Then, unlike Herod and the priests, they actually finished the journey and saw Jesus, who was then a little child. All three ways of finding God helped the wise men finish their journey.

If you want to find God, see his glory in nature, learn of his promises in the Bible, and discover Jesus by getting to know him personally.

---

**2:3 When Herod the king heard this, he was troubled, and all Jerusalem with him.**NKJV The wise men traveled to Jerusalem, the capital city, expecting to find a young king there. However, Herod the Great did not even know about the birth of someone who was to be king. This obviously *troubled* him for several reasons:

- Herod was not the rightful heir to the throne of David. He was partly Jewish, but descended not from Jacob but from Esau. He was an Idumean Arab, but honestly considered himself Jewish by religion. His people had been forcefully converted a century earlier (126 B.C.), but Herod considered himself a faithful Jew. He reigned by appointment from Rome. Many Jews hated Herod as a usurper, even though Herod attempted to boost his popularity among the Jews by doing much for their country (see Josephus's *Antiquities* 13.258). If this baby really was a rightful heir to the throne, Herod could face trouble from the Jews who might want to make the baby king.

- Herod was ruthless, and because of his many enemies, he was suspicious that someone would try to overthrow him. Many feel he had become mentally unstable by this time in his life.
- Herod didn't want the Jews, a religious people, to unite around a religious figure.
- If these wise men were of Jewish descent and from Parthia (the most powerful region next to Rome), they would have welcomed a Jewish king who could swing the balance of power away from Rome. The land of Israel, far from Rome, would have been easy prey for a nation trying to gain more control.

The wise men's news troubled Herod because he knew that the Jewish people expected the Messiah to come soon (Luke 3:15). Most Jews expected the Messiah to be a great military and political deliverer, like Alexander the Great.

That *all Jerusalem* was troubled along with King Herod indicates that the leaders and lay people also felt concern over word of a child born in the Jewish royal line, the line of David. What would this mean? Any who knew Herod's ruthlessness may have feared his aroused suspicions. Such fear was well founded considering Herod's actions recorded in 2:16.

**THE GREAT TROUBLEMAKER**
When Jesus was born into our world, people immediately began to react. His presence did not soothe and comfort people; instead, it startled and disturbed them. In some, he awakened spiritual longings; in others, fear and insecurity. If it is true that God entered our world when Jesus was born, we dare not sit idly by ignoring and rationalizing our inaction. We must acknowledge Jesus as the rightful King of our lives. He did not stay in the manger.

**2:4 When he had called together all the people's chief priests and teachers of the law, he asked them where the Christ was to be born.**NIV Herod needed some advice from the experts. So he *called together all the people's chief priests and teachers of the law.* While Herod did not call a formal meeting of the Sanhedrin, he probably called together a group of leaders living in Jerusalem who could tell him what he wanted to know. The "chief priests" were probably mostly Sadducees, while the "teachers of the law" (sometimes called "scribes") were mostly Pharisees. These two groups did not get along because of vast differences in their beliefs about the law. The Sadducees believed only the Pentateuch (the first five books of the Old Testament) to be God's Word; the Pharisees and teachers of the law were the professional interpreters of the law, the legal specialists of Jesus' day. They interpreted the law but were especially concerned about the "halakah" or "rules" for life that came to be as binding as God's written law in the Torah. Among these men Herod hoped to find someone who could explain *where the Christ was to be born.* Herod apparently understood that the King of the Jews sought by the wise men was also "the Christ," that is, the Jews' promised Messiah. However, the Jews expected their Messiah to be a political leader, accounting for Herod's interest and concern.

---

SO CLOSE; SO FAR
Herod asked the religious leaders and teachers to tell him what the Scriptures said about the location of the Messiah's birth. These religious leaders and teachers had knowledge of the Scriptures, but they lacked the desire to understand and believe. With so many churches nearby, so many Christian books and Bibles available, so many radio and television programs, so many Christian videos and films—how can anyone not believe? But it happens. Several Bibles on your bedroom shelf and perfect Sunday school attendance do not a Christian make! Like the chief priests and teachers of the law, a person can miss the opportunity to believe in Jesus completely while studying the facts of the Bible meticulously.

Becoming a Christian means giving your life to Jesus Christ in faith. In a simple prayer, give up trying so hard to be so good. Admit to God your need, and accept in faith his promise to save you.

---

**2:5-6 "In Bethlehem in Judea," they replied, "for this is what the prophet has written: 'But you, Bethlehem, in the land of Judah, are by no means least among the rulers of Judah; for out of you will come a ruler who will be the shepherd of my people Israel.'"** NIV The answer to Herod's question was simple, for *the prophet* Micah had given the exact location of the Messiah's birth seven centuries earlier in Micah 5:2. Matthew often quoted Old Testament prophets to show how perfectly Jesus fulfilled the prophecies about the Messiah. The religious leaders quoted from Micah 5:2 and 2 Samuel 5:2. As the grandson of an Idumean Jew,

Herod may have known about messianic prophecies, but he was not trained in knowing anything specific. The Jewish religious leaders understood that the Messiah would be born *in Bethlehem in Judea*. In fact, the Messiah's birth in Bethlehem was well-known to all Jews (John 7:41-42). Ironically, when Jesus was born, these same religious leaders became his greatest enemies. When the Messiah for whom they had been waiting finally came, they wouldn't recognize him.

**2:7 Then Herod secretly called for the wise men and learned from them the exact time when the star had appeared.**<sup>NRSV</sup> Herod had a problem on his hands, and already his troubled mind was making a plan. He called the wise men back to him in order to answer their question (2:2) and send them along to Bethlehem. However, Herod also needed some information from them. He needed to know the age of this "king." Herod deduced that if he knew *the exact time when the star had appeared,* he would know the child's age. We infer from this that the star had appeared a couple of years earlier, for when Herod went on his murderous rampage, he ordered the killing of all boys two years old and under (2:16), although he may have added to the age to make sure the child would be destroyed.

**2:8 He sent them to Bethlehem and said, "Go and make a careful search for the child. As soon as you find him, report to me, so that I too may go and worship him."**<sup>NIV</sup> Discovering that this future king was not in Jerusalem, King Herod sent the wise men down the road to the little village of *Bethlehem* to *make a careful search for the child.* Not knowing the age of the child, nor exactly where he would be found, might make for a difficult and lengthy search. Herod certainly wondered how they would know this child even if they found him. But Herod would not let rumor of a future king go unchecked. So he sent the wise men on their way, instructing them to return to Jerusalem after they found the child. Herod's reason? *So that I too may go and worship him,* he explained. This deceitful ruse fooled the wise men, and they agreed to return and *report to* Herod the whereabouts of the child. The wise men had no reason to expect that Herod would do anything other than pay homage to a king, and Herod had no reason to think that the wise men would not return with the information he needed. But Herod did not want to worship Christ—he was lying. Herod planned to kill Jesus.

**2:9 After they had heard the king, they went on their way, and the star they had seen in the east went ahead of them until it stopped over the place where the child was.**<sup>NIV</sup> Having been told that the child was to be born in Bethlehem, the wise men left Jerusalem, heading south. As *they went on their way,* suddenly they saw once again *the star they had seen in the east.* The wise men had followed this star thousands of miles, traveling west toward Jerusalem. At this point, the star reappeared as they traveled south toward Bethlehem, moving *ahead of them.* Then, the star *stopped over the place where the child was.* Obviously this was no ordinary star (see comments on 2:2). Matthew does not tell us what the star looked like, how it moved, or how the wise men found the child from the movement and stopping of the star. But Matthew made his point that God had purposely sent this star to guide these men to his Son.

> God comes to men in the spheres with which they are most familiar; to Zacharias in the Temple, to the shepherds in the fields, to the wise men by a portent in the heavens. He knows just where to find us. Be sure to follow your star, whatever it be; only remember that it must ultimately receive the corroboration of Scripture.    *F. B. Meyer*

**2:10** **When they saw that the star had stopped, they were overwhelmed with joy.**<sup>NRSV</sup> The star's movement had been constant and visible to these men who studied the sky and watched the stars. They had followed this star across thousands of miles. They had not found the child in the palace in Jerusalem as they had expected. So they had wearily continued on their way, only to once again follow the moving star. No wonder that *when they saw that the star had stopped, they were overwhelmed with joy.* Their journey was completed; they had found the one for whom they were searching.

---

FINDING CHRIST
The wise men were overjoyed at finding the child. If you think becoming a Christian means putting on a long face and behaving like a person in a straitjacket, think again. Finding Christ brings real joy—deeper than winning at sports, more enduring than the first test drive in that new car—this joy fills the soul and makes you glad. This joy comes from knowing all is well, you're OK, God loves you, the future will be secure.
Have you been on a journey to find yourself, to find love, satisfaction, or some sense of what this life is all about? There's joy at the end of that journey when you find Christ.

---

**2:11** **And when they had come into the house, they saw the young Child with Mary His mother, and fell down and worshiped Him. And when they had opened their treasures, they presented gifts to Him: gold, frankincense, and myrrh.**<sup>NKJV</sup> Jesus was probably one or two years old (a *young Child*) when the wise men found him. By this time, Mary and Joseph were married, living in a *house* and intending to stay in Bethlehem for a while. The wise men gave expensive gifts because these were worthy presents for a future king. The wise men were simply bringing customary expensive gifts for a superior, but scholars have seen in the gifts symbols of Christ's identity and what he would accomplish. *Gold* was a gift for a king (Psalm 72:15). *Frankincense* (also simply called "incense"), a glittering, odorous gum obtained from the bark of certain trees, was a gift for deity (Isaiah 60:6). *Myrrh,* a valued spice and perfume (Psalm 45:8), also came from trees and was used in embalming; thus, it was a gift for a person who was going to die (Mark 15:23; John 19:39). These gifts certainly would have provided the financial resources for Joseph and Mary's trip to Egypt and back (2:13-23).

These wise men, astrologers from the east, *fell down and worshiped* the young king of the Jews, indicating a further fulfillment of prophecy. Psalm 72:10-19 speaks of a coming king before whom all will bow and whom all nations will serve.

---

HE ALONE IS WORTHY
The wise men brought gifts and worshiped Jesus for who he was. This is the essence of true worship—honoring Christ for who he is and being willing to give him what is valuable to you. We see in their lives a pattern for worship:

- *They entered.* They had prepared for their journey, studied, and sought out Jesus.
- *They bowed.* They humbled themselves in the presence of their superior. They acknowledged his authority.
- *They gave.* They gave expensive and sacrificial gifts out of respect and honor for the child king.
- *They worshiped.* They recognized God's guidance in bringing them and attested to Jesus' royalty. They exalted Jesus as the rightful king.
- *They obeyed.* Their worship was not empty. They followed the guidance they received from God.

Worship God because he is the perfect, just, and almighty Creator of the universe, worthy of the best you have to give.

---

2:12 **And having been warned in a dream not to go back to Herod, they returned to their country by another route.**<sup>NIV</sup> After finding Jesus and worshiping him, the wise men were warned by God *in a dream* not to return through Jerusalem and take their news *back to Herod* as they had intended. God gave guidance to Joseph at four separate times in dreams (see 1:20; 2:13, 19, 22). The first three times, the angel of the Lord is specifically mentioned as appearing and delivering God's message to Joseph. The angel is not mentioned as appearing to the wise men, but somehow God guided the wise men in a dream. The wise men "wisely" followed the guidance given them; after worshiping the child, they *returned to their country by another route.* Going back through Jerusalem would make it impossible to avoid Herod; so they apparently went out of Bethlehem in another direction, perhaps continuing south and going around the southern end of the Dead Sea before heading back north and east. It took courage to refuse the king's command; it also took courage to follow guidance that added many miles to their already lengthy journey.

In this story, God reveals his care for his Son as the hostile world already was attempting to take the young child's life. Matthew has divine intervention as a major theme. He shows how God superintends Jesus' life in order to accomplish the divine plan.

## THE ESCAPE TO EGYPT / 2:13-18 / **13**

Even before the tiny baby could speak, the worldly powers, led by Satan himself, were moving against him. Herod, a ruthless king who had killed three of his own sons to secure his power, was afraid of losing that power, so he embarked on a plan to kill the tiny child who had been born "king of the Jews." In his madness, Herod murdered innocent children, hoping to kill this one child. Herod stained his hands with blood, but he did not harm Jesus. No one can thwart God's plans.

**2:13-14 When they had gone, an angel of the Lord appeared to Joseph in a dream. "Get up," he said, "take the child and his mother and escape to Egypt. Stay there until I tell you, for Herod is going to search for the child to kill him."** NIV This was

the second dream or vision that Joseph received from God. Joseph's first dream had revealed that Mary's child would be the Messiah (1:20-21). His second dream told him how to protect the child's life. Even though the wise men didn't return to Herod, Herod did not give up on his evil plan. *An angel of the Lord* warned Joseph that *Herod is going to search for the child to kill him.* Joseph had to move immediately; it

> Faith means taking the bare Word of God and acting upon it because it is the Word of God. It means believing what God says simply and solely because He has said it.
>
> *Martyn Lloyd-Jones*

would not be long before Herod would realize that he had been tricked and would unleash his anger. The angel told Joseph exactly what to do, and Joseph obeyed.

**Then Joseph got up, took the child and his mother by night, and went to Egypt.** NRSV Joseph *got up* after this dream, took Jesus and Mary, and began the seventy-five mile journey to Egypt *by night,* escaping from Bethlehem under cover of darkness. The angel instructed Joseph to remain in Egypt until God told him otherwise *(stay there until I tell you)* through another dream (see 2:20). Going to Egypt was not unusual. Egypt had been a place of refuge for Israelites during times of political upheaval (1 Kings 11:40; 2 Kings 25:26). There were colonies of Jews in several major Egyptian cities (Alexandria was a key center of Jewish knowledge and education). These colonies had developed during the time of the great captivity (see Jeremiah 43–44) and may have numbered as many as one million Jews. Egypt was a Roman province, but outside Herod's jurisdiction. Even more important, however, this event fulfilled the prophecy of Hosea (see 2:15).

**2:15** **And remained there until the death of Herod. This was to fulfill what had been spoken by the Lord through the prophet,**

**"Out of Egypt I have called my son."** NRSV Joseph followed the angel's instructions and remained in Egypt *until the death of Herod* (see 2:19-20). Thus, Jesus was kept safe.

There is an interesting parallel between this flight to Egypt and Israel's history. Hosea wrote about God's love for Israel and his promise of a deliverer who would draw them to himself. Matthew viewed Hosea's prophecy in light of Jesus Christ as the one who came as the promised deliverer of Israel and of the entire world. As an infant nation, Israel had gone to Egypt, just as Jesus did as a child. Joseph had been taken as a captive to Egypt when he was sold into slavery by his brothers. His brothers had almost killed him, but he was kept safe in Egypt. There is also a parallel between the Egyptian pharaoh's killing of the baby boys of the Israelites

**The Flight to Egypt**
*Herod planned to kill the baby Jesus, whom he perceived to be a future threat to his position. Warned of this treachery in a dream, Joseph took his family to Egypt until Herod's death, which occurred a year or two later. They then planned to return to Judea, but God led them instead to Nazareth in Galilee.*

and Herod's killing of the baby boys in Bethlehem. Years later, in the Exodus, God led Israel out; God had brought Jesus back. Thus, the prophet Hosea's words, *"Out of Egypt I have called my son"* (Hosea 11:1), see Israel's miracle-filled Exodus from Egypt as foreshadowing Jesus' return from Egypt to Israel. And in Jesus, the restoration of Israel from exile is complete.

**2:16** **When Herod saw that he had been tricked by the wise men, he was infuriated, and he sent and killed all the children in and around Bethlehem who were two years old or under, according to the time that he had learned from the wise men.**[NRSV] The events recorded in 2:7-14 most likely happened over just a couple of days. Bethlehem was only five miles from Jerusalem and was a small village. It would not have taken long for the wise men to find the child. Herod certainly expected the wise men to return within a day. But in the meantime, both the wise men and Jesus' family had escaped the city. Probably by the next evening, *Herod saw that he had been tricked* (literally "outwitted") *by the wise men.* Herod was not just upset, *he was infuriated.* And when this king became infuriated, his anger knew no bounds. History documents the terrible acts of this evil man— especially concerning potential rivals to the throne. In his later years, Herod had three of his sons killed, as well as his wife and many actual or suspected conspirators. It did not bother Herod to spill some blood to secure his power.

At this point, all Herod knew was that a future king, still a child, lived in Bethlehem. After the wise men explained when the star had first appeared (2:7), Herod deduced that the child would not be more than two years old. So *according to the time that he had learned from the wise men,* he dispatched his soldiers, and they *killed all the* (male) *children in and around Bethlehem who were two years old or under.* Scholars have estimated that if this tiny village had about one thousand residents, there may have been about twenty male babies. The record of this atrocity is told only here, so some have doubted its authenticity. Considering Herod's ruthlessness and the murderous acts already listed under his name, apparently the slaughter of a few children in an insignificant village did not make the historical annals. There are examples of Romans having entire towns razed, killing every living creature, just as an example to a region. So while the "slaughter of the innocents" by Herod was terrible, it was not as uncommon as we think. But Matthew saw it as fulfillment of Scripture (2:17-18).

Modern readers question how God could allow such evil to occur even as he allowed Jesus to escape it. Yet Matthew did not ask that question. He, as a Jew, knew all too well that the history of God's people was littered with hatred and evil acts against them. The coming of the Messiah caused Satan to unleash an arsenal of evil. In this instance, Satan used Herod, a willing vessel. Herod, the king of the Jews, killed all the boys under two years of age in an obsessive attempt to kill Jesus, the newborn King.

---

WHO'S ON THE THRONE?
Herod was afraid that this newborn king would one day take his throne. He completely misunderstood the reason for Christ's coming. Jesus didn't want Herod's throne; he wanted to be king of Herod's life. Jesus wanted to give Herod eternal life, not take his present life. Today people are often afraid that Christ wants to take things away when, in reality, he wants to give them real freedom, peace, and joy. Don't fear Christ—allow him to reign on the throne of your life.

---

**:17-18** **Then what was said through the prophet Jeremiah was fulfilled: "A voice is heard in Ramah, weeping and great mourning, Rachel weeping for her children and refusing to be comforted, because they are no more."**NIV Matthew saw that the grieving of the mothers in Bethlehem further fulfilled the words of Jeremiah the prophet in Jeremiah 31:15. *Rachel* was one of the wives of Jacob, one of the great men of God in the Old Testament. From Jacob's twelve sons had come the twelve tribes of Israel. Rachel was the symbolic mother of the nation; she had been buried near Bethlehem (Genesis 35:19). The Jeremiah passage describes Rachel, the "mother" of the nation, *weeping for her children* who had been taken away into captivity. *Ramah* was a staging point of deportation (Jeremiah 40:1). The mothers in Bethlehem also wept and mourned for the little boys killed by the soldiers; certainly their sorrow was so great that they could not be comforted. Matthew compared the grief of the mothers at the time of the Exile to the grief of the mothers of the slaughtered children.

> It is a terrible and awful story, that of his [Jeremiah's] prophesying, and suffering, and tears. But in Jeremiah, as in every other prophecy, there was a gleam of the glory of hope. How great were these Hebrew prophets— so cloudy, so rough, so stormy; but on every storm-cloud there is a rainbow, and the promise of deliverance.
>
> *G. Campbell Morgan*

WHEN WE GRIEVE
With the slaughter of these young children, there was much
grief and suffering. Matthew implies that the weeping of these
mothers connects to a long tradition of grieving. Rachel, the
mother of Israel, weeps with the Bethlehem mothers.

When a loved one dies, feelings of loss are strong and
sometimes overwhelming. How should Christians help a friend
deal with his or her grief?

Some well-meaning comforters advise keeping a "stiff upper
lip" in view of the departed's heavenly reward. "Don't cry, she's
in a better place" is the comforting phrase. In other settings,
where busy people don't know each other well, grief takes its
course until everyone gets back to business. "She needs time"
is the phrase they use to keep a distance.

However, helping someone through grief really means that
we cry together, we share the sadness, we enter the other's
world.

## THE RETURN TO NAZARETH / 2:19-23 / **14**

God carefully protected his Son's life, guiding Joseph as he took
the child away from Israel when he was in danger, and then as
he returned to Israel when it was once again safe. Jesus had not
come to earth to minister in Egypt; he had come to his own
people as their Messiah. Thus, God returned him to Israel and
guided his parents as they raised him in Nazareth. God was working out his plan of salvation for our sakes. Believers ought to
read this story with awe as they watch God working behind
the scenes to protect the life of Jesus Christ on this earth.

**2:19-21** **After Herod died, an angel of the Lord appeared in a dream
to Joseph in Egypt and said, "Get up, take the child and his
mother and go to the land of Israel, for those who were trying
to take the child's life are dead."** NIV The angel of the Lord had
promised that Joseph would be told when it would be safe for
him and his family to return to Israel: "Stay there until I tell you"
(2:13). Israel was not safe while Herod the Great ruled. But *after
Herod died* (in 4 B.C. of an incurable disease), the angel appeared
once again in a dream to direct Joseph. The angel instructed
Joseph to return to Israel because *those who were trying to take
the child's life are dead.* The plural "those" used here was most
likely a generalized term including Herod and all those under his
orders.

If Christ was born one to two years before Herod's death, that
would mean that he was born in 6 B.C., that is, six years "before

Christ." The confusion was caused by a switch from the Roman
to the Christian calendar in the sixth century A.D., based on the
faulty calculations of Dionysius Exiguus, who must not have had
accurate information about the date of Herod's death.

Joseph did as the angel said. **Then Joseph got up, took the
child and his mother, and went to the land of Israel.**NRSV
How long they had been in Egypt is unknown. But when the
angel commanded them to return to Israel, Joseph did not
hesitate.

**2:22** **But when he heard that Archelaus was ruling over Judea in
place of his father Herod, he was afraid to go there. And after
being warned in a dream, he went away to the district of Galilee.**NRSV Rome had trusted Herod the Great but didn't trust his
sons. Herod knew that Rome wouldn't give his successor as
much power, so he divided his kingdom into three parts, one for
each son. *Archelaus* received Judea, Samaria, and Idumea, *ruling
over Judea in place of his father Herod.* Herod Antipas received
Galilee and Perea; Herod Philip II received Traconitis. Archelaus,
a violent man, began his reign by slaughtering three thousand
influential people. He was known for his instability; in fact, he
proved to be such a poor ruler that he was deposed in A.D. 6.
Joseph had heard about Archelaus and was *afraid to go* back to
Bethlehem, which was in the district of Judea. Once again, God
guided Joseph, warning him in a dream not to go into the region
of this evil ruler. So Joseph took the family north to *the district
of Galilee.*

**2:23** **And he went and lived in a town called Nazareth. So was
fulfilled what was said through the prophets: "He will be
called a Nazarene."** NIV Joseph returned to his hometown of
Nazareth (Luke 2:4). *Nazareth* sat in the hilly area of southern
Galilee near the crossroads of great caravan trade routes. The
town itself was rather small. The Roman garrison in charge of
Galilee was housed there. The people of Nazareth had constant
contact with people from all over the world, so world news
reached them quickly. The people of Nazareth had an attitude
of independence that many of the Jews despised. This may
have been why Nathanael later commented, "Nazareth! Can
anything good come from there?" (John 1:46 NIV).

The Old Testament does not record the specific statement *He
will be called a Nazarene.* Many scholars believe, however, that
Matthew was referring to Isaiah 11:1 where the Hebrew word for
"branch" *(netser)* is similar to the word for "Nazarene." Others
say he may have been referring to a prophecy unrecorded in the

Bible, or to a combination of prophecies (because he used the plural *prophets*). Matthew painted a picture of Jesus as the true Messiah announced by God through the prophets; he made the point that Jesus, the Messiah, had unexpectedly humble beginnings and would be despised by those to whom he came, just as the Old Testament had predicted.

# Matthew 3

When John "came preaching" (3:1), the people were excited. They
considered John to be a great prophet, and they were sure that the
eagerly awaited age of the Messiah had come. Indeed, it had, and
God was ushering in a brand-new covenant and a new era in his
dealings with humanity. John spoke like the prophets of old, saying
that the people must turn from their sin to avoid punishment and
turn to God to experience his mercy and approval. This is a message for all times and places, but John spoke it with particular
urgency—he was preparing the people for the coming Messiah
and for his kingdom. Our calling is similar to John's, for we, too,
can prepare the way for others to come to Jesus. How much
urgency do you feel for those who still need to hear the message?

**3:1 In those days John the Baptist came preaching in the wilder-
ness of Judea.**NKJV "In those days" is an Old Testament phrase
that points to a critical period of time. It relates to 2:23, loosely
referring to the days when Jesus lived in Nazareth. However,
twenty-eight to thirty years have elapsed since Joseph returned
with the young Jesus and Mary from Egypt back to Israel. He
did not settle in Judea but moved north instead to Galilee and
the city of Nazareth.

But in *the wilderness of Judea* (the rugged land west of the
Dead Sea), a significant event began to occur: *John the Baptist
came preaching.* In these five words, Matthew summed up the
story that Luke would record in greater detail (see Luke 1:5-25,
39-45, 57-80). John was a miracle child, born to Elizabeth and
Zacharias (Zechariah, in some Bible versions). Elizabeth was
unable to have children, and advanced age rendered her and
Zacharias certain to remain childless.

Zacharias was a priest. One day, while he was carrying out his
duties in the temple, the angel Gabriel appeared to him and
explained that Zacharias and Elizabeth would have a baby boy
whom they should name John. Then he added: "He will turn
many of the people of Israel to the Lord their God. With the spirit

and power of Elijah he will go before him, to turn the hearts of parents to their children, and the disobedient to the wisdom of the righteous, to make ready a people prepared for the Lord" (Luke 1:16-17 NRSV). There had not been a prophet in Israel for more than four hundred years. It was widely believed that when the Messiah came, prophecy would reappear (Joel 2:28-29; Malachi 3:1; 4:5). John was that prophet, preaching a message of repentance. The word translated "preaching" comes from the Greek word meaning "to be a herald, to proclaim." Matthew described John as a herald proclaiming

> To us also John the Baptist must come if we shall properly appreciate the Redeemer. We must expose ourselves to the fire, the ax, the winnowing-fan, that we may learn what we really are, and come, like Paul, to reckon our own righteousness as loss if only we may win Christ and be found in him.
>
> *F. B. Meyer*

news of the coming King, the Messiah. The title "the Baptist" distinguished this John from many other men with the same name—baptism was an important part of his ministry (3:6).

John's mother, Elizabeth, was a cousin to Jesus' mother, Mary. Thus, Jesus and John the Baptist were distant cousins. It is likely that they knew of each other, but John probably did not know that Jesus was the Messiah until Jesus' baptism by John (see 3:16-17).

**3:2 "Repent, for the kingdom of heaven has come near."**NRSV John the Baptist's preaching focused specifically on one message—preparing hearts for the coming Messiah. Preparation could only occur through repentance. John called the people to *repent*—to turn away from sins and turn toward God. To be truly repentant, people must do both. Without apology or hesitation, John preached that the people could not say they believed and then live any way they wanted (see 3:7-8). They had to understand that they were sinners, that sin is wrong, and that they needed to change both their attitude and their conduct. Repentance was a radical concept for Jews who considered themselves already "the people of God." In the Old Testament, "repent" means the radical return to God of those who have broken the covenant with him. John used the word this way.

Why did they need this radical repentance? Because *the kingdom of heaven* had arrived. The kingdom of heaven began when God himself entered human history as a man. Passages referring to God's kingdom appear 50 times in Matthew's Gospel alone; the phrase "kingdom of heaven" occurs 33 times. Mark and Luke refer to it as the "kingdom of God." This is a "kingdom" where God reigns. The phrase indicates a present reality and a future hope. Matthew's use of "kingdom of heaven" relates to his Jewish audience and their reluctance to use the name of God. But there is no theological distinction implied between "kingdom of heaven" and "kingdom of God." Today Jesus Christ reigns in the hearts of believers, but the kingdom of heaven will not be fully realized until all evil in the world is judged and removed. Christ came to earth first as a suffering Servant; he will come again as King and Judge to rule victoriously over all the earth.

The phrase "has come near" portrays that God has interrupted history with a dramatic new revelation of his power. Discussion of the timing of the arrival of God's kingdom fills many pages of scholarly work. The issues seem to fall into three main views:

1. *Futurist*—Since the Old Testament view of the kingdom of God refers to his rule over a geographical area and in a political reality, this rule must be in the future. Thus, Jesus was announcing that the rule was "near" or "at hand." Most Jews held this view and would not accept the message of repentance.
2. *Realized*—This view sees God's kingdom as announced and inaugurated with Jesus' ministry on earth. The rule of Satan's kingdom was broken as Jesus cast out demons. With Jesus' initiation of God's rule on earth, all humanity must carry out his will by living in love and peace on earth.
3. *Two-pronged approach*—This view recognizes the kingdom of God as both present and future. The rule of God transcends all time. God ruled before Christ came to earth, but in the ministry of Christ, new power was released through Christ, requiring people to encounter and decide to follow God. This looks forward both to the Resurrection and to Pentecost for further authentication and enabling. However, God's geographical and political rule will be revealed at a future time when Christ returns.

---

**TURN AROUND**
John the Baptist's theme was "Repent!" Repentance means doing an about-face—a 180-degree turn—from the kind of self-centeredness that leads to wrong actions such as lying, cheating, stealing, gossiping, taking revenge, abusing, and indulging in sexual immorality. A person who stops rebelling and begins following God's way of living prescribed in his Word is a person who has repented. The first step in turning to God is to admit your sin, as John urged. Then God will receive you and help you live the way he wants. Remember that only God can remove sin. He doesn't expect us to clean up our lives before we come to him.

---

This third view integrates the Scriptures and explains the teachings of Christ most satisfyingly. It enables us to see God's kingdom as both present (Matthew 12:28; Luke 7:22-23; 17:20-21) and future (Matthew 6:10; Mark 9:47; Luke 13:28-29).

**3:3  For this is he who was spoken of by the prophet Isaiah, saying: "The voice of one crying in the wilderness: 'Prepare the way of the Lord; make His paths straight.'"**[NKJV] The prophet quoted is *Isaiah* (Isaiah 40:3), one of the greatest prophets of the Old Testament and one of the most quoted in the New. Here Matthew quoted from the Septuagint (often abbreviated as LXX), the Greek version of the Hebrew Old Testament. The second half of the book of Isaiah is devoted to the promise of salvation. Isaiah recorded God's promise to bring the exiles home from Babylon. He also wrote about the coming of the Messiah and the person who would announce his coming, John the Baptist (Isaiah 40:3). Like Isaiah, John was a prophet who urged people to confess their sins and live for God. Both prophets taught that the message of repentance is good news to those who listen and seek the healing forgiveness of God's love, but terrible news to those who refuse to listen and thus cut off their only hope.

Matthew understood that John the Baptist was, in fact, the *voice* that came *crying* out to the people of Israel. The Greek word for "crying" is *boao,* meaning "to cry out with great feeling." John the Baptist's message was full of emotion and came directly from God. John was merely God's mouthpiece for the important message that God was sending to his people: *Prepare the way of the Lord.* How were they to do this?

The word "prepare" refers to making something ready; the word "way" could also be translated "road." The picture could come from the ancient Middle Eastern custom of sending servants ahead of a king to level and clear the roads to make them passable for his journey. The people in Israel needed to prepare their minds to eagerly anticipate their King and Messiah. The verbs are in the imperative, meaning that John spoke them as a military general would speak commands—to be obeyed immediately and without hesitation. Those who accepted John's status as a true prophet from God understood these words as God's words to them, humbled themselves, repented, received baptism, and opened the "way" for their Messiah to take hold of their lives.

John's call to *make His paths straight* meant much the same as preparing the way. The "paths" are the way to people's hearts. For Jesus to be able to reach them, people needed to give up their selfish way of living, renounce their sins, seek God's forgiveness, and establish a relationship with almighty God by believing and obeying his words (Isaiah 1:18-20; 57:15). Again, the verb is in the imperative; John was issuing an impassioned command to his fellow Israelites (see also Luke 7:24-28).

Why did this voice come from *the wilderness?* The word "wilderness," also translated "desert," refers to a lonely, uninhabited place. John preached in the Judean wilderness, the lower Jordan River valley. Isaiah's use of the word "wilderness" alludes to the wilderness experience of the children of Israel on their exodus from Egypt to Canaan. The wilderness represents the place where God would once again act to rescue his people and bring them into fellowship with him.

John the Baptist's powerful, to-the-point preaching and his wilderness living made him a curiosity, separated him from the false piety of many of the religious leaders, and gave him an unmistakable resemblance to the ancient prophets. We can only speculate on John's motives for living in the wilderness. Perhaps he wanted (1) to get away from distractions so he could hear God's instructions; (2) to capture the undivided attention of the people; (3) to symbolize a sharp break with the hypocrisy of the religious leaders who preferred their luxurious homes and positions of authority over doing God's work; and (4) to fulfill Old Testament prophecies that said the Messiah's forerunner would be preaching "in the wilderness."

---

STRAIGHT WAYS
John the Baptist "prepared" the way for Jesus. People who do not know Jesus need to be prepared to meet him. We can prepare them by explaining their need for forgiveness, demonstrating Christ's teachings by our conduct, and telling them how Christ can give their lives meaning. We can "make straight paths for him" by correcting misconceptions that might be hindering people from approaching Christ. Someone you know may be open to a relationship with Christ. Can you be their "John the Baptist"? Are you ready to explain, to challenge, and to win others? Take the first step today.

---

**3:4 Now John wore clothing of camel's hair with a leather belt around his waist, and his food was locusts and wild honey.**<sup></sup>NRSV
John must have presented a strange image! He was outfitted for survival in the wilderness—like a desert monk. He dressed much like the prophet Elijah (2 Kings 1:8). Elijah too had been considered a messenger preparing the way for God (see Malachi 3:1; 4:5). John's striking appearance reinforced his striking message, distinguishing him from the religious leaders, whose flowing robes reflected their great pride in their position (12:38-39). Having

separated himself from the evil and hypocrisy of his day, John lived differently from other people to show that his message was new. John not only preached God's law, he "lived" it. Many people came to hear this preacher who wore odd clothes and ate unusual food. John's appearance and food fit the description of the Nazirite vow (see Luke 1:15; also Numbers 6:1-8). Some people probably came simply out of curiosity and ended up repenting of their sins as they listened to his powerful message. People may be curious about your Christian lifestyle and values. You can use their simple curiosity as an opener to share how Christ makes a difference in you.

His diet, *locusts and wild honey,* was common for survival in the desert regions. Locusts were often roasted and were considered "clean" food for the Jews (Leviticus 11:22); wild honey could be found in abundance, made by the wild bees who nested in the clefts of rocks and in the trees of the valley.

---

BEING WEIRD
John's appearance and lifestyle dramatically contrasted with the people of his day. He looked and lived as he did both out of necessity and to further demonstrate his message. Some people go to great extremes today to demonstrate their loyalty to sports teams: They buy jackets, license plates, ties, and collectibles.

Since the days of the early church, faithful Christians have shown loyalty in many ways. Some have adopted clothes and eating habits similar to John's. Some have tried to imitate Peter or other early Christian leaders.

Today, with so much loyalty evident on any city block (just count the baseball caps), Christians need "caps" to show their commitment to Jesus. And the Bible suggests the most important emblems: attitudes like loving others, being hopeful under stress, and trusting in God for daily needs. Badges like these show others how faith in the living God makes a difference in your life. What loyalties does your life portray?

---

**3:5 People went out to him from Jerusalem and all Judea and the whole region of the Jordan.**<sup>NIV</sup> The verb form of "went out" is in the imperfect tense, indicating continuous action. From *Jerusalem* (the holy city of the Jews) and from *the whole region of the Jordan,* a stream of people constantly flowed into the wilderness to hear John the Baptist preach.

John attracted so many people because he was the first true prophet in four hundred years. His blasting of both Herod and the religious leaders was a daring act that fascinated common people. But John also had strong words for the others in his audience— they too were sinners and needed to repent. His message was powerful and true. The people were expecting a prophet like Elijah (Malachi 4:5; Luke 1:17), and John seemed to be the one!

**3:6 Confessing their sins, they were baptized by him in the Jordan River.**<sup>NIV</sup> Many of the people who "went out" to hear John (3:5) came *confessing their sins.* Confession is more than simply acknowledging one's own sinfulness; it is agreeing with God's verdict on sin and expressing the desire to get rid of sin and live for God. Confessing means more than verbal response, affirmation, or praise; it means agreeing to change to a life of obedience and service.

Then *they were baptized.* When you wash dirty hands, the results are immediately visible. But repentance happens inside with a cleansing that isn't seen right away. So John used a symbolic action that people could see: baptism. The Jews used baptism to initiate Gentile converts, so John's audience was familiar with the rite. Here, John gives baptism a special meaning: It was used as a sign of repentance and forgiveness.

For baptism, John needed water, and he used *the Jordan River,* which is about seventy miles long, its main section stretching between the Sea of Galilee and the Dead Sea. Jerusalem lies about twenty miles west of the Jordan. Many significant events in the nation's history took place by the Jordan River. It was here that the Israelites renewed their covenant with God before entering the Promised Land (Joshua 1–5). Here John the Baptist called them to renew their covenant with God, this time through baptism.

BAPTISM
Christians have long pondered the proper mode and timing for baptism and what it really means. Some churches have nearly abandoned baptism as a "ritual," while others claim you can't go to heaven without it.

Baptism is important for all who say to God, "I belong to you." Baptism tells everybody where your loyalties really are, who you really depend on, and what direction your life is taking. Baptism says, "I follow Jesus."

Churches practice different traditions, but all believe that baptism is the outward sign that separates people from the world and attaches them to Christ. God promises blessing to all who take this step.

**3:7 But when he saw many Pharisees and Sadducees coming for baptism, he said to them, "You brood of vipers! Who warned you to flee from the wrath to come?"**<sup>NRSV</sup> John gladly baptized the many repentant men and women who came to him, confessing their sins and desiring to live for God. But when John *saw many*

*Pharisees and Sadducees coming for baptism,* he exploded in anger at their hypocrisy.

The Jewish religious leaders were divided into several groups. Two of the most prominent ones were the Pharisees and the Sadducees. The Pharisees separated themselves from anything non-Jewish and carefully followed both the Old Testament laws and the oral traditions handed down through the centuries. The Sadducees believed the Pentateuch alone (Genesis—Deuteronomy) to be God's Word. They were descended mainly from priestly nobility, while the Pharisees came from all classes of people. While the two groups disliked each other greatly, they both opposed Jesus.

Most likely, these distinguished men had come to John not to be baptized but simply to find out what was going on. John spoke to them with harsh words. John had criticized the Pharisees for being legalistic and hypocritical, following the letter of the law while ignoring its true intent. He had criticized the Sadducees for using religion to advance their political position. He obviously doubted the genuineness of their desire for baptism and was suspicious of them for even showing up. John called them a *brood of vipers* (Jesus also used this term, see 12:34; 23:33). The term literally means "snakes." It conveys how dangerous and cunning these religious leaders were and suggests that they were offspring of Satan (see Genesis 3; John 8:44). His question stung with sarcasm, *"Who warned you to flee from the wrath to come?"* In other words, "Who said you were going to escape God's coming judgment?" The religious leaders applied the "day of the Lord" to judgment on the Gentiles; John applied it to the religious leaders. The reason for John's harshness is revealed in his words that follow.

---

RIGHTEOUS, AND PROUD OF IT!
The Pharisees and Sadducees were proud of their knowledge and position. Religious people must struggle with their pride over spiritual attainments. Who gets big egos? It can happen to wealthy donors, to popular preachers, and to normal, everyday Joe and Jane Sundayschool—anyone who starts believing that he or she is much better than others.

John warned the most religious people in his region that their version of religion was keeping them from a relationship with God. How odd—people whose minds were packed with knowledge of the Scriptures were cut off from the truth because of their pride over spiritual achievements.

Stay close to friends who will be honest with you, who will check your bloated ego; keep your feet on the ground and your heart humble. Without friends like these, you could become as self-righteous as the esteemed Pharisees and Sadducees.

---

## PHARISEES AND SADDUCEES

The Pharisees and Sadducees were the two major religious groups in Israel at the time of Christ. The Pharisees were more religiously minded, while the Sadducees were more politically minded. Although the groups disliked and distrusted each other, they worked together to oppose Jesus.

| Name | Positive Characteristics | Negative Characteristics |
|---|---|---|
| PHARISEES | • Were committed to obeying all of God's commands | • Behaved as though their own religious rules were just as important as God's rules for living |
| | • Were admired by the common people for their apparent piety | • Often forced others to try to live up to standards they themselves could not meet |
| | • Believed in a bodily resurrection and eternal life | • Believed that salvation came from perfect obedience to the law and was not based on forgiveness of sins |
| | • Believed in angels and demons | • Became so obsessed with obeying their legal interpretations in every detail that they completely ignored God's message of mercy and grace |
| | | • Were more concerned with appearing to be good than obeying God |
| SADDUCEES | • Believed strongly in the Mosaic law and in Levitical purity | • Relied on logic while placing little importance on faith |
| | • Were more practically minded than the Pharisees | • Did not believe that all the Old Testament was God's Word |
| | | • Did not believe in a bodily resurrection or eternal life |
| | | • Did not believe in angels or demons |
| | | • Were often willing to compromise their values with the Romans and others in order to maintain their status and influential positions |

**3:8 "Produce fruit in keeping with repentance."** [NIV] Those who refuse to repent will face judgment; those who repent will escape judgment; however, true repentance is seen by the fruit (actions and character) it produces. The Pharisees and Sadducees thought they had a corner on righteousness, but their fruit revealed their true character. Only if they could *produce fruit in keeping with repentance*—if they truly repented and lived for God—then and only then would they be able to "flee from the wrath to come" (3:7).

John the Baptist called people to more than words or ritual; he told them to change their behavior. If we are to produce fruit in keeping with repentance, our words and religious activities must back up what we say. God judges our words by the actions that accompany them. Do your actions match your words?

---

FALSE SECURITY
The religious leaders trusted in Abraham's faith and in their own genetic and religious history. When your life takes a wicked bounce, you're stressed to the max, and you need help fast, where do you turn? Some people hang charms on their wrist or emblems from a car's rearview mirror. Some people repeat the names of early Christians. Wouldn't John the Baptist be surprised to discover that his own name is used by some people to ward off trouble?

If you trust in knickknacks or depend on long-departed Christians to help you wiggle through a tight spot, give it up. Our faith should not be in objects or people, but in God alone. God is your help in trouble, and Jesus, your Lord forever. Trust in his truth.

---

**3:9 "And do not think you can say to yourselves, 'We have Abraham as our father.' I tell you that out of these stones God can raise up children for Abraham."** NIV The pious Pharisees and Sadducees may have sneered at John's outrage. "After all," they thought to themselves, "we are descendants of Abraham; therefore, we are guaranteed God's blessings." Somewhere over the years, the Jews erroneously decided that the promise given to the patriarchs was guaranteed to all their descendants, no matter how they acted or what they believed. John explained to them, however, that relying on Abraham as their ancestor would not qualify them for God's kingdom. John probably pointed at stones in the riverbed and said *out of these stones God can raise up children for Abraham.* John may have used a play on the Aramaic words for "stone" and "children" in making his point that God can make a nation for himself from whomever he chooses. Only those who "produce fruit in keeping with repentance" (3:8) would qualify for God's coming kingdom. The apostle Paul would later explain this to the

Romans: "Not all who are descended from Israel are Israel. Nor because they are his descendants are they all Abraham's children. . . . It is not the natural children who are God's children, but it is the children of the promise who are regarded as Abraham's offspring" (Romans 9:6-8 NIV).

**3:10** **"Even now the ax is lying at the root of the trees; every tree therefore that does not bear good fruit is cut down and thrown into the fire."** NRSV God's message hasn't changed since the Old Testament—people will be judged for their unproductive lives. Just as a fruit tree is expected to bear fruit, God's people should produce a crop of good deeds (3:8). John compared people who claim that they believe God but don't live for God to unproductive trees that will be cut down. "The kingdom of heaven is near" (3:2); judgment was at hand. *The ax is lying at the root of the trees,* poised and ready to do its work, cutting down those trees that do not bear good fruit. Not only will the trees be *cut down,* but they will be *thrown into the fire,* signifying complete destruction.

Jesus used the same illustration in 7:19, "Every tree that does not bear good fruit is cut down and thrown into the fire" (NRSV). Jesus was describing how to recognize false teachers. He explained that we can know them by their fruits, their lives. In the same way, God has no use for people who call themselves Christians but do nothing about it. Like many people in John's day who were God's people in name only, we are of no value if we are Christians in name only. If others can't see our faith in the way we treat them, we may not be God's people at all.

So how are we to *bear good fruit?* God calls us to be "active" in our obedience. To be productive for God, we must obey his teachings, resist temptation, actively serve others, and share our faith.

**3:11** **"I baptize you with water for repentance, but one who is more powerful than I is coming after me; I am not worthy to carry his sandals. He will baptize you with the Holy Spirit and fire."** NRSV Turning his attention away from the self-righteous religious leaders and back to the sincere seekers who came for baptism, John explained that his baptism with the *water* of the Jordan River demonstrated *repentance*—willingness to turn from sin. This was the beginning of the spiritual process. John baptized people as a sign that they had asked God to forgive their sins and had decided to live as he wanted them to live. Baptism was an "outward" sign of commitment. To be effective, it had to be accompanied by an "inward" change of attitude leading to a changed life. John's baptism did not give salvation; it prepared a person to welcome the coming Messiah and receive *his* message and *his* baptism.

John's statement *He will baptize you with the Holy Spirit and fire* revealed the identity of the *one who is more powerful* coming after John as the promised Messiah. The coming of the Spirit had been prophesied as part of the Messiah's arrival:

- "I will pour out my Spirit on your offspring, and my blessing on your descendants" (Isaiah 44:3 NIV).
- "The time is coming. . . . I will put my law in their minds and write it on their hearts. I will be their God, and they will be my people. . . . For I will forgive their wickedness and will remember their sins no more" (Jeremiah 31:31-34 NIV).
- "I will give you a new heart and put a new spirit in you; I will remove from you your heart of stone and give you a heart of flesh. And I will put my Spirit in you and move you to follow my decrees and be careful to keep my laws" (Ezekiel 36:26-27 NIV).
- "And afterward, I will pour out my Spirit on all people. Your sons and daughters will prophesy, your old men will dream dreams, your young men will see visions. Even on my servants, both men and women, I will pour out my Spirit in those days" (Joel 2:28-29 NIV).

The Old Testament promised a time when God would demonstrate his purifying power among people (Isaiah 32:15; Ezekiel 39:29). The prophets also looked forward to a purifying fire (Isaiah 4:4; Malachi 3:2). This looked ahead to Pentecost (Acts 2), when the Holy Spirit would be sent by Jesus in the form of tongues of fire, empowering his followers to preach the gospel. All believers, those who would later come to Jesus Christ for salvation, would receive the baptism of the Holy Spirit and the fire of purification (one article precedes these words, indicating that they were not two separate baptisms, but one and the same). The experience would not necessarily be like that recorded in Acts 2, but the outcome would be the same. This baptism would purify and refine each believer. When Jesus would baptize with the Holy Spirit, the entire person would be refined by the Spirit's fire. So, for those who believe, "the fire" is positive, but for unbelievers, "the fire" brings awful judgment, as is described in the next verse.

John knew that the Messiah would be coming after him. Although John was the first genuine prophet in four hundred years, Jesus the Messiah would be infinitely greater than he. John was pointing out how insignificant he was compared to the one who would come. John pointed out three main differences between himself and the one coming after him: (1) Jesus' baptism transcends John's because it includes full redemption—John's was limited to repentance; (2) Jesus would be "more powerful," referring to eschatological power; (3) John was not even worthy of doing the most menial tasks for him, like carrying his sandals, an act considered so low that only slaves did it. (Not even disciples were required to carry their rabbi's sandals because the dusty shoes symbolized the sins of life.)

John the Baptist said, "He must become greater; I must become less" (John 3:30 NIV). What John began, Jesus finished. What John prepared, Jesus fulfilled.

**3:12** **"His winnowing fork is in his hand, and he will clear his threshing floor, gathering his wheat into the barn and burning up the chaff with unquenchable fire."** NIV *Threshing* was the process of separating the grains of wheat from the useless outer shell called chaff. This was normally done in a large area called a *threshing floor,* often on a hill, where the wind could blow away the lighter chaff when the farmer tossed the beaten wheat into the air. A *winnowing fork* is a pitchfork used to toss wheat in the air in order to separate wheat from chaff. The *wheat* is the part of the plant that is useful; *chaff* is the worthless outer shell. Chaff is burned because it is useless; wheat, however, is gathered. "Winnowing" is often used in the Bible to picture God's judgment. Jesus used the same analogy in a parable (13:24-30). John spoke of repentance, but he also spoke of judgment upon those who refused to repent. The message is always the same; there is no middle ground and no gray area. Repent, turn to Christ, and be saved; or refuse to repent, refuse to turn to Christ, and be destroyed.

> The wrath of God is like great waters that are dammed for the present; they increase more and more, and rise higher and higher, till an outlet is given; and the longer the stream is stopped, the more rapid and mighty is its course, when once it is let loose.
>
> *Jonathan Edwards*

## JOHN BAPTIZES JESUS / 3:13-17 / 17

The beautiful story of Jesus' baptism by John in the waters of the Jordan River reveals a God of love, who came to earth as a human being, identifying with humanity. If Jesus was going to offer salvation to sinners, he needed to identify with sinners. He did this by submitting to John's baptism for repentance and forgiveness of sins. Then God miraculously showed his love for the Son. The opened heavens, the dove, and the voice revealed to everyone (and to us as readers of this wonderful story) that Jesus was God's Son, come to earth as the promised Messiah to fulfill prophecy and to bring salvation to those who believe. Have you believed in Jesus? Have you made him Lord of your life?

**3:13 Then Jesus came from Galilee to John at the Jordan to be baptized by him.**<sup>NKJV</sup> John had been explaining that Jesus' baptism would be much greater than his (3:11) when suddenly *Jesus came* to him and asked to be baptized! *Galilee* was the name of the northern region of Palestine; the other two regions were Samaria (central) and Judea (southern). At this time, Jesus was probably about thirty years old (Luke 3:23). He traveled the long distance on foot (see map "Jesus Begins His Ministry"), along the dusty roads of Galilee and Samaria and into Judea, to meet John the Baptist and *be baptized by him.*

**3:14-15 But John tried to deter him, saying, "I need to be baptized by you, and do you come to me?" Jesus replied, "Let it be so now; it is proper for us to do this to fulfill all righteousness." Then John consented.**<sup>NIV</sup> When Jesus arrived, John balked at his desire to be baptized. John did not think that Jesus needed to be baptized for repentance. John *tried to deter* Jesus, explaining that he wanted to be baptized by Jesus. There are two main views regarding what John meant. (1) Some scholars suggest that John wanted the Holy-Spirit-and-fire baptism that Jesus would bring (3:11). (2) Others say that John simply knew of Jesus' superiority, so John wanted Jesus to baptize him.

**Jesus Begins His Ministry**
*Jesus launched his ministry from his childhood home, Nazareth. He was baptized by John the Baptist in the Jordan River and tempted by Satan in the wilderness; then he returned to Galilee. Between the temptation and his move to Capernaum (4:12-13), Jesus ministered in Judea, Samaria, and Galilee (see John 1–4).*

Jesus explained that he had come to be baptized because it would be the *proper* way for them to *fulfill all righteousness.* What did this mean? It could not mean to fulfill the law, because no law required baptism. While "fulfill" generally refers to prophecy, there are no clear connections to baptism in prophecy. Most likely it refers to fulfilling a relationship with God by obeying him in every aspect of life. When Jesus said this, *John consented* and baptized him.

Why did Jesus ask to be baptized? Jesus saw his baptism as advancing God's work. While even the greatest prophets

(Isaiah, Jeremiah, Ezekiel) had to confess their sinfulness and need for repentance, Jesus didn't need to admit sin—he was sinless (John 8:46; 2 Corinthians 5:21; Hebrews 4:15; 1 John 3:5). Although Jesus did not need forgiveness, he was baptized for the following reasons: (1) to confess sin on behalf of the nation, as Isaiah, Ezra, and Nehemiah had done (see Ezra 9:2; Nehemiah 1:6; 9:1ff.; Isaiah 6:5); (2) to accomplish God's mission and advance God's work in the world; (3) to inaugurate his public ministry to bring the message of salvation to all people; (4) to show support for John's ministry; (5) to identify with the penitent people of God, thus with humanness and sin; and (6) to give us an example to follow.

John's baptism for repentance was different from Christian baptism in the church. When the apostle Paul taught some of John's followers about Jesus, they were baptized again (see Acts 19:2-5). Jesus, the perfect man, didn't need baptism for sin, but he accepted baptism in obedient service to the Father, and God showed his approval. Jesus wanted to show that his mission was to take on the sin of humanity, and thus to absolve it. Jesus took the baptism seriously, not merely as an object lesson for observers. He acknowledged God's holiness, humanity's sin, and said, "I will take it, and I will clear it." That is the essence of the Good News.

---

**LET GO OF EGO**
Put yourself in John's shoes. Your work is going well; people are taking notice; everything is growing. But you know that the purpose of your work is to prepare the people for Jesus (John 1:35-37). Then Jesus arrives, and his coming tests your integrity. Will you be able to turn your followers over to him? John passed the test by publicly baptizing Jesus. Soon he would say, "He must become greater; I must become less" (John 3:30 NIV). Can you, like John, put your ego and profitable work aside in order to point others to Jesus? Are you willing to lose some of your status so that everyone will benefit?

---

**3:16 And when Jesus had been baptized, just as he came up from the water, suddenly the heavens were opened to him and he saw the Spirit of God descending like a dove and alighting on him.**NRSV Apparently the action of the Spirit of God descending from heaven like a dove was a sign that Jesus was the Messiah and that the age of the Spirit predicted by the prophets was formally beginning (Isaiah 61:1). John knew that the Messiah would come, but it is uncertain when he knew that his cousin Jesus was the one. By recording this miraculous opening of the heavens, Matthew left no doubt for his readers as to Jesus' true identity.

The Bible does not tell us that anyone but Jesus saw *the heavens . . . opened.* It says they were opened *to him.* According to the Gospel of John (1:29-34), this event, and *the Spirit of God descending like a dove,* revealed the Messiah to John. The opening of the heavens presented God's intervention into humanity in the human presence of God in Jesus Christ. It was as if the heavens rolled back to reveal the invisible throne of God (Isaiah 63:19–64:2).

The second sign, "the Spirit of God descending like a dove," was probably visible to all the people, for Luke recounts that "the Holy Spirit descended upon him in bodily form like a dove" (Luke 3:22 NRSV). The descent of the Spirit, and the form of the dove itself, represented to Israel God's mighty workings in the world. At creation, "the Spirit of God was hovering over the waters" (Genesis 1:2 NIV). After the great Flood, the dove carried the news to Noah of the receding waters (Genesis 8:8-12). The descending of the Spirit signified God's workings in the world; therefore the arrival of the Messiah would have been marked by the descending of the Spirit, in this case, in the form of a dove. Later, Jesus would read from the prophet Isaiah (Isaiah 61:1-2), "'The Spirit of the Lord is on me, because he has anointed me to preach good news to the poor. He has sent me to proclaim freedom for the prisoners and recovery of sight for the blind, to release the oppressed, to proclaim the year of the Lord's favor'" (Luke 4:18-19 NIV).

The church uses the dove as a symbol for the Holy Spirit; however, the bird itself was not important. The descent of the Spirit "like" (or "in the form of") a dove emphasized the way the Holy Spirit related to Jesus. The descending Spirit portrayed a gentle, peaceful, but active presence coming to anoint Jesus. It was not that Jesus needed to be filled with the Spirit (as if there was any lack in him) because he was "from the Holy Spirit" (1:20) since his conception. Rather, this was his royal anointing (see Isaiah 11:2; 42:1).

John the Baptist, and we who study this important event, can learn not only who the Messiah was, but also what kind of Messiah he would be (how his power would be demonstrated and used). His nature was revealed not by a thunderclap or lightning bolt, nor by an eagle or a hawk, but with a gentle dove. Jesus the Messiah would have a different way and a different message than even John expected.

**3:17 And suddenly a voice came from heaven, saying, "This is My beloved Son, in whom I am well pleased."** NKJV The Spirit descended like a dove on Jesus, and *a voice came from heaven* proclaiming the Father's approval of Jesus as his divine Son. This voice came from the heavenly realm that had been briefly opened in 3:16. The voice said, *This is My beloved Son.* In Greek, the literal translation of this is "As for you, you are my Son, the beloved one." While all believers would eventually be called "sons of God" (or "children of God"), Jesus Christ has a different, unique relationship with God; he is the one unique Son of God. "This is" means that these words were spoken publicly—to Jesus, John, *and* the crowd.

The phrase "in whom I am well pleased" means that the Father takes great delight, pleasure, and satisfaction in the Son. The verb in Greek conveys that God's pleasure in the Son is constant. He has always taken pleasure in his Son.

The words spoken by the voice from heaven echoed two Old Testament passages. First, Psalm 2:7, "He said to me, 'You are my Son'" (NIV). Psalm 2 is a messianic psalm that describes the coronation of Christ, the eternal King. The rule of Christ described in the psalm would begin after his crucifixion and resurrection and will be fulfilled when he comes to set up his kingdom on earth. Second, Isaiah 42:1, "Here is my servant, whom I uphold, my chosen one in whom I delight" (NIV). Isaiah 42:1-17 describes the Servant-Messiah who would suffer and die as he served God and fulfilled his mission of atoning for sin on behalf of humanity. Thus, in the two phrases spoken, the voice from the throne of heaven described Jesus' status both as the Servant who would suffer and die and as the King who would reign forever. In the intertestamental period, the Jews believed that God no longer spoke directly (as through the prophets), but indirectly by teachers and rabbis. The voice of God, heard by everyone, was a direct sign of the arrival of the messianic age.

In 3:16-17, all three persons of the Trinity are present and active. The doctrine of the Trinity, which was developed much later in church history, teaches that God is three persons and yet one in essence. God the Father speaks; God the Son is baptized; God the Holy Spirit descends on Jesus. God is one, yet in three persons at the same time. This is one of God's incomprehensible mysteries. Other Bible references that speak of the Father, Son, and Holy Spirit are Matthew 28:19; John 15:26; 1 Corinthians 12:4-13; 2 Corinthians 13:14; Ephesians 2:18; 1 Thessalonians 1:2-5; and 1 Peter 1:2.

# Matthew 4

From Jesus' temptation we can learn that following our Lord can
bring dangerous and intense spiritual battles. We won't always
feel good; we will experience times of deprivation, loneliness, and
hostility. Jesus' temptation also shows that our spiritual victories
may not always be visible to the watching world. Above all, it
shows that we must use the power of God to face temptation and
not try to withstand it in our own strength.

**4:1 Then Jesus was led up by the Spirit into the wilderness to be
tempted by the devil.**NKJV The word "then" indicates an important connection of the end of chapter 3 and the beginning of
chapter 4. The same Holy Spirit that sent Jesus to be baptized,
then sent Jesus into the wilderness. The temptation was a divine
necessity to prove Jesus' messianic purpose. *Led up by the Spirit,*
Jesus took the offensive against the enemy, Satan, by going into
the lonely and desolate *wilderness* to face temptation. In the Old
Testament, the "wilderness" (or "desert") was a desolate and
dangerous place where wild animals lived (see, for example,
Isaiah 13:20-22; 34:8-15).

"Devil" in Greek means "accuser"; in Hebrew, the word "Satan"
means the same (4:10). The devil tempted Eve in the Garden of
Eden, and here he tempted Jesus in the wilderness. Satan is a fallen
archangel. He is a real, created being, not symbolic, and is constantly
fighting against those who follow and obey God. The verb "to be
tempted" describes continuous action because Jesus was tempted
constantly during the forty days. The word "tempted" means "to
put to the test to see what good or evil, strengths or weaknesses,
exist in a person." The Spirit compelled Jesus into the wilderness
where God put Jesus to the test—not to see if Jesus was ready, but
to *show* that he was ready for his mission. Satan, however, had
other plans; he hoped to thwart Jesus' mission by tempting Jesus to
do evil. Satan tried to get Jesus to declare his kingship prematurely.
Satan tried to get Jesus to take his messianic power into his own
hands and to forsake his Father's will. If Jesus had given in, his

## KNOW THE ENEMY, KNOW THE METHOD

Satan, the archenemy of all believers, has been tempting people to turn from God since the first woman on earth listened to his lies. Interestingly enough, his methods have never really changed. He tempted Eve in the Garden of Eden, Jesus in the wilderness, and tempts us in our daily lives. When we know how he attacks, we can be prepared.

*How Satan tempted . . .*

| Jesus | Eve | Us (see 1 John 2:16) |
|-------|-----|----------------------|
| Turn stones to bread to eat | Fruit would be good to eat | Lust of the flesh |
| Prove his divine sonship | Gain wisdom so as to be like God | Pride of life |
| Obtain all he could see | Look at the fruit and see that it looks tasty | Lust of the eyes |

mission on earth—to die for our sins and give us the opportunity to have eternal life—would have been lost. For more on Satan, see 1 Chronicles 21:1; Job 1–2; Zechariah 3:1-2; Luke 10:18; Revelation 20.

The devil's temptations focused on three crucial areas: (1) physical needs and desires, (2) possessions and power, and (3) pride (see 1 John 2:15-16 for a similar list). This temptation by the devil shows us that Jesus was human, and it gave Jesus the opportunity to reaffirm God's plan for his ministry. It also gives us an example to follow when we are tempted. Jesus' temptation was an important demonstration of his sinlessness. He faced temptation and did not give in.

TIME OF TESTING
This time of testing showed that Jesus really was the Son of God, able to overcome the devil and his temptations. A person has not shown true obedience if he or she has never had an opportunity to disobey. We read in Deuteronomy 8:2-3 that God led Israel into the desert to humble and test them. God wanted to see whether or not his people would really obey him. You too will be tested. Because you know that testing will come, you should be alert and ready for it. Remember, your convictions are only real if they hold up under pressure!

**4:2 He fasted forty days and forty nights, and afterwards he was famished.**NRSV Jesus *fasted* during his time in the wilderness—going without food and perhaps even water, though some fasts allowed food and water only at night. Fasting was used as a spiritual discipline for prayer and a time of preparation for great tasks that lay ahead.

The number forty brings to mind the forty days of rain in the great Flood (Genesis 7:17), the forty days Moses spent on Mount Sinai (Exodus 24:18), the forty years of Israel's wandering in the wilderness (Deuteronomy 29:5), the forty days of Goliath's taunting of Israel prior to David's victory (1 Samuel 17:16), and the forty days of Elijah's time of fear in the wilderness (1 Kings 19:8). In all those situations, God worked in his people, preparing them for special tasks.

At the end of this forty-day fast, Jesus obviously was *famished.* Jesus' status as God's Son did not make this fast any easier; his physical body suffered the severe hunger and pain of going without sustenance. The three temptations recorded here occurred when Jesus was at his most physically weakened state. But Satan could not weaken Jesus spiritually.

WEAK SPOTS
Jesus wasn't tempted inside the temple or at his baptism but in the desert, where he was tired, alone, and hungry, and thus most vulnerable. The devil often tempts us when we are at our weakest point—under physical or emotional stress (for example, lonely, tired, weighing big decisions, or faced with uncertainty). But he also likes to tempt us through our strengths, where we are most susceptible to pride. We guard against his attacks when we start the day with prayer, build our attitudes around the Bible's truth, and depend on God's Holy Spirit to keep us from spiritual harm.

**4:3 The tempter came and said to him, "If you are the Son of God, command these stones to become loaves of bread."** NRSV "The tempter" is another name for the devil (4:1), Satan. Jesus may have finished his fast, but Satan was not finished with his temptations. In fact, his first effort with Jesus was to tempt him to do the obvious. "You've been fasting and you're famished," Satan said. "Why don't you just turn some of these stones into bread and have yourself a small meal?" What could possibly be so wrong about that? But there was much more going on here than a seemingly compassionate offer for a hungry person to have lunch.

Satan phrased his temptation in an interesting manner. He said, *"If you are the Son of God."* The word "if" did not imply doubt; both Jesus and Satan knew the truth. Instead, Satan tempted Jesus with his own power. If indeed Jesus was the Son of the one true, all-powerful God, then Jesus certainly could *command these stones to become loaves of bread* if he so chose in order to satisfy his hunger. "God's Son has no reason to be hungry," Satan suggested. Satan did not doubt Jesus' sonship nor his ability to turn stones to bread. Instead, he wanted Jesus to use his power in the wrong way at the wrong time—to use his position to meet his own needs rather than to fulfill his God-given mission.

In later miracles Jesus did supply baskets full of bread, but he supplied them for a hungry crowd, not to satisfy himself. And he did the miracles in God's timing for God's purposes as part of his mission (see 14:13-21; 15:32-39).

**4:4 But he answered, "It is written, 'One does not live by bread alone, but by every word that comes from the mouth of God.'"** NRSV Jesus saw through Satan's scheme. Jesus did not attempt to get into a discussion with Satan (as Eve had done); instead, he answered with words from what *is written* in Scripture, quoting Deuteronomy 8:3. The words in Deuteronomy describe God's lesson to the nation of Israel. This testing was designed to help Israel depend on God:

- *Remember the long way that the Lord your God has led you these forty years in the wilderness, in order to humble you, testing you to know what was in your heart, whether or not you would keep his commandments. He humbled you by letting you hunger, then by feeding you with manna, with which neither you nor your ancestors were acquainted, in order to make you understand that one does not live by bread alone, but by every word that comes from the mouth of the LORD. (Deuteronomy 8:2-3 NRSV)*

In all three quotes from Deuteronomy, found in Matthew 4:4, 7, and 10, the context shows that Israel failed each test each time. Therefore, Jesus conveyed to Satan that while the test may have caused Israel to fail, it would not work with Jesus. Matthew showed the spiritual superiority of Christ over the nation.

Jesus, God's Son, humbled himself in the wilderness, voluntarily undergoing the trial of extreme hunger in order to learn obedience through suffering. Jesus came to earth to accomplish the Father's mission. Everything he said and did worked toward that goal; nothing could deter or distract him. Jesus understood that obedience to the Father's mission was more important than food—no matter what his physical body said, no matter what Satan said.

To truly accomplish his mission, Jesus had to be completely humbled, totally self-abased. Making himself bread would have shown that Jesus had not quite set aside all his powers, had not humbled himself, and had not identified completely with the human race. But Jesus refused, showing that he would use his powers only in submission to God's plan and that he would depend on God, not his own miraculous powers, for his daily needs. Jesus lived not *by bread alone;* Jesus truly lived and served *by every word that comes from the mouth of God,* giving himself completely to God's mission. Matthew shows that we should follow Jesus' example and depend on God.

---

NORMAL DESIRES
Jesus was hungry and weak after fasting for forty days, but he chose not to use his divine power to satisfy his natural desire for food. Food, hunger, and eating are good, but the timing was wrong. Jesus was in the wilderness to fast, not to eat. And because Jesus had given up the unlimited, independent use of his divine power in order to experience humanity fully, he wouldn't use his power to change the stones to bread. We also may be tempted to satisfy a perfectly normal desire in a wrong way or at the wrong time. If we indulge in sex before marriage or if we steal to get food, we are trying to satisfy God-given desires in wrong ways. Many desires are normal and good, but God wants you to satisfy them in the right way and at the right time. True discipleship means learning from Christ how to know the right ways and right times. Seek the help of a pastor, youth leader, or mature Christian friend to help you get started.

---

**4:5 Then the devil took him to the holy city and had him stand on the highest point of the temple.**<sup>NIV</sup> This temptation is set in *the holy city,* that is, Jerusalem, the religious and political seat of Palestine. The *temple* was the religious center of the Jewish nation and the place where the people expected the Messiah to arrive (Malachi 3:1). Herod the Great had renovated the temple in hopes of gaining the Jews' confidence. The temple was the tallest building in the area, and this *highest point* was probably the corner wall that jutted out of the hillside, overlooking the valley below. The historian Josephus wrote about the enormous height from the top of the temple to the bottom of the ravine below. From this spot, Jesus could see all of Jerusalem behind him and the country for miles in front of him. Whether the devil physically *took* Jesus to Jerusalem, or whether this occurred in a vision is unclear. In any case, Satan was setting the stage for his next temptation.

**4:6 And said to Him, "If You are the Son of God, throw Yourself down. For it is written: 'He shall give His angels charge over you,' and, 'In their hands they shall bear you up, Lest you dash your foot against a stone.'"**<sup>NKJV</sup> Jesus had quoted Scripture in response to Satan's first temptation. Here Satan tried the tactic with Jesus. Satan used Scripture to try to convince Jesus to sin!

Again Satan began with *"If You are the Son of God."* As in 4:3, Satan was not suggesting doubt, but rather saying, "If you're God's Son, then certainly God will want to protect you from harm. So *throw Yourself down* from this pinnacle so that God will send his angels to protect you." Then Satan quoted words from Psalm 91:11-12 to support his request. The psalm describes God's protection for those who trust him. Psalm 91:11 begins, *He shall give His angels charge over you;* verse 12 continues, *In their hands they shall bear you up, lest you dash your foot against a stone.*

Some scholars believe that Satan wanted Jesus to take advantage of the prophecy in Malachi 3:1; the people believed that this prophecy meant that the Messiah would appear suddenly at the temple. What a spectacular proof of Jesus' messiahship this would be if he suddenly appeared on the pinnacle of the temple before all the people and then jumped off, only to be carefully placed on the ground by God's angels. Surely everyone would believe then.

More likely, however, this temptation did not focus on Jesus proving to the people that he was the Messiah. Instead, Satan was focusing on Jesus' relationship with his Father. Satan wanted Jesus to test that relationship to see if God's promise of protection would prove true.

---

DANGEROUS KNOWLEDGE
What a sobering thought that Satan knows Scripture and knows how to use it for his own purposes! Sometimes friends or associates will present attractive and convincing reasons why you should try something that you believe is wrong. They may even find Bible verses that seem to support their viewpoint. Study the Bible carefully, especially the broader contexts of specific verses, so that you understand God's principles for living and what he wants for your life. Only if you really understand what the whole Bible says will you be able to recognize errors of interpretation when people take verses out of context to make them say what they want them to say. Choose your Bible teachers carefully. We have much to learn from others. Capable and wise teachers often present the broader context to help us grow in our Bible knowledge.

---

Satan was quoting Scripture out of context, making it sound as though God protects even through sin, removing the natural consequences of sinful acts. Neither jumping from the roof in a public display or jumping in order to test God's promises would have been part of God's will for Jesus. In context, the psalm promises

God's protection for those who, while being in his will and serving him, find themselves in danger. It does not promise protection for artificially created crises in which Christians call to God in order to test his love and care. We should not test God, as Jesus will explain (see the following verse).

**4:7 Jesus said to him, "Again it is written, 'Do not put the Lord your God to the test.'"**<sup>NRSV</sup> Jesus would not get into a discussion with Satan about this second temptation, as he had also refused to do in the first. Instead, Jesus quoted from Scripture again, but, contrary to Satan's method, Jesus quoted with an understanding of the true meaning. No matter what the words that Satan quoted may have *sounded* like (that is, they seemed to say that no matter what Jesus did, God would protect him), the facts were that while God promises to protect his people, he also requires that they not put him *to the test.*

Jesus quoted from Deuteronomy 6:16, "Do not put the Lord your God to the test, as you tested him at Massah" (NRSV). In this passage, Moses was referring to an incident during Israel's wilderness wanderings, recorded in Exodus 17:1-7. The people were thirsty and ready to mutiny against Moses and return to Egypt if he did not provide them with water. God supplied the water, but only after the people had "quarreled and tested the Lord, saying, 'Is the Lord among us or not?'" (NRSV).

Jesus could have jumped from the temple; God could have sent angels to bring him safely to the ground. But for Jesus to jump from the pinnacle of the temple would have been a ridiculous test of God's power, and it would have been out of God's will. Jesus knew that his Father could protect him; he also understood that all his actions were to be focused on fulfilling his Father's mission, even if it meant suffering and death (which, of course, it did).

---

KNOW THE WORD
Jesus was able to resist all of the devil's temptations because he not only knew Scripture, but he also obeyed it. Ephesians 6:17 says that God's Word is a sword to use in spiritual combat. Knowing Bible verses is an important step in helping us resist the devil's attacks, but we must also obey the Bible. Note that Satan knew Scriptures, but he failed to obey them. Knowing and obeying the Bible helps us follow God's desires rather than the devil's.

---

**4:8-9 Again, the devil took him to a very high mountain and showed him all the kingdoms of the world and their splendor; and he said to him, "All these I will give you, if you will fall down and worship me."**<sup>NRSV</sup> The obvious impossibility of being able to see the

## THE TEMPTATIONS

As if going through a final test of preparation, Jesus was tempted by Satan in the desert. Three specific parts of the temptation are listed by Matthew. They are familiar because we face the same kinds of temptations. As the chart shows, temptation is often the combination of a real need and a possible doubt that create an inappropriate desire. Jesus demonstrates both the importance and effectiveness of knowing and applying Scripture to combat temptation.

| Temptation | Make bread | Dare God to rescue you (based on misapplied Scripture, Psalm 91:11-12) | Worship me! (Satan) |
|---|---|---|---|
| Real needs used as basis for temptation | Physical need: Hunger | Emotional need: Security | Psychological need: Significance, power, achievement |
| Possible doubts that made the temptations real | Would God provide food? | Would God protect? | Would God rule? |
| Potential weaknesses Satan sought to exploit | Hunger, impatience, need to "prove his Sonship" | Pride, insecurity, need to test God | Desire for quick power, easy solutions, need to prove equality with God |
| Jesus' answer | Deuteronomy 8:3: Depend on God Focus: God's purpose | Deuteronomy 6:16: Don't test God Focus: God's plan | Deuteronomy 6:13: No compromise with evil Focus: God's person |

entire world from one mountaintop makes little difference to this story, but it supports the view that this experience may have been visionary. The focus is not on the mountain, but on the *kingdoms of the world* that were (and are) under Satan's dominion. Presently, Satan is "ruler of this world" (John 12:31 NRSV). Luke records Satan's words at this temptation as: "To you I will give their glory and all this authority; for it has been given over to me, and I give it to anyone I please" (Luke 4:6 NRSV). Satan offered to "give" dominion over the world to Jesus. Satan knew that one day Jesus Christ would rule over the earth (see Philippians 2:9-11). The offer wasn't evil, but it challenged Jesus' obedience to God's timing and will. Satan's temptation was, in essence, "Why wait? I can give this to you *now!"* Of course, he would never really give them away because the offer had a catch. Jesus would have to *fall down and worship* Satan.

Satan tempted Jesus to take the world as an earthly kingdom right then, without carrying out his plan to save the world from sin. For Jesus, that meant obtaining his promised dominion over the world without experiencing the suffering and death of the cross. Satan offered a painless shortcut. But Satan didn't understand that suffering and death were a part of God's plan that Jesus had chosen to obey. Satan hoped to distort Jesus' perspective by making him focus on worldly power, not on fulfilling God's plans. In addition, Jesus would have to denounce his loyalty to the Father in order to worship Satan. Satan's goal always has been to replace God as the object of worship.

**4:10  Then Jesus said to him, "Away with you, Satan! For it is written, 'You shall worship the LORD your God, and Him only you shall serve.'"** NKJV Jesus once again met temptation with Scripture. Quoting from Deuteronomy, Jesus dismissed Satan with the words "away with you." The temptations boiled down to a choice between God and Satan. No one can worship and serve both. For Jesus to take a shortcut to the goal, ruling the world by worshiping Satan (4:9) would be to break the first commandment, "Hear, O Israel: The Lord our God, the Lord is one! You shall love the Lord your God with all your heart, with all your soul, and with all your strength. . . . You shall fear the Lord your God and serve Him . . ." (Deuteronomy 6:4-5, 13 NKJV). Jesus would take the path of submission to God. Jesus would *worship* and *serve* the Lord alone. Only by doing so would he be able to accomplish his mission of bringing salvation to the world.

---

ENTICED
The devil offered the whole world to Jesus if Jesus would only bow down and worship him. Today Satan offers us the world by trying to entice us with materialism, sex, and power. The devil would like us to believe that "life is short, get all you can!" Even Christian leaders find themselves tempted to build empires here on earth. But Satan requires people to pay for such success by selling their souls to him. We must resist temptations in the same way that Jesus did. If you find yourself craving something that the world offers, quote Jesus' words to the devil: "Worship the Lord your God, and serve him only." Then follow that advice, with the support and prayers of Christian friends.

---

**4:11  Then the devil left him, and angels came and attended him.** NIV The devil could not stay when Jesus told him to go away (4:10).

Jesus is Satan's superior; Satan must do as Jesus commands. So *the devil left* Jesus. Luke records that Satan "left [Jesus] until an opportune time" (Luke 4:13 NIV). This would only be the first of many encounters that Jesus would have with Satan's power.

That *angels came and attended him* in no way lessens the intensity of the temptations that Jesus faced. The angels may have given Jesus food and drink because the Greek word *diekonoun,* usually translated "ministering" or "attending," can also mean "serving food" (see 1 Kings 19:5 where angels ministered to Elijah). More likely, the angels' ministry was spiritual in nature—attending to Jesus' spiritual needs. The verb indicates continuous action. As Satan's temptations lasted continuously during the forty days, so did the ministrations of the angels.

Angels, like these who waited on Jesus, have a significant role as God's messengers. These spiritual beings were involved in Jesus' life on earth by (1) announcing his birth to Mary, (2) reassuring Joseph, (3) naming Jesus, (4) announcing Jesus' birth to the shepherds, (5) protecting Jesus by sending his family to Egypt, and (6) ministering to Jesus in Gethsemane. Angels are continuously present. Hebrews 1:14 defines angels as messengers for God and ministers to people. They show compassion for human beings. Passages such as Matthew 18:10; Luke 15:10; Acts 12:14-15; and Revelation 19:10 support the idea of guardian angels. As agents of God, angels bring special help to believers (Acts 5:19-21; 12:7-10).

---

SOURCE OF STRENGTH
Jesus was tempted by the devil, but he never sinned! Although we may feel dirty after being tempted, we should remember that temptation itself is not sin. We sin when we give in and disobey God. Remembering this truth will help us turn away from the temptation. Hebrews 4:15 says that Jesus "has been tempted in every way, just as we are—yet was without sin" (NIV). He knows firsthand what we are experiencing, and he is willing and able to help us in our struggles. When tempted, turn to God for strength by a short prayer, make a phone call to a Christian friend, or find a quiet place to pull out your Bible and read a psalm.

---

## JESUS PREACHES IN GALILEE / 4:12-17 / 30

Jesus moved from Nazareth, his hometown, to Capernaum, about 20 miles farther north. Capernaum, on the northwest shore of the Sea of Galilee, became Jesus' home base during his ministry in Galilee. The Gospels do not say why Jesus moved, but Capernaum offered better possibilities for ministry. (1) It was farther away from the intense opposition of the Pharisees in Nazareth. (2) It was a busy city, so Jesus' message could reach more people and spread more quickly. (3) It was home to several of the disciples and could provide extra resources and support for his ministry. Matthew explained how Jesus' move had been prophesied in Scripture. Jesus' actions, words, and movements showed his obedience to God's will and fulfilled the Scriptures about him. Matthew continued to assure his Jewish readers that Jesus' life fulfilled Scripture and that Jesus truly was the promised Messiah.

**4:12-13 When Jesus heard that John had been put in prison, he returned to Galilee. Leaving Nazareth, he went and lived in Capernaum, which was by the lake in the area of Zebulun and Naphtali.**[NIV] Matthew mentioned the arrest of John the Baptist as merely a signal for the ministry of Jesus into *Galilee,* his home region. He moved from *Nazareth* (where his family had settled, 2:23) to *Capernaum.* Luke explained that John *had been put in prison* because he had publicly rebuked King Herod for taking his brother's wife (Luke 3:19-20). John's public protests had greatly angered Herod, so he put John in prison, presumably to silence him. The Herods were renowned for their cruelty and evil; Herod the Great had ordered the murder of the babies in Bethlehem (2:16). The Herod who had imprisoned John was Herod Antipas; his wife was Herodias, Herod Antipas's niece and formerly his brother's wife. The imprisonment of John the Baptist was only one evil act in a family filled with incest, deceit, and murder. (The full story is told in 14:1-12.)

*Zebulun and Naphtali* were two of the original twelve tribes of Israel. They had been allotted this territory and had settled it during the conquest of Canaan under Joshua (see Joshua 19:10-16, 32-39). "By the lake" refers to the area around the Sea of Galilee (also called Sea of Tiberias or Lake of Gennesaret).

**4:14-16 That it might be fulfilled which was spoken by Isaiah the prophet, saying: "The land of Zebulun and the land of Naphtali, by the way of the sea, beyond the Jordan, Galilee of the Gentiles: The people who sat in darkness have seen a great light, And upon those who sat in the region and shadow of death Light has dawned."**[NKJV] Matthew continued to show how all of Jesus' life, even his travel, followed God's plans and fulfilled Scripture. Some Jewish readers may have wondered why Jesus' ministry was not focused in Jerusalem— wouldn't the promised Messiah begin by speaking in the temple itself? However, Matthew explained that Jesus' move to the region of Galilee where Capernaum was located *fulfilled [that] which was spoken by Isaiah the prophet* in Isaiah 9:1-2. Isaiah had prophesied that the Messiah would be a *Light* to *the land of Zebulun and the land of Naphtali.*

As noted above, this area had been the territory of these two tribes of Israel after the conquest of Canaan. When the Assyrians invaded and captured the northern kingdom of Israel, these tribes to the north were among the first to fall. "In the time of Pekah king of Israel, Tiglath-Pileser king of Assyria came and took Ijon, Abel Beth Maacah, Janoah, Kedesh and Hazor. He took Gilead and Galilee, including all the land of Naphtali, and deported the people to Assyria" (2 Kings 15:29 NIV). After conquering a nation, usually Assyria would deport all the people living there and then repopulate the area with others. All who resettled the area were pagans, Gentiles—thus Isaiah called the area *Galilee of the Gentiles.* While Jews eventually moved back into the area, the spiritual *darkness* over the land would continue for centuries until *a great light,* in the form of the Jews' Messiah, would come to live among the people. These words foreshadow Jesus' mission: He came to preach salvation by grace even to those in the deepest spiritual darkness, and he brought that message to the entire world—Jews *and* Gentiles.

**4:17 From that time on Jesus began to preach, "Repent, for the king-dom of heaven is near."** NIV Jesus started his ministry with the very word that people had heard John the Baptist say: *Repent.* The message is the same today. Becoming a follower of Christ begins with repentance, turning away from our self-centeredness and self-control. The next step is to turn the right way, to turn toward Christ and believe in him.

The "kingdom of heaven" means the same as the "kingdom of God" in Mark and Luke. Matthew used "heaven" instead of "God" because the Jews, out of their intense reverence and respect, did not pronounce God's name. The Old Testament prophets often spoke of the future kingdom, ruled by a descendant of King David, that would be established on earth and exist for eternity. Thus, when Jesus said, "The kingdom of heaven is near," the Jews understood him to mean that the Messiah had come to inaugurate his long-awaited earthly king-dom (see the notes on Matthew 3:1-2).

Of course, this caused great excitement among the people. The problem arose, however, in misunderstanding the nature of this kingdom and in timing its arrival. The kingdom of God began when God entered history as a human being. But the culmination of the kingdom of God will not be fully realized until all evil in the world has been judged and removed. Christ came to earth first as the suffering Servant. When he returns, he will come as King and Judge to rule over all the earth. The kingdom begun with Jesus' birth would not overthrow Roman oppression and usher in universal peace. The kingdom of God that began quietly in Palestine was God's rule in people's hearts. Thus, the kingdom was as "near" as people's willingness to make Jesus king over their lives. As Jesus said, "The kingdom of God is within you" (Luke 17:21 NIV). The culmination of the kingdom may still be many years away for us, yet its spiritual reality is as near as accepting Jesus as Savior.

## FOUR FISHERMEN FOLLOW JESUS / 4:18-22 / 33

Jesus told Peter, Andrew, James, and John to leave their fishing business and become "fishers of men," to help others find God. Jesus was calling them away from their productive trade to be productive spiritually. All of Christ's followers need to fish for souls. Those who practice Christ's teachings and share the gospel will be able to draw those around them to Christ like a fisherman who pulls fish into the boat.

**4:18 As he walked by the Sea of Galilee, he saw two brothers, Simon, who is called Peter, and Andrew his brother, casting a net into the sea—for they were fishermen.**NRSV Located 650 feet below sea level, the *Sea of Galilee* is a large lake— 150 feet deep and surrounded by hills. Fishing was the main industry for the approximately thirty towns surrounding the Sea of Galilee during Jesus' day. Capernaum, where Jesus settled (4:13), was the largest of these fishing towns. Simon and his brother Andrew came from Bethsaida, another town on the shore (John 1:44), but they had made their home in Capernaum (Mark 1:21, 29).

Jesus, walking by the sea, *saw two brothers.* Jesus did not approach *Simon* (whom we know as *Peter*) and *Andrew* as strangers. We know from the Gospel of John (1:35-49) that they had had previous contact. Jesus was walking on the beach with a purpose— to find certain *fishermen* whom he wanted to call to follow him. Jesus found them *casting a net into the sea.* Using nets was the most common method of fishing. A circular net (ten to fifteen feet in diameter) would be thrown into the sea. Then it would be drawn up, and the catch hoisted into the boat. Fishermen on the Sea of Galilee were strong and busy men.

FOLLOW ME
When Jesus entered Peter's life, this plain fisherman became
a new person with new goals and new priorities. He did not
become a perfect person, however, and he never stopped
being Simon Peter. We may wonder what Jesus saw in Simon
that made him give this potential disciple a new name: Peter,
the "rock." Impulsive Peter certainly didn't act rock solid much
of the time. But Jesus was looking for real people. He chose
people who could be changed by his love; then he sent them
out to communicate that his acceptance was available to
anyone—even to those who often fail. We may wonder what
Jesus sees in us when he calls us to follow him. But we know
Jesus accepted Peter. We also know that despite his failures,
Peter went on to do great things for God. Keep following Jesus,
even when you fail.

**4:19** **Then He said to them, "Follow Me, and I will make you fishers of men."** NKJV The first pair of men Jesus called to follow
him were brothers, Simon and Andrew. Andrew had been a
disciple of John the Baptist, who, when introduced to the
"Lamb of God," turned and followed Jesus (John 1:35-39).
Then Andrew brought his brother Simon to Jesus. When Jesus
met Simon he said, "'You are Simon son of John. You will be
called Cephas' (which, when translated, is Peter)" (John 1:42
NIV). These men understood and believed who Jesus was. Jesus
arrived on the shore that day to change their lives forever. Jesus
told Simon (Peter) and Andrew to leave their fishing business
and to *follow* him. To "follow" means to accept Jesus as authority, to pursue his calling, to model after his example, to join
his group. Jesus was asking these men to become his disciples
and to begin fishing for people. "Follow" is the major term
for discipleship in the Gospels. Disciples in Jesus' day literally
followed their masters around and imitated them. Jesus required
his disciples to give him their allegiance, daily count the cost
of commitment, and serve others as he did.

The Old Testament pictures God fishing for men, harvesting
them for judgment (Jeremiah 16:16; Ezekiel 29:4-5; 38:4; Amos
4:2; Habakkuk 1:14-17). Gathering souls is urgent because judgment is coming, so Christ's faithful followers were to bring
people in while there was still time. These disciples were adept
at catching fish, but they would need special training before they
would be able to become *fishers of men*—to fish for people's
souls. The words "I will make" portray Jesus as the empowering
agent; these men were simply to follow. Jesus was calling them
away from their productive trade to be productive spiritually by

helping others believe the Good News and carry on his work after he was gone. This was a radical change from the usual rabbi/disciple relationship. In Judaism, the disciples simply would observe the master and memorize his teaching. Jesus' disciples would have an active role. They would participate in the kingdom as *fishers of men.*

**4:20** **They immediately left their nets and followed Him.**NKJV After their previous meeting with Jesus, Simon Peter and Andrew had returned to fishing. But when Jesus called them to follow him as disciples, *they immediately left their nets.* These men already knew Jesus, so when Jesus called them, they were willing to follow him. The judgment was coming; they had to respond right away. Their lives had changed; their allegiance was now to their teacher. Their action indicated radical discipleship, total surrender. This first pair left their occupation; the second pair (4:22) also left their father. When Jesus calls, people must be willing to realign previous plans and goals, sometimes leaving something important in order to follow Jesus. Jesus is not satisfied with half-hearted Christians.

**4:21-22** **As he went from there, he saw two other brothers, James son of Zebedee and his brother John, in the boat with their father Zebedee, mending their nets, and he called them. Immediately they left the boat and their father, and followed him.**NRSV Not far down the beach were *two other brothers, James* and *John.* Zebedee, their father, owned a fishing business where they worked with Peter and Andrew (Luke 5:10). James and John were sitting in their moored boat *with their father Zebedee, mending their nets.* The weight of a good catch of fish and the constant strain on the nets meant that fishermen had to spend a lot of time keeping their nets repaired and in good shape. Holes had to be mended in preparation for the next night's fishing.

John had met Jesus previously. In his Gospel, John records that he and Andrew were following John the Baptist and that then they began to follow Jesus (John 1:35-39). We have no record of James previously meeting Jesus, but he probably knew about Jesus from his brother. The fact that James's name is always mentioned before John's indicates that James was the older brother. When Peter, Andrew, and John left Galilee to see John the Baptist, James stayed back with the boats and fishing nets. Later, when Jesus called them, James was as eager as his partners to follow. James and John were ready for Jesus' call.

Both sets of brothers *immediately* left behind the lives they had known and embarked on an adventure. Surely Jesus must have made a great impression on them, and knowing that Jesus had chosen them must have motivated them to follow without hesitation. James and John left their father in the boat. They did not leave their father to manage for himself; Mark records that he already had hired men who helped him (Mark 1:20). Zebedee must have been a very understanding father; perhaps he too believed and would have gone along himself in younger days.

**TIME TO GO**
James and his brother, John, along with Peter and Andrew, were the first disciples that Jesus called to work with him. Jesus' call motivated these men to get up and leave their jobs—immediately. They didn't make excuses about why it wasn't a good time. They left at once and followed. We do not know if such a radical decision is required of each person alive today. Are we all to leave our jobs and homes to follow Christ in ministry? Apparently not, for Jesus had many believers and disciples, but he chose only twelve to leave all and follow him. Even those twelve did not abandon wives or their responsibility to their parents. But we must all evaluate our service and do what Christ requires. Some students may need to change majors and go into ministry; Christ may choose some to change livelihoods and enter different fields of service for him. All of us must be willing and prompt to respond when Jesus calls.

## JESUS PREACHES THROUGHOUT GALILEE / 4:23-25 / *36*

**4:23 Jesus went throughout Galilee, teaching in their synagogues, preaching the good news of the kingdom, and healing every disease and sickness among the people.**<sup>NIV</sup> Jesus traveled *throughout Galilee,* visiting the various towns and villages. He was *teaching, preaching,* and *healing,* the three main aspects of his ministry. "Teaching" shows Jesus' concern that people learn; "preaching" shows his concern for commitment; and "healing" shows his concern for physical wholeness. Jesus' healing miracles authenticated his teaching and preaching; they proved that he truly was from God.

When Jesus arrived in a town, he first went to the synagogue. *Synagogues* were established during the Exile to give Jews places to assemble and worship because they couldn't go to the temple. Synagogues later became centers for teaching and preaching. Most towns that had ten or more Jewish families had a synagogue. The building served as a religious gathering place on the

Sabbath and as a school during the week. The leader of the synagogue was more an administrator than a preacher. His job was to
invite rabbis to teach and preach. In the synagogue, there were
two types of messages: (1) exposition or teaching—done while
the leader sat; (2) exhortation or preaching—done while the
leader stood. Thus, Jesus had opportunity to share *the good news
of the kingdom* with the Jews who came to the synagogues. The
"good news" was that the kingdom of heaven had arrived. It was
customary to invite visiting rabbis like Jesus to speak, but Jesus'
earthshaking message and powerful miracles (*healing every disease and sickness among the people* in each village) set him apart
from the others.

**4:24 So his fame spread throughout all Syria, and they brought
to him all the sick, those who were afflicted with various diseases and pains, demoniacs, epileptics, and paralytics, and he
cured them.**NRSV Jesus' teaching and healing caused a stir among
the people. Those who heard him told family and friends, who
told others, so that the news *spread throughout all Syria.* "Syria"
may refer to the area to the north of Galilee, indicating that Jesus'
fame had spread beyond the borders of Palestine. The Romans
used "Syria" to refer to all of Palestine, except for the region of
Galilee, which was under the independent administration of
Herod Antipas. Thus, Jesus' fame spread through Galilee and
throughout all of Palestine.

Jesus became well known very quickly. Certainly his acclaimed
ability to heal people of diseases caused people to bring sick family
and friends to him. Jesus *cured various diseases and pains* (probably undiagnosed by doctors), *demoniacs* (people possessed by
demons), *epileptics* (those having seizures or other unexplained
behavior not related to demon possession), and *paralytics* (those
who had become paralyzed).

Why did Jesus perform physical healings? As Creator, Jesus
wanted people to have health and wholeness rather than illness.
The healings also showed Jesus' compassion for suffering people
and revealed that the kingdom had arrived in power and presence.
Although Jesus refused to do "signs" at the whim of doubting
religious leaders, he did perform miracles of healing that caused
many to believe in him.

**4:25 Large crowds from Galilee, the Decapolis, Jerusalem, Judea
and the region across the Jordan followed him.**NIV *Large
crowds* came to Jesus from all over the region of *Galilee* where
Jesus was concentrating his ministry. "The Decapolis" refers to
a league of ten Gentile cities east of the Sea of Galilee that had

joined together for trade and mutual defense. "The region across the Jordan" most likely refers also to Gentile territory. The city of *Jerusalem* was in the region of *Judea.* People came from this region to the south as well as from its leading city. The news about Jesus was out, and Jews and Gentiles were coming long distances to hear him. The words "followed him" may or may not refer to becoming disciples. Some simply followed him from place to place to hear him speak and see his miracles. Some who followed surely also came to believe in him, accepting the Good News about the kingdom.

# Matthew 5

Matthew 5–7 is called the Sermon on the Mount because Jesus gave it on a hillside near Capernaum. This "sermon" probably covered several days of preaching. In it, Jesus revealed his attitude toward the law of Moses, explaining that he requires faithful and sincere obedience, not ceremonial religion. The Sermon on the Mount challenged the teachings of the proud and legalistic religious leaders of the day. It called people back to the messages of the Old Testament prophets who, like Jesus, had taught that God wants heartfelt obedience, not mere legalistic observance of laws and rituals.

The most well-known and provocative portion of the Sermon on the Mount is known as the Beatitudes (5:3-10). These are a series of blessings promised to those who exhibit the attributes of God's kingdom. Over the centuries since Jesus first presented the Beatitudes, many interpretations of them have been offered. There are strengths in each one, and combinations of elements from several can create new interpretations. Five of the main interpretations are as follows:

1. *Perfectionist legalism.* This view was developed during medieval times and teaches that there are higher standards for "disciples" (clergy and the monastic orders). It teaches that true followers should live on a level of righteousness above normal Christians. However, Jesus' sermon does not teach two different standards for Christians, and we must not read into the sermon salvation by works.

2. *Impossible ideal.* Widely accepted after Martin Luther, this view states that the sermon functions like the Old Testament law, forcing people to realize their sinfulness and helplessness and so turn to God. However, Jesus provides enablement to fulfill his requirements, so these demands are not impossible. Scholars also see the use of hyperbole (overstatement to make a point, as in "If your right hand causes you to sin, cut it off" in 5:30) as an accepted teaching method during Jesus' time to stress moral urgency.

3. *Only for Jesus' disciples.* Albert Schweitzer said that this teaching was only for the disciples, who thought that Jesus would return in their lifetime and that the moral demands were not for all time. However, Jesus makes no reference to the end of the world or to his return in this sermon.

4. *Kingdom age.* Dispensationalism teaches that these laws are for the kingdom age (Millennium) and are only an example for us and our day. Jesus offered the kingdom to the Jews, but they rejected it. Thus, the reality was postponed until the Second Coming. However, nothing in Jesus' teaching ever exempted the disciples then or now from these principles. They are principles for disciples for all ages.

5. *Social gospel.* Protestant liberals have used the ethics of the sermon as a mandate for the church to usher in the kingdom of God by means of reforming society. However, the teachings of Jesus here cannot be isolated from all his other teachings about himself, evangelism, personal faith, and devotion.

There is another way to understand the sermon in light of a double-pronged interpretation. The kingdom has been inaugurated (beginning), but not yet realized (completion). So there remains a creative tension between the "already" and the "not yet" aspects. Those who obey Jesus now experience, in a partial way, the wonderful benefits he described.

We must not let the promise of future blessing deter us from the radical demands for discipleship that Jesus presented. We must ask what the Beatitudes meant in the Jewish milieu in which Christ delivered them. We must also interpret the phrases in their historical (cultural) and logical (the developing message) contexts.

So then, the Beatitudes

- present a code of ethics for the disciples and a standard of conduct for all believers,
- contrast kingdom values (what is eternal) with worldly values (what is temporary),
- contrast the superficial "faith" of the Pharisees with the real faith that Christ wants, and
- show how the future kingdom will fulfill Old Testament expectations.

**5:1-2 Now when he saw the crowds, he went up on a mountainside and sat down. His disciples came to him, and he began to teach them, saying: . . .**[NIV] Large *crowds* were following Jesus—he was the talk of the town, even of the entire province, and everyone wanted to see him. Jesus had already been preaching throughout Galilee (4:12-25). During that preaching mission, Jesus had healed several

people: a government official's son in Cana (John 4:46-54), Peter's
mother-in-law and many others in Capernaum (Matthew 8:14-17),
a man with leprosy (Matthew 8:1-4), and a paralyzed man also in
Capernaum (Matthew 9:1-8). (See the Harmony of the Gospels
included in the back of this commentary.) These events happened
prior to this sermon. (Matthew's Gospel is arranged topically rather
than chronologically.) The many miracles that Jesus had performed
throughout Galilee accounted for his immense popularity. When
people learned of this amazing preacher with healing words and
healing power, they sought him out and followed him.

Jesus often presented his teaching *up on a mountainside.* Jesus
did not have access to public address systems or acoustical amphi-
theaters. So he used what he himself had created—the natural stage
of a sloping hill, which were plentiful on the western coast of the
Sea of Galilee. The people sat on the slope below him. After Jesus
went up, he *sat down* (a typical teaching position for a rabbi).

Matthew then reported that *his disciples came to him, and he
began to teach them.* Some scholars say that the word "disciples"
refers to the crowds, many of whom were Jesus' followers (and
therefore, his disciples). However, others say that this refers
specifically to the Twelve, whom Jesus had just chosen (see the
Harmony of the Gospels and Mark 3:13-19). Most scholars agree
that Jesus gave these teachings primarily to the disciples, but that
the crowds were present and listening (see 7:28). Much of what
Jesus said referred to the ideas that had been promoted by the
religious leaders of the day.

The disciples, the closest associates of this popular man, might
easily have been tempted to feel important, proud, and posses-
sive. Being with Jesus gave them not only prestige, but also
opportunity for receiving money and power. However, Jesus told
them that instead of fame and fortune, they could expect mourning, hunger, and persecution. Jesus also assured his disciples that
they would receive rewards—but perhaps not in this life.

**5:3 "Blessed are the poor in spirit, for theirs is the kingdom of
heaven."**[NKJV] The Beatitudes are not multiple choice—pick what
you like and leave the rest. We must take them as a whole. The
Beatitudes describe how Christ's followers should live. Each
beatitude tells how to be *blessed.* "Blessed" means more than happiness; it means singularly favored, graciously approved by God.
Jesus' words throughout this sermon seem to contradict each other.
According to worldly standards, the types of people whom Jesus
described don't seem to be particularly "blessed." But God's way
of living usually contradicts the world's. The Beatitudes don't
promise laughter, pleasure, or earthly prosperity. To Jesus, a person

## THE UNBEATITUDES

We can understand the Beatitudes by looking at them from their opposites. Some, Jesus implied, will not be blessed. Their condition could be described in this way:

- Wretched are the spiritually self-sufficient, for theirs is the kingdom of hell.
- Wretched are those who deny the tragedy of their sinfulness, for they will be troubled.
- Wretched are the self-centered, for they will be empty.
- Wretched are those who ceaselessly justify themselves, for their efforts will be in vain.
- Wretched are the merciless, for no mercy will be shown to them.
- Wretched are those with impure hearts, for they will not see God.
- Wretched are those who reject peace, for they will earn the title "sons of Satan."
- Wretched are the uncommitted for convenience's sake, for their destination is hell.

who is "blessed" experiences hope and joy, independent of his or her outward circumstances. The disciples, riding on the wave of Jesus' popularity, needed to first understand kingdom priorities.

Jesus explained that the *poor in spirit* are blessed. The poor in spirit realize that they cannot please God on their own. They are "poor" or "bankrupt" inwardly, unable to give anything of value to God and thus must depend on his mercy. Only those who humbly depend on God are admitted into *the kingdom of heaven.* In this beatitude and in the very last one (5:10) the reward is the same. And in both places the reward is described in the present tense—"theirs *is* the kingdom of heaven." The intervening beatitudes describe the reward in the future tense. The final consummation of all these rewards, and of the kingdom itself, lies in the future. However, believers can already share in the kingdom (as far as it has been revealed) by living out Jesus' words. It must be remembered, one is not rewarded for being virtuous; virtue is its own reward.

ACTING STRANGELY
People who want to live for God must be ready to say and do what seems strange to the world. Christians must be willing to give when others take, to love when others hate, to help when others abuse. By putting aside our selfish interests so that we can serve others, we will one day receive everything God has in store for us. To find hope and joy, the deepest form of happiness, we must follow Jesus no matter what the cost.

**5:4 "Blessed are those who mourn, for they will be comforted."** NRSV
In another seeming contradiction in terms, Jesus explained that
*those who mourn* are *blessed.* Jesus reminded his disciples that the
prophet Isaiah had promised that the Messiah would "comfort all
who mourn" (Isaiah 61:2 NIV). Scholars differ on the exact nature
of this mourning. Some say that Jesus was referring to the nation
of Israel mourning for its sins; others interpret this more personally,
explaining that it refers to those who mourn for their own sins or
even for personal grief or oppression. Tied with the beatitude in
verse 3, this means that humility (realization of one's unworthiness
before God) also requires sorrow for sins. Still other scholars see in
the word mourning a picture of God's people who suffer because of
their faith in him.

Whether Jesus' followers mourn for sin or in suffering,
God's promise is sure—*they will be comforted.* Only God can
take away sorrow for sin; only God can forgive and erase it.
Only God can give comfort to those who suffer for his sake
because they know their reward in the kingdom. There he will
"wipe away every tear from their eyes" (Revelation 7:17 NIV).
Jesus explained to his disciples that following him would not
involve fame, popularity, and wealth. Instead, it could very
well mean sorrow, mourning, and suffering. But they would
always know that God would be their comfort.

**5:5 "Blessed are the meek, for they will inherit the earth."** NRSV
The word translated "meek" *(praeis)* occurs only three other
times in the New Testament (Matthew 11:29; 21:5; 1 Peter 3:4).
In all three other places, it is translated "gentle." The meaning
conveys humility and trust in God rather than self-centered
attitudes. The psalmist, contrasting the destinies of the meek
and wicked, wrote, "For evildoers shall be cut off; but those
who wait on the Lord, they shall inherit the earth. For yet a
little while and the wicked shall be no more; indeed, you will
look carefully for his place, but it shall be no more. But the
meek shall inherit the earth, and shall delight themselves in the
abundance of peace" (Psalm 37:9-11 NKJV).

Meek people realize their position before God (5:3) and
gladly live it out before their fellow humans. They do not look
down on themselves, but they do not think too highly of themselves either. Such people exemplify the Golden Rule. They
are not arrogant; they are the opposite of those who seek to
gain as much for themselves as possible. Ironically, then, it
will not be the arrogant, wealthy, harsh people who get everything. Instead, the meek *will inherit the earth.* To the Jews,
this implied the Promised Land; Jesus used the "earth" to refer

to the future inheritance of the kingdom. According to Revelation 21–22, believers will enjoy a new heaven and a new earth. God will one day freely give his true disciples what they did not grasp for themselves on earth.

**5:6 "Blessed are those who hunger and thirst for righteousness, for they will be filled."** NRSV The words "hunger and thirst" picture intense longings that people desire to satisfy—necessities that they cannot live without. The psalmist wrote, "As a deer longs for flowing streams, so my soul longs for you, O God. My soul thirsts for God, for the living God. When shall I come and behold the face of God?" (Psalm 42:1-2 NRSV). Those who have an intense longing for *righteousness* are *blessed.* What kind of righteousness? Most likely, this refers to personal righteousness—being so filled with God that the person completely does God's will, without tripping up, sinning, making mistakes, and disappointing God. Righteousness refers to total discipleship and complete obedience. It may also refer to righteousness for the entire world—an end to the sin and evil that fill it. In both cases, God's promise is sure—*they will be filled.* He will completely satisfy their spiritual hunger and thirst.

Regarding the longing for personal righteousness, John, one of Jesus' disciples, later wrote, "Dear friends, now we are children of God, and what we will be has not yet been made known. But we know that when he appears, we shall be like him, for we shall see him as he is" (1 John 3:2 NIV). Regarding the longing for a righteous world, Peter, another of Jesus' disciples hearing this message, later wrote to persecuted believers: "But in keeping with his promise we are looking forward to a new heaven and a new earth, the home of righteousness" (2 Peter 3:13 NIV).

The fourth beatitude bridges the God-centered concerns of the first three and the neighbor-centered focus of the last four. The appetites and satisfaction Jesus promised were directed at both external and internal desires. Those who hunger and thirst for righteousness experience that longing in at least three forms:

1. *The desire to be righteous*—to be forgiven and accepted by God; to be right with God.
2. *The desire to do what is right*—to do what God commands; imitating and reflecting God's righteousness.
3. *The desire to see right done*—to help bring about God's will in the world.

**STARVED**
Hungry for hamburgers, maybe; hungry for victory on the tennis court, normally; hungry for the love of that special someone, usually . . . but hungry for righteousness? We don't hear about that one too often.

We must proceed carefully here. Christians are not to get hungry for self-righteousness. We're not to be prickly and perfect and proud about our morals. That just feeds the ego.

Christians growing closer to the Lord Jesus want what he wants. When evil happens, they hurt for victims and long for the end of evil's influence and strength. They want God's victory over evil to be complete soon—even now. They hunger for the end of trouble, for the full measure of God's peace and righteousness.

Whenever you pray for God's will to be done, you are getting hungry for righteousness. Pray often, until the little pangs become a passion and your heart becomes centered on what God wants most.

**5:7** **"Blessed are the merciful, for they will be shown mercy."** NIV *Merciful* people realize that, because they received mercy from God, they must extend mercy to others. The word "merciful" implies generosity, forgiveness, and compassion, and it includes a desire to remove the wrong as well as alleviate the suffering. Jesus repeated this warning several times in this Gospel (see 6:12, 14-15; 18:21-35). We must be people who show mercy. That *they will be shown mercy* is not contingent upon how much mercy they showed; it is not that God will be merciful because these people have been merciful. Instead, believers understand true mercy because they have received mercy from God. Also, this promise does not guarantee mercy in return from people. The believers' comfort comes in the knowledge that, no matter how the world treats them, God will show them mercy both now and when he returns.

**5:8** **"Blessed are the pure in heart, for they will see God."** NRSV People characterized as *pure in heart* are morally pure, honest, and sincere. They are people of integrity and single-minded commitment to God. Moral purity, honesty, and integrity come only through such a commitment. In turn, people committed totally to God will seek to be morally clean. Because of their sincere devotion to Christ, *they will see God,* here and now through the eyes of faith (Hebrews 11:27), and finally face-to-face (1 John 3:2).

**5:9** **"Blessed are the peacemakers, for they will be called children of God."** NRSV Jesus came as "the Prince of Peace" (Isaiah 9:6-7) and gave the ultimate sacrifice to bring peace between

God and humanity (Ephesians 2:14-18; Colossians 1:20). God calls his children to be *peacemakers.* This involves action, not just passive compliance. Peacemakers do more than just live peaceful lives; they actively seek to "make peace," to cause reconciliation, to end bitterness and strife. This peace is not appeasement but dealing with and solving problems to maintain peace. Arrogant, selfish people do not concern themselves with peacemaking. Peacemakers *will be called children of God* because they reflect their Father's character. This has a royal sense—they will share the glories of the Messiah's kingdom.

---

MAKING PEACE
How do you resolve conflict? Most people use different means for different settings.

Making peace with your children includes defining the boundaries between right and wrong, enforcing discipline, and affirming each child with love and affection.

- Making peace with friends includes broadening your mind to include the possibility that someone else's ideas make sense. It means accepting your friend's explanation at face value and applying the least hurtful meaning to the offensive words you heard. It means taking a step toward trust, away from anger, and onto an unmarked playing field called vulnerability. That's the risky price of friendship.
- Making peace with your spouse can be the most difficult of all. Sometimes it requires outside help, often a lot of listening, mutual confession, and rebuilding of love that's been burned. Too often today, the alternative is to quit.

Make peace your aim. Not sloppy acquiescence—the Milquetoast peace of people without backbone or principle. But strong peace—hard won, committed to the other, centered on God, ready for the wear and tear that another day may bring.

---

**5:10** **"Blessed are those who are persecuted for righteousness' sake, for theirs is the kingdom of heaven."** NKJV Unfortunately, people who exemplify the characteristics already mentioned, who put others before themselves and who attempt to make peace, will seldom receive applause and honors. Often, they will be *persecuted* instead. Because they are "righteous," having oriented their lives around God and his will (see 5:6), they stand out from the world and become marks for enemy attacks. The world is under Satan's control, and believers belong to the opposing army. Persecution should not surprise Christians. Later, when Peter wrote to persecuted believers, he urged them to be sure that their persecution was truly for *righteousness' sake* and not for wrongdoing on their part (1 Peter

## KEY LESSONS FROM THE SERMON ON THE MOUNT

In his longest recorded sermon, Jesus began by describing the traits he was looking for in his followers. He called those who lived out those traits "blessed" because God had something special in store for them. Each beatitude is an almost direct contradiction of society's typical way of life. In the last beatitude, Jesus pointed out that a serious effort to develop these traits would create opposition. Jesus gives us the best example of each trait. If our goal is to become like him, the Beatitudes will challenge the way we live each day.

| Beatitude | Old Testament anticipation | Clashing worldly values | God's reward | How to develop this attitude |
|---|---|---|---|---|
| Poor in spirit (5:3) | Isaiah 57:15 | Pride and personal independence | Receive kingdom of heaven | James 4:7-10 |
| Mourning (5:4) | Isaiah 61:1-2 | Happiness at any cost | Receive comfort | 2 Corinthians 1:4; James 4:7-10 |
| Meekness (5:5) | Psalm 37:5-11 | Power | Inherit the earth | Matthew 11:27-30 |
| Righteous-ness (5:6) | Isaiah 11:4-5; 42:1-4 | Pursuit of personal needs | Be filled (satisfied) | John 16:5-11; Philippians 3:7-11 |
| Mercy (5:7) | Psalm 41:1 | Strength without feeling | Be shown mercy | Ephesians 5:1-2 |
| Pure in heart (5:8) | Psalm 24:3-4; 51:10 | Acceptable deception | See God | 1 John 3:1-3 |
| Peacemaker (5:9) | Isaiah 57:18-19; 60:17 | Pursuit of personal peace, unconcern about the world's problems | Be called sons of God | Romans 12:9-21; Hebrews 12:10-11 |
| Persecuted (5:10) | Isaiah 52:13; 53:12 | Weak commitments | Inherit the kingdom of heaven | 2 Timothy 3:12 |

4:12-19). The reward for these believers will be *the kingdom of heaven.* God will make up for the suffering that his children have undergone because of their loyalty to him. The reward here matches the reward in 5:3, rounding out this list of characteristics of those who belong to God.

TEN STEPS OF BLESSING
The order and orientation of the Beatitudes provide several key insights. The Beatitudes begin and end with the promise of the kingdom of heaven (5:3, 10). They progress from the point of greatest need (spiritual bankruptcy) to the point of greatest identification with Christ (experiencing rejection for his sake). The first four beatitudes outline a deepening relationship with God; the second four depict the impact of our relations to others. Clearly, the Beatitudes are not stages through which we pass and go on, but responses that we must keep on making. Each day we must utilize our opportunities to show mercy, practice peacemaking, and purify our intentions.

**5:11** **"Blessed are you when people insult you, persecute you and falsely say all kinds of evil against you because of me."** NIV The Beatitudes end at 5:10, despite the word "blessed" at the beginning of this verse. This thought expands on 5:10, that the persecuted are blessed. Up to this point, the beatitudes were spoken in the third person: "Blessed are those." Here Jesus switched to the second person, focusing his comments directly at his listening disciples. Jesus was telling his disciples that they shouldn't be surprised *when people insult you, persecute you and falsely say all kinds of evil against you because of me.* Jesus would face such treatment. Later he explained to his followers that they should expect nothing different (10:18; 24:9; John 15:20). In 5:10, the persecution is because of righteousness; here it is *because of me.* To imitate Jesus is to live righteously, and, as explained above, this evil world hates righteous living.

> Discipleship means allegiance to the suffering Christ, and it is therefore not at all surprising that Christians should be called upon to suffer. In fact it is a joy and a token of his grace.
> *Dietrich Bonhoeffer*

**5:12** **"Rejoice and be glad, for your reward is great in heaven, for in the same way they persecuted the prophets who were before you."** NRSV Jesus clearly described the way the disciples should respond to this kind of treatment: *Rejoice and be glad.* The word translated "be glad," *agalliasthe* (also translated "exult"), refers to deep, spiritual joy (see Luke 1:46-47; Acts 16:34; 1 Peter 4:13). This type of rejoicing is eternal—unhindered and unchanged by what happens in this present life.

How can anyone rejoice when being insulted, persecuted, or slandered? While that would not be the first and most natural response, a person with righteous character can rejoice and be glad because of the promise: *Your reward is great in heaven.* When God judges the world, the persecution will pale in comparison to the great reward that awaits. The reward is heaven itself. See 16:24-27 and 19:28-30 for more on rewards.

Besides that, the disciples had good company. The Old Testament described many *prophets* who had come with God's message and had faced persecution, rejection, and even death (see 21:33-46). Jesus placed his disciples in a long line of God's followers who lived righteously and spoke truthfully— only to suffer for it. The Jews held the ancient prophets of God in high esteem; to be placed among them was a great honor. Jesus explained that to live and speak for God in the face of unjust persecution, as did the ancient prophets, would bring great reward in heaven.

---

**IN GOOD COMPANY**
Jesus said to rejoice when we're persecuted. There are four reasons that persecution can be good: (1) It can take our eyes off earthly rewards, (2) it can strip away superficial belief, (3) it can strengthen the faith of those who endure, and (4) our attitude through it can serve as an example to others who follow. We can take comfort in knowing that God's greatest prophets endured persecution (Elijah, Jeremiah, Daniel). Persecution proves that we have been faithful; faithless people would be unnoticed. In the future, God will reward the faithful by receiving them into his eternal kingdom, where there is no more persecution. No matter what you face today, if you remain faithful to Christ, one day you will receive a joyful reward.

---

## JESUS TEACHES ABOUT SALT AND LIGHT / 5:13-16 / **50**

In these verses, Jesus explained to his disciples the true nature of their calling. They would be salt in a dreary world, light in a dark and evil world. But they would do this only because of the one who came as "the Light of the World." This handful of men brought salt that we can taste and light that we can see even today. We, in turn, must pass "salt" and "light" along to others.

**5:13** **"You are the salt of the earth; but if salt has lost its taste, how can its saltiness be restored? It is no longer good for anything, but is thrown out and trampled under foot."** NRSV In the ancient world, *salt* was used for flavoring and as a preservative. Instead of being made by evaporation of salt water, the salt came mostly from salt marshes in the area southwest of the Dead Sea. Salt had commercial value, but the impure salt taken from the sea and its environs was susceptible to deterioration that left only useless crystals. Jesus' question *How can its saltiness be restored?* did not expect an answer—for once salt has deteriorated, it cannot be used as a preservative. Jesus warned them against being defiled by impurities. Even today in Israel, people scatter such salt on the flat roofs of their homes to harden the soil and prevent leaks. These roofs are still used for children to play and for group gatherings, so the salt is still literally *trampled under foot.*

As salt preserves and brings out the best flavor of food, so believers should affect others positively. If a seasoning has no flavor *(has lost its taste),* it has no value. Jesus clearly told his disciples (the word "you" is emphatic, meaning "you, my followers") that if they wanted to make a difference in the world, they would have to *be* different from the world. God would hold them accountable to maintain their "saltiness" (that is, their usefulness). If we are too much like the world, we are useless. Christians should not blend in with everyone else. Jesus tells us, as he told the disciples, that we must be different if we want to make a difference. We dare not allow the world to dilute our effectiveness. If we do, we are of no value to him.

---

### WORKING

How can we be salt when we're working? Most jobs, even the humdrum kind, provide opportunities for saltiness. We can solve problems, keep equipment working, and serve human needs. Christians ought to be proud of their work.

Next time you think you are going nowhere in a boring job, consider your work as a "thank you" to God for the salvation Christ gave you. Do your job with skill and commitment as a missionary in the marketplace, salting your small corner of the world with God's message of renewal and joy.

---

**5:14** **"You are the light of the world. A city that is set on a hill cannot be hidden."** NKJV As salt makes a difference in people's food, so *light* makes a difference in their surroundings. Jesus came as "the light of all people" (John 1:4 NRSV) and would later explain, "I am the light of the world. Whoever follows me will never walk in darkness, but will have the light of life" (John 8:12 NIV). Christ's disciples must live for Christ, shining like lights in a dark world, showing clearly what Christ is like. Who could hide a city that is sitting on top of a hill? Lanterns glowing from behind its walls send a light at night that can be seen for miles. Because Jesus is the Light of the World, his followers must reflect his light. If we live for Christ, we will glow like lights, showing others what Christ is like.

WHO TURNED OUT THE LIGHTS?
"Why would anyone try to hide a light?" Jesus asked.
Unfortunately many Christians do just that. We hide our light by
- being quiet when we should speak
- going along with the crowd
- denying the truth
- letting sin dim our witness for Christ
- not explaining the truth to others
- ignoring the needs of others
Be a beacon of truth—don't shut off your light from the rest of
the world.

**5:15** **"Neither do people light a lamp and put it under a bowl.
Instead they put it on its stand, and it gives light to everyone in
the house."**[NIV] How absurd it would be to *light a lamp* and then *put
it under a bowl* (referring to a clay jar that would conceal the light).
People light lamps to spread light, enabling them to see what they
are doing or where they are going. Thus people place lights on
stands in the best location for them to spread their warm glow.

Jesus emphasized that the disciples would continue to reflect
the light of their Master, the Light of the World. They could no
more hide the light than a city on a hill can hide. They must not
try to conceal their light any more than one would light a lamp
and then conceal it under a clay jar. Being Christ's disciples
means being distinctive. Being Christ's disciples means spreading the light *to everyone in the house*—that is, everyone with
whom they have contact.

**5:16** **"In the same way, let your light shine before others, so that they
may see your good works and give glory to your Father in
heaven."**[NRSV] *In the same way* that a light shines from a lampstand,
Christ's disciples must let their *light shine before others.* The very
reason for the existence of that light is to illuminate—helping show
people what to do and where to go. How would people see this
light? Through the *good works* of Christ's followers. Jesus made
it clear that there would be no mistaking the source of a believer's
good works. *Others* will see and *give glory to your Father in
heaven.* This contrasts with the attitude of the people he will chas-
tise in 6:1, the ones who do good works for their own glory. The
believer's light shines not for himself but to reflect the light back
to the Father and so direct people to him.

In an attempt to steer clear of works for gaining righteousness,
good works are often neglected in church life today. But clearly the
Bible supports the importance of doing good (see Ephesians 2:8-10;
4:12; 1 Timothy 5:10; 6:18; 2 Timothy 2:21; 3:17; Titus 3:1, 8, 14;

James 1:22; 2:14-26; 3:13). Good works are important not only as a witness to others but as a continuation of the work Christ began on earth.

---

**IN THE SPOTLIGHT**
Who gets the spotlight when you witness for Jesus—God or you? When you work all day on a service project, give testimony on Sunday, or lead the church building campaign, whose image and reputation is most important?

Your life is what people see, but the spotlight is all God's. Not that God needs an image boost, but the focus of your witness should always point beyond you to the one you represent. Give your ego a break and give the honor to God.

---

## JESUS TEACHES ABOUT THE LAW / 5:17-20 / **51**

God gave moral and ceremonial laws to help people love him with all their hearts and minds. Throughout Israel's history, however, these laws had been often misquoted and misapplied. By Jesus' time, religious leaders had turned God's laws into a confusing mass of rules. When Jesus talked about a new way to understand the law, he was trying to bring people back to its original purpose. Jesus did not speak against the law itself, but against the abuses and excesses to which it had been subjected.

**5:17 "Do not think that I have come to abolish the law or the prophets; I have come not to abolish but to fulfill."** NRSV Jesus did not come as a rabbi with a brand-new teaching that he had thought up and hoped to convince people was true. Instead, he came as the promised Messiah with a message heard from the beginning of time. He came not to *abolish the law or the prophets,* but to *fulfill* the promises in those Scriptures. The meaning for "fulfill" has been taken three ways: (1) to accomplish or obey the Old Testament laws; (2) to bring out the full meaning of the law and prophecy, showing how Christ is the fulfillment of all to which they pointed; (3) to bring the Old Testament law and promises to their destined end or intended completion. Most likely, "fulfill" contains the thrusts of

> Our Lord's mission was not to destroy, but to construct. As noon fulfills dawn and summer spring, as manhood fulfills childhood and the perfect picture the rude sketch, so does Jesus gather up, realize, and make possible the highest ideals ever inspired in human hearts or written by God's Spirit on the page of inspiration.
>
> *F. B. Meyer*

both (2) and (3). Jesus fills to fullness; he completes and transcends the law. The Old Testament law is not rescinded but now must be reinterpreted and reapplied in light of Jesus. God does not change his mind. He did not send his Son to repeal, abolish, or annul what he had told his people previously. Instead, the Father sent his Son as the fulfillment. Jesus' coming had been part of God's plan from creation (see Genesis 3:15). The disciples would not thoroughly understand how Jesus fulfilled the Scriptures until after his death and resurrection (Luke 24:25-27).

Jesus' reference to *the law* means the commands in the Pentateuch—the books of Genesis through Deuteronomy. In synagogues on the Sabbath, a rabbi would read a portion from the Law and a portion from the Prophets. Unfortunately, many of the learned men of the day who should have seen in Jesus the fulfillment of their Scriptures completely missed him. The Pharisees attempted to follow meticulously the law and saw Jesus only as a lawbreaker. The Sadducees revered only the Pentateuch but missed the promises of the coming of the one through whom all nations on the earth would be blessed (Genesis 22:18).

THE SPIRIT OF THE LAW
What did Jesus have in mind when he claimed to fulfill the law? He illustrated his claim in the paragraphs that follow. Jesus repeated traditional applications of God's law and showed them to be shallow. He taught the principle of true application: understanding the deepest and broadest implications of a command in order to take immediate action. Jesus emphasized that the law wasn't simply "letter," but also "spirit." In the language of today Jesus might have said, "Don't believe those who try to deal with God by using legal technicalities. God knows your heart and will reject rationalizations." Unless we face the truth that God's standards will not be met by our halfhearted efforts, we will never recognize our need for a Savior. Jesus clarified the intent of the law; then he claimed to be our only way of escape from the judgment we deserve for our failure to obey God's commands.

**5:18** **"I tell you the truth, until heaven and earth disappear, not the smallest letter, not the least stroke of a pen, will by any means disappear from the Law until everything is accomplished."** [NIV] Jesus used the words "I tell you the truth" (also translated, "Truly I say to you," or "Verily, verily") several times in his speaking. They signal that what he said next is of vital importance. In these words Jesus ascribes the highest authority to God's Law. Not only did Jesus fulfill the law, but *until heaven and earth disappear* (meaning until the end of the

age) the Law will not change. There are two "until" clauses:
(1) "until heaven and earth disappear"—the eternal validity of
the law is established; (2) "until everything is accomplished"—
probably means the total plan of God.

*Not the smallest letter, not the least stroke of a pen,* will
be set aside or will disappear from the law book. In Hebrew
writing, some letters are very small (the Hebrew letter "yod"
is the smallest letter). Others are distinguished by just a slight
stroke of the pen (for example, a small dot above the double
"s" distinguished "s" from "sh"). Jesus upheld the truth of
every letter of every word in God's Law. Furthermore, Jesus'
statement certifies the absolute authority of every word and
letter of Scripture. God's plan will never change. God's Law
recorded in Scripture looked forward to and prepared people
for the One who would come and fulfill it. Everything prophesied in God's Law will take place. No promise or prophecy in
the Law will remain unfulfilled. Everything will be *accomplished.*

**5:19** **"Therefore, whoever breaks one of the least of these commandments, and teaches others to do the same, will be called least in
the kingdom of heaven; but whoever does them and teaches
them will be called great in the kingdom of heaven."** NRSV Jesus
will fulfill and accomplish the entire Law and the Prophets (5:17-18).
He explained, therefore, that his followers must also keep and practice the commandments included in the Law and the Prophets—
even *the least of these commandments.* No one has the authority to
set aside or alter any of God's laws. In addition, teachers have the
responsibility to live correctly and to teach correctly so that they
do not influence others to break even the smallest law. Jesus was
using hyperbole to make a point and, most likely, was not referring
to minutiae of the law for which the Pharisees were contending
so scrupulously. In the rabbinic debate, some would distinguish
between "greater" and "lesser" commandments. Christ did this
only for illustration.

Because the Law and the Prophets point forward to Jesus and
his teaching, people can "do" and "teach" the commandments by
following Jesus and adhering to his teachings. Those who do so,
Jesus explained, *will be called great in the kingdom of heaven.*
This may refer to degrees of rewards in heaven, but it most likely
does not mean rewarding of status in heaven. Neither breaking
(and teaching others to break), nor practicing and teaching even
"the least of these commandments" ultimately determines a person's inclusion in the kingdom of heaven, so Jesus was simply
indicating how people who treated the law in those ways would

be regarded by God. Those who treated any part of the law as "least," and therefore breakable, would themselves be called "least" and, presumably, be excluded. Jesus explained to his disciples, the men who would be responsible to carry on his message, that they must live carefully and teach carefully, not taking God's will lightly. Jesus' followers must respect and obey even the least commandment if they want to accomplish great things for God.

If Jesus did not come to abolish the law, does that mean all the Old Testament laws still apply to us today? Did Jesus mean that Christians today must follow every law recorded in the Old Testament? Not even Jesus stood for law keeping that was void of heartfelt worship (see the next verse, 5:20). Jesus was emphasizing an attitude of respect toward God's Word and God's will. The Old Testament includes three categories of law: ceremonial, civil, and moral.

1. The "ceremonial law" related specifically to Israel's worship (see Leviticus 1:2-3, for example). Its primary purpose was to point forward to Jesus Christ; these laws, therefore, were no longer necessary after Jesus' death and resurrection. While we need not follow all these ceremonial laws, the principles behind them—to worship and love a holy God—still apply. The Pharisees often accused Jesus of violating ceremonial law.
2. The "civil law" applied to daily living in Israel (see Deuteronomy 24:10-11, for example). Because modern society and culture differ so radically from that time and setting, we need not keep all of these guidelines specifically. However, the principles behind the commands are timeless and should guide our conduct. Jesus demonstrated these principles by example.
3. The "moral law" (such as the Ten Commandments) is the direct command of God; thus, it requires strict obedience (see Exodus 20:13, for example). The moral law reveals the nature and will of God, and it still applies today. Jesus obeyed the moral law completely and expects his followers to do the same.

**5:20 "For I say to you, that unless your righteousness exceeds the righteousness of the scribes and Pharisees, you will by no means enter the kingdom of heaven."** NKJV Jesus' words in 5:19 may have sounded exceedingly difficult ("How can anyone keep all the commandments perfectly?"), but here Jesus made it seem even more difficult. Not only did he expect his followers to keep every part of the law, but he also expected them to be more righteous than the scribes and Pharisees, an almost impossible task. The *Pharisees* were exacting and scrupulous in their attempts to follow God's Law as well as hundreds of traditional laws. They

spent their lives in rigid devotion to keeping every commandment. In Old Testament times, *scribes* prepared new scrolls of
Scripture. By New Testament times, they had become teachers
and lawyers in Jewish courts. How could Jesus reasonably call
his followers to a greater righteousness than theirs?

Jesus was not placing impossible demands on his followers,
expecting them to be even more pious and careful to scrupulously
obey every law; however, Jesus was speaking about the attitude of
the heart, the *righteousness* found on the inside when God works in
a person. The Pharisees were content to obey the laws outwardly
without humbly looking to God to change their hearts (or attitudes).
Jesus was saying, therefore, that the quality of our righteousness
should exceed (abound more than) that of the scribes and Pharisees,
who looked pious, but were far from the kingdom of God. True followers of God know that they cannot *do* anything to become righteous enough to *enter the kingdom of heaven,* so they count on God
to work his righteousness within them. Their righteousness *exceeds*
that of the scribes and Pharisees because it rests on a relationship
with God. That kind of righteousness fulfills the Law and the
Prophets; Jesus will describe that kind of righteousness in the
following verses. The disciples could not see how this would all
work out. They could not yet understand Jesus' teaching from
the perspective of the Cross. But Jesus made it clear to them that
external piety, fine robes, and rigid law keeping was not the way.
Instead, he himself was the only "way" (John 14:6) to enter God's
kingdom. To know how to have righteousness exceeding that of the
experts would require following Jesus.

---

RIGHTEOUSNESS CHECK
Jesus was saying that his listeners needed a different kind
of righteousness altogether (love and obedience), not just a
more intense version of the Pharisees' righteousness (legal
compliance). Our righteousness must (1) come from what
God does in us, not what we can do by ourselves, (2) be God-
centered, not self-centered, (3) be based on reverence for God,
not approval from people, and (4) go beyond keeping the law
to loving God who gave the law.

---

## JESUS TEACHES ABOUT ANGER / 5:21-26 / **52**

Following from 5:20, the question most likely hung in people's
minds, "How can we possibly be more righteous than the law-
abiding Pharisees?" In the following verses, Jesus outlined some
examples of the "how." Six times he will say, "You have heard

## JESUS AND THE OLD TESTAMENT LAW

What seems to be a case of Jesus contradicting the laws of the Old Testament deserves a careful look. God wrote much mercy into the Old Testament laws. What God designed as a system of justice with mercy had been distorted over the years into a license for revenge. It was this misapplication of the law that Jesus attacked. (Verses are quoted from NIV.)

| Reference | Examples of Old Testament mercy in justice |
| --- | --- |
| Leviticus 19:18 | "Do not seek revenge or bear a grudge against one of your people, but love your neighbor as yourself. I am the Lord." |
| Proverbs 24:28-29 | "Do not testify against your neighbor without cause, or use your lips to deceive. Do not say, 'I'll do to him as he has done to me; I'll pay that man back for what he did.'" |
| Proverbs 25:21-22 | "If your enemy is hungry, give him food to eat; if he is thirsty, give him water to drink. In doing this, you will heap burning coals on his head, and the Lord will reward you." |
| Lamentations 3:27-31 | "It is good for a man to . . . offer his cheek to one who would strike him, and let him be filled with disgrace. For men are not cast off by the Lord forever." |

that it was said . . . but I say to you" (5:21-22, 27-28, 31-32, 33-34, 38-39, 43-44). With these words he explained that his teaching went beyond what the Ten Commandments and the Torah said. Jesus showed the true intent of God's Law. The people did not need to be more righteous than the Pharisees by the number of laws that they kept; they had to be more righteous in the *way* they kept the laws. To truly keep the law as God intended, the people could not get by with lip service and with obeying the letter of the law alone. Instead, Jesus' teaching reached to the application of the law, into people's motives and attitudes, showing people's utter inability to keep the law without a relationship with God, who made the laws.

**5:21 "You have heard that it was said to the people long ago, 'Do not murder, and anyone who murders will be subject to judgment.'"** NIV
"You have heard that it was said" is an understatement— Jesus was quoting from the Ten Commandments in 5:21 and 5:27. Moses had brought these commandments to *the people long ago* in the nation of Israel. The Pharisees were teaching that the command against *murder,* found in Exodus 20:13, referred just to taking

another person's life. Murderers were *subject to judgment* (death—see Exodus 21:12; Leviticus 24:17) through certain legal proceedings, also described in the Law.

---

NAME-CALLING
It's not the words that put us in jeopardy of hellfire. We could think of a lot worse names than "you fool" to call people. It's the attitude. By calling someone a fool, you write that person off as worthless, a zero, nothing, nobody.
  And what is the problem with that? That worthless nobody (in your judgment) is someone made in the image of God. If God's image is a fool, doesn't that make God a fool too?
  Next time you write someone off, think about whom you're really talking about.

---

**5:22 "But I say to you that if you are angry with a brother or sister, you will be liable to judgment; and if you insult a brother or sister, you will be liable to the council; and if you say, 'You fool,' you will be liable to the hell of fire."** NRSV When Jesus said, "But I say to you," he was not doing away with the law or adding his own beliefs. Rather, he was giving a fuller understanding of why God made that law in the first place. For example, Moses said, "You shall not murder" (Exodus 20:13). The Pharisees read this law and, not having literally murdered anyone, felt righteous. Yet they were angry enough with Jesus that they would soon plot his death, though they would not do the dirty work themselves.

Jesus, however, taught that his followers should not even become *angry* enough to murder, for then they would already have committed murder in their heart. Killing is a terrible sin, but anger is a great sin too because it also violates God's command to love. "Anger," here, refers to a seething, brooding bitterness against *a brother or sister,* which could refer to a fellow believer. It is a dangerous emotion that always threatens to leap out of control, leading to violence, emotional hurt, increased mental stress, spiritual damage, and, yes, even murder. Anger keeps us from developing a spirit pleasing to God. We may not go to court because of our anger, but it does make us *liable to judgment.* While "judgment" in 5:21 referred to human court, in this verse it refers to divine judgment. "Council" refers to a local council, probably not to the Sanhedrin. To stoop to insulting or calling a fellow believer a derogatory name makes one liable to such judgment as ends in *the hell of fire.* Angry words and name-calling reveal a heart far from God: "All who hate a brother or sister are murderers, and you know that murderers do not have eternal life abiding in them" (1 John 3:15 NRSV). The rabbis used the word "Raca" (translated, "you fool" or "idiot") to excommunicate people; common people used it as an insult.

The word translated "hell" is *Gehenna*. The name derived from the Valley of Hinnom, south of Jerusalem, where children had been sacrificed by fire to the pagan god Molech (see 2 Kings 23:10; 2 Chronicles 28:3; Jeremiah 7:31; 32:35). Later, during the reign of good king Josiah, the valley had become the city's garbage dump where fire burned constantly to destroy the garbage and the worms infesting it. Gehenna, hell, is the place of "fire that shall never be quenched" (Mark 9:43, 45, 47-48 NKJV) prepared for the devil, his angels, and all those who do not know Christ (25:41; Revelation 20:9-10). This is the final and eternal state of the wicked after the resurrection and the Last Judgment.

---

ANGER
Jesus put anger and murder in the same category. He saw a direct connection that we usually deny. In this and other relational matters, like adultery, Jesus taught that intention is a significant part of wrongdoing. Anger leads quickly to a whole range of emotions and actions. When anger is not righteous (see Ephesians 4:26; James 1:19), it becomes destructive. Anger tends to be like a gushing spring that quickly floods its surroundings unless it has a clear channel through which to flow. Anger can destroy its host as well as anything or anyone against which it is directed. Anger may require the following controls:
- *Confrontation*—expressing anger in appropriate ways
- *Contemplation*—examining why we are angry
- *Confession*—asking God and others for help in dealing with our anger
- *Condemnation*—revising inappropriate expectations that lead to anger

Based on Jesus' warning, we cannot assume that anger will go away by itself. It must be directed, controlled, and resolved.

---

**5:23-24** **"So when you are offering your gift at the altar, if you remember that your brother or sister has something against you, leave your gift there before the altar and go; first be reconciled to your brother or sister, and then come and offer your gift."** NRSV At certain times of the year, especially during Passover, Jews brought gifts (referring to animal sacrifices) that they offered *at the altar* in the temple in Jerusalem. This "altar" stood in the Court of the Priests; the person bringing the gift entered this inner court to worship God and offer a specific sacrifice (these are described in the book of Leviticus). The Jews brought their gifts as a matter of course, as part of keeping God's Law. But Jesus explained that those who come into God's presence to worship must come with pure hearts, not hindered by broken relationships that they had the power to mend. Interestingly, this verse focuses not on the worshiper's anger, but on the anger someone else feels toward the worshiper. Jesus explained that if the worshiper remembered someone's anger against him or her, that person should leave the gift and go immediately to *be reconciled to* the offended *brother or sister.* Then he should come back to worship and *offer* his or her gift.

The Old Testament prophets repeatedly told the people that "to obey is better than sacrifice" (1 Samuel 15:22 NRSV). Love for God and for fellow believers is more important than gifts brought to the altar (Isaiah 1:11; Hosea 6:6; Micah 6:6-8). Jesus said that even such a solemn occasion as worship in the inner courts of the temple should be interrupted in order to bring reconciliation among believers.

---

GRUDGES
You've tried your best to patch things up with your friend, but she's still torn. She can't let it go. She won't talk to you and doesn't answer your calls. What do you do . . .

- when friendship requires your complete surrender to her point of view?
- when it's clear you have to give up a different friend to win her friendship back?
- when her pout is unreasonable and childish?

It is time to bring your worries to God in prayer. In relationships where nothing looks hopeful, where every contact digs the hole deeper, try prayer. Pray for your friend daily—for her happiness, recovery, and immediate needs. Time is a healer and miracles can happen—especially when God is at work bringing people together.

---

**5:25-26** **"Settle matters quickly with your adversary who is taking you to court. Do it while you are still with him on the way, or he may hand you over to the judge, and the judge may hand you over to the officer, and you may be thrown into prison. I tell you the truth, you will not get out until you have paid the last penny."** NIV
While 5:24 referred to a believer dealing with the anger of a fellow believer, this verse focuses on dealing with an *adversary.* In Jesus' day, a person who couldn't pay a debt would be *thrown into prison* until the *last penny* was paid. A "penny" was one of the smallest Roman coins, worth two-fifths of a cent. This shows that the debt had to be fully paid. Debts were repaid by selling property or going

into contract as an indentured servant or slave. If he or she had no way to earn money to pay back the debt, the debtor could very well die in prison. Jesus recommended that his followers take immediate action to either reconcile with the angry person (5:24) or *settle matters quickly* in the best way possible before the angry person handed them over to the judge. Under Roman law, the plaintiff went with the defendant to court. On the way, they could settle matters however they wished. But once a legal verdict was reached, it stood.

It is practical advice to resolve our differences with our enemies before their anger causes more trouble (Proverbs 25:8-10). You may not get into a disagreement that takes you to court, but even small conflicts mend more easily if you try to make peace right away. In a broader sense, these verses advise us to get things right with our brothers and sisters before we have to stand before God.

---

COURTS AND JUSTICE
In the first century, courts were controlled by the army of occupation, the Romans. Appealing a court decision meant seeking the favor of some Roman stiff-shirt and, eventually, the emperor himself in Rome. At every turn, the justice system meant power, compromise, and submission to paganism.

Today in democratic societies, courts are accountable to law and to the people. Trial by jury and rights protected by constitutional agreements make our courts as fair as any in the history of human law. But still, should Christians use them?

Christians should try to settle disputes without the intervention of the state as third party. (Even our courts encourage such settlements.) Many Christian attorneys and counselors help people avoid formal court action.

When a lawsuit appears necessary, remember, parties go to court as antagonists, doing battle, seeking a victory. The process can be emotionally exhausting. So pray for justice and for your "enemies" across the courtroom.

---

## JESUS TEACHES ABOUT LUST / 5:27-30 / **53**

In his teaching about lust, Jesus literally got to the heart of the matter by explaining that sin begins in the heart. With strong language Jesus described how his followers must rid themselves of sin. While we cannot be sinless until we finally are with Christ, we must keep a watch on our thoughts, motives, and temptations in the meantime. When we find a destructive habit or thought pattern, we need to "cut it out and throw it away."

5:27-28 **"You have heard that it was said, 'You shall not commit adultery.' But I say to you that everyone who looks at a woman**

**with lust has already committed adultery with her in his heart."** NRSV Again Jesus quoted one of the Ten Commandments, *You shall not commit adultery* (Exodus 20:14). According to the Old Testament law, a person must not have sex with someone other than his or her spouse. Jesus said, *but I say to you* that even the "desire" to have sex with someone other than your spouse is mental adultery and thus sin. Jesus emphasized that if the act is wrong, then so is the desire to do the act. For a man to look at a woman (or a woman to look at a man) and *lust* is virtually the same as committing adultery. The word "lust" means the desire for an illicit relationship. Jesus explained that adultery *begins* in the heart that harbors lust. To simply avoid the act of adultery but to have a mind filled with lustful thoughts and desires for someone else misses the point of God's law.

To be faithful to your spouse with your body but not your mind is to break the trust so vital to a strong marriage. Jesus was not condemning natural interest in the opposite sex or even healthy sexual desire, but the deliberate and repeated filling of one's mind with fantasies that would be evil if acted out.

Some think that if lustful thoughts are sin, why shouldn't a person go ahead and do the lustful actions too? Acting out sinful desires is harmful in several ways: (1) it causes people to excuse sin rather than to stop sinning; (2) it destroys marriages; (3) it is deliberate rebellion against God's Word; (4) it always hurts someone else in addition to the sinner. Sinful action is more dangerous than sinful desire. Nevertheless, sinful desire is just as damaging to righteousness. Left unchecked, wrong desires will result in wrong actions, hurt others, and turn people away from God.

---

SECOND LOOK
"Private sins" have a fatal attraction by appearing to be internal, hidden, secret. Jesus declared lustful looks to be sin. God is not bound by our privacy—our thoughts and emotions are as visible to him as our actions. From the divine perspective, they *are* actions. This, in part, explains their sinfulness. Lust also creates an offense before God by misusing one of his most powerful gifts—the capacity to reflect. That part of us most able to consider and appreciate our Creator, his Word, and his world, becomes increasingly toxic as we use it to consider sin. Unlike an offending eye or hand, a sinful mind cannot be removed. Don't give in to lustful desires.

---

**5:29-30** **"If your right eye causes you to sin, gouge it out and throw it away. It is better for you to lose one part of your body than for your whole body to be thrown into hell. And if your right**

**hand causes you to sin, cut it off and throw it away. It is bet-
ter for you to lose one part of your body than for your whole
body to go into hell."** NIV When Jesus said to get rid of your *eye*
or your *hand,* he was speaking figuratively. He didn't mean literally to gouge out an eye because even a blind person can lust.
But if that were the only choice, it would be better to go into eternal life with one eye or hand than to go to hell physically intact.
This strong language describes how Jesus' followers should
renounce anything that would cause them to sin or turn away
from the faith. The action of surgically cutting sin out of our lives
should be prompt and complete to keep us from sin. Believers
must get rid of any relationship, practice, or activity that leads to
sin. A person would submit to losing a diseased part of the body
in order to save his or her life. In the same way, believers should
willingly *cut off* any temptation, habit, or part of their nature that
could lead them away from Christ. Just cutting off a limb that
committed sin or gouging out an eye that looked lustfully would
still not get rid of sin, however, because sin begins in the heart
and mind. Jesus was saying that people need to take drastic
action to keep them from stumbling. Self-denial is preferable to
sin and its consequences.

The reason? Jesus explained that it would be better to have
lost some worldly attitude or possession than *to be thrown into
hell* because of it. (The word for "hell" is *Gehenna,* also used
in 5:22—see the explanation above.) This is radical discipleship. While none of us will ever be completely free from sin
until we get a new glorified body, God wants an attitude that
renounces sin instead of one that holds on to it.

---

GET RID OF IT
Sometimes we tolerate sins in our lives that, left unchecked,
could eventually destroy us. It is better to experience the pain
of removal (getting rid of a bad habit or something we treasure,
for instance) than to allow the sin to bring judgment and
condemnation. Examine your life for anything that causes you
to sin, and take every necessary action to remove it.

---

### JESUS TEACHES ABOUT DIVORCE / 5:31-32 / **54**

Divorce is as hurtful and destructive today as in Jesus' day. God
intends marriage to be a lifetime commitment (Genesis 2:24).
People should never consider divorce an option for solving
problems or a way out of a relationship that seems dead. In these

verses, Jesus was also attacking those who purposefully abused the marriage contract, using divorce to satisfy their lustful desire to marry someone else. Make sure your actions today help your marriage grow stronger rather than tear it apart.

---

UNFAITHFUL*MESS*
Jesus said that divorce is not permissible except for unfaithfulness. This does not mean that divorce should automatically occur when a spouse commits adultery. The word translated "unfaithfulness" implies a sexually immoral lifestyle, not a confessed and repented act of adultery. Those who discover that their spouse has been unfaithful should first make every effort to forgive, reconcile, and restore their relationship. We should always look for reasons to restore the marriage relationship rather than for excuses to leave it.

---

**5:31** **"It has been said, 'Anyone who divorces his wife must give her a certificate of divorce.'"** NIV Jesus again pointed out a law from the Old Testament that his listeners knew well. The law, given by Moses in Deuteronomy 24:1-4, said, "If a man marries a woman who becomes displeasing to him because he finds something indecent about her, and he writes her a certificate of divorce, gives it to her and sends her from his house . . ." (Deuteronomy 24:1 NIV). The subject of divorce was hotly debated among the Jews at this time. Some religious leaders (those who followed Rabbi Hillel) took this to mean that a man could divorce his wife for almost any reason. They explained that "something indecent" could refer to anything that "displeased" the husband. In a culture where husbands viewed their wives as "property," divorce was fairly easy to obtain. However, other leaders (who followed the teachings of Rabbi Shammai) said that divorce could be granted only in cases of adultery.

**5:32** **"But I tell you that anyone who divorces his wife, except for marital unfaithfulness, causes her to become an adulteress, and anyone who marries the divorced woman commits adultery."** NIV The religious leaders permitted easy divorce, as well as remarriage after divorce. But Jesus said that the sacred union of marriage should not be broken and that to remarry after divorce was committing adultery. However, Jesus here gave one exception regarding divorce, an exception not included in the same teaching recorded in Mark 10:1-12. The Greek word translated "marital unfaithfulness" is *porneia*. It has a broad range of definitions, referring to (1) committing adultery (one offense); (2) unfaithfulness during the betrothal (engagement) period; (3) an illegitimate or incestuous marriage (the man and wife were later discovered to be near relatives); or (4) continued and unrepented unfaithfulness. Any of these reasons would mean that a rupture had already occurred in the marriage. For a man to divorce his wife for one of these reasons was simply a recognition that his union with her had been ended by her sexual union with another. It would be possible then that adultery would be an exception to the prohibition against remarriage.

However, Jesus would not stand for men tossing aside their wives. Marriage is so sanctified in God's eyes that remarriage after divorce amounts to adultery. Notice that while the divorced woman would *become an adulteress,* the man who divorced his wife would be at fault—he *causes* her to become an adulteress. Jesus will explain his strong words in 19:3-12 on the grounds that God originally intended marriage to be for life.

God created marriage to be a sacred and permanent union and partnership between a man and a woman. When the husband and wife both enter this union with that understanding and commitment, they can provide security for each other, a stable home for their children, and strength to weather life's storms and stresses.

---

MAY A DIVORCED PERSON REMARRY?
Jesus would seem to prohibit divorced persons from remarrying, forcing them to live either in celibacy or in sin. Jesus' main point was that people should not use the divorce laws to dispose of a partner in order to get another one.

The nagging question for Christians remains: May a divorced person, who truly repents of a sinful past and commits his or her life to God, remarry?

We long for a simple, direct reply to that question, but we have only biblical context as an answer. We have Jesus' high view of marriage and low view of divorce recorded in the Gospels. Jesus proclaimed new life—full forgiveness and restoration—to all who would come to God in repentance and faith. Spiritual discernment is essential here, but the gospel—God's promise of wholeness and full healing—includes the sacred bond of marriage. Churches should be ready to give a repentant, formerly married person the opportunity to marry another believer.

---

## JESUS TEACHES ABOUT VOWS / 5:33-37 / **55**

In Jesus' day, people commonly made oaths, or vows. Although God's law took these vows very seriously, many of the religious leaders had invented legal maneuvers to get around keeping their oaths. Jesus told his followers not to use oaths—their word alone should be enough (see James 5:12). Are you known as a person of your word? Truthfulness seems so rare that we feel we must end our statements with "I promise." If we tell the truth all the time, we will have less pressure to back up our words with an oath or a promise.

**5:33** **"Again, you have heard that it was said to the people long ago, 'Do not break your oath, but keep the oaths you have made to the Lord.'"** NIV This fourth example focuses on people's words. Jesus did not refer to any specific commandment, but he summed up Old Testament teachings on the subject of *oaths* and vows (see Exodus 20:7; Leviticus 19:12; Numbers 30:2; Deuteronomy 5:11; 6:13; 23:21-23). When a person made an oath, it bound him or her to keep it, whether it was an oath to another person or an oath *made to the Lord.*

**5:34-36** **"But I say to you, do not swear at all: neither by heaven, for it is God's throne; nor by the earth, for it is His footstool; nor by Jerusalem, for it is the city of the great King."** NKJV However, Jesus told his followers not to *swear* (or make oaths) *at all.* The religious leaders had designed an elaborate system indicating how binding an oath was depending on how the oath had been made. Such a system was a contradiction in terms (an oath by definition is binding), and it made light of God's Law. The leaders said that if they swore *by heaven* or *by the earth* or *by Jerusalem,* they could get out of their oath without penalty because they did not make the vow in God's name. Jesus explained that an oath is an oath. A promise is binding before God, no matter what words are used. It would be ridiculous for a person to say that he or she didn't really invoke God's name on the oath. Heaven *is God's throne,* the earth *is His footstool,* and Jerusalem *is the city of the great King.* Furthermore, Jesus added, **"Nor shall you swear by your head, because you cannot make one hair white or black."** NKJV Even the hairs on people's heads belong to God, so a person cannot get around an oath by swearing *by your head.* In other words, because people had made oaths into an elaborate system allowing for deceit, Jesus explained that his followers ought not make oaths at all. They ought to be so well known for their honesty and truthfulness that they would not need to make oaths. Jesus was not condemning the use of oaths in a court of law, nor vows made to God (such as Paul fulfilled, see Acts 18:18), but the kind of statements that added an "I promise" or "Honest!" Christ's followers did not need to say that. Jesus explained why in 5:37.

Each time Jesus used the pattern "You have heard it said . . . but I say to you," he was presenting a traditional standard upon which to base a higher one. Rather than let people off the hook, he set the hook deeper. Jesus spoke about oaths in order to point out that they were not the main problem—integrity was. Oaths are no substitute for personal integrity. A liar's vow expresses a worthless promise. But when a person of integrity says yes or no, that person's simple word can be trusted. Make integrity your standard.

**5:37** **"Simply let your 'Yes' be 'Yes,' and your 'No,' 'No'; anything beyond this comes from the evil one."** NIV Jesus simply emphasized that his followers should tell the truth: When they say *yes* they mean *yes,* and when they say *no* they mean *no.* Consequently, people can trust and believe anything else they say as well. Those who add to their words with an oath imply that their words cannot be trusted. The phrase "from the evil one" is also translated "from evil," revealing the sinful one's need to back up words with a vow. People need oaths only when telling lies is a possibility. Believers, however, know that they are accountable to God for every word they speak, so they will speak truthfully and do what they promise. Keeping promises builds trust and makes committed human relationships possible.

---

SAY YES, SAY NO
Are you the kind of person who
- can't say no when a caller asks for a donation?
- takes on too much at church?
- worries over whether people like you?
- worries over whether God likes you?

If so, this verse is your first lesson in assertiveness training. You need to learn how to say yes and mean it, and how to say no and stick to it, as a child of God.

Try this. Next time someone asks you to do something you cannot accept, resist the urge to launch into a twenty-minute explanation of your schedule conflict, and just say, "I'm sorry, but no." Wow! Does that feel good?

Pretty soon, you will start believing in your own yes and no as genuine reflections of your intentions. You'll be *you* again, and not someone else's image of you.

---

## JESUS TEACHES ABOUT RETALIATION / 5:38-42 / **56**

When people hurt us, often our first reaction is to get even. Instead, Jesus said we should do good to those who wrong us! Instead of keeping score, we should love and forgive. This is not natural—it is supernatural. Only God can give us the strength to love as he does. In the following illustrations, Jesus used hyperbole (extreme examples) to make a point about the attitudes of his followers.

**5:38** **"You have heard that it was said, 'An eye for an eye and a tooth for a tooth.'"** NKJV This example came from God's Law as recorded by Moses in Exodus 21:23-25; Leviticus 24:19-20; and Deuteronomy 19:21. While the law sounds severe to us, in its time it set guidelines against what may have been escalating personal vendettas among people. The principle of retribution, *lex talionis,* gave judges a formula for dealing with crime. That is, "Make the punishment fit the crime." The law limited vengeance and helped the court administer punishment that was neither too strict nor too lenient.

**5:39** **"But I tell you not to resist an evil person. But whoever slaps you on your right cheek, turn the other to him also."** NKJV The word "resist" translates the word *anthistemi,* also used for "take legal action against." Not only did Jesus command against getting back at someone physically, but he commanded against "getting back" by any other means as well. Jesus focused on the attitudes of his followers when dealing with evil individuals. The world advocates getting even, looking out for oneself, and protecting one's "personal rights." Jesus' followers, however, were to hold loosely to their "personal rights," preferring to forgo those rights for the sake of bearing witness to the gospel and the kingdom. Being willing to set aside one's personal rights does not mean that believers have to sit passively while evil goes unhindered (see how Paul dealt with this matter in Acts 16:37; 22:25; 25:8-12).

"A slap on the right cheek" was literally a blow from the back of someone's hand, an act that even today shows the greatest possible contempt. A person who slapped another in this way was giving a great insult. According to Jewish law, the one who slapped another faced punishment and a heavy fine. Thus, the law was on the side of the victim, and the victim would have every right to take this offense to court. Jesus said not to take the legal channels, however, but to offer the *other* cheek for a slap as well. Jesus did not ask his followers to do what he would never do—he received such treatment and did as he had commanded (26:67; see also Isaiah 50:6; 1 Peter 2:23). Jesus wanted his followers to have an unselfish attitude that willingly follows the way of the Cross instead of the way of personal rights. They should entrust themselves to God who will one day set all things right.

To many Jews, these statements were offensive. Any Messiah who would turn the other cheek was not the military leader to revolt against Rome. Because the Jews were under

Roman oppression, they wanted retaliation against their enemies whom they hated. But Jesus suggested a new, radical response to injustice: Instead of demanding rights, give them up freely! According to Jesus, it is more important to give justice and mercy than to receive it.

---

THE CYCLE OF REVENGE

The "eye for an eye, tooth for a tooth" formula expresses the harsh standards of justice. When the principle was applied in the Old Testament (Exodus 21:24; Leviticus 24:20; Deuteronomy 19:21), the context involved punishment administered by society at large in response to a personal crime. Practicing this principle on a personal level leads to revenge. Far from settling offenses, revenge escalates them. This is because we don't just get mad and we don't just get even; we get "just-a-little-more-than-even."

In the face of this human dilemma, Jesus proposed a better way—the radical response of love. His standard was not an attack on the necessity for justice. Rather, Jesus was presenting a practical, rational, and holy way to deal with personal conflict and offense. The apparent impossibility of our generating love and concern for our enemies on our own directs us to God for help. Rely on him for strength to give the appropriate response.

---

**5:40** **"If anyone wants to sue you and take away your tunic, let him have your cloak also."** NKJV Under God's law, no one could take a person's *cloak.* "If you take your neighbor's cloak in pawn, you shall restore it before the sun goes down; for it may be your neighbor's only clothing to use as cover; in what else shall that person sleep? And if your neighbor cries out to me, I will listen, for I am compassionate" (Exodus 22:26-27 NRSV). The cloak was a most valuable possession. Making clothing was difficult and time-consuming. As a result, cloaks were expensive, and most people owned only one. A cloak could be used as a blanket, a sack to carry things in, a pad to sit on, a pledge for a debt, and, of course, clothing.

In this case, the person was suing for the *tunic,* an inner garment worn next to the skin. Jesus said to let the person take both. Again Jesus focused on the attitude expected of his followers. They should hold their possessions very loosely.

**5:41** **"And if anyone forces you to go one mile, go also the second mile."** NRSV This is an allusion to the forced labor that soldiers could demand of ordinary citizens, commandeering them to carry their loads a certain distance (*one mile,* the term for one thousand paces). The Jews hated this law because it forced them to show their subjection to Rome. Yet Jesus said to take the load and willingly go two miles. Jesus called for a serving attitude (as he himself exemplified throughout his life and especially at the cross). Jesus' words probably shocked his hearers. Most of the Jews, expecting a military Messiah, would never have expected to hear Jesus issue a command of non-retaliation and cooperation with the hated Roman Empire. By these words, Jesus was revealing that his followers belong to another kingdom. They need not attempt to fight against Rome (as did the Zealots, a militant group of Jews), which could only end in defeat. Instead, they should work on behalf of God's kingdom. If doing so meant walking an extra mile carrying a Roman soldier's load, then that was what they should do.

THE SECOND MILE

In an unequal power situation, you have no choice about the first mile. The soldier has the sword, so you carry his gear. And it's a mile and an hour you can never get back. You're the loser. What's to be done?

The second mile is your choice. It's your way of saying, "God is in control here. He gives me energy, and a mere mile does not exhaust me. That sword is nothing; God is everything. Do you want to know where the real power lies? Try to keep up with me and I'll tell you."

**5:42** **"Give to the one who asks you, and do not turn away from the one who wants to borrow from you."** NIV Jesus' followers should have a generous spirit. Because they loosely hold on to their personal rights and possessions (as illustrated above), they can freely *give* when the need arises and won't *turn away from the one who wants to borrow.* While people should not blindly give away their possessions (the book of Proverbs makes recommendations about this, see Proverbs 11:15; 17:18; 22:26), Jesus illustrated the heart attitude that he expected of his followers. They must willingly put other's needs before their own and other's rights before their own.

## JESUS TEACHES ABOUT LOVING ENEMIES / 5:43-48 / **57**

By telling us not to retaliate against personal injustices (5:38-42), Jesus keeps us from taking the law into our own hands. This also keeps our focus on him and not on our own rights. By loving and praying for our enemies, we prove our relationship to our Father, show his love in an unlovely world, and overcome evil with good.

## SIX WAYS TO THINK LIKE CHRIST

We are, more often than not, guilty of avoiding the extreme sins
while regularly committing the types of sins with which Jesus was
most concerned. These six examples expose our real struggle
with sin. Jesus explained how he required his followers to live. Are
you living as Jesus taught?

| Reference | Example | It's not enough to: | We must also: |
|---|---|---|---|
| 5:21-22 | Murder | Avoid killing | Avoid anger and hatred |
| 5:23-26 | Offerings | Offer regular gifts | Have right relationships with God and others |
| 5:27-30 | Adultery | Avoid adultery | Keep our hearts from lusting and be faithful |
| 5:31-32 | Divorce | Be legally married | Live out our marriage commitments |
| 5:33-37 | Oaths | Make an oath | Avoid casual and irresponsible commitments to God |
| 5:38-47 | Revenge | Seek justice for ourselves | Show mercy and love to others |

**5:43-44** **"You have heard that it was said, 'You shall love your neighbor
and hate your enemy.' But I say to you, Love your enemies
and pray for those who persecute you."** NRSV The Pharisees
interpreted Leviticus 19:18 as teaching that they should love only
those who love in return, "neighbor" referring to someone of the
same nationality and faith. While no Bible verse explicitly says
*hate your enemy,* the Pharisees may have reinterpreted some of the
Old Testament passages about hatred for God's enemies (see, for
example, Psalms 139:19-22; 140:9-11). But Jesus explained that
his followers would do the true intent of God's law by loving
their *enemies* as well as their neighbors. When a Pharisee asked
Jesus, "Who is my neighbor" (Luke 10:29), Jesus told the parable
of the Good Samaritan. In that parable, Jesus explained that his
followers must show love to all kinds of people—no matter what
faith, nationality, or personality—enemies included. If you *love
your enemies* and *pray for those who persecute you,* you truly
show that Jesus is Lord of your life.

Jesus explained to his disciples that they must live by a higher standard than what the world expects—a standard that is impossible to

reach on mere human strength alone. People who have experienced God's love understand what it means to be loved undeservedly. Only with the help of God's Spirit can his people love and pray for those who seek to do them harm (see Romans 12:14-21).

**5:45** **"So that you may be children of your Father in heaven; for he makes his sun rise on the evil and on the good, and sends rain on the righteous and on the unrighteous."** NRSV The *Father in heaven* shows undiscriminating love to all people, allowing the sun to rise and rain to fall on both the evil and the good, the righteous and the unrighteous. Therefore, his *children* (those who believe in him) must reflect his character and show undiscriminating love for both friends and enemies. This verse refers to physical blessings on earth, not spiritual blessings. Obviously God's children will receive far more in the future. In the meantime, God's love reaches out to all people. God's people must do the same.

**5:46-47** **"For if you love those who love you, what reward do you have? Do not even the tax collectors do the same? And if you greet only your brothers and sisters, what more are you doing than others? Do not even the Gentiles do the same?"** NRSV Jesus has been explaining the much higher standards that are expected of his followers, standards higher than those the world or even their religion accepted. "Why the command to love enemies?" someone might ask (5:44). Jesus would answer, "Because that will mark my followers as different, with hearts and minds turned over to God alone, who can help them do just that." Anybody can love those who love them—that comes naturally, even for *tax collectors* (who were among the most hated people among the Jews of Jesus' day; see more on 9:9-13). In the same way, if Jesus' followers greeted only their fellow believers, they would be no different from the *Gentiles* (non-Jews who did not believe in the one true God). Those disciples who live for Christ and are radically different from the world will receive their *reward.*

**5:48** **"Be perfect, therefore, as your heavenly Father is perfect."** NRSV The word translated "perfect" is *teleios,* a word that can also be translated "mature" or "full-grown" (as in Ephesians 4:13; Hebrews 5:14–6:1). Jesus' followers can *be perfect* if their behavior is appropriate for their maturity level—perfect, yet with much room to grow. Considering all that Jesus had said in this chapter, the perfection Jesus required of his followers did not include strict and flawless obedience to minute laws. It called instead for an understanding of how the law pointed to the *heavenly Father* who is himself *perfect.* The law itself was not the standard of perfection, God was. Those who loved God and desired to follow him would

keep his law as *he* required. But they did this not on their own
strength or to put themselves above others. They did this not
because they were already perfect, but because they were striving
to be perfect, to reflect their Father's character.

As followers of Jesus Christ, how can we be perfect?

- *In character.* In this life we cannot be flawless, but we can
  aspire to be as much like Christ as possible.
- *In holiness.* Like the Pharisees, we are to separate ourselves
  from the world's sinful values. Unlike the Pharisees, we are to
  devote ourselves to God's desires rather than our own and
  carry his love and mercy into the world.
- *In maturity.* We can't achieve Christlike character and holy
  living all at once, but we must grow toward maturity and wholeness. Just as we expect different behavior from a baby, a child,
  a teenager, and an adult, so God expects different behavior
  from us, depending on our stage of spiritual development.
- *In love.* We can seek to love others as completely as God
  loves us.

Lest any of the previous standards of righteousness fail to
humble us and show us our spiritual bankruptcy apart from
God's grace, Jesus drove home his point with the piercing
demand for perfection. People often use the declaration "No
one's perfect" as their basis for self-justification: "No one's
perfect, and God must know I'm doing the best I can." In reality, "No one's perfect, and no one does the best they can either"
(see Romans 3:9-20). As long as we give credibility to our own
feeble efforts at righteousness, we will never recognize our
desperate need for a Savior.

Our tendency to sin must never deter us from striving to be
more like Christ. Obedience is the key to discipleship. The
message of the Sermon on the Mount is that Christ calls all of
his disciples to excel, to rise above mediocrity, and to mature
in every area, becoming like him. Christ's demands cannot be
met by those who attempt to do so on their own strength—only
through the Holy Spirit. Those who strive to become like Christ
will ultimately experience sinless perfection, even as Christ is
perfect (1 John 3:2-3).

# Matthew 6

It's easier to do what is right when we gain recognition and praise.
To be sure our motives are not selfish, we should do our good
deeds quietly or in secret, with no thought of reward. Jesus says we
should check our motives in three areas: generosity or almsgiving
(6:4), prayer (6:6), and fasting (6:18). Those acts should not be self-
centered, but God-centered, done not to make us look good but to
make God look good. God does not promise a material reward.
Doing something only for ourselves is not a loving sacrifice. Check
the motives behind your next good deed by asking, "Would I still
do this if no one would ever know that I did it?"

**6:1** **"Be careful not to do your 'acts of righteousness' before men,
to be seen by them. If you do, you will have no reward from
your Father in heaven."** NIV At first reading, these words seem
to contradict what Jesus had just told his disciples in 5:14-16,
"Let your light shine before others, so that they may see your
good works" (NRSV). No contradiction exists, however, because
in 5:16, Jesus gave his disciples the correct motive: that people
might "give glory to your Father in heaven" (NRSV). Jesus
warned that doing good works *(acts of righteousness)* so that
others might see and praise you for what you do would earn *no
reward from your Father in heaven.*

The phrase "acts of righteousness" can be translated different
ways, but it means "to do what is right." Jesus pointed out three
specific types of acts of righteousness that the Pharisees completed—
many with great fanfare and notice—almsgiving, prayer, and fasting. These three were central to their expression of obedience to
God. While all of these acts could glorify God, some of the Pharisees did them only to bring honor to themselves. In these words,
Jesus was focusing on the motive behind any good deed. God
rewards good deeds done for his glory alone. He does not reward
good deeds done for recognition, display, applause, or honor. In
fact, as Jesus explains in 6:5, the valued "reward" from others is the
only reward that will be received.

**6:2 "So whenever you give alms, do not sound a trumpet before you, as the hypocrites do in the synagogues and in the streets, so that they may be praised by others. Truly I tell you, they have received their reward."** NRSV The first "act of righteousness" Jesus used as an example was "almsgiving." The Jewish law commanded that the people give to those in need: "Give liberally and be ungrudging when you do so, for on this account the LORD your God will bless you in all your work and in all that you undertake. Since there will never cease to be some in need on the earth, I therefore command you, 'Open your hand to the poor and needy neighbor in your land'" (Deuteronomy 15:10-11 NRSV).

Jesus expected his followers to do likewise, following God's law. He said not "if," but *whenever you give alms* (that is, give to the needy). However, Jesus' followers were to have a different motive for their giving than did *the hypocrites.* "Hypocrite" was the Greek word for "actor," one who wore a mask and pretended to be someone he or she wasn't. The term "hypocrites," as used here, describes people who do good acts for appearance only, to *be praised by others*—not out of compassion or other good motives. (Many of the religious leaders did just this; later Jesus calls the Pharisees *hypocrites,* see 23:13-29.)

> Probably the vast majority of people are more influenced by what men will say, than by what God Almighty thinks.
> *G. Campbell Morgan*

The phrase *sound a trumpet before you* probably is not literal, but it pictures people calling attention to themselves, people who "blow their own horns." Their actions may be good, but their motives are hollow. Like actors in a play, they give their gifts in front of an audience, hoping for praise. These empty acts and whatever human praise is received are the only reward the hypocrites will receive for their trouble. God will reward those who are sincere in their faith and whose motive in all their good deeds is to glorify him.

---

GIVE ANYWAY
Jesus emphasized the importance of giving to those in need. Assuming the giving even as he was directing how the giving should be carried out, his repeated phrase was *"When* you give," not *"If* you give." Helping other people becomes a real adventure if we remain anonymous. Regardless, we still must help others. We may have to live through times when our acts of generosity are neither recognized nor appreciated. What can you do to give to those in need?

---

**6:3-4** **"But when you give to the needy, do not let your left hand know what your right hand is doing, so that your giving may be in secret. Then your Father, who sees what is done in secret, will reward you."** NIV In 6:2, Jesus explained how his disciples were *not* to give alms; these verses describe how he wanted them to give. In the phrase *do not let your left hand know what your right hand is doing,* he was teaching that motives for giving to God and to others must be pure.

The phrase is a hyperbole (extreme example) to emphasize the total lack of ostentation. No one should call attention to the act. It is easy to give with mixed motives, to do something for someone if it will benefit us in

> God has given us two hands—one for receiving and the other for giving.
> *Billy Graham*

return. Jesus advised, however, that giving be done *in secret*. Jesus' words do not forbid record keeping, receipting, or reporting procedures used in good stewardship. But he condemned practices to impress others. Jesus' followers should give generously, out of compassion, when there is a need. God rewards such giving. The word for "reward" used here is different from the word used in 6:2, for the reward is very different. The hypocrites receive praise from humans alone as their only "reward." Those who give in secret, however, will receive a reward from the Father—a reward of greater value because it will be perfect and eternal.

---

KEEPING DONOR SECRETS
It's nearly impossible to keep secret the amount of charitable giving you do today. Donors are required by tax authorities to keep very accurate records, and the larger the gift, the more people must keep a record of it. When Jesus said to keep your gifts a secret from even yourself, he was using hyperbole to warn against self-glorifying demonstrations.

Yet Christians can and should apply the spirit of Jesus' teaching, even while they keep accurate financial accounts. Jesus tells us:
- Don't get proud of your generosity. You are only a steward of resources that belong to God already.
- Don't give for the honor bestowed on donors. Instead, give in gratitude for what God has given you.
- Don't count your gifts as merit points for heaven. God will reward you generously, but not on your invoice.

Every time you give, count it as a reminder of your freedom from the power of money and of your trust in Jesus alone for all good things.

---

## JESUS TEACHES ABOUT PRAYER / 6:5-15 / **59**

**6:5** **"And whenever you pray, do not be like the hypocrites; for they love to stand and pray in the synagogues and at the street corners, so that they may be seen by others. Truly I tell you, they have received their reward."** NRSV A second act of piety Jesus addressed was prayer. Some people, especially the religious leaders, wanted the people to think they were very holy, and public prayer was one way to get attention. Jesus saw through their self-righteous acts. He called these men *hypocrites* for praying not to God but to an audience of people who revered them for their apparent holiness. Jesus assumed that his followers would pray *(whenever you pray)*. Prayer *in the synagogues* was not unusual; however, those who prayed *at the street corners* certainly had motives other than piously observing the exact prayer time (although prayers in the streets were acceptable on fasting days). When people prayed in those locations, not to God but merely *so that they may be seen by others,* they were not praying at all. Jesus taught that we find the essence of prayer not in public but in private communication with God. There is a place for public prayer, but to pray only where others will notice you indicates that your real intention is to please people, not God. For these hypocrites, people's praise will be their only reward.

---

PUBLIC PRAYER
Do Jesus' words question the appropriateness of all public prayer? Can public prayer draw attention to God without drawing attention to the one praying? Did Jesus himself practice "closet praying" exclusively? No, the Gospels record Jesus at prayer both privately (14:23) and publicly (14:18-19). Later, his disciples carried on a tradition of corporate prayer from the earliest days of the church (Acts 1:14). As he did with giving, Jesus drew attention to the motives behind actions. The point really wasn't a choice between public and private prayer but between heartfelt and hypocritical prayer. We must learn to pray in private so that we might eventually lead others in effective prayer in public. When asked to pray in public, focus on addressing God, not on how you're coming across to others.

---

**6:6** **"But when you pray, go into your room, close the door and pray to your Father, who is unseen. Then your Father, who sees what is done in secret, will reward you."** NIV The prayer life of Jesus' followers would be radically different from that of the hypocritical religious leaders. Jesus did not condemn public prayer. Such prayer was vitally important to the early church, as it is to churches today. Corporate prayer has powerful results. Jesus' point, however, was that people who prayed more in public than in private should consider their motives. If they really wanted to fellowship with God, Jesus suggested that they go alone into a room, *close the door and pray.* This "room" was probably some inner room without windows, a storeroom, a "secret" place. Prayer in public is subject to concern over correct word usage, political correctness, even pride. Private prayer enables believers to pour out their hearts to God *(your Father, who is unseen),* express their true feelings, and listen in the quietness for God's answer. Jesus called God the "Father," an intimate word describing the relationship believers have with him.

> The self-sufficient do not pray, the self-satisfied will not pray, the self-righteous cannot pray. No man is greater than his prayer life.
> *Leonard Ravenhill*

**6:7-8 "And when you pray, do not keep on babbling like pagans, for they think they will be heard because of their many words. Do not be like them, for your Father knows what you need before you ask him."**[NIV] Repeating the same words over and over *(babbling)* like a magic incantation will not ensure that God hears these prayers. The *pagans* (or Gentiles) focused on how they delivered their prayers, repeating the right words in the right order. They often repeated the names of their gods as a way to get a blessing (as in Acts 19:34). Jesus was not condemning prayer any more than he was condemning giving in 6:1-4. In fact, Jesus encouraged persistent prayer (Luke 18:1-8) and soon would give a pattern for prayer (see 6:9-13). Instead, Jesus was condemning the shallow repetition of words by those who did not have a personal relationship with the Father. Jesus told his followers not to be like the pagans but to come to God as to their Father, bringing their needs. The believers did not pray to idols of wood or stone with incessant babbling. They prayed to the one living and true God who knew what they needed even before they asked! This does not excuse believers from prayer, but they needn't spend a long time telling God their needs because he already knows. God doesn't *need* our prayers; but he *wants* our prayers and knows that *we* need them.

**6:9 "In this manner, therefore, pray: Our Father in heaven, hallowed be Your name."**[NKJV] This prayer is called the Lord's Prayer because Jesus gave it to the disciples to pray, as well as to be a pattern for their prayers. Jesus did not give this prayer as an incantation to be recited over and over—that would render it as ineffective as the "babblings" of the pagans (6:7). Jesus said, *"in this manner, therefore, pray."* In other words, this is how I want you to pray—praise God (6:9), intercede for his work in the world (6:10), ask for provision of individual daily needs (6:11), and request help in daily struggles (6:12-13). Jesus gave the prayer to his disciples; therefore, those who follow Christ should pray it as well. The first person plural pronouns indicate that the believers could pray it corporately. The pattern of praise, intercession, and request helps believers understand the nature and purpose of their personal prayers in their relationship with their Father.

WHY PRAY?

If God knows what we need, why bother praying?

Because prayer is not like sending an order form to a supplier. Prayer develops an intimate personal relationship with an abundantly loving God, who also happens to know us deeply. His knowledge of us should encourage us toward confident and focused prayer. A child may feel an immediate need for candy; a parent considers the child's long-term needs. Stretch that parent's concern and perspective to an infinite dimension, and there you find God's loving care.

Prayer does not beg favors from a reluctant shopkeeper. Prayer develops the trust that says, "Father, you know best." Bring your requests confidently to God.

The phrase "our Father in heaven" indicates that God is majestic and holy; he transcends everything on earth. But he is also personal and loving. The first line of this model prayer is a statement of praise and a commitment to "hallow," or honor, God's holy name. Christians, who bear the holy name of Christ, must be responsible to "hallow" him in every aspect of their lives. These words remind us that God wants to hear and listen as a loving Father, but that coming to him is an awesome privilege. We must enter the King's throne room respectfully. When we pray for God's name to be "hallowed," we pray that this world will honor his name, and we look forward to Christ's return when that will be a reality.

**6:10** **"Your kingdom come."** NKJV The phrase "Your kingdom come" refers to God's spiritual reign, not Israel's freedom from Rome. God announced his kingdom in the covenant with Abraham (8:11; Luke 13:28), and pious Jews were still waiting for it. Jesus' followers recognize that the kingdom began with his coming to earth. Matthew's readers understood the kingdom to be present in believers' hearts as Christ reigned there (Luke 17:21). To say "your kingdom come" is to pray that more and more people will enter the kingdom. It also reaffirms belief that one day all evil will be destroyed, that God will establish the new heaven and earth, and that his glory will be known to all the nations (Psalm 110:1; Revelation 21:1).

**"Your will be done on earth as it is in heaven."** NKJV Praying
*your will be done* does not imply resignation to fate; rather, it is
a prayer that God's perfect purpose will be accomplished in this
world *(on earth)* as it already is in heaven's throne room. The
phrase "on earth as it is in heaven" could apply to the three prior
requests. Each previous request—that God's name be hallowed,
that his kingdom come, and that his will be done—desires that
these will take place on earth while looking forward to complete
fulfillment when Christ returns.

ONE FOOT IN HEAVEN, ONE ON EARTH
How does God accomplish his will on earth? He does it largely
through people willing to do it.
   We must not make this prayer as an abstract wish. Without
personal commitment, the prayer would mean, "Let someone
else do your will, or just get it done miraculously. I have other
business today." When you make this prayer, you're saying,
"I'll do it, Lord. Lead me, guide me, and give me the shovel (or
whatever I need) to get it done."

**6:11**  **"Give us this day our daily bread."** NKJV These last two (verses
11 and 12) are requests for personal needs. "Bread" refers to
food in general, although it also could refer to spiritual "food."
We must trust God *daily* to provide what he knows we need. The
word "daily" suggests that we should not worry about what God
already knows we need (6:8). The adjective translated "daily"
*(epiousios)* occurs only here in the New Testament and carries
several possible meanings: (1) "for the day," perhaps recalling
the daily provision of manna in the wilderness (Exodus 16:15-26);
(2) "necessary," what I need for today in order to survive, "sufficient for today"; (3) "for the coming day," pointing to the coming
kingdom.

DAILY BREAD
Every component of the Lord's Prayer can be described as
"daily," yet only bread was given that specific adjective. God's
Fatherhood, will, and kingdom are all worthy of our daily
attention. God's forgiveness and our forgiveness of others
require daily application. Our continual need for bread points
to our deeper, daily need for God. The request for today's
bread keeps our relationship with God in the present tense.
We will be just as much in need of God tomorrow as we are in
need of his provision of nourishment, protection, and guidance
today. Each day, present your needs to him.

Believers must trust God for provision and not worry. That God "gives" daily bread does not negate people's responsibility to work and earn the food they eat. Instead, it acknowledges that God is Sustainer and Provider. It is a misconception to think that we provide for our needs ourselves. God gives us our ability to work and earn money to buy our food.

**6:12** **"And forgive us our debts, as we forgive our debtors."** NKJV The word "debts" is probably a literal rendering of an Aramaic word, the language Jesus used in preaching. It means "sin," picturing sin as something that requires reconciliation with God. Some have taken this sentence to mean that God's forgiveness of our sins is dependent on our forgiveness of others' sins against us; however, the rest of Scripture shows us that no one can earn God's forgiveness. The meaning, therefore, focuses on the true repentance of a believer who understands the greatness of the forgiveness that he or she has received. This believer willingly extends such forgiveness to others for their wrongs. The flip side of this thought reveals the selfishness of a person who seeks God's forgiveness yet willfully refuses to forgive others. Jesus expands on this in 6:14-15.

---

FORGIVING OTHERS
To forgive completely requires one of the most difficult of all adjustments, but Jesus describes it so simply. Just as we need forgiveness, so we must forgive others.
- You were abused and abandoned. Can you forgive the abuser?
- You were the victim of political oppression or military terror. Can you forgive those who inflicted the pain?
- You thought it was love, but the object of your love has found another. Can you ever forgive that person?

Jesus knows our hurts and wounds. Through the tears, God's love begins to heal. That's why forgiveness is complicated but simple. And it's always the direction God wants your heart to turn, never toward revenge or hate. Forgiving others bears witness to the power of God over the worst that life can deal.

---

**6:13** **"And do not lead us into temptation, but deliver us from the evil one."** NKJV God doesn't *lead us into temptation,* for he does not tempt people to do evil (James 1:13). The Greek word translated "temptation" *(peirasmos)* does not mean "enticement to do evil" but "testing." Sometimes God allows his people to be "tested" by temptation. But this testing is never without a purpose: God is always working to refine his people, teach them to depend on him, and strengthen their character to be more like him. How he does this differs in every person's life.

Why would Jesus encourage us to ask God to avoid tempting or testing us? There are some interesting parallels between this prayer and Jesus' prayer in the Garden of Gethsemane (26:36-46). The Lord's Prayer affirms the will of God ("your will be done"), then asks for relief and delivery from trials. In the garden, Jesus asked the Father to remove the cup of trial while immediately declaring his willingness to cooperate with his Father's will. Soon after, when Jesus discovered the disciples asleep, he encouraged them to pray not to fall into temptation. Jesus knew, however, that they would indeed fall and fail within moments.

The end of the Lord's Prayer reminds us of the importance of testing, even though we seldom *desire* it. Our prayer should be: "And lead us not into further testing even while you are leading us out of evil." Jesus both taught and modeled a freedom in prayer that dared to ask almost anything, fully knowing that the Father will do what is best.

Jesus wanted his followers to place their trust in God during trying times and to pray for deliverance from Satan *(the evil one)* and his deceit. All Christians struggle with temptation. Sometimes it is so subtle that we don't even realize what is happening to us. God has promised: "No testing has overtaken you that is not common to everyone. God is faithful, and he will not let you be tested beyond your strength, but with the testing he will also provide the way out so that you may be able to endure it" (1 Corinthians 10:13 NRSV). Believers who pray these words realize their sinful nature and their need to depend on God in the face of temptation. Some scholars suggest that these words may also include prayer regarding the coming final conflict between God and Satan. If so, the believers' prayers are that they may be spared from the trials surrounding it.

> Once our eyes have been opened to see the enormity of our offence against God, the injuries which others have done to us appear by comparison extremely trifling. If, on the other hand, we have an exaggerated view of the offences of others, it proves that we have minimized our own.
> *John R. W. Stott*

**"For Yours is the kingdom and the power and the glory forever. Amen."** NKJV This doxology does not appear in most ancient manuscripts, nor does it appear in Luke's version of this prayer (Luke 11:2-4), leading scholars to conclude that it was not in the original text. The early church, when using this prayer, may have added this closing sentence of praise.

**6:14-15 "For if you forgive others their trespasses, your heavenly Father will also forgive you; but if you do not forgive others,**

**neither will your Father forgive your trespasses."** NRSV Jesus'
words reinforce the petition in 6:12. Jesus gave a startling warning about forgiveness: If we refuse to *forgive others,* God will
also refuse to forgive us. This does not refer to salvation because
salvation is not dependent on anything people can do. The foundation of God's forgiveness builds upon his own character. In
love he regards the death of Christ as sufficient to pay our penalty. Forgiving others is not a meritorious work for earning salvation. However, living in relationship with God requires constant
repentance of the sins that plague us. Because believers must
come to God constantly for confession and forgiveness, refusing
to forgive others reveals a lack of appreciation for the mercy
received from God. All people are on common ground as sinners
in need of God's forgiveness. If we don't forgive others, we are
in fact denying and rejecting God's forgiveness of us (see Ephesians 4:32; Colossians 3:13). Later, Jesus told a parable depicting
such a situation (18:23-35).

### JESUS TEACHES ABOUT FASTING / 6:16-18 / 60

6:16 **"And whenever you fast, do not look dismal, like the hypocrites, for they disfigure their faces so as to show others that
they are fasting. Truly I tell you, they have received their
reward."** NRSV Jesus here addresses the third "act of piety"—
fasting. People *fast* (go without food) so that they can spend
more time in prayer. This act is both noble and difficult. Fasting was mandatory for the Jewish people once a year, on the
Day of Atonement (Leviticus 23:32); however, people could
fast individually or in groups while praying for certain requests
(see, for example, Esther 4:16). The purpose of fasting is to
provide time for prayer, to teach self-discipline, to remind
God's people that they can live with a lot less, and to help them
appreciate what God has given. In Jesus' day, the Pharisees
fasted twice a week, on Mondays and Thursdays (Luke 18:12).
Fasting could have great spiritual value, but some people,
such as the Pharisees, had turned it into a way to gain public
approval. During a fast, they would *look dismal* and *disfigure
their faces* so that people would know they were fasting and
be impressed by their "holiness." Jesus was condemning
hypocrisy, not fasting. The Pharisees may have felt truly con-
trite; but were they spending time with God in prayer during
their fast? They negated the purpose by making sure others
knew when they were fasting. Public recognition would be
their only reward.

FAST
Most people who practice fasting would say that the word
"slow" presents a clearer picture of this discipline than "fast."
Time slows down during a fast as energy levels decline with the
absence of food.

Fasting presents a physical example of the painstaking
aspects of spiritual growth. Jesus expected his disciples to fast,
but he forbade self-centered and attention-seeking exercises.
This kind of discipline may, in fact, be a key to the renewal of
the church today. Are you willing to give up a mealtime or set
aside other major activities to devote to prayer? What sacrifice
would you be willing to make to spend even one day alone with
the Lord?

**6:17-18** **"But when you fast, put oil on your head and wash your face,**
**so that your fasting may be seen not by others but by your**
**Father who is in secret; and your Father who sees in secret**
**will reward you."** NRSV Jesus did not condemn this third act of
piety any more than he did the first two. As he assumed that his
followers would give (6:2) and pray (6:5), so he assumed that
they would fast. *When you fast,* Jesus was saying, go about your
normal daily routine; don't make a show of it. Putting olive *oil*
on one's head was like putting on lotion; it was a common part of
daily hygiene like washing one's face. No one but God would
know they were fasting. Jesus commended acts of self-sacrifice
done quietly and sincerely. He wanted people to adopt spiritual
disciplines for the right reasons, not from a selfish desire for
praise. As with the other disciplines, the reward would come
from God, not from people.

FASTING
Fasting is a spiritual discipline, like prayer and giving. All three
remind us of a primary relationship—God and us. All three
require that we give up something to gain something better.

The first time you voluntarily give up the pleasure of food, it
may hurt. Start with just a one-meal fast, advises author Richard
Foster. Treat fasting like an athletic exercise. If you're a novice,
don't try to swim the English Channel.

During your fast, pray often. Be sure not to make a big public
event of it, telling friends or moaning to your family about hunger
pangs. Just pray. Open yourself to God. Tell him how much you
want his love and guidance. Read some psalms, refreshing
your heart with food from God's Word. Let your fast bring you
joy before you turn again to the food that you need to run the
next mile.

## JESUS TEACHES ABOUT MONEY / 6:19-24 / **61**

Jesus had been teaching about how his followers should live
quite differently from those in the current religious establishment.
The remainder of this chapter presents Jesus' description of the
attitudes of his followers that would set them apart from the
world. The section about money focuses on true discipleship and
how wealth is often the most common distraction from such discipleship. Jesus demands undivided commitment—no divided loyalties, no part-time disciples. Our attitude toward money is often
the pulse of the heart of our discipleship.

**6:19 "Do not lay up for yourselves treasures on earth, where
moth and rust destroy and where thieves break in and
steal."** NKJV Jesus' followers do not concern themselves with
amassing possessions and wealth; they refuse to *lay up . . .
treasures on earth.* Those treasures by their very nature cannot
be secure, and death would cause a person to lose them. Such
treasures can be eaten away by moths or *rust* (the Greek word
*brosis* can refer to anything that "eats away"), and they can be
stolen by *thieves.*

Jesus did not condemn saving money for the future or having
certain "treasures" in your home that you value. But he condemned
the attitude toward money and possessions that makes these things
more important than eternal values.

**6:20-21 "But lay up for yourselves treasures in heaven, where neither
moth nor rust destroys and where thieves do not break in and
steal. For where your treasure is, there your heart will be
also."** NKJV How does a person *lay up . . . treasures in heaven?*
Laying or storing up treasures in heaven includes, but is not limited
to, tithing our money. It is also accomplished through bringing
others to Christ and all acts of obedience to God. That "treasure"
is the eternal value of whatever we accomplish on earth. Acts of
obedience to God, laid up in heaven, are not susceptible to decay,
destruction, or theft. Nothing can affect or change them; they are
eternal.

The final sentence points out the significance of Jesus' words.
Wherever our focus lies, whatever occupies our thoughts and our
time—that is our "treasure." Jesus warned that people's hearts
tend to be wrapped around their treasures, and few treasure God
as they ought. In this startling challenge we again face the tension between actions and words in following Christ. Words
become cheap when we tell ourselves we can act one way and
believe another. Jesus exposed those who claim to value eternity
while living as if there were nothing beyond this world.

Our *heart* will be with our *treasure*. The "heart" refers to the mind, emotions, and will. What we treasure most controls us, whether we admit it or not. (This is not limited to financial treasure. Some people treasure their house, car, or children almost to the point of idolatry.) For example, if we lay up treasures on earth in the form of money, our "heart" will be with our money. If our focus is our money, then we will do all we can to make more and more, and we will never have enough. We feel great when our stocks are up; we might feel despair if the stock market declines. We may become stingy, unwilling to give a cent of our amassed fortune, for then we would have one cent less. In short, we forget whose money it really is, the good purposes for which he gave it to us, and the fact that it will not last.

Jesus contrasted heavenly values with earthly values when he explained that our first loyalty should be to those things that do not fade, cannot be stolen or used up, and never wear out. We should not be fascinated with our possessions, lest *they* possess *us*. This means that we may have to cut back if our possessions become too important to us. Jesus calls for a decision that allows us to live contentedly with whatever we have because we have chosen what is eternal and lasting.

---

FINANCIAL PLANNING
Do you have a will? a living trust? a diversified porfolio? a broker you can call?

Christians might ask, "Why all the fuss over financial security, given Jesus' warning here?" But Jesus was not teaching people to be sloppy and careless about money. We need solid financial plans to be good stewards of the earthly resources that God has entrusted to us.

Jesus was also saying that money is a means to an end, not an end in itself. Money ought never to be any Christian's goal. Financial plans should not drive our lives. Believers should focus on God's purposes, God's goals, and God's plan.

Everyone needs money. Every Christian ought to share money. Financial planning is a sign of careful management. But hopes and dreams that rise to heaven are the only ones worth living for.

---

**6:22-23** **"The eye is the lamp of the body. If your eyes are good, your whole body will be full of light. But if your eyes are bad, your whole body will be full of darkness. If then the light within you is darkness, how great is that darkness!"** NIV Jesus described the "spiritual vision" his disciples should have. Proper spiritual vision requires us to see clearly what God wants us to do and to see the world from his point of view. "The eye is the lamp of the body" means that through the eyes the body receives light, allowing it to move. In the Old Testament, the "eye" denoted the direction of a person's life. "Good" eyes focus on God. They are generous to others and convey the single focus of a true disciple. They receive and fill the body with God's light so that it can serve him whole-heartedly. "Bad" eyes represent materialism, greed, and covetousness. Those with "bad" eyes may see the light, but they have allowed self-serving desires, interests, and goals to block their vision. Those with "bad eyes" think they have light; in reality, they are in spiritual darkness. This could mean a sort of "double vision"—trying to focus on God *and* earthly possessions. It will lead to gloom in life and darkness in eternity. *How great is that darkness* for those who see the light but are not focused on God. Materialism destroys the whole self. In these words, Jesus was calling his followers to undivided loyalty—eyes fixed and focused on him.

**6:24** **"No one can serve two masters; for a slave will either hate the one and love the other, or be devoted to the one and despise the other. You cannot serve God and wealth."** NRSV Continuing the theme of his disciples having undivided loyalty, Jesus explained that *no one can serve* (that is, be a slave of, belong to) *two masters.* A slave could belong to two partners but not to two separate individuals because his or her loyalty would be divided. While slaves have their earthly master chosen for them, from a spiritual standpoint all people must choose whom they will serve. They can choose to serve themselves—to pursue *wealth* and selfish pleasures—or they can choose to serve *God.* The word translated "wealth" is also translated "mammon," referring to possessions as well. Either we store our treasures with God (6:20-21), we focus our "eyes" on him (6:22-23), and we serve him alone—or else we do not serve him at all. There can be no part-time loyalty. Jesus wants total devotion.

---

WHO'S YOUR MASTER?
Jesus says we can have only one master. We live in a materialistic society where many people serve money. They spend all their lives collecting and storing it, only to die and leave it behind. Their desire for money and what it can buy far outweighs their commitment to God and spiritual matters. Even Christians spend a great deal of time trying to create heaven on earth. Whatever you store up, you will spend much of your time and energy thinking about. Don't fall into the materialistic trap, because "the love of money is a root of all kinds of evil" (1 Timothy 6:10). Does Christ or money occupy more of your thoughts, time, and efforts? Ask yourself, "Have I taken Christ or financial security as my master?"

---

## JESUS TEACHES ABOUT WORRY / 6:25-34 / **62**

**6:25** **"Therefore I tell you, do not worry about your life, what you will eat or drink; or about your body, what you will wear. Is not life more important than food, and the body more important than clothes?"** NIV The command "do not worry" does not imply complete lack of concern, nor does it call people to be unwilling to work and supply their own needs. Instead, Jesus was continuing to highlight kingdom priorities—the attitude toward life that his disciples should exemplify. They need not be overly concerned about food or clothing because they know that God will care for them. Worrying about food and clothing should never take priority over serving God. Food and clothes are less important than the life and body that they supply. Because God sustains our lives and gives us our bodies, we can trust him to provide the food and clothing he knows we need.

When we worry over lack of food or inadequate clothing, we immobilize ourselves and focus on the worry. We refuse to trust that God can supply these most basic needs. Worry immobilizes us, but trust in God moves us to action. We work for our money to supply food and clothing, but we must always remember that these ultimately come from God's hands. When the need arises, we need not worry, for we know that our God will supply.

WORRY
Worry presents us with the dual temptation to distrust God and to substitute fear for practical action. Worry means paying attention to what we cannot change instead of putting our energies to work in effective ways. Jesus made it clear that worry takes away from life rather than adding anything to it. We can counteract worry by doing what we can and trusting where we can't. When we work for God and wait on his timing, we won't have time to worry. When we seek first to honor God as king and conform our lives to his righteousness, worry will always finds us otherwise occupied.

**6:26** **"Look at the birds of the air, for they neither sow nor reap nor gather into barns; yet your heavenly Father feeds them. Are you not of more value than they?"** NKJV Perhaps as he spoke these words, Jesus gestured to several birds passing overhead. The birds need food, and the heavenly Father knows it. The birds are dependent upon God's daily provision because they cannot grow, prepare, or store their food. They work—they hunt for it and then bring it back to their families—

but they don't worry. If God cares for the birds, making sure that the natural order of his creation supplies food for them, how much more will he care for a hungry human being? Jesus was teaching total dependence upon God as opposed to humanity's self-sufficiency. How much more should his followers, who know him personally, trust that he will provide their needs? Jesus was not prohibiting his followers from sowing, reaping, and gathering food (that is, working for it); but he was prohibiting worry about having enough food. All that we have ultimately comes from God's hand. Whether we have much or little, we must remember that God provides for our needs.

WHY IS ANYONE HUNGRY?
What about starving families in African refugee camps? If God supplies food for birds, why not food for street kids in Rio?

- Jesus *is not teaching* that every case of hunger will be satisfied with food. Not every hungry person in his own day was fed, and surely in the course of human history many people would go hungry. Unfortunately, some would die for lack of food.
- Jesus *is teaching* us to focus our minds, channeling our efforts and directing our energies not to mere bodily maintenance but to God's eternal purposes.

Ask yourself: How can I spend less time worrying about my bank account and more time serving the church? less time worrying about mortgages and more time visiting the sick? less time worrying about kids' college tuition payments and more time learning the Bible?

Now you're thinking!

**6:27** **"And can any of you by worrying add a single hour to your span of life?"** NRSV Many of us would do well to ask ourselves this question every morning. Daily we face new challenges, concerns, problems, and choices. Will we worry, or will we pray? Will worrying be of any help whatsoever? Because of the ill effects of worry, Jesus tells us not to worry about those needs that God promises to supply. Worry may damage our health, cause the object of our worry to consume our thoughts, disrupt our productivity, negatively affect the way we treat others, and reduce our ability to trust in God. Worry may, in reality, take time away from our span of life rather than adding to it. It accomplishes nothing.

**6:28-30** **"So why do you worry about clothing? Consider the lilies of the field, how they grow: they neither toil nor spin; and yet I say to**

you that even Solomon in all his glory was not arrayed like one of these. Now if God so clothes the grass of the field, which today is, and tomorrow is thrown into the oven, will He not much more clothe you, O you of little faith?"[NKJV] Sitting on the grassy hillside, Jesus may have gestured to the *lilies of the field,* probably referring generally to the bountiful flowers in Israel. As in 6:26, Jesus was not condoning laziness while waiting for God to supply. Instead, he wanted his disciples to place their lives and needs in God's hands, refusing to worry over basic needs. To *worry about clothing* is to show *little faith* in God's ability to supply. If his creation feeds the birds (6:26) and clothes the earth with beauty and color so rich that even King Solomon's glorious garments could not match it, *will He not much more clothe you?* God "clothes" the flowers and grass of the field, neither of which endures for long *(today is, and tomorrow is thrown into the oven).*

The phrase "thrown into the oven" could refer to the hot wind (called the sirocco) that came off the desert southeast of Israel that would wilt flowers. Also, dry and dead grass was cut and used for fuel in the ovens when baking.

**6:31-32** **"Therefore do not worry, saying, 'What shall we eat?' or 'What shall we drink?' or 'What shall we wear?' For after all these things the Gentiles seek. For your heavenly Father knows that you need all these things."**[NKJV] *Therefore,* Jesus said, because God provides food and clothing not only for birds and flowers but even more for his precious human creation, *do not worry.* Do not spend energy fretting over what you will eat, drink, or wear. Worry has no place in the lives of Jesus' disciples; it is *the Gentiles* (unbelievers) who seek after, fret over, and worry about such things. They have no sense of God's care for them, no reason to focus their energies elsewhere. Jesus' followers, however, have kingdom priorities, a favored relationship with the king, and a promise that their *heavenly Father knows* that they need *all these things.*

**6:33** **"But seek first the kingdom of God and His righteousness, and all these things shall be added to you."**[NKJV] Jesus' followers must settle the question of priorities. They must be different from unbelievers whose priorities are comfort, security, money, fashion, etc. Jesus' followers *seek first the kingdom of God and His righteousness.* The word "seek" is a present imperative, a command to fulfill a continuing obligation. To "seek the kingdom" means both to submit to God's sovereignty here and now and to work for the future coming of his kingdom. To "seek His righteousness" means to seek to live as God requires, to truly seek these "first" calls for total loyalty and commitment. It means to turn to God first for help, to fill our thoughts with his desires, to take his character for our pattern, and to serve and obey him in everything.

What is most important to you; what do you "seek first"? People, objects, goals, money, pleasure, and other desires all compete for priority. Any of these can quickly bump God out of first place if we don't actively choose to give him first place in every area of life. Strangely enough, when we get our priorities right, Jesus promised that *all these things shall be added to you.* When Jesus' followers seek his kingdom first, God takes care of their needs.

But how can we truly be undistracted by materialistic pursuits? We all have to work, dress, drive, pay taxes—these responsibilities take up most of our days. We may not be materialistic; we just have to live. Should we leave it all and become monks? If there is no middle road, how do we do both—seek the kingdom and provide for our needs? Disciples of Jesus must understand the action (seek, strive), the priority (first), and the objectives (the kingdom of God and his righteousness). Priorities and sequence, however, are quite different matters. We determine sequences of work, rest, prayer, and worship according to time available, the cooperation of others, and many variables. But there can be only one central priority, which by its nature affects all others. The central priority determines the ways we pursue all our priorities.

---

**KEEPING PRIORITIES**
Good grades are important, and physical fitness is better than frailty, but neither are top-of-the-list priorities. A loving marriage makes life happy, and workplace promotions affirm our skills, but neither constitutes the last word.

Jesus put all the good we seek to do in divine perspective here: *Seek God's kingdom!* Here are some ways to do that:
- Realize that your church, for all its faults, is your extended Christian family. Serve it well. Give it your energy and time.
- Eagerly tell people how much Jesus means to you personally.
- Direct your work to projects and purposes that God would approve.
- Keep promises made to family and friends.
- Show a lot of love to the people God puts in your life.
- Get with a group of Christian friends and add three specific items to this list that you will work on during the next month. These friends can hold you accountable.

---

When we attempt to assign the appropriate amount of time to the kingdom of God and his righteousness so that we can figure out how much time we have left to do other activities, we reduce Jesus' words to a lesson in sequence and planning rather than a command about the whole of life. But if we think of "seek first" as "consistently look for, honor throughout, represent constantly, and remember always," then the ways we deal with family, friends, work, leisure, etc., will all be transformed. The rule of God and God's rules will determine and direct our efforts in every area of life. If this is not the case, we are not seeking first God's kingdom or righteousness.

**6:34** **"Therefore do not worry about tomorrow, for tomorrow will worry about itself. Each day has enough trouble of its own."** [NIV] Because God cares for his people's needs, *do not worry about tomorrow.* In an appeal to common sense, Jesus explained that what we worry about happening tomorrow may not happen, so we will have wasted time and energy worrying. We need to reserve that energy for today because *each day has enough trouble.* We only add to today's burdens when we worry about the future. All the anxieties about tomorrow will not change the outcome, and it will have enough anxieties of its own. The burdens of today are enough, so let God take care of them. God's certain promises of care for our needs do not mean that life will be without trouble. Trouble comes, so we must trust that God will provide through his grace. We must trust him for today without worrying about tomorrow.

Planning for tomorrow is time well spent; worrying about tomorrow is time wasted. Sometimes it's difficult to tell the difference. Careful planning is thinking ahead about goals, steps, and schedules and trusting in God's guidance. When done well, planning can help alleviate worry. Worriers, by contrast, are consumed by fear and make it difficult to trust God. They let their plans interfere with their relationship with God. Don't let worries about tomorrow affect your relationship with God today.

## SEVEN REASONS NOT TO WORRY

| | |
|---|---|
| 6:25 | The same God who created life in you can be trusted with the details of your life. |
| 6:26 | Worrying about the future hampers your efforts for today. |
| 6:27 | Worrying is more harmful than helpful. |
| 6:28-30 | God does not ignore those who depend on him. |
| 6:31-32 | Worry shows a lack of faith in and understanding of God. |
| 6:33 | There are real challenges God wants us to pursue, and worrying keeps us from them. |
| 6:34 | Living one day at a time keeps us from being consumed with worry. |

### DAILY TROUBLES

One of the best ways to avoid dealing with today's challenges and difficulties is to get wrapped up in tomorrow's. It seems easier to worry about what might not happen in the future than to deal with what *is* happening in the present! Tomorrow may require plans and forethought, but not worry. Today requires work and trust. Worry immobilizes us today and reveals a lack of trust in God's ability to hold tomorrow and preserve us. Jesus left no doubt that troubles of one kind or another will be part of the daily routine. But he also described those troubles as "enough" for each day. Can we not also trust God to provide whatever we need for the day? When we worry about tomorrow, we misuse the strength God has provided for today. We need to take "one day at a time" in our relationship with God.

# Matthew 7

**7:1-2** **"Judge not, that you be not judged."** NKJV The word "judge" (Greek, *krino*) can mean evaluate or analyze. It also refers to private, judgmental attitudes that tear down others in order to build up oneself. The command "judge not" does not refer to judging in a court of law, nor is it a blanket statement against critical thinking. Believers should be discerning and make certain judgments. For example, Jesus said to expose false teachers (7:15-23) and to admonish others in order to help them (18:15). Paul taught that we should exercise church discipline (1 Corinthians 5:1-5). But followers of Christ should not be critical or condemning in their attitudes toward others. A judgmental, critical spirit differs radi-

> They have a right to censure that have a heart to help.      *William Penn*

cally from love. Believers' special position with Christ does not give them license to take God's place as judge. Those who judge in that manner will find themselves *judged* likewise by God. As God will have mercy on the merciful (5:7) and forgive those who forgive (6:14-15), he will condemn those who condemn: **"For in the same way you judge others, you will be judged, and with the measure you use, it will be measured to you."** NIV The way Jesus' followers treat others is the way God will treat them. The religious leaders taught that God judged the world by two "measures"— mercy and justice. Each person receives what he or she measures out, either with mercy or with severity.

"Judge not, that you be not judged" may be the most-often-misquoted text from the Bible. People frequently apply it as if it were a flat command against all moral judgment. In fact, people use it to judge what they consider a judgmental attitude on the part of another. Jesus, however, gave these words as one negative application of the Golden Rule. That is, we should not treat others as we do not want to be treated. We should seek to measure ourselves and others by the same standards.

Jesus declared as unacceptable excusing personal sin while

holding others accountable for similar behavior. When you perceive a fault in others, your first impulse may be to confront or reject that person. But ask yourself first if your awareness of the failure mirrors your own life. Your effort to help will be in vain if the person can point out the same fault in you. Practice your own remedy before you ask others to do it.

---

CRITIC'S CORNER
Jesus tells us to examine our motives and conduct instead of judging others. The traits that bother us in others are often the habits we dislike in ourselves. Our untamed bad habits and behaviors are the very ones that we most want to change in others. Do you find it easy to magnify others' faults while excusing your own? If you are ready to criticize someone, check to see if you deserve the same criticism. Judge yourself first, and then lovingly forgive and help your neighbor.

---

**7:3-5** **"Why do you see the speck in your neighbor's eye, but do not notice the log in your own eye? Or how can you say to your neighbor, 'Let me take the speck out of your eye,' while the log is in your own eye?"** NRSV The word "speck" is also translated "splinter"; "log" is also translated "plank" or "beam." Many have taken this metaphor to mean that Christians should never correct anyone—one's personal sins before God are too great to even consider dealing with others' sins. However, Jesus' point was that while we all have sin in our lives (some as small as a speck; some as large as a log), we are responsible to both deal with our own sin and then help others. **"You hypocrite, first take the log out of your own eye, and then you will see clearly to take the speck out of your neighbor's eye."** NRSV Jesus revealed incredible understanding of human nature. How easy it is for us to overlook our own sins yet easily spot sin in others. How true that the sin we most clearly see in others is also present in us. Believers should first deal with their own sins, but they also must correct and guide erring brothers and sisters. James wrote, "My brothers and sisters, if anyone among you wanders from the truth and is brought back by another, you should know that whoever brings back a sinner from wandering will save the sinner's soul from death and will cover a multitude of sins" (James 5:19-20 NRSV).

It would be ludicrous and hypocritical, however, for a believer to attempt to help a brother or sister with a "speck" while carrying around a "log." That believer would be guilty of criticizing another without personally applying the same critical standards. While the person with the "speck" may certainly need help, that help must come from one who can *see clearly* to take out that speck. Paul wrote to the Galatians, "My friends, if anyone is detected in a transgression, you who have received the Spirit should restore such a one in a spirit of gentleness. Take care that you yourselves are not tempted" (Galatians 6:1 NRSV). Only those who are spiritually mature can discern when and how to confront sin in others.

---

IN-SPECK-TION
As Jesus described the person with a log in his eye trying to assist someone dislodge a painful speck, did his audience notice the twinkle in Jesus' eyes? The humor gets inside our defenses before we realize Jesus has given us a valuable insight. As we visualize the ridiculous caricature of someone with a log lodged in his eye, we may overlook the identity of those with the problem—us.

Jesus, however, didn't point out our sinfulness so we would simply let each other off more easily. He made it clear that a problem noticed usually requires more than one person's response. Both speck and log must be removed. The person with the speck-sized problem may actually be in a better position to help remove the log than the other way around. This means that when you notice a problem in someone else's life, you may have to ask that person to help you with the same problem in your own. A problem in common can be an excellent starting point for accountability.

---

**7:6 "Do not give dogs what is sacred; do not throw your pearls to pigs. If you do, they may trample them under their feet, and then turn and tear you to pieces."** NIV While believers were not to judge others (7:1-5), Jesus warned against a complete lack of discernment about people's attitudes toward the gospel. The *dogs* to which he was referring were not household pets, but wild, scavenger dogs. According to Old Testament law (Leviticus 11:7; Deuteronomy 14:8), *pigs* were "unclean" animals, meaning that Jews were not to eat or even touch them. Anyone who touched an unclean animal would become "ceremonially unclean" and could not go to the temple to worship until he or she had the uncleanness removed.

Because the Jews sometimes used the word "dogs" to refer to Gentiles, some have taken this to be a directive against evangelizing Gentiles. But that theory does not stand up against the rest of Matthew's teaching and, indeed, against the later actions of the apostles. So who are these "dogs" and "pigs"? They are unholy or "unclean" people who, when presented with the gospel, treat it with scorn and contempt. "What is sacred" refers to the special, consecrated food that only the priests and their families ate (Exodus 29:33-34; Leviticus 22:10-16; Numbers 18:8-19). It would be unthinkable to give this sacred food to scavenger dogs. In the same way, it would also be futile to give *pearls* to pigs. "What is sacred" and "pearls" picture the teaching of the gospel of the kingdom (see 13:45-46 where the kingdom of heaven is compared to a pearl of great value). Jesus explained the futility of teaching the gospel to people who do not want to listen; such people will only tear apart what we say. Pigs do not realize the value of pearls; all they know is that they cannot eat them, so they spit them out and then trample them into the mud. Contemptuous, evil people cannot grasp the value of the gospel, so they scornfully cast it away. We should not stop giving God's Word to unbelievers, but we should be wise and discerning so as not to bring scorn to God's message.

---

WHEN IS EVANGELISM WRONG?
Is evangelism ever inappropriate? Sometimes our witnessing requires discretion. There are times and places when witnessing can be rude and offensive. As a result, the gospel will be ridiculed.

When you witness, there will always be resistance to the message. Don't be put off. Resistance is normal. But when your witness provokes anger, slander, or ridicule, consider another time and place. All people need to hear the gospel, but effective witnessing occurs in appropriate settings.

---

## JESUS TEACHES ABOUT ASKING, SEEKING, KNOCKING / 7:7-12 / **64**

**7:7-8** **"Ask, and it will be given to you; seek, and you will find; knock, and it will be opened to you."** NKJV Beginning in chapter 5, the Sermon on the Mount has thus far explained to Jesus' followers the lifestyle and life attitudes that he expected from them. Some may have heard and thought the demands to be impossible. Here Jesus gave the answer to those thoughts and questions—*ask, seek, knock.* The ability to live for God is only a prayer away. The verbs are in the present tense, indicating continuous activity. Jesus' followers can keep on asking, keep on seeking, and keep on knocking, indicating the importance of persistent, consistent prayer in their lives. Only through prayer can believers stay in contact with God, know what he wants them to do, and then have the strength to do God's will in all areas of life. God will answer believers who persistently ask, seek, and knock. Jesus promised, **"For everyone who asks**

receives, and everyone who searches finds, and for everyone
who knocks, the door will be opened." NRSV God had told the
prophet Jeremiah, "You will seek me and find me when you seek
me with all your heart" (Jeremiah 29:13 NIV). The three words (ask,
seek, knock) combine to emphasize the truth that those who bring
their needs to God can trust that they will be satisfied. All three are
metaphors for praying. Sometimes God does not answer our
prayers immediately; sometimes we must keep on knocking, await-
ing God's answer. However, if we continue to trust God through
prayer, Jesus promised that we will receive, find, and have an open
door.

Believers, however, must not take Jesus' words as a blank
check; prayer is not a magical way to obtain whatever we want.
Jesus had already explained some conditions on this promise:
His followers were to show mercy and forgiveness to others (5:7;
6:12), avoid praying in order to get attention (6:5-6), and be willing to persevere in prayer. Our requests must be in harmony with
God's will ("your will be done," 6:10), accepting his will above
our desires.

---

KEEP KNOCKING
Jesus tells us to persist in pursuing God. People often give up
after a few halfhearted efforts and conclude that they cannot
find God. Knowing God takes faith, focus, and follow-through,
and Jesus assures us that we will be rewarded. Don't give up
in your efforts to seek God, even when the doors seem closed.
Continue to ask him for more knowledge, patience, wisdom,
love, and understanding. He will give them to you.

---

**7:9-11** "Is there anyone among you who, if your child asks for bread,
will give a stone? Or if the child asks for a fish, will give a
snake? If you then, who are evil, know how to give good gifts
to your children, how much more will your Father in heaven
give good things to those who ask him!" NRSV Jesus explained
that his followers can depend on God to answer their prayers
(7:7-8) by arguing "from the lesser to the greater." In other
words, if human beings *who are evil* would not think of giving
a child a *stone* that looked like a piece of *bread* or a dangerous
*snake* instead of a *fish,* then *how much more* will a holy God
acknowledge and answer our requests? The phrase "you then,
who are evil" refers to our human condition in comparison to a
holy God. In these words, Jesus revealed the heart of God the
Father. God is not selfish, begrudging, or stingy; his followers
don't have to beg or grovel when they come with their requests.

He is a loving Father who understands, cares, comforts, and willingly gives *good things to those who ask him.* "Good things" could refer to the Holy Spirit but does not exclude material provision. If humans can be kind, imagine how kind God can be. He created kindness!

---

SOMETHING BETTER
How often do people use their God-given sense of justice to question God's fairness without seeing the contradiction? Those who demand that God be accountable for his actions are, in the words of the first verse in this chapter, measuring with a standard they really would not want used on themselves. Don't you expect a loving parent to act lovingly? In spite of notorious failures, don't you still count on parents to behave decently? Why, when it comes to the heavenly Father, are you so ready to question his concern?

Jesus gave a delightful dignity to good parents in his description. He didn't portray them as giving their children whatever they asked. Good parents give good gifts, but they are not hostages to their children's wishes. Neither is God. We can ask God for anything. We ought to remember, however, that our heavenly Father may well have something even better in mind. How much trust do you demonstrate by the way you pray?

---

**7:12** **"So in everything, do to others what you would have them do to you, for this sums up the Law and the Prophets."** NIV This is commonly known as the Golden Rule. Many religions teach a negative version of this statement. Confucius said, "What you do not want done to yourself, do not do to others." The well-known Rabbi Hillel, when challenged to teach the entire Law while standing on one foot, said, "Whatever angers you when you suffer it at the hands of others, do not do it to others, this is the whole law." By stating this positively, Jesus made the statement even more significant. It may be easy to refrain from harming others, but it is much more difficult to take the initiative in doing something good for them. A person may be able to keep the negative form of the law by avoiding sin, but to keep the positive form requires action. This is the key to the radical discipleship that Jesus wants. The Golden Rule is the foundation of active goodness and mercy—the kind of love God shows to us every day. The word "so" links Jesus' words "do to others what you would have them do to you" with the teachings presented thus far in the Sermon on the Mount (beginning at 5:1). Not only does this rule describe briefly the behavior expected of Jesus' followers, it also *sums up the Law and the Prophets,* as Rabbi Hillel said. When we follow the Golden Rule, we keep the rest of God's commands.

## JESUS TEACHES ABOUT THE WAY
## TO HEAVEN / 7:13-14 / **65**

In the closing verses of the Sermon on the Mount, four different
contrasts represent four warnings that focus on future final judgment. There are two ways (7:13-14), two types of trees (7:15-20),
two kinds of followers (7:21-23), and two ways to build (7:24-27).
Jesus was still speaking about the kingdom of heaven, describing
clearly that some will enter it and some will not. The basis for a person's final destination begins with that person's decisions about
Jesus himself.

**7:13-14** **"Enter through the narrow gate; for the gate is wide and
the road is easy that leads to destruction, and there are
many who take it. For the gate is narrow and the road is
hard that leads to life, and there are few who find it."** NRSV
People are presented with two ways, represented by two gates—
one *gate* is *narrow,* the other is *wide.* This was a Jewish teaching (see, for example, Deuteronomy 30:19; Psalm 1:1-2;
Jeremiah 21:8). Jesus commanded his followers to *enter
through the narrow gate.* This "narrow gate" refers to a confined space with little room. One needs careful directions to
find the "one way" to get through the gate. The hard road refers
to the road of discipleship often filled with persecution and
opposition. However, this hard road alone *leads to life*—eternal
life. (See also Luke 13:24.)

Through the wide gate, however, *the road is easy.* This gate is
easy to find; the path is easy to follow. There is plenty of room
for *many* people to wander in and continue in whatever direction
they wish. This road *leads to destruction*—to hell itself.

We don't know whether the "gate" is at the beginning of the
way, opening onto a road that leads to a certain destination, or
whether people follow certain roads that ultimately lead to one
of two gates. Passing through that final gate, people then receive
life or destruction. The Sermon on the Mount's stress on the kingdom makes the latter (the gate at the end of the road) more natural. The "gate" refers to the final judgment.

This gate leading to life is narrow not because it is difficult to
become a Christian but because there is only one way and only a
*few* decide to walk that road. Believing in Jesus is the only way
to eternal life because he alone died for our sins and made us
right before God. The road is hard because true discipleship calls
for sacrifice and servanthood. Following the crowd along life's
easy path results in destruction. Choosing the narrow way of
difficulty and sacrifice ultimately leads to eternal life.

Sometimes Christians receive harsh treatment from people

who don't understand or are plainly hostile. Sometimes Christians give up a lot in order to follow Christ. Sometimes Christians are called to endure terrible pain, even death. But through it all we have God's promise: Jesus is with us, hour by hour, hand in hand. That is the secret of a Christian's strength.

---

TWO GATES
One of Jesus' self-descriptions was of a gate: "I am the gate; whoever enters through me will be saved" (John 10:9 NIV). In Jesus' invitation to enter the narrow gate, he described two lives. Each life has a "gate" consistent with its "way." People *take* the wide gateway, but they *find* the narrow gateway. The wide gateway that leads to destruction defines the normal human experience, except for the few who find and enter the narrow gateway. Jesus' invitation to enter confronts the disciples with the gate itself. They have *found* the gate; he is standing before them. They can enter by trusting him completely.

The invitation still stands. Those who recognize that they have entered the wide gateway that leads to destruction may still enter the way to life through Jesus Christ. Which gateway represents your life right now?

---

## JESUS TEACHES ABOUT FRUIT IN PEOPLE'S LIVES / 7:15-20 / **66**

Jesus warned against false teachers. Many powerful speakers claim to have important ideas for Christians to hear. These speakers range from political reactionaries to extreme environmentalists. There are literally hundreds of cults vying to recruit new members. Add to the list those who present special angles on church doctrine coming from big and small denominations—there's a dazzling array of choices. How do we separate the good (teaching that leads to Christ), the bad (off-center but benign ideas tacked on to the gospel), and the ugly (false teaching)?

It's a complicated problem, but the following safeguards will help along the way:

*Use condemnation sparingly.* An off-center idea may be way out but is not necessarily heresy. A sincere but misguided teacher may not be a "false" teacher. None of us understands God perfectly, so we must be generous and helpful long before we condemn and cast out.

*Pay attention to the teacher's ethical and moral behavior.* The Bible stresses that false teachers will have immorality in their lives. Watch how they treat people and money. Do their lives contain or condone immoral practices? Is money the teacher's or group's prime motivation? Is the leader offended when you ask for the scriptural backing behind his or her statements? Don't excuse or cover up bad behavior.

*Choose your church carefully.* Is the living Christ at the center of your church's ministry? Do leaders pray? Is the Bible honored and taught? Is God at work there? "False" churches may be very busy, but their teaching reveals the void when Christ and the Bible are pushed to the side. If that is the case, go somewhere else.

**7:15 "Watch out for false prophets. They come to you in sheep's clothing, but inwardly they are ferocious wolves."** NIV The Old Testament frequently mentions *false prophets* (see 2 Kings 3:13; Isaiah 44:25; Jeremiah 23:16; Ezekiel 13:2-3; Micah 3:5; Zechariah 13:2). False prophets claimed to receive messages from God, but they prophesied only what the king and the people wanted to hear. False teachers are just as common today. Jesus says to *watch out for* those whose words sound religious but who are motivated by money, fame, or power. These false prophets will come in among the believers like wolves covered in sheep pelts, pretending to be sheep, hoping to go unnoticed as they do their damage. But Jesus described these people as *ferocious wolves.* Just as the false prophets arose from God's people, Israel, so false prophets and false teachers would later come out from among the believers and from the church. Jesus warned his followers that false prophets would come (see also 24:11; Mark 13:22-23). Very shortly, these words began to come true. False teachers infiltrated the early churches just as the gospel message was spreading (see Acts 20:29; 2 Corinthians 11:11-15; 2 Timothy 2:14-19; 2 Peter 2:1-3, 17-22; 1 John 2:18, 22; 4:1-6). While Jesus did not elaborate on the form of their false teaching, it follows from the context that they would teach a way of salvation that did not include a narrow gate and a hard road (7:13-14). Indeed, many of the false teachers about whom Peter, John, and Paul later warned were teaching such a message.

Jesus' followers would need the ability to discern true sheep from wolves *in sheep's clothing.* How could they do this? Jesus explained how in the following verses.

> We must not be dazzled by a person's outward clothing—his charm, learning, doctorates and ecclesiastical honours. We must not be so naive as to suppose that because he is a Ph.D. or a D.D. or a professor or a bishop he must be a true and orthodox ambassador of Christ. We must look beneath the appearance to the reality. What lives under the fleece: a sheep or a wolf?      *John R. W. Stott*

WOLVES

By comparing false teachers to wolves, Jesus exposed a type of deadly spiritual predator. These "teachers" practice hit-and-run tactics among Christians. They appear to be spiritual, but their motive turns out to be greed. They often leave the scene of their attack before the damage becomes apparent. How can we guard against "wolves in sheep's clothing"? We can use the images that Jesus employed on this occasion to establish one important guideline: Newcomers shouldn't be teachers. Christians don't need to be suspicious; just wisely cautious. When we insist that a new teacher first demonstrate integrity and maturity, we create an atmosphere resistant to attacks. A newcomer isn't proven. Time will allow other believers to examine the quality of this person's life. What guidelines are in place in your church to encourage good teaching but guard against "wolves"?

**7:16-18** **"You will know them by their fruits."** NRSV "Fruit" is a Jewish metaphor for both character and conduct. Jesus' followers would be able to discern false prophets by looking at their lives and conduct. In the Old Testament there were tests for a true prophet. The law found in Deuteronomy 13:1-5 required a prophet to be put to death if he promoted rebellion against God. Deuteronomy 18:14-22 taught the Jews to reject a prophet who contradicted previous revelations from God or whose message failed to come true. Jesus may have included the Pharisees among the false teachers because they trusted God's truth to satisfy their own interests. But his warning was against false prophets of any kind.

When the apostles later wrote letters warning about false teachers, they often pointed out their evil actions. Peter would later write, "There will be false teachers among you. . . . Many will follow their shameful ways. . . . Bold and arrogant, these men are not afraid to slander celestial beings. . . . These men blaspheme. . . . Their idea of pleasure is to carouse in broad daylight. . . . With eyes full of adultery, they never stop sinning" (2 Peter 2:1, 2, 10, 12, 13, 14 NIV). The evil character and conduct of these false teachers would reveal that they were no more than wolves in sheep's clothing. No matter what a person claims to be, his or her true character will eventually reveal itself.

**"Are grapes gathered from thorns, or figs from thistles?"** NRSV Jesus' question begins with the Greek word *meti,* which expects a negative answer: "People don't gather grapes from thorns or figs from thistles, do they?" *Grapes* and *figs* were two of the main agricultural products of Israel; no one would misunderstand Jesus' meaning. A person knows a tree by its fruit: **"In the same way,**

**every good tree bears good fruit, but the bad tree bears bad fruit. A good tree cannot bear bad fruit, nor can a bad tree bear good fruit."** NRSV Fruit is good or bad depending on the health of the tree. Healthy trees bear good fruit, and unhealthy trees bear bad fruit. It cannot be any other way. (The positive and negative repetition of this teaching in these verses was a common Jewish teaching method.) Jesus' followers would be able to discern false teachers because in their teaching they minimize Christ and glorify themselves. Their *fruit* would be bad, revealing a bad character. False prophets would not speak the truth; God's true prophets would not speak falsely.

Claims are easier to make or fake than results. Even Jesus' claims would have been ludicrous or insane if he hadn't backed them up with results. He understood the relationship between claim and proof. And he pointed out that the principle applies universally: You can tell a lot about a tree from its fruit! Jesus warned that prophets and teachers are like trees: Examine them and their "fruit" closely. Bad characters frequently attempt to pass as believers. But no matter how well a false prophet might cover his tracks for a while, eventually his "fruit" would make him known.

**7:19 "Every tree that does not bear good fruit is cut down and thrown into the fire."** NKJV This picture of the final judgment of false prophets repeats a similar statement made by John the Baptist: "Even now the ax is lying at the root of the trees; every tree therefore that does not bear good fruit is cut down and thrown into the fire" (3:10 NRSV). A person's mere profession of faith will be meaningless at the final judgment. Any who claim his name but do *not bear good fruit* will be like worthless trees, *cut down and thrown into the fire.* In fact, some will have professed faith, only to face judgment in the end (as explained in the following verses, 7:21-23).

**7:20 "Thus, by their fruit you will recognize them."** NIV Repeating from 7:16 the method of discerning false prophets, Jesus explained that his followers should evaluate teachers' words by examining their lives. Just as trees are consistent in the kind of fruit they produce, good teachers consistently exhibit good behavior and high moral character as they attempt to live out the truths of Scripture. This does not mean we should throw out church school teachers, pastors, and others who are less than perfect. Every one of us is subject to sin, and we must show the same mercy to others that we need for ourselves. When Jesus spoke about bad trees, he meant teachers who deliberately teach false doctrine. We must examine the teachers' motives, the direction they are taking, and the results they are seeking. Those who should not be teaching will be recognizable *by their fruit.*

Jesus never avoided the subject of judgment. He even based his earlier teaching against judgmentalism (7:1-2) on the inevitable final judgment. The certainty of judgment undergirds the entire Sermon on the Mount (see, for example, 5:13, 20, 22, 29-30; 6:15; 7:1-2, 13, 19, 21-23). Jesus drove his teaching home with the warning that a failure to apply his words would expose his hearers to judgment (7:24-27). The standards of the kingdom overwhelm us! Having heard, we can no longer use ignorance as an excuse.

Obedience begins when we acknowledge Jesus as Lord. We don't *earn* his acceptance by our success in obeying him, but we grow in our obedience as we recognize his gracious, saving love toward us. In this sense, the Sermon of the Mount functions as the law did in the Old Testament—it leads us to Christ. We haven't *heard* the teaching of Jesus if we simply admire him or even give some effort to obeying his commands. Half measures pave the way to judgment. His teaching drives us to submit to him even as we seek to obey. Have you met the Guide, Shepherd, and Lord through his Sermon on the Mount?

---

DISCERNMENT
Discerning truth from error, wisdom from falsehood, and right from wrong takes lots of time and maturity, yet we are called to make such judgments daily. Here's a plan:

- Avoid firm opinions made alone. It is better to run your ideas through a group of intelligent, trustworthy Christian friends and mentors. Friends keep us from crackpot ideas and guide our maturing mind and heart.
- Never form a life commitment without reference to the Bible, God's Word. The Bible is silent on lots of subjects (calculus, computer programming, brain surgery, etc.), but it speaks clearly on God's purpose for your life. Consult it daily.
- Be generous in your judgments, but don't compromise with evil. Some fussy Christians today still think beards are a sign of degradation. Many other dos and don'ts trivialize spiritual development. Give your brother and sister in Christ a break. But don't give evil a wedge in your heart.

---

## JESUS TEACHES ABOUT THOSE WHO BUILD HOUSES ON ROCK AND SAND / 7:21-29 / **67**

**7:21** **"Not everyone who says to me, 'Lord, Lord,' will enter the kingdom of heaven, but only the one who does the will of my Father in heaven."** NRSV The two phrases (that Jesus called himself *Lord* and referred to God as *my Father in heaven*) thinly veiled his claim to be the Messiah. While the word "Lord" could also be translated "rabbi" or "teacher," Jesus knew who he was and revealed his part in the coming final judgment in these words. Because people's "fruit" reveal who they really are (7:20), then it follows that simply calling Jesus "Lord" is not enough. It is not wrong to call Jesus "Lord"—Jesus was distinguishing between lip service and real discipleship. It is much easer to *profess* Christianity than to *possess* it.

Those who *will enter the kingdom of heaven* are only those who do *the will of my Father in heaven.* To do God's will implies a relationship with God—the ability to communicate with him, know his will, and then be able to perform it. Such "fruit" reveals one who will enter the kingdom of heaven.

---

LIP SERVICE
Jesus is not impressed by thoughtless and heartless piety. Superficial religion might satisfy the casual observer, but Jesus demands obedience from the inside out. Saying "Lord, Lord" without really obeying Christ simply breaks the third commandment: "You shall not misuse the name of the LORD your God" (Exodus 20:7 NIV).

Many are tempted toward pretense and dishonesty. A shell of spirituality may preserve our reputation with others, but it undermines real growth. We are deluded if we think that God might be fooled by fake holiness. God desires "truth in the inner parts" (Psalm 51:6 NIV). What does God find under the surface of your life? Do your actions live up to your words?

---

**7:22-23** **"Many will say to me on that day, 'Lord, Lord, did we not prophesy in your name, and in your name drive out demons and perform many miracles?' Then I will tell them plainly, 'I never knew you. Away from me, you evildoers!'"** NIV Jesus exposed those people who sounded religious and did religious deeds but had no personal relationship with him. Not sincere followers who had come to him for salvation, they were masquerading as disciples. These people knew in their hearts that they were false. False prophets will even be able to *prophesy* (referring not just to telling the future, but to teaching), *drive out demons,* and *perform many miracles.* Jesus warned that "false Christs and false prophets will appear and perform signs and miracles to deceive the elect—if that were possible" (Mark 13:22 NIV). Paul warned against counterfeit miracles, signs, and wonders in 2 Thessalonians 2:9. Claims to great power, invoking the name of Christ (*in your name,* see Mark 9:38; Acts 19:13-20), and powerful deeds will be no guarantee for heaven. Jesus will send away those who do not know him personally. They may have done impressive deeds, but they are *evildoers.* Jesus will say, *I never knew you. Away from me* (see Psalm 6:8). In other words, "I never had a personal relationship with you, and I never went with you to do these deeds you claim. You can have no part in my kingdom."

*On that day* (the day of judgment), only a person's relationship with Christ—acceptance of him as Savior and obedience to him—will matter. "That day" is the final day of reckoning when God will settle all accounts, judging sin and rewarding faith. Notice that Jesus placed himself as judge—many will say to *me.* Here is another claim to messiahship. Many people think that if they are good people and say religious things, God will have to reward them with eternal life. In reality, faith in Christ is what will count at the judgment.

**7:24-25** **"Everyone then who hears these words of mine and acts on them will be like a wise man who built his house on rock."** NRSV Jesus' true followers not only hear his words, but they act on his words, allowing his message to make a difference in their lives. The key to this parable (as with all parables) is the central message, not the peripheral details. In this teaching, Jesus explained that his true followers, by acting on his words, are *like a wise man who built his house on rock.* The one who builds "on rock" is a hearing, responding disciple, not a phony, superficial one. The apostle James would later write, "But be doers of the word, and not merely hearers who deceive themselves. For if any are hearers of the word and not doers, they are like those who look at themselves in a mirror; for they look at themselves and, on going away, immediately forget what they were like. But those who look into the perfect law, the law of liberty, and persevere, being not hearers who forget but doers who act—they will be blessed in their doing" (James 1:22-25 NRSV).

WALKIE-TALKIE
Some athletes can "talk" a great game, but that tells you nothing about their athletic skills. And not everyone who talks about heaven belongs to God's kingdom. Jesus is more concerned about our "walk" than our "talk." He wants us to do right, not just say the right words. Your house (which represents your life, 7:24) will withstand the storms of life only if you do what is right instead of just talking about it. Some people wonder if they are really Christians. If that's you—start acting like one. Some people jabber about their intense faith. If that's you—just show your faith in faithful living.

Practicing obedience builds on the solid foundation of Jesus' words to weather the storms of life: **"The rain came down, the streams rose, and the winds blew and beat against that house; yet it did not fall, because it had its foundation on the rock."** NIV Jesus pictured Palestine's climate in these words. While there were few rainfalls all year, during the rainy season, heavy rains with excessive flooding could wash away poorly grounded homes. But those houses with their foundations on solid rock would be unaffected by the rising waters and beating winds. When the "storms of life" come (we cannot press the details of the *rain, streams,* and *winds*), only the one who builds his or her life on the *foundation* of Jesus Christ will *not fall.*

---

A LITTLE NUDGE
Like a house of cards, the fool's life crumbles. Most people do not deliberately seek to build on a false or inferior foundation; instead, they just don't think about their life's purpose. Many people are headed for destruction, not out of stubbornness but out of thoughtlessness. Part of our responsibility as believers is to help others stop and think about where their lives are headed and to point out the consequences of ignoring Christ's message. Some people just need a little prodding to come over to Jesus' side. They have heard the gospel, but they're not sure or not convinced or not ready. Often they just haven't met anyone for whom that decision has made a difference.

---

When you meet someone close to a decision to follow Jesus, give a word of encouragement. Offer to help, to pray, to be there with your friend. Everyone feels a certain spiritual inertia, and your simple word may help overcome it.

**7:26-27** **"And everyone who hears these words of mine and does not act on them will be like a foolish man who built his house on sand."** NRSV In contrast to the wise man (7:24), the *foolish man* is the person *who hears these words of mine and does not act on them.* While both the wise man and the foolish man built houses, and while those houses may have even looked identical, only one house would stand the test. Only the man who hears and does God's word will receive God's reward. The house built *on sand* will collapse. **"The rain came down, the streams rose, and the winds blew and beat against that house, and it fell with a great crash."** NIV This time when the storms came, the person turned away, life crumbled, and the end was *a great crash*—final judgment, destruction (7:13-14), separation from God (7:22-23). As character is revealed by fruit (7:20), so faith is revealed by storms. The wise person, seeking to act upon God's Word, builds to withstand anything. It will be the foundation, not the house, that will determine what happens on the Day of Judgment.

What action did Jesus expect as a result of his words? What "building" did he expect to happen? Radical discipleship—people whose lives revealed the characteristics that he had been describing in this sermon (beginning at 5:1).

---

### AUTHORITY

People today accept the concept of individual autonomy. Truth has been relegated to "whatever is true for you is true." Because the possibility of absolute truth has been widely rejected, people now depend on "personal truth." But we can't make up for the loss of absolute truth by creating our own truth. We are simply wrong too often.

Jesus concluded his sermon with a challenge about foundations. Those who heard him were impressed by his authority. But amazement doesn't equal acceptance or submission. People who agree in theory that a house should be built on a solid foundation may still go out and construct their lives on a swamp. Part of sharing the gospel with someone involves helping them really look at the foundation of their lives. We must also be able to demonstrate our own foundation. People need to hear and see that we have made Jesus' teaching the basis of our lives.

---

**7:28-29 Now when Jesus had finished saying these things, the crowds were astounded at his teaching, for he taught them as one having authority, and not as their scribes.**NRSV The words "now when Jesus had finished saying these things" signal the end of Jesus' teaching on discipleship and a return to the narrative in Matthew. Words like these come at the end of each of the major discourses (see 11:1; 13:53; 19:1; 26:1).

The Greek word translated "astounded" is a strong word; it could also be translated "astonished" or "amazed." Jesus completely amazed the *crowds* by his teaching. The Jewish teachers (the *scribes*) often quoted from well-known rabbis in order to give their words more authority. But Jesus didn't have that need. Because Jesus was the Son of God, he knew exactly what the Scriptures said and meant. He was the ultimate *authority*. He didn't need to quote anyone because he was the original Word (John 1:1). The people had never heard such teaching. Jesus created the urgency and alarm that a real prophet would cause, not the discussion and arguments of scribal tradition. He confronted the people with the claims of God on their lives.

The scribes (called "teachers of the law" or "lawyers" in some Bible versions) were the legal specialists in Jesus' day.

They interpreted the law but were especially concerned about the *halakah* or rules for life that came to be as binding as God's written law in the Torah. The scribes were the forerunners of the office of rabbi. Their self-assured authority, in fact, became a stumbling block for them, for they denied Jesus' authority to reinterpret the law, and they rejected Jesus as the Messiah because he did not agree with or obey all of their traditions.

IN CONCLUSION

We must read the Sermon on the Mount with its final application in mind. These words of Jesus set before us two choices described in Matthew 7:24-27. The "wise and foolish builders" share two traits in common: Each were builders and each had "heard" Jesus' instructions. What matters, Jesus declared, is not familiarity with his teaching but putting it into practice. Which is your greater reason for studying what Jesus taught: to increase your knowledge or to improve your obedience?

# Matthew 8

Matthew arranged the following accounts topically, not chronologically. Mark and Luke recorded some of the following events, but placed them in different locations, probably in the chronological sequence of events. The following section features a series of miracles (chapters 8 and 9 have ten). Jesus' miracles demonstrated the power of the kingdom in action. This first miracle involved a man who had been estranged from the Jews because of a dreaded disease.

**8:1 When he came down from the mountainside, large crowds followed him.**NIV In 5:1 we read that Jesus "saw the crowds . . . [and] went up on a mountainside" in order to teach them. After finishing his "Sermon on the Mount" (recorded in chapters 5–7), Jesus *came down from the mountainside*. Whenever we see Jesus, we usually see *large crowds* following him. The people were astonished at Jesus' authority in his teaching (7:28-29); it captivated them, so they followed him to see and hear more.

**8:2 A man with leprosy came and knelt before him and said, "Lord, if you are willing, you can make me clean."**NIV *Leprosy,* like AIDS today, was a terrifying disease because there was no known cure. In Jesus' day, the Greek word for "leprosy" was used for a variety of similar skin diseases, and some forms were contagious. If a person contracted the contagious type, a priest declared him a leper and banished him from his home and city. This also excluded him from participating in any social or religious activities (according to the law in Leviticus 13–14). The leper went to live in a community with other lepers until he either got better or died. This was the only way the people knew to contain the spread of the contagious forms of leprosy.

This man took a great risk when he *came and knelt before* Jesus. The word for "knelt" can also mean "worshiped." His kneeling reveals his desperation, humility, and recognition of Jesus' authority. His words to Jesus reveal his faith. If his disease were to disappear, a priest could declare him clean (or cured), but only Jesus could *make* him *clean.*

The words "if you are willing" reveal the man's faith in Jesus' authority in this matter of healing; Jesus' ability was never in question. This man wanted to be clean—a huge request. The man wanted to become a person again, to be reunited with his family and community. He knew Jesus could do it. He apparently had heard of Jesus' healing power (see 4:24). The question was, *would* Jesus heal him?

---

POINT OF NEED
The leper's actions and words expressed his complete reliance upon Christ. This leper was a broken person. He may not have fully understood who Jesus was, but he regarded Jesus as his source of hope. Perhaps the leper had just stood at a distance, straining to listen to parts of the Sermon on the Mount. He must have thought that surely a man with such powerful words from God might also wield God's power to heal. The leper wanted so badly to be clean.

This desperate man had a point of need; a part of his life was clearly beyond his control. God often uses our point of need as the place in which to make himself known. Until we honestly cry, "Help," any knowledge we have about God will be incomplete. Our point of need may be physical illness, loneliness, or the defeat of recurring sin. God can use that need to make us aware of our deeper need for him.

Has God used your need to draw your attention to himself? Have you turned to him? Let your trust in God deepen as you honestly confess your need to him.

---

**8:3 Jesus reached out his hand and touched the man. "I am willing," he said. "Be clean!"**[NIV] Jesus' love and power work together. Matthew revealed Jesus' heart of compassion. All people shunned lepers, but Jesus *reached out his hand and touched* this man covered with a dreaded, contagious disease. That Jesus' touch precedes his pronouncement of healing indicates his sovereignty over the Jewish law not to touch a leper (Leviticus 5:3; 13:1-46; Numbers 5:2). In touching the leper, Jesus became "unclean." He did not worry about becoming ritually unclean when there was a genuine need.

When Jesus answered the man, *I am willing,* he showed his willingness and ability to meet this social outcast's most basic need. With the words "Be clean," the leprosy immediately disappeared. The words and the touch were simple but effective, revealing Jesus' divine authority over sickness.

**Immediately he was cured of his leprosy.**[NIV] When Jesus spoke the words, the leper was cured *immediately.* We do not know the stage of this man's leprosy—he may have already lost portions of his body to the disease. But when Jesus spoke, the man's health was restored completely and instantly. The man had his life back; he could return to his community, to his family, and to the synagogue.

---

**TELL AND SHOW**
Jesus' touch communicated both to the leper and to the watching people. What communicates with people? What gets through? What cracks the crust and reaches a person beneath the surface?

If all we do is speak (preach or witness), many people will wonder if our words carry much weight. Having words without work seems cheap. Most people prefer the words of someone whose life they trust, and trust requires a tangible demonstration of a person's values.

If all we do is work (touch people with good deeds), many will wonder what all the effort means. Works accomplished but never celebrated may add health or comfort to a person's life (and this is important), but in the end, for what higher purpose?

Jesus speaks and touches, and so should we. In your actions, you show the love of God. In your words, you celebrate God by answering the *how* and the *why* questions connected with your service. For Jesus' sake, *tell* others about him, and *show* others how much you care.

---

**8:4 Then Jesus said to him, "See that you say nothing to anyone; but go, show yourself to the priest, and offer the gift that Moses commanded, as a testimony to them."** NRSV Jesus healed the man, but also gave him two warnings: First, *see that you say nothing to anyone.* The warning was an earnest and forceful admonition—words that Jesus commanded the man to obey. But why would Jesus ask this man not to tell anyone about his healing? Wouldn't this have been great advertising for Jesus, bringing more people to hear his message? While we might think so, Jesus knew better (John 2:24-25). Jesus' mission was to preach the Good News of the kingdom of God. He did not want the crowds descending on him to see miracles or to benefit from his power. Such people would not be receptive to hear and to respond to the gospel. Jesus did not want to be a miracle worker in a sideshow; he wanted to be the Savior of their souls. This verse and others in Matthew (9:30; 12:16; 16:20; 17:9) have been referred to as the "messianic secret," meaning that Jesus wished to keep his full messiahship hidden until after the Resurrection. Different reasons have been given, such as that Jesus did not want to arouse political messianic expectations or that Jesus wouldn't accept the full acclamation until he finished his saving work on the cross. Most likely, there were several and different reasons for each situation. Here perhaps the obvious meaning is that the cleansed man would not be distracted by talking to people until he followed the law and went to the priest.

The law required a priest to examine a healed leper (Leviticus 14). Then the healed leper was to give an offering at the temple, called the guilt offering in Leviticus 14:12. Jesus adhered to these laws by sending the man to the priest, thereby demonstrating high regard for God's law. Jesus wanted this man to give his story firsthand to the priest to prove that his leprosy was completely gone so that he could be restored to his family and community. This would be *a testimony to them.*

Some think that "them" refers to the priests. Jesus would show the religious authorities that he was not anti-law, but the only one who could truly fulfill the law. If the priest declared that the healing had taken place but refused to accept the person and power of Christ who had done it, that priest would be condemned by the evidence. On the other hand, Jesus may have intended the testimony to be a positive one to the people who witnessed the healing. Jesus' meaning would be, "Don't you proclaim it. Instead, let the priest's pronouncement witness for me and for the healing." The priest's words would testify to everyone that the man had recovered and that Jesus did not condemn the law. Most important, however, the testimony would reveal that the one who heals lepers had come. People believed that healing leprosy was a sign of the Messiah's arrival (see 11:5).

Mark records that the man disobeyed Jesus' warning and "went out and began to talk freely, spreading the news. As a result, Jesus could no longer enter a town openly but stayed outside in lonely places" (see Mark 1:45 NIV).

## A ROMAN CENTURION DEMONSTRATES FAITH / 8:5-13 / **68**

This event is also recorded in Luke 7:1-10. This miracle occurred to a person who, because of his race and occupation, was not close to the Jewish faith. In this story and the previous one (the healed leper), Jesus willingly dealt with people the Jews shunned.

**8:5-6 When he entered Capernaum, a centurion came to him, appealing to him and saying, "Lord, my servant is lying at home paralyzed, in terrible distress."** NRSV *Capernaum,* located on the northwestern shore of the Sea of Galilee, was the largest of the many fishing towns surrounding the lake. Jesus had recently moved to Capernaum from Nazareth (4:12-13). Capernaum was a thriving town with great wealth as well as great sin and decadence. Near a major trade route, it housed a contingent of Roman soldiers even though Galilee was not under Roman occupation until after the death of Herod Agrippa in A.D. 44. Because Capernaum had the headquarters for Roman troops, the city was filled with heathen influences from all over the Roman Empire. This was a needy place for Jesus to challenge both Jews and non-Jews with the gospel of God's kingdom.

A *centurion*—a career military officer in the Roman army— had control over one hundred soldiers. Often the sons of Roman senators or powerful figures would begin their careers at this level. The Jews hated Roman soldiers for their oppression, control, and ridicule and considered them "unclean" because they were despised Gentiles.

---

CROSSING BARRIERS
The centurion asked Jesus for help, not for himself but for some-one else. He crossed racial, social, and political barriers to present his servant's plight. But he didn't tell Jesus what he wanted. He simply described his servant's condition: paralyzed and in excruciating pain. He allowed Jesus to decide if and how he would help. The centurion practiced wisdom in what he did and what he didn't do.

God honors us with the gift of prayer. This privilege does not give us permission to make demands but freedom to express our needs, gratitude, and praise. Use the centurion as a model for prayer, and pray for those beyond your immediate circle of relatives and friends. Such praying will not only bring God's resources to bear on that person's life; it also will greatly help to deepen your own compassion.

---

Why did this centurion come to Jesus? Luke records that the man himself didn't come but that he sent "some elders of the Jews" (Luke 7:3). In those days, dealing with a person's messen-gers was considered the same as dealing with the one who had sent them. Because of his Jewish audience, Matthew emphasized the man's race and faith. This Roman centurion was apparently different from many other Roman soldiers who despised the Jews. He may have been a "God-fearer" who worshiped the God of Israel but was not circumcised (see Acts 2:5; 10:2). Luke also explains that the elders reported to Jesus that "this man deserves to have you do this [healing], because he loves our nation and has built our synagogue" (Luke 7:4-5 NIV). This centurion had appar-ently heard about Jesus' healing powers. He may have known about the healing of the Roman official's son (which probably occurred earlier, see John 4:46-54). He knew that Jesus had the power to heal. While this soldier's concern about a *servant* may seem unusual, the Jewish historian Josephus wrote that Roman soldiers had many servants who actually trained and fought with them. So this servant may have been the centurion's personal attendant with whom he felt a close bond. This centurion made an appeal on behalf of his servant who had become paralyzed, was in pain *(terrible distress),* and was near death (Luke 7:2). The centurion, a military authority, addressed Jesus as *Lord.* This Roman officer showed respect for Jesus' authority in this area of healing (see also 8:2).

**8:7** **And Jesus said to him, "I will come and heal him."** NKJV The Roman centurion may have been surprised at Jesus' quick and willing response. Yet this was the same loving person who reached out and touched a leper. He would not hesitate to go to a Gentile's home to heal a sick servant. The Gospels never record an incident of Jews entering a Gentile home. Jews generally did not do so because it made them ceremonially "unclean." However, as Jesus willingly touched a leper (which was against the law) to heal him, so Jesus would willingly enter a Gentile home if needed (however, there is no record that he did). For Jesus, doing good always transcended both Levitical regulations and Sabbath tradition.

**8:8-9** **The centurion answered, "Lord, I am not worthy to have you come under my roof; but only speak the word, and my servant will be healed. For I also am a man under authority, with soldiers under me; and I say to one, 'Go,' and he goes, and to another, 'Come,' and he comes, and to my slave, 'Do this,' and the slave does it."** NRSV The centurion surely knew of the Jewish insistence upon not entering Gentile homes, so he protested Jesus' willingness to go right away to see the servant. The centurion's protest, *"Lord, I am not worthy to have you come under my roof,"* may refer to his being a Gentile. Luke 7:7 seems to show, however, that he was thinking more of his own moral unworthiness. He saw that Jesus' authority was greater than his own and that Jesus need not personally visit his home. The centurion understood that Jesus need *only speak the word* to heal the servant. He understood the power of Jesus' words.

Because of his position, the centurion could delegate responsibility with a word and know that the job would be done. He himself was *a man under authority* because final authority rested with the Roman emperor. The emperor delegated responsibility to various officials, such as this centurion. Thus, when the centurion gave orders to soldiers under him, he spoke with the authority of the emperor. The centurion was accustomed both to obeying and to being obeyed. He may have applied his understanding of military orders to Jesus—realizing that Jesus' power and authority came from God. When Jesus spoke, God spoke. Jesus did not need rituals or medicines or even his touch or presence to accomplish a healing. Whatever he understood, the centurion had absolutely no doubt that Jesus could merely speak the word and heal the servant.

---

WORDS' WORTH
Spoken words were thought to carry much more power in ancient days than now. Most people dust off advertising messages as hype, and radio talk shows as trash. Today, much talk has made spoken words seem trivial.
    We need to recover the power of words. Here are a few suggestions:
- On Sunday, listen to the preacher's sermon, and talk about it afterward.
- At dinnertime on Monday, for even just a few minutes, direct the conversation away from casual chitchat toward some lesson on life or even toward this chapter of Scripture.
- Resist telling lies. Of course, don't rehearse all your ailments whenever someone asks, "How are you?" But on the job, with kids, at church, and with your spouse, speak the truth as clearly as you can.
- Instead of losing your temper—saying things you'll regret—control your anger, speaking what's on your heart in a manner that will lead to healing and correction.

When your words begin to carry more weight than we typically give them today, you'll begin to understand the faith this Roman officer had in Jesus' words, which were filled with divine power, a power that Jesus gives to those who follow him.

---

**8:10 When Jesus heard this, he was astonished and said to those following him, "I tell you the truth, I have not found anyone in Israel with such great faith."** NIV This man's genuine faith *astonished* Jesus. He said to those gathered around him (the disciples, as well as other onlookers and followers) that he had not found *such great faith* in *anyone in Israel.* In other words, this Gentile's faith put to shame the stagnant piety that had blinded many of the Jewish religious leaders. Without the benefit of growing up to memorize the Old Testament Scriptures and to learn from esteemed Jewish leaders, this Gentile had understood the need to depend totally on Jesus' power. He knew, without a doubt, that Jesus could do what seemed impossible. Such faith both astonished and pleased Jesus.

CHAIN OF COMMAND
What did Jesus find in this man's life that astonished him?
The centurion grasped the principle of authority—what he
had learned from his own experience. Great leaders rarely
accomplish all their work by hands-on effort. They direct others.
Wise delegation transforms a leader's plans and desires into
action. The centurion knew how the chain of command worked.
He was a link. He correctly concluded that the same laws
applied to spiritual power. The greater Jesus' authority, the less
necessary his physical presence to accomplish his will. Jesus'
words indicated much more than his authority; they revealed
his concern. Is your faith able to overcome your hesitation and
doubt? Are you willing to act upon his words? If you appreciate
his power and love, give him your full service and obedience.

**8:11-12** **"I say to you that many will come from the east and the west,
and will take their places at the feast with Abraham, Isaac and
Jacob in the kingdom of heaven. But the subjects of the kingdom will be thrown outside, into the darkness, where there will
be weeping and gnashing of teeth."**[NIV] Most Jews looked forward
to the day when the diaspora Jews would return to Jerusalem—
from the east and the west—to enjoy the company of the Messiah
and the patriarchs in a great banquet (Psalm 107:3; Isaiah 25:6;
43:5-6). It was predicted that some Gentiles would also return to
witness this great event and to partake of it vicariously (Isaiah 2:2-3).
But Jesus speaks of the Gentiles' direct participation, for the *many*
who *will come from the east and the west* are the Gentiles who will
come to believe in Jesus. These Gentiles *will take their places at the
feast*. This "feast" is the banquet of celebration in *the kingdom of
heaven*. Few Jews understood, however, that Gentiles would also take
their places at the feast with the patriarchs of the Jewish nation—
*Abraham, Isaac, and Jacob.* A Jew who would sit at a table with a
Gentile would become defiled. Yet Jesus pictured the patriarchs
themselves sitting down with Gentiles at the great feast. No wonder
Jesus' teachings caused such a stir among the religious leaders of
the day! In addition, Jesus explained that while many Jews believed
that their lineage in the Jewish race assured their reservations at the
banquet, this simply was not the case (see also John the Baptist's
words in 3:7-10). In fact, unbelieving *subjects of the kingdom*
(referring to Jews), instead of having assured seats at the banquet,
would find themselves *thrown outside, into the darkness*. In fact,
Gentiles, not Jews, would sit at the head table (a seating arrangement
denoting status, just like today). This passage is one of the strongest
passages in Matthew on God's rejection of the unbelieving Jewish
people (see Romans 9–11). The "darkness" is a place *where there will*

*be weeping and gnashing of teeth*—a common biblical description of hell. These words do not mean that all the "subjects of the kingdom" (that is, all Jews) would be excluded—for Jesus' disciples and many early believers were Jews. The point is that the central focus of God's kingdom will not be only the Jewish race. Some Jews will *not* be included. Many religious Jews who should be in the kingdom will be excluded, however, because of their lack of faith. Entrenched in their religious traditions, they could not accept Jesus Christ and his new message. We must be careful not to become so set in our religious habits that we expect God to work only in specific ways. Don't limit God by your mind-set and lack of faith.

> Faith declares what the senses do not see.
> *Blaise Pascal*

The Gospel of Matthew emphasizes this universal theme—Jesus' message is for everyone. The Old Testament prophets knew this (see Isaiah 56:3, 6-8; 66:12, 19; Malachi 1:11), but many New Testament Jewish leaders chose to ignore it. Each individual has to choose to accept or reject the gospel, and no one can become part of God's kingdom on the basis of heritage or connections. Having a Christian family is a wonderful blessing, but it won't guarantee our eternal life. Each person must believe in and follow Christ.

---

**RSVP**
The centurion's faith astonished Jesus, who then used it as an opportunity to reaffirm the inclusion of many foreigners in the kingdom of God. Although both Matthew and Luke recorded this event, only Matthew added Jesus' comment about the diverse crowds that would flock to the final banquet, while those who assume they are guests of honor would be turned away at the gate. Matthew directed his Jewish readers to two truths:
1. Jesus fulfilled all the foretold descriptions of the Messiah, and
2. Jesus was the Savior of the entire world, not just the Jews.
   The first truth defines Jesus' identity as Messiah; the second truth defines his relationship to us. The first states a fact; the second offers a personal invitation to us. Will we be among the varied multitudes celebrating with Abraham the triumph of Jesus? Your RSVP is required.

---

**8:13 Then Jesus said to the centurion, "Go your way; and as you have believed, so let it be done for you." And his servant was healed that same hour.**<sup>NKJV</sup> Jesus then told the centurion to return home; Jesus would grant his request. The centurion believed that Jesus merely needed to speak the word to heal the servant (8:8). When Jesus spoke the word, the *servant was healed that same hour* (see also 9:22; 15:28; 17:18). "That same hour" means immediately.

## JESUS HEALS PETER'S MOTHER-IN-LAW AND MANY OTHERS / 8:14-17 / *35*

Jesus' compassion reached out to a third category of people viewed as "second-class citizens"—women.

**8:14-15 When Jesus entered Peter's house, he saw his mother-in-law lying in bed with a fever; he touched her hand, and the fever left her, and she got up and began to serve him.**NRSV Mark and Luke have this incident placed after the healing of a demon-possessed man in Capernaum (Mark 1:29-34; Luke 4:38-41). Mark recorded that Jesus, along with James, John, Simon Peter, and Andrew, arrived at Peter's home, where he lived with his wife (mentioned in 1 Corinthians 9:5), his *mother-in-law,* and his brother Andrew. Peter and Andrew had lived in Bethsaida (John 1:44), but now lived in Capernaum where they were fishermen. Jesus and the disciples probably stayed in Peter's home during their visits to Capernaum (see Mark 2:1; 3:20; 9:33; 10:10).

Simon Peter's mother-in-law was *lying in bed with a fever.* A malaria-type fever was common to this region because of marshes near the mouth of the Jordan River. We don't know for sure what this fever signified, but the Greek word for "fever" in the noun form is also the word for "fire"; thus, she was burning with a severe fever. Luke (the doctor) wrote in his Gospel that she "was suffering from a high fever" (Luke 4:38 NIV).

Jesus went to the mother-in-law's bedside and *touched her hand.* For a rabbi to touch a woman who was not his spouse was against Pharisaic regulations; for him to touch a person with a fever was prohibited by Jewish law. Jesus did both in order to heal a sick person, as well as to show his authority. Jesus' touch on the woman's hand brought complete healing. In fact, she *got up and began to serve him,* as protocol required a woman to serve food. Matthew recorded this detail to show that her healing was instant and complete. She didn't need time to recuperate from her illness; she was immediately well enough to serve her guests.

The Gospel writers wrote from different perspectives; thus, the parallel accounts in the Gospels often highlight different details. In Matthew, Jesus touched the woman's hand. In Mark, he helped her get up. In Luke, he spoke to the fever, and it left her. The accounts do not conflict. Each writer chose to emphasize different details of the story in order to emphasize a specific characteristic of Jesus.

**8:16 When evening came, many who were demon-possessed were brought to him, and he drove out the spirits with a word and healed all the sick.**NIV The people came to Jesus on Saturday *evening* after sunset. According to Mark 1:21 and Luke 4:31, the day had been the Sabbath, the Jews' day of worship and rest, lasting from sunset Friday to sunset Saturday. Jewish law prohibited traveling and carrying burdens on the Sabbath, so they waited until evening, after the sun went down. When the Sabbath had ended, the people searched for Jesus.

News had spread quickly about Jesus' healing powers, so the people *brought to him* all who were sick and *many who were demon-possessed.* The Greek word for "brought" is *phero,* meaning "to carry a burden or to move by carrying." Since there were no ambulance services, many people literally carried the ill to Peter's home so Jesus could heal them. The verb is in the imperfect tense, signifying continuous action. A steady stream of sick and demon-possessed people were being carried to Jesus. Jesus *drove out the spirits with a word* and *healed all the sick,* just as he had healed the centurion's servant with a word (8:11-12). The "word" of Jesus stresses his authority over the demonic realm. With just a word, Jesus could eliminate sickness and evil spirits.

**8:17  This was to fulfill what had been spoken through the prophet Isaiah, "He took our infirmities and bore our diseases."** NRSV While Mark 1:34 and Luke 4:41 stress the demons' witness to Jesus' authority, Matthew pointed again to Jesus' fulfillment of prophecy. Quoting from Isaiah 53:4, Matthew used a text that followed the Hebrew closely, speaking of *infirmities* and *diseases.* The Septuagint (the Greek translation of the Old Testament), on the other hand, translates the Hebrew as "bears our sins and suffers anguish for our sake." Isaiah 53 does deal with the suffering Servant bringing deliverance from sin, but Matthew was emphasizing Jesus' healing activity.

Jesus has authority over all evil powers and all earthly disease. He also has power and authority to conquer sin. If we think of sickness as one of the painful and somewhat random side effects of sin in the world, then we can better appreciate Jesus' power to heal. While Jesus was present in the world, he often chose to correct the symptoms that indicated the presence of sin even as he was preparing to defeat the root infection. Sickness is not always the punishment for sin. Rather, sickness can best be seen as a real and constant possibility of life in a fallen world. Physical healing in a fallen world is always temporary. Lazarus was revived from death (John 11:1-44), but later he died again. In the future, when God removes all sin, there will be no more sickness and death. Jesus' healing miracles were a taste of what all believers will one day experience in God's kingdom.

**OUTCASTS**
Notice who gets the help in these three miracles in Matthew 8: a leper, a Roman soldier, and a woman. All three were victims of social stigma and prejudice in their day. "Good people," especially good religious leaders, avoided close contact with those types. Yet Jesus served them all.

Who are the outcasts in your community—the people least liked and most criticized? Inviting what kind of person to church would draw the most flack from the "good people" there? Those are the people Jesus would help and heal. You'd better be there, too.

## JESUS TEACHES ABOUT THE COST OF FOLLOWING HIM / 8:18-22 / 122

According to the Harmony of the Gospels (found at the back of this commentary), this crossing of the lake didn't actually occur after the events just recounted. Matthew chose to include it here to set the stage for the events in the remainder of the chapter. Crossing to the other side and stilling the storm occurred after the second period in Capernaum, according to Mark (see Mark 4:35ff.). The testing of the followers is recorded in Luke 9:57-62 as being after Peter's confession, part of the "road to Jerusalem" travel narrative. Matthew grouped the events thematically to show Jesus' impact on people.

**8:18 When Jesus saw the crowd around him, he gave orders to cross to the other side of the lake.**<sup>NIV</sup> Jesus healed many people in Capernaum, and his ministry attracted a lot of attention. Crowds continued to gather around him, but Jesus had ministry to do in other places as well. So *he gave orders to cross to the other side of the lake.* Capernaum sat on the northwestern shore of the Sea of Galilee (also called a "lake" because it is an inland body of water). So Jesus and the disciples got into a boat (perhaps Peter's fishing boat) and began to cross to the eastern shore.

**8:19-20 A scribe then approached and said, "Teacher, I will follow you wherever you go."**<sup>NRSV</sup> That *a scribe* (also called a "teacher of the law") approached Jesus would be unusual because the scribes were often Jesus' opponents in the Gospels (see 7:29). The scribes were legal specialists and interpreters of the law. However, as part of his evangelistic purpose, Matthew showed that at least one scribe recognized Jesus' authority and wanted to be a disciple.

This scribe addressed Jesus as *teacher* (or "rabbi") and explained that he wanted to *follow* Jesus wherever he went. The words "I will follow you" were not just the words of a disciple to a rabbi. A rabbi's disciples "followed" him by observing the rabbi in his daily tasks, as well as sitting under and living by his teachings.

**And Jesus said to him, "Foxes have holes, and birds of the air have nests; but the Son of Man has nowhere to lay his head."** NRSV Jesus' words to the scribe were more like a challenge than a rebuke or invitation. Jesus focused on the requirements of true discipleship. Jesus did not dash about the countryside attempting to get as many followers as possible. He wanted true followers who understood the cost of following him. People were certainly enthusiastic about Jesus' miracle-working ability. Jesus did not want them following him without commitment. To be Jesus' disciple, a person must willingly put aside worldly security. To follow Jesus *wherever* he would go (as this scribe said) would mean a willingness to give up home and security. In the context of Jesus' present ministry, to follow him meant to be constantly on the move, bringing his message to people in many places. We do not know whether this scribe actually chose to follow. Matthew was focusing on Jesus' words about radical discipleship.

Here, for the first time, Matthew recorded Jesus calling himself *Son of Man.* This was an Old Testament name for the Messiah and was Jesus' favorite designation for himself. The expression occurs eighty-one times in the Gospels, always said by Jesus (twice others said it, but they were quoting Jesus). Calling himself *the* Son of Man, Jesus was pointing to himself as the Messiah (see Daniel 7:13), without using that term, which had become loaded with militaristic expectations in the minds of many Jews.

---

COUNT THE COST
Following Jesus is not always easy or comfortable. Often it involves great cost and sacrifice, with no earthly rewards or security. Jesus did not have a place to call home. You may find that following Christ costs you popularity, friendships, leisure time, or treasured habits. While the cost of following Christ is high, the value of being Christ's disciple is even higher. If you desire to follow Christ, you must be willing to face hardship. Would you be willing to give up your home to follow Christ?

---

**8:21-22 Then another of His disciples said to Him, "Lord, let me first go and bury my father." But Jesus said to him, "Follow Me, and let the dead bury their own dead."** NKJV The scribe wanted to follow Jesus, but Jesus reminded him of the cost of discipleship (8:19-20). This man also expressed commitment (as he was called *another* disciple), but Jesus tested his level of commitment. This man apparently also wanted to follow Jesus (whom he called *Lord,* another polite way of addressing a leader or senior), but he wanted to first return home to *bury* his father. In ancient cultures, this was a sacred responsibility.

It is possible that this disciple was not asking permission to go to his father's funeral, but rather to put off following Jesus until after his father had died. Perhaps he was the firstborn son and wanted to be sure to claim his inheritance. Perhaps he did not want to face his father's wrath if he left the family business to follow an itinerant

> Would you be a disciple of Jesus? Then count the cost, sense the urgency, make the effort to concentrate. And all of this actually comes down to following Jesus.
>
> *Morris Inch*

preacher. Whether his concern was fulfilling a duty, financial security, family approval, or something else, he did not want to commit himself to Jesus just yet. Jesus sensed this reluctance in his follower and challenged him to consider that his commitment had to be completely without reservation. If this man truly desired to follow

Jesus, he would not wait until he had fulfilled all his traditional responsibilities. Jesus was not advising that children disregard family responsibilities. Rather, Jesus was responding to this disciple's qualifying use of "first." Jesus must always come "first," then all other human loyalties. Jesus' directive was not heartless, but it called the man to examine his primary loyalty.

Jesus' response is part of the radical discipleship theme: *Let the dead bury their own dead.* Jesus made sure those who wanted to follow him counted the cost and set aside any conditions they might have. "The dead" in Aramaic can also mean "the dying." So Jesus may have been saying "Let the dying bury the dead." In other words, let those who are spiritually dying (those who have not responded to the call to commitment) stay home and handle responsibilities such as burying the dead. While to us this may sound heartless, it was not without precedent. A high priest and those who had taken the Nazirite vow were required by the law to avoid the corpse of even a

**Jesus' Miraculous Power Displayed**

*Jesus finished the sermon he had given on a hillside near Galilee and returned to Capernaum. As he and his disciples crossed the Sea of Galilee, Jesus calmed a fierce storm. Then, in the Gentile Gadarene region, Jesus commanded demons to come out of two men.*

parent (Leviticus 21:11; Numbers 6:6). A later Jewish precedent says that if there were enough people in attendance, a student of the Torah should not stop his study to bury the dead. Jesus placed commitment to God even above these precedents. As God's Son, Jesus did not hesitate to demand complete loyalty. Even family loyalty was not to take priority over the demands of obedience. His direct challenge forces us to ask ourselves about our priorities in following him. We must not put off the decision to follow Jesus, even though other loyalties compete for our attention.

---

DEATH, THE INTERRUPTER
The disciple's conditional commitment appears reasonable to us. After all, the death of a parent ought to be given honor. Would God actually forbid a disciple to do something good? Would God say no to a sincere action or innocent pleasure? A closer look, however, helps us understand what Jesus heard. The disciple insisted on a delay. Jesus knew that where there's a "first" there also lies a "second" and a "third." Only an unconditional commitment meets the demands of Christ.

Most of us are guilty of using delay tactics with God. His will fits somewhere below the top of our agenda. But, if our assumption boils down to "I'll do what God won't let me do before I surrender," we are revealing a lack of trust in God. We should acknowledge our Creator as our Lord and Savior today, or never. Discipleship means that God has veto power even over actions in our lives that are otherwise acceptable and good.

---

## JESUS CALMS THE STORM / 8:23-27 / **87**

This miracle shows Jesus' power over the natural world.

**8:23-25** **Then he got into the boat and his disciples followed him. Without warning, a furious storm came up on the lake, so that the waves swept over the boat.**[NIV] Jesus and the disciples *got into the boat* to cross to the other side of the Sea of Galilee, as had been planned (8:18). Matthew emphasized that Jesus got into the boat and the disciples *followed*. This may have been a wordplay by Matthew to connect this miracle with the preceding episode and give it a discipleship focus. In other words, this is what discipleship might involve!

This boat probably was a fishing boat because many of Jesus' disciples were fishermen. Josephus, an ancient historian, wrote that there were usually more than three hundred fishing boats on the Sea of Galilee at one time. This boat was large enough to hold Jesus and his twelve disciples.

Mark explained that it was evening when they finally set sail

(Mark 4:35). The boat may have belonged to one of the fishermen among the group, most likely Peter. Setting sail in the evening was not unusual because Peter was used to fishing at night (see John 21:3). Fishing was best then; storms usually came in the afternoon.

The Sea of Galilee is an unusual body of water. It is relatively small (13 miles long, 7 miles wide), but it is 150 feet deep, and the shoreline is 680 feet below sea level. Storms can appear suddenly over the surrounding mountains, stirring the water into violent twenty-foot waves. The disciples had not foolishly set out in a storm. They usually did not encounter storms at night and did not see this one coming. Even though several of these men were expert fishermen and knew how to handle a boat, they had been caught without warning in this *furious storm*. Their danger was real as *the waves swept over the boat.*

**But Jesus was sleeping. The disciples went and woke him, saying, "Lord, save us! We're going to drown!"** NIV While the waves swept over the boat, *Jesus was sleeping.* He probably had lain down on the low bench in the stern where the helmsman (or pilot) would sit and had fallen asleep on the leather cushion. That Jesus could sleep during this storm indicates his complete exhaustion and reveals his human nature. That the noise, the violent rocking of the boat, and the cold spray of the water did not awaken him gives us a glimpse of the physical drain on Jesus throughout his earthly ministry.

The disciples had embarked on this journey at Jesus' request after a long day. Then, of all things, a storm blew in—and not just any storm, but a "furious" one that was threatening to sink the boat and drown them. Worst of all, Jesus was sleeping through it! Didn't he realize that they all were *going to drown?* So they *went and woke him.* They cried above the crashing water, *"Lord, save us! We're going to drown!"* The title "Lord" is used often in Matthew's Gospel, stressing Jesus' lordship over the physical and natural realms.

---

STORMY SEAS
Although the disciples had witnessed many miracles, they panicked in this storm. As experienced sailors, they knew its danger; what they did not know was that Jesus could control the forces of nature. Often our souls are troubled because we feel there is a problem where God can't or won't work. When we truly understand who God is, however, we will realize that he controls both the storms of nature and the storms of the troubled heart. Jesus' power that calmed this storm can also help us deal with the problems we face. Jesus is willing to help if we only ask him. Never discount his power even in terrible trials.

---

**8:26** **He replied, "You of little faith, why are you so afraid?" Then he got up and rebuked the winds and the waves, and it was completely calm.**[NIV] Abruptly awakened from a deep sleep, Jesus arose and rebuked his frightened disciples. The disciples had seen Jesus do wonderful miracles, but they had not taken their knowledge of his power and applied it to every situation. So he asked them, *"You of little faith, why are you so afraid?"* They wanted him to do something; he wanted them to trust him! There is no place in true discipleship for fear—which itself arises out of lack of faith (disbelief). The Greek word for "afraid" *(deiloi)* means "cowardly fear." The disciples were acting like cowards when they should have acted with faith in their teacher. Despite all that the disciples had seen and heard thus far, they still had not grasped that Jesus was himself God, with God's power and authority over all of creation. In Mark, the miracle is recorded as occurring before Jesus rebuked the disciples; in reality, the miracle and the rebuke probably happened almost simultaneously. Matthew's emphasis was on Jesus' words more than the miracle.

> Ye fearful saints,
>    fresh courage take
> The clouds ye so
>    much dread
> Are big with mercy
>    and shall break
> In blessings on
>    your head.
>                    *William Cowper*

Standing in the stern of the rocking ship, Jesus *got up and rebuked the winds and the waves.* This shows Jesus' confidence in himself and his faith in the Father's care. Just as Jesus had healed and cast out demons with only a word, so his words calmed the furious storm. The effect of Jesus' words was that suddenly *it was completely calm.* Anyone who has been in a frightening storm at sea and has watched walls of water toss the ship can understand what an incredible sight it must have been to have the sea suddenly become calm. The forces of nature, when unleashed—whether as a tornado, hurricane, earthquake, or waves of water on a rough sea—can be terrifying because we are completely at their mercy. The power of the Teacher to speak and control the waves shocked the disciples. The storm was out of control, their fears were out of control, but Jesus was never out of control. He may have had no home and no place to lay his head (8:20), but he had power over all the forces of nature.

**8:27** **They were amazed, saying, "What sort of man is this, that even the winds and the sea obey him?"**[NRSV] Jesus' power *amazed* the disciples; however, they still did not completely understand, as their question betrayed: *What sort of man is this, that even the winds and the sea obey him?* They should have known because this miracle clearly displayed Jesus' divine identity. Being with the human, compassionate Jesus was fine for these men; being with the powerful and supernatural Son of God terrified them.

BOAT MATES

Jesus' disciples could certainly be described as a motley crew. They were a mixture of "landlubbers" and seasoned sailors. The storm had them all frightened. The fishermen, like Peter and John, knew those waters well, and their fear came from experience. They had probably lost friends to such storms. Nonsailors like Matthew were simply terrified. Perhaps the fear in the eyes of their mates frightened them as much as the storm itself.

In the storms of life, Jesus is still the master. He shares our boat. Sooner or later, the wind and waves will offer us several key lessons:

- Sometimes, no one but Jesus can do anything.
- No matter how bad the circumstances, God is in control.
- When we reach the end of our resources, Jesus has not even started.
- Hopeless situations make the clearest occasions to trust in God's preserving power.

Jesus wants us to have a full picture of faith. That includes bravery under duress. We cannot learn to be brave in a classroom, but only as we get out and live in our broken world. The faith that Jesus admires is tested by crisis and struggle and emerges confident in God's power. If you face a crisis today, pray for bravery and trust completely in God.

Perhaps those near to you would be helped if you encouraged them to trust in Christ. This story might help you introduce them to Jesus.

When Matthew recorded this event, persecution against Christians had begun. Thus, the story had become an analogy of the persecution and trials of the early church. The disciples were surrounded by a sea that threatened to sink them; the church was surrounded by enemies who threatened to destroy it (first the Jews who tried to undermine the Christian faith, then the Roman empire and its eventual widespread persecution of Christians). Storms will come. Our peace and faith come with the knowledge that Jesus has power over all storms, whatever their source or strength. He can quiet them if he chooses. Often the early Christians hoped for Jesus to quiet the storm of persecution, but he did not. So in the middle of the storm, they relied, instead, on their faith in the power of their Savior and the eternal rest promised to them.

When we become Christians, we enter a cosmic struggle because Satan hates for people to believe in Jesus. Satan launches his limited power against believers individually and the church in general, hoping to sink us to the depths of the sea. But we have the ultimate power on our side, and we will have the final victory. Jesus should not be a mystery to us, causing us to fearfully ask, "What sort of man is this?" He should be our Savior, to whom we turn with all our needs and fears because he cares for us and will help us.

## JESUS SENDS THE DEMONS INTO A HERD OF PIGS / 8:28-34 / **88**

Matthew recorded the following miracle to show Jesus' power over the supernatural realm.

**8:28 When he arrived at the other side in the region of the Gadarenes, two demon-possessed men coming from the tombs met him. They were so violent that no one could pass that way.**[NIV] The boat and its occupants arrived safely *at the other side.* The *region of the Gadarenes* is located southeast of the Sea of Galilee, near the town of Gadara, one of the most important cities of the region (see map, "Jesus' Miraculous Power Displayed"). The precise location is uncertain because this country (or region) is sometimes written as "Gerasenes," "Gergesenes," or "Gadarenes" in various manuscripts. However, some scholars cite evidence that favors "country of the Gerasenes," probably referring to a small town called Gersa (modern-day Kersa or Kours). Others prefer "Gadarenes," citing the town of Gadara, one of the most important cities of the region. Gadara was a member of the Decapolis, or Ten Cities. These ten cities with independent governments were largely inhabited by Gentiles. Whatever the exact location of their landing, the point is that Jesus had planned to go there. This was Gentile territory, revealing a new direction for his ministry.

Matthew says there were *two demon-possessed men,* while Mark and Luke refer to only one. Apparently Mark and Luke mention only the man who did the talking or the one who was the most severe (with a legion of demons, Mark 5:9). Mark's account is more graphic than the others, emphasizing what the demons had done to the men. These men were bloody, out of control, and apparently strong and frightening (Mark 5:4-5). *They were so violent that no one could pass that way.* Demon-possessed people are controlled by one or more demons. Although we cannot be sure why demon possession occurs, we know that evil spirits can use the human body to distort and destroy a person's relationship with God. Demons had entered these men's bodies and were controlling them, trying to destroy or distort God's image. Demons are fallen angels who joined Satan in his rebellion against God and are now evil spirits under Satan's control. They help Satan tempt people to sin and have great destructive powers. These men were clearly hopeless without Christ.

These men came *from the tombs;* Mark explained that they lived there. In those days it was common for cemeteries to have many tombs carved into the hillside, making cavelike mausoleums. There was enough room for a person to live in such tombs. Tombs of wealthy people had more than one chamber for later family members to be buried, so there were empty chambers available for shelter. Such graveyards were often in remote areas. Tombs were unclean places and regarded by the Jews as fit only for lepers and the demon-possessed. People with hopeless conditions, such as these men, could find shelter in the caves.

These men *met* Jesus as he landed. They may have rushed out to see who was coming ashore, or perhaps even to apply for mercy. Most likely, however, the demons wanted to confront Jesus and scare him away, as they had already done to anyone else who had ventured into their territory.

---

UNCLEAN
According to Jewish ceremonial laws, the men Jesus encountered were unclean in three ways: They were Gentiles (non-Jews), they were demon-possessed, and they lived in a graveyard. Jesus helped them anyway. We should not turn our backs on people who are "unclean" or repulsive to us, or who violate our moral standards and religious beliefs. Instead, we must realize that every human individual is a unique creation of God, needing to be touched by his love.

---

**8:29** **"What do you want with us, Son of God?" they shouted. "Have you come here to torture us before the appointed time?"** NIV Though aware of who Jesus was and of his power over them, the demons still attempted to defend themselves by *shouting* and by calling Jesus by his divine name. The loud voice shows the demons' fierce and violent nature.

The demons' first question, *What do you want with us?* is a request that Jesus leave them alone. A more literal translation would be "What to you and to me?" or "What do we have in common?" In other words, the demons asked Jesus to leave them alone, for they had nothing to do with each other. Such a question shows the demons' ultimate rebellion. Jesus and the demons were as far separated as anything could be. Jesus' purpose was to heal and give life; the demons', to kill and destroy. But Jesus would not leave these men in such a condition.

Like the demon who had possessed the man in Capernaum

(Mark 1:24), the demons tried using Jesus' divine name to control him. At this time, people believed that to know an adversary's full name was to be able to gain control over the person. The demon in the synagogue had called Jesus "the Holy One of God," but this demon referred to him as *Son of God.* The demons recognized Jesus as God's divine Son. How ironic that people in Jesus' day were so blind, while the demons were so clear about Jesus' true identity.

The demons asked if Jesus had come to *torture* them. The word for "torture" is graphic and correct. The Bible says that at the end of the world, the devil and his demons will be thrown into the lake of fire (Revelation 20:10). The demons' question revealed that they knew their ultimate fate. The demons hoped that Jesus would not send them to their fate *before the appointed time.* Jewish literature written between the time of the Old and New Testaments taught that demons have permission to oppose mankind only until the Judgment Day. This statement by the demons shows God's power over Satan's forces.

**8:30-31 Now a large herd of swine was feeding at some distance from them. The demons begged him, "If you cast us out, send us into the herd of swine."** NRSV According to Old Testament law (Leviticus 11:7), pigs were "unclean" animals. This meant that they could not be eaten or even touched by a Jew. This incident took place southeast of the Sea of Galilee in a Gentile area. This explains how there could be *a large herd of swine.* Mark tells us there were two thousand in this herd (Mark 5:13).

The demons recognized their ultimate doom (8:29), and they knew that Jesus could seal their fate by returning them to the abyss (the place of their confinement) or sending them far away (Mark 5:10). They evidently wanted a "home" and wanted to possess a living being. On the hillside were enough physical animal hosts for all these demons to inhabit. Pigs were unclean animals, so they provided a fitting habitation for the demons. So the demons asked to be sent into the herd of swine.

Why did the demons ask to enter the swine? We can only speculate. Perhaps the demons thought they could return to the tombs and caves later. Maybe they sought to delay their final destruction. Evidently they did not want to be without a physical body to torment, so they would rather enter the pigs than be idle. Their action seems to portray their ultimate destructive intent.

Why didn't Jesus just destroy these demons—or send them away? Because the time for such work had not yet come. Jesus healed many people of the destructive effects of demon possession, but he did not yet destroy demons. In this situation, Jesus wanted to show Satan's destructive power and intent. Many ask the same question today—why doesn't Jesus stop all the evil in the world? His time for that has not yet come. But it will come. The book of Revelation portrays the future victory of Jesus over Satan, his demons, and all evil.

RECEIVE BY FAITH
Whenever demons were confronted by Jesus, they lost their power. These demons recognized Jesus as God's Son (8:29), but they protested against the power that made them submit and would one day destroy them. Just believing is not enough (see James 2:19 for a discussion of belief and devils). Faith is more than belief. By faith, you must accept what Jesus has done for you, receive him as the only one who can save you from sin, and live out your faith by obeying his commands.

**8:32 He said to them, "Go!" So they came out and went into the pigs, and the whole herd rushed down the steep bank into the lake and died in the water.**<sup>NIV</sup> In every case when confronted by Jesus, demons lost their power. Jesus' simple command, *Go!* showed the extent of his authority over the demons. One word was enough. He did not need to perform a lengthy exorcism. God limits what evil spirits can do; these demons could do nothing without Jesus' permission. During Jesus' life on earth, confrontations with demons were frequent, demonstrating his power and authority over them. Jesus did not command the demons to go into the swine; he gave them permission to *go* and do what they requested.

When the demons entered the pigs, *the whole herd rushed down the steep bank into the lake and died in the water.* Perhaps Jesus let the demons destroy the pigs to demonstrate his superiority over a very powerful yet destructive force. He could have sent the demons away, but he did not because the time for judgment had not yet come. In the end, the devil and all his angels will be sent into eternal fire (25:41). Jesus granted the demons' request to enter the swine and destroy the herd, but he stopped their destructive work in people, particularly the men they had possessed.

Jesus also taught a lesson by giving the demons permission to enter the pigs. He showed his disciples, the townspeople, and even us who read these words today the absolute goal of Satan and his demons. They want total and complete destruction of their hosts.

The sight must have been amazing. A rather peaceful herd of

pigs suddenly became a stampeding horde that ran straight to its destruction.

**8:33-34** **Those tending the pigs ran off, went into the town and reported all this, including what had happened to the demon-possessed men. Then the whole town went out to meet Jesus. And when they saw him, they pleaded with him to leave their region.**[NIV] When Jesus performed this miracle, he again gained immediate publicity. *Those tending the pigs,* astonished and doubtless upset at what had happened, *ran off* and told the amazing story. Their story seemed unbelievable. Two thousand pigs floating on the edge of the lake would certainly be a sight, so *the whole town went out to meet Jesus.* Among these would have been the owner of the herd who, doubtless, was not pleased at the loss of the livestock.

The people could have responded in several ways. They could have been overjoyed to see Jesus on their own shore. They also could have responded with joy that Jesus had healed the demon-possessed men. They could have been thrilled to have seen a healing of such magnitude with their own eyes. Instead, they *pleaded with him to leave their region.* Mark tells us that they were afraid (Mark 5:14-20).

What were they afraid of? Perhaps such supernatural power as Jesus had displayed frightened them. Perhaps they thought that Jesus would be bad for their economy (losing two thousand pigs in one day certainly cost someone). Perhaps they did not want Jesus to change their status quo. Their fear caused them to make a terrible mistake in asking Jesus to leave them. How foolish and yet how easy it is to value possessions, investments, and even animals above human life. Unfortunately for them, Jesus did as they asked. And there is no biblical record that he ever returned. Sometimes the worst that can happen to us is for Jesus to answer one of our poorly considered requests.

# Matthew 9

**9:1 Jesus stepped into a boat, crossed over and came to his own town.**<sup>NIV</sup> The events in 8:28-34 had occurred on the other side of the Sea of Galilee (Jesus and the disciples had gotten there by boat, 8:18, 23). The events Matthew placed at the end of chapter 8 and the beginning of chapter 9 are not in chronological sequence (see the Harmony of the Gospels at the end of this commentary). Matthew continued his story by placing Jesus back into a boat and crossing over the sea to return to *his own town,* Capernaum. This city became Jesus' base of operations while he was in Galilee. This event may have occurred at Simon Peter's house (8:14-17). Matthew may have been preserving his topical arrangement, keeping several of Jesus' miracles together in this section.

Capernaum was a good choice for Jesus' base of operations. It was a wealthy city due to fishing and trade. Situated on the Sea of Galilee in a densely populated area, Capernaum housed the Roman garrison that kept peace in the region. The city was a cultural melting pot, greatly influenced by Greek and Roman manners, dress, architecture, and politics.

**9:2 Some men brought to him a paralytic, lying on a mat. When Jesus saw their faith, he said to the paralytic, "Take heart, son; your sins are forgiven."** <sup>NIV</sup> *Some men,* remembering that Jesus had healed many people in Capernaum on an earlier visit (8:14-17), *brought* a friend who needed Jesus' help. The friend was *a paralytic,* and the men carried him, *lying on a mat,* to Jesus. The "mat" was like a stretcher that the men could carry.

Matthew's Gospel explains how *Jesus saw their faith.* There was such a crowd gathered around the door to the house that these men carrying the man on the mat could not get through to the house. So they went up on the roof and took off enough tiles to lower their friend through the roof to Jesus below (Mark 2:1-4). Jesus "saw their faith" acted out in their determination. They knew that if they could just get near Jesus, Jesus could heal. Jesus referred to the faith of all the men who came but spoke only to the paralytic. *Son* (Greek, *teknon*) was simply a term of affection, used even with adults.

Matthew omitted some of the details of this story to focus on Jesus' words that revealed a new aspect of his authority. Thus far, Matthew has shown Jesus' authority in his teaching (7:28-29), in healing of diseases (8:1-17), over any other allegiance (8:18-22), over nature (8:23-27), and over demons (8:16, 28-34). In this miracle, Matthew showed Jesus' authority to forgive sins.

Jesus said to the paralyzed man, *"Take heart . . . your sins are forgiven."* Several verses in the Old Testament indicate that sickness and death result from humanity's sinful condition (see, for example, Psalms 41:3-4; 103:2-3; and James 5:13-18 for the New Testament parallel). So God works forgiveness and healing together. That does not mean that we can measure a person's spiritual health by looking at his or her physical health. But all sickness and death are the result of evil and sin. This man was paralyzed because of sin (in the world and in every human heart)—that was the root cause. Jesus spoke first to that condition. The man needed spiritual healing, so Jesus forgave his sins. Then Jesus healed the man. Both the man's body and his spirit were paralyzed; he could not walk, and he was not yet one of Jesus' disciples. But the man's spiritual state was Jesus' first concern. If God does not heal us or someone we love, we need to remember that physical healing is not Christ's only concern. We will all be completely healed in Christ's coming kingdom; but first we must become his disciples.

God offers the same forgiveness given to the paralytic to all who believe. The Greek word *aphientai,* translated "forgiven," means to leave or let go, to give up a debt, to send away from oneself. When we say we have forgiven a person, we mean that we have renewed our relationship despite the wrong that the person did. But we cannot erase or change the act itself. But the notion of *aphiemi* goes far beyond our human forgiveness, for it includes the "putting away" of sin in two ways: (1) The law and justice are satisfied because Jesus paid the penalty that our sins deserved; thus, they can no longer be held against us. (2) The guilt caused by our sin is removed and replaced with Christ's righteousness. We are so forgiven that, in God's eyes, it is as if we had never sinned. If Jesus had done this and nothing more for the man, the man should have been satisfied. If Jesus had healed his body and had not dealt with his sinful condition, the man would have been ultimately worse.

TO BE FORGIVEN
Spiritual sickness is Jesus' primary concern. He wants people
to enjoy a right relationship with God—faithful discipleship,
sturdy assurance of God's love for them, freedom from spiritual
oppression. So Jesus intentionally relieved the paralytic of the
burden of his sins first, and then, second, of his physical
paralysis.
    When you think of the good things Jesus brings to you, thank
him for forgiveness first of all. With sins forgiven, you are made
right with God. With sins forgiven, your biggest problem—
beyond your own skill to correct—has been solved. Jesus has
become your Savior, the greatest gift of all. Bring others to
Jesus, so they may experience his blessings upon their lives.

**9:3 Then some of the scribes said to themselves, "This man is
blaspheming."** NRSV These *scribes* (also called teachers of the
law) were the legal specialists in Jesus' day. Jesus' teaching and
popularity had led to special investigation by the powerful leaders of the Jewish faith. These scribes had come from Jerusalem
to Capernaum (Luke 5:17). Jealous of Jesus' popularity and
power, these men hoped to find something to criticize or even
condemn in Jesus' teaching. When they heard Jesus tell the
paralyzed man that his sins were forgiven, they were shocked.
The people in Jesus' day took blasphemy very seriously.
Offenders died. Even an unproven accusation of blasphemy
could prove life-threatening. In such a climate, the charge of
blasphemy worked almost as well as a contract for murder.
Blasphemy meant to curse, revile, or insult the name of God.
Innocent persons could be accused, convicted, and killed without having a chance to defend themselves. In fact, the public
cause of Jesus' death was blasphemy. Those directly responsible
for his execution wanted the charge posted: "This man said, I
am King of the Jews" (John 19:21 NRSV).
    The religious leaders hotly debated the offense of blasphemy in
the first century. Some said that a person had to use the divine name to
be accused. These scribes, however, took the assumption of divine
prerogatives (forgiving sins) as also constituting blasphemy.
    Therefore, because only God can forgive sins, Jesus was claim-
ing to be God. In Jewish law, blasphemy was punishable by death
(Leviticus 24:16). In labeling Jesus' claim to forgive sins as blasphemous, the religious leaders showed they did not understand
that Jesus *was* God. Jesus had God's power and authority to heal
bodies and forgive sins. Forgiveness of sins was a sign that the
messianic age had come (Isaiah 40:2; Joel 2:32; Micah 7:18-19;

Zechariah 13:1). Unfortunately, it did not occur to these Jewish leaders that perhaps this man was their Messiah.

**9:4** **But Jesus, perceiving their thoughts, said, "Why do you think evil in your hearts?"** NRSV God is all-knowing, and Jesus is God. He had access to all the information; he knew every person's thoughts (see 12:25; 22:18). Hebrews 4:13 says, "Nothing in all creation is hidden from God's sight. Everything is uncovered and laid bare before the eyes of him to whom we must give account" (NIV). Jesus' glory and divinity were veiled by his humanity and mortality. While Jesus walked as a human on this earth, he never ceased to be God. When Jesus was born, God became a man. Jesus was not part man and part God; he was completely human and completely divine. Jesus Christ is the perfect expression of God in human form. As a man, Jesus was subject to place, time, and other human limitations. He did not give up his eternal power when he became human, but he did set aside his glory and his rights. In response to the Father's will, he limited his power and knowledge.

When Jesus became human, he restrained the full use of his powers, yet he could still see each person's thoughts, intents, and motives. Jesus perceived the *thoughts* of these scribes, who were accusing him of blasphemy. Jesus may have read their minds, or he may have read the questions in the expressions on their faces. In any case, they could not hide their hostility at Jesus' words. Their thoughts of Jesus as a blasphemer were *evil.*

---

DEALING WITH SKEPTICS
When people dust off your witness, dismiss you as a fanatic, or quickly change the conversation from faith to furniture, you might feel offended. "Forget them!" you might say. "Hopeless!"
  Jesus' response to skeptics was to engage them. His question showed that he was interested *in them.* Even though they were often severely accusatory, Jesus kept talking to them. He did not write them off. Sincere questions have a way of keeping a conversation going.
  In your witness, don't be discouraged by skeptics. Just show compassion as Jesus did, and keep the conversation open, honest, and friendly.

---

**9:5** **"For which is easier, to say, 'Your sins are forgiven,' or to say, 'Stand up and walk'?"** NRSV It would take someone of great power and authority to forgive sins. Yet the statement concerning forgiveness of sins could be said without verification. Healing the paralyzed man would be open to immediate public verification.

Jesus was offering to do an easier task (healing the man) as
public evidence that the more difficult, "secret" task was also
accomplished. The scribes understood sickness to be the result of
sin. Jesus then proposed the converse—if he could heal a person,
then could he not also forgive sins? Jesus wanted to show that he
had the power to forgive sins by showing that he had the power
to make a paralytic *stand up and walk.*

Jesus accepted the premise that words matter. He repeatedly
made claims that were outrageous, arrogant, and deceptive
unless absolutely true. But he backed up his words with his work.
He rested his claim to be God on his statements and actions. Confronted with undeniable evidence, people still refused to believe.

Unfortunately, people today reject Jesus with practically no
evidence. Sometimes, we are so worried about presenting ourselves
as Christians that we fail to present Jesus himself to those around
us. We should seek to gain a hearing. But when we have their
attention, our subject ought to be Jesus. When people actually find
out what he did and said, they will have a clearer reason to respond
to the invitation to believe. They may still reject Jesus. But they
won't be able to say to us, "You never told me."

---

**BACKUPS**
It's easy to tell someone his sins are forgiven; it's a lot more
difficult to reverse a case of paralysis! Jesus backed up his
words by healing the man's legs. Jesus' action showed that his
words were true; he had the power to forgive as well as to heal.
Talk is cheap; our words lack meaning if our actions do not
back them up. We can say we love God or others, but if we are
not taking practical steps to demonstrate that love, our words
are empty and meaningless. How well do your actions back up
what you say?

---

**9:6-7** **"But so that you may know that the Son of Man has authority
on earth to forgive sins"—he then said to the paralytic—"Stand
up, take your bed and go to your home." And he stood up and
went to his home.**<sup>NRSV</sup> Jesus again used the term "Son of Man"
(an Old Testament name for the Messiah), a favorite designation
for himself (alluding to Daniel 7:13; see also Matthew 8:20). The
name claimed authority, for only one of highest authority (God
himself) could forgive sins. The use of the title also reveals that
Jesus was anticipating his future role as Judge. Only here and in
Luke 7:48 does Jesus talk about forgiving sins. He came to do
just that (Matthew 1:21), and his death would make forgiveness
available to all people. But with those whom Jesus met and

## JESUS AND FORGIVENESS

Jesus not only taught frequently about forgiveness, he also demonstrated his willingness to forgive. Here are several examples to remind us that he wants to forgive us also.

| Jesus forgave . . . | Reference |
| --- | --- |
| the paralytic lowered on a mat through the roof | Matthew 9:2-8 |
| the woman caught in adultery | John 8:3-11 |
| the woman who anointed his feet with oil | Luke 7:47-50 |
| Peter, for denying he knew Jesus | John 18:15-18, 25-27; 21:15-19 |
| the criminal on the cross | Luke 23:39-43 |
| the people who crucified him | Luke 23:34 |

touched, he also had the authority to forgive their sins when he perceived that they would understand and accept.

Jesus' authority extended from spiritual healing to physical healing. The physical healings revealed this to the world. One who could heal a paralytic could also forgive sins. Jesus spoke to the doubtful scribes, *so that you may know that the Son of Man has authority on earth to forgive sins.* But Jesus didn't even finish his sentence. He broke off part of the way through and allowed the miracle to speak for itself.

Jesus spoke with commanding authority, showing that he expected immediate obedience. He *said to the paralytic—"Stand up, take your bed and go to your home."* Jesus told the paralytic to stand up on his previously useless legs, to take his mat with arms that may also have been previously useless, and to go home. Jesus' mission was to preach the gospel. His great power served to reveal his authority. Thus, Jesus sent the man back to his home with a new life because he had forgiven the man of his sins. The man did as Jesus said. He *stood up* and *went to his home.*

The healing unmistakably revealed Jesus' power and authority. The scribes who questioned Jesus' ability to forgive sins (9:3) saw the formerly paralyzed man get up and walk. Jesus' question in 9:5 forced their answer: Jesus had the power to make the paralyzed man walk; thus, he also had the authority to forgive his sins.

**9:8 When the crowd saw this, they were filled with awe; and they praised God, who had given such authority to men.**[NIV] Jesus did this miracle in front of *the crowd* that had gathered in this home to hear Jesus speak (Mark 2:2). The phrase "they were filled with awe" implies amazement as well as fear. Such fear was appropriate in the presence of one who displayed *such authority* (that is, authority to forgive sins). What was the result of this awe? The people *praised God.* While the scribes had previously called Jesus a blasphemer, the people recognized God's power and realized that Jesus had authority from God. (Matthew does not tell us if some of the scribes changed their minds.) The difference between the scribes' rejection and the crowd's awe is a major theme in Matthew (see 9:33-34; 12:13-15; 14:34–15:2; 15:29-31 compared to 16:1-4). That God had given such authority *to men* probably means that the people were recognizing that a man—Jesus—displayed God's power.

## JESUS EATS WITH SINNERS AT MATTHEW'S HOUSE / 9:9-13 / 40

**9:9 As Jesus went on from there, he saw a man named Matthew sitting at the tax collector's booth. "Follow me," he told him, and Matthew got up and followed him.**[NIV] *Matthew* (the author of this Gospel) was a Jew who worked for the Romans (specifically for Herod Antipas) as the area's tax collector. (In Mark and Luke, he is called "Levi." Most people in this day had two or three names: a Jewish name, a Roman name, and possibly a Greek name. Levi was his Jewish name, Matthew his Roman name.) He collected custom duties from the citizens as well as from merchants passing through town. (Capernaum was a customs post on the caravan route between Damascus to the northeast and the Mediterranean Sea to the west.) Tax collectors took a commission on the taxes they collected, so most of them overcharged and kept the profits. Thus, most Jews hated tax collectors because of their reputation for cheating, their support of Rome, and their constant contact with "unclean" Gentiles. A Jew who accepted such an office shamed his family and friends and was excommunicated from the synagogue.

The *tax collector's booth* was an elevated platform or bench. Everyone knew who Matthew was, and anyone passing through the city who had to pay taxes could find him easily. Matthew's tollbooth taxed commercial goods being transported from the sea to land routes (his booth was "by the sea," Mark 2:13-14 NKJV). This would not have been the first time that Jesus had seen Matthew, for Jesus had often walked along the shore of the Sea of Galilee. Apparently Jesus saw in Matthew what he could use in his ministry. For example, we can see Matthew's attention to detail and careful record-keeping skills in the way that he wrote this Gospel.

Certainly Matthew had seen Jesus before and, with the crowds, probably had been impressed and intrigued with this man.

Then one day Jesus walked right up to Matthew's booth and said two simple words: *"Follow me."* The words are in the imperative mood, meaning this was a command, a call to discipleship, not an invitation (see 4:19; 8:22; 9:9; 10:38; 16:24; 19:21). Jesus called Matthew to "follow"—that is, to walk the same road. That Jesus called such a notorious person into his circle of disciples certainly must have shocked the other disciples, as well as the trailing crowd. Following upon the discussion of Jesus' ability to forgive sins (9:1-8), this episode dramatically demonstrated the range of sinners that Jesus could and would forgive.

Matthew recognized that Jesus was not inviting him; Jesus was calling him. So *Matthew got up and followed him.* Matthew's radical obedience would cause a great change in his life. Already ostracized by fellow Jews, Matthew's decision to follow Jesus would make no difference in this regard. But Matthew was probably very wealthy—tax collecting was a lucrative occupation; so when Matthew walked away from his booth, he snubbed Rome and a lifetime of potentially great wealth. Several of the other disciples could always return to fishing, but Matthew could never turn back.

GET UP AND GO
When Jesus called Matthew to be one of his disciples, Matthew got up and followed, leaving a promising career and a wealthy lifestyle. When God calls you to follow or obey him, do you do it with as much abandon as Matthew did? Sometimes the decision to follow Christ requires difficult or painful choices. Like Matthew, we must decide to leave behind those things that would keep us from following Christ.

**9:10 While Jesus was having dinner at Matthew's house, many tax collectors and "sinners" came and ate with him and his disciples.**[NIV] Matthew responded as Jesus would want all his followers to do—he followed his Lord immediately, and he called his friends together to meet Jesus too. Matthew held a *dinner* for his fellow *tax collectors* and other notorious *sinners* so they also could meet Jesus. Matthew, who left behind a material fortune to gain a spiritual fortune, was proud to be associated with Jesus.

*At Matthew's house* there gathered a crowd that Jesus could not reach in the synagogues. The tax collectors had been excommunicated. The term "sinners" referred not only to immoral and pagan people, but also to the common people who were not learned in the law and did not abide by the rigid standards of the Pharisees. The Pharisees regarded these people as wicked and opposed to the will of God because they did not observe the rituals for purity, which enabled them to eat with others. These people gathered at Levi's house, where they knew they had a welcome, and they *ate with [Jesus] and his disciples* and listened to the message this marvelous teacher had for them. As portrayed in the call of Matthew, this message may have been that in the kingdom of heaven the distinctions between people break down.

**9:11  When the Pharisees saw this, they said to his disciples, "Why does your teacher eat with tax collectors and sinners?"** NRSV
According to the *Pharisees,* contact with these *tax collectors and sinners* made a Jew unclean; to sit and *eat* with such people was particularly heinous. Sharing fellowship around a meal indicated close association and identification with that person. The Pharisees would have nothing to do with such people, expecting them to change before dealing with them. But not so with Jesus.

The Pharisees were the legal specialists of the time. They interpreted the law but were especially concerned about the "rules" for life that became as binding as God's written law in the Torah. Their job was to teach the Scriptures and the Law and to protect them against anyone's willful defiance. They saw themselves as righteous and everyone else as sinners.

Then along came this man, Jesus, who was popular, taught with great authority from the Scriptures, and claimed to speak for God himself. Yet, he also ignored their laws and seemed to condone sin by keeping company with sinners. They watched Jesus and followed his every move, and their anger continued to boil as he flouted their man-made rules, which they often elevated above the laws of God (see, for example, 15:1-20).

The Pharisees, so strict in their observance of their laws as they attempted to retain their "purity," refused to eat with common people because the sins of the commoners might make them ceremonially impure. So it surprised the Pharisees when Jesus sat down to a meal with these *tax collectors and sinners.* Here was a man who seemed to have the entire law at his fingertips, who taught with great authority, yet who stooped to the level of the poor, unlearned, common people—even sinners! Thus, the Pharisees pulled his disciples aside and asked why Jesus did this. They fashioned their question as an accusation. In this instance, Jesus probably stepped on every Pharisaic regulation about eating—and the Pharisees were not happy about it!

SEPARATISM
The Pharisees were noted for their separatism. Today, separatism promotes the idea that Christians should show the world the value of the gospel by being "separate" from the world—that is, don't mix, don't adopt the world's bad habits (smoking, drinking, playing cards, going to movies, and dancing have all been on various churches' lists of no-no's). Some churches have expanded the idea of separatism to include keeping apart from anyone (including other Christians) who are not as "separate" as they should be. (For example, in the 1950s some white Protestant churches refused to associate with Billy Graham when Catholic and black church leaders first appeared on the evangelist's podium.)

This story teaches us to be very careful of separatism. True, Christian disciples are called to a different lifestyle. But it's wrong to think that we witness to Jesus' gospel when we refuse to associate with people who don't believe, or believe in ways not quite to our preferences. In fact, the disciple who sits in a tavern with a friend, or goes to the office party, would appear to be more like Jesus than the one who righteously stays away. Don't be afraid to reach out to people who sin; God's message can change anyone.

**9:12-13** **When Jesus heard that, He said to them, "Those who are well have no need of a physician, but those who are sick. But go and learn what this means: 'I desire mercy and not sacrifice.' For I did not come to call the righteous, but sinners, to repentance."** NKJV The Pharisees' question apparently made its way to Jesus' ears, and Jesus had an answer for the self-righteous, influential religious leaders. The first part of Jesus' answer was from a common proverb on the healthy and the sick. Those *who are well* do not seek out a *physician;* the physician's waiting room is filled with those *who are sick.* They recognize their need and come to the one who can make them well. The physician, in turn, spends his time helping the sick get well.

> Mere outward correctness and attention to forms and ceremonies will not do. God must have reality.
>
> *Harry A. Ironsides*

Jesus then told these self-righteous Pharisees to *go and learn what this means,* implying that they did not understand their own Scriptures. Rabbis said, "Go and learn," to students who did not understand or apply correctly God's Word and needed to go back and study more. The Pharisees thought they knew Scripture perfectly; Jesus told them to go back and study again the words of God spoken through the prophet Hosea, *I desire mercy and not sacrifice* (Hosea 6:6). Hosea's words were not a blanket condemnation of the sacrificial

## OBEDIENCE VERSUS SACRIFICES

God says many times that he does not want our gifts and sacrifices when we ignore the reasons behind them. God wants us first to love and obey him.

| | |
|---|---|
| 1 Samuel 15:22-23 | Obedience is better than sacrifice. |
| Psalm 40:6-8 | God does not want burnt offerings; he wants our lifelong service. |
| Psalm 51:16-19 | God is not interested in penance; he wants a broken and contrite heart. |
| Jeremiah 7:21-23 | God does not want sacrifices; he wants our obedience. He promises that he will be our God and we will be his people. |
| Hosea 6:6 | God does not want sacrifices; he wants our loving loyalty. He does not want offerings; he wants us to acknowledge him. |
| Amos 5:21-24 | God hates pretense and hypocrisy; he wants to see justice roll on like a river. |
| Micah 6:6-8 | God is not satisfied with offerings; he wants us to be fair and just and merciful and to walk humbly with him. |
| Matthew 9:13 | God does not want sacrifices; he wants us to be merciful. |

system of the Jewish nation at the time; rather, God was condemning a thoughtless, mechanical approach to sacrifice. A religious ritual helps when carried out with an attitude of love for God. If a person's heart is far from God, ritual will become empty mockery. God did not want the Israelites' rituals; he wanted their hearts. Jesus challenged the Pharisees to apply Hosea's words to themselves. The Pharisees' rigid guidelines had created an artificial distinction between the "righteous" and "sinners." As a result, the religious leaders, who should have guided and taught the people, had instead separated themselves. Thus, the "worship" of the religious leaders was as empty as a sacrifice given without thought of God. God wants a heart attitude that includes a right relationship with him and with others, an attitude that reaches out to those in physical and spiritual need.

Jesus carried the proverb a step further and explained his messianic mission. "I am here because these are the people who realize their need and welcome me." Jesus did not come to *call the righteous* (used ironically—those, like these Pharisees, who thought they were righteous) *to repentance,* for the self-righteous do not recognize their sinfulness. But these *sinners* saw their need. This was Jesus' audience. Jesus, the Great Physician, healed people of physical illnesses, but he knew that all people are spiritually sick and in need of salvation. Luke recorded Jesus' words about his mission as, "For the Son of Man came to seek out and to save the lost" (Luke 19:10 NRSV).

THOUGHTLESS WORSHIP AND WILLFUL DISOBEDIENCE Perhaps the greater proof of Matthew's conversion wasn't his willingness to follow Jesus but his immediate invitation to others to also meet the Lord. The people each of us tries to reach with the gospel usually have limits and boundaries. Most often, these limits are self-imposed. Like the Pharisees, we may conclude that a person's reputation or past behavior cuts him or her off from even the opportunity to meet Christ. If so, we are wrong. People still need to hear. The gospel gets compromised more often by our failure to express it than by our failure to express it in the "right context." Is your approach to non-Christians more like Matthew's or like the Pharisees'? Invite someone outside your "world" into your home or church.

## RELIGIOUS LEADERS ASK JESUS ABOUT FASTING / 9:14-17 / **41**

The Pharisees questioned Jesus about those with whom he had fellowship at meals. They also questioned why Jesus and his disciples feasted instead of fasting on the customary days. Jesus showed the need for joy because the Messiah had come.

**9:14 Then the disciples of John came to him, saying, "Why do we and the Pharisees fast often, but your disciples do not fast?"** NRSV *The disciples of John* were the remaining disciples of John the Baptist, a group that lasted into the second century (see Acts 19:1-9). These men and *the Pharisees* were fasting— that is, they were going without food in order to spend time in prayer, repenting and humbling themselves before God. The Old Testament Law set aside only one day a year as a required day of fasting for all Jews—the Day of Atonement (Leviticus 16:29). The Pharisees, however, fasted on Mondays and Thursdays (see Luke 18:12) as an act of piety, and most likely they promoted this among the people.

The tense of the verb for "fast" indicates that the feast at Matthew's house happened at the very time that these people were fasting, apparently on one of the weekly fasting days. John's disciples fasted as a sign of mourning for sin and to prepare themselves for the Messiah's coming. John the Baptist was in prison, and these disciples found themselves siding with the Pharisees on this issue; they were fasting when they should have been feasting with Jesus. Naturally this caused a question: *Why do we and the Pharisees fast often, but your disciples do not fast?*

**9:15 And Jesus said to them, "The wedding guests cannot mourn as long as the bridegroom is with them, can they? The days will come when the bridegroom is taken away from them, and then they will fast."** NRSV In the Bible, people would fast in times of disaster and as a sign of their humility and repentance. Fasting represented mourning. During that time, the people approached God with humility and sorrow for sin. Fasting focused their attention on God and demonstrated their change of heart and their true devotion (see, for example, Judges 20:26; 1 Kings 21:27; Ezra 8:21; Joel 1:14; Jonah 3:5). While Jesus walked the earth, his presence was a cause for celebration—the Messiah had come! The people did not need to mourn; they needed to rejoice. Jesus' presence was as joyous as the presence of the *bridegroom* at a wedding feast. The picture of Jesus as a "bridegroom" comes from the Old Testament description of the wedding feast that God will prepare for himself and his people (Isaiah 54:5-6; Hosea 2:16-20). *Wedding guests* do not mourn or fast; a wedding is a time of celebration and feasting. Likewise, Jesus' coming was a sign of celebration, not mourning and fasting. Jesus did not condemn fasting—he himself fasted (Luke 4:2). He emphasized that fasting must be done at the right time for the right reasons.

Jesus knew, however, that soon he *(the bridegroom)* would be *taken away from them.* The Greek word translated "taken away from" is *aparthe;* a similar verb is used in the Septuagint (a Greek translation of the Old Testament) in Isaiah 53:8, a verse prophesying the Messiah's violent death. "The days [that] will come" refers to the days of Jesus' crucifixion and death. Jesus' disciples would indeed *fast* and *mourn* during those days. John 16:20 says, "You will weep and mourn while the world rejoices. You will grieve, but your grief will turn to joy" (NIV). The disciples would grieve for their crucified Master, and the world (the mass of people opposed to Jesus) would rejoice. But the disciples' grief would not last long; their sorrow would turn to joy when they saw their risen Lord.

CELEBRATE!
When you gather to worship, count it all joy. Jesus is with you there, and where he is, let no one be droopy or melancholy. Severe religion wants people to be excessively sober, serious, and quiet. But Jesus invites us to worship happily, cheerfully, with an enthusiasm that accompanies the reunion of best friends. Let your worship be like a wedding celebration.

**9:16** **"No one sews a piece of unshrunk cloth on an old cloak, for the patch pulls away from the cloak, and a worse tear is made."** NRSV There are several interpretations of the "old versus the new" (see 9:17 which speaks of the "new wineskins" and the "new wine"):

- *Law versus grace.* The old cloth and old wineskins represent people under the Old Testament Law, and the new cloth and new wineskins represent people under grace. This view, preserved by dispensationalists, stresses the complete break of the Old Testament view of obedience with the New Testament.
- *Old covenant versus new covenant.* The old cloth and old wineskins represent the older and partial understanding of God's will that had only a glimmer of understanding of God's grace as exemplified in the gospel. The new covenant would reflect a new way of understanding what true faithfulness to the law would be under Christ's authority. This view does justice to "so both are preserved" (9:17) because it sees the revealed will of God as present in both old and new. But limiting Jesus' words to apply to time in history alone misses his point.
- *Old system of spirituality versus new system.* This view sees continuity in the revealed will of God, both in the Old Testament Scripture and in the New Testament message of Christ. The old cloth and wineskins referred to the old system of application of the law (rigid, legalistic) as typified by the worst teaching of the Pharisees. The old forms and traditions were characterized by the sorrow of fasting. The new attitude of spirituality is characterized by the joy of feasting as seen in Christ and his disciples. New attitudes and methods would be needed. When new attitudes are present, both the understanding of the will of God in Scripture and the new forms will be preserved.

Jesus' arrival on earth ushered in a new time, a new covenant between God and people. The new covenant called for a new way of expressing personal faith. The newness of the gospel could not be combined with the legalism of the Pharisees any more than *a piece of unshrunk cloth* should be used as a patch on *an old cloak.* When the garment is washed, the patch will shrink, pull away from the old garment, and leave a *worse tear* than before.

The Christian church was never meant to be a sect or adaptation of Judaism; rather, Christ fulfills the intent of the Old Testament Scripture. The Jews, patiently waiting for their Messiah, should have recognized Jesus as the Messiah and should have believed the Good News. The apostle John wrote, "The law was given through Moses, but grace and truth came through Jesus Christ" (John 1:17 NKJV). Both law and grace express God's nature. Moses' law emphasized God's law and justice; Jesus Christ came to express God's mercy, love, and forgiveness. Moses could only give the law; Christ came to fulfill the law perfectly (5:17). The law reveals the nature and will of God; Jesus Christ reveals the nature and will of God. But while the law could only point out sin and condemn us, Jesus Christ gave his life to bring us forgiveness of sin and salvation. The parables of the cloth and the wineskins (9:17) apply to more than just fasting or to the Pharisees. They speak of Jesus' entire mission and the new era he inaugurated by his entrance into human history.

**9:17** **"Neither is new wine put into old wineskins; otherwise, the skins burst, and the wine is spilled, and the skins are destroyed; but new wine is put into fresh wineskins, and so both are preserved."** NRSV In Bible times, people stored wine in goatskins sewn around the edges to form watertight bags (called *wineskins*). New wine expanded as it fermented, stretching its wineskin. After this wine had aged, old and brittle wineskins would burst if fresh wine was poured into them. *New wine,* therefore, would always be put into *fresh wineskins.* The new wine was the newness of the gospel as exemplified in the person of Jesus Christ (John 2:1-11). Like old wineskins, the Pharisees and indeed the entire religious system of Judaism had become too rigid to accept Jesus. They could not contain him or his message in their traditions or rules. Their understanding of faithfulness to the law had become unsuitable for the fresh, dynamic power of Christ's message. They were the self-appointed guardians of the "old cloak" and the "old wineskins."

Jesus did not come to abolish or annul the Law and the Prophets but to fulfill them (5:17). But this fulfillment required new approaches and new structures. Jesus' words *and so both are preserved,* reveal that the new wine needed to be preserved in new forms. The new way of obedience to the law would be found in the authoritative teaching of Jesus. Jesus did not come to patch up the old religious system of Judaism with its rules and traditions. If he had, his message would have damaged it.

His purpose was to bring in something new, though God's prophets had told about it centuries before. This new message said that God's Son would come to earth to offer all people forgiveness of sins and reconciliation. The gospel did not fit into the rigid legalistic system that had become the Jewish religion.

---

**FULFILLED WINESKINS**
Jesus repeatedly challenged the thought of the day that moved from timeless truth to wooden, thoughtless practice. He pointed out that a rigid application often contradicts the original truth from which it came. He openly charged people with rejecting God's Word by substituting tradition for truth.

In the present context, Jesus was using the cloth and wineskin illustrations to roll back worn-out applications. Jesus didn't reject fasting; he rejected fasting without purpose and fasting for the wrong reasons. We must ensure that our attitudes and methods for ministry convey the same commitment to the eternal truth of God's Word but portray flexibility in how we communicate it. Are we locked into worn-out traditions for worship and ministry? Are we open to fresh new ways to bring Christ to the world?

---

## JESUS HEALS A BLEEDING WOMAN AND RESTORES A GIRL TO LIFE / 9:18-26 / **89**

In this new kingdom, joy predominates (9:15) and love in action takes the place of rigid law keeping. Matthew followed the previous account of Jesus' words to the questioning Pharisees and disciples of John the Baptist with the account of Jesus reaching out to two more unclean people—a woman with a bleeding disorder and a dead child—healing one and raising the other to life. His compassion outweighed legalism.

**9:18-19 While he was saying these things to them, suddenly a leader of the synagogue came in and knelt before him, saying, "My daughter has just died; but come and lay your hand on her, and she will live." And Jesus got up and followed him, with his disciples.**<sup>NRSV</sup> Jesus was interrupted at his meal by a man who came with a need. Mark and Luke say this man's name was Jairus (Mark 5:22; Luke 8:41). He was *a leader of the synagogue*. The synagogue was the local center of worship, and Jairus was a lay person elected as one of the leaders (a synagogue could have more than one leader or ruler, see Acts 13:15). The synagogue leaders were responsible for supervising worship services, caring for the scrolls, running the daily school, keeping the congregation faithful to the Law, distributing alms, administering the care of the building, and finding rabbis to teach on the Sabbath. The leader of the local synagogue exerted great influence in his community, yet he *knelt* before Jesus, indicating homage and courtesy as he came with his urgent request. Neither position nor pressure could stop Jairus from coming to the one man who could help his daughter. (Mark and Luke add that she was twelve years old— see Mark 5:42 and Luke 8:42; Luke also adds that this was his only daughter.)

Matthew abbreviated this story by quoting the father as saying, *"My daughter has just died."* In Mark's account, we read that the daughter was dying, but while Jesus was on the way, news came that the little girl had died. Matthew intended to stress Jesus' authority over death, so he shortened the story, retaining Jesus' words and focusing on his power.

While Jesus could have healed (or raised) this young girl by speaking the word (as he had done with the centurion's servant, 8:5-13), that was not Jairus's request. Still, Jesus responded to his faith. Jesus apparently heard the urgency in Jairus's voice and saw the strain of worry on his face, so he *got up and followed him, with his disciples.* Mark adds that there was also a large crowd who went along. Thus, so many people filled the streets that they pressed around Jesus (Mark 5:24).

---

### AN EQUALIZING NEED

Shock and grief made the synagogue leader bold. A long series of disappointments had created a similar result in the suffering woman. The first came to Jesus for his child's life; the second came to Jesus to make her whole. The ruler couldn't bear to lose his twelve-year-old child, while the woman couldn't wait to lose her twelve-year-old problem. They were two of many people driven to Jesus by their needs.

Jesus met people in their need. His response was neither calculated nor mechanical. He never ignored people because of their status or position. He clearly wanted people to acknowledge his lordship, but he willingly helped them with no assurance of their gratitude or understanding.

We imitate Christ when we help people any way we can while also offering them the gospel. We must do so lovingly and generously, even if they do not respond to the message.

---

**9:20-21** **Just then a woman who had been subject to bleeding for twelve years came up behind him and touched the edge of his cloak. She said to herself, "If I only touch his cloak, I will be healed."** NIV In the crowd pressing on Jesus was another desperate person in need of divine help. A woman *had been subject to bleeding for twelve years.* This bleeding was painful and may have been a menstrual or uterine disorder. She had been to many doctors, had spent all her money, but had received no cure (Mark 5:26). The bleeding caused the woman to be in a constant condition of ceremonial uncleanness (see Leviticus 15:25-33). She could not worship in the synagogue, and she could not have normal social relationships, for under Jewish law, anyone who touched her also became unclean. Thus, the woman had been treated almost as severely as a leper.

In these two stories we find two people who sought Jesus out—Jairus on behalf of his daughter, and this woman for her incurable disease. Both came in faith, knowing that Jesus could take care of their particular problem. Jairus had already petitioned Jesus, and Jesus was on his way. This woman had heard about Jesus' miracle-working power (apparently for the first time) and had come to Capernaum to find him (tradition says she was from Caesarea Philippi). She worked her way through the crowd and *came up behind* Jesus. She believed that she only had to touch *the edge of his cloak* (the tassels) and she would be healed. Tassels were attached to the outer garment to remind Jews to follow God (Numbers 15:37-38; Deuteronomy 22:12). The effort to touch Jesus' garment was due to the popular belief that the clothes of a holy man imparted spiritual and healing power (see Mark 6:56; Acts 19:11-12). She may have feared that Jesus would not touch her if he knew her condition, that Jesus would not risk becoming unclean in order to heal her. Or she may have feared that if her disease became known to the crowd, the people who had touched her would be angry at having become unclean unknowingly. The woman knew she could receive healing, but she tried to do it as unobtrusively as possible. She thought that she would just be healed and go away.

---

**TOUCHING HIM**
Lots of people were touching Jesus that day, bumping against him, reaching out to shake his hand (or the equivalent), moving alongside the crowd. But one person touched him in faith. That person discovered Jesus' healing power.

Mere curiosity, merely following the crowd, or casually brushing up against Jesus does not represent the faith Jesus looks for, the faith he responds to. The woman was desperate; she believed Jesus could help; and she was determined, even if a bit bashful. We follow her example when we truly lay our needs before Jesus in prayer, believing he can help us. Do that today with your worries and cares. Divine help will be there for you.

---

**9:22 Jesus turned, and seeing her he said, "Take heart, daughter; your faith has made you well." And instantly the woman was made well.**NRSV Mark describes in detail the process of this

healing (Mark 5:25-34) and places the healing before Jesus'
words to the woman. Characteristically, Matthew was focusing
instead on Jesus' authoritative words. Someone had touched
him in order to be healed. Clearly Jesus healed the woman; her
faith appropriated the healing, and Jesus perceived what had
happened. He *turned,* saw the woman who had been healed
(in Mark he asked who had touched him, but he already knew).
Then he spoke words of comfort to the woman, *"Take heart,
daughter; your faith has made you well."* Jesus spoke to the
woman in gentle words, calling her *daughter,* revealing a father-
child relationship. She came for healing and received it, but
she also received peace and a relationship with God himself
because of her faith. Jesus explained that it was not his clothing
that had healed her; rather, her faith in reaching out to the one
person who could heal her had allowed that healing to take
place. Not only did she have faith, but she had also placed her
faith in the right person. She was *instantly* delivered from her
bleeding and her pain.

NEVER GIVE UP
God changed a situation that had been a problem for years.
Like the leper and the demon-possessed men, this diseased
woman was considered unclean. For twelve years, she too had
been one of the "untouchables" and had not been able to lead
a normal life. But Jesus changed that and restored her. Sometimes we are tempted to give up on people or situations that
have not changed for many years. God can change what seems
unchangeable, giving new purpose and hope.

**9:23-24** **When Jesus came to the leader's house and saw the flute players and the crowd making a commotion, he said, "Go away;
for the girl is not dead but sleeping." And they laughed at
him.**[NRSV] Mark explains that messengers then arrived to tell Jairus
that his daughter had died. But this did not stop Jesus. He took
Peter, James, and John and continued on *to the leader's house.*
The *flute players* and the *commotion* (loud crying and wailing)
were all part of the customary ritual of mourning. Lack of weeping and wailing was the ultimate disgrace and disrespect. Some
people, usually women, made mourning a profession and were
paid by the dead person's family to weep over the body. Jairus,
the leader of the synagogue, was an important person in the town.
Thus, at the death of his only daughter, the townspeople demonstrated their great love and respect for Jairus and his family by
weeping and wailing.

Jesus spoke words of encouragement, only to be *laughed at.* His words, *the girl is not dead but sleeping,* probably made Jesus appear rather stupid—certainly anyone could tell death from sleep. Neither was she just in a coma from which Jesus would awaken her as some have proposed. The girl was indeed dead, and everyone from the family to the mourners knew it. Jesus knew it too, but his words tested the faith of the crowd and revealed to Jairus the hope beyond all hope of what Jesus was about to do. She was dead, but Jesus would bring her back to life, as if awakening her from sleep. Jesus used the image of sleep to indicate that the girl's condition was temporary and that she would be restored. Luke explained that when Jesus lifted her up, her spirit returned to her (Luke 8:54-55).

**9:25-26 But when the crowd was put outside, He went in and took her by the hand, and the girl arose. And the report of this went out into all that land.**NKJV Jesus' words sounded ridiculous to the faithless crowd. Their laughter became their judgment—they would not witness the miracle, for Jesus put them all *outside* of the room. Then Jesus took the child's father and mother and the three disciples who had come and *went in* where the child was, in an inner part of the house. Jesus had come to earth to conquer sin and death, and in this dramatic but quiet miracle, he would show his disciples that power. And two bereaved parents would receive back their beloved daughter.

Jesus did no incantations and spoke no magic words, as other healers of the day normally did. He simply went to the girl's bedside and *took her by the hand.* The fact that Jesus touched the girl's hand would have amazed the proper synagogue leader and the disciples. Touching a dead body meant to become unclean. But Jesus had already dealt with a demon-possessed man and a woman with an incurable issue of blood and had touched and healed them. Touching the dead girl confirmed once again that to Jesus, compassion was more important than the letter of the law.

Jesus took the girl's hand in his, he issued a command (Mark 5:41), and the dead child *arose.* Just as the healings Jesus performed were always complete, so the rising of this young girl from the dead was complete.

This was not the first time the disciples had witnessed the raising of a dead person. Luke 7:11-15 records Jesus raising a boy near the village of Nain. Yet, even in this instance, the disciples were amazed. When the girl came back to life, perhaps the disciples may have wondered (as they did after Jesus calmed the storm), "Who then is this, that the dead can be brought back to life?" Jesus would raise yet another person— his friend Lazarus (dead and buried for four days—recorded in John 11). Then finally, most dramatic of all, Jesus himself would rise from the grave and spend time with the disciples before returning to his Father. Jesus had authority and power over humanity's greatest enemy—death.

Mark explained that Jesus had commanded the parents not to advertise the miracle (Mark 5:43). However, despite Jesus' command to the contrary, *the report of this went out into all that land.*

---

**HOPE**
It's terrific to heal, preach, feed, and help people, but still there lingers death as our last and greatest enemy. Here Jesus shows his power over that problem too.

"What is your only hope in life and in death?" asks the first question of the Heidelberg Catechism. "That I am not my own, but belong—body and soul, in life and in death—to my faithful Savior Jesus Christ."

When you approach death, be confident in Jesus' saving power. When loved ones die, treasure the hope of eternal life. Jesus' power will surely carry us through that last portal to our home in heaven.

---

## JESUS HEALS THE BLIND AND MUTE / 9:27-34 / **90**

**9:27 As Jesus went on from there, two blind men followed him, crying loudly, "Have mercy on us, Son of David!"**NRSV Jesus and the disciples returned from *there* (that is, from Jairus's house, 9:23), most likely with a crowd continuing in their wake. *Two blind men* also *followed him.* These men cried out for *mercy,* meaning that they wanted Jesus to help them. Isaiah had prophesied that a day would come when God would open the eyes of the blind (Isaiah 29:18; 35:5-6; 42:7). These men called Jesus *Son of David,* a popular way of addressing Jesus as the Messiah. It was known that the Messiah would be a descendant of David (Isaiah 9:7). This is the first time this title is used in Matthew.

**9:28 When he had gone indoors, the blind men came to him, and he asked them, "Do you believe that I am able to do this?" "Yes, Lord," they replied.**NIV Jesus didn't respond immediately to the blind men's pleas, but they persisted, following Jesus *indoors,* right into the house where Jesus was staying. They knew Jesus could heal them, and they brought their request to him.

The focus of this story is the power of faith. Jesus asked these blind men first if they had faith *(Do you believe . . . ?).* Then he healed them according to their faith (9:29). These men answered Jesus' question about their belief, saying, *"Yes,*

*Lord."* The use of the word "Lord" reveals their faith in Jesus' power and authority to heal them.

---

**"YES, LORD"**
How simple and profound. The blind men showed their faith in plain talk that says, "Yes, Lord, you can do it!"

The "Amen" that closes our prayers is like saying "Yes, Lord." "Amen" is not just a period at the end of a sentence, or a courtesy closing at the end of a letter. It is our vote of confidence that Jesus, our Lord, can do it. Let your *Amen* be as strong and simple, direct and plain, as if you had followed Jesus into the house and asked him for help, person to person. Occasionally, to help remind you of its meaning, say at the end of your prayers, "Yes, Lord, you can do it!"

---

**9:29-31** **Then he touched their eyes and said, "According to your faith let it be done to you." And their eyes were opened.**NRSV These blind men had proven their faith in Jesus to heal them by coming to him with their need and following him right into a house in order to receive healing. Because these men believed, Jesus *touched their eyes* and *their eyes were opened.* The words "according to your faith" do not mean "in proportion to," but "in response to." This healing was a powerful example that Jesus was the Messiah. Healing of the blind had never occurred in the Old Testament or in Judaism before Jesus.

**Then Jesus sternly ordered them, "See that no one knows of this."**NRSV Jesus told these men to be quiet because he was concerned for his ministry. Jesus did not want to be known as just a miracle worker; he wanted people to listen to his words that would heal their broken spiritual lives. Jesus' mission was to preach the Good News of the kingdom of God. If crowds descended on him to see amazing healings and dead people raised, they would not be coming with the heart attitude needed to hear and respond to the gospel. The disciples would understand Jesus' miracles and talk about them after his resurrection—then they could write them down for all of us to read and marvel at as well. But these blind men were too excited to heed Jesus' words. Jesus had *sternly ordered them* to keep quiet **but they went away and spread the news about him throughout that district.**NRSV Obviously the blind men would not be able to hide their healing for long. The power of God and the miracle were so great that no one could keep silent. What, exactly, did Jesus expect? Jesus simply wanted these men to keep the details to themselves and think about them. He wanted them to worship quietly and treasure in their hearts what Jesus had done. He wanted them to focus on the spiritual aspect. Above all, he did not want more advertisement of his healing power. But the men could not contain themselves; they told everyone in that area what Jesus had done.

---

EASY DISOBEDIENCE
Sometimes we think that conversion will solve the world's problems because converted people will obey Jesus and live under his commands. But here we see two faith-filled blind men, newly healed, who receive a direct command and almost immediately disobey. How easy it is!

Sometimes we mistakenly let joyous feelings become our guide, instead of listening to Jesus' word. Or we think we know better ("He can't be serious?!") and so disregard Jesus' words. Thus, gospel-preaching churches have supported slavery, apartheid, oppression, and bigotry—failing to obey the words of Jesus.

Take Jesus' words seriously, and live by them. Give Jesus priority over your own hunches, preferences, and exuberance. Show your commitment to Jesus by obeying him.

---

**9:32 While they were going out, a man who was demon-possessed and could not talk was brought to Jesus.**<sup>NIV</sup> Jesus could hardly come or go without someone in need coming to him! This time, as Jesus and his disciples were leaving, *a man who was demon-possessed and could not talk was brought to Jesus.* The word translated "could not talk" is *kophos,* which can mean deaf, unable to talk, or both. Such disabilities are not always the work of demons, because Jesus healed many people of illness and disability without casting out demons. Matthew wanted his readers to understand, however, that in this situation a demon was at work. While Jesus was on earth, demonic forces seemed especially active. Although we cannot always be sure why or how demon possession occurs, it causes both physical and mental problems. In this case, the demon made the man unable to talk. (For more on demons and demon possession, see commentary on 8:28-34.)

**9:33-34 And when the demon had been cast out, the one who had been mute spoke; and the crowds were amazed and said, "Never has anything like this been seen in Israel."**<sup>NRSV</sup> Matthew avoided detail about the exorcism of the demon (he had already established Jesus' authority over demonic powers, see 8:16, 28-34) and focused instead on the reaction of the crowd. After Jesus *cast out* the demon, the mute man was able to speak.

Once again, the ever-present *crowds were amazed.* They had never seen *anything like this.* The teachings Matthew recorded in chapters 5–7 established Jesus' authority; the miracles grouped in chapters 8 and 9 revealed Jesus' power and divinity. The crowds saw God's power at work in Jesus and began to realize that he was one of the greatest prophets.

The religious leaders, however, saw something entirely different: **But the Pharisees said, "It is by the prince of demons that he drives out demons."** NIV In these words of the *Pharisees,* Matthew was showing the full extent of their rejection of Jesus. This chapter has the Pharisees accusing Jesus of four different sins: blasphemy, befriending outcasts, impiety, and serving Satan, *the prince of demons.* In Scripture Satan is constantly portrayed as the imitator of God, so the Pharisees may have been referring to this belief. They tried to explain Jesus away by saying that he was only imitating God but was really in league with Satan—and that's why the demons obeyed him.

Matthew showed how Jesus was maligned by those who should have received him most gladly. Why did the Pharisees do this? (1) Jesus bypassed their religious authority. (2) He weakened their control over the people. (3) He challenged their cherished beliefs. (4) He exposed their insincere motives. While the Pharisees questioned, debated, and dissected Jesus, people were being healed and lives changed right in front of them. Their skepticism was based on jealousy of Jesus' popularity. The opposition to Jesus was intensifying; Jesus was far too powerful and popular for the Pharisees' comfort.

## JESUS URGES THE DISCIPLES TO PRAY FOR WORKERS / 9:35-38 / **92**

From 9:35 through 10:42, Matthew recorded a second discourse of Jesus, focusing on mission. (The first discourse was the Sermon on the Mount, recorded in chapters 5–7.) Jesus continued to share the Good News of the kingdom to all who would listen, and he exemplified the task and pattern his disciples would follow after his return to heaven.

**9:35** **Then Jesus went about all the cities and villages, teaching in their synagogues, preaching the gospel of the kingdom, and healing every sickness and every disease among the people.**NKJV This verse introduces the next discourse that Matthew recorded (from 9:35 through 10:42). This verse also mirrors 4:23, a verse that introduced the last recorded discourse in chapters 5 through 7.

Jesus *went about all the cities and villages.* Again, Jesus'

ministry is described as *teaching, preaching,* and *healing.*
These were the three main aspects. "Teaching" shows Jesus'
concern for understanding; "preaching" shows his concern for
commitment; and "healing" shows his concern for wholeness.
His miracles of healing authenticated his teaching and preaching, proving that he truly was from God.

The Good News of the kingdom was that the promised and
long-awaited Messiah had finally come. His healing miracles
were a sign that his teaching was true.

**9:36** **But when He saw the multitudes, He was moved with compassion
for them, because they were weary and scattered, like sheep
having no shepherd.**NKJV Wherever Jesus went, crowds gathered.
But when Jesus saw these *multitudes,* he
was *moved with compassion for them.*
The word "compassion" describes the
deep inner mercy of God, often described
in the Old Testament. The prophet
Ezekiel compared Israel to sheep without a shepherd (Ezekiel 34:5, 6; see also
Numbers 27:17; 1 Kings 22:17); Jesus
saw the *weary and scattered* people as
*sheep having no shepherd.* The word for
"weary" can also mean "troubled,"
"bewildered," or "despondent." The
word for "scattered" is also "prostrate"
or "thrown to the ground." The two
words are near synonyms that stress
man's helplessness without God. Jesus
came to be the Shepherd, the one who
could show people how to avoid life's
pitfalls (see John 10:14; 1 Peter 2:25).
Jesus considered the Pharisees to have failed in leading the people
to God, who were therefore left without a shepherd.

> Today I noticed for the
> first time that Jesus'
> compassion on the
> multitudes was not only
> because they were many,
> but because they were
> scattered, divided,
> and distressed . . .
> So it is among our tribes
> [of Auca Indians]—
> scattered, but not many.
> Yet they merit His mercy.
> Thus God confirms my
> way with these encour-
> agements from His Word.
>                    *Jim Elliott*

**9:37-38** **Then He said to His disciples, "The harvest truly is plentiful, but the laborers are few. Therefore pray the Lord of the
harvest to send out laborers into His harvest."** NKJV Jesus
looked at the crowds following him and referred to them as a
field ripe for harvest, but *the laborers* to bring in the harvest
*are few.* These "laborers" were the disciples, then few in number.
Jesus commanded his disciples to *pray the Lord of the harvest
to send out laborers.* The "Lord of the harvest" refers to God.
The verb translated "send out" is a strong term, meaning to
"thrust forth." In this context it speaks of a strong push to get

workers into the field. These laborers must warn people of coming judgment and call them to repentance. Many people are ready to give their lives to Christ if someone would show them how. We are to pray that people will respond to this need for workers. Often, when we pray for something, God answers our prayers by using *us*. Be prepared for God to use you to show another person the way to him. Chapter 10 will describe this mission and what it will involve in more detail.

### MISSIONS

Missions finds its motive in the heart of Jesus ("He was moved with compassion") and its strength in the prayers of the church.

Churches which prefer projects to prayer are missing the power, and missions will eventually fizzle there. Churches where zeal comes from "saving the lost" or "rescuing the perishing"—with emphasis on hurry and efficiency because time is short—miss the heart of Jesus' own motives.

The keys to success in missions are to grow closer to Jesus' heart for people and to pray. Whatever else your church does, learn to love and learn to pray.

# Matthew 10

This chapter continues Jesus' second discourse recorded by Matthew. This second discourse began at 9:35 and ends at 10:42. Matthew 10:1-16, closely parallel to Mark 3:13-19 and 6:7-13, describes Jesus' appointment of the Twelve for their first apostolic mission. Though this was the first time they went out on their own, they had been given authority from Jesus to carry on the work of preaching and healing.

**10:1** **He called his twelve disciples to him and gave them authority to drive out evil spirits and to heal every disease and sickness.**<sup>NIV</sup>
Jesus had many disciples (learners), but he appointed twelve to whom he gave authority and special training. The twelve disciples had already joined Jesus (Mark 3:14-19, see also the Harmony of the Gospels at the back of this commentary), but Matthew waited until writing his missionary discourse to introduce these twelve *disciples.* This records the first time Jesus sent them out on their own. These men were his inner circle. Many people followed and listened to Jesus, but these twelve received the most intense training. We see the impact of these men throughout the rest of the New Testament. They started the Christian church. The Gospels call these men the "disciples" or the "Twelve"; the book of Acts calls them apostles. The choice of *twelve* men is highly symbolic. The number twelve corresponds to the twelve tribes of Israel (19:28), showing the continuity between the old religious system and the new one based on Jesus' message. Jesus looked upon his mission as the gathering of the true people of God. These men were the righteous remnant (the faithful believers throughout the Old Testament who never abandoned God or his law) who would carry on the work the twelve tribes were chosen to do—to build the community of God. These were the righteous remnant chosen out of the apostate nation and given a twofold responsibility: (1) to represent the nation before God; (2) to reach the nation for God. The Gospels and Epistles stressed the ministry of the twelve men together and its significance. The number was so important that when Judas

Iscariot killed himself, the disciples chose another man to replace him (see Acts 1:15-26).

These twelve men had Jesus' *authority* over the forces of evil. Jesus empowered his disciples *to drive out evil spirits.* The disciples could speak the word, and God's power would cast out the demons. Jesus also gave these disciples power *to heal every disease and sickness.* It was important that they have these powers because Jesus was extending his mission through them. Jesus directly confronted demons and sicknesses. The disciples carried Jesus' purpose and his power.

---

CALLED AND CHOSEN
Jesus "called" his twelve disciples. He didn't draft them, force them, or ask them to volunteer; he chose them to serve him in a special way. Jesus did not choose these twelve to be his disciples because of their faith—it often faltered. He didn't choose them because of their talent and ability—no one stood out with unusual ability. The disciples represented a wide range of backgrounds and life experiences, but apparently they may have had no more leadership potential than those who were not chosen. The one characteristic they all shared was their willingness to obey Jesus. Christ calls us today. He doesn't twist our arms and make us do something we don't want to do. We can choose to join him or remain behind. When Christ calls you to follow him, how do you respond? Have you given him only a halfhearted commitment or your whole heart?

---

**10:2-4** **These are the names of the twelve apostles: first, Simon (who is called Peter).**[NIV] In verse 1, these men are called "disciples"; here, the word "apostles" is used to stress their role as messengers, "sent ones."

The first name recorded was *Simon,* to whom Jesus had given the name *Peter* (see John 1:42). Jesus "surnamed" him Peter, meaning that he had given him a name in addition to the one he already had—he did not change Simon's name. Peter was also called Cephas. "Peter" is the Greek equivalent of the Aramaic *Cephas*—a word meaning "stone" or "rock." Peter had been a fisherman (4:18). He became one of three in Jesus' core group among the disciples. He also confessed that Jesus was the Messiah (16:16). Although, later, Peter would deny ever knowing Jesus, he eventually would become a leader in the Jerusalem church, write two letters that appear in the Bible (1 and 2 Peter), and be crucified for his faith.

**His brother Andrew.**[NIV] *Andrew* was Peter's *brother* and also a fisherman (4:18). Andrew had been a disciple of John the Baptist and had accepted John the Baptist's testimony that Jesus was "the

Lamb of God." He had left John to follow Jesus and then had brought his brother Simon Peter to Jesus (John 1:35-42). Andrew and John were Jesus' first disciples (John 1:35-40); Andrew then had brought Peter to Jesus (John 1:41-42).

**James son of Zebedee, and his brother John.**[NIV] James and John had also been fishermen (4:21). James would become the first apostle to be martyred (Acts 12:2). John would write the Gospel of John, the letters of 1, 2, and 3 John, and the book of Revelation. The brothers may have been related to Jesus (distant cousins); thus, at one point their mother requested special places for them in Christ's kingdom (20:20-28).

**Philip.** Philip was the fourth to meet Jesus. John 1:43 states, "The next day Jesus decided to leave for Galilee. Finding Philip, he said to him, 'Follow me'" (NIV). Philip then brought Nathanael (also called Bartholomew)—see John 1:45. Philip probably knew Andrew and Peter because they were from the same town, Bethsaida (John 1:44).

**Bartholomew.** Scholars think that Bartholomew is the same person as Nathanael. In the list of disciples here and in Mark, Philip and Bartholomew are listed together (Mark 3:18); in John's Gospel, Philip and Nathanael are paired up (John 1:45). Thus, it stands to reason that since John does not mention Bartholomew and the other Gospels do not mention Nathanael, then Nathanael and Bartholomew must be the same person. Bartholomew was an honest man; indeed, Jesus' first words to him were, "Here is a true Israelite, in whom there is nothing false" (John 1:47 NIV). Bartholomew at first rejected Jesus because Jesus was from Nazareth. But upon meeting Jesus, his attitude changed, and he exclaimed, "Rabbi, you are the Son of God! You are the King of Israel!" (John 1:49 NRSV).

**Thomas.** We often remember this disciple as "Doubting Thomas" because he doubted Jesus' resurrection (John 20:24-25). But he also loved the Lord and was a man of great courage. When Jesus determined to return to Judea and enemy territory, Thomas said to the disciples, "Let us also go, that we may die with him" (John 11:16 NIV). Thomas was tough and committed, even if he tended to be pessimistic. Thus, when the other disciples said that Jesus was alive, Thomas did not believe them. However, when Thomas saw and touched the living Christ, doubting Thomas became believing Thomas.

**Matthew the tax collector.** Matthew, author of this Gospel, described himself by his former profession, probably to show the change that Jesus had made in his life. Also known as Levi, he had been a *tax collector* (9:9). Thus, he had been a despised out-cast, but he had abandoned that corrupt (though lucrative) way of life to follow Jesus.

**James son of Alphaeus.**<sup>NIV</sup> This disciple is designated as *son of Alphaeus* to differentiate him from James the son of Zebedee (and brother of John) in 10:2. He is also called "James the younger" (Mark 15:40). Matthew is also called "son of Alphaeus" in Mark 2:14, but James and Matthew were probably not related.

**Thaddaeus.**<sup>NIV</sup> Thaddaeus is also called "Judas son of James" (see Luke 6:16; Acts 1:13).

**Simon the Zealot.** <sup>NIV</sup>Some versions of Scripture call this disciple Simon the Canaanite. Simon was probably not a member of the party of Zealots, for that political party did not appear until A.D. 68. Most likely the word "Zealot" that is used here indicates zeal for God's honor and not extreme nationalism; it was an affectionate nickname.

**Judas Iscariot, who betrayed him.**<sup>NIV</sup> The name "Iscariot" is probably a compound word meaning "the man from Kerioth." Thus, Judas's hometown was Kerioth in southern Judea (see Joshua 15:25), making him the only one of the Twelve who was not from Galilee. It was Judas, son of Simon Iscariot (John 6:71), who would betray Jesus to his enemies and then commit suicide (27:3-5; Luke 22:47-48).

---

NO LITTLE PEOPLE
The list of Jesus' twelve disciples does not give us many details—probably because there were not many impressive details to tell.

Jesus called people from all backgrounds and occupations—fishermen, religious activists, tax collectors. He called common people and uncommon leaders; rich and poor; educated and uneducated. Today, many people think only certain people can follow Christ, but this was not the attitude of the Master himself. God can use anyone, no matter how insignificant he or she appears. When you feel small and useless, remember that God uses ordinary people to do his extraordinary work.

---

**10:5-6** **These twelve Jesus sent out with the following instructions: "Do not go among the Gentiles or enter any town of the Samaritans. Go rather to the lost sheep of Israel."** <sup>NIV</sup> Jesus *sent out* the twelve disciples on a mission to preach the coming of the kingdom (10:7) and exercise the authority over demons and sickness that Jesus gave them (10:1). Jesus gave specific *instructions,* however, regarding the focus of their ministry: *"Do not go among the Gentiles or . . . Samaritans."* A "Gentile" was anyone who was not a Jew. The "Samaritans" were a race that resulted from intermarriage between Jews and Gentiles after the Old Testament captivities (see 2 Kings 17:24). When the Jews returned from exile, they refused to allow the Samaritans to help them rebuild the temple (Ezra 4). As a result, the Samaritans developed their own religion, accepting only the Pentateuch as God's authoritative word. In 109 B.C., the Jews burned the Samaritan temple on Mount Gerizim.

This did not mean that Jesus opposed evangelizing Gentiles and Samaritans; in fact, Matthew had already described Jesus' encounter with Gentiles (8:28-34), and John 4 recounts his conversation with a Samaritan woman. Jesus' command to *go rather to the lost sheep of Israel* means that the disciples should spend their time among the Jews (see also 15:24). These words restricted the disciples' "short-term" mission to Galilee. Gentile territory lay to the north and Samaritan territory to the south. Jesus came not to the Jews only, but to the Jews "first" (Romans 1:16). God chose them to tell the rest of the world about him. Later, these disciples would receive the commission to "go and make disciples of all nations" (28:19 NIV). Jewish disciples and apostles preached the gospel of the risen Christ all around the Roman empire, and soon Gentiles were pouring into the church. The Bible clearly teaches that God's message of salvation is for all people, regardless of race, sex, or national origin (Genesis 12:3; Isaiah 25:6; 56:3-7; Malachi 1:11; Acts 10:34, 35; Romans 3:29, 30; Galatians 3:28).

"Sheep" was an affectionate term used often of God's people in the Old Testament, as in Isaiah 53:6; Jeremiah 50:6; Ezekiel 34. We can see their "lostness" in the thoughtless rituals and man-made laws commanded by their religious leaders. Jesus, the Good Shepherd, came to regather the lost sheep.

**10:7-8** **"And as you go, preach, saying, 'The kingdom of heaven is at hand.' Heal the sick, cleanse the lepers, raise the dead, cast out demons. Freely you have received, freely give."** NKJV The disciples went out as Jesus' representatives, spreading his message. John the Baptist and Jesus had preached "the kingdom of heaven is at hand" (3:2; 4:17 NKJV), so he sent his disciples out to also *preach* that *the kingdom of heaven* was near. The Jews were waiting for the Messiah to usher in his kingdom. They were hoping for a political and military kingdom that would free

[Missions is] a tale of tears, trials, testings, and triumphs, of opposition, of substituting human devices for divine methods, of candle lights in the darkness, and the bright shining of a new day.
*V. Raymond Edman*

them from Roman rule and bring back the days of glory under David and Solomon. But Jesus was talking about a spiritual kingdom. The gospel today is that the kingdom is still "near." Jesus, the Messiah, has already begun his kingdom on earth in the hearts of his followers. One day the kingdom will be fully realized. The disciples were also to use the authority and power he had given them (10:1) to *heal the sick, cleanse the lepers, raise the dead,* and *cast out demons,* just as they had seen Jesus do. These four miracles were exactly the miracles Jesus had done and would demonstrate that the disciples had Jesus' power.

Jesus gave the disciples a principle to guide their actions as they ministered to others: *Freely you have received, freely give.* The disciples had received salvation and the kingdom without cost; they should give their time under the same principle. Because God has showered us with his blessings, we should give generously to others of our time, love, and possessions.

---

FREELY GIVE
Pastors, teachers, and missionaries should not plan on getting rich by their pastoring or teaching. Full-time Christian workers deserve a reasonable wage for their labors, but not an enriching one, nor should profit play a part in anything they provide or do. The spirit of capitalism—maximum profit for minumum investment—has no place in the church's ministry.

Beware of well-heeled ministries, preachers who parade diamond rings or tailored suits, mission agencies overly dependent on Western wealth, and churches where six-figure salaries chair all the committees. Jesus sets the precedent for kingdom work: It is to be more humble than showy, more economically marginal than heavily endowed, more trustful in God than in upscale donors.

---

**10:9-10** "Do not take along any gold or silver or copper in your belts; take no bag for the journey, or extra tunic, or sandals or a staff; for the worker is worth his keep." NIV These instructions seem, at first, to be contrary to normal travel plans, but they simply reveal the urgency of the task and its temporary nature. Jesus sent the disciples in pairs (Mark 6:7), expecting them to return with a full report. This was a training mission; they were to leave immediately and travel light, taking along only minimal supplies. They were to depend on God and on the people to whom they ministered (10:11). Most people leaving on a journey would carry money in their *belts.* Normally each one would carry a *bag for the journey* to carry supplies, an *extra tunic* for added warmth at night, *sandals* to protect feet on rough terrain, and *a staff* for help in walking. But Jesus forbade them to take along any of these things.

Mark recorded that Jesus instructed the disciples to take nothing with them *except* staffs, while the accounts in Matthew and Luke say that Jesus told them *not* to take staffs. One explanation for this difference is that Matthew and Luke were referring to a club used for protection, whereas Mark was talking about a shepherd's crook used for walking. Another explanation is that according to Matthew and Luke, Jesus was forbidding them to acquire an *additional* staff or sandals, but instead to use what they already had. The point in all three accounts is the same: The disciples were to leave at once, without extensive preparation, trusting in God's care rather than in their own resources. Jesus' instructions pertained only to this particular mission. Indeed, just after Jesus and the disciples ate the Last Supper, Jesus would ask them: "'When I sent you without purse, bag or sandals, did you lack anything?' 'Nothing,' they answered. He said to them, 'But now if you have a purse, take it, and also a bag; and if you don't have a sword, sell your cloak and buy one'" (Luke 22:35-36 NIV). Different times and situations would call for different measures, but Christian workers still can reveal the simplicity of Christ when they carry out ministry without excessive worldly entanglements.

Jesus said *"the worker is worth his keep,"* meaning that those who minister are to receive care from those to whom they minister. The disciples could expect food and shelter in return for the spiritual service they provided. These words are paralleled in Luke 10:17 and were quoted by Paul in 1 Timothy 5:18, where they are given the ascription, "the Scripture"—alongside a quotation of Deuteronomy 25:4. Thus, this Scripture was used by Paul to urge the churches to financially support the workers among them.

**10:11** **"Whatever town or village you enter, find out who in it is worthy, and stay there until you leave."** NRSV Each pair of disciples would enter a *town or village* and *stay* in a *worthy* person's house (that is, the home of a believer who had invited them to lodge there during their ministry). The command to *stay there* until they left the city cautioned them never to offend their hosts by looking for "better" lodging in a home that was more comfortable or socially prominent. To remain in one home would not be a burden for the home owner because the disciples' stay in each community would be brief. The "worthy" were those who would respond to and believe the gospel message.

Jesus instructed the disciples to depend on others while they went from town to town preaching the gospel. Their purpose was to blanket Galilee with Jesus' message, and by traveling light they could move quickly. Their dependence on others had three other good effects: (1) It clearly showed that the Messiah had not come to offer wealth to his followers; (2) it forced the disciples to rely on God's power and not on their own provision; and (3) it involved the villagers, making them more eager to hear the message. Staying in homes was an excellent approach for the disciples' short-term mission; this was not to be a permanent way of life for them. Yet the faith and simplicity that this way of life portrayed would serve them well in the future.

**10:12-13** **"And when you go into a household, greet it. If the household is worthy, let your peace come upon it. But if it is not worthy, let your peace return to you."** NKJV As the disciples entered a *household,* they were to *greet it.* The actual words of this greeting are recorded in Luke 10:5, "When you enter a house, first say, 'Peace to this house'" (NIV). At this time, people believed that blessings could be given as well as taken back. The disciples would bless the household upon entering. *If the household is worthy* (that is, had accepted them and their message), then the blessing of peace would remain upon that house. But if the household *is not worthy* (that is, did not accept their message), then the blessing of peace would *return to* the disciples, who would then leave that house. The peace returning from that house also indicated judgment to come (10:15). The words of blessing that the disciples had given would not be fulfilled there. These words mean that those who would receive the disciples also would receive the Messiah. Those who cared for God's emissaries would receive blessing in return: "Whoever welcomes you welcomes me, and whoever welcomes me welcomes the one who sent me" (10:40 NRSV).

**10:14** **"If anyone will not welcome you or listen to your words, shake off the dust from your feet as you leave that house or town."** NRSV The disciples should also expect rejection, such as Jesus had faced in Decapolis (8:34). So Jesus further instructed that *if anyone* did not *welcome* them (that is, take them in and offer hospitality) and refused even to *listen to* them, then they should *shake off the dust* from their feet as they left.

Shaking off dust that accumulated on one's sandals showed extreme contempt for an area and its people, as well as the determination not to have any further involvement with them. "Dust" was so common on highways that it came to signify that which clings to one's life (such as sin). To shake the dust off one's feet was a gesture of total repudiation. Pious Jews shook dust from their feet after passing through Gentile cities or territory to show their separation from Gentile influences and practices. When the disciples shook the dust from their feet after leaving a *Jewish* town, it would be a vivid sign that they wished to remain separate from people who had rejected Jesus.

Shaking off the dust of a place, Jesus said, would be a testimony against the people. Its implications were clear and had eternal consequences. The act showed the people that the disciples had discharged their duty, had nothing further to say, and would leave the people to answer to God. We should not take this verse to mean that if one member of a family refuses to accept Christ, we should abandon effort to the other members. Nor should we stop ministry to others in a community if there are some who reject our words. Jesus was saying that if the disciples were rejected by nonbelieving Jews, they should treat those Jews the same as nonbelieving Gentiles. By this statement, Jesus was making it clear that the listeners were responsible for what they did with the gospel. As long as the disciples had faithfully and carefully presented the message, they were not to blame if the townspeople rejected it. Likewise, we are not responsible when others reject Christ's message of salvation, but we do have the responsibility to share the gospel clearly and faithfully.

**10:15** **"Assuredly, I say to you, it will be more tolerable for the land of Sodom and Gomorrah in the day of judgment than for that city!"**NKJV God had destroyed the cities of Sodom and Gomorrah by fire from heaven because of their wickedness (Genesis 19:24-25). To Jews, the judgment of these cities was a lesson not only in punishment of great evil, but also in the finality of divine judgment. Those who reject the gospel will be worse off *in the day of judgment* than the wicked people of these destroyed cities who never had heard the gospel at all.

**10:16** **"I am sending you out like sheep among wolves. Therefore be as shrewd as snakes and as innocent as doves."**NIV The disciples would go out with the message *like sheep among wolves* (the "wolves" were the enemies of the believers—in this context probably the Jewish religious leaders). The solution? *Be as shrewd as snakes and as innocent as doves.* These words may have come from a local proverb. To be "shrewd as snakes" speaks of prudence or cleverness. The Egyptian symbol of wisdom is a serpent, which has great skill in avoiding danger. They were also to be "innocent as doves," that is, to be sincere and to have pure intentions. Shrewdness can become no more than cunning without the balance of innocence. However, innocence can become naïveté, or even ignorance if not balanced with shrewdness. Jesus' followers would need both to be prepared for the battles that lay ahead. They would need to be unafraid of conflict but also able to deal with it in integrity. Jesus warned them that the gospel would not be warmly welcomed in all places. At times there would be outright antagonism, as Jesus describes in the following verses.

---

SENSIBLE SHEEP?
The opposition of the Pharisees would be like ravaging wolves. The disciples' only hope would be to look to their Shepherd for protection. We may face similar hostility. Like the disciples, we should not be sheeplike in our attitude (thoughtless and unprepared), but sensible and prudent. We are not to be gullible pawns, but neither are we to be deceitful connivers. We must find a balance between wisdom and vulnerability in order to accomplish God's work.

---

## JESUS PREPARES THE DISCIPLES FOR PERSECUTION / 10:17-42 / **94**

**10:17-18** **"Beware of them, for they will hand you over to councils and flog you in their synagogues; and you will be dragged before governors and kings because of me, as a testimony to them and the Gentiles."** NRSV The danger of arrest and persecution would come from without *(governors, kings, Gentiles)* and from within *(councils, synagogues).* The "councils" were the local courts that settled small problems among the Jews. In the early days of the church, these were the prosecutors. "Flogging" was a form of punishment where a person was whipped with a leather whip across the back; the law allowed a maximum of forty lashes. These floggings often occurred in the synagogues themselves. The "governors and kings" referred to the pagan rulers who alone could demand the death penalty. The persecution, and perhaps death, that the disciples would face *because of* their relationship with Christ would be *a testimony to* the religious leaders and to the Gentiles. These persecutions would provide opportunities for presenting the gospel. Later, the disciples experienced these hardships (Acts 5:40; 12:1-3; 22:19; 2 Corinthians 11:24). Interestingly, the word "martyr" comes from this Greek word "witness" or "testimony."

Why would this happen? The new movement of Christianity would eventually face great opposition—from Jews and Gentiles alike. While it may not have seemed possible as these disciples roamed the hillsides with the popular teacher, a day would come when some would have to choose between their faith and

persecution (or death). Jesus warned that they would need to
focus on their mission and turn their defense into a testimony
for their faith. In times of persecution, we can be confident and
hopeful because Jesus has "overcome the world" (John 16:33).

---

**BEWARE**
Christians are not called to naïveté. We shouldn't be thoughtless and needn't be conned. We're not fools and don't have to
play the sucker to anyone's shell game.

It's one thing to suffer persecution, and another to walk
stupidly into the middle of a fire. "Beware" alerts us to study
human nature, know the world we live in, and exercise caution
without cynicism. If you're basically clueless about how the
world works, find a mature Christian who can teach you street
smarts without compromising standards. There is no harm in
knowing the other party's game plan.

---

**10:19-20** **"When they hand you over, do not worry about how you are
to speak or what you are to say; for what you are to say will
be given to you at that time; for it is not you who speak, but
the Spirit of your Father speaking through you."** NRSV Jesus
told the disciples that *when* (not "if") they were arrested and
handed over to the authorities, they should not worry about what
to say in their defense. The thought of being brought before Gentile rulers terrified any Jew, but Jesus warned his disciples not to
be afraid. *What you are to say will be given to you at that time*—
God's Spirit would speak through them. The phrase "Spirit of
your Father" is Old Testament language and recalls the inspiration of the prophets. Jesus described the Holy Spirit as a defense
lawyer coming to the disciples' aid. This verse and 3:11 are the
only places in which Matthew mentions the Holy Spirit. This
promise of an infilling of the Holy Spirit was fulfilled in Acts 2,
where the Spirit empowered the disciples to speak. Some mistakenly think this means believers do not have to prepare to present
the gospel because God will take care of everything. Scripture
teaches, however, that we are to make carefully prepared,
thoughtful statements (Colossians 4:6). Jesus was telling his followers to prepare but not to worry. He promised special inspiration for times of great need.

**10:21-22** **"Brother will betray brother to death, and a father his child,
and children will rise against parents and have them put to
death; and you will be hated by all because of my name."** NRSV
Jesus detailed some aspects of the coming persecution. The Jews
considered family denunciations and betrayals a sign of the end

times. These words may allude to Micah 7:6, "For the son treats the father with contempt, the daughter rises up against her mother, the daughter-in-law against her mother-in-law; your enemies are members of your own household" (NRSV). This passage speaks of internal corruption in Israel; Jesus said this was a sign of the last days. Not only will faith in Jesus tear families apart, but believers will also find that they will be *hated by all* types of people. As Jesus' disciples share his authority, they will also share his sufferings.

---

FAMILY BETRAYAL
When those closest to you become your worst enemies, you may wonder if faith is worth the hassle. Consider these four questions:
  1. Who's closest to you really?
  2. Whom can you count on when even a parent thinks you're on the wrong track?
  3. Who demands first priority in your life?
  4. Who can work miracles to mend a disrupted family?
If your response to all four questions is "Jesus," then you also know who loves your family more than you can and who wants to reach them with God's love, probably through you. Trust the Lord for each relationship you think is lost. Jesus is in the miracle business.

---

**"But the one who endures to the end will be saved."** NRSV These words have received a variety of interpretations. (1) *The one who endures to the end* of persecution (that is, keeps the faith through suffering) will be delivered from physical suffering. This we know can't be true because some have been martyred for their faith. (2) "The one who endures to the end" of life's trials will *be saved* into eternal life. That person will not face spiritual harm. This view tends to support a "salvation by works" viewpoint. (3) The one who endures until *the end* (meaning wholly, completely) will enter into Christ's kingdom. This view is more likely because standing firm to the end is not a way to be saved but the evidence that a person is really committed to Jesus. Persistence is not a means to earn salvation; it is the by-product of a truly devoted life. Jesus' point was that persecution will come and his followers must be patient and faithful through it. Their reward is certain.

> Besides being put to death they [Christians under Nero's persecution] were made to serve as objects of amusement; they were clad in the hides of beasts and torn to death by dogs; others were crucified; others set on fire to serve to illuminate the night.
> *Tacitus, Roman historian*

**10:23** **"When they persecute you in one town, flee to the next."** NRSV
While Jesus told the disciples to expect persecution, he also warned
them against foolhardiness. If they faced persecution in one town,
they were to *flee* to the next. They ought not cast their pearls before
swine (7:6), nor should they abort their ministry in fear. They were
to leave and move on if the persecution became too great. Perhaps
this is part of being "shrewd as snakes" (10:16). Persecution was
a regular experience of the early church. The apostle Paul faced
intense persecution. He fled Damascus by going down over the
wall in a basket (Acts 9:25). After being stoned and left for dead
outside of Lystra, Paul got up and moved on to Derbe (Acts 14:19-20).
Persecution did not halt the mission of the early church; in many
instances, it forced the believers to move out into the world to
spread the gospel (Acts 11:19).

**"For truly I tell you, you will not have gone through all the
towns of Israel before the Son of Man comes."** NRSV This difficult sentence has received many interpretations. Following are
five:

1. Some have understood this to focus on the immediate context
   of verses 5-16. The disciples would not have time to go
   through all the towns before Jesus would catch up with them.
   This interpretation is too simple, however, given the language
   in the text that refers to events after the resurrection of Christ.
   At the time of Matthew's writing, the disciples had completed
   the mission, so Jesus obviously was referring to something else.
2. Some suggest that the coming of the Son of Man refers to his
   coming judgment against the Jews, fulfilled in the destruction
   of Jerusalem in A.D. 70. But it is an unlikely interpretation to connect the destruction of Jerusalem with the return of the Son of
   Man.
3. Albert Schweitzer made this the key to his interpretation of
   Jesus, explaining that Jesus expected the end of time to happen
   before the disciples finished this mission. When it did not happen, said Schweitzer, Jesus switched to a more active role and
   tried to force it to come through his crucifixion. This view mis-
   interprets Jesus' words to apply only to the immediate context
   (as does number 1 above).
4. Still others explain that the "coming" refers to Jesus' appearance
   in triumph after his resurrection.
5. Because of the events of the book of Acts, it seems more likely
   that Jesus was referring to events after his resurrection. The
   meaning of his words would be that the task of the mission to
   the Jews would be so great and so difficult (for many would

refuse to believe) that it would not be accomplished even by the time of his second coming.

**10:24-25** **"A student is not above his teacher, nor a servant above his master. It is enough for the student to be like his teacher, and the servant like his master. If the head of the house has been called Beelzebub, how much more the members of his household!"** NIV Jesus used a common proverb stated two ways (*student* and *teacher; servant* and *master*) to show that both must share the same experiences. A student or servant is not *above* the teacher or master. In Judaism, a student (disciple) shared the daily experiences of his teacher; in pagan cultures, a servant fought beside his master. Both receive the same treatment.

Jesus used a play on words by saying *if the head of the house has been called Beelzebub* because "Beelzebub" meant "lord of the dwelling." Beelzebub was the god of Ekron (2 Kings 1:2-3, 6, 16). *Beelzeboul* (Greek) may have been a term coined on the spot by Jesus' accusers. The word has two parts: "Baal" which was the name for local Canaanite fertility gods in the Old Testament, and "Zebul" which means "exalted dwelling." This became a name for Satan himself, prince of the demons. The Pharisees did this very act, accusing Jesus of using Beelzebub's power to drive out demons (see 12:24). If Jesus, who is perfect, was called evil, *how much more the members of his household.* Jesus' followers should expect that they would face similar accusations. God promises to vindicate those who stand firm (10:22).

---

STICKS AND STONES
Jesus was accused of being Beelzebub, and he told his followers to expect the same treatment. Words are powerful weapons, and Jesus' disciples can count on hearing a good number of bad ones slung at them.
When you're the victim of intimidation or slander, keep your cool. Jesus took those knocks too. Instead of getting testy, try laughing a little, and if that doesn't quiet the name-calling, try a solid, forthright, clear-eyed comeback such as, "Would you please stop? That hurts, and it's not true."
Trading insult for insult is never Jesus' way.

---

**10:26** **"Therefore do not fear them. For there is nothing covered that will not be revealed, and hidden that will not be known."** NKJV Jesus' followers can expect persecution, but they must never be afraid. *"Do not fear,"* Jesus said. The gospel mission must be accomplished. The parallel in the phrases (*nothing covered* or *hidden* that will not be *revealed* or *known*) stresses that the truths entrusted to the disciples will be known no matter what the opposition. There is also a hint that the knowledge of the kingdom was presently vague or known in only a limited way, but would later be openly revealed by God. Although the truth may be "hidden" or kept secret for a while, it will not remain so. One day the truth will be "revealed" and "known." Jesus was speaking of the days of his ministry as the time of using parables, concealing the truth, and being rejected by many. The time of revelation would be either Jesus' resurrection and ascension (when his followers would fully understand Jesus' words) or the Second Coming. Jesus' followers did not understand everything about Jesus at that time, but one day all their questions would be answered.

**10:27** **"What I say to you in the dark, tell in the light; and what you hear whispered, proclaim from the housetops."** NRSV The *dark* is not a picture of sin, but of privacy. What Jesus had told them privately they were to proclaim publicly. These parallel phrases (*dark* and *light; what you hear whispered* and *proclaim from the housetops*) describe bold, public proclamation of the truths that Jesus had taught the disciples privately. To "proclaim from the housetops" pictured the common practice (since roofs were flat) of using roofs as platforms for making public announcements. The disciples had a mission and a responsibility to teach what they learned from Jesus.

**10:28** **"Do not be afraid of those who kill the body but cannot kill the soul. Rather, be afraid of the One who can destroy both soul and body in hell."** NIV The disciples might face death, yet Jesus warned them not to *be afraid.* People might be able to *kill the body,* but they would not be able to *kill the soul.* The only One worthy of our fear is God *who can destroy both soul and body in hell.* It is far more fearful to disobey God than to face martyrdom. The worst that people can do (kill the body) does not compare with the worst that God can do. While the Greeks believed that only the soul lived on after death, Jesus says unmistakably that hell is a place of destruction for soul *and* body—the whole person. (For more on hell, see commentary on 5:22.) Some have interpreted this as annihilation, the complete destruction of the person. But that conclusion is unwarranted by this verse. More likely, it is hyperbole, representing the fearful judgment of God. We are not to be afraid of people, but we are to be afraid of (that is, in awe of) God.

**10:29-31** **"Are not two sparrows sold for a penny? Yet not one of them will fall to the ground apart from the will of your Father. And even the very hairs of your head are all numbered. So don't be**

**afraid; you are worth more than many sparrows."** ᴺᴵⱽ This awe-some God whom we are to fear (10:28) is also the God who cares about the smallest sparrow. When we fear him, we have nothing to worry about because he loves us. *Sparrows* were the cheapest type of living food sold in the market; a *penny* was the smallest copper coin. Sparrows were not of high value in the world—a penny could buy two of them. Yet God is so concerned for them that *not one* falls to the ground without God's consent. That God knows the number of *the very hairs* on our heads shows his concern about the most trifling details about each of us. Because God is aware of everything that happens to sparrows, and because he knows every tiny detail about us, Jesus concludes that his followers need never *be afraid.* Sparrows *will* fall to the ground; God's people *will* die, sometimes by martyrdom. Yet we are so valuable that God sent Jesus, his only Son, to die for us (John 3:16). Because God places such value on us, we need never fear personal threats or difficult trials. God our Father is in control. He sees the sparrow fall; he knows and controls everything that happens to us. God cares not only about the "big" problems and situations of life, but also about the tiniest details.

---

WHEN BAD NEWS COMES
During the Vietnam war, the worst sight in the world (State-side) was two dress uniforms walking up to a door. It meant a casualty at that house, and many tears were shed at those doorsteps.

Bad news comes. People without an anchor—without God—are shaken to the foundations. Grief strikes us all with bitter arrows, but God's people rest in hope, respond with courage, and live on by faith. God's care for each of us is greater than the enemy's hatred. Grieve when bad news comes, but don't fear.

---

**10:32-33** **"Everyone therefore who acknowledges me before others, I also will acknowledge before my Father in heaven; but who-ever denies me before others, I also will deny before my Father in heaven."** ᴺᴿˢⱽ People have a clear choice. *Everyone who acknowledges* Jesus Christ (that is, publicly confesses faith in or declares allegiance to him) will be acknowledged by Christ before his *Father in heaven.* Jesus' followers would face earthly courts of law where they would have to publicly claim to belong to Jesus Christ, usually at their peril (10:17-25). But for the disciple to acknowledge Jesus means that Jesus will claim that disciple as his own before the Father in heaven.

On the other hand, the person who *denies* their relationship to

Jesus Christ would in turn face denial by Jesus before the Father. These words refer to those whose true allegiance would be revealed under pressure. Jesus probably did not refer to those who formerly believed and fell away (for no profession of faith has been mentioned or implied). Matthew stressed the Last Judgment and the relationship between the Father and the Son. Jesus was making the astounding statement that each person's standing before God is based on his or her relationship to Jesus Christ. Jesus is the advocate whose intercession before God will depend on one's faithfulness in acknowledging him.

It has never ceased to amaze me that we Christians have developed a kind of selective vision which allows us to be deeply and sincerely involved in worship and church activities and yet almost totally pagan in the day-in, day-out guts of our business lives . . . and never realize it.

*Keith Miller*

**10:34** **"Do not think that I came to bring peace on earth. I did not come to bring peace but a sword."**[NKJV] The Jews believed that when the Messiah came, he would usher in a time of world peace. Jesus' first arrival would not bring that universal peace. The very nature of Jesus' claims forces people to make a choice. They must choose to believe who he said he is, or they must choose to reject him. Jesus did not come to bring *peace* but a *sword* (that is, "division") that separates families, friends, and nations. Conflict and disagreement will arise between those who choose to follow Christ and those who do not. In saying this, Jesus was not encouraging disobedience to parents or conflict at home. Rather, he was showing that his presence demands a decision. Because some will follow Christ and some will not, conflict will inevitably arise. As his followers take their crosses and follow him, their different values, morals, goals, and purposes will set them apart. Do not neglect your family, but remember that your commitment to God is even more important than they are. God should be your first priority. Ironically, those who accept him *do* find inner peace because of their restored relationship with God. One day, however, there *will* be universal peace (Isaiah 9:5-7), for the Prince of Peace will resolve all conflict. For more on Jesus as peacemaker, see Zechariah 9:9-10; Matthew 5:9; John 14:27.

**10:35-36** **"For I have come to set a man against his father, and a daughter against her mother, and a daughter-in-law against her mother-in-law; and one's foes will be members of one's own household."**[NRSV] Jesus was quoting from Micah 7:6 (already alluded to in 10:21, see commentary above). In Micah, these divisive conditions led to a yearning for the Messiah; in this context they were caused

## COUNTING THE COST OF FOLLOWING CHRIST

Jesus helped his disciples prepare for the rejection that many of them would experience by being Christians. Being God's person will usually create reactions from others who are resisting him.

| Who may oppose us? | Natural response | Possible pressures | Needed truth |
|---|---|---|---|
| GOVERNMENT 10:18-19 | | Threats 10:26 | The truth will be revealed (10:26). |
| | | Physical harm 10:28 | Our soul cannot be harmed (10:28). |
| RELIGIOUS PEOPLE 10:17 | Fear and worry | Public ridicule 10:22 | God himself will acknowledge us if we acknowledge him (10:32). |
| FAMILY 10:21 | | Rejection by loved ones 10:34-37 | God's love can sustain us (10:31). |

by the Messiah's coming. Jesus explained the response to his call—there will inevitably be conflict between those who respond and those who do not. Sometimes the reaction is violent, and angry family members become like *foes*. In the early church, Jews who became Christians were excommunicated from the synagogues and often shunned by their families. Even today, the road is difficult for Jews or Muslims who turn to Christianity. Their own family members become their worst enemies. Jesus did not *come* to make such divisions happen; instead, his coming, his words, and his call inevitably will cause conflict between those who accept him and those who reject him.

**10:37** **"Whoever loves father or mother more than me is not worthy of me; and whoever loves son or daughter more than me is not worthy of me."** NRSV Jesus did not force his followers to break family ties to follow him (as opposed to some present-day cults). Jesus was pointing out that his disciples must have singular loyalty to him. When discipleship conflicts with family loyalty, following Jesus must take the priority over natural love of family. If one must choose, one must take Jesus. Christ calls us to a higher mission than to find comfort and tranquillity in this life. Love of family is a law of God (see Ephesians 6:1-4; 1 Timothy 5:8), but even this love can be self-serving and used as an excuse not to serve God or do his work. We must not be so devoted or enmeshed in family love that we push Christ into the background.

**10:38** **"And whoever does not take up the cross and follow me is not worthy of me."** NRSV These words applied to the disciples and to all who want to be *worthy of* Jesus ("worthy" meaning willing to follow and serve, as in 10:11). To *take up the cross* was a vivid illustration of the humility and submission that Jesus asked of his followers. When Jesus used this picture of his followers taking up their crosses to follow him, the people knew what "taking up the cross" meant. Death on a cross was a form of execution used by the Roman Empire for dangerous criminals and political prisoners. A prisoner carried his own crossbar to the place of execution. Jesus' followers faced social and political oppression and ostracism; yet he warned them against turning back. For some, taking up the cross might indeed mean death; for all, it means denying self. Jesus' words meant that his followers had to obey God's Word, spread the gospel, and follow his will, no matter what the results were for them personally. Soon after this, Jesus would take up his own cross. Jesus was speaking prophetically here as well. Jesus' words became graphically clear after his crucifixion.

To *follow* Christ is a moment-by-moment decision, requiring denial of self and taking up one's cross. Following Jesus does not mean walking behind him, but taking the same road of sacrifice and service that he took. The blessing for us is that he walks with us along the way.

**10:39** **"Those who find their life will lose it, and those who lose their life for my sake will find it."** NRSV This verse is a positive and negative statement of the same truth: Clinging to this life may cause us to forfeit the best from Christ in this world and in the next. The Christian life is a paradox: To attempt to *find* (or save) your life means only to *lose* it. The Greek word for "life" is *psuche;* it refers to the soul, the total person, the self, which includes the personality with all its dreams, hopes, and goals. A person who "finds" his or her life to satisfy desires and goals apart from God ultimately "loses" life. Not only does that person lose the eternal life offered only to those who believe and accept Christ as Savior, but he or she loses the fullness of life promised to those who believe.

By contrast, those who willingly "lose" their lives for the sake of Christ actually "find" them. They will receive great reward in God's kingdom. To lose one's life for Christ's sake refers to a person refusing to renounce Christ, even if the punishment were death.

Jesus preached on this theme more often than we may wish to acknowledge:

- "Those who find their life will lose it, and those who lose their life for my sake will find it" (Matthew 10:39 NRSV).
- "For those who want to save their life will lose it, and those who lose their life for my sake will find it" (Matthew 16:25 NRSV).
- "For those who want to save their life will lose it, and those who lose their life for my sake, and for the sake of the gospel, will save it" (Mark 8:35 NRSV).
- "For those who want to save their life will lose it, and those who lose their life for my sake will save it" (Luke 9:24 NRSV).
- "Those who try to make their life secure will lose it, but those who lose their life will keep it" (Luke 17:33 NRSV).
- "Those who love their life lose it, and those who hate their life in this world will keep it for eternal life" (John 12:25 NRSV).

It would be easier to give one's life in battle or in martyrdom than to do what Christ actually asks of us. Not only does Christ demand loyalty over family, he also demands loyalty over every part of our lives. The more we love this life's rewards (leisure, power, popularity, financial security), the more we will discover how empty they really are. The best way to "find" life, therefore, is to loosen our greedy grasp on earthly rewards so that we can be free to follow Christ. We must risk pain, discomfort, conflict, and stress. We must acknowledge Christ's claim over our destiny and our career. In doing so, we will inherit eternal life and begin at once to experience the benefits of following Christ.

PATH TO GREATNESS
The gospel takes us by surprise. We think we have life pretty well figured; then God upsets our schemes and shows us a better way.

Take your life, for example. Ambitious life goals are without a doubt one of the best aspirations a person can have—incentive, drive, challenge, direction. Then God announces, "Wrong! This is not my way!"

Without Christ, ambition is pointless and challenge misdirected. But a life surrendered to Christ gains eternal focus and divine incentive.

Want to find your life? Put Jesus first, let his Word be your guiding light, and get close to others who know him well. Welcome to a new path to greatness!

**10:40-42** **"Whoever welcomes you welcomes me, and whoever welcomes me welcomes the one who sent me."** NRSV In 10:11-14, Jesus described how the disciples should go about their ministry—staying in homes of worthy people. Those who would *welcome* the disciples would receive great reward. The word "welcomes" may refer both to hospitality (receiving the messenger) as well as conversion (receiving the message). Jesus' representatives carry all his authority. Those who welcome the disciples welcome Jesus; those who welcome Jesus welcome *the one who sent Jesus*—God the Father. Again Jesus unmistakably claims his relationship to God. Jesus spoke these words to his twelve disciples, but then repeated the saying three more times using prophets, righteous people, and little ones. **"Whoever welcomes a prophet in the name of a prophet will receive a prophet's reward; and whoever welcomes a righteous person in the name of a righteous person will receive the reward of the righteous; and whoever gives even a cup of cold water to one of these little ones in the name of a disciple—truly I tell you, none of these will lose their reward."** NRSV To give *a cup of cold water* was an important act of courtesy and hospitality. It would not be out of the ordinary and, therefore, would deserve no *reward*. The disciples definitely were "little ones" who were insignificant and despised in the eyes of the world. Those who would *receive* (welcome) the disciples merely because they were disciples would not lose their reward. Because the disciples would come with God's authority, their acceptance by people would test the people's attitudes toward God. It is *that* attitude that leads either to reward or loss of reward. For more on rewards, see 16:24-27; 19:28-30.

# Matthew 11

Opposition against Jesus began to grow as Jesus prophesied in chapter 10. Even John the Baptist had some misunderstanding. At first the opposition is implicit; later it will be explicit.

**11:1 After Jesus had finished instructing his twelve disciples, he went on from there to teach and preach in the towns of Galilee.**NIV This verse forms a transition from chapter 10. Jesus *finished instructing his twelve disciples* (for the time being) and *went on from there to teach and preach in the towns of Galilee*. The constant separation between "teach" and "preach" in Matthew may prepare for *didache* (instruction) and *kerygma* (proclamation) in the early church.

Mark's Gospel describes the sending out and return of the disciples (following Jesus' instructions outlined in the previous chapter). Matthew, however, maintains his focus on Jesus' ministry and teaching.

**11:2-3 When John heard in prison what Christ was doing, he sent his disciples to ask him, "Are you the one who was to come, or should we expect someone else?"**NIV King Herod, also known as Herod Antipas, had imprisoned John the Baptist (4:12). Herod Antipas was known for his insensitivity and debauchery. He had married his own sister-in-law, and John the Baptist had publicly rebuked Herod's blatant sin (more on this incident in 14:1-12).

While John sat in prison, word came to him about *what Christ was doing*. John the Baptist had his own *disciples* who apparently remained close to him during his imprisonment.

> The first step back from doubt to faith is to bring one's plight to the Lord Jesus Himself. It is no sin to ask a question if our heart attitude is right.
>
> *V. Raymond Edman*

They brought news of Jesus' activities, most likely those deeds that reflected that he was the Messiah (such as those described in chapters 8 and 9). This caused John to wonder, so he sent his disciples back to Jesus with a question, *Are you the one who was to come?* John was referring to the promised Messiah. This statement provides a glimpse of John's human side. He had baptized Jesus, had seen the heavens open, and had heard the voice of God (3:13-17), yet he was experiencing periods of doubt and questioning. Perhaps John was wondering why Jesus brought blessing but little judgment, for John had preached that Jesus would baptize with fire and separate the "wheat" from the "chaff" (3:11-12). Jesus' peaceful teaching and healing ministry may not have seemed to measure up. Perhaps John was wondering about the veiled terms in which Jesus was giving his teachings.

Whatever the reason, John's question functions as a conclusion to all that has happened so far in this Gospel, summarizing the necessary reaction to Jesus' deeds and the mission of his disciples. It was not John's question alone; the question highlights what every person must decide when he or she encounters Jesus. Matthew used the name "Christ" to show his readers that while John may have doubted, Jesus was unmistakably showing that he was indeed "the one who was to come."

---

**HONEST QUESTIONS**
Never be embarrassed when asking a sincere question. And never make anyone else feel ashamed to ask one. Even John the Baptist, God's special messenger, had questions. To live is to discover, and no one learns without raising questions. Good questions indicate good listening.

Wonder about something the pastor said on Sunday? Ask. Wonder about something you read in Matthew's Gospel? Ask. How does faith relate to the problems you face this week? Keep asking until you make some solid discoveries.

---

**11:4-6 Jesus answered them, "Go and tell John what you hear and see: the blind receive their sight, the lame walk, the lepers are cleansed, the deaf hear, the dead are raised, and the poor have good news brought to them. And blessed is anyone who takes no offense at me."** NRSV Jesus answered John's doubts by telling John's disciples to *go and tell John what you hear and see.* Jesus pointed to his acts of healing the blind, lame, deaf, and leprous, raising the dead, and preaching the Good News to the poor. With so much evidence, Jesus' identity should have been obvious—Jesus expected his courageous forerunner to come to the correct conclusion. These words reflect Isaiah 35:5-6, Isaiah's prophecy of the final kingdom. The Messiah's arrival was the first phase of this coming kingdom. Jesus fulfilled these words even though Matthew had not yet recorded any healings of lame or deaf people, and Matthew added the cleansing of lepers and raising of dead people to Isaiah's list. That *the poor have good news brought to them* reflects Isaiah 61:1. "The poor" are the small group of faithful followers, the oppressed and afflicted, who respond to the Good News. They are *blessed* because they take *no offense* at Jesus, willingly accepting him as the promised Messiah.

Many Jews, however, *did* take offense at Jesus. Some versions say "cause to stumble," referring to Jews "stumbling" over Jesus because he did not meet their messianic expectations. While Jesus' words and deeds were worthy of the Messiah, he did not meet the Jewish leaders' political and nationalistic interpretations of him. So Jesus warned John and all the Jews not to allow their expectations to drive a wedge between them.

**11:7-8 As they went away, Jesus began to speak to the crowds about John: "What did you go out into the wilderness to look at? A reed shaken by the wind? What then did you go out to see? Someone dressed in soft robes? Look, those who wear soft robes are in royal palaces."** NRSV As John's disciples left with Jesus' message, Jesus took the opportunity to address the crowds. He asked three questions and gave three answers. John the Baptist came preaching in the wilderness, and people went out to listen to him (3:1, 5). Jesus asked if the people had gone into the wilderness to see *a reed shaken by the wind*. A "reed" is the canelike grass that grows on the banks of the Jordan River. To compare a person to a reed was to say that the person was without moral fiber or courage, easily tossed about by various opinions, never taking a stand on anything. Obviously, they did not go to see a "reed"—John's fiery preaching was anything but that. The people who went out to see him had been attracted by the opposite quality.

Second, Jesus asked if they had gone out to see *someone dressed in soft robes*. Obviously, John's rough attire (clothes made of camel's hair, 3:4) hardly qualified as "soft robes." If the people wanted to go look at someone dressed like that, they should go to the *royal palaces* (such as King Herod occupied), not to the wilderness. The people who went out to see John appreciated his prophetic power.

**11:9-10 "Then what did you go out to see? A prophet? Yes, I tell you, and more than a prophet. This is the one about whom it is written: 'I will send my messenger ahead of you, who will prepare your way before you.'"** NIV In this third question, Jesus asked if the people had gone out into the wilderness to see *a prophet*. That was, in fact, true—they had. The people knew that John's appearance meant that something new was about to happen; many believed the age of the Messiah had come. They went out to see a prophet and had seen one; in fact, they had seen, Jesus said, *more than a prophet*. Jesus described John as "more" because he had inaugurated the messianic age and had announced the coming kingdom of God (see also 3:3). More than being a prophet, John had been the subject of prophecy, fulfilling Malachi 3:1 (and Exodus 23:20 in the Septuagint). Jesus changed the words "before me" to "before you" so the wording refers to Jesus as the Messiah.

**11:11** **"Truly I tell you, among those born of women no one has arisen greater than John the Baptist; yet the least in the kingdom of heaven is greater than he."** [NRSV] The words "truly I tell you" indicate that Jesus was about to say something of supreme importance. The words "no one has arisen" use Old Testament language for the coming of a prophet. John the Baptist's role as forerunner of the Messiah put him in a position of great privilege, described as "more than a prophet" (11:9) with *no one . . . greater*. No man ever fulfilled his God-given purpose better than John. Yet in God's coming kingdom, all members will have a greater spiritual heritage than John because they will have seen and known Christ and his finished work on the cross. The *least in the kingdom of heaven* are those of the faithful followers who participate in the kingdom. John would die before Jesus would die and rise again to inaugurate his kingdom. Jesus' followers, because they will witness the kingdom's reality, will have privilege and place *greater* than John's.

**11:12** **"From the days of John the Baptist until now the kingdom of heaven has suffered violence, and the violent take it by force."** [NRSV] There are several views about the meaning of this verse. The interpretation hinges on the meaning of *biazetai,* "suffered violence" and *biastai* "the violent." The NIV gives this verse a more positive meaning by understanding *biazetai* to be in the middle voice rather than in the passive—thus, the rendering, "the kingdom of heaven has been forcefully advancing, and forceful men lay hold of it." This would mean that entering God's kingdom takes aggressive, assertive action. The NRSV takes the verb as passive, indicating that the kingdom has suffered violence. This means that evil, violent forces have worked against the kingdom. Some have suggested that Jesus' words had a temporal meaning, that they referred to Herod's opposition to John as well as to the Jewish opponents of John and Jesus. Others interpret the entire phrase timelessly in reference to the word "kingdom," implying the antagonism of satanic forces or the attempts of Jewish zealots to force the coming of the kingdom by overthrowing Rome. Most likely, this is a reference to Jesus' opponents. Jesus was explaining that as his kingdom advanced, attacks against it by violent people would increase. He referred not to just one type of opposition, but to opposition in general. John the Baptist, as herald of the arrival of the kingdom of heaven, was already experiencing the "forcefulness" of evil men (Herod) against God's kingdom. The conflict had begun.

**1:13-15** **"For all the Prophets and the Law prophesied until John. And if you are willing to accept it, he is the Elijah who was to come. He who has ears, let him hear."**[NIV] *All the Prophets and the Law* had prophesied about the coming of God's kingdom. The Jews called the Old Testament by its three main sections—the Prophets, the Law, and the Writings. In reality, all three point to Jesus' coming (see 5:17-20). John fulfilled prophecy, for he himself was *the Elijah who was to come,* prophesied in Malachi 4:5. John was not a resurrected Elijah, but he took on Elijah's prophetic role—boldly confronting sin and pointing people to God (Malachi 3:1). Jesus understood how difficult it was for the people to grasp all that they were seeing and hearing, for he said, *"If you are willing to accept it."* Indeed, many would be unwilling. Only those who had *ears* would be able to truly *hear* what Jesus meant by the words he said. Only those with the desire of true disciples could truly understand Jesus' words. He spoke in words that could easily put off the half-hearted follower. These were important words that could be easily misunderstood (see also 13:9, 43; 24:15).

---

**REALLY LISTENING**
Jesus said that those who have ears should "hear." Sometimes you can hear words, even understand words, and still not get the message. That often happened to the Pharisees, who knew the Bible better than anyone but didn't really know it at all. Great listening requires

- *Understanding the context of a message.* Words taken out of context are often misunderstood. Learn as much as you can about the whole situation.
- *Understanding the messenger.* Who's talking? What's his or her credibility? What are the biases and presuppositions? Is the messenger trustworthy?
- *What's the purpose of the message?* "I have a dream" can be a stirring call to social justice or an appeal for help on a psychiatrist's couch. What are the words doing to people?

Much of Jesus' ministry was helping people listen better—to the Old Testament prophets and to God himself speaking through Jesus. Listen carefully!

---

**11:16-19** **"But to what shall I liken this generation? It is like children sitting in the marketplaces and calling to their companions, and saying: 'We played the flute for you, and you did not dance; we mourned to you, and you did not lament.'"** NKJV The phrase "to what shall I liken" was a common rabbinic introduction to a metaphor. Matthew used the word *generation* for Jews who rejected both John the Baptist and Jesus. Jesus condemned the attitude of his generation. No matter what he said or did, they took the opposite view. They were cynical and skeptical because he challenged their comfortable, secure, and self-centered lives. Jesus compared them to *children sitting in the marketplaces,* playing games in the public square where the city's business was conducted. These games may copy the adults (such as playing instruments for a wedding or mourning at a funeral procession). The thrust is that some of the children called out to others to join them, but their companions ignored their invitation and went on playing their own games. Jesus' generation, like the children in the square, was unresponsive to the calls issued by John the Baptist and by Jesus. Jesus continued: **"For John came neither eating nor drinking, and they say, 'He has a demon'; the Son of Man came eating and drinking, and they say, 'Look, a glutton and a drunkard, a friend of tax collectors and sinners!'"** NRSV The one "mourning" refers to John the Baptist, who brought the message of confession and repentance to avoid the wrath of God. He came *neither eating nor drinking,* yet that did not satisfy the Jews. John was an ascetic; he did not seek out social occasions. They assumed that he had *a demon* (or was merely deranged). In contrast, the one "playing the flute" referred to Jesus (here he called himself *Son of Man*), who came *eating and drinking.* He joined in social occasions, and his diet was like other people's. But that did not satisfy the Jews either. They simply labeled him as a *glutton and a drunkard* who hung out with the lowest sort of people. Many of the Jews in Jesus' generation, including most of the religious establishment, simply refused to listen and went about their own "games."

**"Yet wisdom is vindicated by her deeds."** NRSV This is God's *wisdom,* personified as a woman *(her deeds).* (See also Proverbs 1:20; 4:6; 7:4; 8:1 for more verses personifying wisdom.) God's wisdom is seen in Jesus' deeds. People could see the kingdom's power through Jesus' miracles. These miracles *vindicated* (justified) Jesus' teaching. People might reject both the miracles and the teaching, but that will not change their truth nor will it hinder the kingdom's arrival.

THE BEST APOLOGETICS
The truth of Jesus' words were vindicated by miracles, both the
healings and the transformed lives of his followers. "Apologetics"
is the discipline of setting out proofs for biblical truth. Why do
we believe? People who "do apologetics" help us with that
question.

Here, however, Jesus surprises us. The best proof that his
words are true: It's *you!* Your life changed from the inside out
by Jesus' power is the best evidence to a skeptical world that
Jesus speaks the truth.

It's a big responsibility, but go easy on yourself. Being a
"perfect" person is impossible and self-defeating. Instead, just
let Jesus work inside your heart and mind. The changes he
brings will speak volumes to a watching world.

## JESUS PROMISES REST FOR THE SOUL / 11:20-30 / 71

**11:20** **Then Jesus began to denounce the cities in which most of his
miracles had been performed, because they did not repent.**[NIV]
Matthew's thematic structure places Jesus' denunciation of these
cities immediately after he had spoken of being rejected by his
own people (11:16-19). In Luke, these words are part of the mission
discourse to the seventy-two disciples (Luke 10:13-16); Matthew
used them to illustrate the rejection of the multitudes. *The cities*
Jesus denounced were those *in which most of his miracles had been
performed.* Because his words were vindicated by his deeds (11:19),
those people should have been eager to *repent* and believe. Instead,
they rejected Jesus, the Messiah. Many had followed Jesus and had
eagerly come to him to be healed or to watch him heal, but few had
repented and believed in him as the "one who was to come" (11:3).

**11:21-22** **"Woe to you, Korazin! Woe to you, Bethsaida! If the miracles that
were performed in you had been performed in Tyre and Sidon,
they would have repented long ago in sackcloth and ashes. But
I tell you, it will be more bearable for Tyre and Sidon on the
day of judgment than for you."**[NIV] For their unbelief, the unrepen-
tant cities would receive judgment, and "woe" is an expression of
grief or regret. The people of *Korazin* (also spelled "Chorazin")
and *Bethsaida* had seen Jesus firsthand (both cities were in Galilee);
yet they stubbornly refused to repent of their sins and believe in
him. Matthew recorded no miracles in either of these cities
although, obviously, Jesus had done miracles there. The Gospel
writers were necessarily selective in what they recorded. As John
wrote at the end of his Gospel, "Jesus did many other things as

well. If every one of them were written down, I suppose that even
the whole world would not have room for the books that would be
written" (John 21:25 NIV).

*Tyre and Sidon* were ancient Phoenician cities with a long-
standing reputation for wickedness (Isaiah 23; Ezekiel 27–28; Amos
1:9-10). God destroyed each city for its opposition to his people
and for its wickedness as a center of Baal worship. (Destruction
for Sidon had come at the hands of the Assyrians in 67 B.C.; for
Tyre it had come at the hands of Alexander the Great who had built
a causeway out to the island fortress and had destroyed it in 332
B.C.) Herod the Great partially restored Tyre. Citizens from there
may well have heard these very words of Jesus.

Jesus said, however, that if he had *performed* the same miracles
in those wicked cities, the people *would have repented . . . in sackcloth and ashes.* "Sackcloth and ashes" were symbols of humiliation, grief for sin, and repentance. Sackcloth was a cheap cloth
made of camel or cattle hair, worn under or in place of garments
during times of grief. For extreme grief, a person might also wear
ashes on his or her head, or sit and wallow in ashes. Such would
have been the display of repentance in these evil cities.

Because Korazin and Bethsaida had rejected Jesus, they would
suffer even greater punishment than that of the wicked cities who
did not see him. Those people had less opportunity to believe;
therefore, they would be accountable for less. The *day of judgment* would be *more bearable* for them. Similarly, nations and
cities with churches on every corner and Bibles in every home
will have no excuse on Judgment Day if they do not repent and
believe.

**11:23-24** **"And you, Capernaum, will you be exalted to heaven? No,
you will be brought down to Hades. For if the deeds of power
done in you had been done in Sodom, it would have remained
until this day. But I tell you that on the day of judgment it
will be more tolerable for the land of Sodom than for
you."** NRSV Jesus singled out the city of *Capernaum* for special
denunciation. Jesus had made his home in this city (4:12-13) and
had performed countless miracles there (8:5-17; 9:2-8, 18-33;
Mark 1:23-28). But would it *be exalted to heaven* for that reason?
*No,* Jesus said, in fact, just the opposite. Instead of being
"exalted," it would be "brought down." Instead of "heaven," it
would experience "Hades." These words allude to one of Isaiah's
prophecies against Babylon (Isaiah 14:13-15). The word "Hades"
is used in the Septuagint (Greek version of the Hebrew Old Testament) for "Sheol," which is the Old Testament word for the

grave, the abode of the dead. Here Jesus used it in a general sense for God's judgment.

As in 11:21-22 above, Jesus was comparing a city that he personally had visited (in this case, had lived in) with one of the most evil cities in the Old Testament. Indeed, if the city of *Sodom* had seen Jesus' *deeds of power,* Sodom *would have remained until this day.* God had destroyed the cities of Sodom and Gomorrah for their extreme wickedness (Genesis 18–19). Jesus implied that the city would have repented of its sin and therefore would not have been destroyed by God. Sodom and Gomorrah were already mentioned in 10:15 as being better off on the Day of Judgment than those cities who would refuse the disciples' message. Even Capernaum itself would be worse off than the worst of the Old Testament cities, simply because it was the home of the Messiah. Its people had seen Jesus, and they had rejected him.

---

**CLOSE TO HOME**
Capernaum, Jesus' adult hometown, should, of all cities, have been keen to see the truth of God's Good News. But it wasn't. And on Judgment Day, a person will be happier to be from Sodom than from Capernaum.

How disastrous when those closest to truth turn away! Some churches do that when they move from faith to doubt, from a focus on Jesus to a focus on everything but Jesus. When selecting a church, look beyond the architecture, the greeting committees, and the nursery facilities. Is Jesus at the heart of it?

---

**1:25-26** **At that time Jesus said, "I praise you, Father, Lord of heaven and earth, because you have hidden these things from the wise and learned, and revealed them to little children. Yes, Father, for this was your good pleasure."** NIV Jesus' response to his rejection, however, was to *praise* his Father. "Praise" is a strong term for worship, signifying acceptance and thanksgiving for God's act. The word for "Father" is the Aramaic *Abba,* signifying close relationship. "Lord of heaven and earth" is a Jewish title for God, stressing his lordship of the universe.

For what did Jesus praise the Father? He praised God for hiding the significance of his words and miracles *from the wise and learned* (that is, those arrogant in their own knowledge) and for revealing these to *little children* (those humbly open to receive the truth of God's Word, a euphemism for his disciples). While this contrasted all self-sufficient and proud people with the humble, it was also a contrast between the self-righteous religious leaders and the humble and unlearned disciples. That God had revealed himself in this way was not an accident; it was his *good pleasure.* Spiritual understanding is not dependent on status, race, or education—it is God's gift. (See also Isaiah 29:14; 1 Corinthians 1:19-20; James 4:6.) God is sovereign. He also hides and reveals as he chooses. Jesus delighted in this—what pleased the Father pleased the Son (as Jesus clearly stated in the next verse).

**11:27 "All things have been committed to me by my Father. No one knows the Son except the Father, and no one knows the Father except the Son and those to whom the Son chooses to reveal him."** NIV Jesus clearly stated his relationship to the Father of whom he spoke in 11:25. He made three unmistakable claims to special relationship with God:

1. *All things have been committed to me by my Father.* These words explain shared knowledge. There are no secrets between Father and Son and never have been. The present perfect tense of "have been committed" indicates that this has been the case from eternity past into eternity future. Jesus is the only source of the revelation that is hidden or revealed (11:25-26).
2. *No one knows the Son except the Father.* In the Old Testament, "know" means more than knowledge; it implies an intimate relationship. The communion between God the Father and God the Son is the core of their relationship. Jesus claimed an intimate relationship that no one else can ever have. Those who make Jesus out to be nothing more than a great teacher have ignored such statements as this, statements that force us to a decision as to whether Jesus really is who he claimed to be.
3. *No one knows the Father except the Son and those to whom the Son chooses to reveal him.* For anyone else to know God, God must reveal himself to that person, by the Son's choice. How fortunate we are that Jesus has clearly revealed to us God, his truth, and how we can know him. People can only approach God through Jesus—he truly is the only way (John 14:6). That Jesus praised the Father for making this choice (11:26) and then explained that the Father had given the Son this authority again emphasizes Jesus' true identity.

**11:28 "Come to Me, all you who labor and are heavy laden, and I will give you rest."** NKJV While those wise and learned in their own eyes are blinded to the truth (11:25-26), Jesus invites those who *labor and are heavy laden.* The "wise and learned" Pharisees had placed so many rules and regulations on the people that religion had become like "labor," and a life of devotion to the law had become a burden to carry (see 23:1-4). But Jesus invited the "little ones," true disciples with eyes open to see the truth, to *come to* him and find relief from these labors. Jesus was clearly admonishing them to abandon Pharisaic legalism and join him.

Jesus' gracious invitation extends to all. No one is omitted or neglected. All we must do is acknowledge our need and come to him. Jesus frees people from these burdens. The rest that Jesus gives equals eternal life (Hebrews 4:9) and brings love, healing, and peace with God, not the cessation of work, effort, worship, or service. To the Jews, rest reminded them of the Promised Land given to their ancestors. Jesus applied the word "rest" to himself spiritually, *"I will give you rest,* I will refresh you" (see Jeremiah 31:25). Those who follow Christ will find refreshment in their renewed relationship with him, freedom from guilt over sin, deliverance from fear and despair, and the promise of continued help and guidance from the Holy Spirit. (See Hebrews 3–4 for more on the New Testament view of rest.)

> Ah, downcast soul, who art writing hard things of thyself, it may be that thy merciful Lord is viewing thy life more accurately and estimating it more lovingly than thou knowest!          *F. B. Meyer*

---

**ONLY JESUS**
"Pluralism" is a recent trend that seeks to promote respect for all points of view, all faiths, all ethnic traditions.

On the one hand, Christians should respect and care for all people, regardless of differences. There is no holy excuse for nastiness or prejudice.

But, on the other hand, Jesus alone is the world's Savior. There is no other. You cannot worship a hundred gods, or two—there's only one! Put all your trust in Jesus. Depend on him alone.

---

**1:29-30** **"Take My yoke upon you and learn from Me, for I am gentle and lowly in heart, and you will find rest for your souls. For My yoke is easy and My burden is light."** NKJV A yoke is a heavy wooden harness that fits over the shoulders of an ox or oxen. It is attached to a piece of equipment that the oxen are to pull. Since Jesus was a carpenter and since carpenters in those days produced and repaired farm equipment, Jesus was quite familar with yokes.

The Law was a "yoke" that was considered hard to bear (as Peter noted in Acts 15:10). Jesus used the familiar phrasing used of the law as an invitation to discipleship. "Take off the burdensome yoke of the Pharisee-styled law," Jesus said, "and *take My yoke upon you.*" Following Jesus would not be a free ride; Jesus had already described the persecution and rejection his followers could expect

(10:17-42). They were not free from all constraints; they would carry a yoke, but it would be *easy* and *light.* Again, this did not belittle the importance or difficulty of carrying out his mission; indeed, Jesus asked for *more* than mere obedience to the law. Discipleship required extraordinary effort. These words focused on Jesus' care and concern for his followers, his promise of guidance and presence (28:20), and the ultimate future rewards. The efforts of Jesus' followers would not result in dead-end toil or drudgery or in frustrating cycles of guilt and depression from trying to please God by being good enough. Jesus' yoke would result in fruitful service. Jesus had God's ultimate authority (11:27), and he was calling them to him. These images come from Old Testament prophecy about the Messiah (see Isaiah 42:2-3; 53:1-2; Zechariah 9:9). He would not be an unkind taskmaster; instead, he would bring *rest* to the souls of his followers (quoted from Jeremiah 6:16).

Jesus said, *"Learn from Me."* Jesus, their leader and example, was also the ultimate servant, *gentle and lowly in heart.* His path of humble service is the pattern for us to follow. So much of our fatigue and burdensome toil stems from pride. If we are successful, our egos are inflated and we try for more. If we falter, the rejection of others and our self-condemnation weigh us down in guilt and self-doubt. It is much more freeing to take Christ's attitude of serving others.

---

EASY DOES IT!
Responsibilities weigh us down, even the job of staying true to God. It's a tough grind, and you're tired. You may be trying hard and still falling short of the mark. Jesus says, "My yoke is easy."
Jesus doesn't offer you a lawn chair and soda—the yoke is still an oxen's tool for working hard. But it's a special kind of yoke, with weight falling on bigger shoulders than yours. Someone with more pulling power is up front helping. Suddenly you're sharing life's responsibilities with a great Partner—and now that frown is turning into a smile, and that gripe into a song.

---

# Matthew 12

At this point, Matthew returned to an order of events matching
Mark's Gospel. The sections included in 9:18–11:30 are out
of order chronologically, but placed thematically according
to Matthew's focus on Jesus' teachings. Matthew 12:1-14
contrasts with 11:25-30 by comparing the yoke of the Law
and the rest Jesus brings. To the Jews, "rest" meant observing
the Sabbath.

**12:1-2** **At that time Jesus went through the grainfields on the Sabbath.
And His disciples were hungry, and began to pluck heads of
grain and to eat. And when the Pharisees saw it, they said to
Him, "Look, Your disciples are doing what is not lawful to do
on the Sabbath!"** NKJV Jesus and his disciples, still in Galilee (most
likely outside of Capernaum, 9:1), went out walking *through the
grainfields.* The fields were not fenced off but separated by stones
set at intervals (Deuteronomy 19:14). Roads often went right
though the fields, so this scene is not unusual. What made it of
special mention was that this stroll and the subsequent actions of
the disciples occurred *on the Sabbath.* The disciples *were hungry,*
so they *began to pluck heads of grain and to eat.* On any other day,
this would have been acceptable. They were not stealing grain; God's
law called for this kind of sharing among his people (Deuteronomy
23:25). Reaping grain was forbidden on the Sabbath (Exodus
34:21). The disciples, however, were picking grain because they
were hungry, not because they wanted to harvest the grain for a
profit. Thus, they were not breaking God's law. The Pharisees, however,
had established thirty-nine categories of actions forbidden on the
Sabbath, based on their own interpretations of God's law and on
Jewish customs. According to the religious leaders, the disciples
were technically "harvesting," because they were picking wheat
and rubbing it in their hands. The Pharisees were determined to
accuse Jesus of wrongdoing. They even followed him around on
the Sabbath in order to do so!

**12:3-4 He answered, "Haven't you read what David did when he and his companions were hungry? He entered the house of God, and he and his companions ate the consecrated bread—which was not lawful for them to do, but only for the priests."** NIV Jesus' answer to the Pharisees (12:3-8) contains four arguments explaining why his disciples' actions were lawful to do on the Sabbath (12:2): (1) David's example (12:3-4), (2) the priests' example (12:5-6), (3) proof from the prophets (12:7), and (4) proof from who he was (12:8).

First, Jesus reminded the Pharisees of an example from the life of David. This story is recorded in 1 Samuel 21:1-6. Each week twelve *consecrated* loaves of *bread,* representing the twelve tribes of Israel, were placed on a table in the *house of God,* here meaning the tabernacle. (This bread was called the bread of the Presence or showbread.) After its use in the temple, it was to be eaten only by priests. On one occasion, when fleeing from Saul, David and his men had been given this consecrated bread to eat by Abiathar, the high priest. The loaves given to David were the old loaves that had just been replaced with fresh ones. Although the priests were the only ones allowed to eat this bread, God did not punish David because his need for food was more important than the priestly regulations. Need alone, however, would not normally supersede the law because only danger of death could override Sabbath regulations. The people involved made the difference: David could break the law because he was David; Jesus could break the law because he was the Messiah, in authority over the law. While the story in 1 Samuel does not relate to the question of the Sabbath, the principle is the same. Jesus was explaining that if the high priest, David, and his followers could break a law, how much more could the Son of David—the Messiah.

The Pharisees knew the Scriptures thoroughly, yet Jesus' question *"Haven't you read?"* reveals their ignorance of the true meaning of the Scriptures. Yes, they had read this story many times, but they had obviously not discerned or applied its meaning. Jesus justified his disciples' action on the grounds that his authority superseded the requirement of ceremonial law. When Jesus compared himself and his disciples to David and his men, Jesus was saying, in effect, "If you condemn me, you must also condemn David." Jesus was not condoning disobedience to God's laws. Instead, he was emphasizing discernment and compassion in enforcing the ceremonial laws, something the self-righteous Pharisees did not comprehend.

**12:5 "Or have you not read in the law that on the sabbath the priests in the temple break the sabbath and yet are guiltless?"** NRSV Jesus responded to the Pharisees' accusation with a second answer, using an example from the priests who served in the temple. Jesus again repeated the question *"Have you not read in the law?"* to show these self-righteous Pharisees that while they had the law memorized, they really didn't understand it. The Ten Commandments prohibit work on the Sabbath (Exodus 20:8-11). That was the "letter" of the law. But because the purpose of the Sabbath is to rest and to worship God, the priests had to perform sacrifices and conduct worship services—in short, they had to "work." Their "Sabbath work" was serving and worshiping God, which God allowed. Thus, even though they technically *break the sabbath,* God holds them *guiltless.* Jesus always emphasized the intent of the law, the meaning behind the letter. The Pharisees had lost the spirit of the law and were rigidly demanding that the letter (and their interpretation of it) be obeyed.

---

READING THE BIBLE
A casual reader of the Bible can find evidence for almost any argument there. Just take a verse out of context, just isolate a passage, just make a story into an edict, and you can make the Bible say anything. The Pharisees, for example, were about to use the Bible (Old Testament) to make Jesus an ally of the devil.
    The Bible must be read correctly, from the vantage point of faith, with a hunger to find in it the truth of God as revealed in Jesus. To aid your reading, find faithful Christian friends (and a trustworthy church) who can guide your understanding. Read your Bible as if it were a conversation between you and God. Then begin to live what you're learning.

---

**12:6 "I tell you, something greater than the temple is here."** NRSV
The use of the neuter gender *(something greater)* indicates that Jesus may have been referring to the kingdom. Yet to refer to the supremacy of the kingdom highlights the supremacy of Jesus. Just as the priestly duties in the temple surpass Sabbath regulations about work, so Jesus' ministry transcends the temple.

The Pharisees were so concerned about religious rituals that they missed the whole purpose of the temple—to bring people to God. And because Jesus Christ is even greater than the temple, how much better can he bring people to God. Our love and worship of God are far more important than the created instruments of worship. If we become more concerned with the means and methods of worship than with the one we worship, we will miss the true purpose for worship—to glorify God.

**12:7 "If you had known what these words mean, 'I desire mercy, not sacrifice,' you would not have condemned the innocent."** NIV

Third, Jesus used proof from the Old Testament prophets to answer the Pharisees. Jesus repeated to the Pharisees words the Jewish people had heard time and again throughout their history (1 Samuel 15:22-23; Psalm 40:6-8; Isaiah 1:11-17; Jeremiah 7:21-23; Hosea 6:6). He had also used this same example in 9:13 when the Pharisees had criticized the people with whom he was spending time ("tax collectors and sinners"). The Old Testament statement "I desire mercy, not sacrifice" means that rituals and obedience to the law are valuable only if carried out with an attitude of love for God. If a person's heart is far from God, ritual and law keeping are no more than empty mockery. God did not want the Israelites' rituals; he wanted their hearts. Jesus challenged the Pharisees to apply the prophets' words to themselves. The Pharisees' rigid guidelines had caused them to be unable to see beyond the letter of the law. So in condemning Jesus and his disciples, they had *condemned the innocent.* The disciples were no more guilty of breaking the law than priests who did their duty on the Sabbath. The disciples were doing "priestly work" by spreading the Good News of the kingdom on the Sabbath. God's mercy takes precedence over legal restrictions. If only the Pharisees *had known* and had understood the words of the prophets, they would have understood the love and compassion behind God's laws. Their condemnation would then have been only to those who deserved it, not to those who were truly innocent of disobedience.

---

CHOOSING A CHURCH
Jesus amazed his listeners when he told them that he, the carpenter's son, was supreme over biblical law—in fact, the only sure authority on biblical law. The point is clear: If Jesus is at the center, all is well; but if anything else becomes the focus of worship (even keeping biblical laws with rigor and diligence), then something is wrong.

When you're choosing a church, be sure that the church keeps Jesus at the center. When you're reading the Bible (or hearing it taught), be sure of the same. Lots of other authorities compete for our attention, but no other authority will do.

---

**12:8 "For the Son of Man is Lord of the Sabbath."** NIV Jesus' fourth answer to the Pharisees' accusation (12:2) focused on who he was. When Jesus said that he (again, calling himself *Son of Man*) was *Lord of the Sabbath,* he was claiming to be greater than the law and above the law. To the Pharisees, this was heresy. They did not realize that Jesus, the divine Son of God, had created the Sabbath. The Creator is always greater than the creation; thus, Jesus had the authority to overrule their traditions and regula-

tions. Jesus claimed the authority to correctly interpret the meaning of the Sabbath and all the laws pertaining to it. Who created
the Sabbath? God did. Therefore, because Jesus, the Son of Man,
is God's Son, given authority and power by God himself, then he
is also Lord of the Sabbath.

## JESUS HEALS A MAN'S HAND ON THE SABBATH / 12:9-14 / 46

As if to illustrate that the commandment to love takes precedence
over the law, Jesus went to the synagogue where he healed a man
with a shriveled hand.

**12:9-10** **Going on from that place, he went into their synagogue, and a
man with a shriveled hand was there. Looking for a reason to
accuse Jesus, they asked him, "Is it lawful to heal on the Sabbath?"** NIV It was the Sabbath (12:1), and according to his regular
custom, Jesus went to the *synagogue.* This may have been any
synagogue in Galilee although it was most likely in Capernaum.
In the synagogue, there was *a man with a shriveled hand.* He had
been born with this defect or had acquired it by an accident or
disease. The hand was useless. Luke adds the detail that it was
the man's right hand (Luke 6:6).

Jesus' reputation for healing (even on the Sabbath, see Mark
1:21-26) had preceded him, but would he dare heal on the Sabbath
with Pharisees watching? (Most likely, the Pharisees had followed
him from the grainfield; 12:1-2). God's law prohibited work on
the seventh day of the week (Exodus 31:14-17); thus, the religious
leaders allowed no healing to be done on the Sabbath unless a
person's life was in danger. Healing, they argued, was practicing
medicine, and they had a law that a person could not practice this
profession on the Sabbath.

The Pharisees did not regard the man's need; instead, they
seized the opportunity to accuse Jesus as a Sabbath breaker. As
they pointed to the man with the shriveled hand, the Pharisees
tried to trick Jesus by asking him if it was *lawful* (legal) *to heal
on the Sabbath.* Their motive, however, was not to gain information; they were *looking for a reason to accuse Jesus.* Their
Sabbath rules said that people could be helped on the Sabbath
only if their lives were in danger. Jesus healed on the Sabbath
several times, and none of those healings were in response to
emergencies. If Jesus had waited until another day, he would
have been submitting to the Pharisees' authority, showing that
their petty rules were equal to God's law. If he healed the man
on the Sabbath, the Pharisees could claim that because Jesus

broke their rules, his power was not from God. But Jesus made it clear how ridiculous and petty their rules were. God is a God of people, not rules. The best time to reach out to someone is when he or she needs help.

---

RULE KEEPING
The Pharisees placed their laws above human need. They were so concerned about Jesus breaking one of their rules that they did not care about the man's shriveled hand. What is your attitude toward others? If your convictions don't allow you to help certain people, those convictions may not be in tune with God's Word. Don't allow rule keeping to blind you to human need.

---

**12:11-12 He said to them, "Suppose one of you has only one sheep and it falls into a pit on the sabbath; will you not lay hold of it and lift it out? How much more valuable is a human being than a sheep! So it is lawful to do good on the sabbath."** NRSV Instead of answering the Pharisees' question, Jesus responded with an illustration and a question of his own. A sheep that had fallen into a pit was in danger. If this occurred on the Sabbath, the sheep's owner was allowed to *lay hold of it and lift it out,* even though this constituted work. If it is acceptable to do good to a sheep on the Sabbath, doesn't it also follow that people can do good for other people on the Sabbath? Because people are *more valuable* than sheep, they are even more worthy of help.

Mark recorded that Jesus asked a rhetorical question: "'Which is lawful on the Sabbath: to do good or to do evil, to save life or to kill?' But they [the Pharisees] remained silent" (Mark 3:4 NIV). The Pharisees knew that giving an answer would have left them without an accusation to pin on Jesus. Their own laws allowed people to do good and to save life on the Sabbath—the farmer who could rescue his only lamb from a pit on the Sabbath knew that. So Jesus made the pronouncement: *So it is lawful to do good on the sabbath.* Doing good fulfills Sabbath intentions.

**12:13 Then he said to the man, "Stretch out your hand." He stretched it out, and it was restored, as sound as the other.**NRSV Jesus refused to play by the Pharisees' rules. After pronouncing that it was lawful to do good on the Sabbath (12:12), Jesus did exactly that. He told the man to stretch out his hand. In response to Jesus' command and with all eyes focused on him, the man stretched his hand out in front of him. The moment he did so, *it was restored, as sound as the other.* "Restored" means that it became like it had been before. As with the leper (8:3) and the paralytic (9:6-7), Jesus

gave this man his life back. The man could work again, and he no
longer had to face the embarrassment of his deformity.

No particular action of Jesus is recorded; he told the man
to move, and with that movement, healing arrived. Jesus did
nothing that could be called "work," but the Pharisees would
not be swayed from their purpose. Jesus had embarrassed them.
He had overruled their authority (Luke 6:11) and had exposed
their evil attitudes in front of the entire crowd in the synagogue,
showing that the Pharisees were more loyal to their religious
system than to God. That was enough to cause them to get on
with their mission of destruction (see 12:14).

---

CARING FOR PEOPLE
Jesus said that if a lost animal is worth saving, people are
worth more. Jesus puts a priority on the care of people. Better
to err (against rule keeping) by caring for people than to err
by a stringent interpretation of biblical law (while people suffer).
    Where are your loyalties? Are you able to use Christian
judgment in cases of a conflict between human need and
law keeping? Ask your Bible study group to take up some
hypothetical situations, and try together to discern how Jesus
would respond.

---

**12:14** **But the Pharisees went out and plotted how they might kill
Jesus.**[NIV] The Pharisees were outraged. Jesus had openly confronted their authority and had placed himself above them. Their
curiosity about Jesus turned to hatred because he had challenged
and exposed their proud attitudes and dishonorable motives. In
their fury, the only option they saw was to *kill Jesus*. Ironically,
the Pharisees had accused Jesus of breaking their law about healing on the Sabbath, yet they were planning (on the Sabbath) to
*kill* him. Their hatred, combined with their zeal for the law, drove
them to plot murder—an act that was clearly against the law.

Mark records that the Pharisees plotted with the Herodians
(Mark 3:6). This was an unlikely alliance. The Herodians were
a Jewish political party that hoped to restore Herod the Great's
line to the throne. Thus, their support of Rome's leadership over
Palestine brought them into direct conflict with the Jewish religious
leaders. The Pharisees and Herodians had little in
common—until Jesus posed a threat to them both. Jesus threatened the Pharisees' authority over the people; Jesus threatened
the Herodians' political ambitions because his talk of a "kingdom" caused them to think that this popular and powerful man
was planning to set himself up as a ruler. This would jeopardize

their authority derived from Herod's power. To get rid of Jesus, the Pharisees needed the support of people with some influence with the secular leaders. Thus, the Pharisees and Herodians, normally enemies, joined forces to discuss how to get rid of Jesus.

The way Jesus kept the Sabbath irritated his critics to the point of fury. To us, their reaction seems overstated. We must remember that the religious leaders, by imposing a bewildering system of Sabbath laws, had in fact made themselves lords of the Sabbath and thus lords over the people. By claiming the title of Lord of the Sabbath (12:8), Jesus was stating his own divinity, and this claim was an affront to the position of the religious leaders. His remaking the Sabbath into a day of refreshment, worship, and healing pried open the tight-fisted control the Pharisees held on the people. No wonder Jesus' approach to the Sabbath led his enemies to plot his death.

---

HOW TO MAKE FRIENDS AND INFLUENCE PEOPLE
Dale Carnegie's famous book by this title taught a generation of people how to get one's way and be friendly at the same time. Carnegie, no doubt, would have counseled Jesus to "take it easy" on the Pharisees. Today we might say, "Lighten up!"
But some conflict must be faced head-on. In Jesus' time and ours, people become angry when told that sin requires a special savior—in fact, the *only* savior. Don't placate people by conceding that any savior will do or that decent people are OK before God on their own. Tell the truth with compassion, even when it generates conflict.

---

## LARGE CROWDS FOLLOW JESUS / 12:15-21 / 47

**12:15-16 Aware of this, Jesus withdrew from that place.**[NIV] Jesus, *aware* that the religious leaders were plotting to kill him (12:14), *withdrew from that place* (presumably Capernaum). Jesus was not afraid of the religious leaders. Up to this point, Jesus had been aggressively confronting the Pharisees' hypocrisy. At this point in time, however, he decided to withdraw from the synagogue before a major confrontation developed. Jesus did this because it was not time for him to die. He still had many lessons to teach his disciples and the people.

**Many followed him, and he healed all their sick, warning them not to tell who he was.**[NIV] Despite his withdrawal, Jesus could not escape the crowds. Many continued to follow him, and Jesus had compassion on those who were sick, and he healed them; however, he also gave them a *warning . . . not to tell who he was.* Jesus did not want those he healed to tell others about his miracles because he didn't want people coming to him for the wrong reasons. A popular following of miracle seekers would hinder his teaching ministry and arouse false hopes about an earthly kingdom (see also 8:4; 9:30). But the news of Jesus' miracles spread, and many came to see for themselves (see Mark 3:7-8).

**2:17-21** **This was to fulfill what had been spoken through the prophet Isaiah.**<sup>NRSV</sup> In the following verses, Matthew gets to the focus of this chapter—Jesus as the one who fulfilled prophecy. The people expected the Messiah to be a king. This quotation from Isaiah's prophecy (Isaiah 42:1-4) showed that the Messiah was indeed a king, but it illustrated the kind of king he would be—a quiet, gentle ruler who brings justice to the nations. Like many in Jesus' day, we may want Christ to rule as a king and bring great and visible victories in our lives. But often his work is quiet, and it happens according to *his* perfect timing, not ours.

This is the longest Old Testament quotation in Matthew. The words don't match exactly any existing Old Testament text from the time, indicating that Matthew may have paraphrased the words for emphasis.

**Here is my servant whom I have chosen, the one I love, in whom I delight.**<sup>NIV</sup> The word for "servant" *(pais)* can also mean "son." The word "chosen" may have also been picked up from Isaiah 43:10 or 44:1 to focus on this "chosen" one as the Messiah. The phrase "the one I love, in whom I delight" echoes words spoken by God at Jesus' baptism and transfiguration (3:17; 17:5).

**I will put my Spirit on him.**<sup>NIV</sup> The coming of the Spirit was a sign of the messianic age. These words also echo Isaiah 61:1, quoted by Jesus in Luke 4:18. After reading the words aloud, Jesus had said, "Today this scripture is fulfilled in your hearing" (Luke 4:21 NIV).

**And he will proclaim justice to the nations.**<sup>NIV</sup> "Proclaim justice" refers to restoring justice and order and bringing judgment on sinners. The Messiah would offer justice to all *nations,* not just to the Jews (some versions use the word "Gentiles").

**He will not quarrel or cry out; no one will hear his voice in the streets.**<sup>NIV</sup> The Messiah pictured in these words differs dramatically from the person the Jews expected—a military leader calling the nation to battle against the Roman foe. Instead, this man *will not quarrel or cry out.* These words follow Matthew's report

## THE HOLY SPIRIT IN MATTHEW

For further study on the Holy Spirit in Matthew, study the following passages:

| | |
|---|---|
| Matthew 1:18, 20 | The Spirit was involved in Jesus' conception. |
| Matthew 3:11 | John promised judgment and referred to the work of the Spirit. |
| Matthew 3:16 | Jesus received the Spirit heralding his ministry and empowering him. |
| Matthew 4:1 | Jesus was led into the wilderness by the Spirit to defeat Satan's temptations. |
| Matthew 12:18 | The Spirit anointing Jesus was an indication that he was the Messiah. |
| Matthew 12:28 | Exorcism and healing were accomplished by the Spirit. |
| Matthew 12:31-32 | Blasphemy against the Holy Spirit is an unforgivable sin. |
| Matthew 28:19 | The Holy Spirit is promised as a gift to those who believe (see also 10:20). |

of Jesus' withdrawal from conflict with the Pharisees (12:15). The Messiah will not be silent (he will "proclaim" justice, see above), but neither will he publicize himself and seek attention. These words suggest gentleness and humility (see 11:29; see also Isaiah 53:7).

**A bruised reed he will not break, and a smoldering wick he will not snuff out, till he leads justice to victory.**<sup>NIV</sup> The "bruised reed" refers to the fragile lives of the "little ones" to whom the Servant ministers. He will not *break* (or destroy) them. The "smoldering wick" pictures a strip of linen cloth with little oil left in the lamp. The wick smolders, on the verge of going out, but the Servant *will not snuff out* the little wick. These words suggest a Savior who comes to heal, not to destroy. The phrase "till he leads justice to victory" seems to paraphrase parts of Isaiah 42:4 and 44:3-4 (see also Habakkuk 1:4). Justice will finally triumph when the Servant-Messiah comes. He may be gentle and meek, kindly healing the sick and teaching those who want to understand, but one day he will bring complete justice.

**In his name the nations will put their hope.**<sup>NIV</sup> In the NRSV, the word *ethne* ("the nations") is translated "Gentiles." People from all nations, not just Jews, will one day *put their hope* in the name of Jesus. "God exalted him to the highest place and gave him the

name that is above every name, that at the name of Jesus every
knee should bow, in heaven and on earth and under the earth, and
every tongue confess that Jesus Christ is Lord, to the glory of
God the Father" (Philippians 2:9-11 NIV). Jesus pointed out his
universal mission; he wanted his message to reach all nations. It
is a further indication of his messianic role that would culminate
in the Great Commission (28:19-20). God would ultimately rescue the oppressed and bring salvation to all who trust him.

---

THE LITTLE GUYS
Jesus cares a lot about people who don't have a Ph.D., don't
own golf clubs, and don't drive a late model car. Jesus cares
about the boring people in your town, the sick and the mentally
retarded, and the people on welfare. Because he cares about
them, they—and not merely the upwardly mobile types—are
the truly important people of this world.
   Do you ever wonder if you matter? Does your nondescript
life make a difference to anyone? Do your modest talents count
for anything? If so, you're exactly the kind of person Jesus
wants to know, his favorite kind of friend. Trust him with your
life. He deals gently with those who come to him in need.

---

## RELIGIOUS LEADERS ACCUSE JESUS OF BEING UNDER SATAN'S POWER / 12:22-37 / 74

Leaving the chronology in these verses, Matthew gives an example
of the intensifying conflict between Jesus and the religious leaders.
(See the Harmony of the Gospels at the back of this commentary;
Mark records this incident early, in Mark 3:22.) The religious leaders had already decided that they wanted to kill him (12:14), so
they began looking for any opportunity to accuse him.

**12:22 Then one was brought to Him who was demon-possessed, blind
and mute; and He healed him, so that the blind and mute man
both spoke and saw.**[NKJV] Matthew downplayed this miracle in order
to highlight the confrontation that followed. A man who was *demon-
possessed, blind and mute* was brought to Jesus for healing. The
Greek wording suggests that the blindness and inability to speak
were a direct result of demon possession. Jesus *healed* the man,
casting out the demon and restoring his ability to speak and see.

**12:23 All the crowds were amazed and said, "Can this be the Son
of David?"**[NRSV] The crowds *were amazed* when they saw the
man healed. This is the only time that the word *existanto* (also
translated "astonished") is used in Matthew's Gospel (although it

occurs often in Mark and Luke). The word conveys intense wonder and amazement. The Greek construction of their question expects a negative answer although it allows for the possibility of a positive response: "This couldn't be the Son of David, could it?" The title "Son of David" is another name for the Messiah. The Jews understood that the promised Messiah would be a son (descendant) of King David (see Isaiah 9:6-7; 11:1; Jeremiah 23:5-6). "Could this man be the one?" they wondered. They were puzzled because, despite all his miracles, Jesus just did not seem to be the Messiah they were expecting.

**12:24 But when the Pharisees heard this, they said, "It is only by Beelzebub, the prince of demons, that this fellow drives out demons."** NIV Apparently another delegation of Pharisees had come from Jerusalem. The people were "amazed," *but . . . the Pharisees* refused to believe that Jesus' power was from God. They could not deny the reality of Jesus' miracles and supernatural power, for he had indeed been driving out demons. So in an attempt to undermine Jesus' authority and popularity among the people, the Pharisees accused him of having power from Satan.

The name "Beelzebub" occurs only in the New Testament (in 10:25 and Luke 11:15) and not in other Jewish literature. In Greek, the term is *beelzeboul.* The Vulgate and Syriac versions tried to clarify the term by changing it to *beelzebub,* the god of Ekron (see 2 Kings 1:2-3, 6, 16). The religious authorities may have invented the term by combining two Hebrew words: *ba'al* ("lord," Hosea 2:16-17) which stood for the local Canaanite fertility god; and *zebul* ("exalted house," 1 Kings 8:13 NRSV) to call Jesus "the lord of heaven." Everyone would have understood this term as referring to Satan, the *prince* (or leader) *of demons.*

**12:25-26 He knew what they were thinking and said to them, "Every kingdom divided against itself is laid waste, and no city or house divided against itself will stand. If Satan casts out Satan, he is divided against himself; how then will his kingdom stand?"** NRSV Jesus *knew what* the Pharisees *were thinking.* In the Incarnation, Jesus gave up the complete and unlimited use of his supernatural abilities, but he still had profound insight into human nature (see 9:4). His discernment stopped the religious leaders' attempts to trick him.

Jesus responded to them in a parable—a simple example from life that would reveal the absurdity of their charge that he was in league with Satan. Following the obvious conclusion of the accusation—that Satan was driving himself out of people—

Jesus indicated that if that were true, it would then mean that there was civil war in the kingdom of evil. No king would throw his own soldiers out of his kingdom; neither would Satan throw his soldiers out because his kingdom would then be *divided against itself.* Such a kingdom would be *laid waste.* In the same way, people in a *city or house,* divided about their goals and working against one another, will not be successful. Jesus implied that it would be impossible for Satan to cast out himself (or his demons).

Obviously Satan is still very powerful and active; thus, his end had not come—not in Jesus' day, nor in ours. So Satan is not opposing himself, nor is he divided. The teachers' charge that Jesus was driving out demons by Satan's power was obviously false. But Jesus wasn't finished.

---

**DRIVING WEDGES**
The worst kind of sin involves driving a wedge between Jesus and the people whom he wants to reach. Pharisees sought to do that by accusing Jesus of partnership with the devil. Today we see it happen when learned professors cynically dismiss religion, when talk-show hosts smirk about religious hypocrites, and when pastors take their sermon cues from psychology instead of the Bible.

Give no encouragement to people who try to undermine Jesus. They are in great danger, and spoiled faith rides in their wake.

---

**12:27** **"And if I drive out demons by Beelzebub, by whom do your people drive them out? So then, they will be your judges."** [NIV] Jesus was not the first person in that area to exorcise demons. In the first century, exorcism was a thriving business, both in pagan and Jewish societies (Mark 9:38; Acts 19:13-14). Some were effective and some were frauds. Exorcists would employ complex incantations, magical charms, and even visual effects. (Jewish exorcists came only from the Pharisees because the Sadducees denied the existence of spirit beings.) Jesus, however, needed only his authoritative word. His constant success, the ease with which he cast out demons, and the reactions of the demons made Jesus' exorcisms notable. Jesus was saying, "If it takes Satan's power to drive out demons, then those of your own group who claim to drive out demons must also be demon-possessed." The Pharisees who had cast out demons would "judge" these other Pharisees for implying that being able to exorcise demons meant being in league with Satan.

**12:28** **"But if it is by the Spirit of God that I cast out demons, then the kingdom of God has come to you."** NRSV The word "if" means "since." There is no question that *it is by the Spirit of God* that Jesus cast out demons. Luke's version of this account says "finger of God" (Luke 11:20). Both mean the same, focusing on the power of God. That *the kingdom of God has come to you* shows that Jesus' exorcisms were specific evidence of the presence of kingdom power.

The kingdom of God came not with a mighty military leader, but with a gentle and compassionate Servant. The real enemy to be conquered was not the Romans but Satan. That Jesus was powerfully casting out demons and plundering Satan's kingdom revealed that the kingdom of God had begun.

---

GET REAL

If the kingdom of God has come, take a reality check. If you live your days without much reference to God, with a few passing words of prayer, your mind consumed with earning and buying, your eyes dashing from one advertisement to another, your heart longing for one more nice purchase—then wake up!

There's a reality you haven't seen or paid much attention to. It's the kingdom of God, right here, and it's very, very important to you. Unless you check in, life will be a dash—and then gone. But people of the kingdom live forever in God's peace and love. Take time today, right now. Live one day regarding your life as being in God's kingdom and yourself as his true servant.

---

**12:29** **"Or how can one enter a strong man's house and plunder his property, without first tying up the strong man? Then indeed the house can be plundered."** NRSV This picture reflects a situation in the ancient world where wealthy people's homes were virtual fortresses, and their servants could form a small army. Jesus called Satan *a strong man* in this parable. His *house* is the realm of evil where there is sickness, demon possession, and death (it also refers to a possessed individual in whom Satan's demons live). Satan's *property* are the demons—those beings through whom he carries out his work in the world. The only way his property could be "plundered" would be for someone to first tie up the strong man; the only way for the demons to be cast out is for someone to first overpower Satan. Jesus' advent into the world did just that (1 John 3:8). Jesus' actions reveal that Satan can never overcome him.

Although Satan still works in our world, God is in control. Jesus, as God, has "tied up" Satan in one sense; Satan's ultimate doom is sure, and his power over death was broken at Christ's resurrection. Jesus and his disciples were able to drive out demons and end their terrible work in people's lives. As such, every exorcism was a binding of Satan; one day Satan will be bound forever (Revelation 20:10). Jesus was not in league with Satan, as the Pharisees tried to claim; rather, he had overpowered Satan by refusing his temptations and by constantly freeing people held in Satan's grasp—either through demon possession or through the power of sin.

**12:30** **"Whoever is not with me is against me, and whoever does not gather with me scatters."** NRSV It is impossible to know about Christ and remain neutral indefinitely. Anyone who is not actively following him has chosen to be *against* him. Any person who tries to remain neutral in the struggle of good against evil is choosing to be separated from God, who alone is good. "Gathering" and "scattering" are Old Testament pictures of faithful and apostate people, respectively. To refuse to follow Christ is to choose to follow Satan.

---

THE NEUTRAL ZONE
Separating North Vietnam from South during more than a decade of battle was the demilitarized zone, a kind of no-man's-land, burned over and barren. Rivers, mountains, and man-made walls have served the same purpose—neutral, open space where both sides watch and neither stakes out a claim. No such space exists in the spiritual battle waged between God and Satan.

Get over to God's side if you're wandering in the middle. Stay on God's side when you're curious about life on the edge. Take your part in the struggle on the front lines, where witnessing hurts and few Christians are strong enough to support a church. But don't be fooled about finding a neutral zone claimed by no side at all.

---

**12:31** **"Therefore I tell you, people will be forgiven for every sin and blasphemy."** NRSV "Therefore I tell you" (also translated, "Wherefore I say unto you" in KJV, "And so I tell you" in NIV, and "Therefore I say to you" in NKJV) is a recurring phrase used by Jesus only prior to a solemn warning or pronouncement. It is like the Old Testament statement, "Thus saith the Lord." The words are divinely self-authenticating and guarantee the truth and importance of what Jesus would say next. Jesus would no longer reason with his accusers; he was giving them a solemn warning. Jesus had just been accused of being in league with Satan and had soundly refuted those charges. Here he had a few words for these so-called teachers of the law, the Jewish leaders.

First, he made the reassuring promise, *people will be forgiven for every sin and blasphemy.* Too often people miss this promise and worry about the warning that follows. But the fact is, those who believe in Jesus will be forgiven of all sins (evil acts, wrong actions, good actions not done, evil thoughts, evil motives, etc.) and of all blasphemies (evil words said against God). When there is confession and repentance, no sin is beyond God's forgiveness.

**"But blasphemy against the Spirit will not be forgiven."** NRSV There is one sin that cannot be forgiven—blasphemy against the Holy Spirit. "Blasphemy against the Spirit" refers not so much to a single action or word as to an attitude. Those who defiantly deny Jesus' power and persistently refuse to believe that he is the Messiah are blaspheming the Holy Spirit. Jesus was not talking about rejecting him, but of rejecting the power behind him.

Jesus' words were addressed directly to the Pharisees. They had blasphemed the Spirit by attributing the power by which Christ did miracles to Satan instead of to the Holy Spirit. This is the unforgivable sin—the deliberate refusal to acknowledge God's power in Christ. It indicates an irreversible hardness of heart. Deliberate, ongoing rejection of the work of the Holy Spirit is blasphemy because it rejects God himself. The Pharisees' stubborn refusal to believe demonstrated an impenetrable hardness of heart; thus, forgiveness would not be possible because it never would be sought. The religious leaders accused Jesus of blasphemy (see Luke 5:21; John 10:33-36), but ironically they were the guilty ones because they looked Jesus in the face and accused him of being possessed by Satan.

---

UNFORGIVABLE?
Jesus said that one sin could not be forgiven. Sometimes believers worry that they have accidentally committed this unforgivable sin. But only those who have turned their back on God and rejected all faith have any need to worry. If you are worried about this sin, realize that your worry is your strongest evidence that you have *not* made this tragic mistake. Use this prompting from the Spirit to repent and turn to Jesus.

---

12:32 **"Whoever speaks a word against the Son of Man will be forgiven, but whoever speaks against the Holy Spirit will not be forgiven, either in this age or in the age to come."** NRSV These words may mean that speaking against the person of Jesus can be forgiven because the insult may be based in ignorance of who he is (at that time not even Jesus' disciples completely understood who he was). But speaking *against the Holy Spirit*—to deny the power behind Jesus' ministry—is unforgivable. (Some versions use the word "blasphemy," meaning extreme slander.) The rejection of a messenger (even of

the Son himself) can be forgiven, but not the rejection of God himself through the Holy Spirit. The mighty works done by the Spirit
were unmistakable announcements that the kingdom had arrived.
Those who dared to attribute these works to Satan were not ignorant;
instead, they had made up their minds *not* to believe. Jesus said that
those who slander the Holy Spirit *will*
*not be forgiven*—not because their sin is
worse than any other, but because they
will never ask for forgiveness. Whoever
rejects the prompting of the Holy Spirit
removes himself or herself from the only
force that can lead anyone to repentance
and restoration with God. Those who have seen the light and
yet prefer the darkness are blaspheming the Holy Spirit. This sin
cannot be forgiven *in this age or in the age to come* because its
consequences are eternal.

> The only sin that God is unable to forgive is the unwillingness to accept forgiveness.
>
> *Robert H. Mounce*

**12:33** **"Make a tree good and its fruit will be good, or make a tree**
**bad and its fruit will be bad, for a tree is recognized by its**
**fruit."** NIV Just as a good tree bears good fruit and a diseased (or
*bad*) tree bears inedible fruit, so the fruits of a person's life will
show the quality of his or her character. *Fruit* is a comprehensive
word, referring to teaching, character, and action. (See also 7:16-18.)
Our character is revealed by our conduct.

**12:34-35** **"You brood of vipers, how can you who are evil say anything good?**
**For out of the overflow of the heart the mouth speaks."** NIV Jesus
called the Pharisees a *brood of vipers* (see also 3:7; 23:33), rebuking them for their hypocritical accusation against him (12:24).
Jesus called them *evil;* their nature and character were completely
evil as seen by their words (their "fruit," 12:33). Because they were
evil, how could they possibly *say anything good* (or wise or truth-
ful)? The words "out of the overflow of the heart" indicate that a
person's words reveal his or her character ("heart" referring to the
inner person). The Pharisees could not hide their evil behind their
status, robes, and position; their words betrayed their true character.
    Restating this same principle, Jesus continued: **"The good**
**person brings good things out of a good treasure, and the**
**evil person brings evil things out of an evil treasure."** NRSV
The word "treasure" is another metaphor for the "heart"—that
is, the inner person. (See also 6:19-21.)

**12:36-37** **"I tell you, on the day of judgment you will have to give an**
**account for every careless word you utter."** NRSV These verses
are found only in Matthew. Jesus explained that words matter—
each person will *have to give an account for every careless*

*word.* The word "careless" refers to words that we might consider insignificant or innocuous. "Careless" means inactive, idle, worthless. This refers not to mindless small talk or carefree jokes, but to broken promises, unkept commitments, and unpaid vows. Such words are better indicators of a person's true character than his or her carefully planned and prepared statements and speeches. No word is insignificant to God, because every spoken word reveals what is in the heart. Because God knows our hearts, our words are vitally important to him. Words will be a basis for judgment because words reveal who a person truly is: **"For by your words you will be acquitted, and by your words you will be condemned."** NIV

## RELIGIOUS LEADERS ASK JESUS FOR A MIRACLE / 12:38-45 / **75**

**12:38** **Then some of the scribes and Pharisees said to him, "Teacher, we wish to see a sign from you."** NRSV Apparently some *scribes* joined the *Pharisees.* They asked Jesus for *a sign*—that is, some miracle proving that he was the Messiah. But they were not sincerely seeking to know Jesus. Jesus knew they had already seen enough miraculous proof to convince them that he was the Messiah if they would just open their hearts. But they had already decided not to believe in him, and more miracles would not change their minds. The Pharisees (here joined by the scribes) wanted Jesus to authenticate by a sign the special relationship he claimed to have with God. In a separate incident recorded in 16:1-4, the Pharisees and Sadducees would ask Jesus for "a sign from heaven." Jesus responded to both requests in the same way.

STUDY THE EVIDENCE
Many people have said, "If I could just see a real miracle, then I could really believe in God." But Jesus' response to the Pharisees applies to us. We have plenty of evidence—Jesus' birth, death, resurrection, and ascension, and centuries of his work in believers around the world. Instead of looking for additional evidence or miracles, accept what God has already given and move forward. He may use your life as evidence to reach another person.

**12:39-40** **He answered, "A wicked and adulterous generation asks for a miraculous sign! But none will be given it . . ."** NIV Jesus refused to give the scribes and Pharisees a sign as they requested.

Instead, he gave them an answer, explaining that a sign would come in *his* timing and that the sign would be unmistakable. Jesus had already called the religious leaders "evil" (12:34); the words "wicked" and "adulterous" are synonyms for evil. "Adulterous" applies to the apostasy of Israel. Marriage and adultery are images used in the Old Testament for God's love and the nation's unfaithfulness. By these words Jesus was showing that the religious leaders were not alone in their rejection of Jesus. Instead, they were representative of most of the nation who had chosen to reject him, just as the nation had chosen to reject God's guidance and love in the past.

**". . . except the sign of the prophet Jonah. For as Jonah was three days and three nights in the belly of a huge fish, so the Son of Man will be three days and three nights in the heart of the earth."** NIV No sign would be given to them *except the sign of the prophet Jonah.* Jonah was a prophet sent to the Assyrian city of Nineveh (see the book of Jonah). Because Assyria was such a cruel and warlike nation, Jonah tried to run from his assignment and ended up spending three days in the *belly of a huge fish.* When Jonah got out, he grudgingly went to Nineveh, preached God's message, and saw the city repent.

There are two possible meanings for this "sign of Jonah":

1. This may refer to a sign of judgment. God will not grant the religious leaders the miracle they asked for but will only point to their rejection of the message. In Jonah's day, Nineveh was the capital of the Assyrian empire, and it was as powerful as it was evil (Jonah 1:2). The extremely wicked city of Nineveh repented at Jonah's preaching; by contrast, when Jesus came to his people, they refused to repent.
2. The "sign" granted to them may refer to the Resurrection. Jesus' resurrection would prove that he is the Messiah. Three days after his death Jesus would come back to life, just as Jonah had been "brought back" to life after spending three days in the fish. Both had been delivered from death. Jonah's presence was a sign to the people of Nineveh; they repented at his teaching. Jesus' return to his people after his death will also be a sign to the people of his generation. Some will repent; many will not. Because of the strong emphasis on the Resurrection as a "sign" in the early church (Acts 2:22-36; 4:10-11), most likely the church took Jesus' words to mean his resurrection. So this is the preferable meaning.

Some have been troubled with the statement "three days and three nights" because it seems to contradict the fact that Jesus died on Friday and was raised on Sunday. In Jewish reckoning, the inclusive days make the time span from death to resurrection three days, but not three nights. But such questioning is unnecessary. The Jews would have taken "three days and three nights" as an idiom for "three days" and would have seen no contradiction.

**12:41** **"The people of Nineveh will rise up at the judgment with this generation and condemn it, because they repented at the proclamation of Jonah, and see, something greater than Jonah is here!"** NRSV The people of Nineveh will condemn those of Jesus' generation *at the judgment.* The pagans repented at the preaching of Jonah, but the Jews and their religious leaders refused to repent at Jesus' preaching. "Something greater than Jonah is here" refers to Jesus himself and his proclamation of the kingdom's arrival (compare to 12:6, "something greater than the temple is here"). Jesus was their promised Messiah. The Jews should have recognized him. The religious leaders who knew prophecy should have been the first to proclaim Jesus as God's Son. Instead, they rejected him; thus, they will face condemnation for their refusal to believe. (See also 11:21-24.)

**12:42** **"The Queen of the South will rise at the judgment with this generation and condemn it; for she came from the ends of the earth to listen to Solomon's wisdom, and now one greater than Solomon is here."** NIV *The Queen of the South* (also called the Queen of Sheba) had traveled from southern Arabia to see Solomon, king of Israel, and to learn about his great wisdom (1 Kings 10:1-10). This unbelieving Gentile recognized the truth about God when it was presented to her, unlike the Jewish religious leaders who refused the truth even though it was staring them in the face. The Queen of the South, along with the people of Nineveh (12:41) will *rise at the judgment* and condemn those who refused to believe *one greater than Solomon*—the Messiah himself.

---

GOD WORKS IN STRANGE WAYS
Who would imagine that a caravan organized by an Arabian queen would become a symbol of God's powerful Good News to millions of listeners and readers down through the ages? But it was, and the queen is rightly honored for her pursuit of God's truth.

Don't box God in. Wonderful things come from his often mysterious plan. Don't box God's purposes for your life. Surprises may come, turns in the road, odd moments you could not predict or plan. Take such events as opportunities, not problems. Regard the people in your life as willing listeners; treat each problem as an opportunity for prayer.

---

**2:43-44** **"When the unclean spirit has gone out of a person, it wanders through waterless regions looking for a resting place,
but it finds none. Then it says, 'I will return to my house
from which I came.' When it comes, it finds it empty, swept,
and put in order."** NRSV To further describe how it will be with
this evil generation (12:39, 45), Jesus told a parable focusing
on the attitude of the nation of Israel and the religious leaders
in particular. There is danger in attempting to be neutral about
Jesus. Unfilled and complacent people are easy targets for
Satan, as Jesus described in this parable. We cannot press the
details of the parable as teaching doctrinal truth about demons
(for example, the picture that demons liked to live in the desert
was based on popular belief, not biblical fact). Jesus may have
been only using popular beliefs in this parable to make his point.

*The unclean spirit* was not "cast out" but for some reason
had *gone out of a person.* The desert *(waterless regions)* was
believed to be the habitation of demons. Because demons need
*a resting place* (that is, someone or something living that they
can enter and torment), this demon returned to its former *house*
when it could find nothing suitable in the desert. This sentence
is probably conditional: "if" the demon decided to return.
Demons do not always repossess people after they leave or are
cast out. That would make exorcisms both worthless and an
invitation to greater disaster (12:45). Jesus was making a point
about the spiritual destiny of his listeners.

In its absence, the demon's "house" had been cleaned up. But
it was still *empty.* Therein lay the problem and the crux of Jesus'
teaching. The problem is not so much with the demons as it is
with the condition of the "house."

**12:45** **"Then it goes and brings along seven other spirits more evil
than itself, and they enter and live there; and the last state
of that person is worse than the first. So will it be also with
this evil generation."** NRSV The nation had been "swept clean"
by the teaching and preaching of John the Baptist and of Jesus.
Many had come to repent. But if the nation did not turn around,
truly repenting from sin and turning to Jesus as their Messiah
and Savior, they would be no better off than a clean but empty
house. Into that house comes worse evil than before. Jesus
pictured the demon finding seven others and returning to the
clean house. But the "owner," now filled with eight demons
instead of one, is definitely *worse* off than before. *So it will be
also with this evil generation.* God's people, privileged with
prophecy and promises, would be faced with horrible judgment
for rejecting their Messiah.

**12:46-47** **While Jesus was still talking to the crowd, his mother and brothers stood outside, wanting to speak to him. Someone told him, "Your mother and brothers are standing outside, wanting to speak to you."** NIV Jesus' mother was Mary (Luke 1:30-31), and his brothers were probably the other children Mary and Joseph had after Jesus (see also Mark 6:3-4). Some Christians believe the ancient tradition that Jesus was Mary's only child. If this is true, the "brothers" were possibly cousins (often called brothers in those days). Some have offered yet another suggestion: When Joseph married Mary, he was a widower, and these were his children by his first marriage. Based on 13:55, these were Jesus' half brothers, Mary and Joseph's other children, because Jesus' father was God, not Joseph.

Apparently Mary had gathered her family, and they had gone to find Jesus. Mark explained that "Jesus entered a house, and again a crowd gathered, so that he and his disciples were not even able to eat. When his family heard about this, they went to take charge of him, for they said, 'He is out of his mind'" (Mark 3:20-21 NIV). Mary hoped to use her personal relationship with Jesus to influence him. She saw her son in a busy ministry that was taking its toll on him. Perhaps she hoped to get him to come home; maybe she brought the brothers along to drag Jesus away from the crowd if necessary.

*While Jesus was still talking to the crowd,* the message from his family was relayed to him. Jesus' family thought that because of their relationship with him, he would answer their request.

**12:48** **He replied to him, "Who is my mother, and who are my brothers?"** NIV Instead of going outside to see what his family members wanted, Jesus looked at the crowd and asked an odd question, *"Who is my mother, and who are my brothers?"* Jesus knew why his family had come, yet he used their visit as a lesson in discipleship. A relationship with Jesus was not limited to those in his immediate family. Jesus opened this relationship to all people. His question could be rendered, "Who are the types of people who can have a family relationship with me?"

**12:49-50** **Pointing to his disciples, he said, "Here are my mother and my brothers. For whoever does the will of my Father in heaven is my brother and sister and mother."** NIV Jesus *point[ed] to his disciples* and answered his own question. The types of people who can have a relationship with him are those who do the Father's will. They listen, learn, believe, and follow. Obedience is the key to discipleship. In these words, Jesus

explained that in his spiritual family, the relationships are ultimately more important and longer lasting than those formed in
his physical family.

Jesus was not denying his responsibility to his earthly family.
On the contrary, he would criticize the religious leaders for not
following the Old Testament command to honor their parents
(Matthew 15:1-9). He would provide for his mother's security
as he hung on the cross (John 19:25-27). His mother and brothers
would be present in the upper room at Pentecost (Acts 1:14).
Instead, Jesus was pointing out that spiritual relationships are
as binding as physical ones, and he was paving the way for a
new community of believers to be formed as Jesus' spiritual
family. This family would be characterized by love; the members
should desire to be together, work together, and share one
another's burdens.

# Matthew 13

Jesus left the synagogue and began to teach outdoors. He left those opposed to him and reached out to the responsive people. Jesus had already made unmistakable claims about his true identity, and there was increasing division between those who accepted and those who rejected. The religious leaders had already decided that Jesus was not the Messiah. The crowds who followed Jesus, listening to his teaching and observing his miracles, wondered if this could be the "Son of David" (12:23), but their leaders told them he was not.

So "that same day" (13:1), Jesus began teaching a series of parables about the kingdom of heaven. Prior to this time he had spoken clearly, but he used the parables to get listeners to think. These "parables" hid the truth from those who had their minds made up, having already chosen to reject Jesus. Those who truly wanted to know Jesus and listened carefully would understand his words.

Chapter 13 includes seven different parables:

- In 13:1-23 is the parable of the sower and the soils, focusing on receptivity to the gospel message.
- In 13:24-35 are three "little power" parables about the weeds, seeds, and leaven.
- In 13:44-50 are three "end time" parables about the treasure in a field, the pearl, and the net.

**13:1-2 That same day Jesus went out of the house and sat beside the sea. Such great crowds gathered around him that he got into a boat and sat there, while the whole crowd stood on the beach.**NRSV Earlier *that same day,* Jesus had been accused of being under Satan's power (12:22-37), had turned down the religious leaders' request for a miracle (12:38-45), and had dealt with his family who had come to take him home (12:46-50; Mark 3:31-35). Having had enough of the conflict, he decided to go *out of the house* in Capernaum and sit *beside the sea* (that is, on the shore of the Sea of Galilee).

As often happened wherever Jesus went, *great crowds gathered.* In fact, these were such great crowds that Jesus *got into a boat* anchored a little way offshore (probably a fishing vessel). Matthew recorded that Jesus *sat there,* a reference to Jesus' teaching style. The boat was surrounded by water; it was not moored to a dock. From that position, Jesus sat and taught *while the whole crowd stood on the beach.*

**13:3 Then he told them many things in parables, saying: "A farmer went out to sow his seed."** NIV Jesus used many illustrations, or *parables,* when teaching the crowds. Parables are short stories that use familiar scenes and everyday objects and relationships to explain spiritual truths. A parable compares something unfamiliar with something familiar. It compels listeners to discover truth, while at the same time concealing the truth from those too lazy or too stubborn to see it. Jesus' insights were hidden from those who refused to seek the truth and from those who would not come back and inquire. To those who were honestly searching, the truth became clear. We must be careful not to read too much into parables, forcing them to say what they do not mean. All parables have one meaning unless otherwise specified by Jesus. In this parable, the farmer represents Jesus, the soil represents Israel, and the seed represents the proclamation of the kingdom. The parable shows the contrast between the results of acceptance and rejection of the gospel message.

This "kingdom parable" gave a familiar picture to Jesus' audience—a *farmer* sowing *seed,* with the resulting increase dependent on the condition of the soil. In ancient Israel, farmers sowed seed by hand. As the *farmer* walked across the field, he would *sow* the seeds by scattering (13:4) handfuls of seed onto the ground from a large bag slung across his shoulders. The plants did not grow in neat rows, as is accomplished by today's machine planting. No matter how skillful, no farmer could keep some of his seed from falling by the wayside, from being scattered among rocks and thorns, or from being carried off by the wind. So the farmer would throw the seed liberally, and enough would fall on good ground to ensure a good harvest. The yield depended on the condition of the soil where the seed fell. A farmer in Palestine could possibly have all four types of soil Jesus described on his farm.

Jesus spoke to the crowds about the kingdom, explaining through this parable that while their religious leaders might reject the Messiah, that did not change the truth. Jesus himself and the gospel were truth; there was no problem with them as there was no problem with the farmer or his seed. The only variable was the land where the seed fell.

**13:4 "As he was scattering the seed, some fell along the path, and the birds came and ate it up."** NIV Some of the seeds *fell along the path* (on the road). Paths (the "roads" in Bible times) ran right through the fields. The hard and compacted soil of the road made it impossible for the seed to penetrate. So it sat on top, as tempting morsels for *birds* that *came and ate it up.* In 13:19 we learn that the "birds" represent Satan. For more on the path representing "hardness of heart" see 13:19.

**13:5-6 "Other seeds fell on rocky ground, where they did not have much soil, and they sprang up quickly, since they had no depth of soil. But when the sun rose, they were scorched; and since they had no root, they withered away."** NRSV Some of that seed *fell on rocky ground.* Unlike the path, rocky ground had some soil to accept the seed, but not much. The seed *sprang up quickly* in the shallow soil. Most of the land in Palestine is rocky. The soil is filled with rocks of all sizes. Such soil traps the moisture so that plants can grow quickly, but the sun takes the moisture out so rapidly that a young plant withers. Thus, *when the sun rose, they were scorched* and *withered away.* See 13:20-21 for a discussion on rocky soil representing hearers who lack real depth.

**13:7 "Other seeds fell among thorns, and the thorns grew up and choked them."** NRSV Some of the farmer's seed *fell among thorns.* No farmer would intentionally scatter the seed into an area filled with thorns and briers; this probably refers to the seed falling among seeds or roots of thorns that cultivation had not destroyed. Thorns rob the sprouts of nutrition, water, light, and space. Thus, when *the thorns grew up,* the good seed was *choked* out and could not grow to maturity and yield a crop.

**13:8 "Still other seed fell on good soil, where it produced a crop— a hundred, sixty or thirty times what was sown."** NIV However, some of the seed landed in plowed and readied soil. This seed had the depth of soil, space, and moisture to grow and produce a crop. This seed multiplied and yielded thirty, sixty, or even up to a hundred times the amount of seed sown. A farmer would be happy indeed to see his crop multiply even ten times. Thirty, sixty, or a hundred would be a marvelous (although not unheard of ) yield, for it would mean even more seed to plant and harvest in the coming year.

---

NO FORMULAS
This parable should encourage spiritual "sowers"—those who teach, preach, and lead others. The farmer sowed good seed, but not all the seed sprouted, and even the plants that grew had varying yields. There are so many factors involved with the process of believing in the truth of the gospel that we should be reluctant to use percentages and ratios (of numbers of presentations to numbers of responses) as an application of this parable. Rather, it is a miracle of God's Holy Spirit as he uses your words to lead others to him. Don't be discouraged if you do not always see results as you faithfully teach the Word.

---

**13:9 "Let anyone with ears listen!"** NRSV Jesus' audience must have wondered at these strange words. Didn't they all have ears, and hadn't they all heard? But Jesus wasn't talking about the act of simply hearing his words. Human ears hear many sounds, but there is a deeper kind of listening that results in spiritual understanding. Jesus was speaking of the response of the mind and heart necessary to gain spiritual understanding. Some people in the crowd were only curious about Jesus; a few were looking for evidence to use against him; others truly wanted to learn and grow. Jesus' words were for the honest seekers. Those who honestly seek God will have spiritual hearing. Jesus pointed out that listening makes fertile soil. If we bear fruit, it is proof that we have listened. If others bear fruit, it shows that the seed we have planted has taken root in their heart.

Jesus purposely spoke in parables to weed out the half-hearted and curiosity seekers from the true seekers. His words, like the farmer's seed, fell on various types of hearts. Those who truly heard and understood would become his followers. Those not ready for Jesus would not understand his words, would lose interest, and finally would either fade away or become his avowed enemies (as did most of the religious leaders).

It is easy for us to hear Jesus' words on others' behalf. We hear what Jesus says and may even understand a deeper meaning, but we are quick to apply the message to someone else's need. When we hear Jesus' words, we should apply them to our lives, not to someone else. If you honestly seek God, you have spiritual hearing, and these parables will give you new perspectives.

## JESUS EXPLAINS THE PARABLE OF THE FOUR SOILS / 13:10-23 / **78**

**13:10** **The disciples came to him and asked, "Why do you speak to the people in parables?"** NIV When Jesus got away from the crowd and was alone with his true followers (the twelve disciples and the larger group of believers from whom the Twelve had been chosen), a more intimate question-and-answer period followed. Perhaps these close followers did not want to reveal their ignorance about Jesus' words in front of the entire crowd. More likely, they were noticing that many people in the crowd were not understanding Jesus' message. So, when they were alone with Jesus, his followers asked him why he spoke to the people *in parables,* in stories that seemed to confuse his listeners and obscure the message. A parable is an extended metaphor to express a moral or spiritual truth. It can be a proverb, riddle, complex story, or extended comparison. The purpose for using them was to get people to think.

**13:11** **He replied, "The knowledge of the secrets of the kingdom of heaven has been given to you, but not to them."** NIV Jesus revealed that understanding the truth of the gospel comes as a gift of God to those he has chosen. The *you* to whom Jesus spoke was the group of his true followers, including the twelve disciples and others who believed in him. God had given them a special gift. That this knowledge is *given* reveals that both grace and judgment are God's prerogative. God had given this *knowledge of the secrets of the kingdom of heaven* to these disciples as a permanent possession, a distinguishing mark of discipleship. They understood, though only partially, the "secret" that God's kingdom had arrived among them in the person of Jesus. Those who have not been given this knowledge *(not to them)* are those who willfully reject the gospel message.

When speaking in parables, Jesus was not hiding truth from sincere seekers, because those who were receptive to spiritual truth understood the illustrations. To others they were only stories without meaning. This allowed Jesus to give spiritual food to those who hungered for it while preventing his enemies from trapping him sooner than they might otherwise have done.

The word translated "secrets" is also translated "mysteries." The Aramaic word *raz* was used in the intertestamental writings to refer to the "hidden" revelation of God, unknown to the apostates, but "given" to his true people at the proper time. In this context, they are the "secrets of the kingdom" given to the disciples through Jesus' teaching.

**13:12** **"For to those who have, more will be given, and they will
have an abundance; but from those who have nothing, even
what they have will be taken away."** NRSV *To those who have*
the knowledge given by God (13:11), God will give even more
knowledge and understanding so that *they will have an abundance.* In contrast are *those who have nothing*—no knowledge
or understanding from God (as explained in 13:11). From these
people, *even what they have will be taken away.* How can
people "have nothing" yet lose what they have? Jesus' words
meant that those who had rejected him and his message had
no knowledge and therefore would lose their privileged status.
Those who "have nothing" were the religious leaders and the
vast majority of the Jews. They thought they were privileged
and secure as God's chosen people, but they would lose that
position. They would never understand the secret because they
would not come to God for the answer. Choosing not to believe
in Jesus as their Messiah, they would not be able to understand
the kingdom. This phrase means that we are responsible to use
well what we have. When people reject Jesus, their hardness
of heart drives away or renders useless even the little understanding they had.

**13:13** **"The reason I speak to them in parables is that 'seeing they
do not perceive, and hearing they do not listen, nor do they
understand.'"** NRSV The parable of the sower accurately pictured
the people's reaction to all of Jesus' parables. Jesus would not
explain them to the people; rather, he would answer questions
about his parables with other parables because *seeing they do not
perceive, and hearing they do not listen, nor do they understand.*
(See the next verse.)

   Mark, also writing about this teaching, used the Greek *hina*
(meaning "in order that") to introduce the statement "seeing
they do not perceive, and hearing they do not listen, nor do
they understand." *Hina* conveys the concept that the parables
were being used to blind those refusing to know the truth.
Matthew's rendering uses the Greek *hoti,* meaning "because."
*Hoti* conveys the meaning that the people were already blind
and spiritually insensitive. Both phrases ("in order that" and
"because") could indicate either: (1) *purpose,* that is, Jesus'
parables would remain unclear to those refusing to understand
in order to keep them from perceiving; or (2) *result,* that is,
the parables resulted in the people being unable to perceive
or understand. The second option is best because it seems too
harsh of Jesus to use the parables to keep people from believ-

ing. While the parables may have been intended to be a means of God's judgment on unbelievers, they also could not penetrate the hard soil of unbelief already characterizing unbelievers' hearts. This was originally given as a prophecy for Isaiah's own day about how his fellow Israelites would receive God's messages through him. Jesus witnessed the same reaction to his words.

These unbelievers had already rejected Jesus; no amount of explaining or talking would make any difference. The soil of their heart was hard; the seed of the word would not grow; the parables would be nothing more than strange stories to them. Jesus was not hiding truth from sincere seekers because those who were receptive to spiritual truth understood the illustrations. To the "path," "thorn patch," or "rocky soil" people, the parables were only stories without meaning. The parables allowed Jesus to give spiritual food to those who hungered for it; but for the others, Isaiah's prophecy explained their situation.

**13:14** **"With them indeed is fulfilled the prophecy of Isaiah that says: 'You will indeed listen, but never understand, and you will indeed look, but never perceive.'"** NRSV God told Isaiah that people would listen without understanding and look without perceiving (Isaiah 6:9); Jesus witnessed the same reaction to his teaching. By quoting from the prophet Isaiah, Jesus was explaining to this inner group of followers that the crowd resembled the Israelites about whom Isaiah had written. God had told Isaiah that the people would listen but not learn from his message because their hearts had hardened beyond repentance. Yet God still sent Isaiah with the message because even though the nation itself would not repent and would reap judgment, some individuals *would* listen. Jesus came to the Israelites hundreds of years after Isaiah, but the scenario was the same. Most would not repent because their hearts were hardened; but a few would listen, turn from their sins, and believe. The deafness to the message did not mean that the message was false or that the messenger was somehow at fault.

> One of the moral diseases we communicate to one another in society comes from huddling together in the pale light of an insufficient answer to questions we are afraid to ask.
> *Thomas Merton*

**13:15** **"'For this people's heart has grown dull, and their ears are hard of hearing, and they have shut their eyes; so that they might not look with their eyes, and listen with their ears, and understand with their heart and turn—and I would heal them.'"** NRSV

Neither Isaiah's nor Jesus' audiences were denied the opportunity to *turn* and receive healing (forgiveness). Instead, refusing to listen would mean inability to perceive and understand anything Jesus had to say. The Pharisees had already accused Jesus of being in league with Satan (12:24). Such an accusation revealed their stubborn blindness and their refusal to believe. Jesus used these words from Isaiah to refer directly to the Pharisees' accusation. The verbs are singular, meaning that they would not be forgiven of their sin of blasphemy. No matter how much they saw of Jesus' miracles or heard of his teaching, they never would be able to understand because they had deliberately chosen to reject. So Jesus was saying that this hardness was, in effect, divine judgment.

**13:16 "But blessed are your eyes for they see, and your ears for they hear."** NKJV The images of "seeing" and "hearing" refer to knowledge of God's revelation. The contrast with 13:13 is striking— Jesus spoke to "them" (that is, the crowds at large) in parables because they refused to understand. However, the disciples ("you") were blessed because they wanted to understand (even if they didn't always completely understand). The same division between the unbelieving and believing was recorded in 11:25-26, "At that time Jesus said, 'I praise you, Father, Lord of heaven and earth, because you have hidden these things from the wise and learned, and revealed them to little children. Yes, Father, for this was your good pleasure'" (NIV). The disciples were *blessed* above the people in the crowd because they were seeing and hearing what the prophets had foretold. God gave them spiritual enlightenment to understand and accept the person and the message of Jesus.

---

BELIEVERS' MODESTY
Jesus takes the pride out of believing when he reminds us that faith is a gift. It's God who saves us and God who opens our eyes to see. Christians inclined to say, "Yea for me—I believe!" need to change their cheer to "Yea God! You've opened my heart to Jesus!"

The New Testament calls this gift "grace." Grace tells us that God is in charge and he keeps us from falling away. We don't deserve God's grace. That's why believers, of all people, should be very modest about their contribution to being a Christian.

---

**13:17 "Truly I tell you, many prophets and righteous people longed to see what you see, but did not see it, and to hear what you hear, but did not hear it."** NRSV The kingdom of God was a mystery to the prophets of the Old Testament because, though they wrote about it, they did not understand it (as Paul explains in Romans

16:25-26). The believers who knew Jesus personally received spiritual insight that illuminated the mystery so that it was no longer a mystery to them. In these words, Jesus was explaining that *he* was the fulfillment of the prophecies given and heard by the *prophets and righteous people* of Old Testament days. Peter later wrote

- *Concerning this salvation, the prophets, who spoke of the grace that was to come to you, searched intently and with the greatest care, trying to find out the time and circumstances to which the Spirit of Christ in them was pointing when he predicted the sufferings of Christ and the glories that would follow. It was revealed to them that they were not serving themselves but you, when they spoke of the things that have now been told you by those who have preached the gospel to you by the Holy Spirit sent from heaven. Even angels long to look into these things. (1 Peter 1:10-12 NIV)*

---

**BELIEVERS' PRIVILEGE**
Old Testament believers saw and heard about a lot of important events pointing to God's loving care (for example, the Exodus, the Goliath battle, the temple being built and rebuilt), but still God's greatest news was murky and distant.

Disciples and followers who saw and heard Jesus were highly privileged. They were firsthand, eye-to-eye witnesses. They saw the Lord, heard him, walked with him.

But the real benefit belongs to us. We have Jesus, the rest of the New Testament, and nearly two thousand years of the Holy Spirit working through the church. What a privilege! Be grateful and glad. Make good use of the knowledge available to you.

---

**3:18-19** **"Hear then the parable of the sower. When anyone hears the word of the kingdom and does not understand it, the evil one comes and snatches away what is sown in the heart; this is what was sown on the path."** NRSV The *sower* was Jesus (see also 13:37) and, by extension, anyone after him who would teach and preach *the word* (represented by the seed). Jesus was telling the parable and exemplifying it; as he spoke of the farmer sowing the seed, he was sowing the word among the crowd of followers. Jesus was revealing his mission while teaching the disciples about theirs. The parable revealed people's varying responses to the gospel message. The attitude or condition of their hearts would govern their response.

The word makes no impression on some people. For those who hear and do not understand, the seed lands on a hard heart (like the hardened soil of the path). Then Satan (like the birds, 13:4) snatches it away. Perhaps the person feels no need in his or her heart, no desire for anything other than this life, no guilt of sin or need of forgiveness. Satan has no trouble with these people.

**EXCUSES**
Today people might say, "It's not my fault if I don't understand Jesus' message!" They may have a variety of excuses:
- "It's too difficult. I can't grasp these abstract concepts." Our responsibility is not to become theologians, just willing listeners.
- "I'm not old enough to make life-changing decisions." But even children understand love, doing right, and spiritual authority.
- "I know too many 'Christian' phonies, jerks, and nerds."
The name "Christian" is used today by racist hate groups, political revolutionaries, and fraudulent money-making schemes. It's sad that the name is detached so far and so often from the reality. But the reality is Jesus' message, and that comes right from God to you, today, with life-changing power. Don't fool with excuses. Embrace and receive Jesus' message as the foundation of your life.

**13:20-21** **"As for what was sown on rocky ground, this is the one who hears the word and immediately receives it with joy; yet such a person has no root, but endures only for a while, and when trouble or persecution arises on account of the word, that person immediately falls away."** NRSV The seed *sown on rocky ground* had some soil to accept the seed, but not much. These people joyfully receive the Good News of the gospel because of the promises offered. They grow a bit initially. These people understand some of the basics but do not allow God's truth to work its way into their souls and make a difference in their lives. They have *no root* and thus endure *only for a while. When trouble or persecution* comes (the scorching heat, 13:5-6), they decide not to believe the gospel or its promises and so fall away. Satan can always use sorrow, trouble, and persecution to draw people away from God. Ironically, those who let the message take root in good soil find that sorrow, trouble, and persecution bring them closer to God.

**13:22** **"As for what was sown among thorns, this is the one who hears the word, but the cares of the world and the lure of wealth choke the word, and it yields nothing."** NRSV This is Satan's most subversive tactic of all. These people hear and accept the word and allow it to take root in their hearts, giving hope of a harvest. But *thorns* grow up and choke out the growing seed. Thorns rob nutrition, water, light, and space from newly sprouting seeds.

Distractions and conflicts rob new believers of time to reflect on and digest God's Word to grow from it, as well as robbing them of guidance and support from interaction with other Christians. Jesus described the "thorns": *cares of the world* and *lure of wealth.*

Worldly worries, the false sense of security brought on by prosperity, and the desire for material things plagued first-century disciples as they do us today. Daily routines overcrowd and materialistic pursuits distract believers, choking out God's Word so that it *yields nothing.*

---

**WHAT'S IN IT FOR ME?**
Sometimes Jesus' message is phrased today like a television commercial, and we "buy into it" on those terms—a product that will make us happier. Then troubles come, and we wonder what went wrong.

Jesus promises to help us through life's troubles, not to remove us from them all. Stay with his message because it's true, not because it makes you feel good. When you start to feel discouraged, it's time to get together with a Christian friend for a good talk, maybe a good cry, and prayer.

---

**13:23** **"But as for what was sown on good soil, this is the one who hears the word and understands it, who indeed bears fruit and yields, in one case a hundredfold, in another sixty, and in another thirty."** NRSV But other people are like the *good soil*—they hear the Word and accept it. These are the true disciples—those who have accepted Jesus, believed his words, and allowed him to make a difference in their lives.

Notice that the seed *bears fruit.* Those who preach the word yield others who preach the word to others who preach the word and so on. The call to evangelize the world should naturally follow from a life rebuilt around God's Word.

This parable answered the question of why there were so many opinions about Jesus. Belief ranged from love to hatred and all shades in between. The same is true today. The answer, said Jesus, lies not in the message, for that is always the same. Neither is the problem caused by the preacher or teacher if he or she sows the message appropriately. The answer is that the message falls on hearts that are in varied degrees of readiness. The message will not be accepted in the same way by all who hear it. God had told the prophet Ezekiel, "Whether they hear or refuse to hear . . . they shall know that there has been a prophet among them. . . . You shall speak my words to them, whether they hear or refuse to hear" (Ezekiel 2:5, 7 NRSV).

**HOW EASY**
Jesus said the seed sown among thorns yields nothing. When we don't obey God, soon our lives become unusable to him. How easy it is to agree with Christ with no intention of obeying. It is easy to denounce the worries of this life and the deceitfulness of wealth, and still do nothing to change our ways. Considering eternal life with God, are your present worries justified? If you had everything you could want but forfeited eternal life with God, would those things be so desirable? Don't let worldly cares and the illusion of wealth deter you from obeying God.

## *JESUS TELLS THE PARABLE OF THE WEEDS / 13:24-30 / 80*

While the kingdom message is being sown, it faces a variety of different receptions (13:1-8, 18-23). Some may have thought that the inauguration of the Messiah's kingdom would be accompanied by cataclysmic events. That did not seem to be happening with Jesus. In the Jewish mind, the coming of the Messiah signaled the coming of the kingdom. Jesus stated that the Messiah had arrived with his kingdom, but the fulfillment of the messianic kingdom would be delayed until he comes a second time. What, then, is the kingdom of heaven like? The parables in this chapter answer this question. They show what the kingdom is really like as opposed to people's expectations of it. The kingdom of heaven is not a geographic location but a spiritual realm where God rules and where believers share in his eternal life. We join that kingdom when we trust in Christ as Savior.

**SOILED?**
The four types of soil represent different responses to God's message. People respond differently because they are in different states of readiness. Some are hardened, others are shallow, others are contaminated by distracting worries, and some are receptive. How has God's Word taken root in your life? What kind of soil are you?

**13:24-26** **He put before them another parable: "The kingdom of heaven may be compared to someone who sowed good seed in his field; but while everybody was asleep, an enemy came and sowed weeds among the wheat, and then went away. So when the plants came up and bore grain, then the weeds appeared as well."**NRSV
Jesus explained that the kingdom grows quietly and abundantly, yet

evil still exists in the world. Jesus gives the meaning of this parable in 13:36-43, "The one who sows the good seed is the Son of Man; the field is the world, and the good seeds are the children of the kingdom; the weeds are the children of the evil one, and the enemy who sowed them is the devil" (13:37-39 NRSV). Remember that in parables, not every item needs to be interpreted; some details are added to give color. That the enemy came *while everybody was asleep* does not indicate neglect on anyone's part; that he *went away* does not indicate his absence. Instead, these details merely highlight the stealth and malicious intent of Satan (the *enemy,* "the evil one").

This was a known practice in ancient warfare and feuds—destroy a nation's (or person's) agricultural base and his military might would also be destroyed. The presence of Satan's children among God's people would also serve to weaken them. Because no one recognized the weeds, both grew at the same time. The "weed" Jesus referred to may have been darnel, a poisonous plant that looks very much like wheat in the early stages of growth, but becomes distinguishable when the heads of the wheat appear. Jesus' hearers would have understood how no one would have noticed the weeds until *the plants came up and bore grain.* Only then would the weeds appear. A heavy infestation of darnel (indicated by it being "sowed" among the grain) would cause the roots of both plants to become entangled. To sow darnel in a person's wheat field was punishable by Roman law. This real-life situation gave Jesus' hearers a picture of God's kingdom growing and thriving alongside evil in this world.

Jesus' reference is to the kingdom of heaven and is not limited to the church. However, the church is in the world as well as in the kingdom of heaven, so the truth also applies. There are good seeds and bad seeds, children of God and children of Satan, in the church. At first glance, the works of each may be difficult to distinguish. Jesus appealed to us to be appropriately inclusive (we should avoid exclusiveness and arrogant separatism). We should strive for unity with others even when it may present the risk of "weeds." The work of judgment is God's. Yet we must not be naive. Satan has a strategy and his children *are* at work.

**13:27** **"The owner's servants came to him and said, 'Sir, didn't you sow good seed in your field? Where then did the weeds come from?'"** NIV After the plants have grown, the *owner's servants* report the surprising appearance of the weeds. Jesus did not identify the servants in his explanation of this parable. The servants knew the master had sowed *good seed.* While the servants would expect a few weeds, this heavy infestation was suspect.

How could there be so many weeds? *"Where then did the weeds come from?"* the servants ask.

Who are these "weeds"? Jesus would soon explain that "the weeds are the children of the evil one" (13:38 NRSV). They may be people in the church who appear to be believers but who never truly believe. The apostles later battled the problem of false teachers who came from within the ranks of the believers (see, for example, 2 Peter 2:1-3, 13-22). To interpret the meaning more broadly—the kingdom of God is present and growing in a world full of sin and unbelief. God will not eliminate all opposition until the end of the age.

**13:28** **"'An enemy did this,' he replied. The servants asked him, 'Do you want us to go and pull them up?'"** NIV The enemy, Satan (13:39), is always working to obstruct the growth of God's kingdom. The enemy caused a problem, but the weeds could not stop the growth of the wheat. The wheat just grew alongside the weeds. So the servants dutifully asked if they should *go and pull* up the weeds.

TOUGH QUESTION
The "servants" in this parable raise one of the toughest questions ever posed: If God is good and all-powerful, where does evil come from, and why is evil permitted?
  The answer provided is a simple one. It does not address all the logical difficulties of good and evil coexisting, but it tells us what we need to know: "An enemy did this."

- God does not generate evil. God is good indeed and ought not be identified with evil at all.
- Let God be concerned about understanding evil deeply and thoroughly. When we seek in-depth understanding of evil (through viewing films or reading novels), we risk real damage to the heart, soul, and mind.
- Spiritual "warfare" is normal, not odd or surprising. Enemies actively oppose one another.

When sin and unbelief seem so strong, don't try to figure out where they originated. We know Satan is our enemy. Instead, trust God and determine to follow him.

**13:29-30** **"But he replied, 'No; for in gathering the weeds you would uproot the wheat along with them. Let both of them grow together until the harvest; and at harvest time I will tell the reapers, Collect the weeds first and bind them in bundles to be burned, but gather the wheat into my barn.'"** NRSV In answer to the servants' question, the owner replied that *no,* they should not weed the fields. Instead, the wheat and weeds should *grow together until the harvest.* At the time of harvest, the workers would reap the field—gathering the wheat into the barn and collecting the weeds to be burned. The "harvest" was a common metaphor for the final judgment (Jeremiah 51:33; Hosea 6:11; see also Revelation 14:14-16). Jesus soon explained that "the harvest is the end of the age, and the reapers are angels" (13:39 NRSV).

Again, Jesus was making the point that while his coming signaled the arrival of the kingdom, its consummation would be delayed. The children of God and children of Satan would grow together "until" the harvest; then, God would judge and separate his children from Satan's children ("the children of the evil one," 13:38).

---

GOD DOES THE WEEDING
The young weeds and the young blades of wheat look the same and can't be distinguished until they are grown and ready for harvest. Weeds (unbelievers) and wheat (believers) must live side by side in this world. God allows unbelievers to remain for a while, just as a farmer allows weeds to remain in his field so that the surrounding wheat won't be uprooted with them. At the harvest, however, the weeds will be uprooted and thrown away. God's harvest (judgment) of all people is coming. Make yourself ready by remaining faithful to Christ and obeying him.

---

## JESUS TELLS THE PARABLE OF THE MUSTARD SEED / 13:31-32 / **81**

**3:31-32** **He told them another parable: "The kingdom of heaven is like a mustard seed, which a man took and planted in his field. Though it is the smallest of all your seeds, yet when it grows, it is the largest of garden plants and becomes a tree, so that the birds of the air come and perch in its branches."** NIV No one parable can completely describe God's kingdom in all its aspects, so Jesus gave several. Through this parable, Jesus explained that his kingdom would have a small beginning. Indeed, it began with Jesus alone and, upon his ascension, was left in the care of twelve apostles and just a few hundred other followers. Jesus compared this beginning to the *mustard seed,* which was the *smallest* seed that a farmer used. The mustard seed was so small that it would take almost twenty thousand seeds to make one ounce. Modern critics have pointed out that the mustard seed is *not* the smallest seed, and they use this to argue against the accuracy of the Bible. Jesus was not making a scientific statement. Though the mustard seed is not the smallest seed in all of creation, it was used in rabbinic proverbs to designate the smallest of things. No other seed so small produced such a large plant.

From this very tiny seed would grow a large shrub—the largest shrub among all the herbs that the farmer would plant in his garden. A mustard shrub could grow ten to twelve feet in just a few weeks. While that is not technically a *tree,* Jesus used hyperbole to stress both the insignificance ("smallest") and magnificence ("largest," "tree") of the kingdom. His point was that just as a tiny seed will grow into the *largest of garden plants,* so God's kingdom will produce many people who truly believe. From this small start, the kingdom will grow into such greatness that when Christ returns, it will take over the entire earth. Jesus stressed the future greatness of the kingdom, which then seemed insignificant. He also showed that the kingdom had small beginnings but would grow and produce great results.

> Sects and ideologies almost always seem stronger than the church. Sects and ideologies fly; the church limps. Sects and ideologies die; the church limps on. Stick with the church.
> *Frederick Dale Bruner*

Jesus' mention of *birds of the air* added color to his parable or described the size of this shrub, but probably did not have any allegorical meaning. Some commentators, however, say that the birds may represent the Gentiles becoming part of God's kingdom (see prophecies such as Ezekiel 17:22-24; 31:6).

For the disciples, and for us, this parable meant that size or relative power does not indicate final results. The disciples needed to understand that while their mission might at times seem unattainable, God's kingdom *would* take root and grow across the world and through the years. This would be no political coup; the kingdom would grow steadily in people's hearts, making a difference in people's lives and preparing them for life to come in God's eternal kingdom.

## JESUS TELLS THE PARABLE OF THE YEAST / 13:33-35 / *82*

**13:33 He told them still another parable: "The kingdom of heaven is like yeast that a woman took and mixed into a large amount of flour until it worked all through the dough."** NIV
In other Bible passages, "yeast" is used as a symbol of evil or uncleanness (see 16:6). Here it is a positive symbol of growth. Like the parable of the mustard seed, this parable stresses small beginnings with great growth. While the seed grows, however, the yeast permeates and transforms; thus, we see another aspect

of the kingdom. Although yeast looks like a minor ingredient, it permeates the whole loaf. Although the kingdom had small beginnings, it would grow to have a great impact on the world. What the Jews saw as insignificant (the man Jesus and his little band of followers) was actually the start of a great and world-changing event. Like leaven working its way through the dough, the kingdom message would spread across the entire world.

---

SMALL IS BEAUTIFUL
Massive churches are exciting, but small churches are the norm. Huge choirs led by trained conductors are thrilling, but little backwoods quartets are the norm. Stereo sound systems make worship acoustically exhilarating, but simple human voices are the norm. It's fine for the church to be small, struggling, and simple—it's normal.

Don't be fooled into thinking that wealth, prestige, and a huge donor base are typical of God's church. The movement Jesus started (and his followers today continue) more often has a humble look to it—not very impressive at all, by modern standards. But the church endures while other movements disappear, and it grows while others crest and fall.

---

**3:34-35 Jesus spoke all these things to the crowd in parables; he did not say anything to them without using a parable. So was fulfilled what was spoken through the prophet: "I will open my mouth in parables, I will utter things hidden since the creation of the world."** NIV The first half of the quoted verse follows the first part of Psalm 78:2. The second half *(since the creation of the world)* seems to be an independent rendition of the end of Psalm 78:2. Psalm 78 reviews Israel's history from the time of slavery in Egypt to David's reign. This psalm was told over and over to each generation so they would not forget God and make the same mistakes as their ancestors. The "things hidden" refers to God's mighty acts in redeeming his people despite their sin and unfaithfulness.

This statement shows that Matthew intended to end a major section here. These verses reiterate 13:10-13, that the Jews would receive the kingdom message only in enigmatic form as judgment upon them. "Jesus spoke" is in the aorist tense, indicating the present situation. The phrase "he did not saying anything to them without using a parable" has a verb in the imperfect tense indicating that this was Jesus' custom. *Parables* were an essential part of Jesus' ministry, imparting truth, fulfilling prophecy, and separating the curiosity seekers from the true followers.

## JESUS EXPLAINS THE PARABLE
## OF THE WEEDS / 13:36-43 / **83**

**13:36** **Then he left the crowds and went into the house. And his disci-**
**ples approached him, saying, "Explain to us the parable of the**
**weeds of the field."** NRSV In 13:1, Jesus had gone "out of the house"
to sit beside the sea. There he spoke publicly to the crowds. Jesus'
movement back *into the house* signifies a movement away from the
crowds and to private discussion with *his disciples.* Jesus' followers
had the knowledge of the secrets of the kingdom (13:11) and the
ability to "see" and "hear" (13:16), but they still needed his help in
understanding all his words.

**13:37-39** **He answered, "The one who sows the good seed is the Son of**
**Man; the field is the world, and the good seed are the chil-**
**dren of the kingdom; the weeds are the children of the evil**
**one, and the enemy who sowed them is the devil; the harvest**
**is the end of the age, and the reapers are angels."** NRSV Jesus
described the identity of the important parts of the parable of the
weeds recorded in 13:24-30. Jesus explained to his listening disciples that the good seeds are believers, sown by the Son of Man in
the field of the world. In this world also existed those who were
*not* children of the kingdom; thus, they were children of the
devil, sown by him into this world. At *the end of the age,* the
angels would come and the *harvest* would begin.

**13:40-42** **"Just as the weeds are collected and burned up with fire, so will**
**it be at the end of the age. The Son of Man will send his angels,**
**and they will collect out of his kingdom all causes of sin and**
**all evildoers, and they will throw them into the furnace of**
**fire, where there will be weeping and gnashing of teeth."** NRSV
At this harvest, God will separate his people from Satan's people.
As the harvesters collect *the weeds* into bundles to be destroyed,
so Satan's works and Satan's people will be thrown *into the fur-*
*nace of fire.* "Furnace of fire" is not a
name for hell but is a metaphor for final
judgment (see Daniel 3:6). Jesus often
used the term "weeping and gnashing
of teeth" to refer to the coming judgment (see 8:12; 13:50; 22:13; 24:51;
25:30). The "weeping" indicates sorrow
or remorse, and "gnashing of teeth" shows extreme anxiety or
pain. Those who say they don't care what happens to them after
they die don't realize what they are saying. God will punish them
for living in selfishness and indifference to him. Jesus, who has
already identified himself as the Son of Man (8:20; 9:6; 10:23;

> Toiling will all be ended,
> shadows will flee away;
> Sorrow will be forgotten,
> O what a wonderful day!
> *John W. Peterson*

11:19; 12:8, 32, 40), revealed that he will inaugurate the end of
the age and the final judgment.

---

**TRAGEDY OF EVIL**
Followers of Jesus do not fear God's final judgment, but we
must respond to it with
- *tears,* for the separation and suffering that will fall upon
  evildoers. We must never gloat over or feel indifferent to the
  fate of those facing judgment. God mourns over lost souls,
  and so should we.
- *sharing the gospel,* since many need to hear and all who
  respond in faith will be saved from judgment. Christians
  ought to always be witnessing people.
- *lifelong service,* because no matter what your job, profession,
  or education, all you do should be dedicated to God. God
  uses your work to advance his kingdom and overcome evil.

---

**13:43** **"Then the righteous will shine like the sun in the kingdom of
their Father. Let anyone with ears listen!"** NRSV Reflecting words
from Daniel 12:3, Jesus described the final glory of *the righteous:*
"Those who are wise will shine like the brightness of the heavens,
and those who lead many to righteousness, like the stars for ever
and ever" (NIV). Those who receive God's favor stand in bright
contrast to those who receive his judgment. The "kingdom of their
Father" is another name for the kingdom of God and heaven.
Heaven will be a glorious place! The message is vitally important,
so *anyone with ears* should *listen!* (See also 11:15.)

## JESUS TELLS THE PARABLE OF HIDDEN TREASURE / 13:44 / **84**

The parable of the hidden treasure and the parable of the pearl
merchant (13:45-46) form a pair and belong together (as seen in
the "again" of verse 45). They note a single event in the past, and
teach the inestimable value of the kingdom.

**13:44** **"The kingdom of heaven is like treasure hidden in a field.
When a man found it, he hid it again, and then in his joy went
and sold all he had and bought that field."** NIV To teach the inestimable value of the kingdom of heaven and of being part of that
kingdom, Jesus described it as a *treasure hidden in a field.* The
*man* who found the treasure would have been a day laborer who
could get possession by quitting his job and then returning to
recover his find. According to rabbinic law, if a worker came
across buried treasure in someone else's field and lifted it out, the
treasure would belong to the owner. In this story, the laborer was

careful not to lift out the treasure. To obtain this treasure, which far surpassed the value of *all he had,* he would have to sell everything he had so he could buy the field. He did this joyfully.

The man who discovered the treasure in the field stumbled upon it by accident but knew its value when he found it. Some have wondered about the morality of a man obtaining a treasure in this way, but Jesus was not teaching a moral lesson. He was merely showing the value of this treasure that is worth every sacrifice and commitment to obtain. The kingdom of heaven is more valuable than anything else we can have, and a person must be willing to give up everything to obtain it.

## JESUS TELLS THE PARABLE OF THE PEARL MERCHANT / 13:45-46 / **85**

This parable and the previous parable of the hidden treasure (13:44) are a pair and should be studied together (as noted by the word "again" in verse 45).

**13:45-46** **"Again, the kingdom of heaven is like a merchant seeking beautiful pearls, who, when he had found one pearl of great price, went and sold all that he had and bought it."** NKJV In the previous parable, Jesus described a man stumbling upon a treasure. In this parable, Jesus pictured a wealthy pearl merchant. Pearls were especially valued in the Near East. A *pearl of great price* could obviously set up this merchant for life. Knowing pearls, this merchant searched earnestly for one of great value. When he found it, he sold everything he had to buy it. Some may discover the kingdom (13:44); some may seek earnestly and finally obtain it. In both cases, the men recognized the value of what they had found and willingly invested everything to obtain it. The kingdom of heaven is so valuable that it calls for a total investment (radical discipleship) from those who find it.

---

JOY

The treasure and pearl parables tell of the joy of finding peace with God. There's no other word to express it. Both stories involve people who very happily find the answer to their life's hopes and dreams.

That's what becoming a Christian is about: deepest needs met, deepest longings satisfied, deepest hurts bandaged, and a future and a hope unlike any other. It all adds up to joy!

If your faith is grim and your life bleak, let God put some of this wonderful happiness back where it should be. If you have not yet trusted in Jesus as your Lord, grab this precious pearl today.

---

### JESUS TELLS THE PARABLE OF THE
### FISHING NET / 13:47-52 / **86**

**3:47-48** **"Once again, the kingdom of heaven is like a net that was let down into the lake and caught all kinds of fish. When it was full, the fishermen pulled it up on the shore. Then they sat down and collected the good fish in baskets, but threw the bad away."** NIV The parable of the fishing net deals with the dividing of people much as the parable of the wheat and weeds does. This parable pictures a dragnet perhaps drawn between two boats or a large net with one end attached to shore and the other taken to sea by a boat. The net is dragged in a wide semicircle with the top held up by corks and the bottom slightly weighted. *All kinds of fish* are caught in the net. The fishermen then draw the net to the beach where they sort the fish. They put good fish into *baskets* and throw away the bad (inedible or "unclean" as in Leviticus 11:10-11) ones.

**13:49-50** **"So it will be at the end of the age. The angels will come out and separate the evil from the righteous and throw them into the furnace of fire, where there will be weeping and gnashing of teeth."** NRSV While the parable of the wheat and weeds highlighted the length of time during which good and evil people must coexist before the judgment, this parable focuses on that final judgment. As the net catches all kinds of fish, the gospel message will go out to all kinds of people. *At the end of the age,* the angels will "sort the fish," separating evil people from righteous. Like the wheat that will be gathered and burned, the bad fish will be thrown into the furnace of fire (a metaphor for judgment, see 13:40-42). In real practice, bad fish would not have been put in a furnace. However, Jesus' point in this parable is that the furnace of fire will be the place for the wicked people. Like the wheat that will be gathered into the barns, the good fish will be put into baskets (13:29-30). As in 13:42, "weeping and gnashing of teeth" indicates sorrow, remorse, anxiety, and pain.

**13:51-52** **"Have you understood all these things?" Jesus asked. "Yes," they replied. He said to them, "Therefore every teacher of the law who has been instructed about the kingdom of heaven is like the owner of a house who brings out of his storeroom new treasures as well as old."** NIV After Jesus had given the parable of the weeds in the field, the disciples came asking Jesus to explain what he had told them (13:36). They did not understand. After giving an explanation, Jesus asked if they understood. They answered *"Yes."* Understanding is the core of discipleship, for only Jesus' true followers are given the ability to understand, as Jesus had explained earlier (13:13-15, 19, 23).

Because the disciples understood, *therefore,* Jesus said, they were the "teachers of the law" in his kingdom. In other words, the current teachers of religious law did not understand, so their teaching was invalid. The disciples had been *instructed about the kingdom of heaven.* They understood God's real purpose in the law as revealed in the Old Testament; therefore, they had a real treasure. The disciples would bring this treasure "out of [the] storeroom" in that their responsibility would be to share what they had learned with others. The disciples had gained this treasure through Jesus' instruction, so they were able to understand and use the best of older wisdom as well as the new insights that Jesus brought to them. True teachers see the value of both old and new.

The Old Testament points the way to Jesus, the Messiah. Jesus always upheld the authority and relevance of the Scriptures. Those who understand Jesus' teaching about the kingdom of heaven receive a double benefit. This was a new treasure that Jesus was revealing. Both the old and new teachings give practical guidelines for faith and for living in the world. The religious leaders, however, were trapped in the old and blind to the new. They were looking for a future kingdom preceded by judgment. Jesus, however, taught that the kingdom was *now* and the judgment was future. The religious leaders were looking for a physical and temporal kingdom (brought on by military strength and physical rule), but they were blind to the spiritual significance of the kingdom that Christ had brought.

---

LIFE OF LEARNING
Jesus wants us to understand God's truth, and that is not easily or quickly done. Learning about God's truth (in all its richness and diversity) is a lifelong process. Did you ever imagine that *learning* is also a way to serve God? Let your life be full of inquiry, and let each step you take be a means of deepening your faith and love for God.

---

## THE PEOPLE OF NAZARETH REFUSE TO BELIEVE / 13:53-58 / **91**

**13:53-54** **When Jesus had finished these parables, he moved on from there. Coming to his hometown, he began teaching the people in their synagogue, and they were amazed. "Where did this man get this wisdom and these miraculous powers?" they asked.**[NIV]

After teaching in *parables*, Jesus left *there* (probably Capernaum) and went *to his hometown;* that is, he returned to Nazareth (2:23). Nazareth was about twenty miles southwest of Capernaum.

Jesus had been born in Bethlehem, but he had been reared in Nazareth (Matthew 2:19-23; Luke 2:39-40; 4:16). This was not the first time he had spoken and taught in Nazareth. Luke 4:14-30 states that Jesus went to Nazareth, "where he had been brought up, [and] he went to the synagogue on the sabbath day" to read and teach (Luke 4:16 NRSV). At that time, the response was less than positive; in fact, the people had tried to kill him, but Jesus had walked away unharmed. This trip to Nazareth, therefore, is significant. The people of Nazareth were about to receive a second chance to believe; unfortunately, they again rejected the Lord.

Jesus' forums for speaking included the mountainsides (5:1), people's homes (9:10-13), the seashore (13:1), and the local synagogues (4:23; 9:35; 12:9). Lay people would conduct synagogue services under the leadership of one or more synagogue leaders.

For example, Jairus, the man whose daughter Jesus brought back to life, was a synagogue leader (see 9:18; Mark 5:22). It was common for one of these leaders to ask a visiting rabbi to speak in the local synagogue. Jesus, a well-known and popular speaker, had no trouble gaining an opportunity to teach in the synagogue on the Sabbath.

The synagogue was the center of the town, controlling civic and social as well as religious life. The synagogue was not like a church today—it was not an empty building except on Sabbath days when only the devoted would come. Instead, it seemed that everyone would come to the synagogue, for this was the focal point of Jewish life. This was really a key place for Jesus to meet the people—much like the city gate in the Old Testament.

The people *were amazed* at Jesus' wisdom, teaching ability,

**Nazareth Rejects Jesus**
*Chronologically, this return to Nazareth occurred after Jesus had been in the Gadarene region where he had healed the demon-possessed men (8:28-34) and after he had recrossed the sea to Capernaum. From there he traveled to Nazareth, where he had grown up, only to discover that the people refused to believe he was the Christ.*

and miraculous powers. The Greek verb for "amazed" is *ekplesso,* which literally means "to strike out of one's senses." The people were so amazed that it was as if they had been struck with a blow—stunned. They were flabbergasted. They knew Jesus' miracles were supernatural, but they wondered about their source (the options were either God or Satan—see 12:24) and how Jesus could do them.

**13:55-56** **"Is not this the carpenter's son? Is not his mother called Mary? And are not his brothers James and Joseph and Simon and Judas? And are not all his sisters with us? Where then did this man get all this?"** NRSV Jesus was teaching effectively and wisely, but the people of his hometown saw him as only *the carpenter's son* (referring to Joseph) whose family they also knew well. "He is no better than we are—he is just a common laborer," they said. Jesus was almost thirty years old before he began his public teaching ministry, and he had never been formally trained as a rabbi. For the years before that, he had been at home, learning the trade of carpentry from his father. The absence of mention of the father, Joseph, supports the theory that Joseph had probably died before the time of Jesus' ministry. Jesus' carpentry trade probably helped to support him and his family after Joseph's death. The story of *his mother called Mary* is recorded in Luke 1:26-38.

The listing of the brothers (see also 12:46-49) indicates that the people knew the family well—the mother, the brothers, the sisters. Apparently they were all ordinary people, and Jesus had experienced an ordinary childhood. The residents of Jesus' hometown had known Jesus since he was a young child and knew his family. But they could not bring themselves to believe in his message. They were too close to the situation. Jesus had come to them as a prophet, one who challenged them to respond to unpopular spiritual truth. They did not listen to the timeless message because they could not see beyond the man.

Jesus' brother *James* later became a believer, a leader in the Jerusalem church (Acts 15:13; Galatians 2:9), and the author of the book of James. *Judas* may have been Jude, author of the book of Jude. Nothing else is known of the other brothers and sisters. (See also 12:46-50 for more on Jesus' family.)

**13:57** **So they were offended at Him. But Jesus said to them, "A prophet is not without honor except in his own country and in his own house."** NKJV Jesus' claims caused the people in his hometown to be *offended at Him.* They stumbled over his words and could not accept them. They were offended that others could be impressed by Jesus and follow him. He was one of their peers, and their preconceived notions about who he was made it impossible for them to accept his message. They also may have been jealous. Jesus had come to them as a prophet, but they saw only a hometown boy.

Jesus used a common proverb found in rabbinic literature. It is significant that Jesus applied the word "prophet" to himself, thus specifically claiming to be God's messenger. The word refers not to one who foretells future events (although that may be part of a prophet's ministry), but to one who speaks God's message. Jesus was not the first prophet to be rejected *in his own country.* Jeremiah, for example, experienced rejection in his hometown, even by members of his own family (Jeremiah 12:5-6). Jesus also experienced rejection by members *in his own house* (John 7:5). Some of Jesus' family did believe in him after his resurrection (Acts 1:14).

**13:58 And he did not do many miracles there because of their lack of faith.**[NIV] That Jesus *did not do many miracles* in Nazareth does not mean that his power had been restricted. Jesus could have done greater miracles in Nazareth, but he chose not to because of the people's unbelief. *Lack of faith* blinds people to the truth and robs them of hope. These people missed the Messiah. Jesus performed mighty works to further the kingdom of God, not to try to convince a group of stubborn people who had already thoroughly rejected him. To do miracles would be of no value because the people did not accept his message or believe that he was from God. Therefore, Jesus looked elsewhere, seeking those who would respond to his miracles and message. We need to proclaim the gospel. At times, however, we need to move on, to other towns and people.

---

FAITH AND POWER
Jesus is not limited by people's faith (or lack of it), but there does seem to be a strong connection between faith and God's power actively at work. Christians who pray discover answers to prayer. Churches who worship Christ find Christ active in their fellowship.

Where skeptics and atheists hold court, God seldom intervenes. God seems to like the role of invited guest over that of party crasher. So, let faith grow, pray all the time, and expect to see God at work in and around you.

---

# Matthew 14

Matthew continued to record various responses to Jesus. The Pharisees have accused him of being under Satan's power (12:22-37). Other religious leaders have revealed their rejection by requesting a "sign" (12:38-45). Jesus' own family thought he had gone crazy (12:46-50; see also Mark 3:31-35). Jesus had to speak in parables because of many people's unbelief (13:1-52). Finally, the people of Jesus' hometown had rejected him (13:53-58). This chapter gives the story of a government leader's misunderstanding. Herod thought that Jesus was the resurrected John the Baptist.

John the Baptist had been arrested just prior to the beginning of Jesus' public ministry. Because John had ministered in Perea ("on the other side of the Jordan," John 1:28), he was under Herod's jurisdiction. The arrest marked the end of John's public ministry. He was imprisoned for some time prior to his death (see 11:2-6).

**14:1 At that time Herod the tetrarch heard the report about Jesus.**NKJV "At that time" is only a connecting phrase. The events of this chapter do not follow chronologically from the end of chapter 13. *Herod* ruled over the territories of Galilee and Perea. In 4 B.C., Herod had been named *tetrarch*—one of four rulers over the four districts of Palestine. He was the son of Herod the Great, who had ordered the killing of the babies in Bethlehem (2:16). Also known as Herod Antipas, he would hear Jesus' case before the crucifixion (Luke 23:6-12).

The history of the Herod family is filled with lies, murder, treachery, and adultery. Herod Antipas was known for his insensitivity and debauchery. Though he was popular with his Roman superiors, his unbridled political ambitions eventually led to his exile in A.D. 39 by the Roman emperor Caligula, who removed him on the basis of charges by his nephew (Herod Agrippa I), who ruled Galilee after Herod Antipas.

**HEROD'S TRAGEDY**
Most people dislike having their sins pointed out, especially in public. The shame of being exposed is often stronger than the guilt brought on by the wrongdoing. Herod Antipas was a man experiencing both guilt and shame. Herod's ruthless ambition was public knowledge, as was his illegal (by Jewish law) marriage to his brother's wife, Herodias. One man made Herod's sin a public issue. That man was John the Baptist. Herodias was particularly anxious to have John silenced. But Herod liked John, who was probably one of the few people he met who spoke only the truth to him. But the truth about his sin was a bitter pill to swallow, and Herod wavered at the point of conflict. Eventually Herodias forced his hand, and John was executed.

For each person, God chooses the best possible ways to reveal himself. He uses his Word, various circumstances, our minds, or other people to get our attention. God is persuasive and persistent but never forces himself on us. To miss or resist God's message, as did Herod, is a tragedy. How aware are you of God's attempts to enter your life? Have you welcomed him?

---

**14:2 And he said to his attendants, "This is John the Baptist; he has risen from the dead! That is why miraculous powers are at work in him."** NIV Herod's guilt over John's death led him to think that his worst nightmares had come true: *John the Baptist* had *risen from the dead.* Oddly enough, John had done no miracles (John 10:41); he had simply preached and prepared the way for Jesus. Verses 3 and 4 show that this incident occurred after John's death and are Matthew's flashback to the prior events.

While Herod had succeeded in silencing John, he had not succeeded in silencing his own guilty conscience (see 14:9). When news of Jesus reached the palace, Herod thought that John had come back to trouble him some more. Thus began Herod's great interest in Jesus and his long-standing desire to see him perform a miracle (Luke 23:8).

**14:3-4 For Herod had arrested John, bound him, and put him in prison on account of Herodias, his brother Philip's wife, because John had been telling him, "It is not lawful for you to have her."** NRSV Herod's personal guilt was well placed, for he had ordered John to be arrested. In ancient days, kings had absolute sway; if the king wanted someone arrested, the arrest was carried out by his guards—no questions asked. Herod, empowered by Rome over the region of Galilee, simply had given the orders and John had been *arrested, bound,* and put *in prison.* The Jewish historian Josephus pinpointed this prison as Machaerus, a fortress (combination palace and prison) near the barren northeastern shore of the Dead Sea in the region of Moab.

Ironically, this "powerful" king did this in response to pressure from *Herodias, his brother Philip's wife.* Why did she make a difference? Mark added that Herod had married her (Mark 6:17). Herod's first wife was the daughter of Aretas, king of the Nabateans, whose land was south of Perea. This marriage was arranged by Augustus to keep peace between Arabs and Jews. Philip was Herod's half brother and *not* Philip the tetrarch. According to Josephus, Salome was the one who later married Philip the tetrarch, who was her granduncle. When Herod Antipas met Herodias, his brother's wife, he divorced his first wife and married Herodias.

Herodias was the daughter of Aristobulus, another half brother. Thus, Herodias was a half niece to both Philip and Herod (and they, in turn, were her half uncles). Herodias married her half uncle Philip and then divorced him to marry another half uncle, Herod. Thus, in marrying, Herodias and Herod had committed adultery, as well as a type of incest. John the Baptist condemned Herod and Herodias for living immorally. It was *not lawful* for Herod to be married to his brother's (that is, half brother's) wife (not to mention that she was also his half niece). Leviticus 18:16 and 20:21 describe the laws that Herod was breaking. Herod was Jewish, and whether or not he cared about the Jewish law, he did care about a revolt against him by the Jews.

---

JOHN THE BOLD
John was called the Baptist, but he could have equally been called the Bold. An evangelist who preached about the kingdom, he got in trouble over a too-direct assault on the morals of the ruling family.

Christians are smart to choose their battles. Not every sin can or should be the topic of loud public preaching. But some sins need the boldness of John: his forthright truth telling, his disregard of personal consequences, his call to moral living. Antislavery preachers of the eighteenth and nineteenth centuries were these types (check out the story of Elijah P. Lovejoy as one good example), as well as civil rights preachers of the twentieth century. Choose your battles, but once engaged, don't quiver for fear of a tyrant's power. Jesus is Lord, everywhere and at all times.

---

**14:5 Herod wanted to kill John, but he was afraid of the people, because they considered him a prophet.**[NIV] Rebuking a tyrannical Roman official who could imprison and execute him was extremely dangerous, yet that is what John had done. In addition, there was political tension over Herod's divorce of his first wife—the daughter of the king of a neighboring country. This king eventually would defeat Herod in battle. This was explosive enough without John bringing up the illegal marriage. John's public denunciation of the incest and adultery of Herod and Herodias was too much for them to bear, especially Herodias, whose anger turned to hatred. Mark's Gospel focuses on Herodias, who was both wicked and ruthless in her attempts to kill John the Baptist. While Matthew's account seems to focus on Herod *(Herod wanted to kill John),* we can combine the accounts to see a wicked yet weak ruler who was not in a hurry to kill John because he was *afraid of the people.* The people considered John to be a *prophet,* and for Herod to put to death one of the Jews' prophets could have caused a huge revolt in his territory and certainly would have created great discontent.

> Never before has the need been more urgent for Christians to bring their faith to the front lines. It takes courage to think and act Christianly in times like these. We must demonstrate Christian love and compassion to even those who oppose us most vehemently.
>
> *Charles Colson*

Mark writes that Herodias "nursed a grudge against John and wanted to kill him. But she was not able to" (Mark 6:19 NIV). Apparently her influence was very strong over her husband. Herodias likely made her desires known, so Herod solved his dilemma by keeping John locked away in prison. Perhaps Herod hoped that stopping John's public speaking would end the problem and quiet Herodias.

**14:6-7 But when Herod's birthday came, the daughter of Herodias danced before the company, and she pleased Herod so much that he promised on oath to grant her whatever she might ask.**NRSV That Herod had imprisoned John the Baptist was not enough for the angry Herodias. She continued to nurse her grudge against John for speaking publicly about her sins, biding her time until she would get her way and have John killed. Then on *Herod's birthday,* the opportunity arrived. Mark wrote that Herod gave a banquet for many notable men from governmental, military, and civil positions in Galilee (Mark 6:21). Celebrating birthdays was a Hellenistic custom, not a Jewish one.

Herodias's *daughter* (by her marriage with Herod Philip) provided the bait Herodias would use to get her way with her husband. According to the Jewish historian Josephus, the daughter was

Salome, a young woman in her middle teens. Herodias sent Salome into the banquet hall to dance *before the company* of Herod and his roomful of male (and probably drunken) dinner guests. The dance she performed may have been provocative and sensual. Few women of respectable position would perform in such a way, but Herodias knew that Salome's dance would gain raucous approval from

> Not that it is wrong in itself to give a good party, but such is the propensity of the human mind to wantonness that when the reins are loosed, men easily go astray.          *John Calvin*

the all-male audience. When Salome ended her dance, the king brought her to his side. He offered her *whatever she might ask.* Not only that, but *he promised on oath*—perhaps his word wasn't good enough without that. Herod probably expected his daughter to request jewels or some other favor. He certainly did not expect the request he received.

---

### SENSUAL AND WEAK

What a study in contrasts: John the bold, in prison; and Herod the powerful, subdued by his own sensuality and moral weakness—internal prisons that John never knew. Herod became weak through a lifetime of weak decisions, culminating in this sorry spectacle. His life was tragic and wasted.

Be careful about those small moral compromises that lead to bigger ones. Herod found himself on a slippery slope and could not stop the slide. Examine all your decisions and choices. Does each step you take reflect what God wants for your life? As soon as you exclude his will from your daily decisions, you risk the error of merely pleasing people.

---

**14:8** **Prompted by her mother, she said, "Give me the head of John the Baptist here on a platter."** NRSV Any young woman might be prepared with a thousand possible suggestions to an offer such as Herod's, but Salome was still a fairly young girl and had already been *prompted*. The Matthew account seems to sound as though Salome already knew what she would request; Mark's Gospel says she returned to her mother to find out what she should ask for. The mother's dark desires dominated the situation. Salome responded with the gruesome request, *"Give me the head of John the Baptist here on a platter."* Herodias wanted John killed and the proof of his death returned on a platter. Bringing the head to the one who ordered the execution was common; however, beheading, while a Roman custom, was not a normal form of Jewish execution. Neither was it legal to put a person to death without a trial. But Herod, faced by drunk and smirking officials who waited to see what he would do, was too weak to object. Herodias would have her way. Herod caved in under the social pressure and John's death was sealed.

**14:9-10 The king was distressed, but because of his oaths and his dinner guests, he ordered that her request be granted and had John beheaded in the prison.**NIV When Salome grandly gave her request to Herod in the hearing of all the important officials, Herod suddenly realized what he had done—and he probably knew he had been trapped by Herodias. Herod *was distressed* because he put himself in this position in front of all the people he wanted to impress (14:5), and yet he considered John a holy man whom he both respected and feared (Mark 6:20). Herod had made a promise and had sealed it with an oath. Such words were considered irrevocable. To back out on the promise would show his important guests that Herod was not a man of his word or that he was afraid of this "unimportant" prisoner in a dungeon. So, *because of his oaths* and for his reputation in front of *his dinner guests,* Herod decided to show his authority by immediately fulfilling the girl's request.

---

STUPID PROMISES
It's a good rule to keep your promises. Like most rules, however, sometimes an exception is necessary. It may require a lot of embarrassing backtracking, but some promises need to be rescinded before they lead to greater trouble. Herod failed to swallow his mistake and, instead, violated local criminal procedures and ordered the summary execution of a man undeserving of that fate.

Try not to make promises you cannot keep (Christian parents and politicians, take note!). But when you make a stupid promise, swallow your pride and get out of it. Better to feel embarrassed than to commit a grave sin.

---

**14:11 The head was brought on a platter and given to the girl, who brought it to her mother.**NRSV If Herod was at his usual location in his palace in Tiberias, some time had to elapse between saying he would fulfill Salome's request and the actual return with the gruesome results. Some scholars think that Herod was at the prison fortress of Machaerus by the Dead Sea where John was imprisoned. If so, the event would have taken place almost immediately. An executioner beheaded John and brought the grisly trophy back *to the girl.* The Greek word translated "girl" *(korasion)* means a girl of marriageable age. As suggested above, she was in her early to middle teens, yet young enough to still be under her parents' authority.

Herod fulfilled his oath and saved face before his guests. But he had been manipulated by his wife and was left with great fear over what he had done in killing a holy man. Herod's guilt could not be assuaged. Thus, when Jesus came upon the scene, Herod thought that John had come back to life (14:2).

---

**GRUESOME INSENSITIVITY**
What mother would ask her teenage daughter to do this . . . the head of a dead man on a tray? By any human standards, the consciences of both mother and daughter were totally desensitized.

Are children similarly desensitized today by early exposure to violence on television, in motion pictures, and in popular music? Is sex so commonplace and murder so normal that the "unspeakable" begins to bore? Researchers have gathered lots of data, and the best results point in that direction: the more exposure we have to gruesome media, the less sensitive we become to real-life cruelty.

Check out the themes on your Sunday night television schedule if you want a modern menu of what Herodias must have taught Salome. And be forewarned.

---

**14:12 His disciples came and took the body and buried it; then they went and told Jesus.**<sup>NRSV</sup> John the Baptist apparently still had *disciples,* even though many had left him to follow Jesus (which John was content for them to do, see John 1:35-37). When they heard that John had been beheaded, they came, took away his corpse, and gave it a proper burial (instead of leaving it to be disposed of by the guards in the prison). Then, they *went and told Jesus.* Matthew's mention of this report to Jesus shows the close link between John's and Jesus' ministries. The report could have also been a warning to Jesus about the violence of which Herod was capable, and the danger of public preaching. "Don't let the same thing happen to you," may have been the messengers' warning. John was the first to feel what could follow for Jesus.

## JESUS FEEDS FIVE THOUSAND / 14:13-21 / 96

Apart from Jesus' resurrection, this is the only miracle that appears in all four Gospels, showing its importance to Jesus' ministry and to the early church. While many people have tried to explain away the incident, it is clear that all the Gospel writers saw this as a wonderful miracle. In Matthew and Mark, this miracle follows the account of Herod's tragic feast where John the Baptist was killed. The placement of the event creates a stark contrast between Herod's deadly orgy and the miraculous feast that Jesus provided for the multitude. Like each of Jesus' miracles, the feeding of the five thousand demonstrated his control over creation and showed that God will provide when we are in need.

**14:13-14** **When Jesus heard what had happened, he withdrew by boat privately to a solitary place.**[NIV] News of John's death resulted in Jesus' desire to pull away and be alone for a while with his disciples. Jesus and the disciples got into a boat (probably the same boat that had transported them already on the Sea of Galilee, see 8:23; 9:1) and *withdrew . . . privately to a solitary place.* The disciples apparently knew of a good location where they thought they could get away from the crowds. Luke tells us that they "withdrew privately to a city called Bethsaida" (Luke 9:10 NRSV), probably landing at a solitary harbor apart from the city, or else they went on foot into the hills to find the "solitary place" where they could rest. This location may have been just outside of Galilee and, therefore, away from Herod Antipas's jurisdiction.

---

COMPANION IN PAIN

Jesus performed some miracles as signs of his identity. He used other miracles to teach important truths. But here we read that he healed people because he "had compassion on them." Jesus was a loving, caring, and feeling person. He put aside his own need for rest and retreat from hostility. When you are suffering, remember that Jesus hurts with you. He has compassion on you. Likewise, we must be available to show compassion to others who need Jesus' kindly touch.

---

**Hearing of this, the crowds followed him on foot from the towns. When Jesus landed and saw a large crowd, he had compassion on them and healed their sick.**[NIV] Popularity and recognition have their own pitfalls. Jesus and the disciples needed rest and quiet time, but the crowds would not let them get away. Instead, they *followed him on foot* from all the towns between Capernaum and Bethsaida. The news spread as more and more people joined the crowd that made their way to where Jesus and the disciples would land. Either the people had heard where the boat was headed, or perhaps the boat was sailing not quite out of sight along the horizon so that the people could follow it.

As soon as Jesus landed, the rest was over because *a large crowd* waited on the shore. Far from feeling impatience and frustration toward these needy people, Jesus *had compassion on them.* While Jesus had hoped to be alone with the disciples for a time of rest, he did not send away this needy crowd. He had compassion for the people and took it upon himself to meet their needs. Jesus knew that his time on earth was short, so he took advantage of every opportunity to teach the Good News of the kingdom to those willing to listen.

**14:15** **When it was evening, the disciples came to him and said, "This is a deserted place, and the hour is now late; send the crowds away so that they may go into the villages and buy food for themselves."**<sup>NRSV</sup> Jesus had been teaching the people until *evening* and *the hour* was *late* (after 3:00 P.M.). Sunset was approaching, and the disciples wondered what Jesus planned to do with this crowd that had come far from their homes to be with them. The place where Jesus had been teaching was *deserted,* far from any town or village. It was near Bethsaida, east of the lake about four miles from Capernaum. Note the frustration in the disciples' statement: Without the normally respectful "Lord," they told Jesus where he was, what time it was, and what he should do. The disciples were upset and thought that Jesus would be wise to let the people go before it got dark in order for them to find food and lodging for the night. So they brought their suggestion to Jesus: *send the crowds away.* No doubt, the disciples also hoped to soon get the rest they had anticipated when they had set out on this journey.

---

YOU FEED THEM
Jesus loved the people in a specific and concrete way. They needed food; they received. We learn two important lessons in this miracle:

1. Jesus provides for our needs. If we trust him, we can find full provision for our basic needs. He has the people and the provision in his church to care for his people. He can multiply meager resources to help us.

2. As Christians, we should be concerned to feed others. This miracle finds a place in all four Gospels and reminds us, "You feed them." So quickly we spiritualize the truth away. But the reality remains that millions are starving in our world today. In honor of our Lord, we should be intermediaries for those with such desperate needs. Find a relief organization that provides food and give to it.

---

**14:16** **But Jesus said to them, "They do not need to go away. You give them something to eat."**<sup>NKJV</sup> The disciples were very concerned regarding the people's needs when they suggested that Jesus send them away. After all, they would need to reach the town before sunset if they were going to obtain food. Jesus' answer both astounded and exasperated them: *They do not need to go away. You give them something to eat.* Jesus directly involved his disciples in the miracle so that it would make a lasting impression on them.

**14:17-18** **They replied, "We have nothing here but five loaves and two fish." And he said, "Bring them here to me."** NRSV There was nothing in the crowd *but five loaves and two fish,* common staples for the poor of Jesus' day. These were not large loaves of bread, but small rye buns, and the fish were small dried fish (see John 6:9-11). Apparently, in their hurry, no one else in the crowd had thought to bring along food to eat. A young boy offered his lunch to the disciples (specifically to Andrew, see John 6:8), but the disciples could see only the impossibility of the situation. Andrew asked the obviously redundant question, "But how far will they go among so many?" (John 6:9 NIV). The normal answer: They will feed one hungry young boy. But Jesus had an entirely different answer, and he asked the disciples to *bring* the five loaves and two fish to him.

**14:19** **And he directed the people to sit down on the grass. Taking the five loaves and the two fish and looking up to heaven, he gave thanks and broke the loaves. Then he gave them to the disciples, and the disciples gave them to the people.** NIV Jesus did not answer the disciples or explain what he would do. Instead, he *directed the people to sit down on the grass.* Mark recorded that Jesus gave the disciples the job of organizing the people into groups. This may have been to make food distribution more efficient, or it may have been to emulate what Moses did (see Exodus 18:21). The men were probably separated from the women and children for the meal, according to Jewish custom.

Jesus, acting as the host of the soon-to-be banquet, took the loaves and fish, looked up to heaven, thanked God beforehand for the provision he was about to give, and then *broke the loaves.* As Jesus broke the loaves, the miracle occurred.

The miracle occurred in Jesus' hands. He broke the loaves and gave them to his disciples to then give *to the people.* He did the same thing with the fish. The disciples acted as waiters to the groups of hungry people seated on the grass, taking bread and fish, distributing it, and then returning to Jesus to get more. They continued to serve the crowd until everyone had had enough to eat.

The God who multiplied the bread was authenticating Jesus as his Son and portraying the munificent blessings of the kingdom. Just as God had provided manna to the Hebrews in the wilderness (Exodus 16) and had multiplied oil and meal for Elijah and the widow at Zarephath (1 Kings 17:7-16) and for

Elisha (2 Kings 4:1-7), he was providing bread for the people on this day. It points to the feast that the Messiah will provide for people in the wilderness (Isaiah 25:6).

---

**MORE THAN ENOUGH**
Jesus multiplied five loaves and two fish to feed over five thousand people. What he was originally given seemed insufficient, but in his hands it became more than enough. We often feel that our contribution to Jesus is meager, but he can use and multiply whatever we give him, whether it is talent, time, or treasure. When we give to Jesus, our resources are multiplied.

---

**14:20** **They all ate and were satisfied, and the disciples picked up twelve basketfuls of broken pieces that were left over.**<sup>NIV</sup> The five loaves and two fish multiplied so that every person had his or her fill. Even the leftovers were more than they had begun with. The disciples *picked up twelve basketfuls of broken pieces that were left over.* The number "twelve" could simply indicate that there was one basket for each of the twelve disciples, or it could also signify fullness and completeness. In any event, there would be no waste at this banquet. The disciples may have taken the food to feed themselves later.

**14:21** **The number of those who ate was about five thousand men, besides women and children.**<sup>NIV</sup> If the readers weren't impressed already, now they should be astounded. The Greek word translated "men" is *andres,* meaning not "people" but "male individuals." Therefore, there were five thousand men *besides* the women and children. The total number of people Jesus fed could have been over ten thousand. The number of men is listed separately because in the Jewish culture of the day, men and women usually ate separately when in public. The children ate with the women. We don't know if this was the case at this particular meal. Jesus did what the disciples thought to be impossible. He multiplied five loaves and two fish to feed over five thousand people.

## JESUS WALKS ON WATER / 14:22-33 / 97

The miracles of Jesus walking on the water and calming the storm (8:23-27) were a double demonstration of Jesus' power over nature. Matthew and Mark highlighted the effects of these miracles on those who participated in them.

**14:22** **Immediately he made the disciples get into the boat and go on ahead to the other side, while he dismissed the crowds.**<sup>NRSV</sup> As soon as the crowd had been fed and the disciples had picked up the scraps, Jesus *immediately* got his disciples and the crowd moving. His sudden desire to dismiss the crowd and send the disciples off in their boat is explained in John's Gospel. Upon seeing (and participating in) the miracle of multiplied loaves and fish, the people "intended to come and make [Jesus] king by force" (John 6:15 NIV). Before the crowd could become an unruly mob, Jesus *made the disciples get into the boat and go on ahead to the other side.* The disciples may have wanted to stay and share the crowd's excitement. They may have been tempted to think that Jesus was ready to inaugurate his kingdom. Jesus' kingdom would not be an earthly one, and he didn't want the enthusiasm of the crowd to deter him or his disciples from fulfilling their true mission. It was getting late in the day, so Jesus *dismissed the crowds* with a few final words before going up to the mountainside by himself.

**Jesus Walks on the Sea**
*The miraculous feeding of the 5,000 occurred on the shores of the Sea of Galilee near Bethsaida. Jesus then sent his disciples across the lake. Several hours later, they encountered a storm, and Jesus came to them—walking on the water. The boat then landed at Gennesaret.*

Exactly *where* the disciples were going causes some confusion if one compares the Gospel accounts. Mark records that Jesus told the disciples to go "to the other side, to Bethsaida" (6:45 NRSV). According to Luke 9:10, Jesus and the disciples were in Bethsaida for the feeding of the five thousand. According to John 6:17, the disciples "set off across the lake for Capernaum" (NIV). One solution is that two communities were named Bethsaida. Luke 9:10 identifies Bethsaida (near Julias) on the northeast side of the Sea of Galilee. The reference in Mark 6:45 identifies Bethsaida as a village (near Capernaum) on the western shore.

**14:23-24 After he had dismissed them, he went up on a mountainside by himself to pray.**NIV Jesus *dismissed* the crowd and "made the disciples get into the boat" and leave (14:22); then he went alone up on a mountainside *to pray.* Jesus wanted time to communicate with his Father. During his ministry on earth, Jesus was in constant contact with the Father—he may have gone off alone to pray often, so his desire to do so may not have surprised the disciples, who left in the boat as instructed.

Jesus had just left a crowd that wanted to make him their king. Perhaps the high popularity was a temptation in itself, for it could have threatened to turn Jesus away from his mission—death on the cross to accomplish salvation. Maybe his prayer on the lonely mountainside focused on fulfilling the mission of suffering when it seemed (at least humanly speaking) more credible to accept their offer of kingship. Jesus, in his humanity, may have continued to face the temptation to turn away from the difficult path and take the easier one. He constantly sought strength from God. Going into the wilderness, alone with the Father, helped Jesus focus on his task and gain strength for what he had to do.

**When evening came, he was there alone, but the boat was already a considerable distance from land, buffeted by the waves because the wind was against it.**<sup>NIV</sup> The disciples had left sometime before sunset, so by the time *evening came,* they were *a considerable distance from land.* The disciples often fished during the night, so sailing out into the night was not unusual. However, the disciples were being blown off course, fighting the sea in their boat, *buffeted by the waves.* At least the last time this had happened, Jesus had been in the boat with them (although they had to awaken him to get his help, 8:23-27). This time, Jesus was alone on the land, and the disciples were left to fend for themselves (or so they thought) against another raging storm.

The other Gospel writers record various details of this scenario. The disciples took down the sails and tried to keep control of the boat by strenuous rowing. For the entire night they fought the storm, able to row only about three or four miles (John 6:19). As Jesus prayed on the mountainside, he "saw the disciples straining at the oars" (Mark 6:48 NIV).

---

PLAYING SOLITAIRE
Seeking solitude was an important priority for Jesus (see also 14:13). He made room in his busy schedule to be alone with the Father. Spending time with God in prayer nurtures a vital relationship and equips us to meet life's challenges and struggles. Develop the discipline of spending time alone with God; it will help you grow spiritually and become more and more like Christ.

---

**14:25 Now in the fourth watch of the night Jesus went to them, walking on the sea.**<sup>NKJV</sup> From evening until *the fourth watch of the night* (between 3:00 and 6:00 A.M.), the disciples had been out on the sea, much of that time fighting a strong headwind and rough seas. Jesus *went to them, walking on the sea.* While some might try to explain away this miracle by saying Jesus was simply on the shore, the Gospel writers made it clear that Jesus walked "on" the water. Not only that, but he walked a great distance. John recorded that the disciples had gone three or four miles by the time Jesus came to them (John 6:19). So the waves were indeed fierce.

The Old Testament often describes God's control over the seas. Jesus' walking on the sea was an unmistakable picture of his identity and power (see Job 9:8; 38:16; Psalm 77:19; Isaiah 43:16).

**14:26 But when the disciples saw him walking on the sea, they were terrified, saying, "It is a ghost!" And they cried out in fear.**NRSV The disciples were battling exhaustion even before they got into the boat to head back across the lake. Their anticipated rest in a solitary place had been interrupted by the crowds (14:13-14). They had been battling the buffeting waves for some time. Suddenly, in the predawn mist, Jesus came walking toward them *on the sea.* They reacted in terror, imagining that they were seeing *a ghost.* They all *cried out in fear.* They thought they had left Jesus back on the mountainside.

> He uses the element we dread as the path for his approach. The waves were endangering the boat, but Jesus walked on them. In our lives are people and circumstances we dread, but it is through these that the greatest blessing of our lives will come, if we look through them to Christ.
>
> *F. B. Meyer*

The Greek word for "ghost" used here is *phantasma,* meaning an apparition or specter. The word was associated with magic and charms. The word differs from *pneuma,* also sometimes translated "ghost," meaning the disembodied spirit of someone who had died (Luke 24:37). Jesus was (as far as they knew) alive and well, so they were terrified by what they saw. Once again, Jesus was doing the unexpected and the impossible. Again the disciples were not ready to grasp what it meant.

**14:27 But immediately Jesus spoke to them and said, "Take heart, it is I; do not be afraid."** NRSV Jesus called out to the disciples over the storm, telling them to *take heart.* He identified himself and told them not to be afraid any longer. The literal reading for "It is I" is "I am" (Greek, *ego eimi*); it is the same as saying "the I AM is here" or "I, Yahweh, am here" (see Exodus 3:14; Isaiah 41:4; 43:10; 52:6). Jesus, the "I AM," came with unexpected help and encouragement during the disciples' time of desperate need. Their need was real; their fear was real. But in the presence of Jesus, fear can be dismissed.

**COURAGE!**
When Jesus arrived, he made a huge difference! Because of Jesus—all he taught, all he did—your life is different now! You're not alone, and you're not lost. You have a heavenly Father, a living Savior, and a present helper, the Holy Spirit. All the problems that beset you are now theirs as well.

Lest we forget, try this. At the end of a phone conversation, instead of "good-bye" say "courage!" Gently, softly, remind one another of what Jesus gives us. In the face of every trouble, every heartbreak, every troubling diagnosis . . . *courage!*

**4:28-29** **"Lord, if it's you," Peter replied, "tell me to come to you on the water." "Come," he said. Then Peter got down out of the boat, walked on the water and came toward Jesus.**NIV Peter was not putting Jesus to the test, something we are told not to do (4:7). Instead, he was the only one in the boat who reacted in faith. His impulsive request led him to experience a rather unusual demonstration of God's power. Jesus' presence in the storm caused Peter to exercise a fearless faith. Peter overcame his fear and attempted the impossible. But notice that he did so only with Jesus' command to *come*. Notice also that he asked only to do what Jesus was doing; that is, he wanted to share in Jesus' power, some of which the disciples had already been experiencing (10:1).

**14:30** **But when he noticed the strong wind, he became frightened, and beginning to sink, he cried out, "Lord, save me!"**NRSV Peter started to sink because he took his eyes off Jesus and focused on the high waves around him. His faith wavered. His faith was strong enough to trust that he could walk on the water. But when he realized that he was in a terrifying storm, his faith did not stand up to the storm. Although we start out with good intentions, sometimes our faith is weak. In Peter's faltering faith we can see the path of discipleship. We have to exercise faith to have the power, but often we stumble and fail to grasp it fully. When Peter's faith faltered, he reached out to Christ, the only one who could help. He was afraid, but he still looked to Christ. When you are apprehensive about the troubles around you and doubt Christ's presence or ability to help, remember that he is the only one who can really help.

**14:31** **And immediately Jesus stretched out His hand and caught him, and said to him, "O you of little faith, why did you doubt?"**NKJV Jesus' immediate response showed Peter that divine undergirding and power are present in times of testing. Jesus caught Peter, saving him from drowning in the waves. Peter had taken his eyes off

Christ and was focusing instead on his situation. Jesus' question focused on why Peter allowed the wind and waves to overwhelm his faith. He momentarily despaired and so began to sink. His doubt became his downfall.

**14:32 And when they got into the boat, the wind ceased.**NKJV Jesus and Peter then *got into the boat* with the rest of the disciples, who must have been speechless. Then, as had occurred once before when the disciples had experienced another storm, *the wind ceased* and the sea once again became calm (see also 8:26). Jesus had revealed to them his complete mastery over nature. (See Isaiah 51:9-16 for a dramatic description of God's power over the sea.)

**14:33 Then those who were in the boat worshiped him, saying, "Truly you are the Son of God."** NIV The disciples' declaration, *Truly you are the Son of God,* indicates a progression in faith. In 14:27, Jesus said, "It is I"; in 14:28, Peter said, "If [since] it's you . . ."; and here the disciples exclaimed, *"Truly you are."* Mark's account focuses on the disciples' hardness of heart in understanding Jesus' true identity; Matthew's account focuses on their astonishment over his encounter with Peter. While the disciples *worshiped* and called Jesus *the Son of God,* they still had much to learn about who Jesus was and what he had come to do.

> The first result of walking with God is great joy, abounding joy, and secondly, a great sense of security, of abiding peace.        *R. A. Torrey*

## JESUS HEALS ALL WHO TOUCH HIM / 14:34-36 / **98**

**14:34 When they had crossed over, they landed at Gennesaret.**NIV The storm had blown the disciples off course, so they did not land at Bethsaida as planned (14:22; see also Mark 6:45). The plan had been to meet Jesus in Bethsaida, but Jesus had come to them on the water. So after the storm ceased, *they landed at Gennesaret.* Gennesaret was a small fertile plain located on the west side of the Sea of Galilee, as well as the name of a small town there. Capernaum sat at the northern edge of this plain.

**14:35-36 After the people of that place recognized him, they sent word throughout the region and brought all who were sick to him, and begged him that they might touch even the fringe of his cloak; and all who touched it were healed.**NRSV Jesus was well-known in the region of Galilee, and his presence always created great excitement. Immediately upon getting out of the boat, people *recognized* Jesus, and a flurry of activity began. There still would be no rest for him. The news of Jesus' arrival spread like wildfire through the area. As Jesus moved through the region, people *brought all who were sick to him* so that he might heal them.

Jesus had gained a widespread reputation as a healer; so a great crowd of people came for healing. In a day when medicines and medical help were few and limited, sickness was rampant and constant. Perhaps the story had spread of the woman in Capernaum who had been healed by touching Jesus' cloak. For at this time the people *begged him that they might touch even the fringe of his cloak.* Jewish men wore tassels on the hem of their robes in order to obey God's command in Deuteronomy 22:12. By Jesus' day, these tassels were seen as signs of holiness (Matthew 23:5). It was natural that people seeking healing should reach out and touch these. No one missed out on Jesus' loving compassion, even if they could only touch the fringe of his cloak; and *all who touched it were healed.* But as the woman in Capernaum learned, healing came from faith in Jesus, not from his garment (9:20-22).

What a contrast in receptions! In Nazareth, his hometown, Jesus found no honor (13:54-58), but in pagan Gennesaret he was recognized immediately and swamped with believing citizens. Even Jesus' disciples had not recognized him (14:26) as readily as did these people. At the beginning of Matthew's Gospel, religious leadership felt threatened, but pagan astrologers (the wise men) came to worship. Pedigree and tradition may obscure God's truth for the religiously inclined, while "outsiders" come to Jesus eagerly, and he to them. Jesus loves faith; he is Lord of all peoples; and his church is truly international.

---

**DOES JESUS HEAL TODAY?**
Some Christians say no. Healing was part of the work of Jesus and the early church to establish his authority, but today it's not part of God's plan, they say. That answer takes away a major source of help for reasons that have nothing to do with Jesus at all.

Some Christians say yes, and there's no need for help of any other kind. To consult a doctor is to show a lack of faith, they say. That answer suggests that twenty centuries of medical knowledge (since Jesus' time) somehow violate God's will.

The best answer is to trust Jesus for concrete help when we're sick, to pray in faith, *and* to respect the professionals who administer health to our day and age. Use all the means God has given to promote health and reduce suffering: prayer, science, and healthy habits of eating and exercise.

---

# Matthew 15

Another delegation came from Jerusalem to investigate this new
rabbi who was causing such a stir throughout the country. Again
the Pharisees and teachers of the law (also called "scribes"), Jesus'
main opponents, brought the complaint. In 9:14, the Pharisees had
attacked Jesus through John's disciples by claiming that Jesus and
his disciples had been wrong not to fast (breaking the religious leaders' additions to God's law). In 12:1-2, they had claimed that the
disciples were wrong to pluck heads of grain and eat them on the
Sabbath (again, only breaking one of their additions to God's law).
In 12:24, such a delegation had incorrectly concluded that Jesus
was casting out demons because he himself was demon-possessed.
In this section, another delegation arrived, ready to debate Jesus
about his disciples' disregard of the oral traditions and rituals.

**15:1-2** **Then some Pharisees and teachers of the law came to Jesus from
Jerusalem and asked, "Why do your disciples break the tradition of the elders? They don't wash their hands before they
eat!"** NIV A delegation came *from Jerusalem,* the center of Jewish
authority, and was made up of *Pharisees* (who advocated detailed
obedience to the Jewish law and traditions) and *teachers of the law*
(professional interpreters of the law who especially emphasized the
traditions). Over the centuries since the Jews' return from Babylonian captivity, hundreds of religious traditions had been added to
God's laws. The Pharisees and teachers of the law considered them
all equally important. They believed that these oral traditions (commentaries and exhortation that were memorized and passed on from
generation to generation) went all the way back to Moses. As these
religious leaders scrutinized Jesus and his disciples, they noticed
that some of his disciples were eating without first washing their
hands. This referred not to washing for cleanliness, but to a particular kind of washing that made a person "ceremonially clean"
before eating. This ceremonial washing cleansed a person from
any defilement he or she may have contacted without knowing it.

The origin of this ceremonial washing is seen in the laver of the tabernacle, where the priests washed their hands and feet prior to performing their sacred duties (Exodus 30:17-21). That *was* part of God's law. Oral tradition extended this law to all Jews to be performed before formal prayers and then before eating. Thus, before each meal, devout Jews would perform a short ceremony, washing their hands and arms in a specific way. This ceremonial washing was not part of God's law; instead, it was part of the rules and regulations added later. "The tradition of the elders" refers to the oral interpretation of God's laws, interpretations that affected every aspect of Jewish daily life. The elders of earlier generations (members chosen from the older people to be part of the Sanhedrin, the most powerful religious and political body of the Jewish nation) passed along this oral tradition until, in the third century B.C., it was collected and written down, eventually forming the foundation of the Jewish Talmud. As such, the tradition of the elders consisted of oral laws given by Jewish religious leaders. The Pharisees and teachers of the law considered these religious traditions to be as binding and as unbreakable as God's law itself. Their assumption was wrong, as Jesus would point out.

---

TRADITION
The Pharisees were very concerned about traditions. Traditions have great significance for us also. In your next meeting with friends from church, ask the group for help in understanding the role of tradition in the life of your church. Here are some specific questions:

- What rules have developed over time (and are no longer questioned) concerning proper behavior with respect to the use of alcoholic beverages, playing cards, motion pictures, and dancing?
- Who originated those rules? Who enforces them today?
- How do such rules help spiritual growth or hinder it?
- Why are such "secondary rules" important to your church? How do you keep them from assuming the same importance as biblical rules?

---

Having noticed that Jesus' disciples were eating with defiled hands, the Pharisees and teachers of the law asked Jesus why they hadn't washed their hands. Notice that the Pharisees realized that this was a "tradition of the elders," but they believed that this tradition had the same authority as God's law. Their underlying statement was, "If you are really a rabbi, as holy, righteous, and versed in the law as we are, then you should know that we don't eat without first ceremonially washing our hands. We won't attack you personally, but since your disciples aren't washing, you obviously haven't taught them about what is important. Maybe you don't even know this law. That makes you no better than a common sinner, certainly not a rabbi whom all these people should be following!" Many religious traditions are good and can add richness and meaning to life. But just because our traditions have been practiced for years, we must not elevate them to a sacred standing. God's principles never change, and his law doesn't need additions. Traditions should help us understand God's laws better, not become laws themselves.

**15:3-4 He answered them, "And why do you break the commandment of God for the sake of your tradition? For God said, 'Honor your father and your mother,' and, 'Whoever speaks evil of father or mother must surely die.'"** NRSV Jesus didn't answer their question until 15:10-11. Instead, he dealt with the issue of authority—*your tradition* versus what *God said.* The disciples may have transgressed the tradition of the elders, but Jesus would show that the religious leaders, who had supposedly devoted their lives to protecting the law, had broken God's law *for the sake of* their tradition. They had become so zealous for the traditions that they had lost their perspective and had missed the point of God's law entirely. Jesus did not reject all the traditions (the position of the Sadducees), but he would explain that traditions should never take the place of God's law.

Jesus first quoted Moses, an especially relevant choice because the teachers of the law traced the oral law back to him (see Deuteronomy 4:14). He chose an example about people's duty toward their parents. One of the Ten Commandments, *Honor your father and your mother* (Exodus 20:12; Deuteronomy 5:16), states that people are to respect their parents, honoring them for who they are and what they have done. The commandment did not apply just to young children but to anyone whose parents were living. "Honor" includes speaking respectfully and showing care and consideration.

The same law is written negatively in Exodus 21:17, *Whoever speaks evil of father or mother must surely die* (see also Leviticus 20:9). "Speaking evil" (also translated "cursing") of one's parents is the opposite of honoring them. It means to criticize, to ridicule, to abuse verbally. The natural result of such behavior is that the person will not honor his parents for who they are, will not speak respectfully, and will certainly show no care or consideration to them. Such action carried a severe penalty—a person who cursed his parents could be put to death.

The religious leaders knew Moses' words backward and forward, but Jesus pointed out how they were actually breaking them (see 15:5-6).

**15:5-6 "But you say that whoever tells father or mother, 'Whatever support you might have had from me is given to God,' then**

**that person need not honor the father. So, for the sake of your tradition, you make void the word of God.'"** NRSV Jesus then went on to explain how some of the Pharisees had found a way to completely sidestep God's command to honor parents. This may seem like an example unrelated to the previous discussion, but Jesus was explaining that to break the oral tradition in one place is to invalidate it completely. The words "but you say" demonstrated how their behavior opposed what Moses had written. In their devotion to the law and tradition, their procedural regulations obscured the true intent of God's Word. As Christians today we must beware of the same error. Are we so devoted to our ministries, methods, and programs that we neglect the true intent of the gospel? We must take this challenge to heart and constantly evaluate our own traditions.

The practice of the tradition of "Corban" (literally, "offering") meant that a person could dedicate money or property for God's exclusive use. When this happened, the money would be reserved for sacred use and withdrawn from use by anyone else. But the benefits could be used by the donor, much like an irrevocable trust works today. This vow was grossly misused. A man could use an article vowed to God indefinitely but could not transfer it to anyone else. Unscrupulous people would even use this vow to keep from paying debts. Others, as Jesus noted, used it to circumvent their responsibility to their parents. Their devotion to God had stripped them of their compassion for people.

The Pharisees had allowed men to dedicate money to God's temple that otherwise would have gone to support their parents (based on Deuteronomy 23:21-23 and Numbers 30:1-16). The legal code of the day was strict, and the family was highly honored. People were expected to care for aging parents. Some found a way to keep from doing so and still use their money or property as they chose. Thus, a man could simply take the vow of Corban, saying that all his money was dedicated to God. Although the action— dedicating money to God—seemed worthy and no doubt conferred prestige on the giver, these religious leaders were ignoring God's clear command to honor parents. Even worse, this was an irrevocable vow. If a son were to later decide that he needed to help his parents, the Pharisees would not permit it. Jesus rightly described the Pharisees as going to great pains to *make void the word of God* by directly violating the fifth commandment. They had elevated their tradition above God's revealed law through Moses and thus had nullified it. They had obeyed what they thought was God's will so scrupulously that they had actually violated what God really intended.

**PHONIES**
Jesus blasted the Pharisees for being hypocrites. The trouble with religious phonies is that God is never fooled, though lots of people are. If in your heart you are greedy, sensual, power-hungry, and happy with it, then you are a phony. For your own sake and for the rest of us, please do one of the following: (1) Give up the church. Better to be a full-fledged pagan than a pagan in a religious suit. God isn't fooled anyhow, and fewer people will be discouraged by your hypocrisy. Or, the better decision, (2) give up your hypocrisy and give your life to Jesus. Let his Spirit renew you from the inside out. Be real about faith, starting today.

---

**15:7-9 "You hypocrites! Isaiah prophesied rightly about you when he said: 'This people honors me with their lips, but their hearts are far from me; in vain do they worship me, teaching human precepts as doctrines.'"** NRSV Jesus blasted these self-righteous leaders with one word; he called them *hypocrites*. They must have been enraged to be addressed that way by such a person. The Greek word originally meant "actor." The Pharisees were hiding behind actors' masks (see 6:2). The Pharisees pretended to be holy and close to God, thus judging all other people as sinners. But what they pretended on the outside was not true on the inside.

Jesus answered not their spoken question but their underlying one, by quoting the Scripture that they claimed to know so well. The Greek word translated "rightly" means "beautifully, excellently." The great prophet *Isaiah* had written beautifully correct words describing these religious leaders: *This people honors me with their lips, but their hearts are far from me; in vain do they worship me, teaching human precepts as doctrines.* The Pharisees and scribes also knew this Scripture by memory, but evidently they never had applied it to themselves. The prophet Isaiah criticized hypocrites (Isaiah 29:13), and Jesus applied Isaiah's words to these religious leaders. "This people" begins the quotation from Isaiah 29:13, resembling more closely the ancient Greek translation of the Old Testament known as the Septuagint. It is not exactly the same as the Hebrew text of Isaiah, though the substance is the same. The religious leaders might say all the right words and give lip service to God, but their hearts were far from God. The problem: The authority for their teaching was human. They taught their human-made rules as though they were given by God. Isaiah explained that their worship was "in vain." They worshiped for appearances, not out of love for God. When we claim to honor God while our hearts are far from him, our worship means nothing. It is not enough to act religious. Our actions and our attitudes must be sincere. If they are not, Isaiah's words also describe us. The Pharisees knew a lot about God, but they didn't know God. It is not enough to study about religion or even to study the Bible. We must respond to God himself.

**15:10-11** **Then he called the crowd to him and said to them, "Listen and understand: it is not what goes into the mouth that defiles a person, but it is what comes out of the mouth that defiles."** NRSV *The crowd* had listened to Jesus' stinging accusation of the religious leaders. Next, they heard him tell *them* to *listen and understand,* for he would sum up his teaching. The Pharisees thought that to eat with defiled hands meant to be defiled (15:1-2). Jesus explained that the Pharisees were wrong in thinking they were acceptable to God just because they were "clean" on the outside. Defilement is not an external matter (keeping food laws, washing ceremonially, keeping Sabbath requirements), but an internal one.

> True Christian preaching is extremely rare in today's church. Thoughtful young people in many countries are asking for it, but cannot find it. The major reason is a lack of conviction about its importance.
>
> *John R. W. Stott*

The phrase, "it is not what goes into the mouth that defiles a person," refers directly to the Pharisees' question about the disciples eating with "defiled" hands. A person does not become morally defiled by eating with hands that have not been ceremonially washed. Instead, the opposite is true: *It is what comes out of the mouth that defiles.* That is, the condition of a person's heart will be revealed by his or her words and actions. Sin begins in the heart, just as the prophet Jeremiah had said hundreds of years before: "The heart is devious above all else; it is perverse—who can understand it? I the LORD test the mind and search the heart, to give to all according to their ways, according to the fruit of their doings" (Jeremiah 17:9-10 NRSV).

As believing Jews and students of Scripture, the Pharisees should have known this. Many times in the Old Testament God had told his people that he valued mercy and obedience based on love above mere observation of rules and rituals (see 1 Samuel 15:22-23; Psalms 40:6-8; 51:16-19; Jeremiah 7:21-23; Hosea 6:6; Amos 5:21-24; Micah 6:6-8). Jesus explained his words more fully to his disciples in 15:16-20.

**15:12** **Then the disciples approached and said to him, "Do you know that the Pharisees took offense when they heard what you said?"** NRSV The concept that people were not defiled by "what

goes into the mouth" was revolutionary to the Jews—and especially
to the Pharisees, who had built a whole set of rules governing such
matters. Mark added the parenthesis that by saying this Jesus had
declared all foods clean (Mark 7:19). Thus, Jesus radically reinterpreted the dietary laws and made them defunct. By so doing, he
was establishing himself as the right interpreter of Scripture. Leviticus 11 contains many of the Jewish dietary laws, including a list of
foods considered "clean" and "unclean." Over the years, however,
the laws had become more important than the reasons for them
and the meanings behind them. As the Jews interpreted the dietary
laws, they believed that they could be clean before God because
of what they had refused to eat. But Jesus explained that sin and
defilement do not come from eating the forbidden foods. Rather,
they come from the disobedience that begins in the heart. No
wonder *the Pharisees took offense* at what Jesus said!

**15:13-14** **He answered, "Every plant that my heavenly Father has not
planted will be uprooted. Let them alone; they are blind
guides of the blind. And if one blind person guides another,
both will fall into a pit."** NRSV The Pharisees may have been
offended (15:12), but Jesus explained that they were being
rejected as leaders of God's people. They claimed to be God's
true people, but like a weed growing in a flowerbed, they would
be *uprooted.* In Isaiah, God describes Israel as his "planting"
(Isaiah 60:21; 61:3NKJV), but these Pharisees did not belong to him
and they would be torn out by the roots. Their teaching, which
they so piously elevated, would be discarded. "Let them alone"
means that Jesus' followers were not to follow, listen to, or regard
the hypocritical Pharisees. In our day, there are religious teachers
and preachers who draw large followings. But time may reveal
that their hearts were insincere. Once we know that their true
intent is *not* God's glory, then we should not listen to them.

The Pharisees claimed to be leaders of the people (see Romans
2:19), but Jesus turned this around to show that they themselves
were *blind guides*—blind to the true meaning of God's law. They
were very proud of their wisdom and enlightenment, so Jesus'
indictment would have stung. Their failure to understand God and
his desires for people would prove to be disastrous for them and
for those who followed them. "Both will fall into a pit" is probably
a picture of judgment (see Isaiah 24:18; Jeremiah 48:44).

**15:15** **But Peter said to him, "Explain this parable to us."** NRSV Peter
often would act as spokesman for the disciples, so he asked Jesus
to explain the parable (15:10-11). Later Peter would be faced
with the issue of clean and unclean food (see Acts 10:9-15). Then

he would learn that nothing should be a barrier to proclaiming the gospel to the Gentiles (non-Jews). Even more, he would learn that everything created by God is good.

---

BLIND RELIGION
Jesus told his disciples to leave the Pharisees alone because the Pharisees were blind to God's truth. Thus, anyone who listened to their teaching would risk spiritual harm. Not all religious leaders clearly see God's truth. Religion can lead you into a pit if you follow teachers who are blind to the truth. All teachers who fail to recognize the supreme authority of Jesus, as Savior and chief interpreter of the Scriptures, are heading that way. Follow them, and you'll fall in too. But if you follow teachers who follow Jesus, the daffy ideas of a thousand crackpot religions won't confuse or bother you. Choose your mentors carefully! Make sure that those you listen to and learn from are those who teach and follow the principles of Scripture.

---

**15:16-17** **Then he said, "Are you also still without understanding? Do you not see that whatever goes into the mouth enters the stomach, and goes out into the sewer?"** NRSV Jesus knew the crowd didn't understand, but he may have been saddened again that his disciples had also failed to comprehend. In the miracle stories, the disciples didn't realize Jesus' identity; in this situation, they didn't understand his teaching. The words "still without understanding" emphasize discipleship as a process of growth. Although they knew much about Jesus, they still had more to learn.

Jesus explained that what goes into a person cannot make that person unclean. Thus, to eat food with hands that may have touched a "defiled" person or article did not mean that the person was ingesting defilement. Logically, as Jesus explained, food *goes in the mouth,* down into *the stomach,* and then *out into the sewer.* It has no effect whatever on the moral condition of the heart. Moral defilement has nothing to do with food. Sin in a person's heart is what defiles that person, not the lack of ceremonial cleansing or the type of food eaten.

**15:18-20** **"But what comes out of the mouth proceeds from the heart, and this is what defiles."** NRSV Defilement occurs because of sinful thoughts, attitudes, and actions. Sin begins in a person's heart, and *what comes out of the mouth proceeds from the heart.* In Jewish culture, parts of the body stood for parts of human personality. The "heart" stood for the center of a person's affections and desires. In Romans 6–8, Paul explains how the Holy Spirit needs to control our sinful human desires.

"Defile" means to corrupt or contaminate the purity of

something. Jews who were defiled were ceremonially unclean, meaning that they were forbidden to participate in certain acts of worship until the uncleanness was dealt with or removed. Sinful words and actions defile the person speaking or acting as well as the object of the act. Jesus' words contain a certain ambiguity. Our first impulse is to believe that the source of the action is defiled, but the text leaves open the possibility that the target of evil words and actions is also defiled. That is, we genuinely hurt people by words and actions that spring from evil motives or intentions.

**"For out of the heart come evil intentions, murder, adultery, fornication, theft, false witness, slander. These are what defile a person, but to eat with unwashed hands does not defile."** NRSV To emphasize how all evil comes from within, Jesus listed several examples of sin. The first, "evil intentions," is probably a category under which the others are found. The remaining six follow the order of the sixth through ninth commandments.

Evil intentions begin in *the heart.* Jesus made it clear why people sin—it's a matter of the heart. Our hearts have been inclined toward sin from the time we were born. While many people work hard to keep their outward appearance attractive, what is in their heart is even more important. When people become Christians, God makes them different on the inside. He will continue the process of change inside them if they only ask. God wants us to seek healthy thoughts and motives, not just healthy food and exercise.

These actions and attitudes begin in a person's *heart,* and *these are what defile a person:*

- *Murder*—Killing a person, taking his or her God-given life
- *Adultery*—Having sex with someone other than one's spouse
- *Fornication*—Engaging in various kinds of extramarital sexual activity
- Theft—Taking something that belongs to someone else
- *False witness*—Tricking or misleading by lying
- *Slander*—Destroying another's good reputation through half-truths and lies

## JESUS SENDS A DEMON OUT OF A GIRL / 15:21-28 / *103*

**15:21 Leaving that place, Jesus withdrew to the region of Tyre and Sidon.** NIV Jesus traveled about thirty miles *to the region of Tyre and Sidon.* These were port cities on the Mediterranean Sea north of Israel. Both cities had flourishing trade and were very wealthy. They were proud, historic Canaanite cities. Jesus withdrew to Gentile territory to evade the opposition of the Pharisees. In David's day, Tyre had been on friendly terms with Israel (2 Samuel 5:11), but soon afterward the city had become known for its wickedness. Its king even had claimed to be a god (Ezekiel 28:1ff.). Tyre had rejoiced when Jerusalem was destroyed in 586 B.C. because without Israel's competition, Tyre's trade and profits would increase.

**15:22 Just then a Canaanite woman from that region came out and started shouting, "Have mercy on me, Lord, Son of David; my daughter is tormented by a demon."** NRSV Apparently, a woman had heard about Jesus' miracle-working power and how he could cast out demons, so she wasn't going to miss a chance to see him. Mark records that she "fell at his feet" (Mark 7:25; see below 15:25). Matthew called her a Canaanite; Mark described her as a Gentile, a Syrophoenician. Both descriptions are correct. Mark's designation refers to her political background. His Roman audience would easily identify her by the part of the Empire that was her home. Matthew's description was designed for his Jewish audience; they remembered the Canaanites as bitter enemies when Israel was settling the Promised Land. Matthew's Jewish audience would have immediately understood the significance of Jesus helping this woman. Some Bible translations identify her as a Greek. This is also correct because she was a Greek-speaking native of the Phoenician area which had been converted to Greek language and culture after the conquest by Alexander the Great in the fourth century B.C.

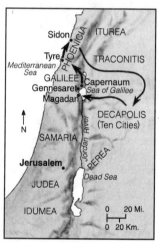

**Ministry in Phoenicia**
*After preaching again in Capernaum, Jesus left Galilee for Phoenicia, where he preached in Tyre and Sidon. On his return, he traveled through the region of the Decapolis (Ten Cities), fed the 4,000 beside the sea, and then crossed to Magadan.*

The woman called Jesus, *Lord, Son of David,* showing her acceptance of Jesus' identity as the Jewish Messiah. She may have been a Greek proselyte. Sometimes Gentiles would convert to Judaism, drawn by the strong moral qualities. This woman came to Jesus on behalf of her daughter, who was *tormented by a demon.* Obviously this woman was greatly distressed over her daughter's suffering.

**15:23 But he did not answer her at all. And his disciples came and urged him, saying, "Send her away, for she keeps shouting after us."** NRSV Jesus' silence seems difficult to understand until we read the lesson of faith that he taught both the woman and his disciples (15:24-28). The woman continued to follow after them, and she continued to shout. Finally, the disciples urged Jesus to *send her away.* This may have meant to get rid of the woman because she was bothering them with her nagging persistence. Or it may have been a request for Jesus to do as she requested, so she would go away and leave them alone. Jesus, always compassionate, would heal the woman's daughter, but not just to make her stop following them. He had a lesson about faith that he needed to teach this woman. In so doing, he would teach the disciples a lesson as well.

It is possible to become so occupied with spiritual matters that we miss real needs right around us, especially if we are prejudiced against needy people or if they cause us inconvenience. Instead of being bothered, be aware of the opportunities that surround you. Be open to the beauty of God's message for all people, and make an effort not to shut out those who are different from you.

**15:24 He answered, "I was sent only to the lost sheep of Israel."** NIV Jesus' words do not contradict the truth that God's message is for all kinds of people (Psalm 22:27; Isaiah 56:7; Matthew 28:19; Romans 15:9-12). After all, when Jesus said these words, he was in Gentile territory. He ministered to Gentiles on many other occasions also, but always in Jewish territory (4:24-25; 8:5-13). Jesus was simply telling the woman that Jews were to have the first opportunity to accept him as the Messiah because God wanted them to present the message of salvation to the rest of the world (see Genesis 12:3). While on earth, Jesus restricted his mission to Jewish people. In doing so, he was doing his Father's will (11:27) and fulfilling the promise God made to Jews in the Old Testament. The restricted mission of Jesus and the disciples echoes the principle recorded in 10:5-6. "I was sent only to the lost sheep of Israel" does not mean Jesus came to the Jews alone; rather, it means that he would go to them first (Mark 7:27). "Sheep" was an affectionate term used often for God's people in the Old Testament.

Jesus was not rejecting the Canaanite woman. Instead, he was explaining that his activities were limited (in his humanity); thus, he had to focus on his goal. Jesus had only a short time on earth. His mission focused on (but was not limited to) the Jews. Jesus tested (in the sense of "probed, challenged, encouraged") this woman's faith and used the situation to teach that faith is available to all people. Matthew alone recorded this interchange. His Jewish audience would have been very interested in Jesus' miracle to help this Gentile woman.

**15:25-26 The woman came and knelt before him. "Lord, help me!" she said. He replied, "It is not right to take the children's bread and toss it to their dogs."** NIV Undaunted by Jesus' apparent unwillingness to respond to her request, the woman *came and knelt before him,* begging for help.

The answer comes in the language of a parable; therefore, we must not press the details too far. Jesus probably spoke Greek to this woman, for she would not have known Aramaic. He used the word *kunarion,* referring to a little dog, a household pet. The simple parable meant that the children at the table should be fed before the pets; it would not be right to take the children's food and give it to the dogs. While it is true that in Jewish tradition Gentiles at times were referred to derogatorily as "dogs," that probably does not apply here. The Greek word used as a derogatory nickname applied to wild dogs or scavenger dogs, not household pets.

> He is not a mere teacher of the way, as some vainly imagine—a teacher of a system of morality, by the observance of which we may be saved. But Christ is truly the Way. He is Himself the Way. The soul is saved by Christ Himself.
>
> *Charles G. Finney*

By these words, Jesus may have meant that his first priority was to spend time feeding his *children* (teaching his disciples), not to take food away from them and throw it to the pets. Jesus was not insulting the woman; instead, he was saying that she must not demand what God had ordained for the Jews. She should wait until God's appointed time when the Gentiles would receive the Good News of the gospel. The point of Jesus' parable is "precedence"—who gets fed first? The children do.

**15:27 She said, "Yes, Lord, yet even the dogs eat the crumbs that fall from their masters' table."** NRSV Unlike many of the Jewish listeners, this Gentile woman understood Jesus' parable. Her answer was wise, for she explained to Jesus, by extending his parable, that the children who love the pets often drop morsels of food to them. Not all the Jews accepted Jesus, while some Gentiles chose to follow him. Why couldn't she have some of those *crumbs* that the Jews didn't want? She adroitly pointed out that *even the dogs* ate with (not after) the children. She did not ask for the entire meal; she was perfectly willing to take second place behind the Jews. All she wanted right then was a few crumbs—or one "crumb" in particular—one miracle of healing for her daughter.

Ironically, many Jews would miss out on God's spiritual healing because they rejected Jesus, while many Gentiles, whom the Jews rejected, would find salvation because they recognized Jesus.

**15:28** Then Jesus answered and said to her, "O woman, great is your faith! Let it be to you as you desire." And her daughter was healed from that very hour.<sup>NKJV</sup> Jesus was delighted by the faith of the woman. He granted her request because of her humility and persistence. She had made her request in faith that Jesus could perform the healing. His words had been meant to challenge her to greater faith, and she had responded. She understood Christ's lordship, and she understood the priorities of his mission. No wonder Jesus exclaimed, *Great is your faith!* On that basis, Jesus healed the woman's daughter. With his words, *her daughter was healed from that very hour.* This miracle showed that Jesus' power over demons was so great that he didn't need to be present physically, or even to speak any word to the demon, in order to free someone. His power transcended distance.

---

GETTING PAST "CHURCH PEOPLE"
One of the obstacles the Canaanite woman had to overcome was the dismissive attitude of the disciples. Likewise, seekers today are advised not to judge the gospel on their first impression of most church folk.

If you are seeking help from Jesus, don't be put off by the airs and attitudes of some people who claim to know him. Christians are not perfect. "Get rid of her," said the disciples. And so today in many different ways people in need of Jesus are put off by the "righteous."

If you're looking for Jesus, don't stop until you find *him.* And when you find him, try your best to be as generous and loving to others as he is.

---

## THE CROWD MARVELS AT JESUS' HEALINGS / 15:29-31 / *104*

**15:29** After Jesus had left that place, he passed along the Sea of Galilee, and he went up the mountain, where he sat down.<sup>NRSV</sup> Then Jesus left the vicinity of Tyre, and went through Sidon, and came down to the Sea of Galilee. He did not go into Jewish regions, however, but traveled to the northeastern shore of the lake instead, into the region of the Decapolis (Ten Cities, see Mark 7:31), a primarily Gentile area.

**15:30-31** Great crowds came to him, bringing with them the lame, the maimed, the blind, the mute, and many others. They put them at his feet, and he cured them, so that the crowd was amazed when they saw the mute speaking, the maimed whole, the lame walking, and the blind seeing. And they praised the

**God of Israel.**[NRSV] A great crowd surrounded Jesus. They wanted to be
healed, and he healed them all: The
lame could walk, the maimed were
made whole, the blind were given sight,
the mute could speak. This list of healings would have reminded Matthew's
readers of Isaiah 35:5-6, "Then will the
eyes of the blind be opened and the ears
of the deaf unstopped. Then will the
lame leap like a deer, and the mute
tongue shout for joy. Water will gush

> Faith is a disposition of
> the heart, without which
> God's most glorious
> blessing is offered to us
> in vain; but by which,
> on the other hand, all the
> fullness of God's grace
> can be most certainly
> received and enjoyed.
> *Andrew Murray*

forth in the wilderness and streams in the desert" (NIV). Matthew
was showing his Jewish readers that the Gentiles would share
with the Jews in the blessings of their Messiah.

The phrase "and they praised the God of Israel" indicates that
this was a Gentile crowd. While Jesus came to the lost sheep of
Israel (15:24), he did not restrict his ministry to the Jews alone.
Other Gentiles had received Jesus' healing touch (the centurion
who had come on behalf of his servant, 8:13; the demon-possessed
men who lived in this same region, 8:33). This scene mirrors the
events in Capernaum: "That evening after sunset the people brought
to Jesus all the sick and demon-possessed. The whole town gathered at the door, and Jesus healed many who had various diseases.
He also drove out many demons" (Mark 1:32-34 NIV).

---

**HEALING TOUCH**
Great crowds came to Jesus to be healed. Jesus still heals
broken lives, and we can bring suffering people to him. Whom
do you know that needs Christ's healing touch? Bring them to
Jesus through prayer or through explaining to them the reason
for the hope that you have (1 Peter 3:15). Then let Christ do
the healing.

---

## JESUS FEEDS FOUR THOUSAND / 15:32-39 / **105**

Differences in details distinguish this miracle from the feeding of
the five thousand described in chapter 14. At that time, those fed
were mostly Jews. At this second feeding, Jesus ministered to a
mixed crowd of Jews and Gentiles in the predominantly Gentile
region of the Decapolis. Also, Jesus began with different quantities
of bread and fish, and he did not require his disciples to admit their
own inability to solve the problem.

**15:32** **Then Jesus called his disciples to him and said, "I have compassion for the crowd, because they have been with me now for three days and have nothing to eat; and I do not want to send them away hungry, for they might faint on the way."** NRSV Jesus was ministering in the region of the Decapolis where he had healed many people (15:30-31), causing his popularity to spread throughout the area. It should come as no surprise, then, that many people were following him. This story sounds very much like the feeding of the five thousand recorded in 14:13-21, but it is a separate event. Both Matthew and Mark include both miracles. Jesus himself referred back to each incident separately when he asked the disciples, "Do you still not perceive? Do you not remember the five loaves for the five thousand . . . or the seven loaves for the four thousand, and how many baskets you gathered?" (16:9-10 NRSV).

In the previous episode, Jesus and the disciples had desired rest, but the crowd had interrupted that rest. Out of *compassion,* Jesus had taught them. Jesus' compassion means that he was deeply moved by the extreme needs of the people. Jesus exhibited God's compassion for his sheep (see Ezekiel 34), not merely human pity for hungry people. (For more on Jesus' compassion, see 9:36; 14:14; 20:34.) The disciples had to come to Jesus, suggesting that the crowd would be getting hungry and that he should send them away to get their own food. In this episode, the crowd had been following Jesus for *three days,* listening to his teaching and observing his miracles. Jesus took the initiative in his concern for their need for food, and he shared his concern with the disciples. The wording probably does not mean that the people hadn't eaten for three days. Instead, whatever supplies they had brought along were depleted, so most of them had nothing left to eat. Thus, Jesus was concerned not to *send them away hungry.* Finally, after the feeding of the five thousand, the people wanted to make him a king. There was no such movement by the people in this episode.

**15:33** **His disciples answered, "Where could we get enough bread in this remote place to feed such a crowd?"** NIV Although the disciples had seen Jesus feed five thousand people, they had no idea what he would do in this situation. Perhaps they didn't expect Jesus to perform the same miracle when the crowd was Gentile and not Jewish (thus revealing their spiritual blindness). This miracle again revealed Jesus' divine power. The crowd was in a *remote place,* and the disciples asked the obvious question: *"Where could we get enough bread . . . to feed such a crowd?"*

Jesus had already found the resources in a previous remote

place for an even larger crowd, yet the disciples were completely perplexed as to how they should be expected to feed this crowd. People often give up when faced with difficult situations. Like the disciples, we often forget God's provision for us in the past. When facing a difficult situation, remember what God has done for you and trust him to take care of you again.

**15:34 Jesus said to them, "How many loaves do you have?" And they said, "Seven, and a few little fish."** NKJV In the Bible, the number seven often signifies perfection or completeness, as in the seven days of creation (Genesis 1) and forgiving seven times (Matthew 18:21). Yet the numbers seven and seventy were also associated with Gentiles. In Jewish tradition, Gentile nations numbered seventy (from Genesis 10:1-32), and Gentiles were sometimes said to be bound, not by the Israelite covenant, but by God's covenant with Noah that was said to have seven commandments (Genesis 9:1-17). In Acts 6:1-7, seven leaders were chosen to minister to the Greek-speaking Christians. Thus, in this passage some have seen the number seven to have symbolic significance. It may hint at the worldwide scope of Jesus' message. Probably the connection to the Gentiles is coincidental, but the church used that connection to enlarge the Gentile mission.

**15:35-36 Then ordering the crowd to sit down on the ground, he took the seven loaves and the fish; and after giving thanks he broke them and gave them to the disciples, and the disciples gave them to the crowds.** NRSV In the previous miracle, Jesus had told the disciples to order the people to sit in groups on the ground; here Jesus himself gave the order for everyone to *sit down.* Perhaps he took over, realizing that the disciples just did not understand. He then *took the seven loaves* and gave thanks to God for the provision he was about to give. In Greek, the term for "giving thanks" is connected with the Christian Eucharist (or Lord's Supper) as in 1 Corinthians 11:24. Later, in 14:22-25, Mark used the verb "to bless" (NRSV) to describe Jesus' prayer over the bread, and the verb "to give thanks" (the same word as used here) to describe his prayer over the cup.

Next Jesus *broke* apart the loaves; then he allowed the disciples to pass them out as before. The verbs for Jesus giving the bread and the disciples' distribution could read, "Jesus kept on giving bread to the disciples, and they kept on distributing it" to the crowd.

In addition to bread, the people received fish. In ancient days, that would form a fairly complete meal. Such a meal certainly would provide enough energy for the people's trip back home.

Like the bread, the fish was blessed and distributed until everyone had enough to eat.

---

**MEALTIME THANKS**
Jews gave thanks before and after a meal. Many people think praying before meals is quaint, out-of-date, or perfunctory. But Jesus never forgot to thank God before a meal. Thanking God before meals reminds us that nourishment, satisfaction, good times—life itself—come from him. If you've become lax, start praying again at your next meal. If you've grown into a habit, keep it up with renewed gratitude.

---

**5:37-38** **They all ate and were satisfied. Afterward the disciples picked up seven basketfuls of broken pieces that were left over. The number of those who ate was four thousand, besides women and children.**[NIV] As had happened before, each person in the crowd had eaten and was filled—no one went away hungry from this banquet. The seven loaves and few fish multiplied so that, again, even the leftovers were more than the food Jesus had started with.

In the previous feeding episode, Jesus had asked the disciples to divide the crowd into a specific arrangement; this time, he did not do so. The Greek word for "basketfuls" provides an interesting twist on this story. In the feeding of the five thousand, there were twelve baskets of leftovers, and the "baskets" were *kophinos,* large baskets. After the feeding of the four thousand, there were seven baskets of leftovers, and the "baskets" were different; these were *spuris*—baskets that were large enough to hold a person. (Paul was let down over the Damascus wall in a *spuris*— Acts 9:25). The abundance of leftovers in these seven baskets may have been more than the leftovers from the twelve baskets in the previous incident.

As before, the number of those who ate, *four thousand,* meant that there were four thousand men in addition to the women and children who were there.

**15:39** **After Jesus had sent the crowd away, he got into the boat and went to the vicinity of Magadan.**[NIV] Once Jesus knew the people had eaten their fill and would not faint from hunger on their journey home (15:32), he *sent the crowd away.* Jesus and the disciples once again *got into the boat* and sailed *to the vicinity of Magadan* (called Dalmanutha in Mark), a town located on the western shore of the Sea of Galilee. This meant a return back to Jewish territory. There Jesus would face further conflict with the Pharisees and Sadducees (16:1-4). Magadan was Mary Magdalene's hometown (Luke 8:2-3).

# Matthew 16

Following the visit to Gentile territories where the Gentiles saw
Jesus' miracles and reacted by praising the God of Israel (15:31),
Jesus returned to Jewish territory, only to face a test from the
unbelieving religious leaders. As recorded in 12:38-39, they had
previously asked for a sign; here they resumed their challenge
to Jesus' authority. Matthew pictured the striking contrast of
responses to Jesus.

**16:1 The Pharisees and Sadducees came, and to test Jesus they
asked him to show them a sign from heaven.**<sup>NRSV</sup> Jesus had been
able to escape the probing Pharisees for a while as he visited in
Gentile areas (15:21-39). His last dealing with them had involved
the issues of the law and ceremonial defilement, and Jesus had
called the Pharisees hypocrites (15:7). But the Pharisees weren't
going to give up in their relentless attempts to discredit Jesus before
the crowds. So, upon Jesus' return to Jewish territory, *the Pharisees
and Sadducees came . . . to test Jesus.* Testing was valid in the Old
Testament to uncover a false prophet, but these leaders were not
seeking the truth. The same Greek word for "test" is used in
Hebrews 3:9 and signifies a test with the intent to discredit. Matthew
may have had this in mind—that these men were tools of Satan and
would be judged for testing the Son of God. Here the word conveys
testing to show that Jesus would fail.

The Pharisees and Sadducees were Jewish religious leaders of
two different parties, and their views were diametrically opposed
on many issues. The Pharisees carefully followed their religious
rules and traditions, believing that this was the way to God. They
also believed in the authority of all the books of Scripture that we
now call the Old Testament and in the resurrection of the dead.
The Sadducees accepted only the books of Moses as Scripture
and did not believe in life after death. In Jesus, however, these
two groups had a common enemy. From their standpoint, this test
would show that Jesus was a false prophet. They demanded that
Jesus *show them a sign from heaven.* What exactly did they

want? They had already seen and heard about many miracles, but evidently, that was not enough for them. They may have wanted something so spectacular that there could be no doubt that Jesus had come from God. More likely, they did not really want to see a sign; they simply hoped to discredit Jesus when he refused to give them one.

A sign was often used by God and his prophets to accomplish two purposes: (1) It showed trustworthiness or reliability—if a prophet said something would happen and it came to pass, this would demonstrate that in all his prophecies he was telling the truth from God. (2) A sign showed power—if a message were accompanied by a sign, this would authenticate the power and authority of the prophet. Jesus would not give them the sign they demanded. He had in mind an even greater evidence of his power.

**16:2-3** **He replied, "When evening comes, you say, 'It will be fair weather, for the sky is red,' and in the morning, 'Today it will be stormy, for the sky is red and overcast.' You know how to interpret the appearance of the sky, but you cannot interpret the signs of the times."** NIV The Pharisees and Sadducees demanded a sign from heaven. This means a sign from above, a miracle with such significance as to be incontrovertible evidence that Jesus was a true prophet. They had tried to explain away Jesus' other miracles as sleight of hand, coincidence, or use of evil power, but they believed that only God could do a sign in the sky. This, they were sure, would be a feat beyond Jesus' power. Although Jesus could have easily impressed them, he refused. He knew that even a miracle in the sky would not convince them that he was the Messiah because they had already decided not to believe in him. So, instead, he spoke to them in a parable.

The earliest and most reliable manuscripts do not include the saying about the weather. Some have thought this was a scribal assimilation to Luke 12:54-56. It is best to consider this quote as possibly coming from Jesus' teaching but not necessarily originally written by Matthew in this context.

Jesus' meaning was that while people (and particularly these religious leaders to whom Jesus was speaking) could discern the signs of the weather by watching the sky and predicting fair weather or storms, they could not *interpret the signs of the times*. That is, they could not interpret the coming of God's kingdom with the appearance of God's Messiah. They asked for a sign from heaven; they had the ultimate sign standing in front of them!

**16:4** **"A wicked and adulterous generation seeks after a sign, and no sign shall be given to it except the sign of the prophet**

**Jonah." And He left them and departed.**<sup>NKJV</sup> This verse
repeats the words that Jesus had given to a group of Pharisees
and teachers of the law who had previously come to Jesus asking for a miraculous sign (see 12:38-42). Jesus refused to give
them the sign they requested. Instead, he gave an answer,
explaining that a sign would come in *his* timing, and that this
sign would be unmistakable. As in 12:39, the words *wicked
and adulterous* are synonyms for evil. "Adulterous" applies
to the apostasy of Israel. Marriage and adultery are used in
the Old Testament to symbolize God's love and the nation's
unfaithfulness.

*No sign* would be given to this generation *except the sign of
the prophet Jonah.* By using the sign of the prophet Jonah, who
had been inside a great fish for three days, Jesus was predicting
his death and resurrection. Jesus' resurrection, of course, would
be the most spectacular sign of all. That sign would come, not
in Jesus' timing or in answer to the Pharisees' demands, but in
God's plan. When it occurred, even that sign would be dismissed
by the religious leaders. (For possible meanings of this "sign,"
see the explanation on 12:39-40.)

Jesus' purpose was not to convince people to come to him
by performing wonders; he came inviting people to come to him
in faith. Then, as a response to their faith, he performed great
miracles. If faith was required, these self-righteous religious leaders had little hope. After this encounter, Jesus *left* abruptly, got
into the boat, and *departed* back toward the northeastern shore
of the Sea of Galilee. This event marked the end of his public
ministry in the region of Galilee.

---

SEEING MIRACLES
Many people, like these Jewish leaders, say they want to see a
miracle so that they can believe. But Jesus knew that miracles
rarely convince the skeptical. Jesus had been healing, raising
people from the dead, and feeding thousands, and still people
wanted him to prove himself by showing them a sign. Do you
doubt Christ because you haven't "seen" a miracle? Do you
expect God to prove himself to you personally before you
believe? Jesus said, "Blessed are those who have not seen and
yet have believed" (John 20:29 NIV). We have all the miracles
recorded in the Old and New Testaments, two thousand years
of church history, and the witness of thousands. With all this
evidence, those who won't believe are either too proud or too
stubborn. If you simply step forward in faith and believe, then
you will begin to see God perform miracles with your life!

---

## JESUS WARNS AGAINST WRONG TEACHING / 16:5-12 / **107**

**16:5 When they went across the lake, the disciples forgot to take bread.**[NIV] Jesus had left his confrontation with the Pharisees abruptly, and the disciples had gone with him. Apparently, at some point out on the sea, they realized that they had forgotten *to take bread.* Perhaps the disciples were feeling guilty for not having planned ahead well enough to have ample supplies on the boat.

**16:6 "Be careful," Jesus said to them. "Be on your guard against the yeast of the Pharisees and Sadducees."**[NIV] The disciples were worrying about bread, so Jesus used the opportunity to teach of the danger of the *yeast of the Pharisees and Sadducees.* Yeast is a key ingredient in bread, for it causes the dough to rise. "Yeast" in this passage symbolizes evil. The Jews were required to celebrate an annual period beginning with the Passover during which no yeast was to be found in their homes; all bread eaten had to be made without yeast ("unleavened," see Exodus 12:14-20). Jesus was teaching that just as only a small amount of yeast was needed to make a batch of bread rise, so the evil teachings and hypocrisy of the religious and political leaders could permeate and contaminate the entire society. Jesus used yeast as an example of how a small amount of evil could affect a large group of people. The wrong teachings of the Pharisees were leading the entire nation astray. Jesus warned his disciples to constantly be on guard against the contaminating evil of the religious leaders (see also 2 Corinthians 13:5; Galatians 5:9).

---

ON GUARD
Jesus told the disciples to be on guard. What does it take to be on guard, in terms of faith?
- *A strong and sure center.* We must keep Jesus at the center of our Christian faith.
- *A developing sense of "what makes sense."* That comes through a lifelong process of learning the Bible, understanding the life of the church, and being open to the Holy Spirit.
- *A core of Christian friends.* A single sentry does not protect a castle. Find friends who will keep you growing. Join a church where Jesus is the center, the Bible is seriously studied, and people are "on the move."

---

**16:7-8 They discussed this among themselves and said, "It is because we didn't bring any bread." Aware of their discussion, Jesus asked, "You of little faith, why are you talking**

**among yourselves about having no bread?"** NIV After hearing
Jesus' warning against wrong teaching, the disciples quietly
talked among themselves. They didn't understand the warning.
They interpreted Jesus so literally that they missed his point
entirely.

Jesus was *aware of their discussion* about having no bread.
These disciples paralleled the problem of the religious leaders,
for they often failed to realize Jesus' true identity. Why did
they talk about bread, something merely temporal, when their
spiritual souls were at stake? Jesus' rebuke, *you of little faith,*
refers both to their lack of faith in realizing that he could supply bread as needed (as he had already done miraculously two
separate times) and to their lack of understanding regarding his
teachings. In these verses, Jesus' rebuke is a series of questions
focusing on the disciples' lack of understanding and lack of
memory regarding all that they had seen and experienced with
him. In Mark 8:17, Jesus was rebuking them for hardness of
heart, but here Matthew focused on their inability to grasp his
true power. These men, closest to Jesus, would carry a huge
responsibility after he was gone. Jesus wanted to be sure that
they were getting the message.

**16:9-10** **"Do you still not perceive? Do you not remember the five loaves
for the five thousand, and how many baskets you gathered? Or
the seven loaves for the four thousand, and how many baskets
you gathered?"** NRSV These are rhetorical questions, not quiz questions. Jesus' question *Do you still not perceive?* emphasized that,
at this point in his ministry, the disciples should have begun to
understand and perceive who Jesus was. After all they had seen
and heard, they should have understood. Jesus rebuked the disciples
for their lack of perception. The two feeding miracles centered
upon the message "God will provide." The disciples did not realize
this truth. These were his trainees—those to whom his mission
would be entrusted once he was gone. Would they ever understand?
Jesus, for all his incredible power, did not and would not force
understanding and belief upon his disciples. They had to comprehend and come to him on their own, in faith. Jesus had shown
compassion on people and had performed miracles to meet their
needs. Thus, the disciples should have understood that Jesus would
meet their needs as well—whether for bread or for spiritual insight
regarding the religious leaders. Jesus wanted the disciples to think
about what they had seen, especially in the two feeding miracles. If
they considered what had happened, they would have to conclude
that Jesus was their Messiah, the Son of God.

**16:11-12** **"How could you fail to perceive that I was not speaking about bread? Beware of the yeast of the Pharisees and Sadducees!" Then they understood that he had not told them to beware of the yeast of bread, but of the teaching of the Pharisees and Sadducees.**<sup>NRSV</sup> The disciples should have realized that Jesus would not talk about bread! Instead, he wanted the disciples to *beware* of the teachings of the Pharisees and Sadducees. Jesus was severing the disciples from all links to their religious past and to the authority of the religious leaders and was attaching them exclusively to himself.

Yet this also may have posed a problem, for the teachings of the Pharisees and Sadducees were diametrically opposed at almost all points. So of what "yeast" were the disciples to "beware"? Probably their incorrect understanding of the Messiah's credentials and of how to get into the kingdom. For the Pharisees, it was rigid law keeping; the Sadducees did not even believe in eternal life. Their wrong understanding caused them to miss the Messiah completely; and their teaching (spreading like yeast through dough) was contaminating the entire nation. The disciples would eventually find that some of the greatest enemies of the Christians were the Jews who refused to believe in Jesus Christ as the Messiah. The need to "beware" would continue long after Jesus' death and resurrection. In addition, the temptation to try to attain the kingdom by rigid law keeping, in order to be good enough (like the Pharisees) or to stop believing in eternal life (like the Sadducees) in the face of persecution and doubts, would, like yeast, be a problem for Jesus' disciples in all ages.

---

YEAST TODAY

Pharisees were the conservatives of their era, and Sadducees were the liberals. Rigidly sure of the proper way to go about religion, Pharisees suffocated true faith in their systems and legalism. Empirically sure of the silliness of most religion, Sadducees trimmed true faith to a skeleton, elevating skepticism to a virtue. Beware of both parties today.

Legalism will bind you. Slowly but surely, your faith will shift from serving and loving Jesus to serving and embracing rules. Your reward will be self-righteousness.

Empiricism will starve you. If everything you believe must be measured, you'll have no place for faith, hope, or love. You will be spiritually gaunt, and with so little room for growth, you'll probably give it up.

Walk with Jesus. Accept no religious substitutes.

---

**16:13** Now when Jesus came into the district of Caesarea Philippi, he asked his disciples, "Who do people say that the Son of Man is?"<sup>NRSV</sup> A beautiful site on the northern shore of the Sea of Galilee, Caesarea Philippi was located about twenty-five miles north of Bethsaida, on the slopes of Mount Hermon. The city lay in the territory ruled by Philip (Herod Antipas's brother, mentioned in Luke 3:1). The influence of Greek and Roman culture was everywhere. The city was primarily non-Jewish, known for its worship of Greek gods and its temples devoted to the ancient god Pan. When Philip became ruler, he rebuilt and renamed the city after Caesar Tiberius and himself. The "Philippi" distinguished the city from another Caesarea located on the Mediterranean seacoast.

As Jesus and the disciples walked toward Caesarea Philippi, Jesus asked his disciples what they had heard from the people regarding his identity: *Who do people say that the Son of Man is?*

**16:14** So they said, "Some say John the Baptist, some Elijah, and others Jeremiah or one of the prophets."<sup>NKJV</sup> The disciples answered Jesus' question with the common view that Jesus was one of the great prophets who had come back to life. This belief may have stemmed from Deuteronomy 18:18, where God said he would raise up a prophet from among the people. (For the story of John the Baptist, see 3:1-17; 4:12; 11:2-15; 14:1-12. For the story of Elijah, see 1 Kings 17–21 and 2 Kings 1–2. Jeremiah's story is told throughout the book of Jeremiah.) Herod had thought that Jesus was John the Baptist come back to life (14:1-2), so apparently this rumor was widespread. The people considered him to be Elijah because Elijah had been a great prophet, and one like him was expected to come before the Messiah arrived (see Malachi 4:5). Jeremiah may have been considered because, according to Jewish legend, he was "immortal" (his death is not

**Journey to Caesarea Philippi**
*Jesus left Magadan, crossed the lake, and landed in Bethsaida. There he healed a man who had been born blind. From there, he and his disciples went to Caesarea Philippi, where Peter confessed Jesus as the Messiah and Son of God.*

mentioned in Scripture); thus, like Elijah, he did not die but was taken to heaven. As were John the Baptist, Elijah, and Jeremiah, Jesus was obviously a spokesman for God. Everyone who heard him understood that his message carried supernatural authority. However, all of these responses were incorrect, revealing that Jesus' true identity was still unrecognized by the people. They didn't realize that Jesus was the Messiah, the Son of God.

---

EXPLAINING JESUS AWAY
Jesus asked his disciples what people were saying about him. Theories still abound concerning the identity of Jesus: good man, remarkable teacher, supreme martyr, etc. All of them miss the point.

Jesus is the Christ: the Answer, the Final Word, the Point. He is in a class by himself—only one Savior, only one Son of God.

Where Jesus is recognized as Lord and Savior, faith grows and the gospel prospers. Where Jesus is esteemed among many other great ones, the "religious buffet" is being served. Pick any entrée besides the living Lord, and you'll discover that they are all equally tasteless. Avoid churches and teachers who haven't learned that Jesus is the Christ.

---

**16:15-16** **He said to them, "But who do you say that I am?" Simon Peter answered and said, "You are the Christ, the Son of the living God."** NKJV The people may have had various opinions and ideas about Jesus' identity, but Jesus was concerned about what his chosen twelve believed about him. So *he said to them, "But who do you say that I am?"* The word "you" is plural; Jesus was asking the entire group.

Peter, often the one to speak up when the others might be silent, declared what he had come to understand, *You are the Christ, the Son of the living God.* "Christ" is from the Greek; and "Messiah" is based on Hebrew—both mean "the Anointed One." Psalm 2:2 mentions "the Lord and his anointed" (NRSV), referring to the Messiah—the King whom God would provide to Israel, the King who would sit on David's throne forever. In his declaration, Peter proclaimed Jesus to be the promised King and Deliverer, *the* one and only *Christ*. This is the core of the gospel message. Matthew interpreted the words in a Jewish framework by adding "the living God."

The disciples needed still further understanding. Although it certainly had already crossed all of their minds that Jesus might be the Messiah (otherwise they probably would not have been following him—see John 1:41, 45, 49), they still needed to learn about their role as agents of the promised Messiah and their role in his kingdom. They did not yet fully understand the *kind* of king Jesus would be. Peter, and indeed all Israel, expected the Messiah to be a conqueror-liberator who would free the nation from Rome. Jesus would be a totally different kind of conqueror-liberator, and he would conquer sin and death and free people from sin's grasp.

---

**SPIRITUAL INSIGHT**
Jesus told Peter that God had revealed the great spiritual truth to him. Often we wonder where certain people get their insight, their faith. If we knew where faith comes from, we could give credit for being faithful.

If it comes from inside us, we get the credit. Jesus did the work that enabled our salvation, but then we could get credit for believing in it.

If it comes from outside us, then God gets the credit. Jesus both did the work that enables our salvation and provides the means of our accepting it. As blind people need help to "see" the world, so spiritually dead people need help to find spiritual life. Jesus gives us that help.

When it comes to bragging about your faith, brag about God. He is the one who gives us faith.

---

**16:17** **And Jesus answered him, "Blessed are you, Simon son of Jonah! For flesh and blood has not revealed this to you, but my Father in heaven."** NRSV All of the disciples may have had glimmers of understanding about who Jesus was, but Jesus perceived the depth of Peter's confession of faith. Thus Jesus called him *blessed.* The Greek word *makarios* (here translated "blessed") is the same word used at the beginning of each beatitude (5:3-10). It means especially favored by God's gracious approval.

Jesus called Peter *Simon son of Jonah.* In John 1:42, at Jesus' first meeting with him, Jesus had said, "'You are Simon son of John. You will be called Cephas' (which, when translated, is Peter)" (NIV). Whether Jesus called him Simon or Peter throughout his ministry is unknown. (That he was called "son of John" in John's Gospel and "son of Jonah" here probably was simply a difference in the transliteration from the Aramaic.) At this point, Peter's new name carried a new meaning.

Peter is pictured as the focus of divine revelation. "Flesh and

> The very man who knows the Word of God also knows that he can bring no capability of his own to this knowledge, but has first to receive all capability.    *Karl Barth*

blood" is a Jewish idiom for people in general. No person showed
Peter the truth he had just spoken (16:16); instead, Jesus' *(my)*
Father in heaven had *revealed* it to him. Then, as now, true understanding of who Jesus is and the ability to confess that fact come
not from our human nature or will, but from God alone. Jesus
emphasized that the Father had revealed this truth to Peter, whereas
Satan prompted Peter (16:23) to talk Jesus out of his upcoming death.
In 16:18, Peter is called a "rock," but in 16:23, he is a "stumbling
block." These contrasting images show Peter's vascillating nature.

**16:18 "And I also say to you that you are Peter, and on this rock I will
build My church."** NKJV The name *Peter* had already been given to
Simon when Jesus first met him (John 1:42). Here Jesus gave the
name new meaning. Jesus said, *"You are Peter [petros], and on this
rock [petra] I will build my church."* While the wordplay is evident,
what did this *rock* refer to? The "rock" on which Jesus would build
his church has been identified in four main ways:

1. *The "rock" refers to Jesus himself (his work of salvation by
   dying for us on the cross).* This would mean that Jesus is the
   divine architect of our faith and that he himself is the chief
   cornerstone. But this truth does not
   seem to be what the language conveys here. The focus was on
   Peter and on Jesus' response to him.
2. *The "rock" refers to Peter as the
   supreme leader or first "bishop" of
   the church.* This view is promoted by
   Roman Catholic scholars. It gives
   authority to the hierarchy of their
   church and regards Peter and each of
   his successors as the supreme pontiff

   > Without a recovery of the
   > spiritual convictions and
   > vitality which marked the
   > church as she came into
   > existence, Christianity
   > is unlikely to remain a
   > serious contender among
   > world religions.
   > *Carl F. H. Henry*

   of the church. There is no mention of succession in these verses,
   however, and while the early church expressed high regard for
   Peter, there is no evidence that they regarded him as final authority. Also, this creates a great problem because such a view
   excludes the churches who do not trace their origin to Peter.
3. *The "rock" refers to the confession of faith that Peter gave and
   that all subsequent true believers give.* This view was promoted
   by Luther and the reformers as a reaction to view number two.
   To regard Peter's confession and discount his leadership makes
   the situation unnecessarily abstract. Peter was looked to as a
   leader in the church. In the phrase, "You are Peter," *you* is
   emphatic, emphasizing Peter's role.
4. *The "rock" refers to Peter as the leader and spokesman (foun-*

*dation stone) of the disciples.* Just as Peter had revealed the true identity of Christ, so Jesus revealed Peter's identity and role. While apostolic succession cannot be found in this context or in any of the epistles, Peter's role as a leader and spokesman of the church must not be discounted. This view has an element from number two in that Peter *is* the forerunner because he is the one who received the revelation of insight and faith concerning Christ's identity, and Peter is the first one who confessed Christ.

The word "church" *(ekklesia)* is found in the Gospels only in Matthew, but the concept is found throughout all four Gospels. Jesus' words reveal that there would be a definite interim period between his death and second coming—the "church age." "Church" means "the called-out people of God." Peter's individual authority became clear in the book of Acts as he became the spokesman for the disciples and for the Christian community. Peter, as the spokesman, became the foundation stone of all believers who would "build" Christ's church.

Later, Peter reminded Christians that they were the church built on the foundation of the apostles and prophets, with Jesus Christ as the cornerstone (1 Peter 2:4-8; see also 1 Corinthians 3:11). All believers are joined into this church by faith in Jesus Christ as Savior, the same faith that Peter expressed here (see also Ephesians 2:20-21; Revelation 21:14). True believers like Peter regard their faith as a revelation from God and are willing to confess him publicly. Jesus praised Peter for his confession of faith. Faith like Peter's is the foundation of Christ's kingdom.

**"And the gates of Hades shall not prevail against it."** NKJV The "gates of Hades" represents Satan and all his minions. These words may be interpreted, in light of other passages on the power of Satan, as Satan's domain in the offensive against the church. Christ promises that Satan will not defeat the church; instead, his sphere of operation (death) will be defeated. In these words Jesus gave the promise of the indestructibility of the church and protection for all who believe in him and become part of his church.

**16:19 "And I will give you the keys of the kingdom of heaven."** NKJV The meaning of this verse has been a subject of debate for centuries. The future tense, *will give,* probably points to the time after Jesus' resurrection and after Peter is reinstated to fellowship with Jesus (John 21). The "binding and loosing" aspect of authority applied to all the disciples (18:18), not just to Peter. However, Jesus gave Peter undeniable authority over the group of disciples,

seen in the leadership he assumed over the Jerusalem believers
(Acts 1:15-26) and over the church after Pentecost.

Some say the "keys of the kingdom" represents the authority
to carry out church discipline, legislation, and administration
(18:15-18); others say the keys give the authority to announce the
forgiveness of sins (John 20:23). Most likely, the "keys" are the
kingdom authority given to the church, including the opportunity
to bring people to the kingdom of heaven by presenting them
with the message of salvation found in God's Word (Acts 15:7-9).
They are also the keys to binding and loosing (18:18-20). Peter
had been told about the foundation of a building that Christ
would build and then was given the keys to that building. The
"keys" suggest not that he was a "doorman," controlling who
would enter the building; rather, they portray a "steward," who
would administer the building.

**"And whatever you bind on earth will be bound in heaven,
and whatever you loose on earth will be loosed in heaven."**NKJV
*Earth* and *heaven* refer not to spatial relationships, but to the divine,
heavenly authority behind the disciples' earthly actions. "Binding"
and "loosing" were a rabbinic concept that could have two meanings: to establish rules or to discipline. The disciples would be
involved in a certain amount of rule making in building God's
community (such as determining what kind of conduct would be
worthy of its members), and they would have authority to discipline
other members of the community. Thus, the words also refer to
the disciples' inspiration as proclaimers of God's new revelation.

The religious leaders thought they held the keys of the kingdom, and they tried to shut some people out. We cannot decide to
open or close the kingdom of heaven for others, but God uses us
to help others find the way inside. To all who believe in Christ
and obey his words, the kingdom doors are swung wide open.

**16:20 Then he sternly ordered the disciples not to tell anyone that he
was the Messiah.**NRSV Jesus *sternly ordered* his disciples *not to tell
anyone that he was the Messiah* because at this point they didn't
fully understand the significance of Peter's confession—nor would
anyone else. Everyone still expected the Messiah to come as a conquering king. But even though Jesus was the Messiah, he still had
to suffer, be rejected by the leaders, be killed, and rise from the
dead. When the disciples saw all this happen to Jesus, they would
understand what the Messiah had come to do. They would have a
difficult time understanding Jesus' work until his earthly mission
was complete. Only then would they be equipped to share the gospel around the world.

## JESUS PREDICTS HIS DEATH THE FIRST TIME / 16:21-28 / **110**

From this point on, Jesus spoke plainly and directly to his disciples about his death and resurrection. He began to prepare them for what was going to happen to him by telling them three times that he would soon suffer and die and then be raised back to life (16:21-28; 17:22-23; 20:17-19).

**16:21  From that time on Jesus began to explain to his disciples that he must go to Jerusalem and suffer many things at the hands of the elders, chief priests and teachers of the law, and that he must be killed and on the third day be raised to life.**NIV The phrase "from that time on" marks a turning point. In 4:17 it signaled Jesus' announcement of the kingdom of heaven. Here it points to his new emphasis on his death and resurrection. The disciples still didn't grasp Jesus' true purpose because of their preconceived notions about what the Messiah should be. While they may have understood that he was the Messiah, they needed to prepare to follow him and to be loyal to him as he suffered and died. So Jesus began teaching clearly and specifically what they could expect so that they would not be surprised when it happened. Contrary to what they thought, Jesus had not come to set up an earthly kingdom. He would not be the conquering Messiah because he first had to *suffer many things . . . and . . . be killed.* For any human king, death would be the end. Not so for Jesus. Death would be only the beginning, for *on the third day,* he would *be raised to life.*

> This cross saved and converted the world, drove away error, brought back truth, made earth Heaven, fashioned men into angels. Because of this cross, the devils are no longer terrible, but contemptible; neither is death, death, but a sleep.
> *John Chrysostom*

Jesus' teaching that he must suffer corresponds to Daniel's prophecies that God's plan for redemption could not be thwarted by any actions people might take: The Messiah would be cut off (Daniel 9:26); there would be a period of trouble (Daniel 9:27); and the king would come in glory (Daniel 7:13-14). The suffering also recalls Isaiah's prophecy of the suffering Servant in Isaiah 53. His rejection looks back to the rejected "stone" in Psalm 118:22.

Jesus knew from what quarters the rejection would come: the *elders, chief priests, and teachers of the law* (also called "scribes"). The "elders" were the leaders of the Jews who decided issues of religious and civil law. Each community had elders, and a group of them was included in the Council (or Sanhedrin) that met in *Jerusalem.* "Chief priests" refers not only to the present high priest, but also to all those who formerly held the title and some of their family members. *Teachers of the law* did just that—taught the law. They were the legal experts. These three groups made up the Sanhedrin, the Jewish supreme court that ultimately sentenced Jesus to be killed (27:1). Notice that opposition came not from the people at large, but from their leaders—the very people who should have been the first to recognize and rejoice in the Messiah's arrival.

---

TRIUMPHALISM
"Triumphalism" is a word that describes the kind of Christianity that seeks political prestige, social recognition, and temporal power. It forces itself on populations and begins to dictate on matters far removed from Jesus' word. It says, "God will not let us lose because God cannot tolerate loss." It presses toward victory by any means. It likes success. It is modern Christianity mimicking Peter's advice to Jesus when he tried to talk him out of his mission.
But Jesus describes the path of faith in much humbler terms: injustice, misunderstanding, suffering, and death. These terms typify true faith for Jesus more than black-tie banquets celebrating multimillion-dollar fund-raising campaigns. When you think of what faith means, focus on Jesus, not on brochures, media presentations, or hyped-up public relations press releases.

---

**16:22 Peter took him aside and began to rebuke him. "Never, Lord!" he said. "This shall never happen to you!"** NIV This was too much for Peter. Having just confessed his heartfelt belief in Jesus as "the Christ, the son of the living God" (16:16) and having been given great authority in Jesus' kingdom (16:18-19), Peter certainly found it most unnerving that the King would soon be put to death. His actions show that he really didn't know what he was saying. If Jesus were going to die, what did this mean for the disciples? If he were truly the Messiah, then what was all this talk about being killed? So Peter took Jesus aside and *began to rebuke him.* The word for "rebuke" is a strong term meaning that Peter was rejecting Jesus' interpretation of the Messiah as a suffering figure.

Peter, Jesus' friend and devoted follower who had just eloquently proclaimed Jesus' true identity, sought to protect him from the suffering he prophesied. But if Jesus hadn't suffered and died, Peter would have died in his sins. Great temptations can come from those who love us and seek to protect us. Be cautious of advice from a friend who says, "Surely God doesn't want you to face this." Often our most difficult temptations come from those who try to protect us from discomfort.

**16:23** **But he turned and said to Peter, "Get behind me, Satan! You are a stumbling block to me; for you are setting your mind not on divine things but on human things."** <sup>NRSV</sup> Peter often spoke for all the disciples. In singling Peter out for rebuke, Jesus may have been addressing all of them indirectly. In his wilderness temptations, Jesus had been told that he could achieve greatness without dying (4:8-9). Peter, in his rebuke of Jesus' words about dying, was saying the same thing. Trying to circumvent God's plan had been one of Satan's tools; Peter inadvertently used Satan's tool in trying to protect his beloved Master. Although Peter had just proclaimed Jesus as Messiah, quickly he turned from God's perspective and evaluated the situation from a human one. This would be a *stumbling block to* Jesus. Peter was speaking Satan's words, thus Jesus rebuked Peter with the words, *Get behind me, Satan!* This didn't make sense to Peter, who, Jesus said, was setting his mind *not on divine things but on human things.* This accusation provides us with an important principle for following Jesus today. We know, from God's Word, Jesus' true identity as God's Son, but it is so easy for us to limit his impact on our life when we are preoccupied with earthly goals. It is so natural and comfortable for us to set our minds on human comfort, security, success, and prosperity that we forget our divine call to sacrifice and service. So we can see that Peter's perspective was wrong. God's plan included suffering and death for the Messiah. Jesus would fulfill his mission exactly as planned.

**16:24** **Then Jesus said to His disciples, "If anyone desires to come after Me, let him deny himself, and take up his cross, and follow Me."** <sup>NKJV</sup> These words applied to the disciples and to all who would *come after* Jesus—that is, become a disciple and enter his fellowship. Recognizing and confessing belief in Jesus as the Messiah is only the beginning of discipleship. Jesus invites every person to follow, but those who desire to follow him must have three attitudes: (1) a willingness to *deny* themselves, (2) a willingness to *take up* the cross, and (3) a willingness to *follow.*

   To deny oneself means to surrender immediate material gratification in order to discover and secure one's true self and God's interests. It is a willingness to let go of selfish desires and earthly security. This attitude turns self-centeredness to God-centeredness. "Self" is no longer in charge; God is. Too often this has been interpreted to mean that we should have no self-esteem. Some discipleship or "deeper life" strategies have advocated stripping ourselves of all dignity or anything that contributes to a sense of self-worth. Jesus' view of denial was immediate and practical. It had to do with the disciples' careers—their future.

To take up the cross was a vivid illustration of the humility and submission that Jesus was asking of his followers. When Jesus used this example of his followers taking up their crosses to follow him, the disciples got the picture. Death on a cross was a form of execution used by Rome for what they considered dangerous criminals. A prisoner carried his own cross to the place of execution, signifying submission to Rome's power. Following Jesus, therefore, meant identifying with Jesus and his followers, facing social and political oppression and ostracism, and no turning back. For some, taking up the cross might indeed mean death. But Jesus' words meant that his followers had to be prepared to obey God's Word and to follow his will no matter what the consequences. We must count the cost and be prepared to pay it. Soon after this, Jesus would take up his own cross. Jesus was speaking prophetically here as well. To *follow* Christ is also a moment-by-moment decision, requiring compassion and service. Following Jesus doesn't mean walking behind him, but taking the same road of sacrifice and service that he took.

---

LOYALTY
Jesus asked for something unique and rare when he suggested that his disciples be loyal to him.

What receives our loyalty today? Sports teams . . . as long as they're winning. Career . . . as long as we're advancing. Marriage . . . as long as one's spouse remains attractive. Basically, the self alone seems to deserve the loyalty of the self. It's each person looking out for number one.

In Christian faith, however, Jesus must be number one, and we must give him our loyalty. Stick with him despite the swift current you're swimming through. Never think that switching loyalties will reckon to your personal advantage. Remain loyal to Jesus and follow him all the way to heaven.

---

**16:25** **"For whoever desires to save his life will lose it, but whoever loses his life for My sake will find it."** NKJV The Christian life is a paradox: To attempt to *save* your life means only to *lose* it. The Greek word for "life" is *psuche,* referring to the soul, the part of the person that includes the personality with all its dreams, hopes, and goals. A person who "saves" his or her life in order to satisfy desires and goals apart from God ultimately "loses" life. Not only does that person not receive the eternal life offered only to those who believe and accept Christ as Savior, but he or she loses the fullness of life promised to those who believe.

By contrast, those who willingly "lose" their lives for the sake of Christ and the gospel (that is, God's kingdom) actually "save" their lives. To lose one's life for Christ refers to a person refusing to renounce Christ, even if the punishment were death. To lose one's life for the gospel implies that the person would be on trial for preaching and circulating the Christian message.

To be willing to put personal desires and life itself into God's hands means to understand that nothing that we can gain on our own in our earthly lives can compare to what we gain with Christ. Jesus wants us to choose to follow him rather than to lead a life of sin and self-satisfaction. He wants us to stop trying to control our own destiny and to let him direct us. This makes good sense because, as the Creator, Christ knows better than we do what real life is about. He asks for submission, not self-hatred; he asks us only to lose our self-centered determination to be in charge.

The possibility of losing their lives was very real for the disciples as well as for Jesus. Real discipleship implies real commitment— pledging our whole existence to his service. If we try to save our physical lives from death, pain, or discomfort, we may risk losing our true eternal lives. If we protect ourselves from pain, we begin to die spiritually and emotionally. Our lives turn inward, and we lose our intended purpose. When we give our lives in service to Christ, however, we discover the real purpose of living.

**16:26** **"For what profit is it to a man if he gains the whole world, and loses his own soul? Or what will a man give in exchange for his soul?"** NKJV To reinforce his words in 16:25, Jesus asked his listeners a rhetorical question. What good would it be for a person to gain *the whole world* (that is, to have power or financial control over the entire world system of which Satan is the head), but lose his or her soul (that is, to lose eternal life with God)? Every person will die, even those most powerful or most wealthy. If they have not taken care to "save" their lives for eternity with God, then they gain nothing and lose everything.

Jesus had faced this exact temptation in the wilderness: "The devil took him to a very high mountain and showed him all the kingdoms of the world and their splendor. 'All this I will give you,' he said, 'if you will bow down and worship me.' Jesus said to him, 'Away from me, Satan! For it is written: "Worship the Lord your God, and serve him only."'" (4:8-10 NIV). Many people spend all their energy seeking pleasure. Jesus said, however, that a world of pleasure centered on possessions, position, or power is ultimately worthless. Whatever a person has on earth is only temporary; it cannot be exchanged for his or her soul. If you work hard at getting what you want, you might eventually have a "pleasurable" life, but in the end you will find it hollow and empty. The answer to the question, then, is that nothing is of enough value that it can be exchanged for one's soul. Even if a person were to gain the world, that person would lose his or her soul—and the soul counts for eternity. No amount of money, power, or status can buy back a lost soul. Believers must be willing to make the pursuit of God more important than the selfish pursuit of pleasure. If we follow Jesus, we will know what it means to live abundantly now and to have eternal life as well.

---

### ETERNITY'S VALUES
When we don't know Christ, we make choices as though this life were all we have. In reality, this life is just the introduction to eternity. What we accumulate on earth has no value in purchasing eternal life. Yet how willing we are to sell our eternal values short for earthly security. How foolish to seek worldly comfort and wealth and ignore the issue of our soul's eternal salvation. How important would a lifetime of pleasure seem when compared to an eternity separated from God and all the blessings of life with him? Even the highest social or civic honors cannot earn us entrance into heaven. Evaluate all that happens from an eternal perspective, and you will find your values and decisions changing.

---

**16:27** **"For the Son of Man is to come with his angels in the glory of his Father, and then he will repay everyone for what has been done."** NRSV Jesus, here again using the self-designation of *Son of Man,* will come again, but at that time he will be in his exalted state as King and Judge. The future tense of the phrase "is to come with his angels in the glory of his Father" indicates Christ's glorious second coming—the time of future judgment when present life ceases and everyone will be repaid *for what has been done.* The idea of repayment is taken from Psalm 62:12, "Steadfast love belongs to you, O Lord. For you repay to all according to their work" (NRSV). The judgment referred to here is positive, involving the Son of Man's loving acceptance of true disciples. While Jesus called his followers to deny themselves, take up their crosses, and follow, he also promised great reward. Their self-denial and discipleship would not be wasted. Their repayment would come in the glorious future kingdom of God.

Jesus Christ has been given the authority to judge all the earth (Romans 14:9-11; Philippians 2:9-11). Although his judgment is already working in our lives, there is a future, final judgment

## JESUS' REWARDS

Jesus had much to say about rewards.

| | | |
|---|---|---|
| 5:12 | "Great is your reward in heaven." | When we are persecuted and remain faithful, our reward in heaven is being with God himself. |
| 6:2, 4 | "They have received their reward in full. . . . Your Father, who sees what is done in secret, will reward you." | Empty acts done for worldly recognition receive human praise, but that is the only reward they get. The acts that God rewards are those done with goodness and kindness as the only motives. |
| 10:41 | "Anyone who receives a prophet because he is a prophet will receive a prophet's reward, and anyone who receives a righteous man because he is a righteous man will receive a righteous man's reward." | Anyone who helps or even shows hospitality to a Christian brother or sister (particularly a Christian worker) will reap the benefit of eternal life. |
| 16:27 | "Then he will reward each person according to what he has done." | Jesus Christ will judge each person's life. As we are reviewed and evaluated for how we utilized the resources God has given us, we will be rewarded. This is not something we can earn, but a by-product of faithful obedience. |
| 19:29 | "And everyone who has left houses or brothers or sisters or father or mother or children or fields for my sake will receive a hundred times as much and will inherit eternal life." | God rewards according to his justice. We who believe will receive eternal life, and it will mean more to us than any sacrifice for the gospel that we made on earth. |
| 20:15 | "Don't I have the right to do what I want with my own money? Or are you envious because I am generous?" | In this parable, Jesus taught that God himself decides the reward he will give. |
| 25:34 | "Then the King will say to those on his right, 'Come, you who are blessed by my Father; take your inheritance, the kingdom prepared for you since the creation of the world.'" | We should love and serve everyone we can, especially the needy people in Christ's church. Our reward is God himself and eternal life with him. |

when Christ returns (25:31-46) and everyone's life is reviewed and evaluated. This will not be confined to unbelievers; Christians too will face a judgment. Their eternal destiny is secure, but Jesus will look at how they handled gifts, opportunities, and responsibilities in order to determine their heavenly rewards. At the time of judgment, God will deliver the righteous and condemn the wicked.

ENIGMATIC PROMISES
It may have been perfectly clear to the disciples, but the meaning of Jesus' promises here is anything but clear to us. We may not see it as clearly as we'd like, but here's what we do know:

- When Jesus begins a statement with "Truly, I tell you . . ." listen hard and long. He emphasized what he said for a reason.
- Jesus holds power over death. While most Christians will die, some will not.
- Jesus' kingdom has a future. The present is not the final chapter. The future will be bright with Jesus in charge.
- Jesus is coming. That should fill us with anticipation, and we should place our hope in Jesus' words.

If quizzical details make the promise enigmatic, this much we know for sure. It's a pretty good start. Trust Jesus' words even when you can't quite figure out all the details.

**16:28** **"Truly I tell you, there are some standing here who will not taste death before they see the Son of Man coming in his kingdom."** NRSV When Jesus said some would *not taste death* (die) before seeing the coming of the kingdom, he may have been referring to

- Peter, James, and John, who would witness the Transfiguration a few days later;
- those who would witness the Resurrection and Ascension;
- the Holy Spirit's coming at Pentecost; and
- all who would take part in the spread of the church after Pentecost.

Some people reading this passage have assumed that Jesus was promising that the disciples would not die before he came back to set up his glorious kingdom. Perhaps the disciples themselves at first thought that Jesus was referring to his glorious rule on earth. But the disciples have died, so this passage must be interpreted differently.

Jesus' transfiguration, which immediately follows (17:1-13), was a preview of that coming glory. At the Transfiguration, Peter,

James, and John saw Jesus' glory, identity, and power as the Son
of God. In 2 Peter 1:16-18, Peter definitely says, "We told you
about the power and coming of our Lord Jesus Christ . . . we
were eyewitnesses of his majesty" (NIV). Thus, certain disciples
*were* eyewitnesses to the power and glory of Christ's kingdom.
Jesus' point was that his listeners would not have to wait for
another Messiah because the kingdom was among them, and it
would soon come in power.

# Matthew 17

**17:1 Six days later, Jesus took with him Peter and James and his brother John and led them up a high mountain, by themselves.**NRSV The time frame of *six days later* probably alludes to Exodus 24:16, where it is recorded that Moses waited for six days before meeting the Lord on Mount Sinai. The words also tie into 16:28, where Jesus had told the people that "some who are standing here will not taste death before they see the Son of Man coming in his kingdom" (NIV). If Jesus had been referring to his coming transfiguration, then three of those with Jesus at the time (Peter, James, and John) *did* get a glimpse of the kingdom during this significant event. While Luke says "about eight days" had passed (Luke 9:28), his was a more general reckoning, measuring partial days as whole days. Mark also wrote that this event occurred six days after Jesus' previous conversation (see Mark 9:2). Jesus singled out Peter and James and John for this special revelation of his glory and purity. Perhaps they were the ones most ready to understand and accept this great truth. These three disciples comprised the inner circle of the Twelve. Seeing Jesus transfigured was an unforgettable experience for Peter (see 2 Peter 1:16).

---

**TIME AWAY**
This was Jesus' retreat—a mountain trip with special friends, a brief taste of glory, then a return to ministry. He took the time for it. So should you. Get away from phones, office, factory, highways, and advertising. Shake the stress out. Read something fun, eat something different. Pray a little longer than usual. Retreats provide a different pace, a change of scenery, adventure, rest, and a chance to meet with God. Take time for it.

---

Jesus took the disciples *up a high mountain*—either Mount Hermon or Mount Tabor. Mount Hermon is about twelve miles northeast of Caesarea Philippi (where Jesus had been in 16:13);

Mount Tabor is in Galilee. A mountain was often associated with closeness to God and readiness to receive his words. God had appeared to both Moses (Exodus 24:12-18) and Elijah (1 Kings 19:8-18) on mountains.

**17:2 And he was transfigured before them, and his face shone like the sun, and his clothes became dazzling white.**<sup>NRSV</sup> The Transfiguration was a glimpse of Jesus' true glory, a special revelation of his divinity to Peter, James, and John. This was God's divine affirmation of everything Jesus had done and was about to do. It reminds us of the experience of Moses on Mount Sinai when, for six days, the glory of the Lord appeared to him in a cloud. Jesus had spoken to the disciples about his impending death, and they had not understood (16:21). He had assured them that those who followed him would receive great reward (16:27). The disciples wondered how this could be true if Jesus were to die. The Transfiguration clearly revealed not only that they were correct in believing Jesus to be the Messiah (16:16), but that their commitment was well placed and their eternity was secure. Jesus was truly the Messiah, the divine Son of God.

The Greek word translated "transfigured" is *metamorphothe,* from which we get our word "metamorphosis." The verb refers to an outward change that comes from within. Jesus' change was not a change merely in appearance; it was a complete change into another form. On earth, Jesus appeared as a man, a poor carpenter from Nazareth turned itinerant preacher. But at the Transfiguration, Jesus' body was transformed into the glorious radiance that he had before coming to earth (John 17:5; Philippians 2:6) and that he will have when he returns in glory to establish his kingdom (Revelation 1:14-15). The glory of Jesus' deity came from within; it was inherent within him because he was divine, God's only Son. The glory shone out from him and *his clothes became dazzling white. His face shone like the sun* recalls Moses' experience recorded in Exodus 34:29-35. The white was not of this earth; it was a white that no human had seen. These were the radiant robes of God, clothing "white as snow" (Daniel 7:9). The expression "dazzling white" suggests supreme glory, purity, and holiness. Mark and Luke also described how Jesus' clothes and face shone (Mark 9:3; Luke 9:29). Peter, James, and John saw what Jesus will look like when he returns to bring his kingdom. See Revelation 1:9-18 for John's description of the glory of Christ.

**17:3 Just then there appeared before them Moses and Elijah, talking with Jesus.**<sup>NIV</sup> Moses and Elijah were considered the two greatest prophets in the Old Testament. They were the primary figures associated with the Messiah (Moses was his predictor and Elijah was his precursor), and they were two people who saw theophanies—that is, special appearances of God (Exodus 24; 1 Kings 19). *Moses* represented the Law, or the Old Covenant. He had written the Pentateuch and had predicted the coming of a great prophet (Deuteronomy 18:15-19). *Elijah* represented the prophets who had foretold the coming of the Messiah (Malachi 4:5-6). Moses' and Elijah's presence with Jesus confirmed Jesus' messianic mission to fulfill God's law and the words of God's prophets (5:17). Their appearance also removed any thought that Jesus was a reincarnation of Elijah or Moses. He was not merely one of the prophets. As God's only Son, he far surpassed them in authority and power. Also, their ability to talk to Jesus supports the promise of the resurrection of all believers. Colossians 3:4 says, "When Christ, who is your life, appears, then you also will appear with him in glory" (NIV).

---

**HEAVEN ISN'T QUIET**
If the Transfiguration was a foretaste of heaven, we should note that these three people were doing something very important: talking together.

In God's world, relationships count highly. People are individuals, with minds and hearts and opinions. People are also part of a wider whole, connected by relationships built on sharing of minds, hearts, and opinions. Friendship is the key.

Find time and opportunity to talk with people, to build friendships, to share yourself with others. Churches bent on doing activities that "count for the kingdom" will not neglect essential time to just talk—it's a taste of heaven here on earth.

---

**17:4** **Peter said to Jesus, "Lord, it is good for us to be here. If you wish, I will put up three shelters—one for you, one for Moses and one for Elijah."**NIV Elijah and Moses were talking with Jesus, and there is no indication that Peter was addressed. But Peter impetuously interrupted to suggest making *three shelters,* one for each of them. He may have had in mind the Feast of Tabernacles, where shelters were set up to commemorate the Exodus, God's deliverance of Israel from slavery in Egypt when the Israelites lived in temporary lean-tos or shelters as they traveled (Leviticus 23:42-43). Peter wanted to build three shelters for these three great men to show how the Feast of Tabernacles had been fulfilled in the coming of God's kingdom. He may have thought that God's kingdom had come when he saw Jesus' glory (as seen in his words *it is good for us to be here*). Perhaps Peter had overlooked Jesus' words that suffering and death would precede glory. He saw the fulfillment of

Christ's glory for a moment and wanted the experience to continue. He wanted to act, but this was a time for worship and adoration. Perhaps Peter was only trying to be hospitable when he offered shelters to all three important people. Regardless of his motives, he had mistakenly made all three men equal. He had missed Jesus' true identity as God himself.

**17:5 While he was still speaking, behold, a bright cloud overshadowed them; and suddenly a voice came out of the cloud, saying, "This is My beloved Son, in whom I am well pleased. Hear Him!"** NKJV Just as God's voice in the cloud over Mount Sinai gave authority to his law (Exodus 19:9), God's voice at the Transfiguration gave authority to Jesus' words. A *bright cloud* suddenly appeared and *overshadowed* this group on the mountain. This was not a vapor cloud, but was, in fact, the glory of God. This was the cloud that had guided Israel out of Egypt (Exodus 13:21), that had appeared to the people in the wilderness (Exodus 16:10; 24:15-18; 34:5; 40:34-38), that had appeared to Moses (Exodus 19:9), and that had filled the temple with the glory of the Lord (1 Kings 8:10).

God's *voice* spoke from the cloud, singling out Jesus from Moses and Elijah as the long-awaited Messiah who possessed divine authority. As he had done at Jesus' baptism, the Father was giving verbal approval of his Son (3:17). God was identifying Jesus as the dearly loved Son and the promised Messiah.

God then commanded Peter and the others to *hear* Jesus, not just their own ideas and desires about what lay ahead. The command recalled the prophecy of Deuteronomy 18:15: "The Lord your God will raise up for you a prophet like me from among your own brothers. You must listen to him" (NIV), and it identified Jesus as the Messiah, the fulfillment of that prophecy. The Greek verb *akouete,* translated "listen," means not merely hearing, but obeying what is heard.

---

WHO IS JESUS?
The voice on the mountain proclaimed Jesus as God's "beloved Son." Many images catch sides of Jesus, from classical art to the musical's Superstar. But at the heart of it, Jesus is God's beloved Son who deserves our worship and obedience. Not just a friend, more than a moralist, greater than a fearless leader—this is the Christ. Follow him, worship him.

---

**17:6-8 When the disciples heard this, they fell facedown to the ground, terrified. But Jesus came and touched them. "Get up," he said. "Don't be afraid." When they looked up, they saw no one**

**except Jesus.**[NIV] When the disciples heard God's voice speaking directly to them as they were enveloped by the luminous cloud, they were *terrified.* Throughout Scripture, the visible glory of deity creates fear (see Daniel 10:7-9). But Jesus, ready always to calm every fear, *came and touched them,* telling them not to be afraid. Peter may have wanted to keep Jesus and Elijah and

> I advise and exhort you, with all love and tenderness, to make Jesus your refuge. Flee to him for relief! Jesus died to save such as you; He is full of compassion.
>
> *George Whitefield*

Moses there in shelters on the mountainside, but his desire was wrong. The event was merely a glimpse of what was to come. Thus, *when they looked up,* the cloud and the prophets were gone. The disciples had to look only to Jesus. He alone was qualified to be the Savior to die on the cross to forgive sin.

**17:9 As they were coming down the mountain, Jesus instructed them, "Don't tell anyone what you have seen, until the Son of Man has been raised from the dead."** [NIV] Jesus instructed Peter, James, and John not to tell anyone about what they had seen, presumably not even the other disciples because they would not fully understand it, *until the Son of Man has been raised from the dead.* This is the only injunction to silence given by Jesus with a time limit. It suggests that once the temporary time limit had expired, the three would not need to keep Jesus' identity secret anymore. Furthermore, after the Resurrection, these disciples would understand the Transfiguration and be able to correctly interpret and proclaim it. They would realize that only through dying could Jesus show his power over death and his authority to be King of all. The disciples could not be powerful witnesses for Christ until they had grasped this truth. It was natural for the disciples to be confused because they could not see into the future. They knew that Jesus was the Messiah, but they had much more to learn about the significance of his death and resurrection.

**17:10 The disciples asked him, "Why then do the teachers of the law say that Elijah must come first?"** [NIV] The appearance of Elijah on the mountain caused a question in the disciples' minds. Based on Malachi 4:5-6, the Jewish scribes believed that Elijah had to appear before the Messiah to usher in the messianic age. Elijah had appeared on the mountain, but he had not come in person to prepare the people for the Messiah's arrival (especially in the area of repentance). The disciples fully believed that Jesus was the Messiah, but they wondered where Elijah was, for he *must come first.*

BIBLE CONUNDRUMS
The question raised in Matthew 17:10 was intelligent and important. The Scriptures seemed to insist that Elijah return prior to the Messiah.

Jesus answered the question in a way that instructs us about this and many other Bible puzzles: He has the answer, and his answer properly interprets all the Scriptures.

Most Christians have a variety of questions about the meaning of this Bible verse or that, this reference or that. Taking Jesus' response here as the cue, the proper answer to all Bible questions emphasizes Jesus as Lord and Savior, His Word as authoritative above all.

The proper way to learn the Bible is to start with Jesus. The proper goal of learning the Bible is to end with Jesus.

**17:11-13** **Jesus replied, "To be sure, Elijah comes and will restore all things. But I tell you, Elijah has already come, and they did not recognize him, but have done to him everything they wished. In the same way the Son of Man is going to suffer at their hands."**NIV Jesus explained to the disciples that the teachers of the law correctly understood that Elijah would come before the Messiah and bring spiritual renewal (see Malachi 4:5-6). But the fact that Elijah would come and restore all things would not change the plan of salvation that would require the suffering and rejection of the Son of Man. That the Messiah would *suffer* was written in Scripture (for example, Psalm 22:14, 16-17; Isaiah 53:1-12). The prophecies would not have been written if they were not going to be fulfilled. Jesus was showing the close connection between the Cross, the Transfiguration, and the messianic passages in the Bible. He was also reminding them that if they rejected the reality of his suffering, they would not have in mind the things of God.

Elijah was supposed to come first, but Jesus explained that, in fact, Elijah had *already come*. Matthew added, **Then the disciples understood that he was speaking to them about John the Baptist.**NRSV Jesus was referring to John the Baptist, not to a reincarnation of the Old Testament prophet Elijah. John the Baptist had taken on Elijah's prophetic role—boldly confronting sin and pointing people to God. Malachi had prophesied that a prophet like Elijah would come (Malachi 4:5). John the Baptist had come and had restored all things just as Malachi had foretold. He had come like Elijah to prepare the way for the Messiah's first coming (3:1-3); Elijah himself will reappear before Jesus' second coming (see Revelation 11).

As "Elijah" then, John the Baptist's work of restoration also involved suffering. Elijah was severely persecuted by King Ahab and Queen Jezebel; later he fled for his life (1 Kings 19). John also suffered when Herod and Herodias did *to him everything they wished,* ultimately leading to his death (14:1-12). The religious leaders rejected John the Baptist (Luke 7:30), the Messiah's herald; thus, they would ultimately reject the Messiah himself. This further supports Jesus' words to the disciples that suffering is the necessary prelude to glory. There is no easy road for true followers of Jesus.

## JESUS HEALS A DEMON-POSSESSED BOY / 17:14-21 / *112*

**7:14-15** **When they came to the crowd, a man came to him, knelt before him, and said, "Lord, have mercy on my son, for he is an epileptic and he suffers terribly; he often falls into the fire and often into the water."** NRSV Jesus, Peter, James, and John came down from the mountain and returned to the other nine disciples (Luke 9:37 says this occurred "the next day"), who apparently were with a *crowd.* Mark explains that a crowd surrounded the disciples and some teachers of the law who were in a heated argument. The nature of the argument is not stated, but we can assume that the religious leaders were arguing with the disciples about their power and authority or about the power and authority of their Master, because the disciples had tried and failed to cast out a demon (17:16).

A man came from the crowd and *knelt before* Jesus. Respectfully calling Jesus *Lord,* he asked for mercy on his son, who was *an epileptic.* Mark gives more detail, for the man explained that he had come looking for Jesus to heal his son who was possessed by an evil spirit, making him unable to utter any sound (also he could not hear, see Mark 9:25). This was not just a case of epilepsy; it was the work of an evil spirit. The demon's destructive intent is seen in that the boy would often fall into the fire or water.

**17:16** **"So I brought him to Your disciples, but they could not cure him."** NKJV Having heard of Jesus' power to cast out demons, the father had come to Jesus, hoping for a cure for his son. He brought his son to the disciples to drive out the spirit, an appropriate request since the disciples had been given this power (10:1). The disciples could not drive out the demon, however, even though they had been given power to do so (10:8). Matthew records the failure of the disciples throughout this section (14:16-21, 26-27, 28-31; 15:16, 23, 33; 16:5, 22; 17:4, 10-22). It serves to teach that the power to heal is God's, not ours. We must appropriate it by faith.

**17:17-18** **"O unbelieving and perverse generation,"Jesus replied, "how long shall I stay with you? How long shall I put up with you?"** NIV Jesus cried out in exasperation, fed up with unbelief and lack of faith. His unusual words carry a biting rebuke. They parallel Moses' frustration as intercessor for God's people (Deuteronomy 32:5, 20) and portray God's frustration with his people (Numbers 14:11; Isaiah 63:8-10). The disciples had been given the authority to do the healing, but they had not yet learned how to appropriate God's power. Jesus' frustration was with the unbelieving and unresponsive generation, including the crowd, the teachers of the law (scribes), the man, and the nine disciples. His disciples merely reflected that attitude of unbelief so prevalent in the society.

**"Bring him here to me." And Jesus rebuked the demon, and it came out of him, and the boy was cured instantly.**NRSV Jesus *rebuked the demon, and it came out of* the boy (Mark's Gospel describes how the demon convulsed the boy terribly one last time before leaving, Mark 9:26). Demons are never pleased to be told to leave their human dwellings, yet they have no choice but to submit to the higher authority. As always when Jesus healed, the cure was complete.

**17:19-20** **Then the disciples came to Jesus in private and asked, "Why couldn't we drive it out?" He replied, "Because you have so little faith."** NIV The disciples had been unable to drive out this demon, and they asked Jesus why. They had cast out demons before; why hadn't this demon responded? Jesus pointed to their lack of *faith.* Perhaps the disciples had tried to drive out the demon with their own ability rather than God's. If so, their hearts and minds were not in tune with God, so their words had no power. Their question revealed their error; they centered on themselves *(we),* not on Christ.

> Obedience is the one sure characteristic of the surrender of faith. Faith that is not coupled with obedience is a pretense.
> *Andrew Murray*

**"I tell you the truth, if you have faith as small as a mustard seed, you can say to this mountain, 'Move from here to there' and it will move. Nothing will be impossible for you."** NIV Jesus pointed to the disciples' lack of *faith.* Jesus wasn't condemning the disciples for substandard faith; he was trying to show how important faith would be in their future ministry. It is the power of God, not our faith, that moves mountains, but faith must be present to do so. The *mustard seed* was the smallest seed known. But like the mustard seed that grew into a large garden plant (13:31-32), even a small "seed" of faith is sufficient. There is great power in even a little faith when God is with us. If we feel weak or powerless as Christians, we should examine our faith, making sure we are trusting not in our own abilities to produce results but in God's. If we are facing problems that seem as big and immovable as mountains, we must turn our eyes from the mountain and look to Christ for more faith. Then, as Jesus promised, *nothing will be impossible.* It is not the "amount" of faith that matters; rather, it is the power of God available to anyone with even the smallest faith. We cannot fail when we have faith.

FAITH
Jesus underlined the importance of faith and suggested that none of our mountains can stand before it. This remarkable statement has been wrongly used to mean:

- If you're sick and prayers do not seem to make a difference, you've got a serious problem with faith.
- Anything you pray for should happen. You've got a magical power over other people and events.
- The Himalayas themselves should be portable, if your faith is strong enough.

So let's get clear: Faith is not a *carte blanche* to supernatural power. Faith does not make God your personal genie. But . . .

Faith is the strongest power in the world, for it connects with God. God rewards faith, even weak faith, and God loves our trust of him, even beginning trust. Where faith is alive and growing, God is present and active. Every day, pray for faith to grow. Every day thank God for the connection that assures us we are not alone.

**17:21** **"However, this kind does not go out except by prayer and fasting."** NKJV This verse does not appear in most modern translations because the best Greek manuscripts do not have it. However, it does occur in Mark 9:29, although the best manuscripts there do not have "and fasting." Jesus explained that *this kind [of demon] does not go out except by prayer and fasting* and that the disciples had not depended on God's power through prayer. God's power must be requested and relied upon in each instance.

Prayer is the key that unlocks and reveals faith. Effective prayer needs both an attitude of complete dependence and the action of asking. Prayer demonstrates complete reliance on God. It takes our mind off ourselves and focuses it totally on God. This helps us deal with difficult situations.

## JESUS PREDICTS HIS DEATH THE SECOND TIME / 17:22-23 / **113**

**17:22-23 As they were gathering in Galilee, Jesus said to them, "The Son of Man is going to be betrayed into human hands, and they will kill him, and on the third day he will be raised." And they were greatly distressed.**<sup>NRSV</sup> The disciples still resisted Jesus' predictions of his suffering and death. This was the second time he clearly told the disciples that he *(the Son of Man)* would suffer (see 16:21). Whereas Jesus had spoken before about being rejected, this time he added the element of betrayal. He again said that he would be killed and that he would rise *on the third day.* There was again the assurance of victory, although the disciples always seemed to miss this point. They never rejoiced or marveled that he would be *raised;* instead, *they were greatly distressed* at his talk of death.

---

SLOW TO UNDERSTAND
The disciples didn't fully comprehend the purpose of Jesus' death and resurrection until Pentecost (Acts 2). We shouldn't get upset at ourselves for being slow to understand everything about Jesus. After all, the disciples were with him, saw his miracles, heard his words, and still had difficulty understanding. Despite their questions and doubts, however, they believed. Don't repress your doubts or questions as if they are wicked— talk about them with Christian friends. And even when you don't have all the answers, look to Jesus for help and direction.

---

## PETER FINDS THE COIN IN THE FISH'S MOUTH / 17:24-27 / **114**

**17:24 When they reached Capernaum, the collectors of the temple tax came to Peter and said, "Does your teacher not pay the temple tax?"**<sup>NRSV</sup> This return to *Capernaum* would be Jesus' last visit prior to his death. All Jewish males (age twenty and older) had to pay a *temple tax* every year (Exodus 30:11-16). The amount was equivalent to about two days' wages for the average worker. The money went for public sacrifices and then for the upkeep of the temple. If any was left over, it would be used for the upkeep of Jerusalem, which was considered part of the temple property. This tax was even collected from Jewish males who lived outside of Palestine. Enormous sums of money came in from such places as Egypt where there were 8 to 10 million Jews. Tax collectors set up booths to collect these taxes. Only Matthew records this incident—

perhaps because he had been a tax collector himself. These *collectors of the temple tax* were probably the temple commissioners who went through Palestine annually (these were not the same people who collected the Roman tax, such as Matthew). These collectors *came to Peter.* He may have been seen as a leader in this band of Jesus' followers, or he may have been approached because he was "head of the household" and a homeowner in Capernaum (Mark's Gospel records that Jesus and the disciples were in the house, presumably Peter and Andrew's; see Mark 1:29; 9:33). These men asked Peter if Jesus *(your teacher)* would be paying the temple tax. To not pay the tax indicated a desire to separate from the religious community.

**7:25-26 He said, "Yes, he does." And when he came home, Jesus spoke of it first, asking, "What do you think, Simon? From whom do kings of the earth take toll or tribute? From their children or from others?"** NRSV Peter answered a question without really knowing the answer, putting Jesus and the disciples in an awkward position. Jesus used this situation, however, to emphasize his kingly role. Jesus' question generalized the issue from the Jewish tax to all taxes. The words "toll" and "tribute" refer to the indirect local tax collected at customs houses by the publicans and to the poll tax or census tax on each family, collected by imperial officers and put directly into the imperial treasury. The *kings of the earth* collected such taxes from *others,* but never from *their children.* The royal family and inner circle of the imperial court were exempt. Thus, it was correct when Peter said, **"From others."** NRSV Likewise, Jesus said to him, **"Then the children are free."** NRSV Children of the king do not need to pay taxes. If the tax is the temple tax, then it belongs to God, and as a royal child of the king, there would be no need for Jesus to pay tax to his Father. By these words, Jesus once again establishes his identity as the Son of God.

Some Christians have used this verse as a license for not paying taxes because they are the children of the king and therefore free from such obligations. But Jesus was applying the metaphor to himself, as is evident by the context. So this passage says nothing one way or the other about our obligation to the government. (See Romans 13:1-7 for further details on this issue.)

**17:27 "However, so that we do not give offense to them, go to the sea and cast a hook; take the first fish that comes up; and when you open its mouth, you will find a coin; take that and give it to them for you and me."** NRSV Just as kings pay no taxes and collect none from their family, Jesus, the King, owed no temple tax because he and his "children" belonged to another "kingdom." But Jesus supplied the tax payment for both himself and Peter rather than offend those who didn't understand his kingship. The word for "give offense" is *skandalizo,* meaning "cause to stumble." Jesus said that he and his followers did not have to pay taxes but should submit to it for the sake of those who did not believe. Jesus taught his disciples that at times it would be important to submit for the sake of their witness. (See also Romans 13:1-7; 1 Timothy 2:1-3; Titus 3:1-3, 8; 1 Peter 2:13-17.)

Although Jesus supplied the tax money, Peter had to go and get it. Ultimately all that we have comes to us from God's supply, but he may want us to be active in the process. God sovereignly controls and answers the needs of his children.

As God's people, we are foreigners on earth because our loyalty is always to our real King—Jesus. Still, we have to cooperate with the authorities and be responsible citizens. An ambassador to another country keeps the local laws in order to represent well the one who sent him. We are Christ's ambassadors (2 Corinthians 5:20). Are you being a good foreign ambassador for him to this world?

---

SMART CHRISTIAN COMPROMISE

Jesus had every right to boycott the temple tax, but he chose instead to pay it. Everywhere Christians live, imperfect laws require us to choose when to go along, when to resist. Jesus made it clear that we must choose our battles, that there is a time to "go along."

But when is compromise acceptable, and when is it contemptible?

Jesus never compromised when the truth of God was at stake, including the truth about his own mission. However, civil or religious procedures that have not caught up to his truth, but that do not challenge or undermine it, are not worth the image of stubbornness that resisting them would provoke.

---

# Matthew 18

The end of chapter 17 is the record of Jesus giving his disciples
a glimpse of his new kingdom and himself as its king. The
special privileges and responsibilities of members of this kingdom led the disciples to question their status as special friends
of the king. All believers are presently part of the kingdom, yet the
consummation of that kingdom is still in the future. In the meantime, we must learn to live together in a way that pleases God.
In this chapter, Matthew included a fourth discourse that deals
with life in the community of believers.

**18:1** **At that time the disciples came to Jesus and asked, "Who
is the greatest in the kingdom of heaven?"** NRSV The opening
phrase "at that time" ties this event to the previous teaching
(17:24-27). The disciples wondered about this coming kingdom of which Jesus would be the king. In addition, Jesus' talk
of his coming death probably made them wonder how they
were to run the kingdom in his absence.

In Jewish culture, a person's rank was of considerable
importance (see Luke 14:7-11 for an example); thus, the
disciples were naturally curious about their position in the
coming kingdom. Jesus' teaching in 5:19 had indicated that
there would be distinctions ("least" and "great") in the kingdom of heaven. Mark explains that this question had caused
an argument among the disciples (Mark 9:33-34). This question also may have been fueled by the special privileges
given to Peter, James, and John at various times, most recently
their trip with Jesus to the mountain and then their silence
about what had happened there (17:1-9). Matthew characteristically abbreviates the story in order to focus on the
teaching. The situation became an occasion for Jesus to teach
about true greatness and the role of competition in the coming
kingdom.

**THE GREATEST**

At first glance, the answer to the disciples' question "Who is the greatest?" is easy: God. But that answer misses their point, which was: Among those who can compete for greatness (God and angels being above competition), who takes the top spot in heaven's all-star rankings?

Now the question becomes much more complicated, since it involves motives contrary to heaven's interests.

Many questions are like that. Phrased simply, they hide attitudes that require an answer quite different from the one anticipated by the question itself. As you listen to the questions of younger Christians, be sure to address matters of faith, of direction and motive, of pride and rebellion—matters implicit in many questions but too often bypassed for the easy answer. Be a real listener. Hear the heart.

**18:2-4** **He called a child, whom he put among them, and said, "Truly I tell you, unless you change and become like children, you will never enter the kingdom of heaven. Whoever becomes humble like this child is the greatest in the kingdom of heaven."** NRSV
To answer the disciples' question, Jesus *called a child.* The Aramaic language has the same word for "child" and "servant." Thus, when Jesus took a little child into his arms, he made the explanation of greatness even more distinct—to be great, one must serve. The disciples needed to *change and become like children.* What did Jesus want them to change? In this instance, it was their attitude toward greatness. The disciples had become so preoccupied with the organization of Jesus' earthly kingdom that they had lost sight of its divine purpose. Instead of seeking a place of service, they were seeking positions of advantage. Jesus used a child to help his self-centered disciples get the point. They were to have servant attitudes, not being "childish" (arguing over petty issues) but "childlike," with *humble* and sincere hearts. As children depend on their parents, so people who come to God must be willing to wholly depend on him. The kind of people whom Jesus described as "blessed" in the first four beatitudes (5:3-6) picture the complete dependence upon God that is needed in order to come to faith.

That Jesus called a child as his example of greatness in his kingdom reveals the nature of this kingdom. God's people are called to humility and unconcern for social status. Those who persist in pride and "ladder climbing" for the sake of status in this world *will never enter the kingdom of heaven.* By contrast, those who, in humility, realize their need of a Savior, accept him, and move into the world to serve, not only enter the kingdom but will be *greatest in the kingdom of heaven.* Jesus would later explain:

"Whoever wants to become great among you must be your servant, and whoever wants to be first must be your slave—just as the Son of Man did not come to be served, but to serve, and to give his life as a ransom for many" (20:26-28 NIV). True humility means to deny oneself, to accept a position of servanthood, and to completely follow the Master.

---

LIKE A CHILD
What did Jesus mean? How do we become like children? Jesus never asks his disciples to be naive simpletons but to trust him with the settled confidence most typical of a child. Here are some ways:
- With your money, avoid schemes which play to your greed (get-rich-quick stock funds) and cooperate with programs that really help the poor, foreigners, and the sick (food pantries, ESL centers, cancer research).
- With your mouth, avoid gossip, backbiting, and lying for advantage. Be someone who tells the truth without exaggeration, who doesn't bad-mouth friends.
- With your mind, avoid teachers whose foundational commitments exclude the possibility of God, sin, or human freedom. Learn all you can about science, the arts, history, literature, and foreign cultures from teachers who respect biblical ideas or, better yet, who embrace the Bible as true.

---

**18:5** **"And whoever welcomes a little child like this in my name welcomes me."** NIV In addition, Jesus taught the disciples to welcome children. This was a new approach in a society where children were usually treated as second-class citizens. Jesus equated the attitude of welcoming children with a willingness to receive him. The principle, as often seen in Matthew, is that God and Christ will consider the way one treats others to be equal to (1) the way one will *be* treated, or (2) the way one treats Jesus (for example, see 6:14-15; 25:31-46). But the meaning here goes deeper, beyond simply welcoming children, as important as that is. An attitude that *welcomes a little child like this in my name,* readily welcomes and embraces believers of little worldly importance and low status. This shows an attitude that also welcomes the Savior, for he too was of little worldly importance and of low status. In God's kingdom, greatness lies in acceptance of and dependence upon the Savior. Together in the church, believers are to welcome and love one another, encourage one another, allow everyone a place to shine according to their gifts, and appreciate one another.

**18:6** **"If any of you put a stumbling block before one of these little ones who believe in me, it would be better for you if a great**

**millstone were fastened around your neck and you were drowned in the depth of the sea."** NRSV As in 18:5, *these little ones* refers not just to children but to Jesus' "little ones"—the disciples. Children are trusting by nature. They trust adults; and because of that trust, their capacity to trust in God grows. God holds parents and other adults who influence young children accountable for how they affect these little ones' ability to trust God. To cause a child or any fellow disciple to sin or fall away from the faith means to purposely put a "stumbling block" in the way to make him or her trip and fall. Jesus warned that anyone who turns believers away from him will receive severe punishment. Jesus' words warn believers that they must not only teach the truth, but live it. If anyone causes young people or new Christians to doubt or fall back into sin, this is a grievous sin with terrible consequences. If they stumble because of wrong teaching, that is a stumbling block as well. Those guilty of such actions or attitudes are putting *a stumbling block before* other believers. Jesus graphically described the harsh consequences of such sin.

With his staff officers around him, Napolean Bonaparte once spread a large map on the table, put his finger on a country colored red, and said, "Messieurs, if it were not for that red spot I could conquer the world." That red spot was the British Isles. The devil gathers his lieutenants about him, points his index finger at Calvary, where the blood of the Son of God is shed, and ruefully moans, "But for that red spot, I could conquer the world!" Why should we surrender to Satan whom Jesus defeated on the cross?

*John Wesley White*

A *millstone* was a heavy, flat stone used to grind grain. There were two common kinds of millstones in use at this time. One was relatively small and was operated by a person. One was large and was connected to an ox or donkey that would walk in a circle, causing the stone to roll and crush the grain. The Gospel writers used the word for the huge animal-operated millstone. To have a millstone tied around one's neck and then be dumped into the sea meant certain death by drowning. Even the horror of such a death was minor compared to what this person would face in eternity.

## JESUS WARNS AGAINST TEMPTATION / 18:7-9 / **117**

**18:7 "Woe to the world because of stumbling blocks! Occasions for stumbling are bound to come, but woe to the one by whom the stumbling block comes!"** NRSV Verses 6-9 are linked together by the words *skandalizo* (meaning "cause to sin") and *skandalon* (meaning "temptation to sin"). *Stumbling blocks* will always be a danger to Jesus' disciples in their time on earth—whether they come from the fellowship (18:6), the world (18:7), or the sinful nature itself (18:8-9). As Jesus had explained in the parable of the wheat and the weeds, the weeds will exist until the end of the age, so evil and its accompanying temptation to sin will be ever-present problems for Jesus' followers.

Jesus described two "woes" in the verse. The first *woe* is *to the world* because of its stumbling blocks; the second *woe* is *to the one* person through whom *the stumbling block comes.* "The world" is used in Matthew to designate unbelieving humanity and relates especially to the Jewish leaders here. Jesus' followers face constant temptations to do evil from the world in general. Yet this does not excuse those individuals who are the cause of stumbling. They face a further "woe." Corporate and individual responsibility are included in the "woes" of those who lead people astray into sin. This responsibility to lead people correctly applies to individuals, churches, and institutions. No person or organization should lead people astray into sin.

**18:8-9** **"If your hand or your foot causes you to stumble, cut it off and throw it away; it is better for you to enter life maimed or lame than to have two hands or two feet and to be thrown into the eternal fire."** NRSV With strong language (not meant to promote self-mutilation), Jesus described how the disciples should renounce anything that would cause them to stumble (sin) or turn away from the faith. The action of surgically cutting sin out of their lives should be prompt and complete in order to keep them from sin. Temptation to sin can come from various sources. In the Bible, "feet" are often associated with traveling to do evil, and "hands" with accomplishments. Jesus continued, **"And if your eye causes you to sin, gouge it out and throw it away. It is better for you to enter life with one eye than to have two eyes and be thrown into the fire of hell."** NIV "Eyes" were associated with vision or desires of the heart, aspirations, or ambitions.

All who desire to follow Jesus must remove any stumbling blocks that cause sin. Jesus did not mean to literally cut off a part of the body; he meant that any relationship, practice, or activity that leads to sin should be stopped. As a person would submit to losing a diseased appendage (hand or foot) or a sense (sight) in order to save his or her life, so believers should be just as willing to "cut off" any temptation, habit, or part of their nature that could lead them to hold on to this world and turn away from Christ and into sin. Just cutting off a limb that committed sin or gouging out an eye that looked lustfully would still not get rid of sin, for that must begin in the heart and mind. Jesus was saying that people need to take drastic action to keep from stumbling.

This also applies to the corporate responsibility of believers and includes excommunicating those who would lead others astray (the Pharisees in Jesus' time; the false teachers in Matthew's time). Anyone who presents a stumbling block to the believers must be "cut off" from the fellowship.

The reason? Jesus explained that it would be better to have lost some worldly possession, attitude, or action than to keep it and *be thrown into the eternal fire* or *the fire of hell* because of it. This is true, radical discipleship. While no person will be completely sin-free until heaven, God wants an attitude that renounces sin instead of one that holds on to sin.

The word translated "hell" is "Gehenna"; it is derived from the Valley of Hinnom, south of Jerusalem, where children had been sacrificed by fire to the pagan god Molech (see 2 Kings 23:10; 2 Chronicles 28:3; Jeremiah 7:31; 32:35). Later, during the reign of good King Josiah, the valley was used as the city's garbage dump (2 Kings 23:10) where fire burned constantly to destroy the garbage and the worms infesting it. Thus, "Gehenna" accurately described the place of "eternal fire" (Matthew 5:22; 10:28; Luke 12:5; James 3:6; Revelation 19:20) that has been prepared for the devil, his angels, and all those who do not know Christ (Matthew 25:46; Revelation 20:9-10). This will be the final and eternal state of the wicked after the resurrection and the Last Judgment.

## JESUS WARNS AGAINST LOOKING DOWN ON OTHERS / 18:10-14 / *118*

**18:10** **"Take care that you do not despise one of these little ones; for, I tell you, in heaven their angels continually see the face of my Father in heaven."** NRSV This verse is found only in Matthew and bridges from the concept of leading the *little ones* astray to seeking them when they do go astray (see also 18:6). "Little ones" can refer to both children and disciples. The words "do not despise" pointed directly at the pious religious leaders who showed nothing but contempt for those below them on the "spiritual ladder" (see, for example, Luke 18:9-14 about the Pharisee and the tax collector). The reason the "little ones" should not be despised is because *their angels continually see the face of my Father in heaven.* Some have seen in these verses the concept of guardian angels. These words neither prove nor condemn the concept. Seeing God's face means having access to God, so these angels are ministering angels (see Hebrews 1:14). The Old Testament does not speak about guardian

angels assigned to God's people, but it does speak of angelic intercession and help (as in Psalm 91:11). Also, in Daniel 10:10-14,
angels watch over nations. The meaning here is that God's people
are constantly represented before the Father; therefore each one of
us has special importance. The writer of Hebrews said, "Are not all
angels ministering spirits sent to serve those who will inherit salvation?" (Hebrews 1:14 NIV). Any investigation of angels should
keep in mind that it is God's care that they administer, so the focus
should be on God, not merely angels (see also Luke 15:10; 16:22).

---

**TOO BUSY FOR CHILDREN?**
Our concern for children must match God's treatment of them.
Angels watch over children, and they have direct access to
God. These words ring out sharply in cultures where children
are taken lightly, ignored, or aborted. If their angels have
constant access to God, the least we can do is to allow children
to approach us easily in spite of our far too busy schedules.

---

**18:11** **"For the Son of Man has come to save that which was lost."** NKJV
This verse is not found in the earliest and best manuscripts; therefore, it is not included in most modern versions. It may have been
encouraged by the words of Luke 19:10, added by a later scribe to
provide a better bridge between 18:10 and the parable in 18:12-14.
In Luke, these words describe Jesus' acceptance of Zacchaeus, who
had been *lost,* but was saved when Jesus found him. Through faith,
anyone who is lost can be forgiven and made new.

**18:12** **"What do you think? If a shepherd has a hundred sheep, and
one of them has gone astray, does he not leave the ninety-nine
on the mountains and go in search of the one that went
astray?"** NRSV The differences between this parable as recorded by
Matthew and by Luke are important. In Luke's context, the words
were addressed to the religious leaders who objected to Jesus' dealings with undesirables (such as Zacchaeus, the tax collector). In
Luke's account, the sheep is "lost"; in Matthew's account, the sheep
*has gone astray.* Here, Jesus was addressing not his opponents but
his disciples, reminding them that God's care extends to each of his
"little ones" (here portrayed as *sheep*). If a sheep should go astray
from the flock, God, like a protective *shepherd,* will *go in search
of the one that went astray.* God is concerned about every single
believer and will actively go in search of those who have "gone
astray" (meaning they have gotten out of a right relationship with
him, are heading toward false teaching, are heading down a dangerous path in life, or are falling into sin).

"SEEKING" MINISTRIES
Many churches around the country (even the world) have begun to adopt creative new means to appeal to nonbelievers. Some have seekers' ministries, bringing the gospel to divorcees, singles, gays, and other groups that feel marginalized in most churches. Often these churches are criticized for glitzy music, peppy sermons, and shallow teaching—by other churches that have forgotten about shepherds.

With all your might and creative methods, go after people who are lost, astray from God. Be the shepherd who searches for the stranger and the straggler. Help your church adapt the message—not its truth but its format—to reach people living around you who don't believe.

**18:13-14** **"And if he finds it, truly I tell you, he rejoices over it more than over the ninety-nine that never went astray."**NRSV The sheep went astray, but the shepherd sought after it. *If he finds it . . . he rejoices over it.* The love for the little lost sheep is not at the expense of the rest of the flock. That the shepherd left the *ninety-nine* behind should not be pressed to mean that he leaves them unprotected. As noted above, not every detail of a parable must be pressed. The point is that the Father does not want any of his flock to wander away. Jesus explained that **"in the same way your Father in heaven is not willing that any of these little ones should be lost."**NIV God so loves each of his followers that, should they go astray, he actively seeks and rejoices when they return to him. Just as a shepherd is concerned enough about one lost sheep to go search the hills for it, so God is concerned about every believer no matter how small or weak his or her faith might be (he is "not wanting anyone to perish," 2 Peter 3:9 NIV). A sheep that is not "found" (that is, one that willingly refuses faith) will face a consequence—that sheep will remain *lost.* But God does not want that to happen. What wonderful love! God rejoicing in us! God rejoicing when a "lost" person is "found!" And God wants faithful believers to be part of the rescue team. Our follow-through care of new Christians, our small group ministry, and our individual contact with fellow believers should demonstrate the Great Shepherd's care for his sheep.

## JESUS TEACHES HOW TO TREAT A BELIEVER WHO SINS / 18:15-20 / **119**

The thrust of the parable in 18:12-14 leads naturally into the area of discipline. Note that the rigid use of excommunication (18:8-9) was muted by the law of love, which seeks to bring the straying believer back into the fold.

**18:15** **"If another member of the church sins against you, go and point out the fault when the two of you are alone. If the member listens to you, you have regained that one."**<sup>NRSV</sup> These are Jesus' guidelines for dealing with those who sin against us. These guidelines were meant for Christians (not unbelievers) and for discipline and conflict resolution in the context of the church, not in the community at large. These steps are designed to reconcile those who disagree so that church members can live in harmony.

The two earliest manuscripts omit the words "against you," and indeed there is a very high degree of doubt about their inclusion. The addition of "against you" focuses the sin in the area of personal offenses; its exclusion means believers could confront other believers when they see sin in their lives, not just when the sin is interpersonal. Of course, since most sin is interpersonal, these offenses must be dealt with properly.

Jesus explained that the person who has been offended must first *go and point out the fault when the two of you are alone.* A personal confrontation, carried out in love, will allow the sinning member the opportunity to correct himself or herself. However, the person doing the confronting ought to be very certain of his or her accusation and that he or she is doing this out of true humility with a view to restoration of the other (see Galatians 6:1-4). This call to confrontation is not a license for a frontal attack on every person who hurts or slights us. Many misunderstandings and hurt feelings can be solved at this stage. This saves church leaders from getting involved in everyone's personal concerns. Personal confrontation also keeps believers from gossiping with one another. Instead, believers are to be mature enough to go directly to the source and deal with the problem at that level.

When someone wrongs us, we often do the opposite of what Jesus recommends. We turn away in hatred or resentment, seek revenge, or engage in gossip. By contrast, we should go to that person first, as difficult as that may be. Then we should forgive that person as often as he or she needs it (18:21-22). This restores relationships.

**18:16** **"But if you are not listened to, take one or two others along with you, so that every word may be confirmed by the evidence of two or three witnesses."**<sup>NRSV</sup> If the personal confrontation yields nothing and the confronter is *not listened to,* then he or she is to proceed to step two. In this step, the confronter takes *one or two others along.* This is backed up by Old Testament law (see Deuteronomy 19:15). It is unclear from the text whether these "others" come along in order to support the confronter by bringing additional testimony about the erring person's sin, or if they are witnesses to this second meeting so as to give testimony should the erring person need to be brought before the church (step three, 18:17). These "others" also ought to help in reconciliation at this second meeting, hoping to settle the matter privately. An erring person might be willing to listen to the wise counsel of these "others."

---

RESOLVING CONFLICTS

Jesus' advice for keeping peace in your relationships:
- Don't ignore conflict; address it.
- Don't exaggerate conflict; solve it with the least possible publicity and public scrutiny.
- Don't abandon conflict; pursue it to resolution.
- Don't fence yourself in by conflict; taking two or three witnesses requires that you also are open to reproof and correction.
- Don't recycle conflict; once resolved, let it go and get back to your life.

---

**18:17** **"If the member refuses to listen to them, tell it to the church."** NRSV If the additional witnesses can accomplish no reconciliation and *the member refuses to listen to them,* then the third step is to *tell it to the church.* (This is the second and last time that the word "church" is used in the Gospels, see 16:18). The objective at this point still is not disciplinary action but helping the sinning person to see his or her fault, repent, and be restored.

**"And if the offender refuses to listen even to the church, let such a one be to you as a Gentile and a tax collector."** NRSV Even the law of love has its limit. The fourth and last step is to disassociate from that person. Some have construed this advice to be the final step of excommunication. The goal, even through this difficult act, is to help the person see his or her sin and repent. Paul recommended such action to the church in Corinth (see 1 Corinthians 5:1-13; 2 Corinthians 2:5-11; 2 Thessalonians 3:14-15). The person should be treated *as a Gentile and a tax collector;* such people were shunned by the Jews. Matthew recorded this saying for his Jewish audience who would understand the metaphor for the kind of avoidance Jesus demanded in this situation. In the phrase "let such a one be to you," the word "you" is singular—while the decision of the church is made corporately, the avoidance is acted out at the individual level.

While all people in the church are "sinners saved by grace," and while no church will ever be free of members who commit sin, the person described here has a huge blind spot to sin, and many people can see it. Yet this person refuses to listen to those whom God sends to help. In the church, believers are to teach, challenge, encourage, admonish, help, and love each other. But there can be no true fellowship with a believer who refuses the loving guidance of his or her fellow church members.

**18:18** **"Truly I tell you, whatever you bind on earth will be bound in heaven, and whatever you loose on earth will be loosed in heaven."** NRSV This verse parallels the similar authority given to Peter and the disciples in 16:19. Here the authority belongs to the church—the words "you" in this verse are plural. The "binding" and "loosing" refer to the decisions of the church in conflicts and discipline. Among believers, there is no court of appeals beyond the church. Ideally, the church's decisions should be God-guided and based on discernment of his Word. Believers have the responsibility, therefore, to bring their problems to the church, and the church has the responsibility to use God's guidance in seeking to discipline members. Handling problems God's way will have an impact now and for eternity.

**18:19-20** **"Again I say to you that if two of you agree on earth concerning anything that they ask, it will be done for them by My Father in heaven. For where two or three are gathered together in My name, I am there in the midst of them."** NKJV In context, the application of this verse applies to matters of church discipline. Other verses apply to prayer in general (21:22; John 14:13-14; 15:7-8, 16). Some scholars explain that the "two or three" who agree refers directly back to the previous verses (especially 18:16)—the people in the confrontation (the offender and the one offended, or the group brought in step two). These people come into the confrontation, and God stands behind them as they work through their disagreement. If the matter must go before the church, God is there helping those in agreement to deal with the sinning member as they ought. Indeed, God may be using the people to "chase down the lost sheep," so to speak, and bring him or her back "into the fold."

Jesus looked ahead to a new day when he would be present with his followers not in body but through his Holy Spirit. In the body of believers (the church), the sincere agreement of two people is more powerful than the superficial agreement of thousands because Christ's Holy Spirit is with them. Two or more believers, filled with the Holy Spirit, will pray according to God's will, not their own; thus their requests will be granted. In context, if the focus of their prayer is the repentance and restoration of the sinning believer, then that meeting of two or three concerned believers will have tremendous power when they realize the promise that God is *there in the midst of them.*

## JESUS TELLS THE PARABLE OF THE UNFORGIVING DEBTOR / 18:21-35 / **120**

At this point, the perspective shifts to showing God's grace and how ridiculous it is for us to withhold forgiveness from those who sin against us.

**18:21 Then Peter came and said to him, "Lord, if another member of the church sins against me, how often should I forgive? As many as seven times?"** NRSV Peter brought to Jesus a question commonly asked in rabbinic debates. The common answer was that it was considered sufficient to forgive three times, but on the fourth time, there should be no forgiveness. Peter may have chosen the number *seven* not only to indicate generosity and charity, but also because the number seven is commonly used in the Bible to communicate completeness.

**18:22 Jesus answered, "I tell you, not seven times, but seventy-seven times."** NIV Jesus' answer did not mean his followers ought to keep count up to *seventy-seven times;* rather, this statement means not to keep track of numbers at all. There ought to be no limit to a believer's willingness to forgive another believer (within the confines of the steps set out above in helping to restore straying believers, 18:15-20). All believers ought to willingly forgive, for all believers have already been forgiven far beyond their comprehension, as the following parable shows.

---

FORGIVENESS
Jesus puts no limits on forgiveness, not even the generous boundaries that Peter implies. No one can ever say, "I've forgiven enough; now it's time to hold a grudge."

If you refuse to work toward forgiveness, you develop handicapped emotions. You'll stunt your growth with grudges, no matter how important they seem to you.

Make a list of your top five hurts. Who must be forgiven to relieve these burdens? How can forgiveness be initiated? Who might help? Participate in Communion next time with a heart free from grudges, your own forgiveness reflecting the greater forgiveness of God toward you.

---

**18:23-24 "Therefore, the kingdom of heaven is like a king who wanted to settle accounts with his servants. As he began the settlement, a man who owed him ten thousand talents was brought**

to him."ᴺᴵⱽ This parable is recorded only in Matthew and illustrates the need for unlimited forgiveness in the body of Christ. The believers, already part of *the kingdom of heaven* must *therefore* forgive in the following manner.

The presiding *king* decides that he wants to go over the books with his accountant and settle up on accounts receivable and accounts payable. These *servants* (some versions say "slaves") probably would be court officials, powerful men in their own right. These were not slaves or servants in the strict meaning of the words, yet they were subservient to the king. Until modern times, kings had absolute power over their subjects. Probably the man first brought before the king was a tax collector who gathered revenue for the king from a certain province. The huge sums of money that passed through his hands might have provided a temptation to borrow or even embezzle. So this man, when called upon, found himself in debt for a huge sum of money. *Ten thousand talents* was an astronomical sum; King David had donated that much for the building of God's temple (1 Chronicles 29:4), and Haman had offered the king of Persia that much to help in destroying the Jews (Esther 3:9). In today's currency, the servant owed his master about 20 million dollars.

**18:25** **"Since he was not able to pay, the master ordered that he and his wife and his children and all that he had be sold to repay the debt."ᴺᴵⱽ** The man *was not able to pay* the king the ten thousand talents that he owed, so the king *ordered that he and his wife and his children and all that he had be sold.* The sale of family as well as possessions to pay debts was common in ancient times. Considering the sum, this would be no more than a drop in the bucket against the debt. Since no family could ever be worth that much money, the illustration reveals the king's anger against one of his officials.

**18:26-27** **"The servant fell on his knees before him. 'Be patient with me,' he begged, 'and I will pay back everything.'"ᴺᴵⱽ** The official humbly *fell on his knees* before the king and *begged* for patience. Although his promise to *pay back everything* shows that he might be willing to try, in reality it would probably be impossible. Yet the merciful king went beyond the servant's request. Instead of merely giving him more time, **"The servant's master took pity on him, canceled the debt and let him go."ᴺᴵⱽ** This highly unlikely turn of events would have surprised Jesus' listeners. No king would forgive such a huge debt. The king set aside a huge debt, rightfully owed to him, and let the man go free. The man's desperate plight caused the king to take *pity* on him. What an incredible load must have been taken from his shoulders! Unfortunately, the story doesn't end here.

**18:28-31** **"But when that servant went out, he found one of his fellow servants who owed him a hundred denarii. He grabbed him and began to choke him. 'Pay back what you owe me!' he demanded."** NIV The king had forgiven a debt of 20 million dollars and had let his servant go free. But when that servant left, he apparently ran into *one of his fellow servants* (probably a subordinate) *who owed him a hundred denarii,* amounting to about twenty dollars. *He grabbed him and began to choke him,* demanding the repayment. Twenty dollars would still be a somewhat significant amount, for it represented about a hundred days' wages for a common laborer. But compared to the millions, it was extremely small. Jesus' point was to show the ungratefulness of this forgiven man to be so cruel and exacting of his fellow servant for such a relatively small sum. **"His fellow servant fell to his knees and begged him, 'Be patient with me, and I will pay you back.' But he refused. Instead, he went off and had the man thrown into prison until he could pay the debt."** NIV This second servant echoed the request of the first servant. He also *fell to his knees and begged* for patience and time. He did not request cancellation of the debt; instead, he promised to repay it. The only difference between these two scenarios was that this second servant's request was not impossible. He *would* be able to repay his debt given a little bit of time.

But the first servant refused, having the man *thrown into prison until he could pay the debt.* This was not unusual. In Bible times, serious consequences awaited those who could not pay their debts. A person lending money could seize the borrower who couldn't pay and force him or his family to work until the debt was paid. The debtor could also be thrown into prison, or his family could be sold into slavery (as the king had planned to do to the first servant) to help pay off the debt. It was hoped that the debtor, while in prison, would sell off his landholdings or that relatives would pay the debt. If not, the debtor could remain in prison for life.

Compared to what the first servant had been forgiven, his refusal to forgive another was appalling. Apparently other *servants* (other court officials) thought his behavior was appalling as well: **"When the other servants saw what had happened, they were greatly distressed and went and told their master everything that had happened."** NIV

**8:32-33** "Then the master called the servant in. 'You wicked servant,' he said, 'I canceled all that debt of yours because you
begged me to. Shouldn't you have had mercy on your fellow
servant just as I had on you?'" NIV For some reason, the first
servant just didn't understand. After being forgiven millions of
dollars, he threw into prison a fellow servant who owed him
twenty dollars. But before he continued too far on his merry
way, he found himself summoned back to the king. The king,
who had been so merciful, angrily reproved the servant for
accepting forgiveness and then being unwilling to extend forgiveness to another. The king's question was rhetorical. Of
course, the servant should have had mercy on his fellow servant (see 6:14-15). In light of all that God has forgiven us, how
can we refuse to forgive the small hurts that we experience?

---

THE GOLDEN RULE REVISITED
Our forgiveness of others should be in proportion to what God
has done for us. If you need a favor, extend the same favor to
someone who needs it from you. If you need help, offer to help
someone else. First, we discover that problems can be solved,
and second, we find that serving others is God's way of helping
us overcome difficulties in our own lives. Because God gives
so generously to us, we ought to give generously to others. Life
goes better when we follow God's lead.

---

**18:34** "In anger his master turned him over to the jailers to be tortured, until he should pay back all he owed." NIV The king was so
angry that he turned the man over to the jailers. While torture was
forbidden by Jewish law, it was widespread in the ancient world
and was used in order to force people to reveal sources of money
that could be used to repay their debts. Getting into debt was serious business in the ancient world. To be forgiven of a debt was
almost unheard of in pagan circles. Because this man would not forgive another, the king decided not to forgive his debt either.
Instead, the man would be tortured until he paid back the millions
he owed. This man effectively received a life sentence.

**18:35** "So my heavenly Father will also do to every one of you,
if you do not forgive your brother or sister from your
heart." NRSV The king in the parable represents the *heavenly
Father* and pictures his role as judge. In the context of inter-
church discipline, the parable could underscore the corporate
responsibility of the church to deal righteously with erring
members. This includes harsh judgment but not torture on those
who hurt the fellowship by refusing to forgive one another

(6:15). Because God has forgiven all our sins, we should not withhold forgiveness from others. Realizing how completely Christ has forgiven us should produce a free and generous attitude of forgiveness toward others. When we don't forgive others, we are saying that we appreciate God's love and forgiveness but that we're unwilling to give it to anyone else.

# Matthew 19

**19:1-2 When Jesus had finished saying these things, he left Galilee and
went into the region of Judea to the other side of the Jordan.
Large crowds followed him, and he healed them there.**<sup>NIV</sup> Both
Matthew and Mark note the geographic shift in Jesus' ministry
from Galilee to *the region of Judea to the other side of the Jordan.*
Traveling to Judea from Galilee meant going through Samaria—a
district that most Jews avoided. Jesus had traveled directly through
Samaria before (see John 4), but this time he crossed the river and
went into the region of Perea. John the Baptist had ministered
there, and crowds had come to Jesus from the region earlier (see
Mark 3:8). Jesus was already well known, and on his arrival there,
*large crowds followed him, and he healed them there.* Jesus continued his ministry, but he was moving toward his death in Jerusalem,
in the region of Judea. We know from the other Gospels that Jesus
had already made several visits to Jerusalem, especially during key
festivals. Matthew records only this final trip to the capital city of
Jerusalem.

**19:3 Some Pharisees came to him, and to test him they asked, "Is
it lawful for a man to divorce his wife for any cause?"** <sup>NRSV</sup>
John the Baptist had been put in prison and killed, at least in part,
because of his public opinions on marriage and divorce. Divorce
was a hot topic of debate among the Shammai and Hillel schools
of the Pharisees. The Pharisees hoped to trap Jesus by getting
him to choose sides in a theological controversy and incriminate
himself in the process.

The debate focused on Moses' words about divorce recorded in
Deuteronomy 24:1-4: "If a man marries a woman who becomes
displeasing to him because he finds something indecent about her,
and he writes her a certificate of divorce, gives it to her and sends
her from his house . . ." (NIV). The religious leaders' controversy
focused around the interpretation of the words "something indecent."
There arose two schools of thought representing two opposing
views. One group (followers of Rabbi Hillel) said a man could

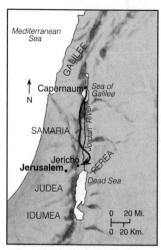

**Jesus Travels toward Jerusalem**

*Jesus left Galilee for the last time—heading toward his death in Jerusalem. He again crossed the Jordan, spending some time in Perea before going on to Jericho.*

give his wife a "certificate of divorce" for almost any reason, even finding another woman more attractive than his wife; "something indecent" could refer to anything that "displeased" him. The other group (followers of Rabbi Shammai) believed that a man could divorce his wife only if she had been unfaithful to him; that is, "something indecent" referred to adultery.

There was another issue, however. In ancient Jewish marriages, when a woman got married, her father gave her a dowry that reflected his wealth. The dowry— money, slaves, or other property—remained the woman's throughout her marriage. If the husband divorced her, he had to return the dowry to her, unless she was guilty of sexual misconduct. To divorce his wife, a man merely had to write a document stating that the wife was free from him and could remarry. No court action would be necessary; it was a very simple process. As a result, some Jewish men were divorcing their wives and claiming infidelity in order to avoid returning a wife's dowry to her.

The Pharisees asked the question *to test* Jesus. Perhaps they hoped that he might have very lax views about divorce (considering his apparent lack of concern for their laws about the Sabbath and fasting) and would depreciate the law of Deuteronomy 24:1-4, or that he would condemn divorce and lose some of his popular following. If Jesus were to support divorce, he would be upholding the Pharisees' procedures; they doubted that Jesus would do that. If Jesus were to choose sides in the controversy, some members of the crowd would dislike his position, for some may have used the law to their advantage to divorce their wives. Or, if he were to speak against divorce altogether, he would appear to be speaking against Moses' law (which allowed divorce). The Pharisees wanted to trap Jesus. They were serving their own desires, not seeking to know his view of God's will based on God's Word. As we examine the divorce issue, our motives must be to do God's will, not to serve our own desires.

**19:4-6** **"Haven't you read," he replied, "that at the beginning the Creator 'made them male and female,' and said, 'For this reason a man will leave his father and mother and be united**

**to his wife, and the two will become one flesh'? So they are no longer two, but one."** NIV Jesus' answer began with the words "haven't you read," implying that they had not truly read their own Scriptures with any understanding (compare to the words "go and learn" in 9:13). They had certainly read the words many times, but they were unable to understand what the words meant. The Pharisees had quoted Moses' writings in Deuteronomy; Jesus also quoted from Moses' writings (Genesis 1:27; 2:24), but he went back to Genesis, *the beginning*. Jesus was referring to Moses' words in Genesis about the ideal state of creation and particularly of marriage. In this answer, Jesus was using a rabbinic technique of arguing from the "weightier" text; in other words, an argument from creation was "weightier" than one from the Law because it had been written prior to the Law.

Jesus focused on God's ideal in creating *male and female*. The Hebrew words for "male" and "female" reveal that the two had been created complementary to each other. God's plan was that in marriage the husband and wife *become one flesh*, an intimate closeness that cannot be separated. The wife is not property to be disposed of but a person created in God's image.

**"So they are no longer two, but one flesh. Therefore what God has joined together, let no one separate."** NRSV Jesus drew a distinction: God's creation of marriage and his absolute command that it be a permanent union versus the provisions written hundreds of years later that tolerated divorce because of people's utter sinfulness (their "hard hearts," 19:8). God permitted divorce as a result of sin, but his command was that husband and wife be *no longer two, but one flesh*, describing an indissoluble union.

The Pharisees regarded Deuteronomy 24:1 as a proof text for divorce. But Jesus focused on marriage rather than divorce. He pointed out that God intended marriage to be a covenant— a permanent promise of love and faithfulness. The Pharisees regarded divorce as a legal issue rather than a spiritual one— marriage and divorce were merely transactions similar to buying and selling land (with women being treated as property). But Jesus condemned this attitude, clarifying God's original intention—that marriage bring unity that *no one* should *separate*.

**19:7 "Why then," they asked, "did Moses command that a man give his wife a certificate of divorce and send her away?"** NIV The Pharisees clearly understood that Jesus was denying the divorce laws with his statement "What God has joined together, let no one separate" (19:6 NRSV). If that were the case, they asked, *why then . . . did Moses command* divorce? Again, the Pharisees were summarizing the law recorded in Deuteronomy 24:1-4. They wondered if Jesus was saying that Moses had written laws contrary to God's commands. Such a comment would be considered heretical.

GOD'S IDEA
What does the Bible teach about marriage?

- *Marriage is a committed partnership between a man and a woman.* God's creative work was not complete until he made woman. He could have made her from the dust of the ground, as he had made man. God chose, however, to make her from the man's flesh and bone. In so doing, he illustrated for us that in marriage, a man and a woman symbolically become one flesh. This is a mystical union of the couple's hearts and lives. Throughout the Bible, God treats this special partnership seriously. If you are married or planning to be married, are you willing to keep the commitment that makes the two of you one? The goal in marriage should be more than friendship; it should be oneness.
- *Marriage is a cooperative effort between equal partners.* God forms and equips men and women for various tasks, but all these tasks lead to the same goal—honoring God. Man gives life to woman; woman gives life to the world. Each role carries exclusive privileges; there is no room for thinking that one sex is superior to the other.
- *Marriage is a gift from God.* God gave marriage as a gift to Adam and Eve. They were created perfect for each other. Marriage was not just for convenience, nor was it brought about by any culture.
- *Marriage was designed by God.* The marriage relationship that God designed has three basic aspects: (1) The man leaves his parents and, in a public act, promises himself to his wife; (2) the man and woman are joined together by taking responsibility for each other's welfare and by loving the mate above all others; (3) the two become one flesh in the intimacy and commitment of sexual union that is reserved for marriage. Strong marriages include all three of these aspects.

Because sinful human nature made divorce inevitable, Moses had instituted laws to help its victims. Under Jewish law, only a husband could initiate and carry out a divorce. The civil laws protected the women, who, in that culture, were quite vulnerable when living alone. Because of Moses' law, a man could no longer just throw his wife out—he had to write a formal letter of dismissal, *a certificate of divorce,* so she could remarry and reclaim her dowry. This was a major step toward civil rights for women, for it made a man think twice before sending his wife away. Moses' words gave protection to the wife and limited abuses of divorce.

**DIVORCE**
Jesus' first word about divorce upholds the sanctity of marriage. Before considering all the qualifications and conditions that may necessitate or permit divorce, Jesus pointed to an over-riding divine preference for stable, long-term monogamous marriage. So strong is the bond that the two persons in it should be regarded as if they are one.

Divorces will happen, some by flimsy choice and others dictated by basic human needs such as survival and avoidance of desperate harm. Some will occur because one partner became attracted to a third party, and then sexual relations outside of marriage spoiled the primary relationship. We need civil procedures for dealing with these troubles.

But above all that, marriage is good, strong, and endurable. That's God's intention and design. To that end we should pray and work. All else is unfortunate—the spoiled result of a good plan turned rotten by greed, lust, and selfishness.

**19:8 He said to them, "It was because you were so hard-hearted that Moses allowed you to divorce your wives, but from the beginning it was not so."** NRSV The change in verbs between these two verses is interesting—the Pharisees asked why Moses "commanded" divorce (19:7); Jesus explained that Moses only *allowed* divorce. The Pharisees had tried to make this concession into a divine law, but this was not God's plan *from the beginning*. As in 19:4-6, Jesus was again arguing from the "weightier" position—the law versus what had been planned when God had created marriage.

In Moses' time, as well as in Jesus' day (as well as today), the practice of marriage fell far short of God's intention. Jesus said that Moses allowed divorce only because the people *were so hard-hearted;* in other words, they were insensitive to God's will for marriage. "Hard-heartedness" refers to a stubborn, willful attitude (for example, see Deuteronomy 10:16). Many refused to follow through with their marriages as God had intended, so God allowed divorce as a concession to their sinfulness. Divorce was not approved, but it was preferred to open adultery. The Ten Commandments include two statements relative to this situation: "You shall not commit adultery . . . [and] you shall not covet your neighbor's wife" (Exodus 20:14, 17 NIV). Jesus explained that divorce was never God's intent; instead, God wants married people to consider marriage to be permanent and to control the desire for someone else's spouse.

Jesus turned the Pharisees' "test" question back on them by

using it as an opportunity to review God's intended purpose for marriage and to expose their spiteful motives in testing Jesus.

---

ONENESS
The union of husband and wife merges two persons in such a way that little can affect one without also affecting the other. "Oneness" in marriage does not mean that a person loses his or her personality in the personality of the other. Instead, it means caring for the spouse as oneself, learning to anticipate his or her needs, and helping the other person become all he or she can be. The creation story tells of God's plan that husband and wife should be one (Genesis 2:24), and Jesus also referred to this plan (Matthew 19:4-6). Are you experiencing oneness in your marriage? Are you caring for your spouse as you should? What can you do to work toward God's perfect plan of oneness with your spouse?

---

**19:9** **"I tell you that anyone who divorces his wife, except for marital unfaithfulness, and marries another woman commits adultery."** NIV Jesus had clearly explained that divorce dissolves a divinely formed union. Some men were divorcing in order to get remarried. The rabbis' interpretation of Moses' law permitted remarriage after divorce, but Jesus explained that marriage after divorce is *adultery.* However, he gave one exception (see also 5:32).

The Greek word translated "marital unfaithfulness" is *porneia.* As noted in 5:32, it has a broad range of definitions (see commentary there). Scholars agree that Jesus' words refer to both husbands and wives; that is, the unfaithfulness of one could be grounds for divorce by the other, because Mark recorded that Jesus then added, "And if she divorces her husband and marries another man, she commits adultery" (Mark 10:12 NIV).

While the application of Jesus' words requires interpretation to specific situations, one truth is inescapable: God created marriage to be a sacred, permanent union and partnership between husband and wife. When both husband and wife enter this union with that understanding and commitment, they can provide security for each other, a stable home for their children, and strength to weather any of life's storms or stresses.

**19:10** **The disciples said to him, "If this is the situation between a husband and wife, it is better not to marry."** NIV The disciples believed Jesus upheld such an impossible standard that it would be better for people not to get married than to enter into the covenant of marriage. It seemed better not to make the vow than to make the vow and not be able to keep it.

CONDITIONS FOR DIVORCE
Churches and Christians struggle to understand the Bible's
tolerance for divorce and remarriage. Is unfaithfulness the
only acceptable condition, or do the conditions here point to
additional conditions not explicitly mentioned but nonetheless
valid?

- First, Jesus spoke to a specific cultural situation: divorce
  as a husband's prerogative. This was only true of the
  Jews. Women could sue for divorce in the Gentile world.
  Today many divorces are initiated by women against their
  husbands.
- Second, in Matthew's account, Jesus addressed the remarriage question from a man's point of view—those were the
  people in his audience. Should we extend his precept to
  women as well? (See Mark 10:12.)
- Third, Jesus mentioned one condition that allows for divorce,
  but there may be others. Jesus was dealing with the traits
  of these specific Pharisees. What about a husband who
  abuses his daughter or habitually beats up his wife, or
  who is missing and declared legally dead by the state,
  or a number of reasons more reflective of the twentieth
  century than the first century? Might Jesus' allowance of
  one condition permit the church today to allow others?

Married people who want to follow the Lord through a thicket of
questions like these are advised to seek counseling rooted
in the Bible and keep their eyes open to the hurts of human life.
Churches struggling with what to do need prayer, wisdom,
compassion, and a dose of tolerance for others who come up
with different answers.

---

**19:11-12** But he said to them, "Not everyone can accept this teaching,
but only those to whom it is given. For there are eunuchs who
have been so from birth, and there are eunuchs who have
been made eunuchs by others, and there are eunuchs who
have made themselves eunuchs for the sake of the kingdom of
heaven. Let anyone accept this who can."<sup>NRSV</sup> Views differ on
which "teaching" Jesus was referring to when he said, *"Not
everyone can accept this teaching."* If he meant the disciples'
words in 19:10, he was saying that their proposal of celibacy was
a good one, but not everyone can be celibate, *only those to whom
it is given.* The problem with this interpretation is that Jesus
would have been setting celibacy above marriage as a "higher
ideal," and this would contradict his teaching in 19:3-9 (and the
high ideal of marriage). A second option is that "this teaching"
referred to his own words in 19:3-9 regarding the high ideal of
marriage, a demanding one, an ideal to which not everyone is
called "but only those to whom it is given." Those "given" that

responsibility are expected to adhere to it, as Jesus described above. This second interpretation fits best.

---

**SINGLE LIFE**
Many Christians are single, chaste, and happy. Marriage is not a prerequisite for a fulfilled life. The question raised here is whether diligent Christians should choose singleness as a way of better serving Christ.

Clearly, the Roman Catholic tradition promotes this. Priests and nuns are single in order to enhance their devotion to Christ. In other traditions, some have chosen singleness for spiritual purposes. Here's some help:

- Jesus' comment on singleness, like his comment on divorce, comes in the context of God's overriding approval of stable marriage. A serious Christian should not, therefore, feel "less spiritual" because of a desire to marry.
- A decision to be single should never be forced (by parents or pastors or anyone) on anyone. Such a decision touches so deeply our personal lives that pressure or guilt should never be imposed.
- Vows of chastity are advisedly taken with an escape clause, in the event that, down the road, the vow becomes a source of deep sadness. Just as we would advise a friend, "Don't marry just to marry," so we would also advise, "Don't set yourself up to burn with emotion, passion, and regret, should God lead you to that special person."

---

There are some to whom this gift of marriage is *not* given. A "eunuch" is an emasculated male—a man with no testicles. Some *are eunuchs . . . from birth,* who perhaps had physical limitations that prevented their marrying. Others were *made eunuchs by others,* such as those servants who, in ancient cultures, were castrated in order to serve the master without sexual distractions or without the ability to create offspring (such as the men who presided over the king's harem). Those *who have made themselves eunuchs for the sake of the kingdom of heaven* are those who voluntarily remained totally abstinent, choosing not to marry because, in their particular situation, they could serve God better as single people. They did not literally castrate themselves. Jesus himself would be in this category, as was the apostle Paul. Some believers throughout history have interpreted this wrongly as a command to remove their testicles. Origen (A.D. 184–254), a Christian scholar in Alexandria, did this in order to give himself more fully to teaching young women, but he later regretted this act. Jesus was not teaching that believers should avoid marriage because it is inconvenient or takes away freedom. That would be selfish. He was teaching that a good reason to remain single would be to use the time and freedom to serve God. Paul elaborates on this in 1 Corinthians 7.

---

TAKING THE PLUNGE
Although divorce was relatively easy in Old Testament times (19:7), it is not what God originally intended. Couples should decide against divorce from the start and build their marriage on mutual commitment. There are also many good reasons for not marrying; for example, single people can focus their energies on working for God's kingdom. Don't assume that God wants everyone to marry. Many may be better off unmarried. Be sure that you prayerfully seek God's will before you plunge into this lifelong commitment.

---

## JESUS BLESSES LITTLE CHILDREN / 19:13-15 / **174**

**19:13** **Then little children were brought to Jesus for him to place his hands on them and pray for them. But the disciples rebuked those who brought them.**NIV It was customary for people to bring their children (the Greek word *paidia* could refer to children ranging in age from babies to preteens) to a rabbi for a blessing. Thus people were bringing children to Jesus so that he could *place his hands on them and pray for them.* The disciples, however, thought the children were unworthy of the Master's time—less important than whatever else he had to do. In the first century, Jewish households were patriarchal—men came first, followed by women and children. Adult men were the key members of society, women quite secondary, and children were to be seen but not heard. The disciples apparently viewed these parents and children as an intrusion and a drain of time and energy. So they *rebuked* those who brought the children.

**19:14** **But Jesus said, "Let the little children come to Me, and do not forbid them; for of such is the kingdom of heaven."**NKJV When Jesus saw his disciples rebuking the people for bringing their children, he spoke to his disciples, telling them in a double command to *let the little children come* and *do not forbid them.* The implicit command is that the disciples should never forbid anyone from coming to Jesus, especially children. Why? Because, Jesus explained, *of such is the kingdom of heaven.* The disciples must have forgotten what Jesus had said about children earlier (see 18:4-6). Jesus wanted little children to come because he loves them and because they have the kind of attitude needed to approach God. He didn't mean that heaven is only for children but that people need childlike attitudes of trust in God. The receptiveness of little children was a great contrast to the stubbornness of the religious leaders who let their education and sophistication stand in the way of the simple faith needed to believe in Jesus. Anyone of any age who exhibits such faith and trust is promised access to Jesus and to the kingdom. The kingdom of God is God's universal, dynamic rule over his people. The trust displayed by children represents the trust that all true disciples need to have. The children came to Jesus in humility and received his blessing as a gift. They had no authority or rights, but they came to him in trust and love.

CHILDREN
Just as Jesus took time for the sick, the poor, and the hungry, so he also took time for little children. Jesus clearly enjoyed the company of the weak. We never read of him courting the favor of the powerful.
With whom do you like to spend time?
Without idealizing children (who are not always perfect company!), give them time. They need many other things from you, too, like discipline, provision, and health care. But don't forget to give them time. Hold them, hug them, tell them you love them. Today.

**19:15 And he laid his hands on them and went on his way.** NRSV One by one, Jesus *laid his hands on them* and blessed them. Jesus took time with each child, blessing each as he or she was brought to him. This certainly took time, but Jesus did not rush through the process or pass it off as unimportant. It probably brought him great joy to spend time with little children whose faith and trust were so pure and simple. Only after he had blessed each child did he then continue *on his way.*

## JESUS SPEAKS TO THE RICH YOUNG MAN / 19:16-30 / 175

While the children came readily to Jesus, a rich young man had difficulty. He wanted to get close, but he wanted to do so on his own terms. Jesus reached out in truth and love; unfortunately, the rich young man turned away.

**19:16 Now a man came up to Jesus and asked, "Teacher, what good thing must I do to get eternal life?"** NIV Jesus continued on his way from Perea, moving south toward Jerusalem. On his way, a man ran up to him (a "young man," see 19:22; Luke referred to him as a ruler in 18:18). This was a relatively young man who was both wealthy (Mark 10:22; Luke 18:23) and of prominent social standing. He called Jesus *teacher* (not the more common "rabbi") and eagerly asked a pressing question. This rich young ruler wanted to be sure he would receive *eternal life,* so he asked what he could *do to get* it. He viewed eternal life as something that one achieves. While the man had kept the commandments (or so he thought, 19:20), he still had some concern about his eternal destiny. He thought Jesus would have the answer.

To this man seeking assurance of eternal life, Jesus pointed out that salvation does not come from good deeds unaccompanied by love for God. The man needed a whole new starting point. Instead of adding another commandment to keep or a good deed to perform, the young man needed to submit humbly to the lordship of Christ.

**9:17-19 "Why do you ask me about what is good?" Jesus replied. "There is only One who is good. If you want to enter life, obey the commandments."** NIV At first, Jesus did not address the man's question but, instead, challenged him to think about God. Goodness is not measured by one's works; in fact, *there is only One who is good*—God alone. Jesus wanted the man to turn his attention from himself and instead think about God's absolute goodness. In Greek the word "me" in Jesus' question to the man is emphasized. Jesus asked why the young man needed to ask Jesus in particular *about what is good.* As a learned Jew, the young man should have already known "what is good."

In response to the young man's question about how to have eternal life, Jesus told him to *obey the commandments.* The young man then **said to Him, "Which ones?" Jesus said, "'You shall not murder,' 'You shall not commit adultery,' 'You shall not steal,' 'You shall not bear false witness,' 'Honor your father and your mother,' and, 'You shall love your neighbor as yourself.'"** NKJV Jesus responded by listing five of the Ten Commandments (numbers five through nine) and adding Leviticus 19:18—all referring to relationships with others. The last command to *love your neighbor as yourself* is not one of the Ten Commandments but was a command that the Jews believed summed up the last six. By rehearsing the commandments, Jesus illustrated that keeping God's commands merely points us to the One who is truly good. People's obedience merely reflects God's goodness.

LIFE INSURANCE
The life insurance industry is selling a misnamed product. Life insurance is a hedge against the economic hurt of a person's inevitable death. But if we could, we would all buy insurance against death itself. That's what this man was looking for.

He went to the right place. Jesus has the agency on real life insurance, long-term and secure. "I am the resurrection and the life," he said (John 11:25). The young man sought the right goal, for Jesus had said, "What good will it be for a man if he gains the whole world, yet forfeits his soul?" (Matthew 16:26 NIV).

Yet the young man muffed on the crucial play. That's because he wanted a mere policy, not a life; he wanted only insurance, not a Lord and Savior.

When you shop around for life, go to Jesus. When you hear his offer of eternal life, take it. When he says, "Follow me," do it.

**19:20** **The young man said to him, "I have kept all these; what do I still lack?"** NRSV The man sincerely believed that he had not broken any commandments, yet he felt that something was lacking. The powerful lesson here is that even *if* a person could keep all these commandments perfectly, which this man claimed to have done, there would *still* be a *lack* of assurance of salvation. The answer was that keeping the commandments perfectly could not save anyone—for obedience is not a matter of law keeping, it is a matter of the heart. This was a mind-bending revelation to this young man and to all of Jesus' listeners. Such is the condition of one who tries to attain eternal life or a relationship with God by his or her own merit. Even if it seems that the person has kept all the laws perfectly, he or she still needs assurance. Jesus would reveal to this man what he lacked.

**19:21** **Jesus said to him, "If you want to be perfect, go, sell what you have and give to the poor, and you will have treasure in heaven; and come, follow Me."** NKJV Jesus' words "if you want to be perfect" parallel his words in 19:17, "If you want to enter life." Matthew is the only Gospel writer to use the word "perfect" *(teleios)* here and in 5:48, "Be perfect . . . as your heavenly Father is perfect." There, as here, the word "perfect" can be translated "mature" or "full-grown." The young man said he had never once broken any of the laws Jesus mentioned, so he may have felt that he had attained a certain level of perfection. But Jesus never asked for strict and flawless obedience to any set of laws as the foundation for "perfection." Instead, he called for an understanding of how the law pointed to the heavenly Father who is himself perfect. The law was not the standard of perfection, God was. Those who loved God and desired eternal life would keep his laws as he required.

So Jesus lovingly broke through the young man's pride by

pointing out that despite his self-proclaimed obedience, he still had a long way to go in understanding what God desired. Jesus told him, *Sell what you have and give to the poor.* This challenge exposed the barrier that could keep this young man out of the kingdom: his love of money. Money represented the young man's pride of accomplishment and self-effort. Ironically, his attitude made him unable to keep the first commandment, one that Jesus did not quote: "You shall have no other gods before me" (Exodus 20:3 NRSV; see also Matthew 22:36-40). The young man did not love God with his whole heart as he had presumed. In reality, his many possessions were his god, his idol. If he could not give these up, he would be violating the first and greatest commandment.

> The way of salvation is the way of downward mobility. It is the call to give up our privilege and power and to identify with the poor. But it is good news, not bad news. It is bad news only for those who worship Mammon.
>
> *Art Gish*

The task of selling all his possessions would not, of itself, give the man eternal life. But such radical obedience would be the first step for this man to become a follower of Jesus. The emphasis is not so much on "selling" as on "following." Jesus' words to this rich young man were a test of his faith and his willingness to obey. The man thought he needed to *do* more; Jesus explained that there was plenty more he could do, but not in order to obtain eternal life. Instead, he needed an attitude adjustment toward his wealth. Only then could he submit humbly to the lordship of Christ. *Follow Me* was a stipulation that required more than mental and spiritual commitment. Jesus was asking this man to abandon his present career and join Jesus' itinerant group as a disciple. By putting his treasure in heaven and following Jesus along the road of selflessness and service to others, the man could be assured of his eternal destiny.

In this story, we see clearly the essence of the gospel—repent and believe. Jesus told the rich young man to turn his back on his past (repent) and to begin following him (believe). The young man may have wanted to believe, but he was unwilling to repent.

**19:22  When the young man heard this word, he went away grieving, for he had many possessions.**NRSV This man's *many possessions* made his life comfortable and gave him power and prestige. When Jesus told him to sell everything he owned, Jesus was touching the very basis of the man's security and identity. The young man did not understand that he would be even more secure if he followed Jesus than he was with all his possessions. He could not meet the one requirement that Jesus gave—to turn his whole heart and life over to God. The one assurance he wanted, eternal life, was unattainable because he deemed the price too high. The man came to Jesus wondering what he could do; he left seeing what he was unable to do. No wonder he *went away grieving*. How tragic—to be possessed by possessions and miss the opportunity to be with Jesus.

---

SELL ALL
Jesus told the rich young man to sell what he had and to give the money to the poor. Should all believers sell everything they own? No. We are responsible to care for our own needs and the needs of our families so as not to be a burden on others. We should, however, be willing to give up anything if God asks us to do so. This kind of attitude allows nothing to come between us and God and keeps us from using our God-given wealth selfishly. If you are comforted by the fact that Christ did not tell all his followers to sell all their possessions, then you may be too attached to what you have.

---

**19:23-24** **Then Jesus said to his disciples, "Truly I tell you, it will be hard for a rich person to enter the kingdom of heaven."** NRSV Jesus looked at his disciples and taught them a lesson from this incident with the rich young man. Jesus explained that it was very difficult for the rich to enter the kingdom of heaven (not impossible, but difficult). Jesus was explaining that wealth can be a stumbling block on the path to discipleship because it engenders self-sufficiency. The rich, with most of their basic physical needs met, often become self-reliant. When they feel empty, they can buy something new to dull the pain that was meant to drive them toward God. Their abundance and self-sufficiency become their deficiency. People who have everything on earth can still lack what is most important—eternal life. They have riches, but they don't have God's kingdom.

Jesus used a common Jewish proverb describing something impossible and absurd to illustrate how *hard* it will be *for a rich person to enter the kingdom of heaven* by saying, **"Again I tell you, it is easier for a camel to go through the eye of a needle than for someone who is rich to enter the kingdom of**

Most Christians in the Northern Hemisphere simply do not believe Jesus' teaching about the deadly danger of possessions. . . . An abundance of possessions can easily lead us to forget that God is the source of all good. We trust in ourselves and our wealth rather than in the Almighty.

*Ron Sider*

**God."** <sup>NRSV</sup> With all their advantages and influence, rich people
may find it difficult to have the attitude of humility, submission,
and service required by Jesus. Because money represents power,
authority, and success, wealthy people often have difficulty realizing their need and their powerlessness to save themselves. Thus,
Jesus explained that it would be easier to get a camel (the largest
animal in Palestine) through the eye of a sewing needle than for a
person who trusts in riches to get into the kingdom of God.

Some commentators have suggested that the "needle" refers to
a certain gate in the wall of Jerusalem, a gate that was too low for
camels to get through. However, the Greek word refers to a needle
that is used with thread, and the Needle's Eye Gate didn't exist in
Jesus' day. It was put in later when the city was rebuilt after its
destruction by the Romans. Thus, Jesus' image was for hyperbolic
effect.

---

MANY POSSESSIONS
This young man may have been very wealthy, but any of us who
own anything could also be considered wealthy by someone
else's standards. Whatever you own could become a barrier to
entering the kingdom if it comes between you and God. Because
it is impossible for a camel to go through the eye of a needle, it
appears impossible for a rich person to get into the kingdom of
God. Jesus explained, however, that "with God all things are
possible" (Matthew 19:26 NKJV). Even rich people can enter the
kingdom if God brings them in. Faith in Christ, not in self or
riches, is what counts. On what are you counting for salvation?

---

**19:25 When the disciples heard this, they were greatly astounded and
said, "Then who can be saved?"** <sup>NRSV</sup> The disciples were *greatly
astounded,* almost to the point of exasperation. Again, they wondered what Jesus meant. The Jews looked upon wealth as a blessing from God, a reward for being good, a sign of his special favor.
The lives of David and Solomon encouraged this view. If the rich—
those who from the disciples' vantage point seemed to be first in
line for salvation—cannot be saved, then *who can be saved?*

**19:26 But Jesus looked at them and said to them, "With men this is
impossible, but with God all things are possible."** <sup>NKJV</sup> The
answer to the disciples' question, "Who can be saved?" turned out
to be quite simple. In reality, it is not just the rich who have difficulty, for salvation is not possible for anyone from a human standpoint. No one can be saved by his or her wealth, achievements,
talents, or good deeds: *With men this is impossible.* But the situation is not hopeless, for God has an entirely different plan: *With*

*God all things are possible.* The Greek word order stresses the contrasts between the words "men" and "God," and between the words "impossible" and "possible." Salvation cannot be earned; God gives it to us as a gift. No one needs money, talent, or advantage to obtain it. Instead, it is offered to all people equally. No one is saved on merit; but all are saved who humbly come to God to receive salvation. As Paul wrote to the Ephesians, "For by grace you have been saved through faith, and this is not your own doing; it is the gift of God—not the result of works, so that no one may boast" (Ephesians 2:8-9 NRSV).

MISSION IMPOSSIBLE
Jesus was forever turning the tables. The last would be first, children are the kingdom, the wealthy would have to squeeze through an impossible gate to heaven. Rightly, the disciples were dazzled. *What's going on here? Who changed the rules?* they must have been thinking.

Whenever you're puzzled about the eternal destiny of a loved one or exasperated at a friend's hardness of heart toward God, remember Jesus' assurance that God has the power to save anyone. Trust God to change and soften people's hearts.

**19:27 Peter answered him, "We have left everything to follow you! What then will there be for us?"** NIV Peter, once again acting as spokesman for the Twelve, contrasted the disciples with the rich young man. He refused to give up what he had, but the disciples had *left everything to follow* Jesus. The Greek word *aphekamen* is in the aorist tense, signifying a once-for-all act. They had done what the rich young man had been unwilling to do. They had abandoned their former lives. Peter's question, *"What then will there be for us?"* emphasizes that the disciples had done the ultimate in self-denial and had followed Jesus' call. So their natural question would seem to be, "Won't we receive some great reward for having done so?" While Peter's question seems somewhat selfish, he was merely thinking about rewards from the standpoint of his Jewish background. In the Old Testament, God rewarded his people according to his justice, and obedience often brought reward in this life (Deuteronomy 28). But Jesus explained to Peter that obedience and immediate reward are not always linked. If they were, good people would always be rich, and suffering would always be a sign of sin. The disciples' true reward (and ours) was God's presence and power through the Holy Spirit. The reward also includes the assurance of salvation and eternal life (an assurance that the rich young man lacked,

19:20). Later, in eternity, God will reward his people for faith and
service (see 5:12).

---

**UPSIDE DOWN**
Jesus turned the world's values upside down. Consider the
most powerful or well-known people in our society—how many
got where they are by being humble, self-effacing, and gentle?
Not many! But in the life to come, the last will be first, if they
came in in last place by choosing to follow Jesus. Don't forfeit
eternal rewards for temporary benefits. Be willing to make
sacrifices now for greater rewards later. Be willing to accept
human disapproval, knowing that you have God's approval.

---

**19:28** **Jesus said to them, "Truly I tell you, at the renewal of all
things, when the Son of Man is seated on the throne of his
glory, you who have followed me will also sit on twelve
thrones, judging the twelve tribes of Israel."** NRSV Peter and the
other disciples had paid a high price—leaving their homes and
jobs and secure futures—to follow Jesus. But Jesus reminded
them that following him has its benefits as well as its sacrifices.
Although they had to leave everything (19:27) to follow Christ,
they would be paid back in this present age (the time period
between Jesus' first and second comings, see Mark 10:29-30;
Luke 18:29-30) as well as *at the renewal of all things* in the age
to come (after Jesus' second coming). Mark and Luke stressed
both present and future rewards; Matthew, perhaps due to persecution of the church in his own time, stressed only the future
side. The word for the "renewal of all things" is found only here
and in Titus 3:5, where it is translated "rebirth". It seems to refer
to the creation of the new heaven and new earth (2 Peter 3:10-13;
Revelation 21–22). The Jews looked forward to this restoration
as the messianic age at the end of the world based on Old Testament prophecy (Isaiah 65:17; 66:22). They believed that a golden
age similar to the days when David ruled the kingdom would be
restored. This would occur when *the Son of Man is seated on the
throne of his glory.* Jesus made it clear that this was an event still
in the future. The disciples had been hoping that it would happen
immediately, but Jesus' constant talk of his coming death made
them wonder what would happen to them in this whole scenario
and who would rule in Jesus' absence.

Jesus clarified that the time would come when he would rule.
They, in turn, would also rule with him. First Corinthians 6:2-3
stresses that all believers will rule the world and the angels. In
Luke 22:28-30, at the end of the Last Supper, Jesus assured the

disciples that they would have a certain role. The *twelve thrones* and *judging the twelve tribes* can be understood in different ways.

- If taken literally, the twelve apostles will rule the tribes of Israel at Christ's return (although this leaves open the question of Judas's betrayal, the addition of Matthias as a disciple to replace Judas, and the role of Paul's apostleship). The exact time and nature of that role is not specified.
- If not taken literally, then the disciples will oversee the church, which will have a prominent place in God's plan.
- This may be a promise to Jesus' closest disciples (probably Paul would be included) who will have a special place of authority in the messianic kingdom. But the entire church, meaning all believers and not just the Jewish branch of God's people, is included (because of the constant juxtaposition of the disciples and the church, 16:17-19; see also 1 Corinthians 6:2-3; James 1:1).

The second understanding (the disciples will oversee the church) seems likely because the "Son of Man" imagery ties to Daniel 7:13-14. The prophet Daniel recorded his vision for the future: "But the saints of the Most High will receive the kingdom and will possess it forever—yes, for ever and ever. . . . The Ancient of Days came and pronounced judgment in favor of the saints of the Most High, and the time came when they possessed the kingdom" (Daniel 7:18, 22 NIV). The "saints of the Most High" are the true Israel, the people ruled by the Messiah. Jesus Christ gave the kingdom to the new Israel, his church—all faithful believers. His coming ushered in the kingdom of God with all believers as its citizens. God may allow persecution to continue for a while, but the destiny of his followers is to possess the kingdom and be with him forever. This amazing teaching not only answered Peter's question about future rewards but also revealed God's will regarding his people.

**19:29 "And everyone who has left houses or brothers or sisters or father or mother or children or fields, for my name's sake, will receive a hundredfold, and will inherit eternal life."** NRSV Jesus assured the disciples that anyone who gave up something valuable for his sake would be repaid a hundred times over, although not necessarily in the same form. It is difficult to say whether Jesus had in mind material as well as spiritual blessings, although his statement probably means that God will give spiritual blessings for material sacrifices. For example, someone may be rejected by his or her family for accepting Christ, but he or she will gain the larger family of believers with all the love it has to offer.

Here is the answer to the rich young ruler's question about how to obtain eternal life. Jesus explained that by submitting to his authority and rule, making him top priority over all else, and giving up anything that hinders following him, each person can *inherit eternal life*. For the rich young man, that meant giving up money as his idol. For each person the sacrifice may be different, though no less difficult. We may have little or much, but are we willing to give it all up in order to have eternal life?

**19:30** **"But many who are first will be last, and the last will be first."** NRSV Jesus had already shown that the "greatest" are like "little children" (18:1-4). In the world to come, the values of this world will be reversed. Those who believe but who still seek status and importance here on earth will have none in heaven. Jesus may have been referring to the disciples' mixed-up motives. They had given up everything and hoped for rewards and for status in God's kingdom. Jesus explained that yearning for position would cause them to lose any position they might have. Christ's disciples who have humbly served others are most qualified to be great in heaven. Rewards in heaven are not given on the basis of merit or "time served" or other earthly standards. What matters in heaven is a person's commitment to Christ. Radical discipleship—a willingness to follow totally and accept the consequences, a willingness to surrender *everything* to and for the service of Christ—is the only path to reward. (For a discussion on rewards, see note on 16:27.)

# Matthew 20

**20:1-2** "For the kingdom of heaven is like a landowner who went out early in the morning to hire laborers for his vineyard. After agreeing with the laborers for the usual daily wage, he sent them into his vineyard." <sup>NRSV</sup> This parable further explains Jesus' words in 19:30 (indicated by the repetition of that verse in 20:16). It explains the "first and last" saying by focusing on the landowner's generosity (God's gracious love) in welcoming everyone into his field.

Jesus further clarified the membership rules of the kingdom of heaven—entrance is by God's grace alone. In this parable, God is the *landowner,* believers are the *laborers,* and the *vineyard* is the *kingdom of heaven.* This parable speaks especially to those who feel superior because of heritage or favored position, to those who feel superior because they have spent so much time with Christ, and to new believers so as to reassure them of God's grace.

The landowner went out *early in the morning* to find some laborers. The workday went from sunup to sundown, so this "early morning" hour was about six o'clock. These laborers agreed to work *for the usual daily wage* (usually a denarius). Bosses and managers should not overlook the fact that laborers had a fair role in the negotiation of wages at the beginning of this story. Owners do not hire workers on a "take it or leave it" basis here. They talk, and as the day's work begins, both sides are pleased with the terms.

Fair bargaining today means that Christian managers talk with labor at a table where both sides recognize mutual interests, needs, and expectations. When the talk is done, both sides should say, "Good deal, let's get to work."

**20:3-4** "When he went out about nine o'clock, he saw others standing idle in the marketplace; and he said to them, 'You also go into the vineyard, and I will pay you whatever is right.' So they went." <sup>NRSV</sup> The landowner *went out about nine o'clock* and hired more workers who were *standing idle in the marketplace.*

(Some versions say "the third hour." The day was divided from sunrise to sunset into twelve hours, so the third hour would be about nine o'clock in the morning; the eleventh hour, mentioned in 20:6, would be five o'clock in the afternoon.) Why the landowner went out and continued hiring people is not explained and is not essential to the point of Jesus' parable. Evidently the landowner needed workers. The marketplace was the public square of the city where most of the business was done. Unemployed laborers could stay there waiting for an opportunity to work. If there was a lot of work to do, they might work right up until sunset, but never beyond, for there would be no light in the fields. So each successive group of laborers worked for less time than the group hired previously. The landowner promised to pay this second group of laborers *whatever is right*—which they probably considered would be the appropriate fraction of the denarius that matched the amount of time they worked.

WORKLESS
How quickly the workers forgot their condition when the landowner found them! None of the "shifts" were found looking for work. Instead, they were standing idle in the marketplace. The landowner approached them with an opportunity. He called; they answered. The original condition of the workers strengthens the point Jesus made. He gave the invitation to people who were doing nothing.

Apart from God's gracious call, life has no ultimate purpose. Before we become servants of Christ, our lives account for little more than standing around in the marketplace. The world passes by, and we're going nowhere. But God finds us idle and offers us work. His love makes contact and gives purpose and direction. Tell someone today about the difference God made in your life when he gave you purpose, direction, and a destination.

**20:5-7** **"When he went out again about noon and about three o'clock, he did the same. And about five o'clock he went out and found others standing around; and he said to them, 'Why are you standing here idle all day?' They said to him, 'Because no one has hired us.' He said to them, 'You also go into the vineyard.'"**NRSV The landowner went out and hired three more groups of workers: some at noon, some at three o'clock, and some at five o'clock. Whether these people were *idle* (which is a later addition) truly because no one had hired them or because they were lazy is an unknown detail and is not important for Jesus' meaning in this parable. If people didn't work, they would likely go hungry. So the landowner hired these people as well. They were willing to work,

even for that last hour which they thought would not earn them
much money at all.

**20:8-10** **"When evening came, the owner of the vineyard said to his
foreman, 'Call the workers and pay them their wages, beginning with the last ones hired and going on to the first.'"**[NIV] At
*evening* (referring to sunset), the workers were called to collect the
day's wages, which was required by Jewish law so that the poor
would not go hungry (see Leviticus 19:13; Deuteronomy 24:14-
15). The landowner purposely asked that the last ones hired get
paid first. This is not a normal reaction; it would have surprised the
workers and it surely surprised Jesus' listeners. So **"when those
hired about five o'clock came, each of them received the usual
daily wage. Now when the first came, they thought they would
receive more; but each of them also received the usual daily
wage."** [NRSV] When those who worked less time received a full day's
wage, the laborers who had worked throughout the day expected to
get paid *more* than that, even though the *daily wage* was what they
had agreed upon when they were hired (20:2). Certainly those listening to the parable expected the same thing, although all would
wonder at the astuteness of a businessman who would pay a full
day's wage to laborers who had worked only an hour.

---

RIGHTS
The workers grumbled, and we can identify with them. They
have a strong point. It's a commonplace principle: more work,
more pay; less work, less pay. It nears the status of a right that
a worker may fairly claim—the right to a wage commensurate
with the market value of one's work. Jesus' point, however, is
that in God's kingdom, grace supersedes rights.
    Grace rewards generously, according to the goodwill of the
giver. Rights claim what's fair. Grace mixes workers together,
young and old, bright and slow, veteran and novice, breaking
down social distinctions. Rights tend to keep people in their
"rightful" slot. Grace means the kingdom includes many joyful
surprises.
    If God's rewards were based on rights, we'd all worry about
collecting "Brownie points"—the focus would be on *me* and *my*
work. Because God rewards on the basis of grace, we can
keep our focus on Jesus and faithful service to him. Be
confident of God's good and generous judgment.

---

**20:11-12** **"When they received it, they began to grumble against the landowner. 'These men who were hired last worked only one hour,'
they said, 'and you have made them equal to us who have
borne the burden of the work and the heat of the day.'"**[NIV]

Everyone who had been hired during the day received the same—
the daily wage. The laborers who had worked all day in the hot sun
received what they had agreed upon. *They began to grumble
against the landowner,* not because he hadn't kept his bargain with
them, but because he had been generous to everyone else. They
thought it wasn't fair that those who had worked *only one hour*
received the same amount of pay as (were made equal to) those
who had *borne the burden of the work and the heat of the day.*

---

THE DIGNITY OF PARTICIPATION
The loving father allows his child to push against the mower
handle while Dad makes it move. Alone, the child could not
budge the machine. Alone, the father would finish the work
much sooner. But this father has a greater purpose than simply
mowing grass. He also desires to help his child grow. The
landowner in Jesus' parable had more than grapes to harvest.
He also wanted to practice generosity. He went looking for
harvesters.

Grace cannot be rightly defined as God doing it all for us.
That would simply display divine power. Rather, God's grace
evokes wonder and growth in us as we recognize that he does
it all *with us!* Our participation is never essential, but it is real!
God doesn't need us. Working in and through us slows the
divine plan to a snail's pace. But therein lies God's grace!
Submitting to Christ's lordship requires that we admit that we
can't do it by ourselves. Nor can we claim that the final results
are due to our efforts. But we have participated. In fact, the
deeper our commitment to working with the Father, the greater
our awareness of how much God does. Ask God to multiply
your efforts to serve him.

---

**20:13-15** **"But he replied to one of them, 'Friend, I am doing you no
wrong; did you not agree with me for the usual daily wage?
Take what belongs to you and go; I choose to give to this last
the same as I give to you.'"** NRSV While the laborers did not address
the landowner with any respectful title, the landowner responded to
*one of them* as *friend.* He pointed out that he had not done wrong
by these laborers who had worked hard all day; he had paid them
the agreed amount. Besides, he added, **" 'Don't I have the right to
do what I want with my own money? Or are you envious
because I am generous?'"** NIV Obviously, the landowner could pay
whatever he chose as long as he cheated no one—it *was* his own
money. So what was the real problem? The early workers were
envious that the landowner had been generous with everyone else.
In this parable, Jesus pointed out that salvation is not earned, but
given freely only because of God's great generosity, which goes far

beyond our human ideas of what is fair. The message of the parable
is that God's loving mercy accepts the lowest member of society on
an equal footing with the elite. This parable may have been addressed
in the presence of the religious leaders who "grumbled" because
Jesus chose the "lowly" disciples and spent time with those considered unclean and sinful (Luke 15:1-2). Those who come to God—
regardless of social strata, age, material wealth, or heritage, and no
matter when in life they come—will all be accepted by him on an
equal footing. All will receive their inheritance in the kingdom of
heaven—no one will get less than what they expect, and some may
receive more. Such generosity, such grace, ought to cause all believers great joy—no one should be in the corner grumbling.

---

REVERSED ORDER
Jesus repeated a principle that is recorded in 19:30. There he
used it to respond to the disciples' amazement that wealth was
not a gauge of acceptance with God. Here he said, "So the last
will be first, and the first will be last" as the moral of the parable
of the workers (20:1-15). Clearly, Christ rejects the widely
accepted notion: "first come, first served." Why? Here are three
possible reasons:

1. *God isn't impressed by our achievements.* The workers
   did no more than they were asked to do. The landowner
   gave them work they did not merit and fulfilled his promise.
   Those who worked all day were not cheated. Those who
   worked an hour had no reason to brag. The idea that God
   "owes" us something is wrong. Instead of complaining, we
   should be grateful that God seldom gives us what we
   deserve.
2. *God rejects our comparisons.* To understand our sinfulness, we should examine our tendency toward discontent
   and ungratefulness. Like children, we demand equal treatment when we think that we have received less than
   others. Yet we are rarely concerned for others when we're
   ahead of them. Like the landowner, however, God holds
   us to our agreement. God keeps his promises. Comparing
   ourselves to others will not help our defense when we
   stand before God.
3. *God's rewards are his domain.* The landowner held the
   right to be generous to whomever he desired. If we are
   not astonished at God's grace toward us, we will miss it
   completely.

Are there areas of ungratefulness in your life? Use this list to
remind yourself of what God has done for you.

---

**20:16** **"So the last will be first, and the first will be last."**[NIV] The
reversal noted in these words (and in 19:30) points out the
differences between this life and life in the kingdom. Many

people we don't expect to see in the kingdom will be there. The criminal who repented as he was dying (Luke 23:40-43) will be there, along with people who have believed and served God for many years. The Jews were promised the kingdom first, but the Gentile believers will share the kingdom along with them. God offers his kingdom to all kinds of people everywhere. God's grace accepts the world's outcasts. No one has a claim to God's generosity; it is by his grace alone. No one has a claim to position in the kingdom; God will make the appointments—the *last* and *first* cannot be earned, bought, or bargained for (see 20:20-23).

## JESUS PREDICTS HIS DEATH THE THIRD TIME / 20:17-19 / *177*

**20:17-19** **Now as Jesus was going up to Jerusalem, he took the twelve disciples aside and said to them, "We are going up to Jerusalem, and the Son of Man will be betrayed to the chief priests and the teachers of the law."**NIV Jesus and the disciples continued toward Jerusalem. Jesus led the way, determined to go to the city where he knew he would die (see also Luke 9:51). Going "up to Jerusalem" refers to the ascent of the land toward the city that sat on the highest point around. Anyone walking toward Jerusalem went "up" in elevation.

---

DENIAL
More than once, Jesus described the horror of his final hours to his disciples. They reacted in different ways: confusion, fear, questions. They refused to accept what would have helped them understand—Jesus told them he would die. They chose denial rather than facing the truth.

On the one hand, Jesus' words leave us no doubt: God surrendered to death intentionally. He planned our salvation, then carried it out. He knew what he was doing all along the way. We may wonder why God doesn't tell us more specifically about the future. He knows we would waste the knowledge by denial or outright rejection. After all, that's what we do with the reality of our own death. We studiously avoid thinking about it. Consequently, we seldom arrive at death prepared or confident. Are you prepared to die? Do the people closest to you know what you think about death? Have you told them what you expect beyond that doorway? Your words may provide your friends with a powerful reason to consider Christ.

---

Jesus had just spoken to them about facing persecution and had told them of his impending death twice before (see 16:21 and 17:22, 23 for the first two times). However, this is the first mention of it occurring in Jerusalem itself, of the involvement

of Gentiles, and of his death coming by crucifixion (see below).
Jesus clearly explained what would happen to him, but the
disciples didn't really grasp what he was saying. Certainly they
did not want to believe that he might die. Jesus said he was the
Messiah, but they thought the Messiah would be a conquering
king. Instead, Jesus clearly explained that he, the *Son of Man,* the
human being who was also the Messiah, God's Son, would be
*betrayed* (someone who had loved him would turn on him) to the
Jewish leaders—*the chief priests and the teachers of the law.*

---

REALITY CHECK
Crowds were following Jesus, people were singing his praises,
miracles were happening, and now Jesus and the disciples
were heading for Jerusalem. Time for a reality check: The
purpose of this trip was to suffer and die, then to rise from the
dead. These predictions greatly disturbed the disciples who
had every reason to expect a triumphant Jerusalem
appearance by their Master.

We need reality checks, too. The Christian life is mostly
identifying with our suffering Savior, mostly misunderstanding
from religious leadership and hostility from secular power,
mostly everything the world counts as a loss. True, some
Christians achieve wealth, prestige, status, and influence. But
those cases are abnormal. Most Christians experience the
suffering side of faith and never receive an honorary degree
from an honorable Christian school to which they have given a
truckload of cash.

We should strive not for honors, but to be faithful followers of
Jesus, wherever he leads. The road heading for Jerusalem
may have looked to the disciples like a royal highway, but
Jesus' royalty is signaled by a crown of thorns.

---

**"They will condemn him to death and will turn him over to
the Gentiles to be mocked and flogged and crucified. On the
third day he will be raised to life!"** NIV The Sanhedrin (or Jewish
supreme court comprised of the Jewish leaders) would *condemn*
Jesus to die. But because Israel was occupied territory, they had
to submit to Rome's authority in cases of capital punishment.
They could punish lesser crimes, but only Rome could execute
an offender. Thus, the Jewish leaders could condemn Jesus, but
they had to *turn him over to the Gentiles* in order to have him
executed. "The Gentiles" refers primarily to Pilate, the Roman
governor, who represented Rome in Palestine. The Gentile
Romans would show great contempt for their prisoner, mocking
and flogging him before killing him.

Jesus added that *on the third day* he would rise again, but the disciples heard only his words about death. Because Jesus often spoke in parables, the disciples may have thought that his words on death and resurrection were another parable they weren't astute enough to understand. The Gospel records of Jesus' predictions of his death and resurrection show that these events were God's plan from the beginning and not accidents. The prophets had predicted what would happen to Jesus (see, for example, Psalm 22:6-8; Isaiah 50:6; 52:13–53:12).

## JESUS TEACHES ABOUT SERVING OTHERS / 20:20-28 / **178**

Matthew created a dual contrast by including Jesus' comment on his impending death between the section on rewards and eternal life and the request from the mother of James and John. The consistent misunderstanding represents a pattern of response to Jesus. He shattered the expectations and interpretations of others. Who could deny the characteristic boldness of a mother in regard to her children? Jesus responded to her request without rebuke. His words read like a gracious correction. "You do not know what you are asking," he said. How often do our prayers evoke the same response from God? We hardly ever know what we're asking. Fortunately, God isn't bound by our requests. He lovingly edits our prayers. So, ask what you will today for yourself and for others, but remember that God will always do what is best.

**20:20 Then the mother of the sons of Zebedee came to him with her sons, and kneeling before him, she asked a favor of him.**NRSV As the disciples followed Jesus toward Jerusalem, they realized that something was about to happen; they certainly hoped Jesus would be inaugurating his kingdom. The disciples knew Jesus believed he would die—he had told them three times. What was to become of his kingdom? Who would be in charge after his death? Among themselves, the disciples were arguing about this issue. Then Salome, *the mother of the sons of Zebedee* (who were James and John, 4:21), came to ask a *favor* of Jesus. She was apparently among Jesus' regular followers who were "disciples" but not part of the Twelve. She was at the cross when Jesus was crucified (27:56). Some have suggested that she was the sister of Mary, the mother of Jesus. Thus, she and her sons may have hoped that, as Jesus' cousins, their close family relationship would lend weight to their request.

James and John were brothers who, along with Peter, made up the inner circle of disciples (17:1). Mark records that James and John came with the request. There is no contradiction in the accounts—mother and sons agreed in this request for honored places in Christ's kingdom, and James and John were present because they directly answered Jesus' question in 20:22.

The mother of James and John came to Jesus, *kneeling before him.* She worshiped Jesus, but her real motive was to get something from him. Too often this happens in our churches and in our lives. We play religious games, expecting God to give us something in return. True worship, however, adores and praises Christ for who he is and for what he has done.

**20:21** **And he said to her, "What do you want?" She said to him, "Declare that these two sons of mine will sit, one at your right hand and one at your left, in your kingdom."** NRSV The mother of these disciples, due to their close family relationship with Jesus and her sons' close fellowship with him in his "inner circle," may have felt that she had a right to make the request that her two sons would sit, *one at your right hand and one at your left, in your kingdom.* Jesus had already promised "thrones" (although the disciples may have misconstrued the meaning) when he said that the twelve disciples would "sit on twelve thrones, judging the twelve tribes of Israel" (19:28 NIV). In ancient royal courts, the persons chosen to sit at the right and left hands of the king were the most powerful people in the kingdom. James and John's mother wanted her sons to sit beside Christ in his glory—these were the most honored places in the kingdom. They all understood that Jesus would have a kingdom; they understood that Jesus would be glorified (James and John had seen the Transfiguration, although they had not told anyone about it, as Jesus had commanded); and they approached him as loyal subjects to their king. However, until after the Resurrection, none of them fully understood that Jesus' kingdom was not of this world; it was not centered in palaces and thrones, but in the hearts and lives of his followers.

The mother of James and John asked Jesus to give her sons special positions in his kingdom. Parents naturally want to see their children promoted and honored, but this desire is dangerous if it causes them to lose sight of God's specific will for their children. God may have different work in mind—not as glamorous but just as important. Thus parents' desires for their children's advancement must be held in check as they pray that God's will be done in their children's lives.

**20:22** **But Jesus answered, "You do not know what you are asking. Are you able to drink the cup that I am about to drink?" They said to him, "We are able."** NRSV Jesus responded to Salome (and through her to James and John who were apparently present, for they directly answered Jesus' question) that in making such a self-centered request, they did not know what they were asking. To request positions of highest honor meant also to request deep suffering, for they could not have one without the other. Jesus had been teaching the concept of glory through suffering since 16:21-28, but the disciples still did not understand. Jesus asked first if they were *able to drink the cup* that he would drink. The verb tense in Greek indicates an event that has not yet occurred but is so certain that it can be spoken of as already having happened. The "cup" to which Jesus referred is the same "cup" that he would mention in his prayer in Gethsemane, "My Father, if it is possible, may this cup be taken from me" (26:39 NIV). It is the cup of suffering that he would have to drink in order to accomplish salvation for sinners. Jesus would not only endure horrible physical pain, but he would also bear the wrath of God's punishment for sin, causing him to be abandoned by God for a time (27:46).

Jesus' "cup" of suffering was unique, for it had a unique purpose, and only he could drink the particular "cup" that would accomplish salvation. Jesus was asking James and John if they were ready to suffer for the sake of the kingdom. James and John replied confidently to Jesus' question. They answered that they were *able* to drink the cup and be baptized with Jesus. Their answer may not have revealed bravado or pride as much as it showed their willingness to follow Jesus whatever the cost, to fight the battle that was before them. As loyal followers, they hoped to receive honor along with Jesus when he would establish his kingdom; however, their desertion of Jesus in the Garden of Gethsemane revealed how unready they really were for what this "cup" entailed (26:56).

---

FIRST AND LAST CUP
The deaths of James and John were dramatic answers to Jesus' question, "Can you drink my cup?" James was first among the apostolic martyrs. His brother outlasted them all and died an exile. Each of their "cups" had its own difficulty. James's cup came with shocking suddenness; John's with wearisome waiting. Each drank from Jesus' cup in his time.

The gift of salvation is priceless and free, but the way of discipleship isn't painless or easy. Life will test our commitment to Christ. Those closest to us will face their own challenges in following Jesus. Far greater benefit will be gained by encouraging one another than by wondering who will be greatest in the kingdom of heaven. Look for a brother or sister in Christ you can encourage today.

---

**20:23 Jesus said to them, "You will indeed drink from my cup, but to sit at my right or left is not for me to grant. These places belong to those for whom they have been prepared by my Father."** NIV James and John said they were willing to "drink the cup," that is, to face any trial for Christ. Jesus replied that they would be called upon to do so: James died as a martyr—he was put to death by the sword (Acts 12:2); John lived through many years of persecution before being forced to live the last years of his life in exile on the island of Patmos (Revelation 1:9).

Although Jesus knew that these two disciples would face great suffering, this still did not mean that he would grant their request for great honor. Suffering is the price of greatness, but it is the price required to follow Christ at all. They would follow and they would suffer, but they would not thereby sit at his right and left in the kingdom. Jesus would not make that decision; instead, those places were reserved for *those for whom they have been prepared by my Father.* This statement, that God already knew who would gain those places of great honor, reveals that God is omniscient (all-knowing).

Jesus' words reveal that, although he will distribute eternal rewards (2 Timothy 4:8), he will do so according to the Father's decisions. Jesus showed by this statement that he was under the authority of the Father, who alone makes the decisions about leadership in heaven. Such rewards are not granted as favors. They are reserved for those whom God selects.

Jesus didn't ridicule James and John for asking, but he denied their request. We can feel free to ask God for anything, but our requests may be denied. God wants to give us what is best for us, not merely what we want.

**20:24-25 When the ten heard about this, they were indignant with the two brothers. Jesus called them together and said, "You know that the rulers of the Gentiles lord it over them, and their high officials exercise authority over them."** NIV The other ten disciples were *indignant* that James and John had tried to use their relationship with Jesus to grab the top positions. Why such anger? Probably because *all* the disciples desired honor in the kingdom. Perhaps Peter, his temper getting the best of him, led the indignant ten disciples, for he had been the third with James and John in the group closest to Jesus. This probably seemed like a real slight to him. The disciples' attitudes degenerated into pure jealousy and rivalry.

Jesus immediately corrected their attitudes, for they would never accomplish the mission to which he had called them if they did not love and serve one another, working together for the sake of the kingdom. So he patiently called his disciples together and explained to them the difference between the kingdoms they saw in the world and God's kingdom, which they had not yet experienced.

The Gentile kingdoms (an obvious example being the Roman empire) have *rulers* and *high officials* who *lord it over* people, exercising authority and demanding submission (see 1 Peter 5:1-3). These Jews knew how very unpleasant it was to live under Rome's oppression. Jesus was delicately saying that the disciples were acting no better than the despised Gentiles and their rulers. In Gentile kingdoms, people's greatness depended on their social standing or family name. But Jesus explained that his kingdom would be like nothing they had ever experienced.

**20:26-28** **"It will not be so among you; but whoever wishes to be great among you must be your servant, and whoever wishes to be first among you must be your slave."** NRSV In a sentence, Jesus taught the essence of true greatness: *Whoever wishes to be great among you must be your servant.* Greatness is determined by servanthood. The true leader places his or her needs last, as Jesus exemplified in his life and in his death. Being a "servant" did not mean occupying a servile position; rather, it meant having an attitude of life that freely attended to others' needs without expecting or demanding anything in return. Seeking honor, respect, and the attention of others runs contrary to Jesus' requirements for his servants. An attitude of service brings

> You won't know what it's like to be a servant until you've been treated like one. *Gerry Fosdal*

true greatness in God's kingdom. Jesus described leadership from a new perspective. Instead of using people, we are to serve them. Jesus' mission was to serve others and to give his life away. A real leader has a servant's heart. Servant leaders appreciate others' worth and realize that they're not above any job.

Jesus' kingdom had already begun right there in that group of twelve disciples, but the kingdom was not set up with some who could lord it over others. Instead, the greatest person would be the servant of all. Jesus used the imagery of both a household "servant" and a "slave" to demonstrate what a servant attitude looked like. The Old Testament often spoke of submission and service, but it usually referred to a person's relationship with God. Jesus applied the concept of the servant attitude to a person's relationship to other people. In so doing, he transformed the ethics of the ancient world. The Greeks considered humility to be the lowest virtue; Jesus made it the highest.

What did this mean for the disciples? A real leader has a

servant's heart, willingly helping out others as needed. Servant leaders appreciate others' worth and realize that they're not above any job. They work together, not trying to gain positions of status or authority. They don't keep count of who did what or why. They aren't jealous of someone else's gifts, but gladly fulfill their duties. Only with such an attitude would the disciples be able to carry out the mission of sharing the gospel across the world.

**"Just as the Son of Man came not to be served but to serve, and to give his life a ransom for many."** NRSV Why should the disciples have to be willing to serve? Because their Master set the example. Jesus explained that he *came not to be served but to serve.* Again Jesus referred to himself as *the Son of Man.* Jesus was the Son of God, but his glory was hidden in the form of a servant who would pay the ultimate price to serve others: he would give his life. Paul later wrote

■ *Your attitude should be the same as that of Christ Jesus: Who, being in very nature God, did not consider equality with God something to be grasped, but made himself nothing, taking the very nature of a servant, being made in human likeness. And being found in appearance as a man, he humbled himself and became obedient to death—even death on a cross! (Philippians 2:5-8 NIV)*

Jesus' mission was to serve—ultimately by giving his life in order to save sinful humanity. His life wasn't "taken"; he "gave" it by offering it up as a sacrifice for people's sins. A *ransom* was the price paid to release a slave from bondage. Jesus paid a ransom for us, and the demanded price was his life. The Greek word translated "for" *(anti)* includes the idea of substitution. The concept of substitutionary atonement did not begin with Paul's writings, but with Jesus. Here and in the words of institution in the Last Supper, Jesus showed awareness of his death as substitution.

Jesus took our place; he died the death we deserved. Peter later wrote that the payment was not in silver or gold, but "the precious blood of Christ" (1 Peter 1:18-19 NIV). That payment freed us from our slavery to sin. The disciples thought that Jesus' life and power would save them from Rome; Jesus said his death would save them from sin, an even greater slavery than Rome's. Jesus told his disciples often that he had to die, but here he told them why—to redeem all (the word "many" does not mean "quite a few," but "all") people from the bondage of sin and death. "Many" is a term used in the Old Testament (Isaiah 53:11-12) to refer to the covenant community, the elect who will inherit the kingdom of God. Jesus' words that he would give his "one" life for "all" people may allude to Isaiah 53:11-12 (see also Romans 5:19). Because Jesus willingly took the lowest place, God gave him the highest seat in God's kingdom. All who repent and believe can come to him.

RANSOM
The concept of Jesus as our substitute creates strong aversion in the modern mind. Some would rather define salvation as an optional lifestyle chosen from enlightened self-interest (that is, neither Christ's work nor our response to it has any ultimate significance; equally good help can be found elsewhere). Others opt for a universalism that avoids accountability for sin by saying that ultimately everyone will be saved. Each of these views guts the gospel by making sin and eternity irrelevant. Ransom, however, speaks bluntly of hopelessness, necessity, and sin. By definition, ransom must be done *for* us. The God who ransoms doesn't save out of whim; God declares us valuable by paying the highest price. But some refuse the ransom offer. They remain in slavery, even when told that a way out has been provided by the death of Jesus on the cross. Don't neglect Jesus' offer to be your ransom! And if you have accepted his offer, don't recoil from presenting it to others, even when they seem unreceptive.

## JESUS HEALS A BLIND BEGGAR / 20:29-34 / *179*

**20:29-31** **As they were leaving Jericho, a large crowd followed him. There were two blind men sitting by the roadside. When they heard that Jesus was passing by, they shouted, "Lord, have mercy on us, Son of David!"** NRSV Jesus and the disciples were on the way out of *Jericho,* continuing southward toward Jerusalem. The Old Testament city of Jericho had been destroyed by the Israelites (Joshua 6:20), but during Herod the Great's rule over Palestine, he had rebuilt the city (about a mile south of the original city) as a site for his winter palace. Jericho was a popular and wealthy resort city, not far from the Jordan River, about eighteen miles northeast of Jerusalem.

As usual, *a large crowd followed him,* probably made up of Jews on their way to Jerusalem for the Passover. Matthew recorded that there were two blind men, while Mark and Luke mentioned only one. This is probably the same event, but Mark and Luke singled out the more vocal of the two men. Mark gave his name, Bartimaeus, an Aramaic name meaning son of Timaeus. These two blind men were *sitting by the roadside.* In ancient times, blind people (and others with infirmities that made them unable to work) had no other option but to beg. So they sat and waited along the roads near cities because that was where they were able to contact the most people. Jericho, with its fairly wealthy inhabitants, was a popular location for beggars. Medical help was not available for their problems, and people tended to ignore their obligation to care for the needy (Leviticus 25:35-38). Thus, beggars had little hope of escaping their way of life.

The blind men could not see, but they *heard* that Jesus of Nazareth was at the head of the approaching crowd. In order to be heard above the din, they *shouted* for Jesus' attention. They had undoubtedly heard that Jesus had healed many (including blind people—see 9:29-31), and they hoped that Jesus would *have mercy* on them and heal their eyes. There were no healings of the blind in the Old Testament; the Jews believed that such a miracle would be a sign that the messianic age had begun (Isaiah 29:18; 35:5).

The men called Jesus *Lord* and *Son of David* because they, along with all Jews, knew that the Messiah would be a descendant of King David (see Isaiah 9:6-7; 11:1; Jeremiah 23:5-6). The fact that they called Jesus "Son of David" showed that they recognized Jesus as the Messiah, for this was a key name for the Messiah. These blind beggars could "see" that Jesus was the long-awaited Messiah, while so many who witnessed Jesus' miracles were blind to his identity, refusing to open their eyes to the truth. Seeing with one's eyes doesn't guarantee seeing with the heart.

---

SHOUT IT LOUDER

There's much to admire in people who go against the grain, who stand against the crowd, who "shout it louder" when they're told to "keep quiet over there." The crowd wants these beggars to behave like respectable beggars: quiet, passive, unobtrusive. But these two would not be silenced.

If you are searching for faith, wondering about Jesus, thinking about commitment—don't let the crowd keep you quiet. God will answer your prayers, and when that happens (when the clarity and power of the gospel starts to move inside your heart and head), shout for all you're worth!

When you're searching for truth, don't settle for anything less. Passive people take the crowd's advice. Finders keep yelling until they get answers.

---

**The crowd sternly ordered them to be quiet; but they shouted even more loudly, "Have mercy on us, Lord, Son of David!"** NRSV The crowd tried to get the men to *be quiet*. It was most natural for the people, even Jesus' disciples, to attempt to shield Jesus from being harassed by beggars. But this only caused the men to shout *even more loudly*. They kept on crying out in an attempt to gain Jesus' attention. And it worked.

> Genuine charity is of such a nature that it is constantly hungering and thirsting after the glory of God and the salvation of all men, even of those who are strangers to us.
>
> *Menno Simons*

**20:32-33 Jesus stopped and called them. "What do you want me to do for you?" he asked. "Lord," they answered, "we want our sight."** NIV Although Jesus was concerned about the coming events in Jerusalem, he demonstrated what he had just told the disciples about service (20:26-28) by stopping to care for the blind men. Blindness was considered a curse from God for sin (John 9:2), but such an idea did not hinder Jesus.

Because Jesus probably knew what the men wanted, his question was not to gain information, but to allow them to specify their need and, in the process, to declare their faith that Jesus could meet that need. *"Lord,"* they called him again, *"we want our sight."* These words literally mean "we want to recover our sight," indicating that they had at one time been able to see.

---

COMPASSION
"What do you want me to do for you?" Jesus asked. Of course, blind men want their sight. Or do they? Jesus frequently asked seemingly obvious questions. They invite a second look.

Could the blind men have answered otherwise? "We want to come with you to Jerusalem," or "Please tell these people to be kinder to us," or "We would like a cup of water." Even obvious questions have a place. They help us clarify our thinking. They can transform general desires into specific requests. The blind men simply stated their greatest need. Jesus' compassion was stirred by their directness. Such moments must have been joyful ones for Jesus.

Jesus healed numerous blind people. His actions underscored a role he expressed most clearly in John 9:39, "I came into this world for judgment so that those who do not see may see, and those who do see may become blind" (NRSV). Faced with Jesus' question, "What do you want me to do for you?" what is your response? Ask him for the great desires of your heart. He is the King; his resources are beyond your imagination. How recently have we called out to God for mercy?

---

**20:34 Jesus had compassion on them and touched their eyes. Immedi-
ately they received their sight and followed him.**[NIV] The result of
the blind men's request was that *they received their sight.* Jesus had
made them well. The restoring of sight led to discipleship, for they
then *followed* Jesus; that is, they remained with the crowd that
followed Jesus to Jerusalem. It could also mean that they followed
Jesus as disciples.

# Matthew 21

This is Passover season, and Jesus has walked all the way from
Galilee with thousands of other Galilean pilgrims. Jesus did
not need to ride the last few miles, but he did so to point to his
identity as the Messiah. Matthew concentrated chapters 21 and
22 in the temple area to show Jesus' authority and superiority
over the Jewish leaders and their way of thinking.

**21:1-2 As they approached Jerusalem and came to Bethphage on the
Mount of Olives, Jesus sent two disciples, saying to them, "Go
to the village ahead of you, and at once you will find a donkey
tied there, with her colt by her. Untie them and bring them to
me."** NIV After passing through Jericho and healing the blind men
(20:29-34), they *approached Jerusalem* and came to the villages
of Bethphage and Bethany. These two villages were about one
mile apart, one and two miles respectively from the eastern wall
of Jerusalem, and sat on the eastern slope of the Mount of Olives.
Bethany was the home of Jesus' dear friends Mary, Martha, and
Lazarus; he often stayed there with his disciples (see John 11:1).
He may have returned to their home each night after his visits to
Jerusalem during the days of this final week.

The Mount of Olives is a ridge about two and a half miles long
on the other side of the Kidron Valley east of Jerusalem. The view
from the top of this twenty-nine-hundred-foot ridge is spectacular—
one can see the whole city. From this site, Jesus discussed the coming destruction of the city and temple (24:1-3). The Mount of
Olives is important in the Old Testament as the place of God's final
revelation and judgment (see Ezekiel 43:2-9; Zechariah 14:1-19).
When Jesus spoke these words, they were probably in Bethphage.
He sent two disciples to Bethany to get the donkey and her colt and
bring them back. Jesus had walked all the way from Galilee; in
fact, it seems that he walked everywhere during the years of his
ministry. So this switch to riding a colt the last mile into Jerusalem
was a deliberate gesture, filled with meaning for the Jews.

Matthew mentions a donkey and a colt, while the other

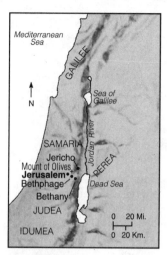

**Preparation for the Triumphal Entry**
*On their way from Jericho, Jesus and the disciples neared Bethphage, on the slope of the Mount of Olives just outside Jerusalem. Two disciples went into the village, as Jesus told them, to bring back a donkey and its colt. Jesus rode into Jerusalem on the donkey, an unmistakable sign of his kingship.*

Gospels mention only the colt. This was the same event, but Matthew focused on the prophecy in Zechariah 9:9, where a donkey and a colt are mentioned, thus affirming Jesus' royalty. He showed how Jesus' actions fulfilled the prophet's words, thus giving another indication that Jesus was indeed the Messiah. When Jesus entered Jerusalem on a donkey's colt, he affirmed his messianic royalty as well as his humility. When Jesus came to Jerusalem, he did not fulfill the people's hopes as the conquering deliverer to drive out the Gentiles, but he nonetheless gave all the signs of a royal person making entrance into the city.

This was Sunday of the week that Jesus would be crucified, and the great Passover festival was about to begin. Jews would come to Jerusalem from all over the Roman world during this week-long celebration to remember the great exodus from Egypt (see Exodus 12:37-51). Many in the crowds had heard of or had seen Jesus and were hoping he would come to the temple (John 11:55-57).

Jesus did come to the temple, not as a warring king on a horse or in a chariot but as a gentle and peaceable king on a donkey's colt, just as Zechariah 9:9 had predicted. Jesus knew that those who would hear him teach at the temple would return to their homes throughout the world and announce the coming of the Messiah.

The parallel accounts of the Triumphal Entry make a good example of the benefits of having four biographies of Jesus. Matthew and John were eyewitnesses of these events; Mark and Luke recorded eyewitness accounts by others. Matthew highlighted the prophetic fulfillment by noting a second donkey, the colt's mother. Jesus didn't ride her, nor is she essential to the story. But she provides a detail of fact. Her calming presence also explains the handling of an unbroken colt. In contrast, John's recollection of the colt is almost incidental. Perhaps he wasn't involved in the errand to fetch it. He was more concerned to indicate to his readers that the disciples understood little of what was happening at the time (John 12:16). While

John viewed the Triumphal Entry in light of its impact on the disciples themselves, Matthew highlighted the crowd's responses, pointed to Jesus as the Messiah, and kept the story in the temple area to show Jesus' authority over Judaism. Further, Mark reported the events in storyteller fashion. Luke focused on Jesus' state of mind. Each of the views helps make a complete picture.

Each of the Gospels presents a variation of the Triumphal Entry. Overall, the Gospel accounts are seldom identical. The differences usually have to do with perspective and priorities. Under the inspiration of the Holy Spirit, each writer told his story. The Gospels maintain a balance between shared similarities and independent entries. The similarities in language indicate that the later writers were aware of and used material from the earlier ones and that they were all writing about the same life. The dissimilarities show that they wrote independently and that each one had a slightly different purpose and audience in mind while composing his version.

**21:3** **"If anyone says anything to you, just say this, 'The Lord needs them.' And he will send them immediately."** NRSV Jesus knew the disciples would be asked why they were taking the colt. Donkeys and their colts were valuable; this could be compared to borrowing someone's car. So Jesus, sensitive to this fact, told them to explain that the colt would be returned. By this time Jesus was extremely well known. Everyone coming to Jerusalem for the Passover feast had heard of him, and Jesus had been a frequent visitor in Bethany. *The Lord needs them* was all the two disciples would have to say, and the colt's owners (Luke 19:33) would gladly let them take the animals.

> Jesus used these words to indicate His universal authority, His Chief Proprietorship of all things—the Lord hath need of them.
> *G. Campbell Morgan*

The disciples went and found everything just exactly as Jesus had said. Those who owned the colt may have been spoken to ahead of time by Jesus; thus, they were expecting this incident. Others suggest that Jesus, who had been a frequent visitor in Bethany, would have been well known enough to be able to commandeer a donkey and colt for a short time. Jesus, who would ride into Jerusalem as a "lowly king," was at the same time master over all his circumstances. Even these details were under his command and control.

**21:4-5** **All this was done that it might be fulfilled which was spoken by the prophet, saying: "Tell the daughter of Zion, 'Behold,**

**your King is coming to you, lowly, and sitting on a donkey, a colt, the foal of a donkey.'"** NKJV When Jesus mounted the colt and headed toward the city, the people recognized that he was fulfilling prophecy. The first part comes from Isaiah 62:11, the rest from Zechariah 9:9, "Rejoice greatly, O Daughter of Zion! Shout, Daughter of Jerusalem! See, your king comes to you, righteous and having salvation, gentle and riding on a donkey, on a colt, the foal of a donkey" (NIV). Matthew omitted the words "righteous and having salvation" from the Zechariah quote—perhaps because he wanted to focus on the "lowliness" and "humility" of this King. His arrival on a donkey was a sign of peace; a conquering king would come on a warhorse. Jesus was indeed king but not in the nationalistic sense. He was the King, but he would bring peace by his own suffering.

---

PARADOXICAL ENTRANCES
Jesus chose a peaceful entrance into Jerusalem. He restrained the crowd's exuberance by his actions. He accepted their joy while recognizing that it was based on false assumptions. Jesus arrived as King, but not by the crowd's definition. Their perspective was limited to the immediate historical moment: They wanted a political Messiah. Jesus insisted on remaining the timeless Savior. His contemporaries couldn't see beyond the Roman occupation; Jesus saw the needs of the world held hostage to sin.

We reduce God when we demand his attention only to our concerns. True, God encourages us to bring our daily needs to him in prayer. But God refuses to be a private deity. When we treat him like a house idol or a village god, he graciously fails our expectations. If we answer the question "How big is your God?" by mere human measures, we will diminish the King of kings and Lord of lords. We can be confident that God can meet our daily needs when we have a clearer picture of his greatness. Have you limited God to your expectations?

---

**21:6-7** **The disciples went and did as Jesus had directed them; they brought the donkey and the colt, and put their cloaks on them, and he sat on them.** NRSV The two disciples went to Bethany and found the donkey and colt just as *Jesus had directed them.* They walked the animals back to Bethphage. The colt, never having been ridden (Mark 11:2), did not have a saddle, so the disciples threw their *cloaks* on its back so that Jesus could sit on it. The mother donkey may have been brought along to help control the colt; she may have been festooned with cloaks as well. The action of placing the cloaks on the donkey and Jesus riding it connotes majesty (see 2 Kings 9:13 where cloaks were spread out for King Jehu).

**21:8 A very large crowd spread their cloaks on the road, and others cut branches from the trees and spread them on the road.**<sup>NRSV</sup> Crowds of people had already gathered on this stretch of road a mile outside of Jerusalem, going to the city for the Feast of Unleavened Bread and Passover. The crowd's spontaneous celebration honored Jesus; it was demonstrated when they *spread their cloaks on the road* for him to ride over (compare with 2 Kings 9:12-13).

In addition, *others cut branches from the trees*. These branches were used as part of the pilgrimage into Jerusalem. Some were spread along Jesus' path; others were probably waved in the air (see Psalm 118:27). The branches, probably from olive or fig trees, were used to welcome a national liberator and symbolized victory. John recorded that they used palm branches (John 12:13). This verse is one of the few places where the Gospels record that Jesus' glory was recognized on earth. Today Christians celebrate this event on Palm Sunday.

---

WORSHIP IN ACTION
The Triumphal Entry included a number of acts of respect. People shouted blessings and Old Testament phrases of praise to God. Some waved branches or placed them on the road. Many removed their coats and spread them under the colt's hooves. The people "rolled out the red carpet" for Jesus. Their spontaneous worship puts much of our worship to shame. How often in your church does the presence of Jesus cause a genuine stir? Are the "rules for worship" defined so narrowly that spontaneous expressions of praise for Christ are frowned upon? Also, lest we blame the church too quickly, how often does your experience with Christ cause you to want to praise?

We can't blame the lack of praise for God on lack of opportunity. Certainly there are appropriate times for formal worship. But a genuine relationship with God ought to find expression beyond "official" structure. Do you use hymns and choruses in your private times with God? Do you look for opportunities to give thanks to God? What does "Hosanna" mean to you? What, in your experience, would be similar to spreading your coat for Jesus to walk on? Make sure your worship includes action and tangible expressions.

---

**21:9 Then the multitudes who went before and those who followed cried out, saying: "Hosanna to the Son of David! 'Blessed is He who comes in the name of the LORD!' Hosanna in the highest!"**<sup>NKJV</sup> This was not a little group of people along the wayside;

this crowd was characterized as "multitudes." The people chanted words from Psalm 118:25-26. Although the word "Hosanna" technically means "save now," the people were probably not asking God to do so. They were using a phrase like "Praise the Lord" or "Hallelujah," not really thinking about the meaning. The expression "Blessed is He who comes in the name of the LORD" may have been recited as part of the Passover tradition—as a blessing given by the people in Jerusalem to the visiting pilgrims. Thus, not all the people saying this would have realized its messianic significance. Of course, others did. They spoke of Jesus as *Son of David* because of God's words to David in 2 Samuel 7:12-14 (see note on 1:1). The people lined the road, praising God, waving branches, and throwing their cloaks in front of the colt as it passed before them. "Long live the King" was the meaning behind their joyful shouts because they knew that Jesus was intentionally fulfilling prophecy.

This was the crowd's acclamation that he was indeed the long-awaited Messiah. He chose a time when all Israel would be gathered at Jerusalem, a place where huge crowds could see him, and a way of proclaiming his mission that was unmistakable. The people were sure their liberation from Rome was at hand. While the crowd correctly saw Jesus as the fulfillment of these prophecies, they did not understand where Jesus' kingship would lead him. The people who were praising God for giving them a king had the wrong idea about Jesus. They expected him to be a national leader who would restore their nation to its former glory; thus, they were deaf to the words of their prophets and blind to Jesus' real mission. When it became apparent that Jesus was not going to fulfill their hopes, many people would turn against him. A similar crowd would cry out, "Crucify him!" when Jesus stood on trial only a few days later.

---

ONE BRIEF MOMENT
For one brief moment in time, lots of people greeted Jesus with enthusiasm and honor, respect and celebration. It's a great experience to be part of such a crowd. Consider attending the national convention of a major Christian organization or movement, volunteering to help in a large-scale evangelistic crusade, or traveling to an overseas missions conference or national church gathering. Every once in a while, it's refreshing to be reminded of how large the church really is, how enthusiastic are today's disciples, how diverse their means of celebrating God's love. Join them. Catch their spirit.

---

**21:10-11 When Jesus entered Jerusalem, the whole city was stirred and asked, "Who is this?" The crowds answered, "This is Jesus, the prophet from Nazareth in Galilee."** NIV The people in

Jerusalem were naturally very interested in who was causing the furor. When Jesus had been born and the wise men had come seeking him, the entire city had been "disturbed" (2:3). Once again, Jesus caused a great disturbance in this great city. So the city leaders asked the crowds, *"Who is this?"* and the crowds gave their reply, *"This is Jesus, the prophet from Nazareth in Galilee."* The description seems almost anticlimactic—why all this fuss over a prophet? But Jesus was not just another prophet; he was *the* prophet who was to come. Moses had prophesied, "The LORD your God will raise up for you a prophet like me from among your own brothers. You must listen to him. . . . I will raise up for them a prophet like you from among their brothers; I will put my words in his mouth, and he will tell them everything I command him" (Deuteronomy 18:15-18 NIV). Who was this "prophet"? Stephen used this verse to support his claim that Jesus Christ is God's Son, the Messiah (Acts 7:37). The coming of Jesus Christ to earth was not an afterthought but part of God's original plan. Jesus was the man for whom they had been waiting. No wonder the city was in an uproar!

## JESUS CLEARS THE TEMPLE AGAIN / 21:12-17 / *184*

**21:12 Then Jesus entered the temple and drove out all who were selling and buying in the temple, and he overturned the tables of the money changers and the seats of those who sold doves.**[NRSV] Jesus entered the great city and went to the temple, entering its outer courts as did many in the crowd. The temple in Jerusalem was already rich with history. There had been three temples on the same site. The first, Solomon's glorious temple, had been built in the tenth century B.C. and was destroyed in 586 B.C when the Babylonians captured Jerusalem. The second, Zerubbabel's temple, was much smaller than Solomon's temple and had been built on the same site by the exiles who had returned from captivity in the sixth century B.C. The second temple, the one Jesus entered, had been enlarged by Herod the Great. Construction on this magnificent structure, much larger and more elaborate than the others, was begun in 20 B.C. and may not have been completely finished before it was destroyed by the Romans in A.D. 70 in response to a Jewish revolt.

What were people *selling and buying* in the temple? People came to the temple in Jerusalem to offer sacrifices, where Jewish sacrifices were only to be offered. The temple was run by the high priest and his associates. All adult male Jews were required to go to Jerusalem for three annual celebrations: Passover in late spring, the Feast of Tabernacles (or Booths) in the fall, and the Feast of Weeks in early summer. God had originally instructed the people to bring sacrifices from their own flocks (Deuteronomy 12:5-7). However, the religious leadership had established four markets on the Mount of Olives where such animals could be purchased. Some people did not bring their own animals and planned to buy one at the market. Others brought their own animals, but when the priests managed to find the animal unacceptable in some way (it was supposed to be an animal without defect, Leviticus 1:2-3), worshipers were forced to buy another.

Next, in an economic move that surely lined many pockets and enriched the temple coffers, the high priest had authorized a market to be set up right in the Court of the Gentiles, the huge outer court of the temple. The Court of the Gentiles was the only place Gentile converts to Judaism could worship. They could go no farther into the temple because they were not "pure" Jews. But the market filled their worship space with merchants so that these foreigners, who had traveled long distances, found it impossible to worship. The chaos in that court must have been tremendous. Josephus, an ancient Jewish historian, wrote that 255,600 lambs were sacrificed at the Passover in A.D. 66. This lack of worship atmosphere didn't seem to bother the religious establishment who saw lots of money to be made in selling animals, grain, oil, and salt for the various sacrifices.

The *money changers* exchanged all international currency for the special temple coins—the only money the merchants would accept. The money changers did big business during Passover with those who came from foreign countries. The inflated exchange rate often enriched the money changers, and the exorbitant prices of animals made the merchants wealthy. The money changers also exchanged Hebrew shekels for Roman drachmas for the temple tax. Because the drachmas had the stamped image of Caesar (who was an idol worshiper) on them, they were considered blasphemous by the Jews.

The mention of *doves* refers to an alternate sacrifice for those too poor to purchase larger animals. Doves were also sacrificed for the cleansing of women and lepers (Leviticus 12:6; 14:22). Imagine money boxes spilling and clattering across the floor as doves escaped from their overturned cages and scattered above the crowd. Jesus became angry because God's house of worship had become a place of extortion and a barrier to Gentiles who wanted to worship.

Because both those who bought and those who sold were going against God's commands regarding the sacrifices, Jesus

*drove out all* of them. This is the second time that Jesus cleared
the temple (see John 2:13-17).

**21:13 And He said to them, "It is written, 'My house shall be called a
house of prayer,' but you have made it a 'den of thieves.'"** NKJV
Obviously Jesus' actions stunned the many people crowded into
the temple area and probably drew spectators from both inside
and outside. Jesus recognized an opportunity to teach, and he
didn't waste it. He quoted from Isaiah 56:7 and used it to explain
God's purpose for the temple. God's "house" was meant to be a
*house of prayer,* but the merchants and money changers were
using it for other purposes. This was judgment on Jerusalem and
the corrupt system that governed the temple. It was meant to be a
place of spiritual worship, but the Jewish leaders had allowed it
to become a market where extortion took place.

Not only that, but all these merchants were no more honest
than *thieves* (the word would be more correctly translated
"robbers," as in Jeremiah 7:11, those in organized bands who
worked on large-scale robberies). Jesus had just come from
Jericho a few days before, along a road known for its dangerous bands of robbers that preyed on travelers. (In the story of
the Good Samaritan, the man was attacked on the road between
Jerusalem and Jericho—see Luke 10:30.) No organized band
of robbers along that treacherous stretch of road could possibly
match the thievery going on in the temple. The merchants had
turned the temple into their *den.* This was a horrible desecration. No wonder Jesus was so angry. Mark records that Jesus
entered the temple and then returned the next morning to perform this cleansing (Mark 11:11, 15-16).

In this instance, Jesus set himself in authority above the religious leaders—the high priest (Caiaphas) and all those on the
Sanhedrin. They were in charge of the temple, and they would
soon have words with Jesus about this episode (21:15-16).

**21:14 Then the blind and the lame came to Him in the temple, and
He healed them.** NKJV It was significant that *the blind and the
lame* came to Jesus in the temple. Usually they were excluded
from worship in the temple based on laws stemming from
2 Samuel 5:8. With the coming of the Messiah, Jesus himself
welcomed them *in the temple* and *healed them,* for he himself
was greater than the temple (12:6). This was also an expected
result of the messianic age (Isaiah 35:5). These are the only
recorded healings inside the temple walls, indicating a new
age when God would accept all people into his presence (the

tearing of the curtain in the temple at Jesus' death was another such indication, 27:51).

**21:15-16** **But when the chief priests and the scribes saw the amazing things that he did, and heard the children crying out in the temple, "Hosanna to the Son of David," they became angry and said to him, "Do you hear what these are saying?"** NRSV It didn't take long for news of Jesus' actions in the temple to reach the ears of the chief priests and scribes. The *chief priests* were mostly Sadducees (the wealthy, upper-class, priestly party among the Jewish political groups); the *scribes* (also called teachers of the law) were usually Pharisees. These two parties had great contempt for each other (see, for example, Acts 23:6-10). That these two groups could agree on anything was highly unusual. But Jesus' actions in the temple brought the wrath of these religious leaders against him. The *children* who were in the temple with their parents were also crying out *Hosanna to the Son of David,* echoing the cries made by the crowd along the road to Jerusalem (21:9). Matthew highlighted these words again to stress Jesus as the Messiah and to show that the children perceived what the religious leaders would not. The religious leaders' question indicated that they objected to the concept of Jesus as "the Son of David."

It is difficult to know whether these religious leaders were angry at the lack of decorum from children, who were expected to be quiet in the temple, or afraid that the Romans might misinterpret the furor and come down on them, or upset at the claims the children were making in their words about Jesus. Probably all three factors were involved in the reaction of the chief priests and scribes. They may also have been angry that the blind and lame had been allowed into the temple and that Jesus had actually performed healings there (21:14). Jesus was becoming a real problem, especially in this instance because he was undermining their authority in the temple.

**Jesus said to them, "Yes; have you never read, 'Out of the mouths of infants and nursing babies you have prepared praise for yourself'?"** NRSV Yes, Jesus heard what the children were saying, and yes, what they were saying was absolutely true. Jesus affirmed his agreement with their shouts of praise. His words "have you never read" were meant to insult these religious leaders who spent much time reading and studying the law. Unfortunately, they read and studied but never understood. Jesus was quoting from Psalm 8:2, a psalm regarded as messianic by the early church.

CHILDREN'S PRAISE
What a delightful experience to hear children in heartfelt praise
to God! The children in the temple repeated the shouts of
praise they had heard. Some of the cries were echoes from
the Triumphal Entry. Others were responses to the cleansing
of the temple. Still others were made by the blind and lame
whom Jesus had healed. As they often do, the children found
a way to participate in the excitement. Their innocent praise
glorified Jesus.

They can still praise God. What place do children occupy where
you worship? Are they recognized as participants? Are they
treated reasonably regarding their attention spans, their ages,
and their ability to understand? Does the order of worship
include a children's sermon? Are children offered "children's
church"? At some point, children will pass into adulthood. In
the meantime, however, can they contribute as children to the
worship in your church? Make some observations about the
way children are involved in your church. Share any suggestions
you have with the church leadership.

**21:17 He left them, went out of the city to Bethany, and spent the
night there.**<sup>NRSV</sup> With the religious leaders plotting to kill him,
Jerusalem would hardly be a safe place for Jesus to spend the
night. Safely outside the city, Jesus could not be surprised and
arrested by the temple priesthood. So when evening came, Jesus
and the disciples left the city and returned to *Bethany.* Most pilgrims who traveled to Jerusalem for the great feasts found lodging outside the city.

A PLACE TO REST
Jesus knew and practiced the discipline of rest, and he honored
his friends by allowing them to host him throughout this final
week. Between days of intense public pressure in Jerusalem,
Jesus found fellowship in Bethany. Jesus balanced stress
with friendship and quietness. His example reminds us to make
time for rest.

A life intent on serving God will meet resistance. Others may
reject or misunderstand our efforts. Evil doesn't give ground
without a fight. Even God's work leads to tired workers. The
fourth commandment has not been canceled. Jesus put it in its
proper context (Mark 2:27) by reminding us that God ordered
us to rest for our benefit, not just to obey a command. Like
Jesus, we may have to leave the place of conflict and stress in
order to rest. Bethany was no escape or retreat; it was refreshment. How often do you rest? Do you plan times of withdrawal
for reflection and renewal? Discipleship will be weary work without the component of rest. We are under orders to include it.

## JESUS SAYS THE DISCIPLES CAN PRAY FOR ANYTHING / 21:18-22 / **188**

**21:18 Early in the morning, as he was on his way back to the city, he was hungry.**NIV After their stay in Bethany overnight (21:17), Jesus and the disciples got up and headed back into Jerusalem. Bethany was about two miles outside of Jerusalem, making it a suburb of the city. Somewhere along the way, Jesus mentioned that he was *hungry.* Jesus' hunger portrays his humanity. He was fully human, just as we are, and can sympathize with our human experience and daily needs. When we pray to him, expressing our weaknesses and troubles, we can be confident that he knows what we are facing. He has faced it too (Hebrews 4:15).

**21:19-20 And seeing a fig tree by the side of the road, he went to it and found nothing at all on it but leaves. Then he said to it, "May no fruit ever come from you again!" And the fig tree withered at once.**NRSV Fig trees were a popular source of inexpensive food in Israel. In March, the fig trees had small edible buds; in April came the large green leaves. Then in May, the buds would fall off and be replaced by the normal crop of figs. This incident occurred in April, and the green leaves should have indicated the presence of the edible buds that Jesus expected to find on the tree. This tree, however, though full of *leaves,* had no buds. Fig trees require three years from the time they are planted until they can bear fruit. The absence of buds indicated that the tree would not produce figs that year. The tree looked promising but offered no fruit.

> Is not everyone who claims to be a Christian but does not bear fruit, in awful danger of becoming a withered fig-tree? So long as a person is content with the mere leaves of religion— with a reputation for being alive while he is dead, a form of godliness without the power—so long his soul is in great peril.        *J. C. Ryle*

Jesus did not curse this fig tree because he was angry at not getting any food from it. Instead, this was an acted-out parable intended to teach the disciples. By cursing the fig tree, Jesus was showing his anger at religion without substance. Jesus' curse did not make the tree barren of figs; instead, it sealed the way the tree had always been (see 13:13-15). Jesus' harsh words to the fig tree could be applied to the nation of Israel and its beautiful temple. Fruitful in appearance only, Israel was spiritually barren. Just as the fig tree looked good from a distance but was fruitless on close examination, so the temple looked impressive at first glance, but its sacrifices and other activities were hollow because they were not done to worship God sincerely (see

Jeremiah 8:13; 24:1-8; Hosea 9:10, 16; Micah 7:1). The temple displayed beautiful architecture, but contained barren ritual; it was ripe for destruction. Most likely, Jesus was not limiting his condemnation of fruitlessness to the temple or Judaism of that day. This action displays his stand against all hypocrisy—any religious people who make a show of bearing fruit but are spiritually barren.

After Jesus spoke these words, the fig tree *withered at once.* Mark told the story in two stages: Jesus cursed the tree on Monday, then the next morning, Tuesday, Jesus and his disciples passed by the same fig tree, and in the morning light, they could see that the tree had died. Jesus had done more than condemn the tree, he had killed it. **When the disciples saw this, they were amazed. "How did the fig tree wither so quickly?" they asked.**[NIV] This parable of judgment on spiritually dead people revealed a severe judgment. The early church later applied this parable to the total destruction of Jerusalem in A.D. 70.

**21:21** **Jesus answered them, "Truly I tell you, if you have faith and do not doubt, not only will you do what has been done to the fig tree, but even if you say to this mountain, 'Be lifted up and thrown into the sea,' it will be done."**[NRSV] Jesus did not explain why he cursed the fig tree, and we don't know whether the disciples understood Jesus' meaning. Yet his words to them could mean that they must have *faith* in God. Their faith should not rest in a kingdom they hoped Jesus would set up, in obeying the Jewish laws, or in their position as Jesus' disciples. Their faith should rest in God alone.

Jesus then taught them a lesson about answers to prayer. Jesus had cursed the fig tree; the fig tree had died; the disciples had expressed surprise. Jesus explained that they could ask anything of God and receive an answer. Jesus again used the words "truly I tell you" to introduce this important message. They should not have been surprised that a fig tree could be withered at Jesus' words. Jesus was using a mountain as a figure of speech to show that God could help in any situation: *This mountain* (referring to the Mount of Olives on which they stood) could be *thrown into the sea* (the Dead Sea, that could be seen from the Mount). Jesus' point was that in their petitions to God they must believe without doubting (that is, without wavering in their confidence in God). The kind of prayer Jesus meant was not the arbitrary wish to move a mountain of dirt and stone; instead, he was referring to prayers that the disciples would need to faithfully pray as they faced mountains of opposition to their gospel message in the years to come. Their prayers for the advancement of God's kingdom would always be answered positively—in God's timing.

MOUNTAIN MOVERS
Many have wondered about Jesus' statement that if we have
faith and don't doubt, we can move mountains. Jesus, of
course, was not suggesting that his followers use prayer as
"magic" and perform capricious "mountain-moving" acts.
Instead, he was making a strong point about the disciples' (and
our) lack of faith. What kinds of mountains do you face? Have
you talked to God about them? How strong is your faith?

**21:22** **"If you believe, you will receive whatever you ask for in
prayer."** NIV This verse was not a guarantee that the disciples could
get anything they wanted simply by asking Jesus and believing.
God does not grant requests that will hurt people or that will violate
his own nature or will. Jesus' statement was not a blank check to be
filled in by believers, not a "name it and claim it" theology. To be
fulfilled, requests made to God in prayer must be in harmony with
the principles of God's kingdom. They must be made in Jesus'
name (John 14:13-14). The stronger our faith, the more likely our
prayers will be in union with Christ and in line with God's will;
then God will be happy to grant them. God can do anything, even
what seems humanly impossible.

## RELIGIOUS LEADERS CHALLENGE JESUS' AUTHORITY / 21:23-27 / **189**

The basic theme of this whole section is that Jesus was taking on
the religious leaders at their own game and defeating them with
their own logic. And Jesus was triumphant in his dealings with
them. This served to anger them even more.

**21:23** **Jesus entered the temple courts, and, while he was teaching,
the chief priests and the elders of the people came to him.
"By what authority are you doing these things?" they asked.
"And who gave you this authority?"** NIV Jesus and the disciples
returned to the temple, where Jesus had thrown out the merchants
and money changers the day before. A delegation of *the chief
priests and the elders of the people* stopped him. This was an
angry official group sent on an official mission to question Jesus
regarding his actions. This group of leaders was already plotting
to kill Jesus (Mark 11:18), but they couldn't figure out how to do
it. His popularity was far too widespread and his miracle-working
powers too well known. The Sanhedrin probably had met on
Monday night in a hastily called session to decide how to handle
this man who was flouting their authority. So they brought him a

question that they hoped would trap him into saying something for which he could be arrested. They asked for his credentials and demanded that he tell them who gave him the *authority* to cast the money changers and merchants out of the temple. That this delegation would even ask these questions indicates that Jesus had not yet publicly declared himself to be the Messiah.

If Jesus were to answer that his authority came from God, which would be tantamount to declaring himself as the Messiah and the Son of God, they would accuse him of blasphemy and bring him to trial (blasphemy carried the death penalty, Leviticus 24:10-23). If Jesus were to say that his authority was his own, the religious leaders could dismiss him as a fanatic and could trust that the crowds would soon return to those with true authority (themselves). Jesus would not let himself be caught; however, turning the question on them, he exposed their motives and avoided their trap.

---

### BY HIS AUTHORITY
The struggle between Jesus and the religious leaders often revolved around the issue of authority. By the final week, only a shell of civility covered the attacks. Faced with Jesus' character, the religious leaders repeatedly tried to pin him down on a technicality. They dared him to make an open claim about himself that they could label blasphemous. Their questions had no other purpose than to gather evidence against Jesus.

But Jesus' authority came from God, and that fact could not be denied. In Jesus' world, as in ours, people looked for the outward sign of authority—education, title, position, connections. But Jesus' authority came from who he was, not from any outward and superficial trappings. As followers of Christ, God has given us authority—we can confidently speak and act on his behalf because he has authorized us. Are you exercising your authority?

---

**1:24-26** **Jesus said to them, "I will also ask you one question; if you tell me the answer, then I will also tell you by what authority I do these things. Did the baptism of John come from heaven, or was it of human origin?"** NRSV To expose the leaders' real motives, Jesus countered their question with a question. This was a common debating technique among rabbis. Jesus explained that his answer would depend on their answer. The questions the religious leaders asked were perfectly valid questions to check for a false prophet or false teacher, but their sinister motives made it an evil test.

Jesus' question seems totally unrelated to the situation at hand, but Jesus knew that the leaders' attitude about John the Baptist would reveal their true attitude toward him. In this question,

Jesus implied that his authority came from the same source as John the Baptist's. So Jesus asked these religious leaders what they thought: *Did the baptism of John come from heaven* [thus, from God] *or was it of human origin?*

**And they argued with one another, "If we say, 'From heaven,' he will say to us, 'Why then did you not believe him?' But if we say, 'Of human origin,' we are afraid of the crowd; for all regard John as a prophet."** NRSV The interchange recorded among these factions of the religious leaders revealed their true motives. They weren't interested in the truth; they didn't want an answer to their question so they could finally understand Jesus—they simply hoped to trap him. But they found themselves in a position of looking foolish in front of the crowd. If they answered that John's baptism had come *from heaven* (with God's authority), then they would incriminate themselves for not listening to John and believing his words. The people knew that the religious leaders had been silent about Herod's murder of John. If they accepted John's authority, they would be accepting his criticism of them as a brood of vipers who refused to repent (see 3:7-10). They would then have to admit that Jesus also had divine authority.

If they rejected John as having any divine authority and said that his baptism was *of human origin,* then they also would be rejecting Jesus' authority and would be in danger of the crowd (see Mark 12:12). Luke recorded that they were afraid the crowd would stone them for such an answer (Luke 20:6), *for all regard John as a prophet.* They would have preferred this answer, but they could not give it because of the crowd.

**21:27 So they answered Jesus, "We do not know." And he said to them, "Neither will I tell you by what authority I am doing these things."** NRSV The Pharisees couldn't win, so they hoped to save face by refusing to take either alternative. Thus, Jesus was not obligated to answer their question. In reality, he had already answered it. His question about John the Baptist implied that both he and John received their authority from the same source. The crowds believed that John was a prophet; Jesus' words should have made them realize that he was victorious over the Pharisees and that his authority was from God. While some in the crowd may have understood and believed, the religious leaders had already decided against Jesus, and nothing would stand in the way of their plan to kill him. They had already rejected both Jesus and John as God's messengers, carrying on a long tradition of the leaders of Israel rejecting God's prophets. This was the point that Jesus made in the following parable (21:28-32).

## JESUS TELLS THE PARABLE OF THE TWO
## SONS / 21:28-32 / **190**

**:28-30** **"What do you think? A man had two sons; he went to the
first and said, 'Son, go and work in the vineyard today.' He
answered, 'I will not'; but later he changed his mind and
went. The father went to the second and said the same;
and he answered, 'I go, sir'; but he did not go."** NRSV Jesus
continued his conversation with the religious leaders who had
attempted to trip him up with a trick question (21:23-27). This
parable was spoken directly to them, and it showed them their
true position in the kingdom of heaven.

The family laws made the father the absolute head over his
children. The *man* in this parable represents God, while the *two
sons* represent, respectively, the "sinners" (or outcasts among the
Jews) and conservative Jews.

The first son said he would not go to the vineyard, but *later he
changed his mind and went.* This son represents the "sinner" and
outcast who rejected the call but "repented" and then obeyed.

---

CHANGED MIND
True beliefs are responses tested by time. Each of the sons in
Jesus' story responded immediately to their father's request.
As it turned out, their first answers were meaningless. Each
changed his mind. What they finally did and said mattered
most. Jesus faced his detractors with a blunt application. Those
considered farthest from God (prostitutes and tax collectors)
were boldly embracing his grace. Meanwhile, those most
familiar with God were rejecting the promised Messiah. Jesus
didn't close the door of the kingdom to the religious leaders,
but he challenged their assumed citizenship. Four lessons flow
immediately from this story:
  1. Those who accept or reject the gospel too easily will be
     tested.
  2. Regardless of how we came to Christ, our present state
     of obedience indicates our spiritual health.
  3. People who resist the gospel may be closer to conversion
     than those who are familiar with it.
  4. Where God is at work, we dare not jump to conclusions.

---

The second son said he would go to the vineyard, but then
*did not go.* This son represents the Jewish leaders of the day
who said yes to the kingdom message (that is, they accepted the
outward call to Jewish piety) but did not obey its intent. They
rejected the call to true obedience. They said they wanted to do
God's will, but they constantly disobeyed. They lacked insight

into God's real meaning, and they were too stubborn to listen to Jesus. It is dangerous to pretend to obey God when our hearts are far from him, because God knows our true intentions. Our actions must match our words.

**21:31 "Which of the two did what his father wanted?" "The first," they answered. Jesus said to them, "I tell you the truth, the tax collectors and the prostitutes are entering the kingdom of God ahead of you."** NIV Jesus directed his question to the religious leaders, and they gave the obviously correct answer. The son who *did what his father wanted* was the son who refused at first but then repented and actually obeyed his father. Jesus' words "I tell you the truth," introduce a solemn truth: The *tax collectors and the prostitutes* would be entering the kingdom of God *ahead of* the religious leaders. These were astounding words. The tax collectors and prostitutes were representative of the despised classes, those who were the most despicable to the self-righteous leaders. The pious religious leaders had said they would "go to the vineyard" but then had refused. The tax collectors and prostitutes had obviously strayed from God and had refused to go to the vineyard. But those who repented of their sin would enter the kingdom of God, instead of pious Jews, who thought they would be the ones to enter.

---

MAKE WAY!
Beware of churches that teach that to enter a relationship with Christ, you must first get a haircut, shave a beard, lengthen your dress, or talk like "the rest of us." Jesus warns religious leaders that the kingdom of heaven has a dramatic appeal to "low-life" types (that is, to people generally shunned by religious types). To the prim and proper, Jesus says, "Make way! God's message is getting through!"

---

**21:32 "For John came to you to show you the way of righteousness, and you did not believe him, but the tax collectors and the prostitutes did. And even after you saw this, you did not repent and believe him."** NIV Why would the tax collectors and prostitutes enter the kingdom of heaven instead of the religious leaders? Jesus explained why in this verse. The total rejection of John the Baptist (and his acceptance by the less-esteemed members of society) spelled out their rejection (or acceptance) of the one John proclaimed—Jesus, the Messiah. Even when the religious leaders *saw* how lives were changed at John's preaching of *the way of righteousness,* even as they saw what happened when these sinful people repented and believed, these leaders still *did not believe* John. Neither, then, would they believe Jesus.

## JESUS TELLS THE PARABLE OF THE WICKED TENANTS / 21:33-46 / *191*

**21:33** **"Listen to another parable: There was a landowner who planted a vineyard. He put a wall around it, dug a winepress in it and built a watchtower. Then he rented the vineyard to some farmers and went away on a journey."**[NIV] The main elements in this parable are (1) the *landowner*—God, (2) the *vineyard*—Israel, (3) the *farmers*—the Jewish religious leaders, (4) the landowner's *servants*—the prophets and priests who remained faithful to God and preached to Israel, (5) the *son*—Jesus, and (6) the *other tenants*— the Gentiles. In this parable, Jesus displayed his knowledge of the religious leaders' murderous plot (21:45).

The imagery follows Isaiah 5:2, which also calls Israel a vineyard. It pictures a landowner who builds a farm and rents it to tenant farmers to run and care for in his absence. In a vineyard such as this, the *watchtower* would have been for guards who would protect the farm from thieves; the *wall* would have kept wild animals out; the *winepress* was for making wine. These building projects were normal parts of a tenant farm.

**1:34-36** **"When the harvest time approached, he sent his servants to the tenants to collect his fruit. The tenants seized his servants; they beat one, killed another, and stoned a third. Then he sent other servants to them, more than the first time, and the tenants treated them the same way."**[NIV] The rent on the farm was paid by crops at harvesttime, a common practice in this culture. So, as expected, *when the harvest time approached,* the landowner *sent his servants* to collect the rent in the form of fruit from the harvest. But *the tenants seized his servants,* beating, killing, and stoning them. More servants were sent, and they received the same treatment. These "servants" refer to the prophets who had been sent to Israel over the centuries. Some had been beaten (Jeremiah 26:7-11; 38:1-28), some had been killed (tradition says Isaiah was killed; John the Baptist had been killed, Matthew 14:1-12), and some had been stoned (2 Chronicles 24:21). Jesus was reminding the religious leaders that God's prophets often had been ridiculed and persecuted by God's people.

**1:37-39** **"Finally he sent his son to them, saying, 'They will respect my son.' But when the tenants saw the son, they said to themselves, 'This is the heir; come, let us kill him and get his inheritance.'**

**So they seized him, threw him out of the vineyard, and killed him."** NRSV After all his servants had been killed, the landowner *sent his son,* thinking that surely the tenants would respect his son. The historical situation behind this section reflects the law that property would go to anyone in possession of it when the master died. So the tenants assumed that by killing the son and *heir* to the property, they would obtain the *inheritance.* So they *killed* the son. (They may have thought that the owner had already died.) With these words, Jesus was revealing to the religious leaders his knowledge of their desire to kill him.

---

CONSCIOUS REJECTION
The tenants in Jesus' story knew exactly what they were doing. They killed the son to take his property. Did the conspirators against Jesus knowingly reject him? The tenants assumed wrongly that they would inherit the vineyard if they eliminated the son of the owner. The religious leaders of Jesus' day assumed they would continue in power if they killed Jesus. In both cases (the story and history), people who should have recognized rightful authority rejected it.

Scripture makes one of its most sobering points when it teaches that we will be responsible for what we know (Romans 2). The results of the tenants' rejection of the son are not immediate. But justice will be served when the landowner arrives. Submit to Jesus' authority. Accepting or rejecting him has eternal consequences.

---

**21:40-41** **"Now when the owner of the vineyard comes, what will he do to those tenants?" They said to him, "He will put those wretches to a miserable death, and lease the vineyard to other tenants who will give him the produce at the harvest time."** NRSV Jesus' question forced the religious leaders to announce their own fate. These words allude to Isaiah 5:5 and continue the same imagery. In their answer to Jesus, the religious leaders announced themselves to be *wretches* who deserved a *miserable death,* and stated that *other tenants* would take over what they thought they had. Jesus explained what this meant in 21:43.

**21:42** **Jesus said to them, "Have you never read in the Scriptures: 'The stone which the builders rejected has become the chief cornerstone. This was the LORD's doing, and it is marvelous in our eyes'?"** NKJV The religious leaders had answered correctly, but they still didn't understand. So Jesus said, *"Have you never read in the Scriptures"*—this was a statement of rebuke, since that's what they did for a living—but Jesus pointed out that they may have read but had never understood. The imagery of the stone rejected by the builders is taken from Psalm 118:22-23, referring to the deliverance of Israel from a situation when it seemed that their enemies had triumphed. Their deliverance could only be attributed to God's miraculous intervention. Various people rejected David (Samuel, David's family), but God chose and used David to deliver the nation. Jesus referred to himself as *the stone which the builders rejected.* Although Jesus had been rejected by many of his people, he will become the *cornerstone* of his new building, the church (see Acts 4:11 and 1 Peter 2:6-7, where it is clear that Peter was impressed with this vivid image of Jesus being the rejected stone). It seemed that Jesus had been rejected and defeated by his own people, the Jews, but God would raise him from the dead and seat him at his own right hand. Jesus would be vindicated, and *it is marvelous in our eyes.*

---

CAPSTONE
Cornerstones and capstones were valued architectural pieces. Stone masons demonstrated their ability by choosing just the right rock. Cornerstones anchored and shaped the foundation of a large building. They had to be square and solid. Capstones required a special shape. They were the final piece in an arch. Jesus is both cornerstone and capstone. Jesus' role gives shape to all of history. His presence defines the church. Though rejected by those who should have known better, Jesus was placed in the honored position by his heavenly Father. Make Jesus the cornerstone of your life.

---

**21:43** **"Therefore I tell you that the kingdom of God will be taken away from you and given to a people who will produce its fruit."** NIV Again Jesus introduced a solemn truth with the words "therefore I tell you." The "other tenants" who will pay their rent refers to the Gentiles who will be added to make up God's people (21:41). By their rejection of the prophets' message and finally of the Son himself, Israel showed that they were incapable of repentance and belief. So the kingdom *will be taken away* from them and given to a unity of Jews and Gentiles, a foreshadowing of the church. The same presentation is given by Paul in Romans 11:11-24, where he used the image of branches being grafted into the olive tree.

**21:44** **"The one who falls on this stone will be broken to pieces; and it will crush anyone on whom it falls."** NRSV Jesus used this metaphor to show that one stone can affect people different ways, depending on how they relate to it (see Isaiah 8:14-15; 28:16; Daniel 2:34, 44-45). Ideally they will build on it; many, however, will trip over it. At the Last Judgment, God's enemies will be crushed by it. At that time, Christ, the "building block," will become the "crushing stone." He offers mercy and forgiveness now, and he promises judgment later. Some versions do not include this verse because many of the older manuscripts omit it. The verse may have been inserted later, copied from the parallel passage in Luke (Luke 20:18).

---

STUNNING REVERSAL

The very people who should most welcome the coming of God's kingdom will be denied its privileges, and the very people most unlikely to succeed spiritually will find it.

So all spiritually satisfied, religiously proud, and biblically astute and learned people should take note. Christ is the center, and no amount of paraphernalia can take his place. You may know Greek and Hebrew, you may hold church office, and you may be a respected Christian philanthropist, but if any of this nudges Christ from the center of your faith and life, beware of some stunning reversals ahead. Others will receive God's blessing.

---

**21:45-46 When the chief priests and the Pharisees heard his parables, they realized that he was speaking about them. They wanted to arrest him, but they feared the crowds, because they regarded him as a prophet.**NRSV It seems that the religious leaders finally understood something, for here *when the chief priests and the Pharisees heard his parables, they realized that he was speaking about them.* What they realized was that they were the "wicked tenants" who were plotting to kill the son and who would have the "vineyard" taken away from them. They must have become very angry, so much so that *they wanted to arrest him.* The Jewish leaders wouldn't do so because *they feared the crowds.* To arrest Jesus would have caused an uprising against them and an uproar that they couldn't afford with the Romans ready to come down on them. The crowds *regarded* Jesus *as a prophet.*

# Matthew 22

Jesus had already told two parables focusing on rejection of him as God's Son and God's resulting judgment. The parable of the two sons (21:28-32) showed how the rewards of the sons were switched according to their ultimate service rendered. The parable of the wicked tenants (21:33-46) explained that "other tenants" would be given the vineyard. The following parable of the wedding feast showed that those least expected, from "the highways," would be invited to the feast.

**22:1-3 Once more Jesus spoke to them in parables, saying: "The kingdom of heaven may be compared to a king who gave a wedding banquet for his son. He sent his slaves to call those who had been invited to the wedding banquet, but they would not come."** NRSV Jesus spoke in parables, but he made his subject clear—the kingdom of heaven. The scenes changed, but the theme remained consistent. Jesus' message was that God extends a gracious invitation to people to participate in his kingdom. Accepting the invitation leads to joy while rejection leads to punishment. When Jesus spoke of God's kingdom, he spoke with authority. His stories convicted because he knew his audience. His parables have a universal character; they make the hearer or reader ask, "If this parable is about everyone, I must fit here somewhere. Which character in the story represents me?" Those for whom the parables were immediately intended usually felt their sting (see 21:45; 22:15).

> This was something completely unnatural; in real life a royal invitation is not refused. . . . Their [invited guests'] outward profession was a long way from glad acceptance of the ways of God. When they were summoned by the King of heaven, they should surely have complied.    *Leon Morris*

In this parable, Jesus pictured the kingdom of heaven being offered to those who might be least expected to enter it. In the story, a *king* gives a *wedding banquet for his son* (clearly this was allegorical and may point to the messianic feast of the last days, described in Isaiah 25:6-8 and Revelation 19:7-9). In this culture, two invitations were expected when banquets were given. The first asked the guests to attend; the second announced that all was ready. When the king *sent his slaves to call those who had been invited,* this referred to the second invitation. These invitees had already accepted the first invitation. At this second one, however, these guests said *they would not come.* Not only that, but they refused yet another invitation, as described in 22:4-6. Like the son who said he would go to the vineyard and didn't (21:30) and the tenant farmers who refused to pay the rent (21:34-39), these guests reneged on an earlier agreement.

DELIVERING THE INVITATIONS
Jesus pictured two equally effective ways of rejecting a summons. Some ignored the invitation while others abused the servants who brought the message. The servants in this parable seldom receive much attention in sermons. They certainly got a mixed reception from those they approached with the Good News. But they delivered their message anyway.

Those who invite others to meet Jesus will still experience rejection. It will take both forms—active and passive. None of us enjoys rejection. We usually take it personally. The more carefully we make the invitation to meet Christ clear and appealing, the more we will feel the impact of a rebuff. Are you a servant? Your challenge remains the same: Faithfully deliver the message God has given you. Trust him for your safety.

**22:4-6** **"Again he sent other slaves, saying, 'Tell those who have been invited: Look, I have prepared my dinner, my oxen and my fat calves have been slaughtered, and everything is ready; come to the wedding banquet.' But they made light of it and went away, one to his farm, another to his business, while the rest seized his slaves, mistreated them, and killed them."** NRSV *Oxen* and *calves* were food only the wealthy could afford. This was a grand feast. In this story the king invited his guests three times; these verses describe the third invitation. After having originally agreed to come, these people refused the last two invitations. The meal was ready, the king had made great preparations, but these guests placed a higher priority on their farms and businesses, deciding not to go to the great banquet. The Messiah had arrived, yet they went about their daily business as if nothing important were happening. In fact, many *made light of it and went away.* The seizing and killing of these *slaves* stretches the imagination for this story, but probably recalls the same meaning as in the parable of the wicked tenants who killed those servants. The servants are the prophets whom God had sent to offer his invitation. Their invitation was rejected, with many of the prophets mistreated and killed (see 21:35-36).

**22:7-8** **"The king was enraged. He sent his troops, destroyed those murderers, and burned their city. Then he said to his slaves, 'The wedding is ready, but those invited were not worthy.'"** NRSV The king's invitation had been refused, even ridiculed and his servants had been murdered, so he *was enraged.* Sending troops and destroying the city has been interpreted as referring to the destruction of Jerusalem in A.D. 70. More likely it refers to the final war between good and evil, a very popular theme in passages about the end times (Isaiah 25:6-8; Ezekiel 39:17-24; Revelation 19:17-21). The feast was ready and waiting, *but those invited were not worthy.* This is similar to the giving of the vineyard to "other tenants" in the previous parable (21:41). The kingdom will go to those whom God has deemed "worthy."

---

WHAT A MIX!
In this parable, invitations are delivered to the whole range of people. The Christian church is multicultural, multicolor, multilingual, multiethnic. Make no mistake. No nation or personality type has a lock on the gate to heaven. Lots of different kinds of people will be there. As a result . . .
- Open your church to the wider world.
- Develop programs to meet a wider set of needs.
- Consider worship services in minority languages.
- Learn simple hymns from other continents.
- Open your heart to people different from yourself. This may be the hardest of all, but if you succeed, the rest will follow.
Let God expand your heart, and sure enough, the church will become a warmer place for strangers.

---

**22:9-10** **"'Go therefore into the main streets, and invite everyone you find to the wedding banquet.' Those slaves went out into the streets and gathered all whom they found, both good and bad; so the wedding hall was filled with guests."** NRSV The king still wanted to share his banquet, so he ordered his servants to go out *into the main streets* and *invite everyone* they found. They did so, bringing *both good and bad* (meaning the servants didn't discriminate with regard to social standing, reputation, or moral character) into the *wedding hall* for the feast. The metaphor focuses on the outcasts and sinners (see also 21:31-32) as well as righteous people. An unlikely scenario in ancient times, this scene pictures God's gracious invitation to all kinds of people—Jew and Gentile, rich and poor, male and

female, good and bad. As the servants gathered all who would
respond, so God gives salvation to all who hear and respond.

---

SPEECHLESS
One ill-prepared guest showed up for the wedding. He failed
to wear wedding clothes. Whether we imagine this person
neglecting to dress for the occasion or refusing the wedding
robes offered at the door, the same results occurred. The
banquet hall was filled with a cross section of humanity ("both
good and bad," 22:10), but that one guest stood out because
he wasn't covered like the other guests. He came to the
banquet without forethought. Others had no better right than he
to be present, but they knew where they were and dressed
accord- ingly. He, however, came as he was, without
acknowledging his unworthiness. When asked about his attire,
he was "speechless" (22:12).
     This speechless character represents a superficial response
to Christ's gospel. Such persons view the gracious invitation
of the gospel as a mere formality. They assume themselves
worthy of the invitation. What others receive as grace, they take
for granted. They are unwilling or incapable of seeing themselves honestly. Therefore, when God confronts their unworthiness, they can say nothing.
     We dare not consider the invitation of Christ lightly. We must
be ready to meet the One who invites us into the kingdom of
heaven.

---

**22:11-12** **"But when the king came in to see the guests, he noticed a man
there who was not wearing wedding clothes. 'Friend,' he asked,
'how did you get in here without wedding clothes?' The man
was speechless."**[NIV] The late arrival of the king was customary, for
often the host did not partake of the banquet but came after the
meal had begun. The *wedding clothes* probably refers to clean,
fresh clothing. It was unthinkable to come to a wedding banquet in
soiled clothes. This would insult the host, who could only assume
that the guest was ignorant, had not truly been invited, or was not
prepared for the banquet. When the king pointed this out, *the man
was speechless.* He had no explanation for his appearance (he had
had plenty of time to get ready), so the king declared him unprepared and unworthy. The man had been invited, but he needed his
wedding garment or he would miss out on the banquet.

     The wedding clothes picture the righteousness needed to enter
God's kingdom—the total acceptance in God's eyes that Christ
provides for every believer (Isaiah 61:10). Christ has provided this
garment of righteousness for everyone, but each person must put
it on (accept Christ's gracious provision of his life given for us) in
order to enter the King's banquet (eternal life). There is an open

invitation, but we must be ready. For more on the imagery of clothes of righteousness and salvation, see Psalm 132:16; Zechariah 3:3-5; Revelation 3:4-5; 19:7-8. Those who refuse God's invitation will face judgment, as the following verse indicates.

**22:13** **"Then the king told the attendants, 'Tie him hand and foot, and throw him outside, into the darkness, where there will be weeping and gnashing of teeth.'"** NIV In Jesus' parable, he moved beyond normal reality (for this would never happen in real life) to teach a spiritual truth. In the final judgment, God's true people will be revealed. Claiming to belong at the wedding feast while refusing to wear the correct garments was like the nation of Israel claiming to be God's people but refusing to live for him. Like the wicked tenants who deserved "a wretched end" (21:41), so this impostor at the banquet found himself tied up and thrown outside *into the darkness, where there will be weeping and gnashing of teeth*—a common biblical description of hell (see also 8:12; 13:42, 50).

---

ETERNAL INSECURITY?
Does this passage in Matthew teach the eternal insecurity of all who claim faith in Christ? No, but neither does it give a blank check for all who march the sawdust trail. That kind of religion reduces faith to a life insurance policy. Once signed, it may be forgotten until death, when its terms come due. This is not Christian faith. Eternal insecurity, however, reduces faith to a guessing game in which we all hope not to be the one tossed away on Judgment Day. This is not Christian faith. Christian faith is living in a new relationship to God, characterized by love and proven by faithful service.

God's love will never let you go, but don't be presumptuous. If you recited the sinner's prayer twenty years ago and haven't thought of God since, wake up—you're fooling no one. God calls you to a life of love and service. Follow it in faith every day.

---

**22:14** **"For many are called, but few are chosen."** NKJV Those who are *called* but reject God's invitation will be punished, as will those who seem to accept the call but fail to follow through. The use of the word "called" means "invited," not the irresistible call of God as Paul used it (see Romans 8:28-29). The invitation had gone out to all Israel, but only a few had accepted and followed Jesus. "Chosen" refers to the elect. Jesus was applying this teaching to the Jews, who believed that because they were descendants of Abraham, they would be sure to share in the blessings of God's kingdom through the Messiah. But Jesus taught that not all those invited would actually be among the chosen of God. As Jesus had noted earlier, "Wide is the gate and broad is the road that leads to destruction, and many enter through it. But small is the gate and narrow the road that leads to life, and only a few find it" (Matthew 7:13 NIV).

## RELIGIOUS LEADERS QUESTION JESUS ABOUT PAYING TAXES / 22:15-22 / **193**

The Pharisees and Herodians who approached Jesus usually were parties in conflict, with one side against Rome and one side pro-Rome. They were young men, sent in the hope that Jesus would not suspect them of trickery. They addressed Jesus as a mediator, inviting him to settle their dispute. Their true purpose, however, was to discredit him.

**22:15-16 Then the Pharisees went out and laid plans to trap him in his words. They sent their disciples to him along with the Herodians.**NIV The Jewish leaders would not be put off—they were so intent on killing Jesus. The *Pharisees* were a religious group opposed to the Roman occupation of Palestine. The *Herodians* were a political party that supported the Herods and the policies instituted by Rome. These groups with diametrically opposed beliefs usually were antagonistic toward each other. It may seem strange that any group of Jews would support Rome and the Herods, but the real hope of the Herodians was to keep the nation together so that one day they might again be free. After Herod the Great's death in 4 B.C., Palestine had been divided among his sons. Although the nation had been split apart, the rulers were still of one family. The Herodians' love was more for country than for Herod; they realized that the only way to preserve their land and national identity was to keep Herod's family in the ruling positions.

These two groups found a common enemy in Jesus. The Pharisees did not like Jesus because he exposed their hypocrisy. The Herodians also saw Jesus as a threat. They had lost political control when, as a result of reported unrest, Rome had deposed Archelaus (Herod's son with authority over Judea) and had replaced him with a Roman governor. The Herodians feared that Jesus would cause still more instability in Judea and that Rome might react by never replacing the Roman leaders with a descendant of Herod.

Despite Jesus' solemn warning to the Jewish leaders in his previous parable, they didn't let up. More delegates arrived whose intentions were simply to *trap* Jesus in his words. These two groups, on different sides of religious and political issues (the Pharisees opposed the Roman tax; the Herodians supported it), hoped to get an answer from Jesus that one of them would be able to use against him.

**"Teacher," they said, "we know you are a man of integrity and that you teach the way of God in accordance with the truth. You aren't swayed by men, because you pay no attention to who they are."** NIV The men in this delegation, pretending to be honest, flattered Jesus before asking him their trick question, hoping to catch him off guard. Their flattering words focused on Jesus' sincerity, his refusal to show deference or partiality toward those in authority, and his truthfulness. These words reek with irony because the reader knows that Jesus was a man of integrity and taught the way of God.

---

GOOD TIMING

The Pharisees and Herodians thought they could trap Jesus by forcing him to choose between two responsibilities. He stunned them by choosing both. He demonstrated that behind many of our conflicts lies a failure to recognize priorities. Should we give time and attention to our families or our work? Can we communicate our relationship with God through the work we do or by setting our work aside and engaging our fellow workers in conversation? Should we support our church or other worthy causes? According to Jesus' handling of this situation, these problems are issues of timing and priority, not right and wrong. The real challenge for most of us concerns whether or not we are doing what we should be doing at the appropriate time.

Citizenship in the kingdom of God doesn't lessen commitments. In fact, it often intensifies them! Marriage duties, parental roles, church involvement, earthly citizenship—all take specific place under God's authority. Make sure your commitment to God stays strong, then all your priorities will be under his authority.

---

**22:17** **"Tell us then, what is your opinion? Is it right to pay taxes to Caesar or not?"** NIV Judea had been a Roman province since 63 B.C. But recently, the Jews had been forced to pay taxes or tribute to Caesar—in A.D. 6, the Sanhedrin (Jewish Council) was made responsible to collect taxes. There were three basic types of taxes: (1) A land or produce tax took one-tenth of all grain and one-fifth of all fruit (or wine); (2) everyone aged fourteen to sixty-five paid a head or poll tax collected when a census was taken—one day's wages; and (3) a custom tax was collected at ports and city gates as toll for goods transported—rates were 2 to 5 percent of the value of the goods. This question may have been focusing on the poll tax or on taxes in general.

This was a hot topic in Palestine. The Jews hated to pay taxes to Rome because the money supported their oppressors and symbolized their subjection. Much of the tax money also went to maintain the heathen temples and luxurious lifestyles of Rome's upper class. The Jews also hated the system that allowed tax collectors to charge exorbitant rates and keep the extra for themselves. The Roman government allowed tax collectors to contract for tax collection by paying the Romans a flat fee for a district. Then the tax collectors could profit from collecting all they could get. Anyone who avoided paying taxes faced harsh penalties. Thus, this was a valid (and loaded) question, and the crowd around Jesus waited expectantly for his answer. Matthew, as a former tax collector, was certainly interested in Jesus' response to this question.

The leaders, however, did not really want an answer; their motives were only to put Jesus in a dilemma between the religious and political implications of their question. The Pharisees were against these taxes on religious grounds; the Herodians supported taxation on political grounds. Thus, either a yes or a no could get Jesus into trouble. If Jesus agreed that it was right to pay taxes to Caesar, the Pharisees would say he was opposed to God, and the people would turn against him. If Jesus said the taxes should not be paid, the Herodians could hand him over to Herod on the charge of rebellion.

**22:18-19 But Jesus, aware of their malice, said, "Why are you putting me to the test, you hypocrites? Show me the coin used for the tax." And they brought him a denarius.**[NRSV] These crafty religious leaders were not able to deceive Jesus. He immediately saw through their flattering words and their pretense to the underlying hypocrisy. He knew it was a trap, so without hesitation he asked them why they were testing him with their question. Jesus knew why, of course, but his question exposed their motives and revealed them to those listening.

Jesus then asked his questioners to produce *a denarius,* which was *the coin used for the tax,* so he could use it to make a point. A denarius, a typical day's wage for a laborer, was a silver coin with Caesar's portrait on it. The tax paid to Rome was paid in these coins.

**22:20-21 And He said to them, "Whose image and inscription is this?" They said to Him, "Caesar's." And He said to them, "Render therefore to Caesar the things that are Caesar's, and to God the things that are God's."**[NKJV] The coin was brought to Jesus. The denarius had a portrait *(image)* of the reigning Caesar, probably Tiberius Caesar who reigned A.D. 14–37. The *inscription* referred to Caesar as divine and as "chief priest." The Caesars were worshiped as gods by the pagans, so the claim to divinity on the coin itself repulsed the Jews. In addition, Caesar's image on the coins was a constant reminder of Israel's subjection to Rome.

The Pharisees and Herodians thought they had the perfect question to trap Jesus. But Jesus answered wisely, again exposing their self-interest and wrong motives. Jesus said, *Render therefore to Caesar the things that are Caesar's*—that is, the coin bearing the emperor's image should be given to the emperor. In their question, the religious leaders used the word *didomi,* meaning "to give." Jesus responded with the word *apodidomi,* meaning "to pay a debt." In other words, having a coin meant being part of that country, so citizens should acknowledge the authority of Caesar and pay for the benefits accorded to them by his empire (for example, peace and an efficient road system). The Pharisees and Herodians tried to make it appear that it was incompatible to be a Jew and pay taxes to a pagan emperor who claimed to be divine. But Jesus explained that no such incompatibility existed because God was ultimately in control. They would lose much and gain little if they refused to pay Caesar's taxes (see Romans 13:1-7; 1 Timothy 2:1-6; 1 Peter 2:13-17).

Paying the taxes, however, did not have to mean submission to the divinity claimed by the emperor. The words on the coins were incorrect. Caesar had the right to claim their tax money, but he had no claim on their souls. The Jews had a responsibility to render *to God the things that are God's*. While they lived in the Roman world, the Jews had to face the dual reality of subjection to Rome and responsibility to God. Jesus explained that they could do both if they kept their priorities straight. The tax would be paid as long as Rome held sway over Judea, but God had rights on eternity and on their lives. To Jesus, this was the crucial issue. Were they giving their lives to God? These Jews (and especially the self-righteous Pharisees) claimed to be God's chosen people, but were they "rendering" to God what truly belonged to him—themselves?

**22:22 When they heard this, they were amazed; and they left him and went away.**NRSV Everyone was once again *amazed.* The Pharisees and Herodians were unable to believe that somehow Jesus had escaped their trap. True to what they had said, Jesus had been sincere, showed no deference or partiality, and truthfully taught God's way even when asked about a hotly debated topic.

CIVIL OBEDIENCE
Jesus taught that Christians should render to Caesar the things that are Caesar's. In this passage, Jesus did not elaborate on all the issues related to a Christian citizen's responsibility to the state, but he did indicate a preference for compliance and civil stability. So . . .

- Choose your battle carefully. No state is perfect. If you refuse to live with moments of unfairness or bureaucratic hassle, you'll need to live by yourself on an island.
- Cooperate and support the state as far as faith will take you. Fortunately in democratic countries (unlike Judea in Jesus' time), we can work for peaceful change through speeches, publications, assemblies, boycotts, and media campaigns. There is no need to be a hermit or a rebel.
- Be wary of radicals on the left and reactionaries on the right. Militia movements have appealed to worried Christians and caused them to become more worried still. Leftist movements have attracted other Christians, who confuse political change with spiritual growth.
- When resistance is required, pray a lot and take counsel from Christian friends. Citizenship requires compromise, but Christians should not compromise Christ or do injustice before God.

## RELIGIOUS LEADERS QUESTION JESUS ABOUT THE RESURRECTION / 22:23-33 / 194

The Sadducees asked Jesus what marriage would be like in heaven. Jesus said it was more important to understand God's power than know what heaven will be like. In every generation and culture, ideas of eternal life tend to be based on images and experiences of present life. Jesus answered that these faulty ideas are caused by ignorance of God's Word. We must not make up our own ideas about eternity and heaven by thinking of it and God in human terms. We should concentrate more on our relationship with God than about what heaven will look like. Eventually we will find out, and it will be far beyond our greatest expectations.

22:23 **That same day the Sadducees, who say there is no resurrection, came to him with a question.**<sup>NIV</sup> The combined group of religious leaders from the Sanhedrin had failed with their first question (21:23-27); the paired antagonists of Pharisees and Herodians had failed with a political question (22:15-22); here the *Sadducees,* another group of religious leaders, smugly stepped in to try to trap Jesus with a theological question. The Sadducees were at odds theologically with the Pharisees (the other major group of Jewish leaders) because they honored only the Pentateuch— Genesis through Deuteronomy—as Scripture and because they rejected most of the Pharisees' traditions, rules, and regulations. The Pharisees expected a cataclysmic restoration of David's kingdom by the Messiah, while the Sadducees were pro-Herod and favored cooperation with political powers and pursuit of earthly prosperity. Little more is known about the Sadducees. We have no writings from them; the only descriptions come from Christian or Jewish sources, both of which put them in a negative light. The group may have originated in the second century B.C.

The Sadducees said *there is no resurrection* of the dead because they could find no mention of it in the Pentateuch. Apparently, the Pharisees had never been able to come up with a convincing argument from the Pentateuch for the resurrection, and the Sadducees thought they had trapped Jesus for sure. But Jesus was about to show them otherwise.

IMPOSSIBILITIES
People who impose human limitations on God shouldn't be surprised when he fails them. Deadly arrogance underlies an attitude which says to God, "If I can't imagine it, you can't do it!" Inventing problems for God may seem like an effective way to delay responsibility before God, but the approach still fails. A camouflaged excuse is still an excuse.

Case studies and hypothetical situations like the one that the Sadducees presented to Jesus often appear to create unsolvable dilemmas. Situation ethics, for instance, largely bases its approach on the assumption that humans must make decisions on their own, apart from any divine help or guidance of absolutes. Thus, when faced with a difficult situation, ask these questions as you work to find an answer: (1) Will God be allowed to help with the solution? (2) How do the guidelines of Scripture relate to this situation? (3) What would Jesus do if faced with this question?

**22:24** **"Teacher," they said, "Moses told us that if a man dies without having children, his brother must marry the widow and have children for him."** NIV This may have been a question the Sadducees always used to argue with others about the resurrection. Because the Sadducees recognized only the books attributed to Moses (Genesis through Deuteronomy), their question referred to Moses' writings. In the Law, Moses had written that when a man died without a son, his unmarried brother (or nearest male relative) was to marry the widow and produce children. The first son of this marriage was considered the heir of the dead man (Deuteronomy 25:5-6). The main purpose of the instruction was to produce an heir and guarantee that the family would not lose their land. The book of Ruth gives an example of this law in operation (Ruth 3:1–4:12; see also Genesis 38:1-26). This law, called "levirate" marriage, protected the widow (in that culture widows usually had no means to support themselves) and allowed the family line to continue.

**22:25-28** **"Now there were seven brothers among us; the first married, and died childless, leaving the widow to his brother. The second did the same, so also the third, down to the seventh. Last of all, the woman herself died. In the resurrection, then, whose wife of the seven will she be? For all of them had married her."** NRSV The book of Tobit (an apocryphal book not accepted by Protestants as part of the Old Testament canon but highly regarded by Jewish scholars at that time) includes the story of a woman who was married to seven men successively without ever having children. In Tobit the men are not brothers.

The law of levirate marriage, written by Moses in Deuteronomy 25:5-10, would cause a real problem for the woman in the situation the Sadducees described, for she had been married seven times to seven different men, all according to the law. The Sadducees reasoned that because this was in the law, there could not be a resurrection. According to Jewish history, this was an ongoing debate among the rabbis. When all eight of them were resurrected (the seven brothers and the woman), *Whose wife of the seven will she be?*

The Sadducees erroneously assumed that if people were resurrected, they would assume physical bodies capable of procreation. They did not understand that God could both raise the dead and make new lives for his people, lives that would be different than what they had known on earth. The Sadducees had brought God down to their level. Because they could not conceive of a resurrection life, they decided that God couldn't raise the dead. And since they thought that Moses hadn't written about it, they considered the case "closed."

**22:29-30** **Jesus replied, "You are in error because you do not know the Scriptures or the power of God. At the resurrection people will neither marry nor be given in marriage; they will be like the angels in heaven."** NIV Jesus wasted no time dealing with their hypothetical situation but went directly to their underlying assumption that resurrection of the dead was impossible. Jesus clearly stated that these Sadducees were wrong about the resurrection for two reasons: (1) They didn't know the Scriptures (if they did, they would believe in the resurrection because it is taught in Scripture), and (2) they didn't know the power of God (if they did, they would believe in the resurrection because God's power makes it possible). Ignorance on these two counts was inexcusable for these religious leaders.

Furthermore, Jesus said, *at the resurrection* (spoken with certainty—it will happen, so the Sadducees were wrong at the very foundation of their beliefs), people will not rise to an extension of their earthly lives. Instead, life in heaven will be different. Believers *will be like the angels in heaven* regarding marriage. Believers do not become angels, because angels were created by God for a special purpose. Angels do not marry or propagate; neither will glorified human beings. On earth where death reigns, marriage and childbearing are important in order to "fill the earth and subdue it" (Genesis 1:28 NKJV); but bearing children will not be necessary in the resurrection life because people will be raised to glorify God forever—there will be no more death. Those in heaven will no longer be governed by physical laws but will be "like the angels"; that is, believers will share the immortal and exalted nature of angels, living above physical needs.

Jesus was not teaching that people will not recognize their spouses in heaven. Jesus was not dissolving the eternal aspect of marriage, doing away with sexual differences, or teaching that we will be asexual beings after death. Nor was he teaching that the angels are asexual. We cannot learn very much about sex and marriage in heaven from this one statement by Jesus. His point was simply that we must not think of heaven as an extension of life as we now know it. Our relationships in this life are limited by time, death, and sin. We don't know everything about our resurrection life, but Jesus was affirming that relationships will be different from what we are used to here and now. The same physical and natural rules will not apply.

Jesus was not intending to give the final word on marriage in heaven. Instead, this response was Jesus' refusal to answer the Sadducees' riddle and fall into their trap. The Sadducees did not believe in angels either (Acts 23:8), so Jesus' point was not to extend the argument into another realm. Instead, he was showing that because there will be no levirate marriage in the resurrection or new marriage contracts, the Sadducees' question was completely irrelevant. But their assumption about the resurrection needed a definitive answer, and Jesus was just the one to give it.

**FACING ARGUMENTS**
The Sadducees tried to trick Jesus with a clever question.
Clever arguments against the Bible and against faith in Christ
are easy to find. If you are faced with such cleverness and
hope to make a meaningful reply . . .

- Don't address all the problems. Instead, cut to the heart of
  the issue, which includes motives and unstated agendas.
- Don't try to embarrass the questioner with your superior
  logic; instead, address the heart issue with compassion.
  Your goal is not to win a contest, but to win a person to faith
  in Christ.
- Stay with clear teachings of Scripture that you understand.
  If you get over your head in theology, you'll be frustrated
  and ill tempered. At the same time, keep learning, keep
  searching, keep growing yourself.

**22:31-32** **"But about the resurrection of the dead—have you not read
what God said to you, 'I am the God of Abraham, the God
of Isaac, and the God of Jacob'? He is not the God of the
dead but of the living."** NIV The Sadducees' underlying comment regarded their view of the absurdity of resurrection. Their
question to Jesus was intended to show him to be foolish. So
Jesus cut right to the point: *But about the resurrection of the
dead.* Because the Sadducees accepted only the Pentateuch as
God's inspired Word, Jesus answered them from the book of
Exodus (3:6). God would not have said, *"I am the God of
Abraham, the God of Isaac, and the God of Jacob"* if he had
thought of Abraham, Isaac, and Jacob as dead (he would have
said, "I *was* their God"). Thus, from God's perspective, they
are alive. This evidence would have been acceptable in any
rabbinic debate because it applied a grammatical argument:
God's use of the present tense in speaking of his relationship to
the great patriarchs who had been long dead by the time God
spoke these words to Moses. God had a continuing relationship
with these men because of the truth of the resurrection.

God had spoken of dead men as though they were still alive;
thus, Jesus reasoned, the men were not *dead* but *living*. God
would not have a relationship with dead beings. Although men
and women have died on earth, God continues his relationship
with them because they are resurrected to life with him in heaven.

Some might argue that this shows only the immortality of the
soul, not necessarily the resurrection of the body. But Jesus' answer
affirmed both. The Jews understood that soul and body had insepa-
rable unity; thus, the immortality of the soul necessarily included a

resurrection of the body. Therefore, the Sadducees were wrong in their mistaken assumption about the resurrection.

**22:33 And when the crowd heard it, they were astounded at his teaching.**[NRSV] These discussions with the Pharisees, Herodians, and Sadducees were public, with crowds standing around as important but silent participants. When they heard Jesus' answers to these difficult questions, *they were astounded at his teaching.* They saw Jesus as much wiser than their religious leaders.

### RELIGIOUS LEADERS QUESTION JESUS ABOUT THE GREATEST COMMANDMENT / 22:34-40 / 195

The questions leading up to the one recorded in this section were intended to trap Jesus rather than to find answers. Here, however, an "expert in the law" asked Jesus to condense the law to a single principle. Because Matthew was highlighting the atmosphere of rejection during the final week, he did not emphasize the cordial exchange between Jesus and this lawyer that Mark included in his account (Mark 12:28-34).

**22:34-36 Hearing that Jesus had silenced the Sadducees, the Pharisees got together. One of them, an expert in the law, tested him with this question: "Teacher, which is the greatest commandment in the Law?"**[NIV] The Pharisees were probably delighted to hear Jesus' definitive answer about the resurrection that had finally *silenced the Sadducees.* So another Pharisee stepped up. Mark portrays him as more sincere than the others, asking his question in order to get an answer. This *expert in the law* asked Jesus, *Which is the greatest commandment in the Law?*

The legal expert was referring to a popular debate about the "more important" and "less important" of the hundreds of laws that the Jews had accumulated. The Pharisees had classified over six hundred laws and would spend much time discussing which laws were weightier than others. Some religious leaders tried to distinguish between major and minor laws; some taught that all laws were equally binding and that it was dangerous to make any distinctions. As a Pharisee, the

> The mind is a gift from God. It may be used for his glory, neglected to its waste or abused idolatrously. It is no exaggeration to say that the process of secularization which had posed so many difficulties for Christians in our century is in considerable measure the result of Christians . . . neglecting questions of the mind.
> *Mark A. Noll*

man had in mind the debates over the relative importance of ritual, ethical, moral, and ceremonial laws, as well as the positive versus negative laws. Jesus' definitive answer about the resurrection caused this man to hope that Jesus might also have the final answer about all these laws.

**22:37-38** **Jesus replied: "'Love the Lord your God with all your heart and with all your soul and with all your mind.' This is the first and greatest commandment."**[NIV] This quote comes from Deuteronomy 6:5, "Love the Lord your God with all your heart and with all your soul and with all your strength" (NIV). Jesus added "with all your mind." Jesus' purpose was to show that a person's total being must be involved in loving God. Nothing must be held back because God holds nothing back. Much of the New Testament focuses on Jesus' addition *(with all your mind)* by strongly emphasizing the renewing of the mind (Romans 12:2; Ephesians 4:23). We need this emphasis every bit as much as this scribe who came to Jesus. Much of modern-day teaching attempts to bypass the mind. Yet the mind is vital, and we need to take every thought captive for Christ (2 Corinthians 10:5).

---

 WHOLE LOVE
Jesus used "heart," "soul," and "mind" to express the dimensions of our love for God. The terms should be taken together to mean, "Love God with your whole being." In life they cannot be completely isolated (such as, "I will love God today with all my heart while my soul and mind are otherwise occupied"). Heart, soul, and mind function in harmony in our love for God.

Take each of these components and meditate on how to express your love. "Heart" refers primarily to our emotional response. When we think about love, we usually stop with emotions. The helpful roles of "soul" and "mind" become clear when our emotions (or heart) fail us. What do we do with the command to love God if we don't feel like it? "Soul" includes the willful, decision-making part of us. Loving God with our soul covers those times when we love God *apart* from our feelings, such as when we truly forgive another while part of us feels like exacting revenge on that person.

"Mind" refers to an active component of our love for God. In a world where faith is often described as characteristic of people who don't think, Jesus' words point to the importance of engaging our mind as a central aspect of what we believe. Of course, loving God with our mind covers much more than the practice of thinking about God. If we place our mind into service for God, it will enjoy its greatest usefulness. Identify what area of your whole love for God needs special attention, and make it a point to involve that part of yourself in loving God.

---

The word for "love" is *agapao,* totally unselfish love, a love of which human beings are capable only with the help of the Holy Spirit. God's Spirit helps us love him as we ought. God wants our warmhearted love and devotion, not just our obedience. The *heart* is the center of desires and affections, the *soul* is a person's "being" and uniqueness, the *mind* is the center of a person's intellect. To love God in this way is to fulfill completely all the commandments regarding one's "vertical" relationship.

---

KEEPING ALL THE COMMANDMENTS
Faith is both freedom and responsibility. In Christ, we are freed from the religious rules and duties that frustrate and consume religious people around the world. At the same time, we are morally responsible to love others.

- Clear biblical rules are part of God's plan for your success in life, but the application of those rules should always consider the supreme need to exhibit our faith in loving ways.
- When you face a decision not so clearly covered by biblical rules (or where rules conflict), let love set a priority.
- If you have a choice between exhibiting faith as a strict rule keeper (straight as an arrow, regimented, unbending) or as someone who loves a lot (sometimes flexible, sometimes firm), better to err on the side of love than on the side of rule keeping. To love a lot, in Jesus' view, is to obey God by reflecting his care for people—his character at its very heart.

---

**22:39-40** **"And the second is like it: 'You shall love your neighbor as yourself.' On these two commandments hang all the Law and the Prophets."** NKJV In addition to the law quoted in 22:37-38, there is a second and equally important law. This second law focuses on "horizontal" relationships—dealings with fellow human beings. A person cannot maintain a good vertical relationship with God (loving God) without also caring for his or her neighbor. For this second law, Jesus quoted Leviticus 19:18: "Love your neighbor as yourself." The word "neighbor" refers to fellow human beings in general. The love a person has for himself or herself (in the sense of looking out for oneself, caring about one's best interests, etc.) should be continued, but it should also be directed toward others.

In answer to the man's question, Jesus explained that *on these two commandments hang all the Law and the Prophets.* The Ten Commandments and all the other Old Testament laws are summarized in these two laws. By fulfilling these two commands to love God totally and love others as oneself, a person will keep all the other commands.

## RELIGIOUS LEADERS CANNOT ANSWER JESUS' QUESTION / 22:41-46 / **196**

**22:41-42 While the Pharisees were gathered together, Jesus asked them, "What do you think about the Christ? Whose son is he?"** NIV This was still presumably Tuesday of Jesus' final week on earth. Jesus had answered questions from various groups of religious leaders: the Pharisees, Herodians, and Sadducees. Then Jesus turned the tables and asked the Pharisees a question that went right to the heart of the matter—what they thought about the Messiah's identity. The central issue of life for these ancient religious leaders (as well as for us) is Jesus' true identity.

**"The son of David," they replied.** NIV The Pharisees expected a Messiah (the *Christ,* the Anointed One), but they erroneously thought he would be only a human ruler who would reign on King David's throne, deliver the Jews from Gentile domination by establishing God's rule on earth, and restore Israel's greatness as in the days of David and Solomon. They knew that the Messiah would be a *son* (descendant) *of David,* but they did not understand that he would be more than a human descendant—he would be God in the flesh. They were correct, but only halfway.

Jesus' question was designed to force the Pharisees to take the extra step that would explain the truth of the Messiah's identity. This first question was rhetorical—the scribes said that the Messiah would be the son of David because the Old Testament Scriptures clearly state this truth.

**22:43-45 He said to them, "How is it then that David, speaking by the Spirit, calls him 'Lord'? For he says, 'The Lord said to my Lord: "Sit at my right hand until I put your enemies under your feet."'"** NIV The Jews and early Christians knew that the Scriptures (our Old Testament) were inspired by God, bearing his authority in its teachings. Jesus quoted Psalm 110:1 to show that David, speaking under the influence of the Holy Spirit, understood the Messiah to be his *Lord* (that is, one who had authority over him), not just his descendant. The Messiah would be a human descendant of David, but he would also be God's divine Son. The religious leaders did not understand that the Messiah would be far more than a human descendant of David; he would be God himself in human form, much greater than David. (Hebrews 1:13 uses the same text as proof of Christ's deity; see also Acts 2:34-35)

Using the same type of rabbinic debate technique that he had used before (22:31-32), Jesus took the specific words of this verse in David's psalm and explained their implications.

- David said, "The *Lord*." This first "Lord" is *Yahweh,* the Hebrew name for God the Father.
- The second "*Lord*" in Hebrew is *Adonai* (in Greek, *Kurios*) and refers to David speaking of the coming Messiah as his "Lord."
- "*Sit at my right hand*" means the Messiah would sit at the right side of God's throne, the place of highest honor and authority in God's coming kingdom. In ancient royal courts, the right side of the king's throne was reserved for the person who could act in the king's place.
- "*Until I put your enemies under your feet*" describes the final conquering of sin and evil. In ancient Oriental battles, the conquered ruler was forced to put his neck under the foot of the triumphant ruler, showing defeat and subjection.

**"If David thus calls him Lord, how can he be his son?"** NRSV If the great King David himself called the coming Messiah his *Lord* in Psalm 110:1, then how could the scribes say that the Messiah would be merely David's *son* (meaning "descendant")? David himself didn't think the Messiah would be just a descendant; instead, David, under the inspiration of the Holy Spirit, had realized that the Messiah would be God in human form and would deserve due respect and honor.

The answer to Jesus' question is that David was clearly saying the Messiah was his *Lord.* Jesus was revealing his divine identity. The divine Messiah had, indeed, come in human form; he was standing among them.

---

SILENCE
Jesus' opponents tried to make him incriminate himself. They missed. Their opposition grew in intensity as their efforts to get rid of him were frustrated. Each of their frontal attacks failed. Matthew recorded that from this point on in the final week, the "trick question" tactic was canceled.

Within the opposition to the gospel there will always be questioners who will refuse to be answered, doubters who will reject any reason, and unbelievers who will be determined to remain such. Compassion and honesty require that we attempt to answer and care for each questioner, doubter, and unbeliever. Sooner or later, however, we may be faced with silence. When all that can be done has been done, silence may well lead to progress. Silence creates a vacuum for reflection. Arguments and debates seldom convince people. But a calm after the storm often leads to reconsideration. Keep silent and give God extra room to work!

---

**22:46 No one was able to give him an answer, nor from that day did anyone dare to ask him any more questions.**<sup>NRSV</sup> The silence of Jesus' opponents shows their total defeat. This was Jesus' last controversy with the religious establishment. It established with finality his victory over his opponents.

# Matthew 23

Chapter 23 serves as a transition between the controversy narra-
tives (which it concludes) and the Olivet Discourse (which it
introduces). This is Jesus' fifth and final discourse. Matthew's
extensive coverage (Mark has only three verses) shows his con-
suming interest in Jesus' words to the religious establishment of
the day. In this section, the theme continues that Jesus' true opponents were not the common people, but the Jewish leaders. Jesus
made many scathing remarks to the religious leaders, but not *all*
of them were evil (consider Nicodemus in John 3 and Joseph in
Mark 15:43). Jesus attacked their legalism that had become a
stumbling block for the Jews.

**23:1-2 Then Jesus said to the crowds and to his disciples, "The scribes
and the Pharisees sit on Moses' seat."** NRSV Jesus turned his attention *to the crowds and to his disciples* as he spoke to them about
the religious leaders. Pointing to their pride and hypocrisy, Jesus
showed them to be far from the type of followers God desires. The
*scribes* (also called teachers of the law) were the legal experts and
the professional copiers of God's Word. Most scribes were also
*Pharisees,* the strict religious group who made a lifetime profession
of keeping all the minute regulations in the law and, especially, in
their oral traditions. The problem came because their interpretations and applications of the laws had become as important to them
as God's law itself. Some of their laws were beneficial, but they
ran into trouble when they (1) took man-made rules as seriously
as God's laws, (2) told the people to obey these rules but did not
do so themselves, or (3) obeyed the rules not to honor God but to
make themselves look good. Usually Jesus did not condemn what
the Pharisees taught, but what they were—hypocrites.

To *sit on Moses' seat* had both literal and metaphorical meanings. Jesus referred to an actual seat in a synagogue on which a
rabbi sat when teaching. It also referred to the authority that
came down to them from Moses himself—as keepers, teachers,
and interpreters of the law. But Jesus' words most likely carried

a sarcastic meaning, for the religious leaders had assumed more authority than they actually possessed.

---

ALOOF INSTRUCTION
The Pharisees laid impossible burdens on the people. What parent tells a child to "fix that bike," then refuses to show how to do it? That would be setting up that child for sure failure.

Likewise in spiritual growth. To teach Bible truths but then refuse to help along the way is to (1) accentuate your own importance in contrast to others' failures, (2) make students needlessly dependent upon you, and (3) create frustration with and eventually resignation from spiritual growth.

If you volunteer to teach, be prepared to help. Yes, it will take time and will create schedule problems for you. If that's unacceptable, give the teaching assignment to someone else.

---

**23:3-4** **"Therefore, do whatever they teach you and follow it; but do not do as they do, for they do not practice what they teach. They tie up heavy burdens, hard to bear, and lay them on the shoulders of others; but they themselves are unwilling to lift a finger to move them."** NRSV Jesus explained that because of the scribes' and Pharisees' authority as teachers of the law, the Jews ought to *do whatever they teach you and follow it.* This seems strange at first because of Jesus' denouncement of much of their teaching (see 12:1-14; 15:1-20; 16:6-12; 19:3-9). Yet Jesus did not toss aside the religious leaders as worthless; he understood the need for their function when they taught correctly. But he did question their actions. Some scholars see irony, even sarcasm, in Jesus' words, "do whatever they teach you." Jesus was now attacking the very system of the Pharisees that stressed minutiae of the law over obedience to God himself. For all their teaching, they did not practice what they taught. The Pharisees were notorious for adding minute details and requirements to the law that made it impossible for the average person, whose life did not revolve around the law, to keep the law. These were the *heavy burdens, hard to bear.* After giving the people all these impossible commands, the leaders were *unwilling to lift a finger to move them.* In other words, they lived in their "ivory towers," teaching their lofty commands and interpretations. Yet, they offered the people no practical advice in working these out in their lives or in building a relationship with the heavenly Father. The scribes and Pharisees misused application. They distorted the law by reducing it to pointless practices and trivial pursuits. In their hands, the law ground people down instead of bringing them up to grace.

The Lord described his way as narrow and hard (7:13-14). But instead of laying an impossible burden on the shoulders of others, he carried the burden of the Cross on his own. He didn't just lend a helping finger; he lifted the load.

**23:5-7 "They do all their deeds to be seen by others."** NRSV As they made their living keeping all their tiny laws, the scribes and Pharisees were very aware of the attention they received from the people—and they loved it. They performed *all their deeds* so that they might *be seen by others.* They did not keep the laws because they loved God, but because they loved human praise.

---

FOR SHOW
Jesus held up both the mixed motives and the hypocritical behavior of his opponents for scrutiny. He accused them of overconcern with appearance and prestige. They expected to be noticed. They relished the perks of their positions. They gave superficial attention to God's demands in order to enjoy special privileges. Their behavior was exactly opposite from what Jesus expects of his followers.

What parallels might we find today? Any time we settle for appearance over truth, we tread a time-worn path. Our culture has made image a higher priority than character. In modern terms, Jesus' charges sound like this: "Contrary to popular opinion, image *isn't* everything. You are far too concerned with how you look and how others see you. You are not concerned with how your heavenly Father sees you." When Jesus holds up a mirror to our character and we see nothing deeper than our image, we need to repent. We need to again read carefully what Jesus expected of his disciples (23:8-12). His directions will lead to character development.

---

**"For they make their phylacteries broad and their fringes long."** NRSV Phylacteries were little leather boxes containing Scripture verses. Very religious people wore these boxes on their forehead (tied around the head by a strap) and on their arms so as to obey—literally—Deuteronomy 6:8 and Exodus 13:9, 16. While it is difficult to know for sure how many of the details in these verses were practices in Jesus' day, the general outline here probably was still the case. To "make their phylacteries broad" could refer either to widening the strap around the forehead (so as to make it more noticeable) or to wearing the phylacteries all day long (instead of just during prayer times). But the phylacteries had become more important for the status they gave than for the truth they contained.

To make "fringes long" referred to the fringe that the law said men should attach to the four corners of a garment (Deuteronomy 22:12). The religious leaders lengthened this fringe (or tassels), again simply to make them more noticeable.

**"They love to have the place of honor at banquets and the best seats in the synagogues, and to be greeted with respect in the marketplaces, and to have people call them rabbi."** NRSV
The *place of honor at banquets* is the seat to the right of the host. Those seated there received special treatment during the meal. *The best seats in the synagogues* were where the elders sat, at the front, near the place where the scrolls of the Torah were kept. Those seats faced the congregation and were reserved for the most important people. *To be greeted with respect in the marketplaces* was a highly treasured honor. Greetings in the Near East then (today as well) meant more than they do in the West today. Custom called for those less learned to greet their superiors; thus, these religious leaders would receive many greetings. To be called *rabbi* (meaning "teacher") was treasured for the status it gave a person as a leading teacher of the Torah. In short, the scribes had lost sight of their priority as teachers of the law and were enjoying their position merely because of the "perks" it offered. Jesus condemned this attitude.

People desire positions of leadership in the community, at work, and in the church. It is dangerous when love for the position grows stronger than loyalty to God. This is what happened to the Pharisees and teachers of the law. Jesus is not against all leadership—we need Christian leaders—but against leadership that serves itself rather than others.

TITLES AND HONORS
Who loves honor today? In churches across the world, it has become courteous (even obligatory) to refer to Christian leaders by their highest titles, often academic or honorary doctorates. Christian leaders have even been known to actively seek an honorary doctorate, in order to be called "Doctor" at the next missions conference. But Jesus wants all that role-playing put aside.

If you hold a title, don't depend on it for self-respect. (Billy Graham, for example, was often introduced as "Doctor Graham," to which he would typically respond, "I'm just Billy.") If you don't hold a title, don't covet one. Leadership in God's kingdom goes to servants first.

**23:8-10** **"But you are not to be called 'Rabbi,' for you have only one Master and you are all brothers. And do not call anyone on**

earth 'father,' for you have one Father, and he is in heaven.
Nor are you to be called 'teacher,' for you have one Teacher,
the Christ." NIV In these words, Jesus described true discipleship. "You are not to be called 'rabbi'" did not mean that Jesus
refused anyone that title. Rather, this means that a learned
teacher should not allow anyone to call him "rabbi" in the
sense of "great one." Why? Because there is only one "Great
One," *one Master,* and all rabbis are under his authority. Rabbis
of Jesus' day tended to have independent spirits, each establishing his own school. True disciples, however, are united
under one authority (*and you are all brothers*) and do not
establish a hierarchy of importance.

"Do not call anyone on earth 'father'" does not mean that we
cannot use the word for a parent. Again, Jesus was speaking in
the context of the rabbi and disciple relationship. Disciples would
call their rabbi "father," and the relationship could be compared
to that between a father and son. This command gives the flip
side of the first one. While rabbis must not accept homage from
disciples, the disciples were not to revere any rabbi or put him
on a pedestal.

The third command repeats the first one, but adds the emphasis
of *the Christ,* the Messiah. All rabbis (all learned teachers) fall
under the authority of *one Teacher.* Jesus, of course, was referring
to himself.

**3:11-12** **"The greatest among you will be your servant. All who exalt
themselves will be humbled, and all who humble themselves
will be exalted."** NRSV The heart of discipleship is not found in
outward appearances or long tassels or places of honor. It comes
from servanthood and humility. Jesus had explained in 20:26 that
true greatness comes from being a servant. The true leader places
his or her needs last, as Jesus exemplified in his life and in his
death. Being a *servant* did not mean occupying a servile position;
rather, it meant having an attitude of freely attending to others'
needs without expecting or demanding anything in return. Trying
to *exalt* oneself by seeking honor, respect, and the attention of
others runs contrary to Jesus' requirements for his servants. Only
those who *humble themselves* in an attitude of service will find
true greatness in God's kingdom. This completely opposed the
attitudes and actions of the Jewish religious leaders. Jesus challenged society's norms. To him, greatness comes from serving—
giving yourself to help God and others. Service keeps us aware
of others' needs, and it stops us from focusing only on ourselves.
Jesus came as a servant. What kind of greatness do you seek?
(See also 5:1-3; 20:25-26.)

## JESUS CONDEMNS THE RELIGIOUS LEADERS / 23:13-36 / **198**

Matthew included seven "woes" (or denunciations) against the scribes and Pharisees whom Jesus unhesitatingly called "hypocrites." Being a religious leader in Jerusalem was very different from being a pastor in a secular society today. Israel's history, culture, and daily life revolved around its relationship with God. The religious leaders were the best known, most powerful, and most respected of all leaders. Jesus made these stinging accusations because the leaders' hunger for more power, money, and status had made them lose sight of God, and their blindness was spreading to the whole nation.

**23:13 "But woe to you, scribes and Pharisees, hypocrites! For you lock people out of the kingdom of heaven. For you do not go in yourselves, and when others are going in, you stop them."** NRSV

"Woe" is a term that warns of judgment to come but also conveys a feeling of regret because the listeners refuse to repent. The formula that begins each "woe" ends in calling the scribes and Pharisees *hypocrites* (a favorite term that Jesus used for his opponents). It then describes their failure to live up to their responsibility as interpreters and teachers of the law. The word "hypocrite," as used against these Pharisees, refers to those who scrupulously obey the small details of the law but have no thought or concern about people's right relationship with God. This first "woe" to the hypocritical scribes and Pharisees concerns the fact that they were locking people out of the kingdom of heaven. Their rejection of Jesus and emphasis on their petty demands had the effect of locking people out of the kingdom and keeping themselves out as well. Anyone who might have gotten in through a saving relationship with God (see also 5:20; 7:21; 18:3; 19:23-24) was stopped by these Pharisees. They made God seem impossible to please, his commands impossible to obey, and thus heaven an impossible goal.

> Hypocrisy is the most difficult and nerve-racking vice that any man can pursue; it needs an unceasing vigilance and a rare detachment of spirit. It is a whole-time job.
> *W. Somerset Maugham*

**23:14 "Woe to you, scribes and Pharisees, hypocrites! For you devour widows' houses, and for a pretense make long prayers. Therefore you will receive greater condemnation."** NKJV This verse is not present in the older manuscripts and is probably borrowed from Mark 12:40, a parallel verse. As such, it should not be considered the second "woe," which occurs in 23:15.

SELECTING TEACHERS
Who will teach you and your family about the Scriptures? This
is one of the most important decisions you make. Jesus offers
some helpful hints at the beginning of the "seven woes":

- People schooled and devoted to the Scriptures deserve our
  ear. To the degree that they teach the Scriptures, we can
  learn from them, even if their own faith is weak or their practice of faith is faulty.
- When it is necessary, separate the teaching of a person
  from the example of his or her life.
- Whenever possible, select teachers whose words illuminate
  the Scriptures and who live in faithful service to God. When
  a teacher lives what he or she teaches, you will learn by
  word and example.

**23:15 "Woe to you, scribes and Pharisees, hypocrites! For you cross
sea and land to make a single convert, and you make the new
convert twice as much a child of hell as yourselves."**NRSV This
second "woe" focuses on the scribes and Pharisees perverting their
own converts. There were two stages for someone converting to Judaism. The first step was for the person to understand the concept of
one God (as opposed to many gods) and to accept the basic tenets
of Judaism. The second step was to become circumcised—circumcision was the unmistakable and irrevocable mark of joining God's
people. The Pharisees restricted their zealous missionary efforts
to God-fearing pagans. "God-fearing" referred to Gentiles who
followed the beliefs of Judaism. They didn't want to mix with the
"unclean" Gentiles. But the Pharisees' zeal was real. They would
go to Jewish communities in other lands, and in addition to handling
legal matters and teaching, they would try to talk the God-fearers
into undergoing the final rite of circumcision.

Unfortunately, many of the Pharisees' converts were attracted
to status and rule keeping, not to God. By getting caught up in
the details of the Pharisees' additional laws and regulations, they
completely missed God, to whom the laws pointed. A religion of
deeds pressures people to surpass others in what they know and
do. Thus, a hypocritical teacher was likely to have students who
were even more hypocritical. Making converts was laudable. But
when the ones doing the converting are "children of hell," then
their converts will likely meet the same end.

**23:16-19 "Woe to you, blind guides, who say, 'Whoever swears by the
sanctuary is bound by nothing, but whoever swears by the
gold of the sanctuary is bound by the oath.' You blind fools!
For which is greater, the gold or the sanctuary that has made**

**the gold sacred?"** NRSV This third "woe" concerns the binding power of oaths. These were vows or binding promises made to God to dedicate service or contribute property. Jesus had used the term "blind guides" for the Pharisees in 15:14. They should have been guides for the blind but instead were blind themselves. Two examples were given of the ridiculous lengths to which the overly legalistic system had gone—swearing by the temple or the gold, and swearing by the altar or the gift: **"And you say, 'Whoever swears by the altar is bound by nothing, but whoever swears by the gift that is on the altar is bound by the oath.' How blind you are! For which is greater, the gift or the altar that makes the gift sacred?"** NRSV In the Near East, people often would "swear by" something or make oaths. However, they would avoid making oaths using God's name or a sacred object (such as the temple or the altar) because they believed that then the oath was binding. Moses' law kept them from swearing by God's name, so an elaborate system was created to make vows less binding. The closer the basis of the vow was to God's name, the more binding it was. The Jew then would swear an oath by peripheral objects, like the *sanctuary* (meaning the temple) or *the altar* in the temple, so he could break his oath if needed. The idea was that a person would be bound if he swore by something greater than himself; so there was an ascending scale of values and of binding power. Jesus illustrated the minute (and ridiculous) distinctions. They were saying that the *gold* was more sacred because it covered the temple and the *gift* was more sacred because it was offered to God.

---

MAJORING IN THE MINORS
The Pharisees confused the externals for the essentials. Likewise, many Christian churches today make major issues of minor personal choices and divert new Christians from Christ to their own version of cultural essentials.

With a group of friends, describe experiences in your past where minor issues were elevated to major concerns. What happened? How did you respond? How did you recover (or did you?) a relationship to Christ amid the pressure to conform to "the list"?

Many Christians need help recovering from the legacy of the Pharisees that many churches practice today. Let your small group be a place where such help is eagerly given.

---

**23:20-22** **"So whoever swears by the altar, swears by it and by everything on it; and whoever swears by the sanctuary, swears by it and by the one who dwells in it; and whoever swears by**

**heaven, swears by the throne of God and by the one who is seated upon it."** NRSV Jesus had explained that his followers should not need to make any oaths at all, for to do so would imply that their word could not be trusted (5:33-37). The scribes were completely blind (23:16-19)—by attempting to make distinctions in oaths, they had lost sight of the fact that all oaths are made before God and should be equally binding. To try to outwit God by swearing by peripherals cannot work even by their own logic. To swear by the altar and the temple and heaven is still to swear by God, for he is the one who receives the gifts on the altar, lives in the temple, and is enthroned in heaven. In other words, anyone making a vow should fulfill that vow, for all vows are binding. No oath should be made with a loophole.

**23:23** **"Woe to you, scribes and Pharisees, hypocrites! For you tithe mint, dill, and cummin, and have neglected the weightier matters of the law: justice and mercy and faith. It is these you ought to have practiced without neglecting the others."** NRSV The fourth "woe" points to the scribes' and Pharisees' hypocrisy concerning their lack of mercy. There is no evidence in God's law demanding a tithe of cooking herbs or medicinal spices, although the Israelites would tithe agricultural products such as fruit (Leviticus 27:30; Deuteronomy 14:22). But since these spices were edible, the scribes and Pharisees carried the law to its extreme and tithed even *mint, dill, and cummin.* Jesus did not condemn this practice, but he condemned their complete neglect of *the weightier matters of the law,* for example, *justice and mercy and faith.* The hypocrisy of the scribes and Pharisees lay in their careful obedience to the small details of the law while they ignored larger issues that were far more important—such as dealing correctly with other people and building a relationship with God.

It is possible to carefully obey certain details of God's laws but still be disobedient in our general behavior. For example, we could be very precise and faithful about giving 10 percent of our money to the church but refuse to give one minute of our time in helping others. Tithing is important, but giving a tithe does not exempt us from fulfilling God's other directives. The last phrase sums up all the "woes." They ought to *have practiced* the *weightier matters* without *neglecting* others, such as tithing. Jesus was not negating faithfulness to God's law; rather, he was condemning a concern for minor details that replaced true piety and discipleship.

**23:24** **"You blind guides! You strain out a gnat but swallow a camel!"** NRSV How *blind* these religious leaders were—*guides* who were leading the people astray! Jesus used a play on words here—the Aramaic words for "gnat" and "camel" are very similar. The Pharisees strained their wine so they wouldn't accidentally swallow a gnat—an unclean insect according to the law. Meticulous about the details of ceremonial cleanliness, they nevertheless had lost their perspective on the matters of justice, mercy, and faithfulness (23:23), symbolized by the camel. The camel was not only the largest creature in the Near East but was also unclean. As the Pharisees took great care of the smallest details in order to remain pure, they had become unclean in the most important areas. Ceremonially clean on the outside, they had corrupt hearts.

STRAINED OBEDIENCE
What did Jesus have in mind when he used the terms "gnats" and "camels"? His statement identifies three items in each category. "Gnats" were like tithing mint, dill, and cummin. "Camels" were justice, mercy, and faith. Two millenia later, the camels remain the same, but the gnats have undergone a remarkable transformation. Jesus did not condemn meticulous obedience. He affirmed the validity of the tithe, saying that the leaders should have practiced these "without neglecting the others."

An application of Jesus' statement would have to address our wider lack of obedience. We disregard the biblical guidelines from "light to weighty." In our case, Jesus might well say, "You strain out nothing, but swallow everything whole!" We can respond positively by giving more thought and taking more specific action in living out our faith. How and what do we tithe? In what ways are we concerned with justice, mercy, and faith? Do we make them part of conversation? The Christian movement becomes anemic when believers overlook the details of faithful living and forget the priorities God holds dear.

**23:25-26** **"Woe to you, scribes and Pharisees, hypocrites! For you clean the outside of the cup and of the plate, but inside they are full of greed and self-indulgence. You blind Pharisee! First clean the inside of the cup, so that the outside also may become clean."** NRSV The fifth "woe" focuses on inner defilement and the scribes' and Pharisees' failure to distinguish between external "correctness" and internal "cleanness." The Pharisees were so obsessed about having contact with only "clean" things that they not only washed the kitchen utensils but also made certain that the utensils were ceremonially clean. Staying ceremonially clean was the central focus of the Pharisees' lifestyle. Jesus pointed out that they had taken care of the external purification but neglected their own internal defilement, for they were *full of greed* (literally "robbery" and "extortion") *and self-indulgence.* These words describe a strong self-interest that cares only for personal needs. Jesus condemned the Pharisees and religious leaders for outwardly appearing saintly and holy but inwardly remaining full of corruption and greed. If the Pharisees' lives were clean from within, they wouldn't need to worry so much about ceremonial cleanness.

---

SOLVING PROBLEMS
How easy it is for us to keep the outside appearances looking good, while ignoring our inside condition. Is your marriage dissolving? Are your friendships hurting? Is your job on the line? Is your attitude toward life disintegrating?

Two routes toward problem solving lie open to you: (1) Live as though nothing were wrong and behave as though all were well, or (2) get to the core issues and deal with them.

- *Your sense of purpose and direction.* What are you living for? What are you trying to do? Evaluate your life's direction.
- *Your conceit, self-centeredness, and jealousy.* Whom do you really love? Whom do you despise? Get honest about your feelings.
- *Your connection to authority.* Whom are you willing to listen to? to obey? Is God the Lord on the inside of your life, or just window dressing?

Christian friends and pastors can help you. Counselors, too. The issues are too important to gloss over. Make a call today, set up an appointment, and start solving those problems. God has some wonderful surprises ahead for the person who will take a step toward honest change.

---

**3:27-28** **"Woe to you, scribes and Pharisees, hypocrites! For you are like whitewashed tombs, which on the outside look beautiful, but inside they are full of the bones of the dead and of all kinds of filth."** NRSV The sixth "woe" describes the Pharisees as *whitewashed tombs.* Jesus may have been referring to the whitewashing of the tombs before Passover. Tombs were located in various places in the hilly countrysides (usually in caves). While the natives might know the locations of these tombs, pilgrims coming from many other cities and nations would not. To keep them from becoming unclean by inadvertently touching a tomb, the tombs were plainly marked by whitewash. Another possibility is that Jesus was referring to tombs that people had decorated with ornamental plaster and whitewash in order to make them look more attractive. In both cases, the beauty on the outside could not change the death and corruption on the inside.

Building on the image of "clean" in the last "woe" (23:26), Jesus used it to contrast internal and external cleanliness. Like a whitewashed tomb, the religious leaders had put on a *beautiful* appearance, but inside they were *full of the bones of the dead and of all kinds of filth.* Jesus referred to the filth of their desire to put him to death, just as leaders of the past, who followed the Pharisees' way of thinking, had killed the prophets. Jesus prepared for his indictment in the verses to follow. Jesus explained, **"In the same way, on the outside you appear to people as righteous but on the inside you are full of hypocrisy and wickedness."** NIV Jesus called his enemies "hypocrites" in each "woe" because they were supposed to be the holy men and instead were filled with *hypocrisy* (in their wrongful application of God's law and their attempts to make others live up to their standards) and *wickedness* (in their evil deeds, such as those described in 15:5-6 and 23:14).

23:29-32 **"Woe to you, scribes and Pharisees, hypocrites! For you build the tombs of the prophets and decorate the graves of the righteous, and you say, 'If we had lived in the days of our ancestors, we would not have taken part with them in shedding the blood of the prophets.'"** NRSV This final "woe" condemned the scribes and Pharisees for murdering the prophets. Continuing the imagery of the whitewashed tombs in 23:27-28, Jesus centered on the *tombs of the prophets* and *the graves of the righteous.* The graves of saints, prophets, and martyrs were revered. People even decorated the graves of those long dead who seemed worthy of such honor. Herod the Great built a marble monument at Solomon's and David's tombs. The veneration of the martyrs' graves was ironic because these martyrs had, in most cases, been killed by the religious establishment of the day. For example, the prophet Zechariah was executed (2 Chronicles 24:20-22) and the prophet Uriah (or Urijah) was killed (Jeremiah 26:20-23). While the current religious leaders said that they *would not have taken part with* their ancestors in murdering God's prophets, Jesus pointed out that they were no different from their ancestors at all. Jesus explained, **"Thus you testify against yourselves that you are descendants of those who murdered the prophets. Fill up, then, the measure of your ancestors."** NRSV In these words, Jesus showed that the religious leaders were no different from their ancestors who had killed God's messengers, for they were plotting to kill another messenger from God—the Messiah himself. "Fill up, then, the measure of your ancestors" means, "Go ahead and finish what your ancestors started by killing me too" (see 23:34). These words may also reflect the Jewish belief that the kingdom will come when the sins of the people have "filled" the cup of God's wrath.

## THE SEVEN WOES

Jesus mentioned seven ways to provoke God's anger. These are often called the "seven woes." Jesus probably spoke these seven statements about the religious leaders with a mixed tone of judgment and sorrow. They were strong and unforgettable. And they still apply anytime we become so involved in perfecting the practice of religion that we forget God's concern with mercy, real love, and forgiveness.

| | |
|---|---|
| 23:13 | Not letting others enter the kingdom of heaven and not entering yourselves |
| 23:15 | Converting people away from God to be like yourselves |
| 23:16-22 | Blindly leading God's people to follow man-made traditions instead of God's Word |
| 23:23-24 | Involving yourselves in every last detail and ignoring what is really important: justice, mercy, and faith |
| 23:25-26 | Keeping up appearances while your private world is corrupt |
| 23:27-28 | Acting spiritual to cover up sin |
| 23:29-36 | Pretending to have learned from past history, but your present behavior shows you have learned nothing |

Therefore, it is a promise of judgment to come and looks forward to Jesus' further discussion of the future in the Olivet Discourse (chapter 24).

**23:33** **"You snakes! You brood of vipers! How will you escape being condemned to hell?"** NIV In 3:7 and 12:34, these leaders were also called *brood of vipers*. Here Jesus also added *snakes* to give his accusation greater impact. By using this description, Jesus called the scribes and Pharisees contemptible and obnoxious creatures. Their punishment evokes the imagery of Gehenna, *hell* and its eternal fires. There will be no escape for these men, for they had already cast aside any hope of salvation.

**23:34** **"Therefore I am sending you prophets and wise men and teachers. Some of them you will kill and crucify; others you will flog in your synagogues and pursue from town to town."** NIV These *prophets, wise men,* and *teachers* were probably leaders in the early church who eventually were persecuted, scourged, and killed, just as Jesus predicted. Flogging in the synagogues was a common Jewish punishment. The people of Jesus' generation said they would not act as their fathers did in killing the prophets whom God had sent to them (23:30), but they were about to kill the Messiah himself and his faithful followers. Thus, they would become guilty of all the righteous blood shed through the centuries.

**23:35-36** **"And so upon you will come all the righteous blood that has been shed on earth, from the blood of righteous Abel to the blood of Zechariah son of Berekiah, whom you murdered between the temple and the altar."** NIV Jesus gave two examples of Old Testament martyrdom. *Abel* was the first martyr (Genesis 4); *Zechariah* was the last mentioned in the Hebrew Bible, which ended with 2 Chronicles. Zechariah is a classic example of a man of God who was killed by those who claimed to be God's people (see 2 Chronicles 24:20-21). In both cases, the call for vengeance is explicit (Genesis 4:10; 2 Chronicles 24:22). The *righteous blood* of the prophets, also mentioned in 23:30, now came *upon* them, for Jesus said, **"Truly I tell you, all this will come upon this generation."** NRSV The current religious establishment would be guilty of all of their deaths, for they would be guilty of murdering the Messiah and would face judgment for that act. The destruction of Jerusalem in 70 A.D. was a partial fulfillment of Jesus' words.

## JESUS GRIEVES OVER JERUSALEM AGAIN / 23:37-39 / **199**

These verses bridge the gap between Jesus' denunciation of the Judaism of the religious leaders (that had become horribly corrupt) and his explicit prediction of the destruction of the temple in chapter 24.

**23:37** **"O Jerusalem, Jerusalem, the one who kills the prophets and stones those who are sent to her! How often I wanted to gather your children together, as a hen gathers her chicks under her wings, but you were not willing!"** NKJV Jerusalem was the capital city of God's chosen people, the ancestral home of David, Israel's greatest king, and the location of the temple, the earthly dwelling place of God. It was intended to be the center of worship of the true God and a symbol of justice to all people. But Jerusalem had become blind to God and insensitive to human need. Jerusalem here stands for all the Jewish people, but this prophecy specifically looks to the city's destruction. The Jewish leaders had stoned and killed the prophets and others whom God had sent to the nation to bring them back to him. By their constant rejection of God's messengers, they had sealed their fate.

Jesus *wanted to gather* the nation and bring it to repentance, but the people *were not willing*. Here we see the depth of Jesus' feelings for lost people and for his beloved city that would soon be destroyed. Jesus took no pleasure in denouncing the religious establishment or in prophesying the coming destruction of the city and the people that rejected him. He had come to save, but they would not let him.

---

GOD'S SOFT HEART
Matthew 23 is so full of denunciation and honest criticism that some find it hard to believe these were Jesus' words—they seem so out of character. But at the end of these "woes," Jesus shows how tenderly he cares for the very people whose religious attitudes he has just criticized. God's plan always includes love, reconciliation, and peace.

Jesus also wants to protect us if we will just come to him. Many times we hurt and don't know where to turn. We reject Christ's help because we don't think he can give us what we need. But who knows our needs better than our Creator? Those who turn to Jesus will find that he helps and comforts as no one else can. Never think that you are so bad, so undeserving, so much a failure that God could not possibly love you. If such thoughts trouble you, read Matthew 23 again. It's filled with bad guys, but Jesus would gather all of them in. He wants to gather you too. Never doubt that.

---

**3:38-39** **"Look, your house is left to you desolate. For I tell you, you will not see me again until you say, 'Blessed is he who comes in the name of the Lord.'"** NIV Jesus may have been alluding to Jeremiah 12:7, "I will forsake my house, abandon my inheritance; I will give the one I love into the hands of her enemies" (NIV). Jeremiah had prophesied the coming destruction of the temple by the Babylonians. The nation's sin sealed their punishment, and God's presence left the temple. When Jesus Christ came, God himself again stood in the temple. But the people's refusal to accept him would have severe consequences, for he would again leave the temple. The temple stood for the people's relationship with God; a desolate temple meant separation from God.

The words "blessed is he who comes in the name of the Lord" echo the words of the crowd during Jesus' triumphal entry into the city (21:9), taken from Psalm 118:26. The words "until you say" could be related to what is said in Romans 11:25-26, where it is said that some of the Jewish nation will recognize Jesus as their true Messiah.

# Matthew 24

**24:1 As Jesus came out of the temple and was going away, his disciples came to point out to him the buildings of the temple.**<sup>NRSV</sup> Chapter 24 of Matthew is the second part of the fifth and final discourse that began in chapter 23. This chapter contains a conversation between Jesus and his disciples as they left the temple and began their walk back to Bethany where they were spending their nights. A casual remark by a disciple led Jesus to make a startling prophetic statement about the fate of the magnificent temple. The group paused on the Mount of Olives, where they could glance back across the valley toward Jerusalem. Perhaps they watched the sun set behind the ancient city. Jesus and the disciples had just left the temple (this may have been either Tuesday or Wednesday evening of the week before the Crucifixion). This was Jesus' last visit to the temple area. He would do no more preaching or public teaching.

One of the disciples pointed out to Jesus the temple buildings, remarking on their incredible beauty (Mark 13:1). Although no one knows exactly what the temple looked like, it must have been magnificent, for in its time it was considered one of the architectural wonders of the world. This was not Solomon's temple, for it had been destroyed by the Babylonians in the seventh century B.C. (2 Kings 25:8-10). This temple had been built by Ezra after the return from exile in the sixth century B.C. (Ezra 6:14-15). Then it had been desecrated by the Seleucids in the second century B.C., reconsecrated by the Maccabees soon afterward, and enormously expanded by Herod the Great after that.

About fifteen years before Jesus was born (around 20 B.C.), Herod the Great had begun a massive reconstruction project to help the Jews remodel and beautify their temple. Herod had no interest in the Jews' God, but he wanted to stay on friendly terms with his subjects as well as build what he thought would be a lasting monument to his dynasty. Though the Jews disliked Herod, they were very proud of the temple. At this time, the temple was still under construction; Herod's reconstruction project would not be finished until about A.D. 64 (just a few years before it was destroyed by Rome).

The temple was impressive, covering about one-sixth of the land area of the ancient city of Jerusalem. It was not one building, but a majestic mixture of porches, colonnades, separate small edifices, and courts surrounding the temple proper. Next to the inner temple, where the sacred objects were kept and the sacrifices offered, there was a large area called the Court of the Gentiles (this was where the money changers and merchants had their booths). Outside these courts stretched long porches. Solomon's porch was 1,562 feet long, and the royal porch was decorated with 160 columns stretching along its 921-foot length. The disciples gazed in wonder at marble pillars 40 feet high, carved from a single solid stone. The temple's foundation was so solid that it is believed that some of the original footings remain to this day. The Jews were convinced of the permanence of this magnificent structure, not only because of the stability of construction but also because it represented God's presence among them.

---

BEHIND APPEARANCES
The disciples were awed by the temple complex—so gleaming, so expansive, such a tribute to architecture, construction skills, and engineering talent. But Jesus saw the complex as a symbol of the emptiness of religion without God.

We stand in awe of certain structures: the Eiffel Tower, the Capitol in Washington, ancient Greek monuments. They speak of perseverance, ingenuity, and endurance. But Jesus sees the technology we treasure as a passing glimmer. The real truth to history and life lies in God's revelation of his kingdom. And Jesus' greatest desire is that we know and believe that truth.

---

**24:2 Then he asked them, "You see all these, do you not? Truly I tell you, not one stone will be left here upon another; all will be thrown down."** NRSV Jesus acknowledged the great buildings but then made a startling statement: This wonder of the world would be completely destroyed. As in the days of the prophet Jeremiah, the destruction of the Jews' beloved temple would be God's punishment for turning away from him. Jeremiah had spoken God's words to the rebellious nation, "I will make Jerusalem a heap of ruins, a haunt of jackals" (Jeremiah 9:11 NIV). Jerusalem had been attacked and leveled before. Here Jesus prophesied that Jerusalem and the beautiful temple would again be completely destroyed. This happened only a few years later when the Romans sacked Jerusalem in A.D. 70. The Romans fulfilled Jesus' words to the letter. After fire raged through the temple, Emperor Titus ordered the leveling of the whole area, so no part of the original walls or buildings remained. Titus considered this as punishment for the Jewish rebellion in A.D. 66.

Gazing at the massive stones, the disciples surely found it difficult to believe that not one of the stones would be left on top of another. Because the temple symbolized God's presence among them, the Jews would be horrified to see it destroyed.

The purpose of Jesus' words was both theological and prophetic. The sovereign judgment of God was to fall upon his unbelieving people; and just as Jesus as Lord of the temple had proclaimed its purification, here he predicted its destruction.

**24:3 As Jesus was sitting on the Mount of Olives, the disciples came to him privately. "Tell us," they said, "when will this happen, and what will be the sign of your coming and of the end of the age?"** [NIV] The *Mount of Olives* rises above Jerusalem to the east. As Jesus was leaving the city to return to Bethany for the night, he would have crossed the Kidron Valley, and then he would have headed up the slope of the Mount of Olives. From this slope, he and the disciples could look down into the city and see the temple. The prophet Zechariah predicted that the Messiah would stand on that very mountain when he returned to set up his eternal kingdom (Zechariah 14:1-4). This place evoked questions about the future, so it was natural for the disciples to ask Jesus when he would come in power and what they could expect at that time.

Mark records that the inner circle of disciples (this time with Andrew added—Andrew was Peter's brother; James and John were brothers) came to Jesus privately (Mark 13:3-4). Matthew did not distinguish the four. Probably all the disciples heard Jesus' answer. They wanted to understand what Jesus meant and when this terrible destruction would happen.

The disciples' question had two parts. They wanted to know (1) *When will this happen?* (referring to the destruction of the temple) and (2) *What will be the sign of your coming and of the end of the age?* The second part of their question referred to the Messiah's reign in God's kingdom. In the disciples' minds, one event would occur immediately after the other. They expected the Messiah to inaugurate his kingdom soon, and they wanted to know the sign that it was about to arrive.

Jesus gave them a prophetic picture of that time, including events leading up to it. He also talked about far future events connected with the last days and his second coming when he would return to earth to judge all people. As many of the Old Testament prophets had done, Jesus predicted both near and distant events without putting them in chronological order. The coming destruction of Jerusalem and the temple only foreshadowed a future destruction that would precede Christ's return.

In order to understand the prophecy, picture yourself standing on a mountaintop looking across a distant mountain range. The mountain peaks appear to be next to each other, while in reality they are miles apart because of the valleys in between. Jesus' prophecy pictured "mountain peaks" (significant future events), looking to us as though they would occur together, when, in reality, they may be thousands of years apart. Some of the disciples lived to see the destruction of Jerusalem in A.D. 70, while some of the events Jesus spoke of have not yet—to this day—occurred. But the truth of Jesus' prediction regarding Jerusalem assured the disciples (and assures us) that everything else he predicted will also happen.

There are three primary views on the Olivet discourse:

1. All of chapter 24 describes *both* the destruction of Jerusalem and the last days before Christ's return;
2. The first part of the prophecy deals only with the destruction of Jerusalem (24:4-35), and then the last part switches to the return of Christ (24:36-51);
3. All of chapter 24 gives a prediction only of the destruction of Jerusalem; it says nothing about the return of Christ.

The first view seems most likely: We may interpret the Olivet discourse, as with most Old Testament prophecies, as having a double fulfillment. Jesus was predicting the destruction of Jerusalem *and* the end times. The references are interwoven so that themes from both the fall of Jerusalem and the Second Coming occur as one expression of God's judgment on unbelievers and deliverance for believers. However, in the first part of the prophecy, the destruction of Jerusalem is more prominent; in the second part, the last days before Christ's return are more prominent.

**24:4-5** **Jesus answered them, "Beware that no one leads you astray. For many will come in my name, saying, 'I am the Messiah!' and they will lead many astray."**[NRSV] Jesus first answered the disciples' second question about the end of the age and the coming kingdom. The disciples wondered what sign would reveal these things, but Jesus warned them against false messiahs: *Beware that no one leads you astray.* "Beware" stresses watchfulness and vigilance. Jesus knew that if the disciples looked for signs, they would be susceptible to deception. There would be many false prophets (24:24) with counterfeit signs of spiritual power and authority. Jesus predicted that before his return, many believers would be misled by false teachers coming in his name—that is, claiming to be Christ. Second Thessalonians 2:3-10, which describes a man of lawlessness who will lead people astray, reflects the teaching of this passage. Throughout the first century, many such deceivers arose (see Acts 5:36-37; 8:9-11; 2 Timothy 3; 2 Peter 2; 1 John 2:18; 4:1-3).

In every generation since Christ's resurrection, individuals have claimed to be the Christ or to know exactly when Jesus would return (remember Jim Jones, Sun Myung Moon, and David Koresh?). Obviously, no one else has been Christ, and no one has been right about the timing of the Second Coming. According to Scripture, the one clear sign of Christ's return will be his unmistakable appearance in the clouds, which will be seen by all people (Matthew 24:30; Revelation 1:7). In other words, believers never have to wonder whether a certain person is the Messiah. When Jesus returns, believers will know beyond a doubt because he will be evident to all.

---

SIGNS OF THE TIMES
The disciples asked Jesus for the sign of his coming and of the end of the age. Jesus' first response was "Watch out that no one deceives you." The fact is that whenever we look for signs, we become very susceptible to deception. Many "false prophets" (24:11, 24) have counterfeit signs of spiritual power and authority. The only sure way to keep from being deceived is to focus on Christ and his words. Don't look for special signs, and don't spend time looking at other people. Look at Christ.

---

**24:6-8** **"You will hear of wars and rumors of wars, but see to it that you are not alarmed. Such things must happen, but the end is still to come. Nation will rise against nation, and kingdom against kingdom. There will be famines and earthquakes in various places. All these are the beginning of birth pains."** NIV
In these words, Jesus prepared his followers for a difficult passage of time before his return. A key phrase in this verse comforts all believers: *see to it that you are not alarmed.* As political situations worsen, as wars ravage the world, Jesus' disciples and all his followers should not be afraid that somehow God has lost control or that his promises will not come true. Just as false messiahs and religious frauds come and go, so do political and natural crises. Even when the world seems to be in chaos, God is in control. *Such things must happen* as part of God's divine plan. However, the wars and rumors of wars do not signal *the end* (the end of the world). The disciples probably assumed that the

temple would only be destroyed at the end of the age as part of God establishing his new kingdom. Jesus taught that horrible events would happen, *but the end is still to come.*

The nations at war and the earth's turmoil, revealed in increased earthquakes and famines, would also not signal the end. Instead, this will be but *the beginning of birth pains;* in other words, these will be preliminary sufferings. Jesus' words indicated to the eager disciples that there would be a span of time before the end of the age and the coming kingdom—it would not come that week, or immediately upon Jesus' resurrection, or even right after the destruction of Jerusalem. First, much suffering would occur as a part of life on earth, while history would move toward a single, final, God-planned goal—the creation of a new earth and a new kingdom (Revelation 21:1-3). The description of sufferings as "birth pains" is a typical biblical metaphor for the beginning of prekingdom travail and suffering (see Isaiah 13:6-8; 26:16-18; Jeremiah 4:31; 22:20-23; Hosea 13:9-13).

While we must never trivialize suffering, all these troubles must not make Christians alarmed. Because Jesus has warned us about them, we know that they must precede the arrival of God's glorious kingdom. Preachers on prophecy who count earthquakes in order to determine when Jesus will return have not read Jesus' words carefully. Everything will happen according to God's divine plan. Our responsibility is to be prepared, to endure, and to continue to preach the Good News to all nations (24:14).

**24:9 "Then you will be handed over to be persecuted and put to death, and you will be hated by all nations because of me."** NIV Jesus personalized his prophecy by explaining that the disciples themselves would face severe persecution; thus, they must be on their guard in order to stay true to the faith. Mark's account is longer; Matthew added a repetition of the danger of apostasy previously stated in 24:4 and reiterated the theme of persecution as a necessary aspect of discipleship (see 5:10; 10:16). As the early church began to grow, most of the disciples experienced this kind of persecution. Luke recorded many of these persecutions in the book of Acts. Being "handed over to be persecuted" refers to the local Jewish courts held in the synagogues (smaller versions of the Sanhedrin in Jerusalem). Jesus didn't say it, but the disciples would learn that loyalty to Christ meant separation from Judaism. Two of the disciples listening to Jesus (Peter and John, Mark 13:3) faced the Sanhedrin not long after Jesus' resurrection (Acts 4:1-12). At that time, they certainly remembered these words of Jesus. *Because of* the disciples' belief in Jesus, the Jews would denounce them as traitors or heretics and pass down the

sentence right in their synagogue. They even would condemn
Christians to death.

---

REMEMBER
You may not be facing intense persecution now, but Christians
in other parts of the world are. As you hear about Christians
suffering for their faith, remember that they are your brothers
and sisters in Christ. Pray for them. Ask God what you can do
to help them in their troubles. When one part suffers, the whole
body suffers. But when all the parts join together to ease the
suffering, the whole body benefits (1 Corinthians 12:26).

---

Not only would the disciples face hatred from religious and
civil leaders and their own families, they would be *hated by all
nations.* For a Jew to convert to Christianity would soon become
very dangerous because it would lead to hatred and ostracism.
And Jesus' words looked forward to a time when hatred of Christians would grow. As believers, we should not be shocked or surprised that the world hates us (see John 15:18-21). On the other
hand, we shouldn't be overly suspicious or totally withdraw from
the world (see 1 Corinthians 5:9-11). To believe in Jesus and stay
strong to the end (24:13) will take perseverance because our faith
will be challenged and opposed. Severe trials will sift true Christians from phony believers.

---

IT GETS MESSY
If you're the type who likes harmony in all relationships, you've
got problems ahead. Jesus indicates in many ways how prob-
lematic relationships will get before he comes again.
- People you considered Christian brothers will turn against you.
- Admiration for your faith will give way to tolerance, then to
  spite, then to hate.
- The justice system you believed would protect you will
  decide to oppress you, then threaten you, and then exter-
  minate you.
What's to be done? Stay faithful to Jesus, loyal to all who
call him Lord, true to your calling as best you understand it.
Stay alert and focused. God's Word is truth, and God will see
you through.

---

**24:10 "Then many will fall away, and they will betray one another and
hate one another."** [NRSV] Jesus warned that such severe persecution
may lead to the defection (falling away) of some members (the verb
translated "fall away" is also used in 5:29-30; 13:21; 18:6-9). It will
lead some to *betray one another and hate one another.* The fear and

persecution will be so intense that people will betray and hate in order to keep themselves safe. It will not be popular or respectable to be a Christian. It will be dangerous.

**24:11 "And many false prophets will arise and lead many astray."** NRSV Not only will believers face defection and betrayal from within the body, but also *false prophets will arise* and their teachings will *lead many astray.* The Old Testament frequently mentions false prophets (see 2 Kings 3:13; Isaiah 44:25; Jeremiah 23:16; Ezekiel 13:2, 3; Micah 3:5; Zechariah 13:2). False prophets claimed to receive messages from God, but they said what the people wanted to hear, even when the nation was not following God. We have false prophets today, popular leaders who tell people what they want to hear—such as "God wants you to be rich," "Do whatever your desires tell you," or "There is no such thing as sin or hell." Jesus said false teachers would come, and he warned his disciples, as he warns us, not to listen to their dangerous words. Second Thessalonians 2:3 mentions "the rebellion" (or the apostasy) when false teachers will use the persecution to influence others to lose hope in the Second Coming or even to abandon their profession of faith.

---

THE FIRST DECEPTION
Truth has many competitors. Each presents its case; each tries for its audience; each has its reasons and attractions. Part of our calling as Christians is to explore the competition, to sift truth from error, to discover, and to understand. Jesus warns us not to displace truth with an impostor.

To whom do you look when you want the truth? In the face of many claims, what's your authority? It is the most important quest of your life. How do you know who speaks truth and who speaks a mix of truth and falsehood? Truth matches the teaching of Jesus Christ—the one who is truth. As God's Son, Jesus has God's power and authority; thus, his words should be our final authority. If a person's teaching is true, it will agree with Jesus' teachings. Test everything you hear against Jesus' words, and you will not be led astray. Don't be hasty to seek advice and guidance from merely human sources and thereby neglect Christ's message.

---

**24:12 "And because of the increase of lawlessness, the love of many will grow cold."** NRSV In this context, this *lawlessness* (also translated "wickedness") will bring judgment to the rebels. It is a way of life totally rejecting God's law. (The Antichrist in 2 Thessalonians 2:3, 8 is called "the man of lawlessness.") False teaching and loose morals bring a particularly destructive disease—the loss of true love for God and others. Love grows *cold* when sin turns our focus on ourselves and our desires.

---

**GREAT TRIBULATION**
Is tribulation to be a short period of intense persecution somewhere in the future, or what? The debate over the time of the Tribulation is a tribute to the church's desire to understand Jesus' words clearly. While debaters hash out the meaning and implications of terms, we have to live as committed believers.

Clearly, some Christians in some parts of the world face intense and life-threatening persecution. Vicious reprisals against entire populations (such as the war in Rwanda) and ongoing, meaningless carnage (such as Liberia's and Bosnia's civil wars) have resulted in the deaths of many believers, some of whom sought refuge in churches and were killed while praying. For these people, great tribulation struck during their lifetimes, and they were called to endure.

In the comfortable and stable West, where religious freedom is written into the fabric of our laws, we cannot imagine such a fate. But impossible things have a way of turning out, and Jesus warns against spiritual unpreparedness. We must be steadfast in our faith, remaining loyal to Christ and to God's truth. We must reject the temptation to rebellion and lawlessness. Above all, we must not let our love for God turn cold.

---

**24:13** **"But the one who endures to the end will be saved."** NRSV Only Jesus' faithful followers will enter God's kingdom. The stress in this verse is not on endurance, but on salvation; the verse offers both a promise and a warning. "The end" refers to the consummation of the kingdom at Christ's return. This became a precious promise to believers who were struggling during intense persecution throughout the history of the church.

Enduring to the end does not earn salvation for us; it marks us as already saved. The assurance of our salvation will keep us going through times of persecution. While some will suffer and some will die, none of Jesus' followers will suffer spiritual or eternal loss.

---

**STAND FIRM**
Jesus predicted that his followers would be severely persecuted by those who hated what he stood for. In terrible persecutions, however, they could have hope, knowing that salvation was theirs. Times of trial serve to sift true believers from false ones. When you are pressured to give up and turn your back on Christ, don't do it. Remember the benefits of standing firm, and continue to live for Christ.

---

**24:14** **"And this gospel of the kingdom will be preached in all the world as a witness to all the nations, and then the end will come."** NKJV Jesus said that before his return, the *gospel of the kingdom* (the message of salvation) would be preached throughout the world. Some have misconstrued Jesus' predictive prophecy; it does not necessarily mean that every last tribe *must* hear the gospel before Christ returns. But this was the disciples' mission—and it is ours. Jesus talked about the end times and final judgment to emphasize to his followers the urgency of spreading the Good News of salvation to everyone. Although persecution is inevitable, Jesus' followers must never give up in their mission to preach the Good News to *all the nations* and to get the Word of God to every language group. Jesus predicted a great missionary expansion to all the world before he would return.

By the time Matthew's readers would hear these words, Jesus' prediction had already begun to be fulfilled. Reaching all the nations occurred at Pentecost (Acts 2:5-11) and was spreading to all the world (Romans 1:5, 8; 15:19; Colossians 1:6, 23; 1 Timothy 3:16).

**24:15-16** **"So when you see standing in the holy place 'the abomination that causes desolation,' spoken of through the prophet Daniel—let the reader understand—then let those who are in Judea flee to the mountains."** NIV Jesus warned against seeking signs, but as a final part of his answer to the disciples' second question (24:3), he gave them the ultimate event that would signal coming destruction. The "abomination that causes desolation" (also translated "desolating sacrilege") refers to the desecration of the temple by God's enemies. The phrase "let the reader understand" was a sort of code. A more precise explanation may have been dangerous for the believers if the letter were to fall into the wrong hands, so Matthew urged his readers to understand Jesus' words in light of the prophecy from the Old Testament prophet Daniel (see Daniel 9:27; 11:31; 12:11). The "abomination that causes desolation" refers to pagan idolatry and sacrifice (see Deuteronomy 29:16-18; 2 Kings 16:3-4; 23:12-14). The "abomination" (pagan idolatry) that would occur in the temple itself would cause the temple to be desolated and abandoned.

The first fulfillment of Daniel's prophecy occurred in 168 B.C. by Antiochus Epiphanes when he sacrificed a pig to Zeus on the sacred temple altar and made Judaism an outlaw religion, punishable by death. This incited the Maccabean wars.

The second fulfillment occurred when Jesus' prediction of the destruction of the temple (24:2) came true. In just a few years (A.D. 70), the Roman army would destroy Jerusalem and desecrate the temple. Matthew's Jewish audience, under Roman oppression for many years, understood the sacrilege that would occur. The Roman army was notorious for its disregard for the religious life and freedom of the peoples it conquered.

Based on 24:21, the third fulfillment is yet to come. Jesus' words look forward to the end times and to the Antichrist. In Mark's Gospel, the Greek reads, "the desolating sacrilege set up where *he* should not be" (Mark 13:14). In the end times, the Antichrist will commit the ultimate sacrilege by setting up an image of himself in the temple and ordering everyone to worship it (2 Thessalonians 2:4; Revelation 13:14-15).

Many of Jesus' followers would live during the time of the destruction of Jerusalem and the temple in A.D. 70. Jesus warned his followers to get out of Jerusalem and Judea and to *flee to the mountains* across the Jordan River when they saw the temple being profaned. The Jewish historian Josephus wrote that from A.D. 66, Jewish Zealots clashed with the Romans. Many people realized that rebellion would bring the wrath of the Empire, so they fled to Pella, a town located in the mountains across the Jordan River. As Jesus had said, this proved to be their protection, for when the Roman army swept in, the nation and its capital city were destroyed.

**24:17-20** **"The one on the housetop must not go down to take what is in the house; the one in the field must not turn back to get a coat. Woe to those who are pregnant and to those who are nursing infants in those days! Pray that your flight may not be in winter or on a sabbath."** NRSV There is undoubtedly a dual reference both to the historical present and to the distant future. First, this section prophesied the profaning of the temple by the Roman armies. The Jewish historian Josephus witnessed these very events and wrote about them in great detail in his *Antiquities* (13.140). Josephus believed that it fulfilled a prophecy regarding the desecration of the temple by Jews (Daniel 9:27). Just before the Roman victory in A.D. 70, the army of Jewish Zealots, driven back into Jerusalem, took over the temple and desecrated it with their presence and their actions. The flight with haste, then, may focus on going to the mountains. The problem with fleeing *in winter* was the swollen rivers that would make passage difficult across the usually small streams, as well as across the Jordan River, as Jews made their way out of Judea. The reference to *the housetop* points to the construction of homes where a flat roof would be used like a family room. People would sit on their housetops and work or converse; in the evening, they would enjoy the cooler air on the roof. Jesus told them to get away immediately (using the outside staircase), not worrying about their possessions.

The destruction of the temple would also be a sign pointing to the final desecration that precedes the second coming of Christ (2 Thessalonians 2:4). They could be fleeing the judgment of God that would fall upon the land of Judea, or fleeing from the Antichrist.

During this terrible event, the people were to leave immediately, not taking time to pack bags or even to return to the city to get a coat (a most basic necessity). They should leave everything behind when they flee from the coming crisis. Jesus expressed sympathy and concern for those who would have difficulty fleeing because they were pregnant or had small children. Jesus told the disciples to pray that the crisis would not break in winter because that would make it difficult for everyone to get away. Matthew added *or on a sabbath* for his Jewish audience. The Sabbath law stated that a person could not go more than two thousand cubits (1,050 yards). They should pray for nothing to hinder their flight. These people literally would be running for their lives.

**24:21** **"For then there will be great distress, unequaled from the beginning of the world until now—and never to be equaled again."** NIV Jesus gave this warning to get out quickly *for then there will be great distress, unequaled from the beginning of the world.* The prophet Daniel wrote, "At that time Michael, the great prince who protects your people, will arise. There will be a time of distress such as has not happened from the beginning of nations until then. But at that time your people—everyone whose name is found written in the book—will be delivered" (Daniel 12:1 NIV). Great suffering is in store for God's people throughout the years ahead. This way of describing the future is also used by Jeremiah (Jeremiah 30:7). The time would be evil and filled with suffering. This language may sound like an exaggeration, but it is not unusual in Scripture when describing an impending disaster. The Jewish historian Josephus recorded that when the Romans sacked Jerusalem and devastated Judea, one hundred thousand Jews were taken prisoner and another 1.1 million died by slaughter and starvation.

Jesus' words could be taken as referring to the destruction of Jerusalem by the Romans in A.D. 70, but they are so emphatic and clear that they must point ultimately to the final period of tribulation at the end of the age because, as Jesus stated, nothing like it had ever been seen or would ever be seen again. Yet the great suffering is tempered by a great promise of hope for true believers.

**24:22** **"If those days had not been cut short, no one would survive,**
**but for the sake of the elect those days will be shortened."** NIV
Many interpreters conclude that Jesus, talking about the end
times, was telescoping near-future and far-future events, as the
Old Testament prophets had done. Many of these persecutions
have already occurred; more are yet to come. While a certain
amount of persecution happened in the destruction of Jerusalem,
Jesus may also have envisioned the persecution (tribulation) of
believers throughout the subsequent years. The persecution will
be so severe that *those days had* to be *cut short*—that is, if they
did not have a specific ending time, *no one would survive.* This
refers to physical survival (as opposed to 24:13, which speaks of
spiritual survival). The time would be cut short *for the sake of the
elect,* God's chosen people. The shortening of the time will limit
their duration so that the destruction will not wipe out God's
people and thus their mission. God is ultimately in charge of history and will not allow evil to exceed the bounds he has set. Jesus
had predicted the Cross for himself; here he was predicting persecution, death, and resurrection for his disciples.

There are three main views regarding the Tribulation, and each
view interprets this verse differently:

1. *Pretribulationism* believes that the "elect" will be Jews who
   will have returned to the Lord in a national revival and will
   join the believers (taken to heaven first) at the end of three and
   a half years.
2. *Midtribulationism* believes that the "elect" refers to the church
   (all true Christians, both Jews and Gentiles). Jesus will return
   in the middle of the Tribulation (mid-Tribulation rapture), as
   recorded in Revelation 11:7-14, where the Tribulation seems to
   be interrupted after "three and a half days" or halfway through
   the tribulation period.
3. *Posttribulationism* believes that the "elect" will be the church
   (all true Christians, both Jews and Gentiles) who will persevere
   throughout the tribulation period, which will be ended by
   God for their sakes (their rapture would occur at the end, see
   Revelation 19).

Who are the "elect"? In the Old Testament, "elect" refers to
Israel, particularly those who are faithful to God (see 1 Chronicles
16:13; Psalm 105:43; Isaiah 65:9, 15; Daniel 12:1). In the New
Testament, "elect" refers to the church—all believers (Romans
8:33; Colossians 3:12; 2 Timothy 2:10; 1 Peter 1:1-2). In this verse,
the words "elect" and "chosen" refer not to Old Testament Jews
but to all faithful believers, whether Jews or Gentiles. Paul wrote,

"For those whom he foreknew he also predestined to be conformed to the image of his Son. . . . Those whom he predestined he also called; and those whom he called he also justified; and those whom he justified he also glorified" (Romans 8:29-30 NRSV). Some believe that these verses mean that before the beginning of the world, God chose certain people to receive his gift of salvation. Others believe that God foreknew those who would respond to him and upon those he set his mark (predestined). What is clear is that God's purpose for people was not an afterthought; it was settled before the foundation of the world.

When the time of suffering comes, the important point for the disciples and all believers to remember is that God is in control. Persecution will occur, but God knows about it and controls how long it will take place. The main thrust of Jesus' teaching is to show God's mercy toward the faithful and to show that God is loving and sovereign. He will not forget his people.

**24:23-25** **"Then if anyone says to you, 'Look! Here is the Messiah!' or 'There he is!'—do not believe it. For false messiahs and false prophets will appear and produce great signs and omens, to lead astray, if possible, even the elect. Take note, I have told you beforehand."** NRSV In times of persecution even strong believers will find it difficult to be loyal. They will so much want the Messiah to come that they will grasp any rumor that he has arrived. Jehovah's Witnesses teach that Christ has already returned. Religious groups in India teach that certain leaders have been reincarnations (avatars) of Jesus Christ. To keep believers from being deceived by false messiahs, Jesus explained that his return will be unmistakable (24:30); no one will doubt that it is he. If believers have to be told that the Messiah has come, then he hasn't. Christ's coming will be obvious to everyone.

Most *false messiahs* build their following from faithful church attendees who have been led astray. Often the cult leader's appeal is based on "I am the true way," "I will fulfill the expectations you have," or "I will be the power you need." Church leaders must be alert and prevent weak Christians from being drawn into such cults.

These false leaders *will appear and produce great signs and omens*. Jesus warned his disciples, as he warns us, not to be swayed by whatever signs and miracles false leaders might produce. These false messiahs will be able to perform great signs designed to convince people that their claims are true. But their "power" will be by trickery or from Satan, not from God. Both false and true prophets can work miracles (see Deuteronomy 13:1-5; 2 Thessalonians 2:1-12; 1 John 4:1-3; Revelation 13:11-18).

Yet will they be so convincing that they might even lead the elect astray (for explanation of "elect," see 24:22)? Is it possible for Christians to be deceived? Yes, and Jesus pointed out the danger (see also Galatians 3:1). The arguments and proofs from deceivers in the end times will be so convincing that it will be difficult to be faithful. If we are prepared, Jesus says, we can remain faithful. With the Holy Spirit's help, the elect will not give in and will be able to discern that what the deceivers say is false.

The disciples had been given special knowledge about the coming kingdom, as well as the coming crises and deceptions preceding it. This gave them all the more reason to *take note* (or "be alert") so as to be aware of the deceptions. While they might not be taken in, they would be responsible to help keep others from being deceived. Spiritual vigilance is a major theme of Jesus' discourse to his disciples as he sat on the Mount of Olives. Jesus' warnings about false teachers still hold true. Upon close examination, it becomes clear that many promises that leaders make don't agree with God's message in the Bible. Only a solid foundation in God's Word can equip us to perceive the errors and distortions in false teaching.

## JESUS TELLS ABOUT HIS RETURN / 24:26-35 / **202**

**24:26-27** **"So, if they say to you, 'Look! He is in the wilderness,' do not go out. If they say, 'Look! He is in the inner rooms,' do not believe it. For as the lightning comes from the east and flashes as far as the west, so will be the coming of the Son of Man."** NRSV Jesus had already warned his followers "beforehand" that false messiahs and false prophets will come and attempt to lead many astray (24:23-25). Others will think they have found the messiah and will try to convince people by saying that he can be found in a certain place. The "wilderness" refers to prophetic expectation regarding an Elijah-prophet, similar to John the Baptist, who would come out of the wilderness (Isaiah 40:3; Malachi 4:5). The "inner rooms" refers to the expectation of a "hidden Messiah" who would appear suddenly, as if emerging from the inner rooms of a large house. Jesus explained that, by contrast, his coming would be as obvious and unmistakable as a flash of lightning bursting across the sky. Lightning may flash in one part of the sky and be seen just as clearly in another part; *so will be the coming of the Son of Man.*

**24:28** **"Wherever there is a carcass, there the vultures will gather."** NIV
This verse, probably quoting a well-known proverb of the culture,
looks to the Second Coming as a time of judgment. Jesus was
telling his audience that, just as you know a carcass must be nearby
if you see vultures circling overhead, so his coming will be unmis-
takenly marked by various signs. This illustration may picture an
invading army (the Romans in A.D. 70 and the Lord's army in Revelation 19:17-19) swarming over its prey.

**24:29** **"Immediately after the suffering of those days the sun will be
darkened, and the moon will not give its light; the stars will fall
from heaven, and the powers of heaven will be shaken."** NRSV
The phrase "of those days" signaled that Jesus was talking specifically about the end times (see similar wording in the Prophets:
Isaiah 34:4; Jeremiah 3:16, 18; 31:29; Joel 3:1; Zechariah 8:23).
After the time of tribulation, nature itself would experience change.
As taught in Romans 8 and 2 Peter 3, the entire universe had
become involved in humanity's fallen predicament; thus, the entire
universe will be changed when humanity is changed.

The changes in the heavens will be an intended contrast to
the pseudo "signs and omens" (24:24) of the false messiahs.
There will be a variety of changes—the *sun* going dark, the
*moon* not being seen, *stars* falling, heavenly bodies being
shaken. These words also recall the words of the prophets
(Isaiah 13:10; Joel 2:10-11). What Jesus described here, John
saw in his vision of the end times recorded in Revelation: "I
watched as he opened the sixth seal. There was a great earthquake. The sun turned black . . . , the whole moon turned blood
red, and the stars in the sky fell to earth. . . . The sky receded
like a scroll, rolling up" (Revelation 6:12-14 NIV).

Mark 13:24-26 and Matthew 24:29-31 form the heart of the
teaching that Jesus' coming will not occur until after the Tribulation (a time of intense persecution of believers). Those who hold
this view believe that Christ will not return until the ultimate
destruction has occurred. But the connection of these verses to
their Old Testament roots in the prophets seems to connect them
more with judgment on the nations and the political powers than
on the destruction of the world.

Coming persecutions and natural disasters will cause great
sorrow in the world. But when believers see these events happening, they should realize that the return of their Messiah is near
and that they can look forward to his reign of justice and peace.
Rather than being terrified by what is happening in our world,
we should confidently await Christ's return to bring justice and
to restore his people.

COMING . . . COMING . . . COME
Well-known speaker Tony Campolo has a famous message titled, "It's Friday, But Sunday's Coming." That's a great summary of the Christian life: a difficult present, but someday Jesus will come to make everything right, to wipe out sin and grief, to bring an eternity of Sundays. From crucifixion comes resurrection; from tribulation comes a wonderful Savior.

Let Jesus reign in your heart today. No reason to put him off. You have every reason to say, "Yes, Lord, I believe. My life is yours. And every day that I live, come whatever, I will trust and serve you."

That decision inaugurates a brand-new relationship with God through Jesus Christ. Now you are part of the future—now you have a day to look forward to.

---

**24:30** **"At that time the sign of the Son of Man will appear in the sky, and all the nations of the earth will mourn. They will see the Son of Man coming on the clouds of the sky, with power and great glory."**[NIV] The *Son of Man* will return from *the sky,* just as he would leave. Although Jesus was still with them, the day would soon come when an angel would tell the disciples, "Men of Galilee . . . why do you stand here looking into the sky? This same Jesus, who has been taken from you into heaven, will come back in the same way you have seen him go into heaven" (Acts 1:11 NIV).

"All the nations of the earth" is an Old Testament metaphor for the universal impact of the Second Coming. *The nations of the earth will mourn* because unbelievers will suddenly realize that they have chosen the wrong side. (This phrase alludes to Zechariah 12:10-12, which centers on the repentance of Jerusalem.) Here the scene centers on God's judgment of his enemies. Everything they have scoffed about will be happening, and it will be too late for them.

After the cosmic events recorded in 24:29, all the people on earth *will see the Son of Man coming on the clouds.* Jesus' return will be unmistakable; no one will wonder about his identity. The "clouds" are pictured as the Son of Man's royal chariot, bringing him from heaven to earth in the Second Coming (to the Jews, clouds signified divine presence; see, for example, Exodus 13:21; 19:9; Psalm 97:1-2; Daniel 7:13). Jesus' second coming will not be as a humble, human carpenter, but as the powerful, glorious, and divine Son of Man. He will arrive to defeat Satan and judge all people, and there will be no doubt as to his identity.

**24:31** **"And He will send His angels with a great sound of a trumpet, and they will gather together His elect from the four winds,**

**from one end of heaven to the other."** NKJV Upon his return to earth, Jesus will *send His angels* out to *gather together His elect from the four winds* (that is, from all across the world, see also Psalm 50:3-5; Isaiah 43:6; 66:18; Jeremiah 32:37; Ezekiel 34:13; 36:24; 37:9; Daniel 7:2; 8:8; 11:4; Zechariah 2:6). This gathering of the chosen ones signifies the triumphant enthronement of the Son of Man, who will be revealed in all his power and glory. The manifestation of the angels and the gathering of the people will gloriously mark the end of Jesus' keeping his divine power and authority a secret. Jesus' second coming marks the core of the Christian hope. The imagery of the *great sound of a trumpet* would have reminded Matthew's readers of Isaiah's prophecy, "on that day a great trumpet will be blown" (Isaiah 27:13 NRSV). The trumpet was used in ancient Israel to gather God's people for religious purposes, as well as to call them for battle. This final trumpet (see also 1 Corinthians 15:52; 1 Thessalonians 4:16) will signal the gathering of God's people. When he comes, the whole world will know that Jesus is Lord, and Christians' hope and faith will be vindicated.

As in 24:22, three main views of the Tribulation interpret this verse in different ways:

1. *Pretribulationists* would say that this "gathering of the elect" refers to the gathering of Jewish saints (also as in 24:22), not the church. The "rapture" (taking believers to heaven) occurred before the Tribulation and concerned only the church.
2. *Midtribulationists* would say that this verse refers to the rapture and that it identifies both the church and the Jewish saints. This event will occur in the middle of the Tribulation, with the outpouring of God's wrath on the world occurring in the last half of that period.
3. *Posttribulationists* would say that the rapture and revelation are a single event, and this pictures the only return of Christ at the end of the Tribulation. There, as here, he will come to gather his saints (the "elect") and to judge unbelievers.

The phrase "from one end of heaven to the other" combines two Old Testament expressions, found in Deuteronomy 13:7 and 30:4, "Whether near or far, from one end of the land to the other, . . . even if you have been banished to the most distant land under the heavens, from there the LORD your God will gather you and bring you back" (NIV). The wording gives special stress to the concept that none of the elect will be overlooked or forgotten. God won't lose track of anyone.

**24:32-33** **"Now learn this lesson from the fig tree: As soon as its twigs get tender and its leaves come out, you know that summer is near.**

**Even so, when you see all these things, you know that it is near, right at the door."** NIV Using a parable, Jesus answered the disciples' question regarding when the events he spoke about would happen (24:3). The disciples, like anyone living in Palestine, knew when summer would come by observing the twigs and leaves of fig trees. The Mount of Olives was known for its fig trees, which were often twenty to thirty feet high. At Passover time, the budding would be just beginning. Jesus and his disciples were probably walking past many fig trees on their way out of Jerusalem as they crossed the Mount of Olives. Fig trees lose their leaves in winter (while most of the other trees in Palestine do not), and they bloom in late spring (many of the other plants bloom in early spring). Jesus chose the fig tree for this peculiarity; since its buds come late, it was a perfect example to picture the delay of the Second Coming. The dry, brittle twigs getting tender with rising sap and the leaves coming out were certain signs that summer was near. Inherent in this process is patient waiting. There is no hurrying the natural cycle of the fig tree. So all believers must patiently await the Second Coming.

In the same way that they could interpret the season by the leaves on trees, so the disciples could know when these significant events would occur. When they saw *all these things* (referring to the events described in previous verses), they would know that the destruction of Jerusalem would soon follow. Some scholars feel that the phrase "it is near" refers to the coming desecration of the temple. But this interpretation makes too abrupt an interjection in Jesus' thought. Because Jesus was reassuring the disciples, it makes more sense to interpret "it" as the Son's second coming. Therefore, this verse means that the second coming of Jesus is both certain and near. The fulfillment of Jesus' prophecy would assure the disciples that the other prophecies he had given regarding the end times would also come true.

**24:34** **"Truly I tell you, this generation will not pass away until all these things have taken place."** NRSV The solemn phrase "truly I tell you" introduces an important truth, an assurance like an oath. There are three views of the meaning of this verse: (1) It refers only to those alive at the time Jesus spoke who still would be alive at the destruction of Jerusalem; (2) it refers to the end times only; (3) it refers both to the destruction of Jerusalem and the end times, the destruction of Jerusalem containing within itself the elements of the final end times.

Jesus singled out *this generation* using the Greek word *genea,* which can refer both to those living at a given time as well as to race or lineage (therefore, he would be speaking of the Jewish race). That makes the third view above most likely. Jesus used "generation" here to mean that the events of 24:1-28 would occur initially within the lifetime of Jesus' contemporaries. Not that all the problems would stop at the end of their lifetimes, but that *all these things* would be under way, verifying what Jesus had said. Jesus explained that many of those alive at that time would witness the destruction of Jerusalem. In addition, the Jewish nation would be preserved and remain on earth, so Jews also would witness the end-time events (see also 16:28).

**24:35** **"Heaven and earth will pass away, but my words will never pass away."** NIV There could be no doubt in the disciples' minds about the certainty of these prophecies. While *heaven and earth* as we know them would eventually come to an end, Jesus' *words* (including all his teachings during his time on earth) would *never pass away* into oblivion. They were true and would remain for all eternity.

THEY COME AND GO
This chapter opened with the disciples admiring the durability and beauty of the temple. But Jesus countered with a different vision of durability: Only his words endure; only the truth of God survives.

History is the story of change, the rise and fall of empires, the coming and going of societies, which, for a time, happened upon some happiness, then floundered upon some folly. What survives all this change?

Not temples, not governments, and not even Christian saints (who get sick and die like everyone else). Only God's Word endures. On that alone we stake everything. God's promises endure forever, and all who belong to Jesus share in them. Take hope. Jesus alone leads through change to a bright and buoyant future, full of everything good.

## JESUS TELLS ABOUT REMAINING WATCHFUL / 24:36-51 / *203*

**24:36** **"No one knows about that day or hour, not even the angels in heaven, nor the Son, but only the Father."** NIV While Jesus had given general "signs" to watch for regarding the coming of the end, he clearly explained to the disciples that the exact day or hour was not known by the angels or the Son (Jesus himself). When Jesus said that even he did not know the time of the end, he was affirming his limitations as a human (see Philippians 2:5-8). Of course, God the Father knows the time, and Jesus and the Father are one. But when Jesus became a man, he voluntarily gave up the unlimited use of his divine attributes. On earth, Jesus laid aside his divine prerogatives and submitted to the Father's will. Thus, *only the Father* knows exactly when Jesus will return.

> Christ designed that the day of his coming should be hid from us, that being in suspense, we might be as it were upon the watch.
> *Martin Luther*

The emphasis of this verse is not on Jesus' lack of knowledge, but rather on the fact that *no one knows*. It is God the Father's secret to be revealed when he wills. No one can predict by Scripture or science the exact day of the Second Coming. Jesus was teaching that preparation, not calculation, was needed.

It is good that we don't know exactly when Christ will return. If we knew the precise date, we might be tempted to be lazy in our work for Christ. Worse yet, we might plan to keep sinning and then turn to God right at the end. Heaven should not be our only goal; we have work to do here. And we must keep on doing it until death or until we see the unmistakable return of our Savior.

**24:37-39** **"For as the days of Noah were, so will be the coming of the Son of Man. For as in those days before the flood they were eating and drinking, marrying and giving in marriage, until the day Noah entered the ark, and they knew nothing until the flood came and swept them all away, so too will be the coming of the Son of Man."** NRSV This verse carries on the theme initiated in 24:36 regarding the unexpected nature of the Second Coming and its connection with the need for vigilance. The first outpouring of God's judgment upon sinful people in *the days of Noah* has a natural connection with the final outpouring at the Lord's return. People will be going about their daily business, just as they were in Noah's time (Genesis 7:17-24). Just as the flood caught them unawares (and after it was too late) and swept them away in judgment, so it will be at *the coming of the Son of Man* (see also 1 Peter 3:20-21).

**24:40-42** **"Then two men will be in the field: one will be taken and the other left. Two women will be grinding at the mill: one will be taken and the other left. Watch therefore, for you do not know what hour your Lord is coming."** NKJV To further illustrate the suddenness of his return, Jesus pictured "business as usual" in Palestine—the men out working in the field; the women doing domestic chores such as grinding grain. The Second Coming and the angels' accomplishment of their task of "gathering the elect" (24:31) will happen so suddenly that in the blink of an eye, one of those people may be taken and the other left. The reason? One was ready and one was not. Because no one except the Father knows when Christ will return (the "you" in "you do not know" points to every one of us), Jesus explained that believers must be on guard and alert, constantly ready for him to come at any time. Christ's second coming will be swift and sudden. There will be no time for last-minute repenting or bargaining. The choice that people have already made will determine their eternal destiny.

Jesus commanded his followers to *watch.* "Watch" is an Old Testament concept, arising out of the necessity of maintaining constant vigil on city walls against marauding bands. It also referred to the spiritual vigilance needed to keep people from wandering away from God. In the context of the Olivet discourse, it is active rather than passive. A person maintains vigilance not by passively waiting, but by engaging in good deeds and active discipleship.

---

VIGILANCE
Jesus urged his followers to be ready and waiting for his return. Why is this spiritual preparation so important in each believer's life?

*Spiritual preparation is commanded by God.* Jesus' purpose in telling about his return is not to stimulate predictions and calculations about the date, but to warn us to be prepared. Will you be ready? The only safe choice is to obey him today (Matthew 24:46).

*Spiritual preparation is active.* Jesus asks us to spend the time of waiting taking care of his people and doing his work here on earth, both within the church and outside it. This is the best way to prepare for Christ's return.

*Spiritual preparation is focused on Christ's coming.* Knowing that Christ's return will be sudden and unexpected should motivate us always to be prepared. We are not to live irresponsibly—sitting and waiting, doing nothing; seeking self-serving pleasure; using his tarrying as an excuse not to do God's work of building his kingdom; developing a false security based on precise calculations of events; or letting our curiosity about the end times divert us from doing God's work.

---

**24:43-44** **"But understand this: if the owner of the house had known in what part of the night the thief was coming, he would have stayed awake and would not have let his house be broken into. Therefore you also must be ready, for the Son of Man is coming at an unexpected hour."** NRSV Jesus' purpose in telling about his return was not to stimulate predictions and calculations about the date, but to warn his people to be ready. In this simple parable, Jesus again pointed out the need for constant vigilance. A homeowner cannot know when a thief might come to break into his home, so he must be always prepared. So with the return of Christ. He will come *at an unexpected hour.*

---

WHEN JESUS RETURNS
At the hour when zealous Christian teachers predict Jesus to return, you can be pretty sure it won't happen. Jesus' schedule is simply not available. No one knows. Yet the uncertainty of the time is no excuse for apathy.

- God's Good News must get everywhere. What role can you play in helping your neighbor, or people far away, come to faith in Jesus?
- God's church should be everywhere, helping people worship and building up their faith. What can you do to help?
- God's people should work everywhere, striving to advance God's interests in public justice, housing, health, environmental maintenance, recreation, etc. What are you doing about it?

This is Jesus' agenda. When he comes, we ought to be caught doing it.

---

**4:45-47** **"Who then is the faithful and wise servant, whom the master has put in charge of the servants in his household to give them their food at the proper time? It will be good for that servant whose master finds him doing so when he returns. I tell you the truth, he will put him in charge of all his possessions." NIV** In ancient times it was a common practice for masters to put one servant in charge of all the household business. The *servant* described as *faithful and wise* parallels the disciples, who were given unprecedented authority by Jesus, sharing in his very ministry. Yet it also describes those appointed to positions of leadership in the church who should

> If God has given you more than your neighbors, dedicate it to Christ, and realize that you are only a steward of that which God has given you—some day you will have to give an account for every penny you spent.
> *Billy Graham*

be found faithfully carrying out their duties when Jesus *(the master)* returns. Such activity explains how Jesus' followers can "watch" and "be ready." These servants will be given great rewards.

**4:48-49** **"But suppose that servant is wicked and says to himself, 'My master is staying away a long time,' and he then begins to beat his fellow servants and to eat and drink with drunkards." NIV** Some servants, however, might decide to take advantage of their leadership positions, bullying others and indulging themselves. Jesus may indeed stay *away a long time,* but that will never be an excuse for laziness, inadequate service, or wickedness.

**24:50-51** **"The master of that servant will come on a day when he does not expect him and at an hour he is not aware of. He will cut him to pieces and assign him a place with the hypocrites, where there will be weeping and gnashing of teeth."** NIV The servant may have thought his master would be gone a long time (and perhaps the master was), but one day, the master will return. It will be sudden and without warning, and the evil servant will be "caught in the act." The master's judgment against his wicked servant will be extremely severe—he will cut the servant to pieces. Even worse than that horrible punishment will be the servant's eternal destiny. No better than a hypocrite, he will be assigned to a place of *weeping and gnashing of teeth* (referring to hell). God's coming judgment is as certain as Jesus' return to earth.

---

HOLY GOD, LOVING LORD
The brutal language of this verse speaks clearly of the judgment of God against phonies and hypocrites. Everywhere in the Bible Jesus is presented as the loving Lord of all who come to him in repentance and faith. But on a few pages, the Bible also points to the holiness side, the side of God completely intolerant of sin, utterly unwilling to compromise with evil.

These fewer pages balance the picture. God is love, and God is holy. All who trust in Jesus are participants in his holiness. The penalty for your sin was paid on the cross. But all who refuse stand in jeopardy of suffering the judgment of a holy God. Don't be there when God's anger strikes. Heed the warning and appeal to Jesus for salvation. He is your only hope.

---

# Matthew 25

Jesus told the following parables to clarify further what it means
to be spiritually vigilant—ready for his return and how to live
until he comes. The ten bridesmaids (25:1-13) teach that every
person is responsible for his or her own spiritual condition. The
story of the talents (25:14-30) shows the necessity of using well
what God has entrusted to us. The parable of the sheep and goats
(25:31-46) stresses the importance of serving others in need. No
parable by itself completely describes our preparation. Instead,
each presents one part of the whole picture.

**25:1** **"Then the kingdom of heaven will be like this. Ten bridesmaids
took their lamps and went to meet the bridegroom."** NRSV The
word "then" reminds us that this parable ties in with Jesus' words
about his return (see chapter 24). This parable about a wedding
describes the need for readiness for the kingdom and explains that
some will be included while others will not. Wedding customs differed from village to village in ancient Israel, but all weddings
included the processional of the bridegroom to the bride's family
home.

The wedding day would be spent in dancing and celebrating,
concluding with the wedding feast at dusk. The bride would be
accompanied with torches to the bridegroom's house for this
feast. These *ten bridesmaids* (also called "virgins" because they
were unmarried) were going out to *meet the bridegroom,* who
was coming to the bride's home to join the procession back to his
house for the ceremony and the wedding banquet. This happened
after dark, and in villages and towns without streetlights, these
torches lit the way (the Greek word translated "lamps" means
torches, not lanterns). Everyone was required to carry his or her
own "lamp"; those who didn't have one were considered party
crashers—those who had not been invited.

**25:2-4** **"Five of them were foolish, and five were wise. When the foolish took their lamps, they took no oil with them; but the wise**

**took flasks of oil with their lamps.**" NRSV The *foolish* bridesmaids were unprepared; *they took no oil with them.* If their lamps burned out, they would be unable to light them again. The *wise* bridesmaids had brought along *flasks of oil,* so they were prepared to relight their *lamps* if necessary. As with any parable, the details ought not to be pressed. For example, that there were five wise bridesmaids and five foolish ones does not mean that half the world will be saved. The parable simply establishes two categories, for there will be only two—those who believe and receive the king, and those who do not.

**25:5-7 "The bridegroom was a long time in coming, and they all became drowsy and fell asleep. At midnight the cry rang out: 'Here's the bridegroom! Come out to meet him!' Then all the virgins woke up and trimmed their lamps."** NIV During the long wait, the bridesmaids *became drowsy and fell asleep.* Again this need not be taken as an allegory; their sleep was not condemned, because both the wise and the foolish slept. "Sleep" simply illustrates the *long time* they waited for the *bridegroom.* The second coming of Jesus will be delayed, as Jesus has already alluded to many times. It will be a longer wait than anyone (especially Jesus' first disciples) expected. The difference was that one group had made preparations early; the other group waited until the last minute, and then it was too late.

Finally *at midnight,* the bridegroom arrived. Everyone *woke up and trimmed their lamps* in anticipation of the procession. (The word translated "trimmed their lamps," *kosmeo,* means "put in order" and could refer to preparing their torches, which were usually made with rags soaked in oil.)

**25:8-9 "The foolish said to the wise, 'Give us some of your oil, for our lamps are going out.' But the wise replied, 'No! there will not be enough for you and for us; you had better go to the dealers and buy some for yourselves.'"** NRSV The foolish bridesmaids realized that their torches were burning low *(going out)* and that they would need more oil to raise the flame higher. But the wise bridesmaids explained that they didn't have enough to share. This was not self-ishness, but rather the realization that if they shared their little oil, then *all* the torches would burn low and there would not be enough light for the wedding procession. They needed all their oil to make their torches burn brightly enough. The suggestion to *go to the dealers and buy some* at midnight was not that unusual. A wedding procession, especially in the small villages of Israel, might cause the whole town to be up and about. The foolish women were able to

buy oil at this late hour. However, Jesus' focus was on their unpreparedness and on engaging in secular pursuits at the moment of
spiritual need. When Jesus returns to take his people to heaven, we
must be ready. Spiritual preparation cannot be bought or borrowed
at the last minute. No one can rely on anyone else. Our relationship
with God must be our own.

**25:10-12** **"And while they went to buy it, the bridegroom came, and
those who were ready went with him into the wedding banquet; and the door was shut."** NRSV While the foolish bridesmaids were off trying to get ready for the bridegroom's arrival,
he came. Everyone proceeded on to the wedding banquet. The
central focus of the parable lies in the words "and the door
was shut." Jesus' point again is that to not be ready at the right
time means to miss out completely. Jesus explained, **"Later
the other bridesmaids came also, saying, 'Lord, lord, open to
us.' But he replied, 'Truly I tell you, I do not know you.'"** NRSV
There is a finality to the shutting of that door. Those outside
will not have another chance to be let in. To have been "part
of the party" will not be enough. Unless correct preparations
are made, some will still lose out.

---

TOO LATE
In Jesus' story, the young women missed their opportunity.
They were foolish and unprepared, and they refused to think
ahead. Surely at a real wedding they would have been admitted.
But in this case, with this lord, there was a limit. When God
orders the gates of heaven sealed, cries from the outside will
be as futile as planting corn in the Sahara Desert.
     Don't be late. Tell God today that you want to follow Jesus,
to be his disciple, to serve him with all your energy. Don't
presume on God's goodness; embrace it now.

---

**25:13** **"Therefore keep watch, because you do not know the day or
the hour."** NIV Jesus concluded with the application that his true
followers must *keep watch* and be ready because he will return
when they will least expect it. God may delay his return longer
than we might prefer or expect. We must be prepared for such a
delay—counting the cost of discipleship and persevering faithfully until he returns. Those who are unfaithful must realize
that neglecting Christ's invitation may lead to irreversible consequences and the time of opportunity to believe may pass. In
the following parable, Jesus described *how* we are to "keep
watch."

## JESUS TELLS THE PARABLE OF THE
## LOANED MONEY / 25:14-30 / **205**

The following parable explains *how* Jesus' followers are to
"keep watch" (25:13) during their wait for his return. While the
previous parable about the wise and foolish bridesmaids stressed
readiness, this parable focused on using the waiting time well.

**25:14-15** **"Again, it will be like a man going on a journey, who called
his servants and entrusted his property to them. To one he
gave five talents of money, to another two talents, and to
another one talent, each according to his ability. Then he
went on his journey."** NIV The *man going on a journey* was obviously wealthy enough to have servants and to have an amount
of money that he wanted invested and multiplied while he was
gone. He would be gone a long time (25:19) and did not want his
assets to lie fallow during his absence. He was characterized as a
"harsh man" (25:24 NRSV).

The master divided the money *(talents)* among his servants
according to their abilities. While the English word "talent" has
come to mean a natural ability, the Greek word *talanton* simply
means a sum of money. Each of three servants received different
amounts of money *according to his ability.* The first received
*five talents of money* (over twelve thousand dollars), the second
*two talents,* and the last *one talent.* No one received more or
less than he could handle. Obviously the master knew his servants well, for the one entrusted with the least was the one who
let him down. The different sums of money point out how God
recognizes each person as a unique individual with varied
circumstances and personality. What he "gives" to each person
is exactly what that person can handle. For these servants, if any
of them failed in the assignment, his excuse could not be that he
was overwhelmed. We can only speculate why the servant with
one talent failed in his responsibility. He could have been lazy,
borne hatred toward his master, made a stupid decision, lacked
self-confidence, or even simply procrastinated. The talents represent any kind of resource that believers are given. God gives us
time, abilities, and other resources according to our abilities, and
he expects us to invest them wisely until he returns.

**25:16-18** **"The one who had received the five talents went off at once and
traded with them, and made five more talents. In the same way,
the one who had the two talents made two more talents. But the
one who had received the one talent went off and dug a hole in
the ground and hid his master's money."** NRSV These "servants"
may have been professional people who were either allowed to

engage in business, paying a fixed amount to their master, or to "trade" (engage in business) on his behalf and share the profits with him. Many slaves earned their freedom this way, saving their share in order to buy their freedom.

The first two servants doubled the money the master had given them. But the third servant *went off and dug a hole . . . and hid his master's money.* This would not have seemed unusual to Jesus' listeners, for in the ancient world, it was not an uncommon way to safeguard one's valuables (see 13:44). We do not know why he did it; he could have been lazy or afraid.

**:19-21** **"After a long time the master of those slaves came and settled accounts with them. Then the one who had received the five talents came forward, bringing five more talents, saying, 'Master, you handed over to me five talents; see, I have made five more talents.'"** NRSV The master returned *after a long time* (again Jesus was making it clear that his return would not be immediate) and *settled accounts with them.* The "settled accounts" indicates that the master had expected his servants to make money with his money. This first slave brought the ten talents, and his master was pleased with his efforts and with the profit. **"His master replied, 'Well done, good and faithful servant! You have been faithful with a few things; I will put you in charge of many things. Come and share your master's happiness!'"** NIV The reward for the servant's fulfilling his responsibilities and faithfulness is even greater responsibility. In addition, the *master's happiness* points to the eternal rewards of heaven (see John 15:11).

---

KEEP ON WORKING
We must give an account of our faithfulness. Jesus is coming back—we know this is true. Does this mean we must quit our jobs in order to serve God? No, it means we are to use our time, talents, and treasures diligently in order to serve God completely in whatever we do. For a few people, this may mean changing professions. For most of us, it means doing our daily work out of love for God. Be faithful in what you have been given.

---

**:22-23** **"The man with the two talents also came. 'Master,' he said, 'you entrusted me with two talents; see, I have gained two more.' His master replied, 'Well done, good and faithful servant! You have been faithful with a few things; I will put you in charge of many things. Come and share your master's happiness!'"** NIV The second servant had also faithfully fulfilled his responsibility. He had been given less money, but he had done everything he could and brought the four talents to the master. Because he had faithfully discharged his responsibility, even though he had less than the first servant, he received the same reward, commendation, and privileges.

We are responsible to use well what God has given us. The issue is not how much we have but how well we use what we have. Each believer should faithfully carry out the duties entrusted to him or her by God and multiply his or her God-given "talents" for the sake of the kingdom.

---

COME SHARE!
Everyone seeks affirmation, someone else to applaud our good work. "Nice hit!" says the Little League coach. "Nice paper," says the college professor. "Nice order," says the sales manager. And we brim with pleasure that our talents are recognized.

The Christian, when all is said and done, wants God to say, "Nice going!" For that reason, we may have to give up some of the other affirmations offered to us, and we may have to wait a bit longer than some of our friends. But that is no cause to fret. When God affirms your life and work, you will feel and know that only his affirmation matters. Deep in your soul, in the race to make your life mean something, you won. And there's a mighty big party waiting to celebrate. Come on in.

---

**25:24-25** **"Then the one who had received the one talent also came forward, saying, 'Master, I knew that you were a harsh man, reaping where you did not sow, and gathering where you did not scatter seed; so I was afraid, and I went and hid your talent in the ground. Here you have what is yours.'"** NRSV Since this is a story, we can only speculate how this last servant reasoned. All we know is that he was afraid. Perhaps this last man was thinking only of himself. He hoped to play it safe and protect himself from his hard master, but he had accomplished nothing for him. His words to the master reveal a self-centered character. He accused his master of being *harsh* and exploiting the labors of others (*reaping* and *gathering* where he *did not sow* or *scatter*). His accusation was an attempt to cover up his own irresponsibility. He knew that if he were to lose the one talent, he would be punished. He may also have been so afraid that he decided to do nothing with it at all.

The servant made excuses instead of realizing that, from the start, his responsibility was to serve his master to the best of his ability. To refuse to serve reveals a lack of love and little desire to accomplish anything for the master. We must not make excuses to avoid doing what God calls us to do. God truly is our Master, so we must obey him. Our time, abilities, and money aren't really ours; we are caretakers, not owners. When we ignore, squander, or abuse what we have been given, we are rebellious and deserve to be punished.

**:26-27** **"His master replied, 'You wicked, lazy servant! So you knew that I harvest where I have not sown and gather where I have not scattered seed? Well then, you should have put my money on deposit with the bankers, so that when I returned I would have received it back with interest.'"** NIV Using the servant's own words, the master pointed out that he had every right to *harvest* and *gather* even if he had not *sown* or *scattered*. He also had every right to require that his servants fulfill their responsibilities. He had not expected much of this servant in the first place; that's why the servant received so little. So even putting the money in the bank to earn interest would have been enough. Yet the *wicked, lazy servant* had not even done that.

**5:28-29** **"'So take the talent from him, and give it to him who has ten talents. For to everyone who has, more will be given, and he will have abundance; but from him who does not have, even what he has will be taken away.'"** NKJV The master severed his relationship with this servant, took away his talent, and gave it to the one who had earned the ten talents. Jesus had already taught the concept of *to everyone who has, more will be given* in 13:12. This parable describes the consequences of two attitudes regarding Christ's return. The person who diligently prepares for it by investing his or her time and talent to serve God will be rewarded. The person who has no heart for the work of the kingdom will be punished. God rewards faithfulness. Those who bear no fruit for God's kingdom cannot expect to be treated the same as those who are faithful.

**25:30** **"'And throw that worthless servant outside, into the darkness, where there will be weeping and gnashing of teeth.'"** NIV To fail to do good with what God has entrusted to us, to fail to use it to increase his kingdom, is a grievous sin that will receive severe punishment—for it means that one never knew or loved the Master. The *outside, darkness,* and *weeping and gnashing of teeth* picture hell (see 8:12; 13:42, 50; 22:13; 24:51).

Watching and waiting for the kingdom means being prepared. Being prepared means making ready for it by increasing the glory of God in this world through good deeds. Good deeds are best performed through the talents God has given us and should be done to the best of our ability.

CAN SALVATION BE LOST?
In this parable, it seems that a servant on the inside is thrown outside when judgment falls. Christian churches are divided on whether a person saved by faith in Jesus can lose his or her salvation. Here's what we can know from the Bible:

- There is no security apart from Jesus. He saves us, keeps us, and promises heavenly happiness after a life of faith and service. Only Jesus can do that. Rest only on him.
- The security we enjoy in God's promises should not make us presumptuous. Don't become cocky with God. Don't assume that God *must* let you in, that you can *demand* entrance, that you have a *right!*
- Live each day in faith, believing in God's great promises, dedicating your time and talent to God's work, loving your Christian brothers and sisters, being generous with the weak and poor. Your life is secure in Christ, but what you do with your day is often your own choice. Make choices that please God.

## JESUS TELLS ABOUT THE FINAL JUDGMENT/ 25:31-46 / *206*

This so-called "parable of the sheep and goats" is not truly a parable but a metaphor around which Jesus builds his message of judgment and salvation.

**25:31-33** **"When the Son of Man comes in his glory, and all the angels with him, he will sit on his throne in heavenly glory."** NIV This verse pictures Jesus when he will return, not as the humble carpenter from Nazareth but *in his glory.* The sight will be spectacular when the angels accompany the Son and we see him *on his throne in heavenly glory* (see also 16:27-28; 24:30-31; Zechariah 14:5). He will come as Judge, for **"all the nations will be gathered before him."** This fulfills Psalm 110:1, "The LORD says to my Lord: 'Sit at my right hand until I make your enemies a footstool for your feet'" (NIV). Jesus had quoted from this psalm in 22:41-45, applying the words to himself. Paul later wrote, "For all of us must appear before the judgment seat of Christ, so that each may receive recompense for what has been done in the body, whether good or evil" (2 Corinthians 5:10 NRSV).

**"And he will separate people one from another as a shepherd separates the sheep from the goats, and he will put the sheep at his right hand and the goats at the left."** NRSV Jesus used *sheep* and *goats* to picture the division between believers and unbelievers. Sheep and goats often grazed together but were separated at night because the goats needed a warm shelter at night (their coats are not nearly as thick) while sheep preferred open air.

In the parable of the wheat and the weeds (13:24-30), Jesus had talked about a final separation at the Last Judgment. The sheep and goats grazed together; the wheat and weeds grew together. At the end, however, Jesus, the Judge, *will separate people one from another.* While all "nations" are before him, he will separate individuals, for each individual is responsible for his or her own salvation (as seen in the parable of the brides-maids, 25:1-13). This "separation" became a picture for the Last Judgment. The gathering and separating, part of the shepherd's duties, further united the concept of the Son of Man as both Shep-herd and Judge. (See also Ezekiel 34:17-23.)

GOD'S PLAN
When Jesus first called his disciples, he said, "Come, follow." Here, at the end, he said to all his disciples, "Come, take." What can we learn about our spiritual pilgrimage during the time in between?

- Jesus is forever calling us closer to himself. We are never too close, never close enough. Jesus invites us closer all the time.
- Spiritual life is movement. We're always approaching (or conversely, retreating from) God, never standing still. All the physical movements in your life (changing jobs, changing homes, traveling to serve others) are pictures of your spiri-tual journey: moving closer to God, finding how faith works, reaching heavenly goals. All the emotional movement in your life (loves found and lost, loved ones dying and new ones born) reflect the need we all have to find a stable place to build our lives. That stable place is a person, the Lord Jesus.

You are God's plan. Since the very moment of creation, the wonderful kingdom of God—you included—has been the goal that now comes to its fullness and finality. You have been part of the world's most important movement—faithfully living as a disciple of Jesus—and now you are part of the world's biggest celebration. Are you lucky? No, you are God's plan, now fulfilled.

**25:34** **"Then the King will say to those on his right, 'Come, you who are blessed by my Father; take your inheritance, the kingdom prepared for you since the creation of the world.'"** [NIV] The "sheep" were at the king's *right* side, referring to a position of honor. Sheep were more commercially valuable than goats, and throughout Scripture they are an image for God's people. Thus here they are identified as "the elect," God's chosen people, as seen in the words "take . . . the kingdom prepared for you since the creation of the world." This kingdom, existing from the beginning of time, is sure and unchangeable. Believers need never doubt its existence, nor the glory of it as their *inheritance*. This inheritance had been God's plan for them *since the creation of the world.*

**25:35-36** **"'For I was hungry and you gave me something to eat, I was thirsty and you gave me something to drink, I was a stranger and you invited me in, I needed clothes and you clothed me, I was sick and you looked after me, I was in prison and you came to visit me.'"** NIV This list describes acts of mercy people can do every day. These acts do not depend on wealth, ability, or intelligence; they are simple acts freely given and freely received. No special "talent" is needed. Jesus demands our personal involvement in caring for others' needs (Isaiah

> The rule for all of us is fairly simple: do not waste time bothering whether you "love" your neighbor; act as if you did.    *C. S. Lewis*

58:7). That this list is repeated four times in this parable indicates its importance as a guide for practical discipleship. The list is not exhaustive; instead, it represents all types of good deeds. This parable is not teaching salvation by good deeds, but evidence of salvation through good deeds.

**25:37-39** **"Then the righteous will answer him, 'Lord, when did we see you hungry and feed you, or thirsty and give you something to drink? When did we see you a stranger and invite you in, or needing clothes and clothe you? When did we see you sick or in prison and go to visit you?'"** NIV The righteous are surprised at the King's words. He commends them for their acts of kindness to him, but they realize that they did not have opportunity to do such kindnesses to him directly.

**25:40** **"And the King will answer them, 'Truly I tell you, just as you did it to one of the least of these who are members of my family, you did it to me.'"** NRSV The basis of reward rests on the acts of kindness each individual believer did for other believers *(these who are members of my family),* for in so doing, they did those kindnesses for the King himself.

> The love of our neighbor is the only door out of the dungeon of self.
> *George MacDonald*

Jesus himself, through the Holy Spirit, is present in even the most humble, lowly, or "insignificant" follower of Christ.

There has been much discussion about the identity of the "family members." Some have said they are the Jews; others say they are

## CONCERN FOR THE POOR

Concern and care for the poor are essential to truly biblical
Christianity.

| | |
|---|---|
| We are not to take advantage of the needy. | Exodus 22:25-27 |
| We are not to charge interest or make a profit on food sold to them. | Leviticus 25:35-37 |
| Every third year the tithe was to be given to poor people. | Deuteronomy 14:28-29 |
| We are instructed to give generously to the poor. | Deuteronomy 15:11; Matthew 6:2-4 |
| Jesus had special concern for the place of the poor. | Luke 4:18-19; 6:20-21 |
| Paul was eager to remember the poor. | Galatians 2:10 |

The Bible teaches that Christians should care for the poor, so
what can you do?

*Feed the poor.*
   Contribute to a food relief organization.
   Volunteer to help in a community program.
   Work through your church to develop a project to help the needy.
   Consider giving extra tithe to help ministries that assist the poor.

*Secure justice for the poor.*
   Help widows, orphans, aliens, and the oppressed.
   Help agencies that work for housing, education, and job opportunities
   for needy people.

*Uphold the cause of the poor.*
   Stand against oppression.
   Intercede for even one person.
   Write to Christian missions and encourage them to support the cause
   of the poor.
   Tell your deacons that you will help a poor person under their super-
   vision.

the apostles and/or all Christians; still others say they are poor and
needy people everywhere. Such a debate is much like the lawyer's
question to Jesus, "Who is my neighbor?" (Luke 10:29). The point
of this parable is not the "who" but the "what"—the importance of
serving where service is needed. Jesus' original intent seems to be
that how we treat lowly and needy fellow Christians determines
how truly we love Jesus. If Christians who have resources would
help needy fellow Christians, non-Christians would be totally per-
suaded of the validity of Christian love. Such love for others glorifies

God by reflecting our love for him. But that does not excuse our broader responsibility to show love and mercy to everyone in need.

---

GOD IS GENEROUS

It appears that God wants to be overly generous even on Judgment Day. You'll be rewarded for good deeds done even if you did not know you were doing them, even if you did not do them during a church-sponsored missions trip, or even if you were not that aware that Jesus was watching. What attitudes should that inspire?

- Develop a loving lifestyle, so that good deeds flow naturally from your normal conduct of life. God is generous; you be generous. God is patient; you be patient. Learn to live that way.
- Don't be so sure about God's will. The deeds you might dismiss as casual and simple (tending the church nursery, cleaning up after a picnic, greeting visitors) God will regard as valuable moments of showing his love and grace to people. The deeds you may regard as highly spiritual God may dismiss as calculating and misconceived.
- Be energetic about the little moments in your ordinary day. Offering a drink to someone is a simple gesture of care and concern. A lot of similar "little gestures" build into a much bigger story: God has changed your life, turning natural selfishness into generosity and compassion. This God is great! Believe in him. That's your message in each of the little gestures that shows God's love.

---

**25:41** "Then he will say to those on his left, 'Depart from me, you who are cursed, into the eternal fire prepared for the devil and his angels.'" NIV For the goats *(those on his left),* however, the story is different. These "goats," mingling every day as they did with the sheep, may have thought that they could get by unnoticed. But God would separate them, and their judgment would be severe. There will be no middle ground at the final judgment—either a person is a "sheep" or a "goat." And the result will be either "the kingdom" (25:34) or *eternal fire* (referring to hell) and separation from God forever (indicated by the words "depart from me").

Eternal punishment takes place in hell (that is, the lake of fire or Gehenna), which is the place of punishment after death for all those who refuse to repent. In the Bible, three words are used in connection with eternal punishment: (1) *Sheol,* or "the grave," is used in the Old Testament to mean the place of the dead, generally thought to be under the earth. (See Job 24:19; Psalm 16:10; Isaiah 38:10.) (2) "Hades" is the Greek word for the underworld, the realm of the dead. It is the word used in the New Testament for Sheol. (See

Matthew 16:18; Revelation 1:18; 20:13-14.) (3) Gehenna, or hell, was named after the Valley of Hinnom near Jerusalem where children had been sacrificed by fire to the pagan gods (see 2 Kings 23:10; 2 Chronicles 28:3). This is the place of eternal fire (Matthew 5:22; 10:28; Mark 9:43; Luke 12:5; James 3:6; Revelation 19:20) prepared for the devil, his angels, and all those who do not believe in Christ (Revelation 20:9-10). This is the final and eternal state of the wicked after the resurrection and the Last Judgment.

**25:42-43** **"'For I was hungry and you gave me nothing to eat, I was thirsty and you gave me nothing to drink, I was a stranger and you did not invite me in, I needed clothes and you did not clothe me, I was sick and in prison and you did not look after me.'"** NIV The sin noted by the King was (as in the parables of the bridesmaids and the talents) not active evildoing but failure to do good. The apostle James later wrote, "Anyone, then, who knows the right thing to do and fails to do it, commits sin" (James 4:17 NRSV). As in 25:35-36, the list is not comprehensive, but it represents good deeds that people often fail to do. Doing wrong in ignorance may be excusable (see Acts 3:17; 1 Timothy 1:13), but when believers neglect to help those in need, they disobey Christ. These actions do not take special talents, gifts, or lifestyles. One need not be rich to carry these out. Failure to do them then, as with the man who buried the talent, shows a lack of love for Christian brothers and, by extension, for the Lord himself.

**25:44-45** **"Then they also will answer, 'Lord, when was it that we saw you hungry or thirsty or a stranger or naked or sick or in prison, and did not take care of you?' Then he will answer them, 'Truly I tell you, just as you did not do it to one of the least of these, you did not do it to me.'"** NRSV The evildoers, also, were surprised at the King's words. How could he say that they had neglected to do acts of kindness to him personally when, in reality, that would seem to be an impossibility? So he explained that in neglecting to do these kindnesses to even *the least* of the Christian brothers and sisters, they had neglected to do so for him. By that neglect, they had shown no true salvation, for their salvation had not manifested itself in good deeds, as it would naturally do. Their failures were not acts of wickedness, but refusals to do good and to show compassion.

**25:46** **"And these will go away into everlasting punishment, but the righteous into eternal life."** NKJV God will separate his obedient followers from pretenders and unbelievers, and their destinies will be vastly different. The real evidence of our belief is the way we act. To treat all persons we encounter as if they are Jesus is not easy, for we may not know if they are believers. What we do for others demonstrates what we really think about Jesus' words to us—feed the hungry, give the homeless a place to stay, look after the sick. How well do your actions separate you from pre- tenders and unbelievers? Will you be sent away to the place of *everlasting punishment* or *into eternal life?*

FINAL SEPARATION

From this judgment, God provides no appeal. There's no higher court set up to adjudicate your case. The judgment is final.

Given the love of God toward you, the offer of eternal life extended to you, and the finality of the Last Judgment against you . . . don't you think it's time to say, "Yes, Lord, I believe. Yes, I will follow."

It is time, right now. If you've never told God these things or are unsure if you ever really meant them, tell him now. Then start living in light of God's invitation to enter his eternal king- dom, prepared for you since the very beginning.

# Matthew 26

Starting in this chapter and through the end of the book, we find
the climax of Jesus' ministry. Matthew recorded little teaching
(as opposed to John who recorded lengthy teaching at the Last
Supper) and instead focused on Jesus' completion of the work
that he had come to do, emphasizing

- God's sovereign control of the events of Jesus' death and
  resurrection;
- the voluntary nature of Jesus' sacrifice—he was not an unfortunate
  victim but went boldly to death in obedience to God;
- the nature of Jesus as Son of God and royal Messiah contrasting
  with his humility in suffering and death;
- the guilt of the Jewish leaders, who even used false witnesses
  against Jesus; and
- the victory of Jesus over his opponents—gaining the ultimate
  victory by rising from the dead.

**26:1-2 When Jesus had finished saying all these things, he said to his
disciples, "You know that after two days the Passover is coming,
and the Son of Man will be handed over to be crucified."** NRSV
"All these things" that Jesus *had finished saying* refers to his teachings about the kingdom, recorded in chapters 23–25. Matthew used
this statement to signal the end of his record of teaching. Next, Jesus
moved into the final days of his earthly ministry and to the act that
he ultimately came to accomplish—death for sins. This was never a
surprise to Jesus—in fact, he had already told his disciples on three
different occasions that he would suffer and die (see 16:21-28;
17:22-23; 20:17-19). As if echoing these warnings, Jesus reminded
his disciples that the time had come for these things to be fulfilled.

That Jesus would die during *Passover* was deeply significant
with respect to Jewish history. The "Passover" commemorated
the night the Israelites were freed from Egypt (Exodus 12), when
God "passed over" homes marked by the blood of a lamb. This
was the last great plague on Egypt when, in unmarked homes, the

firstborn sons died. After this horrible disaster, Pharaoh allowed the Israelites to leave. Annually, Hebrew families would celebrate the Passover meal, a feast with the main course of lamb. The sacrifice of a lamb and the spilling of its blood commemorated Israel's escape from Egypt when the blood of a lamb painted on their doorposts had saved their firstborn sons from death. This event foreshadowed Jesus' work on the cross. As the spotless Lamb of God, his blood would be spilled in order to save his people from the penalty of death brought by sin.

**26:3-5 Then the chief priests and the elders of the people assembled in the palace of the high priest, whose name was Caiaphas, and they plotted to arrest Jesus in some sly way and kill him. "But not during the Feast," they said, "or there may be a riot among the people."** NIV The Jewish leaders *(chief priests and the elders of the people)* plotted secretly to kill Jesus. The opposition against Jesus had been rising for some time. These leaders had already decided that Jesus must die (see John 11:47-53); they just needed the opportunity to *kill him.* Matthew placed this explanation here, immediately after Jesus' words of knowledge regarding coming events, to emphasize that though the leaders might plot and connive, all events would occur according to God's sovereign plan.

So they *assembled in the palace of the high priest. Caiaphas* was the ruling high priest during Jesus' ministry. He was the son-in-law of Annas, the previous high priest. Although the position of high priest was supposed to be held for life, the Roman government had taken over the process of appointing all political and religious leaders. Annas had been replaced by Caiaphas, which was illegal according to the Law; therefore, many Jews still regarded Annas as the true high priest. Caiaphas was the leader of the religious group called the Sadducees. Educated and wealthy, the Sadducees were politically influential in the nation. An elite group, they were on fairly good terms with Rome. Caiaphas served for eighteen years, longer than most high priests, suggesting that he was gifted at cooperating with the Romans. He was the first to recommend Jesus' death in order to "save" the nation (John 11:49-50). The religious leaders hated Jesus because he taught a message and claimed an authority for himself that they could not accept.

The leaders were afraid of Jesus' popularity, so they needed *some sly way* to arrest Jesus and convict him with the death penalty. They did not want to attempt to arrest Jesus *during the Feast.* The day of Passover (recalling the Israelites' escape from Egypt) was followed by a seven-day festival called the Feast of Unleavened Bread, a harvest feast celebrating the gathering of the barley crop

(Deuteronomy 16:9). Eventually the eight days (the day of Passover and the week of the Feast of Unleavened Bread) came to be called the Passover Feast. This holiday found people gathering for a special meal that included lamb, wine, bitter herbs, and unleavened bread. Passover was celebrated on the fourteenth day of the Jewish month of Nisan (by our calendar, the last part of March and the first part of April). All Jewish males over the age of twelve were required to go to Jerusalem for Passover and the Feast of Unleavened Bread (Deuteronomy 16:5-6), although Jews in faraway lands could celebrate there if they faced in the direction of Jerusalem. During this holiday, Jerusalem, a town of about 50,000, would swell to 250,000 people.

Thus, the leaders realized that to arrest Jesus during the Feast days could cause this huge crowd to *riot* on his behalf. They feared that such an uprising might bring the wrath of Rome. While Roman reprisals for riots in its territories were not as automatic as some have thought (politics in Rome at this time favored being tolerant), use of force was a possibility. The religious leaders did not want to take that chance. They may have planned to arrest Jesus after *the Feast* when the vast crowds were gone. Perhaps Judas's unexpected offer (26:14-16) caused them to move sooner than they had planned, but, as this passage implies, all was proceeding according to God's timetable.

---

SUBTLE SECRECY
Jesus was conducting his ministry in public, but opponents were planning behind closed doors. Public works of love made Jesus vulnerable; secret acts of treachery preserved the religious leaders' public reputations.

Today, Christian workers should know that behind many closed doors, evil plots are developed to overturn God's kingdom. Opposition is always present, though not always public. Pray for help and wisdom to work through it, and don't be naive about its intentions. To the forces of evil, you are the enemy.

---

## A WOMAN ANOINTS JESUS WITH PERFUME / 26:6-13 / **182**

Matthew and Mark put this event just before the Last Supper, while John included it just before the Triumphal Entry. Of the three, John placed it in the most likely chronological position. Matthew sandwiched this beautiful event between two sections dealing with the plot to eliminate Jesus. This act of devotion by Mary, who is a true heroine in this narrative, contrasts with the treachery of the villains—the religious leaders and Judas. Matthew and Mark's accounts make thematic use of this event without claiming that it occurred at a certain time in the week. They may have simply placed it here to contrast the devotion of Mary with the betrayal of Judas, the next event recorded in their Gospels.

**26:6-7 While Jesus was in Bethany in the home of a man known as Simon the Leper, a woman came to him with an alabaster jar of very expensive perfume, which she poured on his head as he was reclining at the table.**[NIV] *Bethany* was located on the eastern slope of the Mount of Olives (Jerusalem is on the western side). This town was the home of Jesus' friends Lazarus, Mary,

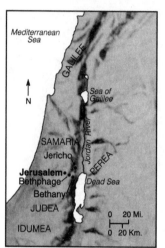

and Martha. Jesus had been returning to Bethany from Jerusalem each night during this final week, probably staying with these dear friends (21:17).

One night, a dinner had been prepared with Jesus as the honored guest (thus his position of *reclining at the table*). The host, *Simon the Leper,* did not have leprosy at this time, for lepers were forced to live separately from people because of the extreme contagiousness of the disease. Jesus may have healed Simon of his leprosy, but he had the nickname as a former leper.

The woman who *came to him* was probably Mary, the sister of Martha and Lazarus, who lived in Bethany (John 12:1-3). An *alabaster jar* was a beautiful and expensive vase with a long, slender neck. It was carved from translucent gypsum. The *perfume* inside the jar is described as "pure nard" (Mark 14:3 NIV), a fragrant ointment imported from the mountains of India. This was pure and genuine ointment, thus very costly. The perfume may have been a family heirloom. The beautiful jar was broken (Mark 14:3), and the costly ointment was poured on Jesus' head. (John records that the oil was poured on Jesus' feet—Mary probably did both, for Jesus was reclining with his legs stretched out behind the table.) It was a common custom at some Jewish meals for the honored guests to be anointed with oil (see Luke 7:44-46), but it would not be expensive nard. Such an anointing, using expensive oil and pouring it

**Visit in Bethany**
*Chronologically, the events of Matthew 26:6-13 precede the events of 21:1ff. In 20:29, Jesus left Jericho, heading toward Jerusalem. Then he arrived in Bethany, where a woman anointed him. From there he went toward Bethphage, where two of his disciples got the donkey that he would ride into Jerusalem.*

on the head as well as the feet, pictured a royal anointing appropriate for the Messiah.

**26:8-9** **When the disciples saw this, they were indignant. "Why this waste?" they asked. "This perfume could have been sold at a high price and the money given to the poor."** NIV Mary's gift to Jesus was worth a year's wages. Perfume such as this was used in burial rites because embalming was not the Jewish custom. Perfume covered the odor of the dead body. The disciples used a pious protest to hide their mixed reactions. They concluded that the expensive ointment had been wasted on Jesus, so they rebuked Mary for such an act because the perfume *could have been sold* and *the money given to the poor.* Where Matthew says *the disciples,* John specifically mentions Judas (John 12:4-5). Judas's indignation over Mary's act of worship would not have been based on concern for the poor, but on greed. Because Judas was the treasurer of Jesus' ministry and had embezzled funds (John 12:6), he no doubt wanted the perfume sold so that the proceeds could be put into his care. It would have brought a nice sum. The disciples were astonished at Mary's action; they resented this gesture as apparent waste. Passover was the time of special giving to the poor (see John 13:27-29), and the sale of this ointment would certainly have provided a generous amount to give. The disciples felt moral outrage at the loss of resources for the poor. But Jesus wanted them to understand that even concern for the poor must never be elevated over devotion to him. Jesus also knew what was in Judas's heart. Judas wasn't interested in helping the poor; he was interested in getting his hands on the money (John 12:6).

CALCULATING VALUE

Efficiency is the relentless taskmaster that drives all our decisions, all our proposals, all parts of our life, said French philosopher and theologian Jacques Ellul. Efficiency (he called it by a special term, *la technique*), pervades the church as well as the corporation. Everything we do is justified by its calculated contribution to established goals. Thus the disciples were quite modern to protest the "waste" of valuable oil.

Jesus alerts us that efficiency is an inadequate governor for at least one crucial encounter: people with God. In worship, let efficiency take its place, but not a primary place. In evangelism, use resources wisely but do not calculate cost-benefits as accountants are trained to do. What appears to be waste may well bring Jesus supreme enjoyment, and that matters most.

**26:10-11** **But Jesus, aware of this, said to them, "Why do you trouble the woman? She has performed a good service for me. For you always have the poor with you, but you will not always have**

me." NRSV Jesus reprimanded the disciples for their lack of insight. Their words criticized Mary's actions, but Jesus' words comforted her. The expensive perfume poured on Jesus had been *a good service* to him—a beautiful, acceptable, appealing act of love and sacrifice—and Jesus declared it to be so. This was a unique act for a specific occasion—an anointing that anticipated Jesus' burial and publicly declared faith in him as Messiah. In saying, *you always have the poor with you,* Jesus was not saying that we should neglect the poor, nor was he justifying indifference to them. Jesus was affirming Mary's unselfish act of worship and highlighting the special sacrifice that Mary had made for him. The essence of worshiping Christ is to regard him with utmost love, respect, and devotion, as well as to be willing to sacrifice to him what is most precious.

> Obedience is all over the Gospels. The pliability of an obedient heart must be complete from our wills right on through to our actions.
>
> *Catherine Marshall*

The phrase "you will not always have me" meant that Jesus would soon be gone from them physically. Jesus' purpose in these words was to explain that the opportunity to show him such devotion and to anoint him with oil (in preparation for burial) would soon pass. However, they should show kindness to the poor, and opportunities to do so would continue until the end of time. There would always be poor people who would need help. Jesus brought to mind Deuteronomy 15:11: "The poor will never cease from the land" (NKJV). This statement does not justify ignoring the needs of the poor. Scripture continually calls us to care for the needy. The passage in Deuteronomy continues: "Therefore I command you, saying, 'You shall open your hand wide to your brother, to your poor and your needy, in your land'" (NKJV). (For Jesus' teaching about the poor, see 6:2-4; Luke 6:20-21; 14:13, 21; 18:22. See also the chart in 25:40.)

Jesus' words should have taught Judas and the disciples the valuable lesson that devotion to Christ is worth more than money. Unfortunately, Judas did not take heed; soon he would sell his Master's life for thirty pieces of silver.

**26:12-13** **"When she poured this perfume on my body, she did it to prepare me for burial. I tell you the truth, wherever this gospel is preached throughout the world, what she has done will also be told, in memory of her."** NIV Mary may not have set out to anoint Jesus *for burial*; she was merely showing great respect for the Teacher she so loved and respected. She may not have understood Jesus' approaching death any more than the disciples, although she was known for truly listening to Jesus (Luke 10:39).

She may have realized something was going to happen to Jesus, for all knew he was in great danger, and thus she sympathized with him and honored him with the greatest gift she could give.

Mary's unselfish act would be remembered forever. This has come true because we read about it today. While the disciples misunderstood Jesus' mission and constantly argued about places in the kingdom and while the religious leaders stubbornly refused to believe in Jesus and plotted his death, this one quiet woman so loved Jesus and was so devoted to him that she considered no sacrifice too great for her beloved Master. She is an example to us all of unselfish devotion to our Savior.

### JUDAS AGREES TO BETRAY JESUS / 26:14-16 / **208**

**26:14-16** **Then one of the twelve, who was called Judas Iscariot, went to the chief priests and said, "What will you give me if I betray him to you?"** NRSV Why would one of Jesus' twelve disciples, Judas Iscariot, want to betray Jesus? The Bible does not reveal Judas's motives other than gaining money. All attempts to explain why he betrayed Jesus are speculation. As treasurer, Judas certainly assumed (as did the other disciples—see 20:20-28) that he would be given an important position in Jesus' new government. But when Jesus praised Mary for pouring out the perfume, thought to be worth a year's salary, Judas finally began to realize that Jesus' kingdom was not physical or political. Other views include the following: Judas became disillusioned when he saw that Jesus' role was to suffer rather than to assume leadership; Judas saw that Jesus' cause was losing impetus so he sought to save himself and cut a desperate deal; Judas thought that by betraying Jesus he could force Jesus to use his power to set up the kingdom, start a rebellion, and overthrow Rome. Although each of these theories is possible, we simply do not know *why* Judas betrayed Jesus.

Judas knew that the religious leaders had it in for Jesus, and he knew they would have the power to arrest Jesus. So that was where he went. Judas's greedy desire for money could not be fulfilled if he followed Jesus, so he betrayed him in exchange for money from the religious leaders. To have discovered a traitor among Jesus' followers greatly pleased the religious leaders. They had been having difficulty figuring out how to arrest Jesus (26:3-5), so when an offer of help came from this unexpected corner, they took advantage of it. Judas hoped for a monetary reward: *What will you give me if I betray him to you?*

**They paid him thirty pieces of silver. And from that moment he began to look for an opportunity to betray him.**<sup>NRSV</sup> Matthew alone has the exact amount of money Judas accepted to betray Jesus—*thirty pieces of silver,* the price of a slave (Exodus 21:32). This also looks ahead to 27:3-10 where Judas returned the money, and the amount fulfills Zechariah 11:12-13 (see also Jeremiah 18:1-4; 19:1-13; 32:6-15). The religious leaders had planned to wait until after the Passover to take Jesus, but with Judas's unexpected offer, they accelerated their plans. Judas, in turn, *began to look for an opportunity to betray him* when there would be no Passover crowds to prevent Jesus' capture and no possibility of a riot. Judas knew where they could find Jesus alone on Passover night and could positively identify him.

## DISCIPLES PREPARE FOR THE PASSOVER / 26:17-19 / **209**

**26:17** **Now on the first day of the Feast of the Unleavened Bread the disciples came to Jesus, saying to Him, "Where do You want us to prepare for You to eat the Passover?"** <sup>NKJV</sup> The Passover took place on one night and at one meal, but the Feast of Unleavened Bread, which was celebrated with it, would continue for a week. The first day of the feast was technically the day after Passover, but the two were combined because they occurred in the same month. Thus, this was either Wednesday night (the day before Passover) or Thursday of Jesus' last week (the night of the Passover meal). Two main questions emerge.

First, *was this Last Supper a Passover meal?* Most likely it was. In John, Jesus seems to have this meal on the evening before Passover. But the synoptic writers (Matthew, Mark, and Luke) identify this meal as a Passover meal (Matthew 26:18; Mark 14:12-16; Luke 22:7-16). Certain descriptions in the Gospels indicate that this was a Jewish Seder:

- Everyone ate in a reclining position (Matthew 26:20; Mark 14:18; Luke 22:14; John 13:23). Jews reclined only at Passover. The rest of the time Jews ate sitting up so as to differentiate themselves from other cultures like the Egyptians and the Romans.
- A traditional Passover contains a hand-washing ceremony that could have been the opportunity for the foot washing (John 13:1-11).
- The symbolic use of bread and wine occurred in the Passover Seder; Jesus used them both with new meaning.

- The dipping of the unleavened bread into the preparation of bitter herbs comes from Passover (Mark 14:20; John 13:26).
- Though eating lamb is not mentioned in any of the Gospels, it was not an exact requirement to complete the celebration. A Passover could be celebrated without eating lamb. Those Jews traveling or living away from Jerusalem could not eat the Passover lambs officially slain at the temple either. So it would be possible for the disciples to eat kosher lamb, but not one ceremonially sacrificed at the temple.

Second, *did this meal take place on Wednesday or Thursday?* Traditionally, Passover was from sundown (6:00 P.M.) on Thursday to sundown on Friday, the fifteenth day of the month of Nisan (April). Matthew, Mark, and Luke seem to indicate that Jesus and the disciples celebrated the Last Supper on Thursday evening. However, several verses in John suggest that the Last Supper occurred on a Wednesday (see John 13:1, 29; 18:28; 19:14, 31, 36, 42).

The following three attempts have been made to solve this apparent problem:

1. There were two calendars being used to determine the day of Passover. The official calendar followed by the Pharisees and Sadducees was lunar. Jesus and the disciples followed a solar calendar, possibly used at Qumran (a monastic Dead Sea community). The two calendars differed by one day, so that Jesus ate the Passover meal one full day before the Jerusalem Passover. There have been no conclusive historic arguments to support this theory.
2. Jesus and his disciples had the Passover meal Wednesday night, one day early, in anticipation of Passover. This view explains John 18:28 and still allows Jesus to be the Passover Lamb—crucified at the same time as the Passover lambs were slaughtered. If Jesus can heal on the Sabbath because he is the Lord of the Sabbath, he certainly could authorize eating the Passover meal one day early. This view harmonizes the chronology of all the Gospel writers and preserves their authority and reliability. Furthermore, it allows for a full three-day period when Jesus was in the grave—not just part of Friday, all of Saturday, and part of Sunday—but from Thursday evening to Sunday morning. This view is plausible, but it has the problem that the Gospels do not tell us that they ate the meal early.
3. Jesus and the disciples did eat the meal on the official day of Passover. In A.D. 30 (the year of Jesus' crucifixion), the Passover was celebrated on Thursday evening (the fourteenth

of Nisan) and was immediately followed by the Feast of Unleavened Bread, which lasted from the fifteenth of Nisan (Friday) to the twenty-first of Nisan. During each day of this celebration, special meals *(chaggigah)* were eaten. According to this view, the other references in John are to the Feast of Unleavened Bread, not the Passover meal (John 13:29; 18:28; 19:14). In John 13:29, after the Passover meal, Judas went out—actually to betray Jesus—but the disciples thought he had left to buy provisions for the upcoming feast. In John 18:28 the Pharisees did not want to make themselves unclean by entering Pilate's palace, thereby disqualifying themselves from partaking of the feast. In John 19:14, "the preparation for the Passover" was not for the Passover meal but for the whole week that followed, which in New Testament times was called both the Passover and the Feast of Unleavened Bread. This view seems most probable.

Therefore, the chronology was as follows:

- *Thursday*—Lambs were slain in the afternoon, Passover began at 6:00 P.M., Last Supper, Gethsemane, arrest
- *Friday*—Official trial, Crucifixion, burial by sundown, Feast of Unleavened Bread and Sabbath began at 6:00 P.M.
- *Saturday*—Jesus' body was in the tomb
- *Sunday*—Early morning Resurrection

Jesus' disciples asked him, *Where do You want us to prepare for You to eat the Passover?* Jesus' disciples assumed that they would eat the Passover meal together with Jesus. The meal had to be eaten in Jerusalem, however, so the disciples asked Jesus where they should go in order to make preparations. Peter and John, the two disciples Jesus sent on this errand (Luke 22:8), had to buy and prepare the unleavened bread, herbs, wine, and other ceremonial food. Families would eat the Passover meal together although a "family" could refer to any integrally related group, so disciples could celebrate together with their rabbi acting as "father" of the group. This was the case with Jesus and the twelve disciples. The Passover meal was characterized by the same hope of salvation that the exodus from Egypt had signified for Judaism—looking to God's final intervention to redeem Israel. The meal was liturgical, centering on the father's Passover prayer and the recitation of the Hallel (Psalms 113–118). Both the drinking of the wine and the partaking of food had ceremonial significance, and Jesus would give each new meaning at this particular Passover meal.

**6:18-19** **He replied, "Go into the city to a certain man and tell him, 'The Teacher says: My appointed time is near. I am going to celebrate the Passover with my disciples at your house.'" So the disciples did as Jesus had directed them and prepared the Passover.**[NIV] Luke tells us that Jesus sent Peter and John (Luke 22:8). Whether Jesus had supernatural knowledge in this instance or if he had made arrangements in advance is unclear (as in the incident with his Triumphal Entry, see 21:1-3). It seems that in this instance a room in this house had been reserved previously and kept secret—none of the disciples knew where they would eat this meal. Jesus already knew that Judas would be looking for an opportunity to betray him without crowds around, so Jesus may have made these arrangements and kept them secret. Jesus was in complete command of the situation and the sequence of events. The *appointed time* to which Jesus alluded referred to his coming death. Previously his time had not yet come (see John 2:4); now it *is near.*

The two disciples were dispatched in the morning from Bethany to Jerusalem to prepare the Passover meal. In Jewish homes, preparation required that the family eat only unleavened bread (bread with no yeast, like matzo today) for seven days before Passover. The house must be dust free lest any yeast remain in the home. The lamb had to be procured and taken to the designated spot near the temple to be slaughtered.

Jesus told the two disciples that as they entered the city, they would meet a *certain man.* In Mark, Jesus explained that this man would be carrying a jar of water (Mark 14:13). Ordinarily women, not men, would go to the well and bring home the water. So this man would have stood out in the crowd. This may have been a prearranged signal, or Jesus may have supernaturally known that this man (most likely a servant) would be there and would lead them to the right house. This private location kept the plans secret and security tight. Tradition says that this may have been Mark's home (the writer of the Gospel). If this speculation is true, the owner of the house would have been Mark's father and one of Jesus' followers. He knew exactly who *the Teacher* was and probably knew the disciples by sight. The disciples did as Jesus directed and made preparations for the others.

### JESUS AND THE DISCIPLES HAVE THE LAST SUPPER / 26:20-30 / *211*

**26:20-22** **When evening came, Jesus was reclining at the table with the Twelve.**[NIV] On that *evening,* Jesus and the disciples arrived in Jerusalem. The Passover meal was supposed to be eaten in

Jerusalem after sunset and before midnight. The disciples and Jesus took their places on the *reclining* couches around the table. During such an important meal as the Passover, everyone would recline at the table, symbolizing the freedom the people had gained after the very first Passover and their subsequent release from slavery in Egypt.

The meal was organized around drinking four cups of red wine, symbolizing the four-part promise of redemption found in Exodus 6:6-7: (1) "I will bring you out"; (2) "I will rescue you from their bondage"; (3) "I will redeem you"; and (4) "I will take you as My people, and I will be your God" NKJV.

There was a traditional program for the meal. First would come a blessing of the festival and the wine, followed by drinking the first cup of wine (this also made the meal special because water was usually served with meals). Next, the food would be brought out. Then the youngest son would ask why this night was distinguished from others. The father would answer with the story of the Exodus and would point to each item on the table as he explained its symbolic significance (for example, bitter herbs symbolized the bitter bondage of slavery in Egypt). This would be followed by praise to God for past and future redemption (taken from the first part of the Hallel in Psalms 113–114). Then the second cup of wine would be drunk. After the second cup, the bread would be blessed, broken, and distributed, and then eaten with bitter herbs and a fruit-paste dish.

This would be followed by eating the meal. The Passover meal included roasted lamb that had been sacrificed in the temple. At the end of the meal, the father would bless a third cup of wine, which would be followed by singing the second part of the Hallel (from Psalms 115–118). A fourth cup of wine would conclude the meal.

Jesus and the disciples were at the point of eating the bread with the sauce of herbs and fruit: **And while they were eating, he said, "I tell you the truth, one of you will betray me." They were very sad and began to say to him one after the other, "Surely not I, Lord?"** NIV Jesus knew who would betray him, and his words caused quite a stir among the disciples. Jesus had told them three different times that he would soon die, but news that one of them was a traitor saddened them greatly. From the accounts of Mark and John we know that the betrayer was Judas Iscariot. Although the other disciples were confused by Jesus' words, Judas knew their meaning. Apparently Judas was not obvious as the betrayer. After all, he was the one the disciples were trusting to keep the money (John 12:4-6). So each disciple asked

Jesus for assurance: *Surely not I, Lord?* The Greek form of the question would be rendered, "It is not I, is it?" and implied a negative answer. Each disciple hoped to clear himself and wondered if he would have the courage to remain faithful.

**6:23-24** **Jesus replied, "The one who has dipped his hand into the bowl with me will betray me. The Son of Man will go just as it is written about him. But woe to that man who betrays the Son of Man! It would be better for him if he had not been born."** NIV
Jesus answered that the betrayer was indeed one of the Twelve, and he added that this betrayer was dipping his bread into the bowl with Jesus. At this time, some food would be eaten from a common dish into which everyone would dip his or her hand. Meat or bread would be dipped into a dish filled with sauce often made from fruit. Jesus' words emphasized the treachery of the betrayer. To eat with a friend and then turn around and betray him was treachery at its worst. Jesus alluded to Psalm 41:9, "Even my close friend, whom I trusted,

he who shared my bread, has lifted up his heel against me" (NIV).

Indeed, Jesus would be betrayed and would die as he had already told his disciples. His death would not occur merely because of the betrayer, for the *Son of Man* had to die to complete God's plan and fulfill Scripture (for example, Psalm 41:9-13; Isaiah 53:1-6). All would happen *as it is written about him.*

But *woe to that man* who would betray Jesus. Again Jesus' words are reminiscent of Psalm 41, this time

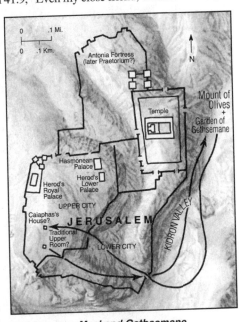

**The Passover Meal and Gethsemane**
*Jesus, who would soon be our Passover Lamb, ate the traditional Passover meal with his disciples in the upper room of a house in Jerusalem. During the meal they partook of wine and bread, the elements of future communion celebrations, and then went out to the Garden of Gethsemane on the Mount of Olives.*

verses 10-12, where the sufferer is vindicated by God and his enemies punished. Jesus felt true pity for this one who would betray him because he was acting as Satan's agent. The betrayer's fate would be so awful that Jesus expressed his pity by saying that it would have been better for that person not to have been born. Jesus knew that Judas was going to betray him, and he also knew that Judas would not repent. Jesus next predicted Peter's denial. The words were not so full of doom, however, for Peter would repent and be forgiven of his sin.

**26:25** **Judas, who betrayed him, said, "Surely not I, Rabbi?" He replied, "You have said so."** NRSV Each of the disciples asked if he were the one who would betray Jesus (26:22), but Matthew set apart Judas's question to state even more clearly that Judas was guilty. Jesus' answer to Judas was ambiguous enough so that only Judas would know that Jesus had identified him as the betrayer. It could mean, "You have said it, not I," and is like Jesus' statement to Pilate (in 27:11).

Luke wrote that "Satan entered Judas, called Iscariot" before Judas went to the religious leaders (Luke 22:3 NIV); however, Satan's part in the betrayal of Jesus does not remove any of the responsibility from Judas. In God's sovereign will and according to his timetable, he uses sinful men, but that doesn't excuse their sin. All people will be held accountable for their choices and actions. Satan tried to end Jesus' mission and thwart God's plan. Like Judas, Satan did not know that Jesus' death and resurrection were the most important parts of God's plan all along.

John wrote that upon this pronouncement, Jesus told Judas to "do quickly what you are going to do" (John 13:27 NRSV). Then Judas went out into the night.

---

GOD'S PLAN AND OUR RESPONSIBILITY
Was Judas to blame, if Jesus' crucifixion was part of God's eternal plan?

The Bible teaches two simultaneous truths about events, and we must live in light of each one:
1. God is in control. We may not know how, what, or why events are happening as they are, but we should remain confident that God knows and that he governs everything.
2. You are responsible for your behavior. You should not say, "I am a puppet, guided by a sovereign hand without a will of my own. Whatever I do, God is doing it." Tyrants and murderers have tried that excuse, but it is not valid.

We must recognize God's all-powerful control. We must make decisions trusting him and following him. Often we will not understand until much later how his will was at work in what we decide. But we must act on the best guidance we have.

---

**26:26 And as they were eating, Jesus took bread, blessed and broke it, and gave it to the disciples and said, "Take, eat; this is My body."** NKJV As Jesus and the disciples were eating, Jesus took the loaf of unleavened bread, blessed, and broke it. This probably occurred with the third cup of the meal (see the notes on 26:20-22). By so doing, Jesus was associating his words with the cup representing, "I will redeem you." The "blessing" of the bread refers to the Jewish practice of giving thanks for bread at a meal by saying, "Blessed are you, Lord, our God, who brings forth bread from the earth." Considered a gift from God, it was irreverent to cut bread with a knife, so it was torn (or broken) with the hands. Jesus gave the bread to the disciples to eat with the sauce. As he did so, he gave this Passover practice an entirely new meaning. Just as the Passover celebrated deliverance from slavery in Egypt, so the Lord's Supper celebrates deliverance from sin by Christ's death.

The Lord's Supper is also called Communion, the Lord's Table, the breaking of the bread, or Eucharist (thanksgiving), and it is still celebrated in worship services today. The celebrations in the Christian church have first a sharing of bread (including a repetition of Jesus' words "This is my body"), and then a sharing of wine (including a repetition of Jesus' words "This is my blood," 26:28). Thus, the Christian celebration incorporates the initial and ending portions of this last supper of Jesus. For more on the significance of celebrating the Last Supper, see 1 Corinthians 11:23-29.

Jesus and his disciples ate a meal, sang psalms, read Scripture, and prayed. Then Jesus took two traditional parts of the Passover meal, the passing of bread and the drinking of wine, and gave them new meaning as representations of his body and blood. He used the bread and wine to explain the significance of what he was about to do on the cross. Jesus told the disciples to *Take, eat; this is My body.* Jesus used visual elements to describe a figurative truth. Just as he had so many times said, "I am" the door, the bread, the light, the vine, so the bread symbolized Jesus' work of salvation on behalf of humanity. By breaking the bread and then saying, "this is My body," Jesus portrayed the sacrifice he would make and the spiritual benefit that would be passed on to those who had a personal relationship with him. This was Jesus' pledge of his personal presence with all his disciples whenever they would partake of this meal.

Christians differ in their interpretation of the meaning of the Lord's Supper. There are three main views: (1) The bread and wine actually become Christ's body and blood; (2) the bread and wine remain unchanged, yet Christ is spiritually present by faith in and through them; and (3) the bread and wine, which remain unchanged, are lasting memorials of Christ's sacrifice. No matter which view they favor, all Christians agree that the Lord's Supper commemorates Christ's death on the cross in our place, paying the penalty for our sins, and that it points to the coming of his kingdom in glory. When we partake of it, we show our deep gratitude for Christ's work on our behalf, and our faith is strengthened.

---

CELEBRATION
Each name we use for this sacrament brings out a different dimension to it. It is the "Lord's Supper" because it commemorates the Passover meal that Jesus ate with his disciples; it is the "Eucharist" (thanksgiving) because in it we thank God for Christ's work for us; it is "Communion" because through it we commune with God and with other believers. As we eat and drink, we should quietly reflect as we recall Jesus' death and his promise to come again, being grateful for God's wonderful gift to us and joyful as we meet with Christ and the body of believers.

---

**26:27-28** **Then he took a cup, and after giving thanks he gave it to them, saying, "Drink from it, all of you; for this is my blood of the covenant, which is poured out for many for the forgiveness of sins."** NRSV Luke mentions two cups of wine, while Matthew and Mark mention only one. In a traditional Passover meal, wine is served four times. Most likely the cup mentioned in this verse was the third cup; verse 28 refers to the fourth cup that Jesus did not drink, vowing first to complete his mission before drinking again of wine. He gave thanks and gave it to them, saying, *Drink from it, all of you.* The Greek word translated "after giving thanks" is *eucharisteo,* from which we get the English term "Eucharist."

As with the bread, Jesus spoke words in figurative language. *This is my blood* means, "this wine represents my blood." It couldn't have been his literal blood because he was sitting there with the disciples as he spoke, with his blood flowing through his veins. Jesus' blood, shed on behalf of *many,* began a *covenant* between God and people. The "many" are those who will become part of the covenant that his death created. According to Isaiah 53:11-12 and rabbinic teaching, "many" is a key word that refers to the chosen people, the elect community of salvation who will inherit the kingdom of God.

The word "covenant" refers to an arrangement established by one party that cannot be altered by the other party. In other words, God established the covenant and humans can only accept or reject it; they cannot alter it in any way. Jesus was saying these words at the drinking of the third cup at the Last Supper, the cup that stands for "I will redeem" (see the commentary on 26:20-22). Jesus' words recall Exodus 24:6-8, where Moses poured half of the blood of the covenant on the altar and sprinkled the people with the other half to seal the covenant. Jesus understood his death as sacrificial, inaugurating and sealing the new covenant.

What did Jesus mean by a new covenant? In Old Testament times, God had agreed to forgive people's sins if they would bring animals for the priests to sacrifice. When this sacrificial system was inaugurated, the agreement between God and human beings was sealed with the blood of animals (Exodus 24:8). But animal blood did not in itself remove sin (only God can forgive sin), and animal sacrifices had to be repeated day by day and year after year.

Jesus instituted a new covenant, or agreement, between humans and God. This concept is key to all New Testament theology and forms the basis for the name of the "New Testament" portion of the Bible. Under this new covenant, Jesus would die in the place of sinners. Unlike the blood of animals, Jesus' blood would truly remove the sins of all who would put their faith in him. And Jesus' sacrifice would never have to be repeated; it would be good for all eternity (Hebrews 9:23-28). The prophets looked forward to this new covenant that would fulfill the old sacrificial agreement (Jeremiah 31:31-34), and John the Baptist called Jesus "the Lamb of God who takes away the sin of the world" (John 1:29 NKJV).

The old covenant was a shadow of the new, pointing forward to the day when Jesus himself would be the final and ultimate sacrifice for sin. Rather than an unblemished lamb slain on the altar, the perfect Lamb of God was slain on the cross, a sinless sacrifice to accomplish *forgiveness of sins* once and for all. Jesus explained that his blood would be *poured out,* referring to a violent death. Once again Jesus was teaching his disciples that he would soon face a violent death, dying on behalf of others.

Those who accept Christ's sacrifice and believe in him receive forgiveness. Now all people can come directly to God through faith because Jesus' death has made us acceptable in God's eyes (Romans 3:21-24).

**26:29** **"I tell you, I will never again drink of this fruit of the vine until that day when I drink it new with you in my Father's kingdom."** NRSV Again Jesus assured his disciples of his victory over his imminent death and of a future in his *Father's kingdom.* The next few hours would bring apparent defeat, but soon they would experience the power of the Holy Spirit, and they would witness the great spread of the gospel message.

Jesus' vow to abstain from wine was made before the fourth cup, which traditionally was drunk after the recitation of these words: "I will take you as My people, and I will be your God" (see commentary on 26:20-22). Jesus reserved the drinking of this cup for the future restoration. This powerful scene is accented by Jesus' taking the third cup, saying, "I will redeem you," sharing it with the disciples, and then pledging that together they would finish this celebration in the kingdom of God (see also Isaiah 25:6; Luke 14:15; Revelation 3:20; 19:6-9). Because Jesus would be raised, so his followers will be raised. One day we will all be together again in God's new kingdom. The *fruit of the vine* in the kingdom will be *new* like Jeremiah's new covenant (Jeremiah 31:31-34). When Jesus celebrates with his people, all God's promises will be fully realized.

FINISHING THAT DRINK
There will be a party someday, and you'll be there. Jesus will be celebrating the wonderful salvation that his crucifixion accomplished, and you'll be there. Sin and suffering will be past—no more cancer, no more auto accidents, no more feeling lonely—and you'll be there. Next to you will be loved ones at whose deaths you cried, but there will be no reason for crying then.

Just when everyone has gathered, Jesus will pick up his cup. It is the one that he didn't finish back in Jerusalem, the one that he said he would wait to drink until all God's work was done. And then he will hold it up, and a whole new world will begin. He will drink at last. A huge cheer will erupt from the biggest, happiest crowd ever gathered. And you will be there!

**26:30** **And when they had sung a hymn, they went out to the Mount of Olives.**NKJV The *hymn* they sang was most likely taken from Psalms 115–118, the second part of the Hallel that was traditionally sung after eating the Passover meal. These were sung antiphonally with the leader (father or rabbi) reciting the text as the others responded with "Hallelujah." These words must have held great significance for Jesus: He pledged to keep his vows (Psalm 116:12ff.), called upon the Gentiles to join in praise (Psalm 117), and concluded with steadfast confidence in his ultimate triumph (Psalm 118:17).

John included a lengthy discourse that Jesus had with his disciples (John 13:31–17:26) before he and the eleven remaining disciples left the upper room and *went out to the Mount of Olives,* located just to the east of Jerusalem. Leaving the room did not surprise the disciples, for they had not been staying in Jerusalem at night and had left the city every evening to return to Bethany. This time, however, Jesus would go only as far as the southwestern slope, to an olive grove called Gethsemane, which means "olive press" (26:36).

## JESUS AGAIN PREDICTS PETER'S DENIAL / 26:31-35 / 222

**26:31** **Then Jesus told them, "This very night you will all fall away on account of me, for it is written: 'I will strike the shepherd, and the sheep of the flock will be scattered.'"** NIV This is the second time in the same evening that Jesus predicted the disciples' denial and desertion. (For Jesus' earlier prediction, see Luke 22:31-34 and John 13:36-38.) That the disciples would *fall away* means they would turn away from him. Fearing what would befall Jesus, they would not want to experience the same treatment. So Jesus explained that they would desert him, deny association with him, and distance themselves from him. Jesus would go to the cross alone.

The disciples might have been tempted to think that Satan and his forces had gained the upper hand in this drama about Jesus' death. But God was in control, even in the death of his Son. Satan gained no victory—everything occurred as God had planned. Jesus himself explained that the disciples' desertion would also occur just as it had been predicted in Scripture, specifically Zechariah 13:7.

In Zechariah, God commanded that the shepherd be struck down. As a result, the sheep would be scattered. Without a shepherd and on their own, the sheep would go through a period of great trial and be refined. The refining process would strengthen them and create a new, faithful people for God. The disciples would be staggered by what would happen to Jesus, but his death ("striking the shepherd") would ultimately produce their salvation and regather the sheep.

**26:32** **"But after I have risen, I will go ahead of you into Galilee."** NIV After predicting the disciples' desertion, Jesus predicted their reunion after his resurrection. Jesus promised that he would *go ahead* of them *into Galilee* and meet them all there. In Galilee, the scattered followers would be reunited; their relationship with their Master would be renewed, their failures forgiven, and their pattern of ignorance and rejection broken. Indeed the angel at the tomb would reassure the women, "Go quickly and tell his disciples, 'He has been raised from the dead, and indeed he is going ahead of you to Galilee; there you will see him'" (28:7 NRSV). Jesus made resurrection appearances in Galilee (28:16-20; John 21:1-23) and in Jerusalem and the surrounding area (Luke 24:13-52; John 20:11-29; 1 Corinthians 15:5-8).

**26:33 Peter replied, "Even if all fall away on account of you, I never will."** NIV Although all the disciples protested Jesus' words (26:35), Peter, always ready to speak up, declared that his allegiance to Jesus would prove to be much stronger than that of all the other disciples. He knew that Jesus had said to him, "On this rock I will build my church" (16:18), and may have assumed that he would be immune to such faithlessness. He seemed to ignore what Jesus had said in 26:31, but he was not rejecting the reality of Christ's suffering as he had in 16:22.

---

PETER'S PROMISE

It was not the night for low-key promises, so Peter made a big one that, despite his best intentions, he could not keep. He might better have said, "Lord, when I fail, and I probably will, please forgive me and keep me close to you." That would have been more honest, though less dramatic.

Peter would learn that God's forgiveness surpasses the guilt we experience when we fail. If guilt dampens your life, take a hint from Peter. He could have moped about that failure his whole life ("I'm such a failure!"). Instead, believing that Jesus truly forgave him, he went on to serve God boldly and well.

Give up your mistakes and start fresh with God.

---

**26:34 Jesus said to him, "Assuredly, I say to you that this night, before the rooster crows, you will deny Me three times."** NKJV However, Peter's very special future (16:18-19) would carry with it great responsibility, something Peter still needed to learn. Jesus' words to Peter were solemn, begun with the phrase "assuredly, I say." Instead of being the only loyal disciple, Peter would in fact prove to be more disloyal than the other ten. Not only would he desert Jesus, but he would also *deny* him *three times.* And this would happen in the space of the next few hours. Before the night was over, that is before the rooster crowed at dawn's first light, Peter would deny the Master to whom he claimed such loyalty.

**26:35 Peter said to Him, "Even if I have to die with You, I will not deny You!" And so said all the disciples.** NKJV Peter did not think it possible for him to actually deny any relationship with Jesus. Perhaps he was worried that *he* was the betrayer whom Jesus had mentioned during their meal (26:21). Not only Peter, but *all the* *disciples,* declared that they would die before denying Jesus. A few hours later, however, they all would scatter.

---

AND SO THEY SAID
Peter vowed that he would remain faithful. Talk is cheap. It is easy to say we are devoted to Christ, but our claims are meaningful only when they are tested in the crucible of persecution. How strong is your faith? Is it strong enough to stand up under intense trial? Learn from Christ's warning. Don't make impulsive promises. Realize your tendency to blend in with the crowd. Stay tied closely to Christian brothers and sisters. Be ready to stand up for Christ.

---

## JESUS AGONIZES IN THE GARDEN / 26:36-46 / **223**

**26:36 Then Jesus went with them to a place called Gethsemane; and he said to his disciples, "Sit here while I go over there and pray."** NRSV After eating the meal, the disciples left Jerusalem and went out to a favorite meeting place (Luke 22:39; John 18:2). This gardenlike enclosure called *Gethsemane,* meaning "olive press," was probably an orchard of olive trees with a press for extracting oil. The garden was in the Kidron Valley just outside the eastern wall of Jerusalem and just below the Mount of Olives. Jesus told eight of the disciples to sit down and wait, probably near the garden's entrance, while he went farther in to pray. The disciples must have been physically and emotionally exhausted from trying to comprehend what would transpire. Instead of watching, however, they gave in to their exhaustion and fell asleep.

---

URGENT PRAYER
When pressed with a difficulty, what's your first instinct: blame your mom? blame your kids? call 9-1-1?
   Jesus prayed.
   When you're sick with grief, worry, or guilt, prayer should be first on the list. In prayer, you settle things with God, and God strengthens you. It takes the sting from an emergency. It shares the burden with a big-shouldered friend. Pray first, especially when trouble is close at hand. Pray with others. There you will find strength and support.

---

**26:37-38 He took Peter and the two sons of Zebedee along with him, and he began to be sorrowful and troubled. Then he said to them, "My soul is overwhelmed with sorrow to the point of**

**death. Stay here and keep watch with me.**"<sup>NIV</sup> Jesus then took the other three disciples, his inner circle (Peter, James, and John), farther into the garden with him. To these closest friends, Jesus revealed his inner turmoil over the event he was about to face. Jesus was *sorrowful and troubled* over his approaching death because he would be forsaken by the Father (27:46), would have to bear the sins of the world, and would face a terrible execution. The divine course was set, but Jesus, in his human nature, still struggled (Hebrews 5:7-9). His coming death was no surprise; he knew about it and had even told the disciples about it so they would be prepared. Jesus knew what his death would accomplish. He also knew that the means to that end would mean taking upon himself the sin of the world, alienating him, for a time, from his Father who would be unable to look upon sin: "God made him who had no sin to be sin for us, so that in him we might become the righteousness of God" (2 Corinthians 5:21 NIV). Jesus bore our guilt by "becoming a curse for us" (Galatians 3:13 NIV). As the time of this event neared, it became even more horrifying. Jesus naturally recoiled from the prospect.

Early in Jesus' ministry Satan had tempted him to take the easy way out (4:1-11); later Peter had suggested that Jesus did not have to die (16:22). In both cases, Jesus had dealt with the temptation soundly. Now, as his horrible death and separation from the Father loomed before him, he was *overwhelmed with sorrow to the point of death.* So he asked Peter, James, and John to stay with him and keep watch. Jesus knew Judas would soon arrive, and Jesus wanted to devote himself to prayer until that time came. Jesus also wanted them to stay awake and participate with him in his suffering. Spiritual vigilance is a vital part of discipleship and a key theme in this book. Jesus wanted these disciples to understand his suffering and to be strengthened by his example when they faced persecution and suffering.

**26:39** **He went a little farther and fell on His face, and prayed, saying, "O My Father, if it is possible, let this cup pass from Me; nevertheless, not as I will, but as You will."**<sup>NKJV</sup> Jesus went still farther into the garden to be alone with God. His agony was such that he threw himself on the ground before God in deep spiritual anguish, praying that if possible *let this cup pass*—in other words, he was asking the Father to let the mission be accomplished some other way not requiring the agony of crucifixion, when he would become sin and be separated from the Father. In the Old Testament, "cup" stood for the trial of suffering and the wrath of God (Isaiah 51:17). So Jesus referred to the suffering that he must endure as the "cup" he would be required to drink. Yet Jesus humbly submitted to the Father's will. He went ahead with the mission for which he had come (1:21).

With the words "let this cup pass from Me," Jesus was referring to the suffering, isolation from God, and death he would have to endure in order to atone for the sins of the world. Jesus, as God's Son, recoiled from sin, yet part of his task would be to take the sins of the whole world upon himself. This was a cup he truly hated to drink. In addition, Jesus, as God's Son, knew constant fellowship with the Father. Yet

> Prayer is a shield to the soul, a sacrifice to God, and a scourge to Satan.
> *John Bunyan*

for a time on the cross he would have to be deprived of that fellowship. This was a bitter cup. The physical suffering would be horrible enough (Hebrews 5:7-9), but God's Son also had to accept the cup of spiritual suffering—bearing our sin and being separated from God (27:46).

Yet Jesus was not trying to get out of his mission. Jesus was expressing his true feelings as a human being, but he was not denying or rebelling against God's will. (Jesus may have been referring to Isaiah 51:22, where God lifted the cup of judgment for the righteous in Jerusalem.) He reaffirmed his desire to do what God wanted by saying, *Nevertheless, not as I will, but as You will.* Jesus' prayer reveals his terrible suffering. Jesus paid for sin by being separated from God. The sinless Son of God took our sins upon himself to save us from suffering and separation.

---

**TRUE PRAYER**
In times of suffering, people sometimes wish they knew the future, or they wish they could understand the reason for their anguish. Jesus knew what lay ahead of him, and he knew the reason. Even so, his struggle was intense—more wrenching than any struggle we will ever have to face. What does it take to be able to say "as God wills"? It takes firm trust in God's plans; it takes prayer and obedience each step of the way. This is the heart of true prayer and should be our basic response to trials. Trust God that his way is best, even when it doesn't seem like it.

---

God did not take away the "cup," for the cup was his will. Yet he did take away Jesus' extreme fear and agitation. Jesus moved serenely through the next several hours, at peace with God, knowing that he was doing his Father's will.

**PEACE**

Some people believe their troubles are caused by bad people, bad germs, or bad luck. But Christians know that God rules, so we rightly make our appeal to his will, which

- takes the bitterness out of the cup we may face, though it doesn't always remove the cup. God's will for each of us includes some pain, some loss, some struggle;
- never breaks us or makes us feel hopeless or abandoned;
- always assures us of God's presence and care; and
- ever promises reunion and relief.

Take comfort in God's will for you. Pray sincerely, "Your will be done!"

**26:40-41 Then He came to the disciples and found them asleep, and said to Peter, "What? Could you not watch with Me one hour? Watch and pray, lest you enter into temptation."** NKJV Jesus got up from his prayer to return to the three disciples. He had told them to stay and keep watch. But instead of showing support for Jesus by remaining awake with him and praying for strength in the coming hours, they had fallen asleep, "exhausted from sorrow" (Luke 22:45 NIV). Also, the hour was very late, perhaps after midnight. Jesus addressed Peter directly. Peter had said he would never leave Jesus; yet when Jesus needed prayer and support, Peter wasn't there for him. Thus, Jesus rebuked Peter for his failure to keep watch for even one hour.

Jesus told the disciples that this was the time to *watch and pray,* for very soon they would face difficult temptations. Jesus was not only asking that they pray for him, but also that they pray for themselves. Jesus knew that these men would need extra strength to face the temptations ahead—temptations to run away or to deny their relationship with him. "Enter into" could also be translated "fall into." Jesus wanted the disciples to pray that their faith would not collapse. The word "temptation" can mean testing or trial. Jesus wanted his disciples to pray for strength to go through the coming ordeal. The disciples were about to see Jesus die. Would they still think he was the Messiah? The disciples would soon face confusion, fear, loneliness, guilt, and the temptation to conclude that they had been deceived.

> More can be done by prayer than anything else. Prayer is our greatest weapon. *Billy Graham*

**"The spirit indeed is willing, but the flesh is weak."** NKJV Many have interpreted "spirit" to mean the "human spirit." Thus, it would mean that while their spirit might be willing, their *flesh* would be weak. Their inner desires and intentions would be, as they had previously boasted, to never deny Jesus and to die with him. Their relationship with Jesus had made the disciples eager to serve him in any way possible. Yet their human inadequacies, with all their fears and failures, would make it difficult to carry out those good intentions. A *willing* spirit (see Psalm 51:12) needs the Holy Spirit to empower it and help it do God's will.

Jesus used Peter's drowsiness to warn him to be spiritually vigilant against the temptation he would soon face. The way to overcome temptation is to stay alert and to pray. This means being aware of the possibilities of temptation, sensitive to the subtleties, and morally resolved to fight courageously. Because temptation strikes where we are most vulnerable, we can't resist alone. Prayer is essential because God's strength can shore up our defenses and defeat Satan.

**26:42** **Again, a second time, He went away and prayed, saying, "O My Father, if this cup cannot pass away from Me unless I drink it, Your will be done."** NKJV Jesus left the three disciples and returned to his conversation with the Father (26:39).

**26:43-45** **And He came and found them asleep again, for their eyes were heavy.** NKJV Jesus came back once again to the three disciples and *found them asleep again.* Despite his warning that they should be awake, alert, and praying not to fall to the coming temptations, *their eyes were heavy,* and all three went back to sleep. **So He left them, went away again, and prayed the third time, saying the same words.** NKJV Jesus continued his conversation with his Father, as before (26:39, 42). During these times of prayer, the battle was won. Jesus still had to go to the cross, but he would humbly submit to the Father's will and accomplish the task set before him.

**Then he came to the disciples and said to them, "Are you still sleeping and taking your rest? See, the hour is at hand, and the Son of Man is betrayed into the hands of sinners."** NRSV Jesus went away to pray a third time, only to come back and find the disciples still asleep. After much time in prayer, Jesus was ready to face his *hour,* which conveyed that all he had predicted about his death was about to happen (see John 12:23-24). The disciples had missed a great opportunity to talk to the Father, and there would be no more time to do so, for Jesus' hour had come. Thus, Jesus did not again tell them to pray. Jesus had spent the last few hours with the Father, wrestling with him, and humbly submitting to him. Now he was prepared to face his betrayer and the *sinners* who were coming to arrest him. "Sinners" was the term used for Jews who did not live according to God's will and for Gentiles, who were viewed collectively as sinners because they didn't live by God's law. Jesus probably used the term to refer to the priestly authorities who were disobeying God in their treachery, and to the Romans who were participating in Jesus' arrest, mockery, and death.

**26:46** **"Rise, let us go! Here comes my betrayer!"** NIV Jesus roused the three sleeping disciples (and perhaps the other eight as well) and called them together. His words "rise, let us go" did not mean that Jesus was contemplating running. Instead, he was calling the disciples to go with him to meet the traitor disciple, Judas, and the coming crowd. Jesus went forth of his own will, advancing to meet his accusers rather than waiting for them to come to him. Jesus' *betrayer,* Judas, had arrived. Judas knew where to find Jesus and the disciples because Gethsemane had been a favorite meeting spot (John 18:1-2). It was to this quiet garden in the very early hours of the morning that Judas brought a crowd to arrest Jesus.

## JESUS IS BETRAYED AND ARRESTED / 26:47-56 / *224*

**26:47** **While he was still speaking, Judas, one of the Twelve, arrived. With him was a large crowd armed with swords and clubs, sent from the chief priests and the elders of the people.** NIV Even as Jesus spoke to his disciples to rouse them from their sleep, *Judas, one of the Twelve,* appeared. Judas, who had left the Last Supper at Jesus' request (John 13:27), had apparently gone to the religious leaders to whom he had spoken earlier (26:14-16). The religious leaders had issued the warrant for Jesus' arrest, and Judas was acting as Jesus' official accuser. Judas led the group to one of Jesus' retreats where no onlookers would interfere with them.

The armed crowd was probably made up of members of the temple guard, who were Jews supervised by the temple authorities and given authority by the Romans to make arrests for minor infractions. The detachment of soldiers mentioned in John 18:3 may have been a small group of Roman soldiers who were not participating in the arrest, but who had accompanied the temple guard to make sure that matters stayed under control. The armed men came in the middle of the night when most of the people were asleep, so they could arrest Jesus without commotion. Although there were no crowds to worry about, Jesus was surrounded by eleven loyal followers who the temple guards feared might put up a fight. So they came armed with *swords and clubs* in addition to lanterns and torches to light their way (John 18:3).

Matthew mentions that these men had been *sent from the chief priests and the elders of the people.* Mark added the scribes (or teachers of the law, see Mark 14:43). These were the three groups that made up the Sanhedrin, the Jewish supreme court. Jesus mentioned these three groups in his predictions of his death (see 16:21; 20:18). The entire religious leadership issued the warrant for Jesus' arrest and was together in the attempt to condemn Jesus to death.

**6:48-49 Now the betrayer had given them a sign, saying, "The one I will kiss is the man; arrest him." At once he came up to Jesus and said, "Greetings, Rabbi!" and kissed him.**NRSV Judas *(the betrayer)* had told the crowd to arrest the man whom he would *kiss.* This would be an arrest by religious leaders, not by Roman soldiers under Roman law. Judas pointed Jesus out because Jesus was hard to recognize in the dark and because Judas had agreed to be the formal accuser in case a trial was called. A kiss on the cheek or hand was a common form of greeting in the Middle East, so this was not unusual. Judas would affectionately greet the man the guards were to arrest and lead away.

Judas had planned to find Jesus and the disciples in Gethsemane, and he was correct. He entered the garden followed by the armed band and went directly to Jesus. In a friendly gesture of greeting and affection, Judas called Jesus *Rabbi* and then gave him a kiss (on the cheek or on the hand). While a rabbi did not have an official ecclesiastical position like a pastor today (the office of rabbi did not begin for another century), the title was an unofficial sign of respect. Judas showed himself to be the ultimate traitor. He had eaten with Jesus only hours before, and here he used a sign of friendship and affection in his betrayal.

**26:50 Jesus said to him, "Friend, do what you are here to do." Then they came and laid hands on Jesus and arrested him.**NRSV The use of the word "friend" for Judas was an act of love on Jesus' part, which shows that God's love never leaves even the apostate. But it carried a twist of irony in that both Jesus and Judas knew of the treachery. Jesus was still in charge, and his words *do what you are here to do* amount to him giving permission for the event to take place.

The religious leaders had not arrested Jesus in the temple for fear of a riot. Instead, they had come secretly at night, under the influence of the prince of darkness, Satan himself. Jesus offered no resistance and was duly arrested. Everything was proceeding according to God's plan. It was time for Jesus to suffer and die.

FACING A TRAITOR

When people hurt us, our first impulse is to strike back. At a minimum, we rescind friendship and regard the traitor as an enemy. But Jesus called Judas "friend" even here.

In most betrayals, the traitor has surrendered integrity and commitment for short-term gain. Often, as in Judas's case, it's money. There's no long-term gain in betraying a friend, so the real victim is the traitor himself. In that sense, a traitor deserves our pity before our rebuke.

If a colleague at work maneuvers at your expense, if a friend passes an unfounded rumor, try Jesus' way: Before you cut all ties, offer a recovery of the bond that once existed between you. Perhaps by calling someone "friend" who no longer deserves it, you will save that person from a huge mistake. Judas could have changed his mind. He had the chance. Jesus didn't reject him but tried once more to help him see.

**26:51 With that, one of Jesus' companions reached for his sword, drew it out and struck the servant of the high priest, cutting off his ear.**[NIV] According to John 18:10, the person who pulled the sword was Peter, who cut off the right ear of a *servant of the high priest* named Malchus. Peter was trying to demonstrate his loyalty as well as prevent what he saw as defeat. He wasn't going to let this crowd arrest Jesus without putting up a fight. Luke 22:51 records that Jesus immediately healed the man's ear and prevented any further bloodshed. Peter was not also arrested because Jesus handled the matter by healing the man and restraining Peter.

**26:52-54 "Put your sword back in its place," Jesus said to him, "for all who draw the sword will die by the sword. Do you think I cannot call on my Father, and he will at once put at my disposal more than twelve legions of angels? But how then would the Scriptures be fulfilled that say it must happen in this way?"**[NIV] Jesus told Peter to put away his sword and allow God's plan to unfold. Peter didn't understand that Jesus had to die in order to gain victory. But Jesus demonstrated perfect commitment to his Father's will. His kingdom would not be advanced with swords, but with faith and obedience.

Jesus' words here, recorded only by Matthew, stress the difference between people's tendency to take matters into their own hands (and suffer the consequences) and God's more far-reaching actions. The reason for putting the sword *back in its place* was that *all who draw the sword will die by the sword* (probably quoting a local proverb). Jesus' words meant that the law of vengeance is below the level of God's plans. To take action into one's own hands is to set oneself against the will of God. Jesus clarified this by

## BETRAYED!

Scripture records a number of occasions in which a person or group was betrayed. The tragedies caused by these violations of trust are a strong lesson about the importance of keeping our commitments.

| | |
|---|---|
| Delilah betrayed Samson to the Philistines. | Judges 16:16-21 |
| Absalom betrayed David, his father. | 2 Samuel 15:10-17 |
| Jehu betrayed Joram and killed him. | 2 Kings 9:14-27 |
| Officials betrayed Joash and killed him. | 2 Kings 12:20-21 |
| Judas betrayed Jesus. | Matthew 26:46-56 |

stating that he could call on his Father who would at once make available to him *more than twelve legions of angels* (in the Roman army, a "legion" had 6,000 infantry and 120 cavalry). Jesus was stating that he was in control—thus, everything was happening with his permission. What is one sword to him who could command an army of angels with one word? He did not need the help of a few sleepy disciples. He could call upon legions of angels, but he refused to do so because he had already settled this matter with God during his previous hours of prayer.

Jesus knew the far-reaching results. If he were to call for protection from legions of angels, *how then would the Scriptures be fulfilled that say it must happen in this way?* The plural "Scriptures" probably continues Matthew's focus on how Jesus fulfilled Old Testament prophecies, and so pointed to many passages describing the suffering Servant (such as Psalms 22; 69; Isaiah 53; Zechariah 13:7). Jesus' suffering would be necessary to God's plan; no one must stand in the way of God's will.

**26:55-56 At that hour Jesus said to the crowds, "Have you come out with swords and clubs to arrest me as though I were a bandit? Day after day I sat in the temple teaching, and you did not arrest me. But all this has taken place, so that the scriptures of the prophets may be fulfilled."** NRSV Jesus pointed out the ridiculous tactics of these people who had come to arrest him. They did not need to come against him with *swords and clubs,* for he voluntarily surrendered himself. Jesus was not a revolutionary *bandit* leading a rebellion; he was a religious teacher who had been teaching in the temple *day after day* during the past week. On one of them, he had emptied the temple of merchants and money changers. Yet no one had arrested him. Instead, they came at night for fear of the crowds. Jesus also mocked their show of worldly power. He who could summon angels was not afraid of swords. Did the guards imagine that swords would intimidate Jesus? They didn't understand who he was.

While Jesus mentioned this to reveal the religious leaders' evil motives and cowardice, he knew why the events were unfolding as they were—*that the scriptures of the prophets may be fulfilled*. Judas's treachery, the coming mockery of a trial against Jesus, and its ultimate outcome had all been prophesied (see, for example, Psalms 22:7-8, 14, 16-17; 41:9; Isaiah 50:6; 53:7-8).

**Then all the disciples deserted him and fled.**<sup>NRSV</sup> Just hours earlier, these disciples had vowed never to desert Jesus (26:35). The "all" who promised total allegiance were now the *all* who fled. Judas's kiss marked a turning point for the disciples. With Jesus' arrest, each one's life would be radically different. For the first time, Judas openly betrayed Jesus before the other disciples. For the first time, Jesus' loyal disciples *deserted him and fled*. Their world was crumbling. The teacher who had held forth in the temple was now under arrest. The treasurer had become a traitor. The garden sanctuary that had always been "safe" was turned into the place of confrontation. What confusion! The disciples' primary loyalty to Jesus should have kept them from running. But fear took its toll. Jesus' growing isolation was now complete; he would face the cross alone.

---

THE UNTHINKABLE
Jesus came to understand his role in God's plan of salvation by reading and understanding the Old Testament Scriptures. So important were these Scriptures that he referred to them as the reason for his own acceptance of the death he was about to face. Better he die on the cross than the Scriptures be wrong. Indeed, the Scriptures cannot be wrong. That would be unthinkable.

Take the Bible seriously. Read it, understand it, and live by it. It is not merely a book of nice thoughts. Rather, it is God's Word to you. That it could be wrong is unthinkable. Give God's Word its rightful place in your life.

---

## CAIAPHAS QUESTIONS JESUS / 26:57-68 / **226**

**26:57 Those who had arrested Jesus took him to Caiaphas, the high priest, where the teachers of the law and the elders had assembled.**<sup>NIV</sup> By then it was very early Friday morning, before daybreak. Jesus was taken under guard from the garden back into Jerusalem. First he was questioned by Annas, the former high priest and father-in-law of *Caiaphas.* Annas had been Israel's high priest from A.D. 6 to 15, when he had been deposed by Roman rulers. Then Caiaphas had been appointed high priest. He held that position from A.D. 18 to 36/37. According to Jewish law, the office of high priest was held for life, but the Roman government had taken over the process of appointing all political and religious leaders. Caiaphas served for eighteen years, longer than most high priests, suggesting that he was gifted at cooperating with the Romans. Caiaphas was the first to recommend Jesus' death in order to "save" the nation (John 11:49-50). Many Jews, however, still considered Annas to be the high priest. Annas may have asked to question Jesus after his arrest and had been given permission to do so. This hearing is described in John 18:12-24.

After that preliminary hearing, Jesus was taken to the home of *Caiaphas,* the ruling *high priest.* That *the teachers of the law and the elders had assembled* shows that this was a trial by the Sanhedrin (the Jewish Council of religious leaders consisting of seventy members plus the high priest). Because of their haste to complete the trial and see Jesus die before the Sabbath, less than twenty-four hours later, the religious leaders first met at Caiaphas's house at night to accomplish the preliminaries before their more formal meeting in the temple at daylight. (John recorded that Jesus was taken to Annas first and then to Caiaphas. Most likely their homes shared a common courtyard.) The leaders finally had Jesus where they wanted him, and they were determined to accomplish their plans as quickly as possible.

The trial by the Sanhedrin had two phases. This first phase occurred during the night (recorded here in 26:57-68); then another meeting was held "early in the morning" (27:1 NIV) to satisfy a law that allowed trials only during the daytime. That meeting was a mere formality held at daybreak, during which the verdict was given and Jesus was led off to the Roman procurator for sentencing. The Sanhedrin was the most powerful religious and political body of the Jewish people. Although the Romans controlled Israel's government, they gave the people power to handle religious disputes and some civil disputes; so the Sanhedrin made many of the local decisions affecting daily life. But a death sentence had to be authorized by the Romans (John 18:31).

**26:58 But Peter followed him at a distance, right up to the courtyard of the high priest. He entered and sat down with the guards to see the outcome.**[NIV] Jesus had been taken immediately to the high priest's house, even though it was not yet daylight. The Jewish leaders were in a hurry because they wanted to complete the execution before the Sabbath and get on with the Passover celebration. The high priest's residence was a palace with outer walls enclosing a *courtyard.* That this trial should occur here was unprecedented. Normally the Sanhedrin would meet in a large hall in the temple area. They could have met there because, during the Passover, the temple opened at midnight rather than at dawn. This meeting at Caiaphas's home may have been to aid in a hasty assembly; however, they still could just as easily have met in a normal location. Most likely, it was their desire to avoid a riot (26:5) that led them to this more private setting.

In the courtyard, a charcoal fire was burning, around which the servants and soldiers were warming themselves against the early morning chill. Although most of the disciples had fled when the soldiers arrested Jesus, two of them, Peter and another disciple (perhaps John), returned to where Jesus had been taken (John 18:15). After securing permission to enter the courtyard, Peter joined the others as they warmed themselves around the fire. Peter's experiences in the next few hours would revolutionize his life. He would change from an impulsive follower to a repentant and wiser disciple, and finally to the kind of person Christ could use to build his church. Peter's story continues at 26:69. Although he would deny Jesus three times, Peter was the only disciple to go all the way to the trial to find out what would happen to Jesus.

**26:59-61** **The chief priests and the whole Sanhedrin were looking for false evidence against Jesus so that they could put him to death. But they did not find any, though many false witnesses came forward.**[NIV] Upstairs in the high priest's palace, *the chief priests and the whole Sanhedrin* (meaning the group of seventy-one leaders of the Jews—priests and respected men) assembled before dawn.

The religious leaders wanted to get this trial under way, but they had a dilemma on their hands. They wanted evidence to convict Jesus of a crime deserving death, but *they did not find any.* The obvious conclusion should have been that Jesus was innocent of any crime. But this was not a trial for justice; it was a trial to accomplish an evil purpose. There were apparent illegalities in this trial: Jews were not to hold trials during the night nor during festivals; Jesus had no counsel nor time to prepare a defense (see the chart, "How Jesus' Trial Was Illegal" on page 536). These leaders held a trial to keep up appearances, while their whole purpose was to kill Jesus. Matthew pointed out the irony of the Sanhedrin breaking the law in order to keep the law.

There was no shortage of witnesses; the problem was in finding two testimonies that agreed. During a trial, each witness would be called upon separately to give his testimony. But the stories these witnesses gave did not agree in the details. According to Moses' law, no one was to be put to death on the testimony of only one witness (Numbers 35:30); there had to be two or three agreeing witnesses (Deuteronomy 19:15). This must have been exasperating for the desperate religious leaders. They weren't going to let Jesus get away on a technicality!

These *false witnesses* were identified by the Sanhedrin; but Matthew knew that any testimony against Jesus would have to be false, and he knew that, in essence, false testimony was exactly what the Sanhedrin needed. Otherwise, they had no grounds to convict Jesus (Mark 14:55). Ironically, these religious guardians of the law were breaking one of the Ten Commandments, "You shall not give false testimony" (Exodus 20:16 NIV).

**Finally two came forward and declared, "This fellow said, 'I am able to destroy the temple of God and rebuild it in three days.'"** NIV *Finally* they found a couple of witnesses who testified regarding Jesus' words about the temple. The witnesses claimed that Jesus had said he could *destroy the temple* in Jerusalem—a blasphemous boast. Such a claim would bring wrath from even the Romans because destroying temples was considered a capital offense throughout the Roman empire. However, Jesus had not spoken in the first person ("I will destroy"); nor had he said anything linking his words with the temple building. Instead, Jesus had spoken in the second person plural, issuing a command, "Destroy this temple, and in three days I will raise it up" (John 2:19 NKJV). Jesus, of course, was talking about his body, not the building. Ironically, the religious leaders were about to destroy Jesus' body just as he had said, and *three days* later he would rise from the dead.

**26:62-64** **Then the high priest stood up and said to Jesus, "Are you not going to answer? What is this testimony that these men are bringing against you?" But Jesus remained silent.** NIV The legal code required that a defendant answer his accusers, so Caiaphas was getting frustrated. His only hope was to get Jesus to say something that would give them evidence to convict him. So he simply *stood up* in this revered group and spoke directly to Jesus. He may have been hoping that Jesus was ignorant enough to not realize that the witnesses had invalidated themselves (Mark pointed out their contradictions, Mark 14:59). Caiaphas tried to make up in intimidation what was lacking in evidence. He asked Jesus to answer his accusers and then to explain the accusations against him.

Jesus, however, refused to say anything. He had nothing to say to the group of liars who had spoken against him, and he did not choose to answer their false accusations. So he *remained silent.* This had been prophesied in Scripture: "He was oppressed and afflicted, yet he did not open his mouth; he was led like a lamb to the slaughter, and as a sheep before her shearers is silent, so he did not open his mouth" (Isaiah 53:7 NIV). With Jesus' silence, the court proceedings ground to a halt.

---

SILENCE

Jesus remained silent at his trial. Historians have asked why Jews at Auschwitz and other camps went to their deaths quietly. Why didn't they fight?

When injustice is so strong that words no longer appeal to the conscience of the oppressor, silence has dignity. Better to suffer in dignity than to squander wasted words before evil people devoted to their cruelty.

Jesus did not mount a legal defense in a proceeding so fraught with injustice and hate. Deitrich Bonhoeffer prayed before being taken to the gallows after a Nazi kangaroo court issued his sentence. So thousands of martyrs have taken the flame or the bullet in dignity without splattering words in futile debate.

Words are vital weapons in the advance of God's kingdom. But sometimes silence is the better testimony. Silence can speak loudly about our confidence in God's righteousness and mercy. It tells the oppressor that the fear he inspires is not all that impressive, that we stand by a power much higher than he.

---

**The high priest said to him, "I charge you under oath by the living God: Tell us if you are the Christ, the Son of God."** NIV But Caiaphas had another tactic up the sleeve of his priestly robe. He decided to ask Jesus point-blank, *Tell us if you are the Christ, the Son of God.* The Sanhedrin must have held their collective breath in anticipation. Here was the question that could make or break the entire plot. Would Jesus outrightly claim to be the Messiah? We may wonder why Jesus refused to answer the first question and then chose to answer this one. Caiaphas put Jesus *under oath* so that Jesus would be forced to answer by law (Leviticus 5:1); thus he would be forced to incriminate himself.

**"Yes, it is as you say," Jesus replied. "But I say to all of you: In the future you will see the Son of Man sitting at the right hand of the Mighty One and coming on the clouds of heaven."** NIV To the first questions, Jesus made no reply because the questions were based on confusing and erroneous evidence. Not answering was wiser than trying to clarify the fabricated accusations. But if

Jesus had refused to answer this second question, it would have been tantamount to denying his deity and his mission. So Jesus answered without hesitation, *Yes, it is as you say.*

Then Jesus gave a startling prophecy. The words "the Son of Man sitting at the right hand of the Mighty One" refer back to Psalm 110:1, and "coming on the clouds of heaven" recall Daniel 7:13-14. The "clouds" represented the power and glory of God. Both verses were considered to be prophecies of the coming Messiah, and Jesus applied them to himself. "The Son of Man" stood for Jesus' role as the divine agent appointed by God to carry out judgment. In Psalm 110:1, the Son is given the seat of authority at the right hand of God. In Daniel 7:13-14, the Son is given "authority, glory and sovereign power" (NIV). Jesus used these verses to predict a powerful role reversal. *Sitting at the right hand* of power, one day he would come to judge his accusers, and they would have to answer to him (Revelation 20:11-13). This represented the highest view of Jesus' deity possible. Jesus used the highest titles for God's deity and then applied them to himself. Jesus declared his royalty in no uncertain terms. In saying he was the Son of Man, Jesus was claiming to be the Messiah, as his listeners well knew. How ironic that this declaration is given to the high priest, Jesus' greatest opponent. He knew this declaration would lead to his conviction, but he did not panic. He was calm, courageous, and determined.

**26:65-66 Then the high priest tore his clothes and said, "He has blasphemed! Why do we still need witnesses? You have now heard his blasphemy. What is your verdict?" They answered, "He deserves death."** NRSV Tearing one's clothing was an ancient expression of deep sorrow (see Genesis 44:13). The law forbade a priest from tearing his garments over personal grief because they were a sign of his special role (Leviticus 10:6; 21:10), but it was appropriate in an instance when blasphemy had been spoken in his presence. Blasphemy was the sin of claiming to be God or of attacking God's authority and majesty in any way. Caiaphas *tore his clothes* to signify his outrage at the audacity of the claims of this mere teacher from Nazareth. Jesus had identified himself with God by applying two messianic prophecies to himself. The high priest recognized Jesus' claim and exclaimed to the Sanhedrin, *He has blasphemed!*

While claiming to be God was blasphemy, there is no evidence that claiming to be the Messiah was blasphemy. So why did the high priest accuse Jesus of blasphemy? A combination of Jesus' words and actions may give the answer. Jesus had prophesied a future exaltation of the Son of Man (26:64), a position next to

## HOW JESUS' TRIAL WAS ILLEGAL

The religious leaders were not interested in giving Jesus a fair trial. In their minds, Jesus had to die. This blind obsession led them to pervert the justice they were appointed to protect. Here are many examples of the actions taken by the religious leaders that were illegal according to their own laws.

- Even before the trial began, it had been determined that Jesus must die (John 11:50; Mark 14:1). There was no "innocent until proven guilty" approach.
- False witnesses were sought to testify against Jesus (Matthew 26:59). Usually the religious leaders went through an elaborate system of screening witnesses to ensure justice.
- No prepared defense or representative counsel for Jesus was sought or allowed (Luke 22:67-71).
- The trial was conducted at night (Mark 14:53-65; 15:1), which was illegal according to the religious leaders' laws for Sanhedrin trials.
- The high priest put Jesus under oath, but then incriminated him for what he said (Matthew 26:63-66).
- Cases involving such serious charges were to be tried only in the Sanhedrin's regular meeting place, not in the high priest's palace (Mark 14:53-65).

God himself. Thus, part of Jesus' offense was this portrayal of his status next to God (on the "right hand" referred to the ability to act on behalf of God). In addition, Jesus' ministry had included teachings and actions that the religious leaders had found to be unlawful (such as his teachings about the Sabbath). Thus, according to them, Jesus claimed divinity, yet taught lawbreaking. These religious leaders thought that Jesus was leading the people astray and bringing dishonor to God's holy name. For any other human being, Jesus' words would have amounted to blasphemy; in Jesus' case, the claim was true.

Blasphemy was punishable by death (Leviticus 24:15-16). *Why do we still need witnesses?* asked Caiaphas without expecting any answer. They needed no more false witnesses (Caiaphas probably was relieved, since the witnesses had been worthless). Jesus had finally said what Caiaphas needed, so he asked for the group's decision. The Jewish leaders had the evidence they wanted, so all of them condemned him as deserving death. Those present, or at least the majority, gave the death sentence, although Nicodemus would not have agreed (John 3:1-21; 19:38-40), nor would Joseph of Arimathea, "who, though a member of the council, had not agreed to their plan and action" (Luke 23:50-51 NRSV).

Of all people, the high priest and members of the Sanhedrin

# Matthew 28

The resurrection of Jesus from the dead is the central fact of Christian history. On it, the church is built; without it, there would be no Christian church today. Jesus' resurrection is unique. Other religions have strong ethical systems, concepts about paradise and afterlife, and various holy scriptures. Only Christianity has a God who became human, literally died for his people, and was raised again in power and glory to rule his church forever.

Why is the Resurrection so important?

- Because Christ was raised from the dead, we know that the kingdom of heaven has broken into earth's history. Our world is now headed for redemption, not disaster. God's mighty power is at work destroying sin, creating new lives, and preparing us for Jesus' second coming.
- Because of the Resurrection, we know that death has been conquered and that we, too, will be raised from the dead to live forever with Christ.
- The Resurrection gives authority to the church's witness in the world. Look at the early evangelistic sermons in the book of Acts: The apostles' most important message was the proclamation that Jesus Christ had been raised from the dead!
- The Resurrection gives meaning to the church's regular feast, the Lord's Supper. Like the disciples on the road to Emmaus, we break bread with our risen Lord.
- The Resurrection helps us find meaning even in great tragedy. No matter what happens to us as we walk with the Lord, the Resurrection gives us hope for the future.
- The Resurrection assures us that Christ is alive and ruling his kingdom. He is not legend; he is alive and real.
- The power of God that brought Christ's body back from the dead is available to us to bring our morally and spiritually dead selves back to life so that we can change and grow (1 Corinthians 15:12-19).

Christians can look very different from one another, and they can hold widely varying beliefs about politics, lifestyle, and even theology. But one central belief unites and inspires all true Christians—Jesus Christ rose from the dead!

**28:1 Now after the Sabbath, as the first day of the week began to dawn, Mary Magdalene and the other Mary came to see the tomb.**NKJV The women could not make the trip to the tomb until *after the Sabbath.* As dawn approached, *Mary Magdalene and the other Mary came to see the tomb.* Both of them had been at Jesus' cross and had followed Joseph so they would know where the tomb was located (27:56, 61). Mark also mentioned that Salome was with them; she had also been at the cross and was probably the mother of the disciples James and John. The women went home and kept the Sabbath as the law required, from sundown Friday to sundown Saturday. In the Jewish reckoning of time, a day included any part of a day; thus, Friday was the first day, Saturday was the second day, and Sunday was the third day. Unlike the Jewish leaders, they certainly had no expectation that the disciples would steal the body (27:62-66). When the women arrived at daybreak on Sunday, the third day, Jesus had already risen.

Mark explained that they had gone back to the tomb to bring spices and perfumes to anoint Jesus' body because they had had no time to do so before the Sabbath (Mark 16:1). Anointing a body was a sign of love, devotion, and respect. Bringing spices to the tomb would be like bringing flowers to a grave today. Since they did not embalm bodies in Israel, they would use perfumes as a normal practice. The women undoubtedly knew that Joseph and Nicodemus had already wrapped the body in linen and spices. They probably were going to do a simple external application of the fragrant spices. Matthew, however, omitted the detail of their visit, explaining only that they *came to see the tomb.*

**28:2-4 There was a violent earthquake, for an angel of the Lord came down from heaven and, going to the tomb, rolled back the stone and sat on it.**NIV Again a supernatural event took place, probably having occurred before the women arrived at the tomb. *There was a violent earthquake* (see also 27:51-52) that occurred as the angel of the Lord descended, or it was the means by which the stone was rolled away from the tomb's entrance. The stone was not rolled back so Jesus could get out, but so others could get in and see that Jesus had indeed risen from the dead, just as he had promised. This is as close a description of the Resurrection as the Bible gives us.

Mark records that the women were concerned about how they would get into the tomb to anoint Jesus' body (Mark 16:3). They had seen Joseph put the stone at its entrance (27:60-61), although they may have been unaware of the sealing of the stone and of the guards who had been posted. When they arrived at the tomb, they saw that the large stone had already been rolled aside. *An angel of the Lord* was sitting on the stone. **His appearance was like lightning, and his clothing white as snow. For fear of him the guards shook and became like dead men.**NRSV The radiance of this angel made him appear *like lightning*. These words recall Old Testament visions like that of Daniel (see Daniel 7:9; 10:6). The angel's beauty and glory, coming from heaven itself, caused the posted guards to faint with fear and caused great fear for the women as well (28:5, 8). Matthew and Mark wrote that one angel met the women at the tomb, while Luke mentions two angels. Each Gospel writer chose to highlight different details as he explained the same story, just as eyewitnesses to a news story may each highlight a different aspect of that event. Matthew and Mark probably emphasized just the angel who spoke.

**28:5-6 The angel said to the women, "Do not be afraid, for I know that you are looking for Jesus, who was crucified. He is not here; he has risen, just as he said. Come and see the place where he lay."** NIV The angel spoke reassuringly to the frightened women. They were looking for Jesus, the human being who had been crucified on the cross. But Jesus was not there; he had risen. Jesus had given the disciples three predictions of both his death and of his resurrection (16:21-28; 17:22-23; 20:17-19). The angel said to the women, "Remember how he told you, while he was still in Galilee, that the Son of Man must be handed over to sinners, and be crucified, and on the third day rise again" (Luke 24:6-7 NRSV).

The angel invited the women to look into the inner burial chamber and *see the place where he lay.* John records that the linen cloths that had been wrapped around Jesus' body were left as if Jesus had passed right through them. The handkerchief was still rolled up in the shape of a head, and it was at about the right distance from the wrappings that had enveloped Jesus' body (John 20:6-7). A grave robber couldn't possibly have made off with Jesus' body and left the linens as if they were still shaped around it. The best explanation was that Jesus had risen from the dead, *just as he said* he would.

COME AND GO
The angel who announced the good news of the Resurrection
to the women gave them four messages:
1. "Do not be afraid." The reality of the Resurrection brings
   joy, not fear. When you are afraid, remember the empty
   tomb.
2. "He is not here." Jesus is not dead and is not to be looked
   for among the dead. He is alive, with his people.
3. "Come and see." The women could check the evidence
   themselves. The tomb was empty then, and it is empty
   today. The Resurrection is a historical fact.
4. "Go quickly and tell." They were to spread the joy of the
   Resurrection. We too are to spread the great news about
   Jesus' resurrection.

**28:7 "Then go quickly and tell his disciples, 'He has been raised
from the dead, and indeed he is going ahead of you to Galilee;
there you will see him.' This is my message for you."** NRSV The
women who had come to anoint a dead body were given another
task—proclaiming the Resurrection to the frightened disciples.
Mark explained that the angel made special mention of Peter to
show that, in spite of Peter's denials, Jesus had not disowned and
deserted him. According to Luke's account, several women ran to
tell the disciples: "Now it was Mary Magdalene, Joanna, Mary
the mother of James, and the other women with them who told
this to the apostles. But these words seemed to them an idle tale,
and they did not believe them. But Peter got up and ran to the
tomb; stooping and looking in, he saw the linen cloths by themselves; then he went home, amazed at what had happened" (Luke
24:10-12 NRSV). John, in his personal account, added that he too
dashed in amazement to the tomb (John 20:3-5).

The disciples had deserted Jesus in the hour of trial, but the
angel's words held hope of renewal and forgiveness. The disciples
had deserted, but they were directed to meet Jesus in *Galilee*. This
was exactly what Jesus had told them during the Last Supper, that
he would go ahead of them into Galilee after his resurrection
(26:32).

## JESUS APPEARS TO THE WOMEN / 28:8-10 / *241*

**28:8 So the women hurried away from the tomb, afraid yet filled
with joy, and ran to tell his disciples.** NIV The women *hurried
away from the tomb,* realizing that they had seen the results of an
awesome miracle in the empty tomb and had been in the presence
of an angel. This revelation from God had filled them with a

mixture of fear and joy. They obeyed the angel's command and *ran* to the eleven disciples with the good news of the empty tomb and Jesus' resurrection.

**28:9 Suddenly Jesus met them and said, "Greetings!" And they came to him, took hold of his feet, and worshiped him.**<sup>NRSV</sup>
As the women ran from the tomb, in their path appeared Jesus himself! The women *took hold of his feet* (a Near Eastern custom for a subject showing obeisance to a king) and *worshiped him,* giving homage to their Savior, Lord, and King.

---

MEETING THE SAVIOR
When Moses met God on Mount Sinai, it was a scene of holy terror: burning bush, awesome voice, brilliant glory-light. But here, Jesus surprises the two Marys and says, "Hello." What a friendly way to greet two devoted followers.
How does Jesus greet us today? Usually in quiet, friendly ways.
- With a moment of deep assurance after a morning prayer.
- Through the touch of a friend come to share a piece of news.
- By the arrival of a letter from an old friend.
- Through a feeling of wonder at the Lord's Supper during morning worship.
How does Jesus greet you? Share your joy with others this week.

---

**28:10 Then Jesus said to them, "Do not be afraid; go and tell my brothers to go to Galilee; there they will see me."**<sup>NRSV</sup> By "brothers," Jesus meant his disciples. This showed that he had forgiven them, even after they had disowned and deserted him, and that he raised them to a new level of fellowship—from disciples to "brothers" (see John 15:15). Jesus told the women to pass a message on to the disciples—that they should *go to Galilee,* as he had previously told them (26:32). Galilee was where Jesus had called most of them and where he had said they would become "fishers of men" (4:19 NIV), and it would be where this mission would be restated (John 21). But the disciples, filled with fear, remained behind locked doors in Jerusalem (John 20:19). Jesus met them first in Jerusalem (Luke 24:36) and later in Galilee (John 21). Then he returned to Jerusalem, where he ascended into heaven from the Mount of Olives (Acts 1:9-12).

> In almost every example of God breaking into life on earth, the opening words are, "Fear not . . . Have no fear, I am with thee." Our Father knows that we need constant reassurance.
>
> *Catherine Marshall*

## RELIGIOUS LEADERS BRIBE THE GUARDS / 28:11-15 / 242

**28:11** **While the women were on their way, some of the guards went into the city and reported to the chief priests everything that had happened.**[NIV] Jesus' resurrection was already causing a great stir in Jerusalem. A group of women was moving quickly through the streets, looking for the disciples to tell them the amazing news that Jesus was alive. At the same time, guards were on their way, not to Pilate, but *to the chief priests.* If these were Roman guards (see commentary on 27:65), under Roman law, they would have paid with their lives for falling asleep on the job (28:13). Since they were assigned to the Jewish authorities, they went to the religious leaders badly in need of a cover-up. They went to the *chief priests,* to tell them *everything that had happened* (at least up to the point where they fainted!).

**28:12-15** **When the chief priests had met with the elders and devised a plan, they gave the soldiers a large sum of money, telling them, "You are to say, 'His disciples came during the night and stole him away while we were asleep.' If this report gets to the governor, we will satisfy him and keep you out of trouble."**[NIV] The religious leaders' worst fears had been realized (27:63-64)—Jesus' body had disappeared from the tomb! Instead of even considering that Jesus' claims had been true and that he truly was the Messiah risen from the dead, the chief priests and elders *devised a plan* and paid a bribe to the soldiers in order to explain away what had happened. What irony that the chief priests were forced to bribe the guards to spread the very lie that the chief priests had tried to prevent! This may have seemed like a logical explanation, but they didn't think through the details. Why would Jesus' disciples, who already had run off on him at his arrest, risk a return at night to a guarded and sealed tomb in an effort to steal a body—an offense that could incur the death penalty? If they had done so, would they have taken the time to unwrap the body and leave the graveclothes behind?

If this had occurred *while* the guards *were asleep,* how could the guards possibly have known that the *disciples came during the night and stole* the body? If this truly happened, why didn't the religious leaders arrest the disciples in order to prosecute them? The story was full of holes and the guards would have to admit to negligence on their part, so getting them to spread this rumor required *a large sum of money.* If *the governor* (Pilate) were to hear the story, the Jewish leaders promised to intervene for the guards, *satisfy* Pilate with the made-up rumor, and keep the guards *out of trouble.*

(Considering their treatment of Judas in 27:4, one ought to wonder at the sincerity of these words!) Nevertheless, the plan worked: **So the soldiers took the money and did as they were instructed. And this story has been widely circulated among the Jews to this very day.**<sup>NIV</sup> Apparently the sum of money paid was worth it, because the soldiers took it and *did as they were instructed.* The story circulated and many people believed the lie, also apparently not thinking through the information long enough to ask the obvious questions. The story was still being circulated in the days of Matthew's writing this Gospel, and even in the days of Justin Martyr (A.D. 130–160).

---

LIES COMPOUNDED
First the religious leaders had to get false accusers to give false reports at Jesus' kangaroo court. Then they had to invent false charges of treason against Roman authority. Here they developed an alibi for the guards, and, if necessary, they would lie to Pilate to protect the guards and themselves.

Lying leads to lying. If you start down that slide, there's a gravity that keeps pulling you down. Invent one story, and you'll have to invent another, sure thing.

■ Take a lesson from these sorry leaders. Tell the truth, and live free from the worry that your cover may be blown. At home, require the truth from your children, and give the truth to them. At work, be up-front and square. The bumps you may feel over the truth are nothing like the boulders you'll have to climb by lying to protect yourself.

---

## JESUS GIVES THE GREAT COMMISSION / 28:16-20 / **248**

**8:16-17** **Now the eleven disciples went to Galilee, to the mountain to which Jesus had directed them. When they saw him, they worshiped him; but some doubted.**<sup>NRSV</sup> Jesus made several appearances to various people after his resurrection (see the chart "Jesus' Appearances after His Resurrection" on page 577). "The eleven" refers to the remaining disciples after the death of Judas Iscariot. Although he first appeared to the disciples in Jerusalem, at his first appearance, Thomas had been absent. He doubted the story of the rest of the disciples, until Jesus appeared to him as well (John 20:24-31). They did go to Galilee, as Jesus had previously directed them (26:32; 28:10). At some point they returned to Jerusalem where Jesus ascended into heaven from the Mount of Olives (Acts 1:9). "The mountain" referred to here in Galilee is unknown; however, mountains figured prominently in Matthew, for they are found sixteen times in connection with divine revelation (at the Temptation, Sermon on the Mount, Transfiguration, etc.).

In an effort to exclude the eleven disciples from having "doubted" Jesus, some scholars have suggested that *they* who *saw him* refers to more than just the eleven disciples—perhaps the "five hundred brothers" mentioned by Paul in 1 Corinthians 15:6 NRSV. But the text doesn't allow for this; among the eleven who saw Jesus there were some who *doubted*—which means, they had hesitations about believing in Jesus' resurrection. Apparently on their walk from Jerusalem to

> This mountain at the conclusion of our Lord's life corresponds to the mountain of temptation at the beginning. There he was offered the empire of the world, if only he would take the easy lower path; here he is acknowledged King of the world because he took the hard one of obedience unto death.
>
> *F. B. Meyer*

Galilee, lengthy discussions were held. Matthew may have been reporting some of the doubts and concerns still lingering in the minds of the eleven chosen disciples. Of course, they would all eventually be fully convinced and believe.

---

**DOUBT**
Matthew's honesty is remarkable. Some of the disciples struggled with doubt.

No Christian grows in faith without some doubt. The five-year-olds who took in every Bible story will become the fifteen-year-olds who want to know how, what, why, when, and where. And they will grow, too, and press for deeper answers along the way.

When you doubt, don't be discouraged. It's not a sin nor a failure. It's a normal part of spiritual growth. Keep talking with thoughtful Christian friends and teachers, keep studying and praying, keep serving the Lord, and keep asking questions and looking for answers. God gave you a mind to discover his truth. Don't let anyone tell you that discovery is wrong.

---

**28:18 And Jesus came and said to them, "All authority in heaven and on earth has been given to me."** NRSV When someone is dying or leaving us, we pay close attention to his or her last words. Jesus left the disciples with these last words of instruction:

- They were under his authority.
- They were to make more disciples.
- They were to baptize and teach these new disciples to obey Christ.
- They would have Christ with them always.

## JESUS' APPEARANCES AFTER HIS RESURRECTION

| | |
|---|---|
| 1. Mary Magdalene | Mark 16:9-11; John 20:10-18 |
| 2. The other women at the tomb | Matthew 28:8-10 |
| 3. Peter in Jerusalem | Luke 24:34; 1 Corinthians 15:5 |
| 4. The two travelers on the road | Mark 16:12-13; Luke 24:13-35 |
| 5. Ten disciples behind closed doors | Luke 24:36-43; John 20:19-25 |
| 6. All eleven disciples (including Thomas) | Mark 16:14; John 20:26-31; 1 Corinthians 15:5 |
| 7. Seven disciples while fishing on the Sea of Galilee | John 21:1-14 |
| 8. Eleven disciples on a mountain in Galilee | Matthew 28:16-20; Mark 16:15-18 |
| 9. A crowd of 500 | 1 Corinthians 15:6 |
| 10. Jesus' brother James | 1 Corinthians 15:7 |
| 11. Those who watched Jesus ascend to heaven | Mark 16:19-20; Luke 24:50-53; Acts 1:3-9 |

God gave Jesus authority over heaven and earth, a sweeping concept that implies divine status. He has "all authority"—that is, nothing is outside of his sovereign control. The major message here and in 28:20 is that Jesus, the one raised from the dead, has the authority of God himself. During Satan's temptation of Jesus, Satan had offered "all the kingdoms of the world and their splendor" (4:8 NRSV). Jesus resisted the tempter, obeyed God to the point of horrible death, and was raised again in victory to receive *all* authority over heaven and earth—something Satan could never have given because it was never his in the first place.

**28:19-20** **"Go therefore and make disciples of all the nations, baptizing them in the name of the Father and of the Son and of the Holy Spirit, teaching them to observe all things that I have commanded you; and lo, I am with you always, even to the end of the age." Amen.**[NKJV] On the basis of his authority, Jesus told his disciples to *go* and *make disciples* as they preached, baptized, and taught. "Making disciples" means instructing new believers on how to follow Jesus, to submit to Jesus' lordship, and to take up his mission of compassionate service. To be a disciple means entering a relationship of learner to Master (Teacher) with Jesus. The church must not merely evangelize, but it also must show new converts how to obey Jesus' commands. Discipleship must be stressed without neglecting evangelism. "Baptism" is important because it unites a believer with Jesus Christ in his or her death to sin and resurrection to new life. Baptism symbolizes submission to Christ, a willingness to live God's way, and identification with God's covenant people. To baptize *in the name of the Father and of the Son and of the Holy Spirit* affirms the reality of the Trinity, the concept coming directly from Jesus himself. He did not say baptize them into the "names," but into the "name" of the Father, Son, and Holy Spirit. While the word "Trinity" does not occur in Scripture, it well describes the three-in-one existence of the Father, Son, and Holy Spirit. (See also Romans 8:11; 1 Corinthians 12:4-6; 2 Corinthians 13:14; Galatians 4:6; Ephesians 4:4-6; 2 Thessalonians 2:13.)

Whereas in previous missions Jesus had sent his disciples only to the Jews (10:5-6), their mission from here forward would be to go to *all the nations.* This is called the Great Commission. The disciples had been trained well, and they had seen the risen Lord. They were ready to teach people all over the world *to observe all things* that Jesus had *commanded* them. This also showed the disciples that there would be a lapse of time between Jesus' resurrection and his second coming. During that time, Jesus' followers had jobs to do—evangelize, baptize, and teach people about Jesus so that they, in turn, could do the same. The good news of the gospel was to go forth to all the nations.

With this same authority, Jesus still commands us to tell others the Good News and make them disciples for the kingdom. We are to go—whether it is next door or to another country—and make disciples. It is not an option, but a command to all who call Jesus "Lord." We are not all evangelists in the formal sense, but we have all received gifts that we can use to help fulfill the Great Commission. As we obey, we have comfort in the knowledge that Jesus is *always* with us. "Always" literally means "all the days" and refers to the presence of Christ with each believer every moment. This would occur through the Holy Spirit's presence in believers' lives. The Holy Spirit would be Jesus' presence that would never leave them (John 14:26; Acts 1:4-5). Jesus continues to be with us today through his Spirit. As this Gospel began, so it ends—Immanuel, "God with us" (1:23).

The Old Testament prophecies and genealogies in the book

of Matthew present Jesus' credentials for being King of the world—not a military or political leader, as the disciples had originally hoped, but a spiritual King who can overcome all evil and rule in the heart of every person. If we refuse to serve the King faithfully, we are disloyal subjects. We must make Jesus King of our lives and worship him as our Savior, King, and Lord.

## 250 EVENTS IN THE LIFE OF CHRIST/ A HARMONY OF THE GOSPELS

All four books in the Bible that tell the story of Jesus Christ—Matthew, Mark, Luke, and John—stand alone, emphasizing a unique aspect of Jesus' life. But when these are blended into one complete account, or harmonized, we gain new insights about the life of Christ.

This harmony combines the four Gospels into a single chronological account of Christ's life on earth. It includes every chapter and verse of each Gospel, leaving nothing out.

The harmony is divided into 250 events. The title of each event is identical to the title found in the corresponding Gospel. Parallel passages found in more than one Gospel have identical titles, helping you to identify them quickly.

Each of the 250 events in the harmony is numbered. The number of the event corresponds to the number next to the title in the Bible text. When reading one of the Gospel accounts, you will notice, at times, that some numbers are missing or out of sequence. The easiest way to locate these events is to refer to the harmony.

In addition, if you are looking for a particular event in the life of Christ, the harmony can help you locate it more rapidly than paging through all four Gospels. Each of the 250 events has a distinctive title keyed to the main emphasis of the passage to help you locate and remember the events.

This harmony will help you to better visualize the travels of Jesus, study the four Gospels comparatively, and appreciate the unity of their message.

## I. BIRTH AND PREPARATION OF JESUS CHRIST

|  | Matthew | Mark | Luke | John |
|---|---|---|---|---|
| 1 Luke's purpose in writing |  |  | 1:1–4 |  |
| 2 God became a human being |  |  |  | 1:1–18 |
| 3 The ancestors of Jesus | 1:1–17 |  | 3:23–38 |  |
| 4 An angel promises the birth of John to Zechariah |  |  | 1:5–25 |  |
| 5 An angel promises the birth of Jesus to Mary |  |  | 1:26–38 |  |
| 6 Mary visits Elizabeth |  |  | 1:39–56 |  |
| 7 John the Baptist is born |  |  | 1:57–80 |  |
| 8 An angel appears to Joseph | 1:18–25 |  |  |  |
| 9 Jesus is born in Bethlehem |  |  | 2:1–7 |  |
| 10 Shepherds visit Jesus |  |  | 2:8–20 |  |
| 11 Mary and Joseph bring Jesus to the temple |  |  | 2:21–40 |  |
| 12 Visitors arrive from eastern lands | 2:1–12 |  |  |  |
| 13 The escape to Egypt | 2:13–18 |  |  |  |
| 14 The return to Nazareth | 2:19–23 |  |  |  |
| 15 Jesus speaks with the religious teachers |  |  | 2:41–52 |  |
| 16 John the Baptist prepares the way for Jesus | 3:1–12 | 1:1–8 | 3:1–18 |  |
| 17 John baptizes Jesus | 3:13–17 | 1:9–11 | 3:21, 22 |  |
| 18 Satan tempts Jesus in the desert | 4:1–11 | 1:12, 13 | 4:1–13 |  |
| 19 John the Baptist declares his mission |  |  |  | 1:19–28 |

| | Matthew | Mark | Luke | John |
|---|---|---|---|---|
| 20 John the Baptist proclaims Jesus as the Messiah | | | | 1:29–34 |
| 21 The first disciples follow Jesus | | | | 1:35–51 |
| 22 Jesus turns water into wine | | | | 2:1–12 |

## II. MESSAGE AND MINISTRY OF JESUS CHRIST

| | Matthew | Mark | Luke | John |
|---|---|---|---|---|
| 23 Jesus clears the temple | | | | 2:12–25 |
| 24 Nicodemus visits Jesus at night | | | | 3:1–21 |
| 25 John the Baptist tells more about Jesus | | | | 3:22–36 |
| 26 Herod puts John in prison | | | 3:19, 20 | |
| 27 Jesus talks to a woman at the well | | | | 4:1–26 |
| 28 Jesus tells about the spiritual harvest | | | | 4:27–38 |
| 29 Many Samaritans believe in Jesus | | | | 4:39–42 |
| 30 Jesus preaches in Galilee | 4:12–17 | 1:14, 15 | 4:14, 15 | 4:43–45 |
| 31 Jesus heals a government official's son | | | | 4:46–54 |
| 32 Jesus is rejected at Nazareth | | | 4:16–30 | |
| 33 Four fishermen follow Jesus | 4:18–22 | 1:16–20 | | |
| 34 Jesus teaches with great authority | | 1:21–28 | 4:31–37 | |
| 35 Jesus heals Peter's mother-in-law and many others | 8:14–17 | 1:29–34 | 4:38–41 | |
| 36 Jesus preaches throughout Galilee | 4:23–25 | 1:35–39 | 4:42–44 | |
| 37 Jesus provides a miraculous catch of fish | | | 5:1–11 | |
| 38 Jesus heals a man with leprosy | 8:1–4 | 1:40–45 | 5:12–16 | |
| 39 Jesus heals a paralyzed man | 9:1–8 | 2:1–12 | 5:17–26 | |
| 40 Jesus eats with sinners at Matthew's house | 9:9–13 | 2:13–17 | 5:27–32 | |
| 41 Religious leaders ask Jesus about fasting | 9:14–17 | 2:18–22 | 5:33–39 | |
| 42 Jesus heals a lame man by the pool | | | | 5:1–18 |
| 43 Jesus claims to be God's Son | | | | 5:19–30 |
| 44 Jesus supports his claim | | | | 5:31–47 |
| 45 The disciples pick wheat on the Sabbath | 12:1–8 | 2:23–28 | 6:1–5 | |
| 46 Jesus heals a man's hand on the Sabbath | 12:9–14 | 3:1–6 | 6:6–11 | |
| 47 Large crowds follow Jesus | 12:15–21 | 3:7–12 | | |
| 48 Jesus selects the twelve disciples | | 3:13–19 | 6.12–16 | |
| 49 Jesus gives the Beatitudes | 5:1–12 | | 6:17–26 | |
| 50 Jesus teaches about salt and light | 5:13–16 | | | |
| 51 Jesus teaches about the law | 5:17–20 | | | |
| 52 Jesus teaches about anger | 5:21–26 | | | |
| 53 Jesus teaches about lust | 5:27–30 | | | |
| 54 Jesus teaches about divorce | 5:31, 32 | | | |
| 55 Jesus teaches about vows | 5:33–37 | | | |
| 56 Jesus teaches about retaliation | 5:38–42 | | | |
| 57 Jesus teaches about loving enemies | 5:43–48 | | 6:27–36 | |
| 58 Jesus teaches about giving to the needy | 6:1–4 | | | |
| 59 Jesus teaches about prayer | 6:5–15 | | | |
| 60 Jesus teaches about fasting | 6:16–18 | | | |
| 61 Jesus teaches about money | 6:19–24 | | | |
| 62 Jesus teaches about worry | 6:25–34 | | | |
| 63 Jesus teaches about criticizing others | 7:1–6 | | 6:37–42 | |
| 64 Jesus teaches about asking, seeking, knocking | 7:7–12 | | | |
| 65 Jesus teaches about the way to heaven | 7:13, 14 | | | |
| 66 Jesus teaches about fruit in people's lives | 7:15–20 | | 6:43–45 | |
| 67 Jesus teaches about those who build houses on rock and sand | 7:21–29 | | 6:46–49 | |
| 68 A Roman centurion demonstrates faith | 8:5–13 | | 7:1–10 | |
| 69 Jesus raises a widow's son from the dead | | | 7:11–17 | |
| 70 Jesus eases John's doubt | 11:1–19 | | 7:18–35 | |
| 71 Jesus promises rest for the soul | 11:20–30 | | | |
| 72 A sinful woman anoints Jesus' feet | | | 7:36–50 | |
| 73 Women accompany Jesus and the disciples | | | 8:1–3 | |
| 74 Religious leaders accuse Jesus of being under Satan's power | 12:22–37 | 3:20–30 | | |

| | Matthew | Mark | Luke | John |
|---|---|---|---|---|
| 75 Religious leaders ask Jesus for a miracle | 12:38–45 | | | |
| 76 Jesus describes his true family | 12:46–50 | 3:31–35 | 8:19–21 | |
| 77 Jesus tells the parable of the four soils | 13:1–9 | 4:1–9 | 8:4–8 | |
| 78 Jesus explains the parable of the four soils | 13:10–23 | 4:10–25 | 8:9–18 | |
| 79 Jesus tells the parable of the growing seed | | 4:26–29 | | |
| 80 Jesus tells the parable of the weeds | 13:24–30 | | | |
| 81 Jesus tells the parable of the mustard seed | 13:31, 32 | 4:30–34 | | |
| 82 Jesus tells the parable of the yeast | 13:33–35 | | | |
| 83 Jesus explains the parable of the weeds | 13:36–43 | | | |
| 84 Jesus tells the parable of hidden treasure | 13:44 | | | |
| 85 Jesus tells the parable of the pearl merchant | 13:45, 46 | | | |
| 86 Jesus tells the parable of the fishing net | 13:47–52 | | | |
| 87 Jesus calms the storm | 8:23–27 | 4:35–41 | 8:22–25 | |
| 88 Jesus sends the demons into a herd of pigs | 8:28–34 | 5:1–20 | 8:26–39 | |
| 89 Jesus heals a bleeding woman and restores a girl to life | 9:18–26 | 5:21–43 | 8:40–56 | |
| 90 Jesus heals the blind and mute | 9:27–34 | | | |
| 91 The people of Nazareth refuse to believe | 13:53–58 | 6:1–6 | | |
| 92 Jesus urges the disciples to pray for workers | 9:35–38 | | | |
| 93 Jesus sends out the twelve disciples | 10:1–16 | 6:7–13 | 9:1–6 | |
| 94 Jesus prepares the disciples for persecution | 10:17–42 | | | |
| 95 Herod kills John the Baptist | 14:1–12 | 6:14–29 | 9:7–9 | |
| 96 Jesus feeds five thousand | 14:13–21 | 6:30–44 | 9:10–17 | 6:1–15 |
| 97 Jesus walks on water | 14:22–33 | 6:45–52 | | 6:16–21 |
| 98 Jesus heals all who touch him | 14:34–36 | 6:53–56 | | |
| 99 Jesus is the true bread from heaven | | | | 6:22–40 |
| 100 The Jews disagree that Jesus is from heaven | | | | 6:41–59 |
| 101 Many disciples desert Jesus | | | | 6:60–71 |
| 102 Jesus teaches about inner purity | 15:1–20 | 7:1–23 | | |
| 103 Jesus sends a demon out of a girl | 15:21–28 | 7:24–30 | | |
| 104 The crowd marvels at Jesus' healings | 15:29–31 | 7:31–37 | | |
| 105 Jesus feeds four thousand | 15:32–39 | 8:1–10 | | |
| 106 Religious leaders ask for a sign in the sky | 16:1–4 | 8:11–13 | | |
| 107 Jesus warns against wrong teaching | 16:5–12 | 8:14–21 | | |
| 108 Jesus restores sight to a blind man | | 8:22–26 | | |
| 109 Peter says Jesus is the Messiah | 16:13–20 | 8:27–30 | 9:18–20 | |
| 110 Jesus predicts his death the first time | 16:21–28 | 8:31–9:1 | 9:21–27 | |
| 111 Jesus is transfigured on the mountain | 17:1–13 | 9:2–13 | 9:28–36 | |
| 112 Jesus heals a demon-possessed boy | 17:14–21 | 9:14–29 | 9:37–43 | |
| 113 Jesus predicts his death the second time | 17:22, 23 | 9:30–32 | 9:44, 45 | |
| 114 Peter finds the coin in the fish's mouth | 17:24–27 | | | |
| 115 The disciples argue about who would be the greatest | 18:1–6 | 9:33–37 | 9:46–48 | |
| 116 The disciples forbid another to use Jesus' name | | 9:38–41 | 9:49, 50 | |
| 117 Jesus warns against temptation | 18:7–9 | 9:42–50 | | |
| 118 Jesus warns against looking down on others | 18:10–14 | | | |
| 119 Jesus teaches how to treat a believer who sins | 18:15–20 | | | |
| 120 Jesus tells the parable of the unforgiving debtor | 18:21–35 | | | |
| 121 Jesus' brothers ridicule him | | | | 7:1–9 |
| 122 Jesus teaches about the cost of following him | 8:18–22 | | 9:51–62 | |
| 123 Jesus teaches openly at the temple | | | | 7:10–31 |
| 124 Religious leaders attempt to arrest Jesus | | | | 7:32–52 |
| 125 Jesus forgives an adulterous woman | | | | 7:53–8:11 |
| 126 Jesus is the light of the world | | | | 8:12–20 |
| 127 Jesus warns of coming judgment | | | | 8:21–30 |
| 128 Jesus speaks about God's true children | | | | 8:31–47 |
| 129 Jesus states he is eternal | | | | 8:48–59 |
| 130 Jesus sends out seventy-two messengers | | | 10:1–16 | |
| 131 The seventy-two messengers return | | | 10:17–24 | |
| 132 Jesus tells the parable of the Good Samaritan | | | 10:25–37 | |
| 133 Jesus visits Mary and Martha | | | 10:38–42 | |
| 134 Jesus teaches his disciples about prayer | | | 11:1–13 | |
| 135 Jesus answers hostile accusations | | | 11:14–28 | |
| 136 Jesus warns against unbelief | | | 11:29–32 | |

| | Matthew | Mark | Luke | John |
|---|---|---|---|---|
| 137 Jesus teaches about the light within | | | 11:33–36 | |
| 138 Jesus criticizes the religious leaders | | | 11:37–54 | |
| 139 Jesus speaks against hypocrisy | | | 12:1–12 | |
| 140 Jesus tells the parable of the rich fool | | | 12:13–21 | |
| 141 Jesus warns about worry | | | 12:22–34 | |
| 142 Jesus warns about preparing for his coming | | | 12:35–48 | |
| 143 Jesus warns about coming division | | | 12:49–53 | |
| 144 Jesus warns about the future crisis | | | 12:54–59 | |
| 145 Jesus calls the people to repent | | | 13:1–9 | |
| 146 Jesus heals the crippled woman | | | 13:10–17 | |
| 147 Jesus teaches about the kingdom of God | | | 13:18–21 | |
| 148 Jesus heals the man who was born blind | | | | 9:1–12 |
| 149 Religious leaders question the blind man | | | | 9:13–34 |
| 150 Jesus teaches about spiritual blindness | | | | 9:35–41 |
| 151 Jesus is the Good Shepherd | | | | 10:1–21 |
| 152 Religious leaders surround Jesus at the temple | | | | 10:22–42 |
| 153 Jesus teaches about entering the kingdom | | | 13:22–30 | |
| 154 Jesus grieves over Jerusalem | | | 13:31–35 | |
| 155 Jesus heals a man with dropsy | | | 14:1–6 | |
| 156 Jesus teaches about seeking honor | | | 14:7–14 | |
| 157 Jesus tells the parable of the great feast | | | 14:15–24 | |
| 158 Jesus teaches about the cost of being a disciple | | | 14:25–35 | |
| 159 Jesus tells the parable of the lost sheep | | | 15:1–7 | |
| 160 Jesus tells the parable of the lost coin | | | 15:8–10 | |
| 161 Jesus tells the parable of the lost son | | | 15:11–32 | |
| 162 Jesus tells the parable of the shrewd manager | | | 16:1–18 | |
| 163 Jesus tells about the rich man and the beggar | | | 16:19–31 | |
| 164 Jesus tells about forgiveness and faith | | | 17:1–10 | |
| 165 Lazarus becomes ill and dies | | | | 11:1–16 |
| 166 Jesus comforts Mary and Martha | | | | 11:17–37 |
| 167 Jesus raises Lazarus from the dead | | | | 11:38–44 |
| 168 Religious leaders plot to kill Jesus | | | | 11:45–57 |
| 169 Jesus heals ten men with leprosy | | | 17:11–19 | |
| 170 Jesus teaches about the coming of the kingdom of God | | | 17:20–37 | |
| 171 Jesus tells the parable of the persistent widow | | | 18:1–8 | |
| 172 Jesus tells the parable of two men who prayed | | | 18:9–14 | |
| 173 Jesus teaches about marriage and divorce | 19:1–12 | 10:1–12 | | |
| 174 Jesus blesses little children | 19:13–15 | 10:13–16 | | |
| 175 Jesus speaks to the rich young man | 19:16–30 | 10:17–31 | 18:15–17 | |
| 176 Jesus tells the parable of the workers paid equally | 20:1–16 | | 18:18–30 | |
| 177 Jesus predicts his death the third time | 20:17–19 | 10:32–34 | 18:31–34 | |
| 178 Jesus teaches about serving others | 20:20–28 | 10:35–45 | | |
| 179 Jesus heals a blind beggar | 20:29–34 | 10:46–52 | 18:35–43 | |
| 180 Jesus brings salvation to Zacchaeus's home | | | 19:1–10 | |
| 181 Jesus tells the parable of the king's ten servants | | | 19:11–27 | |
| 182 A woman anoints Jesus with perfume | 26:6–13 | 14:3–9 | | 12:1–11 |
| 183 Jesus rides into Jerusalem on a donkey | 21:1–11 | 11:1–11 | 19:28–44 | 12:12–19 |
| 184 Jesus clears the temple again | 21:12–17 | 11:12–19 | 19:45–48 | |
| 185 Jesus explains why he must die | | | | 12:20–36 |
| 186 Most of the people do not believe in Jesus | | | | 12:37–43 |
| 187 Jesus summarizes his message | | | | 12:44–50 |
| 188 Jesus says the disciples can pray for anything | 21:18–22 | 11:20–26 | | |
| 189 Religious leaders challenge Jesus' authority | 21:23–27 | 11:27–33 | 20:1–8 | |
| 190 Jesus tells the parable of the two sons | 21:28–32 | | | |
| 191 Jesus tells the parable of the wicked tenants | 21:33–46 | 12:1–12 | 20:9–19 | |
| 192 Jesus tells the parable of the wedding feast | 22:1–14 | | | |
| 193 Religious leaders question Jesus about paying taxes | 22:15–22 | 12:13–17 | 20:20–26 | |
| 194 Religious leaders question Jesus about the resurrection | 22:23–33 | 12:18–27 | 20:27–40 | |
| 195 Religious leaders question Jesus about the greatest commandment | 22:34–40 | 12:28–34 | | |
| 196 Religious leaders cannot answer Jesus' question | 22:41–46 | 12:35–37 | 20:41–44 | |

| | Matthew | Mark | Luke | John |
|---|---|---|---|---|
| 197 Jesus warns against the religious leaders | 23:1–12 | 12:38–40 | 20:45–47 | |
| 198 Jesus condemns the religious leaders | 23:13–36 | | | |
| 199 Jesus grieves over Jerusalem again | 23:37–39 | | | |
| 200 A poor widow gives all she has | | 12:41–44 | 21:1–4 | |
| 201 Jesus tells about the future | 24:1–25 | 13:1–23 | 21:5–24 | |
| 202 Jesus tells about his return | 24:26–35 | 13:24–31 | 21:25–33 | |
| 203 Jesus tells about remaining watchful | 24:36–51 | 13:32–37 | 21:34–38 | |
| 204 Jesus tells the parable of the ten bridesmaids | 25:1–13 | | | |
| 205 Jesus tells the parable of the loaned money | 25:14–30 | | | |
| 206 Jesus tells about the final judgment | 25:31–46 | | | |

## III. DEATH AND RESURRECTION OF JESUS CHRIST

| | Matthew | Mark | Luke | John |
|---|---|---|---|---|
| 207 Religious leaders plot to kill Jesus | 26:1–5 | 14:1, 2 | 22:1, 2 | |
| 208 Judas agrees to betray Jesus | 26:14–16 | 14:10, 11 | 22:3–6 | |
| 209 Disciples prepare for the Passover | 26:17–19 | 14:12–16 | 22:7–13 | |
| 210 Jesus washes the disciples' feet | | | | 13:1–20 |
| 211 Jesus and the disciples have the Last Supper | 26:20–30 | 14:17–26 | 22:14–30 | 13:21–30 |
| 212 Jesus predicts Peter's denial | | | 22:31–38 | 13:31–38 |
| 213 Jesus is the way to the Father | | | | 14:1–14 |
| 214 Jesus promises the Holy Spirit | | | | 14:15–31 |
| 215 Jesus teaches about the vine and the branches | | | | 15:1–17 |
| 216 Jesus warns about the world's hatred | | | | 15:18—16:4 |
| 217 Jesus teaches about the Holy Spirit | | | | 16:5–15 |
| 218 Jesus teaches about using his name in prayer | | | | 16:16–33 |
| 219 Jesus prays for himself | | | | 17:1–5 |
| 220 Jesus prays for his disciples | | | | 17:6–19 |
| 221 Jesus prays for future believers | | | | 17:20–26 |
| 222 Jesus again predicts Peter's denial | 26:31–35 | 14:27–31 | | |
| 223 Jesus agonizes in the garden | 26:36–46 | 14:32–42 | 22:39–46 | |
| 224 Jesus is betrayed and arrested | 26:47–56 | 14:43–52 | 22:47–53 | 18:1–11 |
| 225 Annas questions Jesus | | | | 18:12–24 |
| 226 Caiaphas questions Jesus | 26:57–68 | 14:53–65 | | |
| 227 Peter denies knowing Jesus | 26:69–75 | 14:66–72 | 22:54–65 | 18:25–27 |
| 228 The council of religious leaders condemns Jesus | 27:1, 2 | 15:1 | 22:66–71 | |
| 229 Judas kills himself | 27:3–10 | | | |
| 230 Jesus stands trial before Pilate | 27:11–14 | 15:2–5 | 23:1–5 | 18:28–37 |
| 231 Jesus stands trial before Herod | | | 23:6–12 | |
| 232 Pilate hands Jesus over to be crucified | 27:15–26 | 15:6–15 | 23:13–25 | 18:38—19:16 |
| 233 Roman soldiers mock Jesus | 27:27–31 | 15:16–20 | | |
| 234 Jesus is led away to be crucified | 27:32–34 | 15:21–24 | 23:26–31 | 19:17 |
| 235 Jesus is placed on the cross | 27:35–44 | 15:25–32 | 23:32–43 | 19:18–27 |
| 236 Jesus dies on the cross | 27:45–56 | 15:33–41 | 23:44–49 | 19:28–37 |
| 237 Jesus is laid in the tomb | 27:57–61 | 15:42–47 | 23:50–56 | 19:38–42 |
| 238 Guards are posted at the tomb | 27:62–66 | | | |
| 239 Jesus rises from the dead | 28:1–7 | 16:1–8 | 24:1–12 | 20:1–9 |
| 240 Jesus appears to Mary Magdalene | | 16:9–11 | | 20:10–18 |
| 241 Jesus appears to the women | 28:8–10 | | | |
| 242 Religious leaders bribe the guards | 28:11–15 | | | |
| 243 Jesus appears to two believers traveling on the road | | 16:12, 13 | 24:13–35 | |
| 244 Jesus appears to the disciples behind locked doors | | | 24:36–43 | 20:19–23 |
| 245 Jesus appears to the disciples including Thomas | | 16:14 | | 20:24–31 |
| 246 Jesus appears to the disciples while fishing | | | | 21:1–14 |
| 247 Jesus talks with Peter | | | | 21:15–25 |
| 248 Jesus gives the Great Commission | 28:16–20 | 16:15–18 | | |
| 249 Jesus appears to the disciples in Jerusalem | | | 24:44–49 | |
| 250 Jesus ascends into heaven | | 16:19, 20 | 24:50–53 | |

# BIBLIOGRAPHY

Bauer, Walter, William F. Arndt, and Wilbur F. Gingrich. *A Greek-English Lexicon of the New Testament and Other Early Christian Literature.* Chicago: University of Chicago Press, 1979.

Blomberg, Craig L. *The New American Commentary.* Vol. 22. Nashville: Broadman Press, 1992.

De Dietrich, Suzanne. *Matthew.* The Layman's Bible Commentary. Atlanta: John Knox Press, 1982.

Douglas, J. D., ed. *The New Greek-English Interlinear New Testament.* Robert K. Brown and Philip W. Comfort, trans. Wheaton, Ill.: Tyndale House Publishers, 1990.

France, R. T. *The Gospel According to Matthew: An Introduction and Commentary.* Tyndale New Testament Commentaries. Grand Rapids: William B. Eerdmans Publishing Company, 1985.

Gaebelein, Frank E., ed. *The Expositor's Bible Commentary.* Vol. 8. Grand Rapids: Zondervan Publishing House, 1984.

Green, Joel B., and Scot McKnight, eds. *Dictionary of Jesus and the Gospels.* Downers Grove, Ill.: InterVarsity Press, 1992.

Hagner, Donald A. *Matthew 1-13.* Word Biblical Commentary. Dallas: Word Books, 1993.

*Life Application Bible, New International Version.* Wheaton, Ill.: Tyndale House Publishers, 1991, and Grand Rapids: Zondervan Publishing House, 1991.

Meyer, F.B. *Devotional Commentary.* Wheaton, Ill.: Tyndale House Publishers, 1989.

Morris, Leon. *The Gospel According to Matthew.* Grand Rapids: William B. Eerdmans Publishing Company, 1992.

Mounce, Robert H. *Matthew.* The New International Biblical Commentary Series. W. Ward Gasque, New Testament ed. Peabody, Mass.: Hendrickson Publishers, 1991.

Ogilvie, Lloyd J., ed. *The Communicator's Commentary: Matthew.* Dallas: Word Books, 1982.

Walvoord, John F., and Roy B. Zuck. *Bible Knowledge Commentary. New Testament.* Wheaton, Ill.: Victor Books, 1983.

# INDEX